AF574384

SHD

Super
Holland
Design

New
Graphics

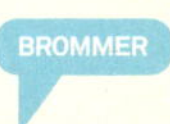

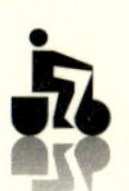

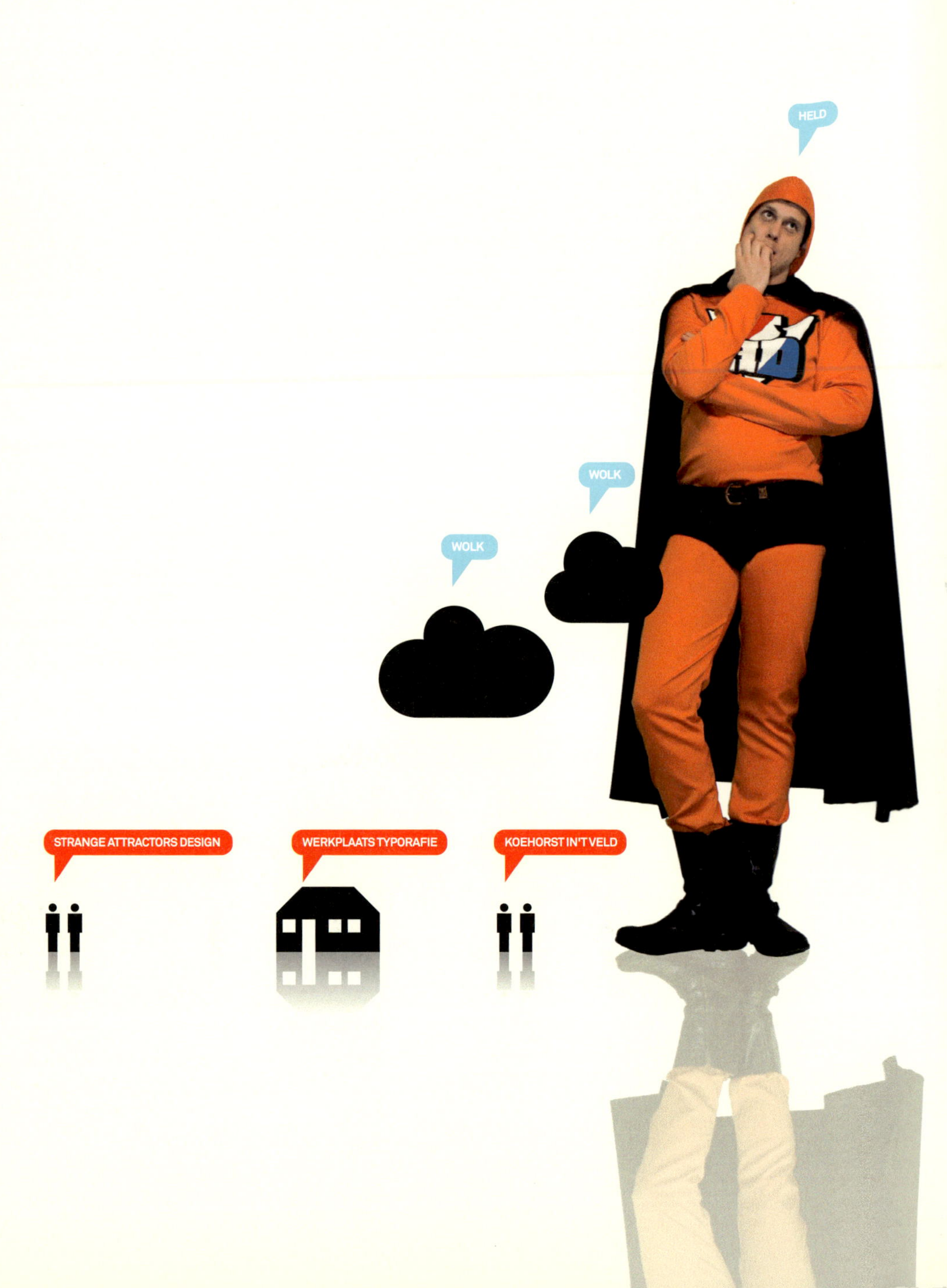
HELD
WOLK
WOLK
STRANGE ATTRACTORS DESIGN
WERKPLAATS TYPORAFIE
KOEHORST IN'T VELD

Contents

9 Introduction
14 Re-Mix
50 Drawing The Letters
86 Statistical Graphics
130 Political Graphics
180 Instruction Manual
202 Story Tellers
224 Read Me
254 2D Space
284 Behave In Digital Language
304 Space Design
337 Postcards from Holland
365 Who's Who
426 Index
432 Credits

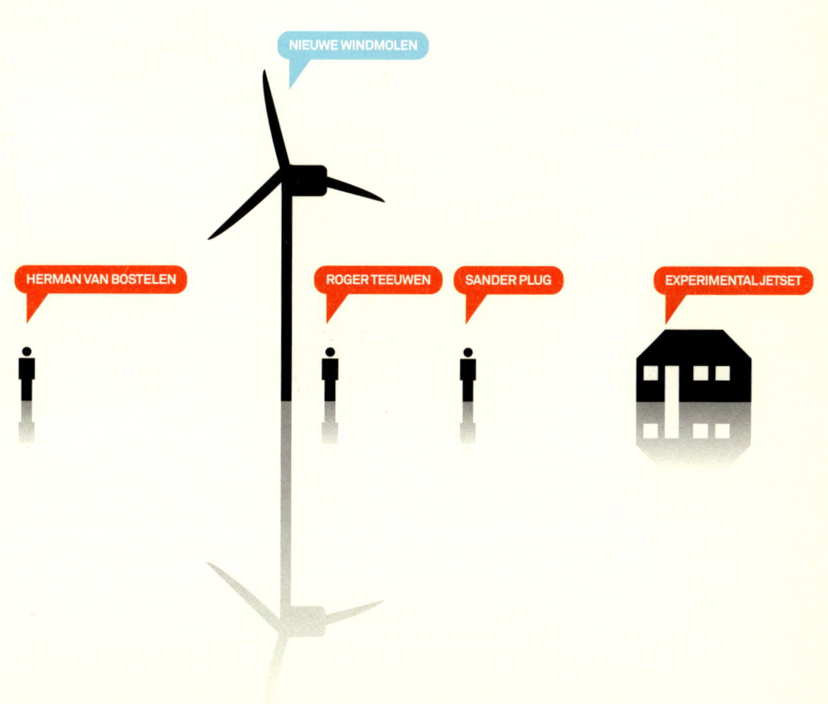

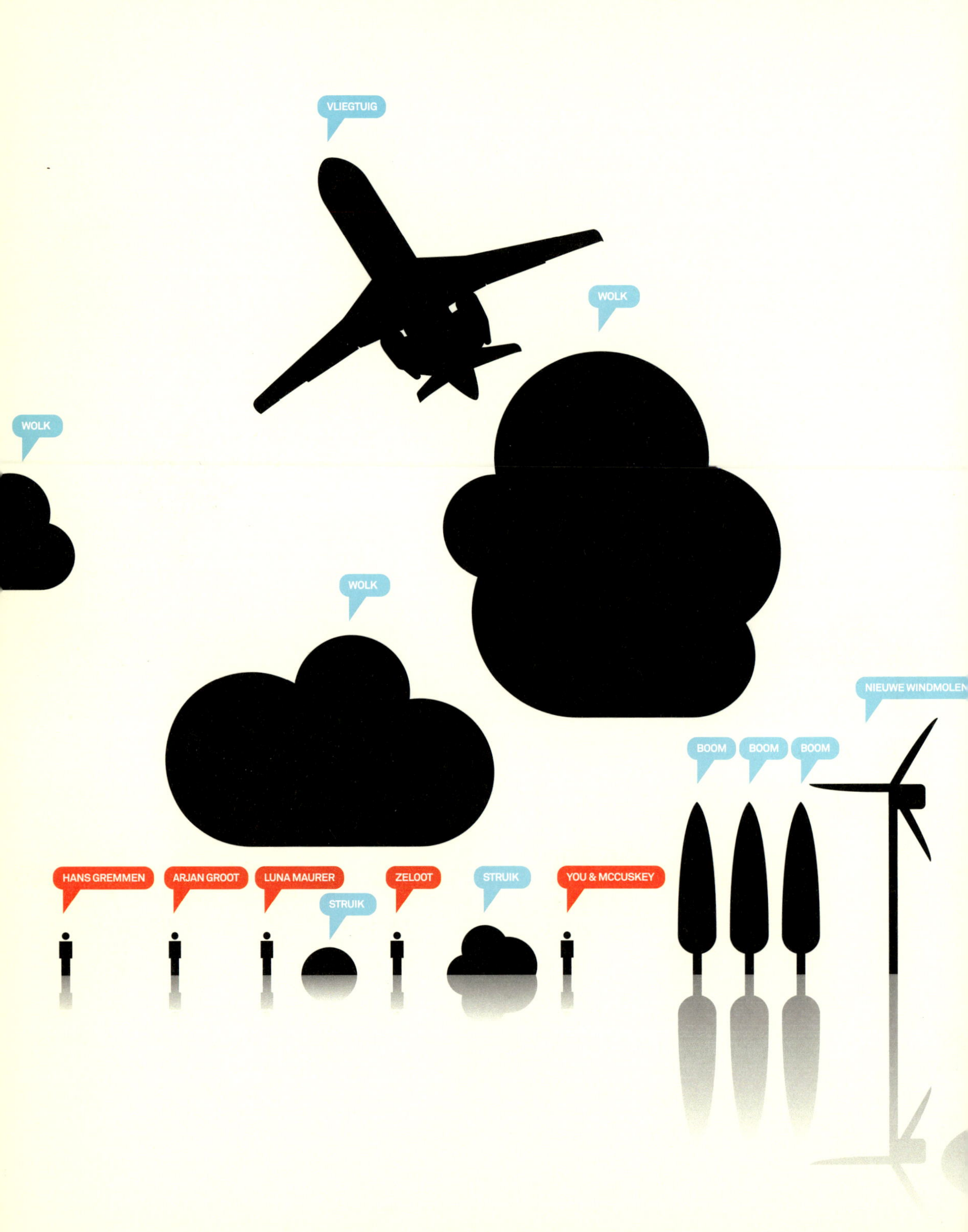

VLIEGTUIG
WOLK
WOLK
WOLK
NIEUWE WINDMOLEN
BOOM
BOOM
BOOM
HANS GREMMEN
ARJAN GROOT
LUNA MAURER
STRUIK
ZELOOT
STRUIK
YOU & MCCUSKEY

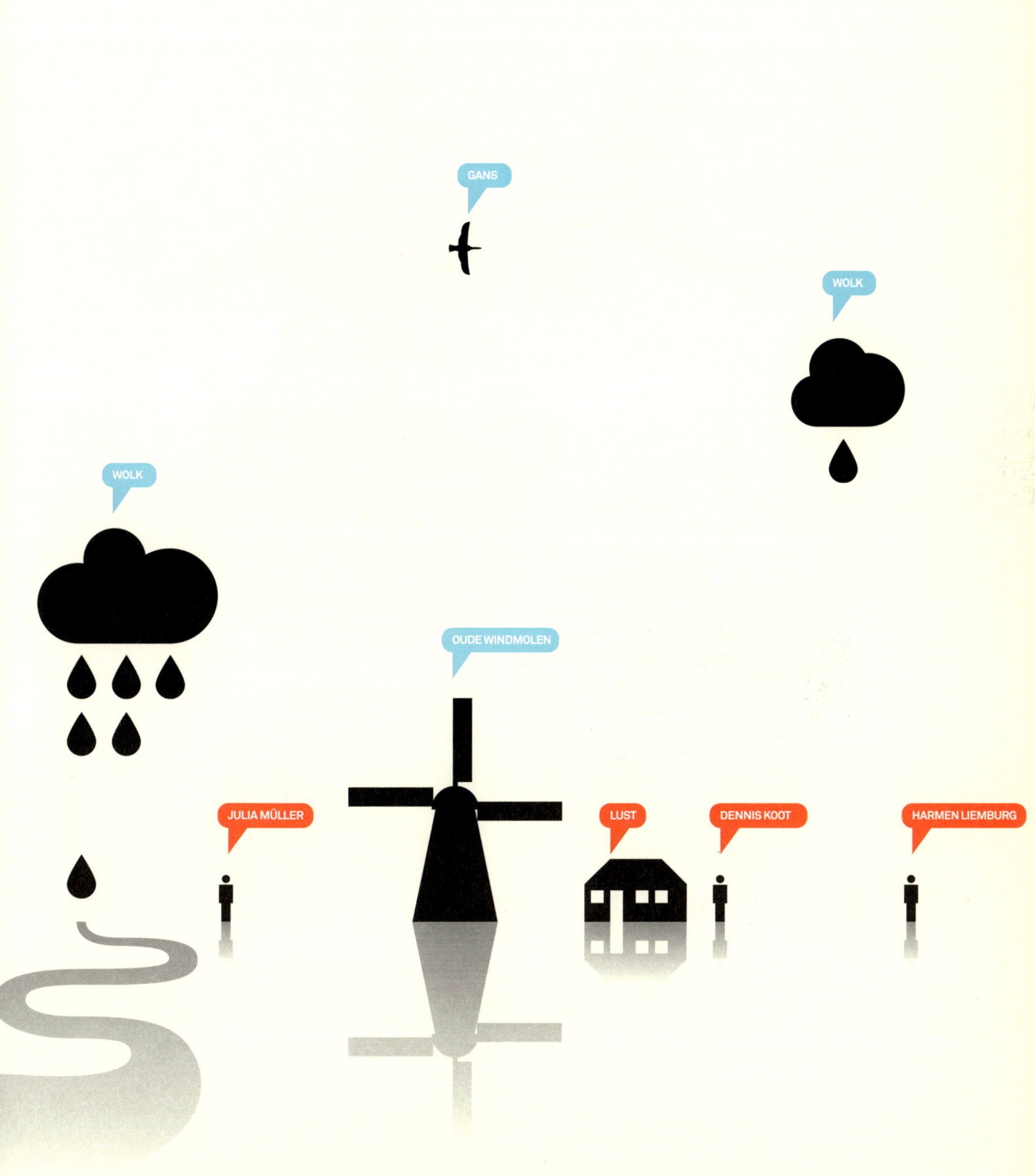
GANS
WOLK
WOLK
OUDE WINDMOLEN
JULIA MÜLLER
LUST
DENNIS KOOT
HARMEN LIEMBURG

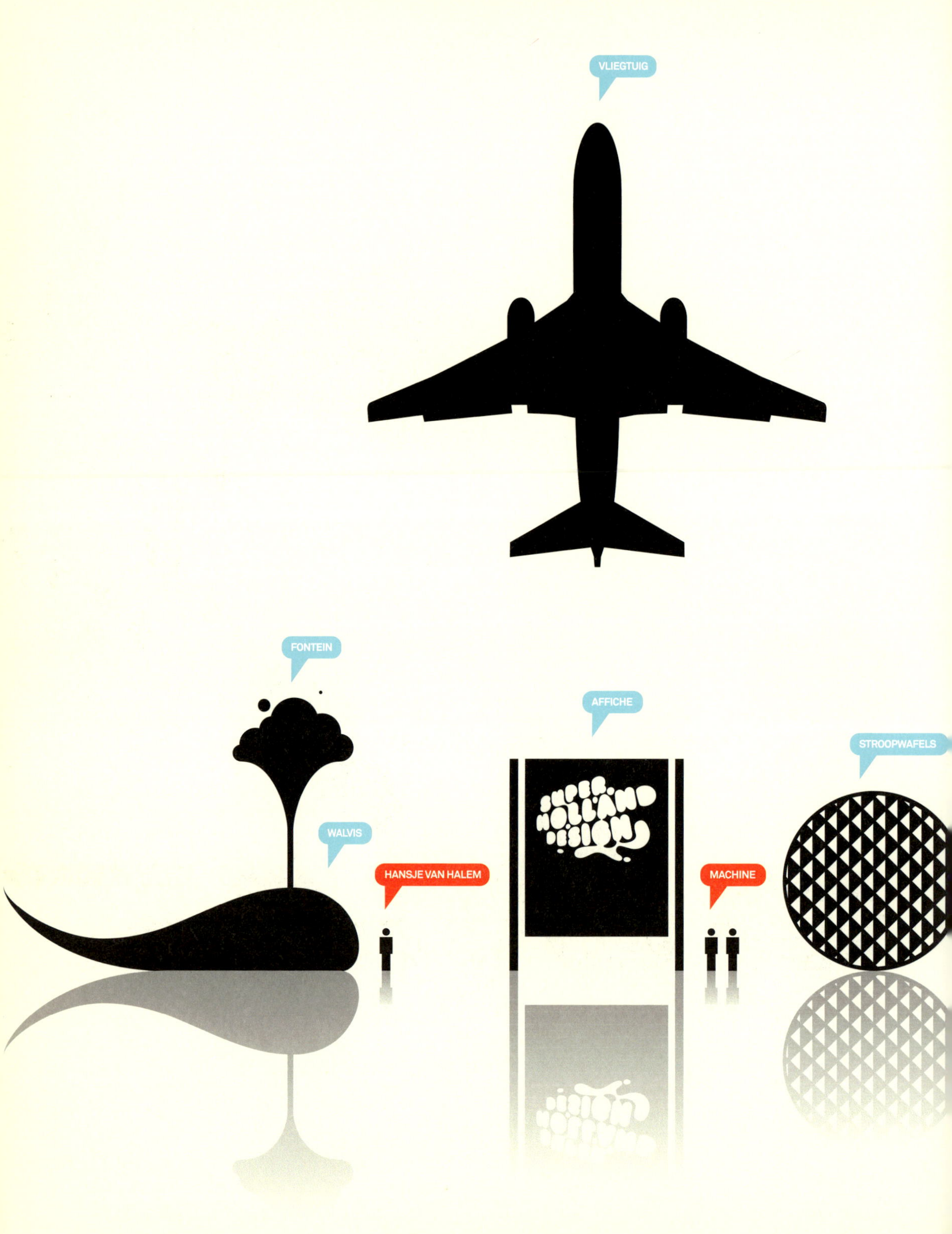

VLIEGTUIG
FONTEIN
AFFICHE
STROOPWAFELS
WALVIS
HANSJE VAN HALEM
MACHINE
SUPER HOLLAND DESIGN

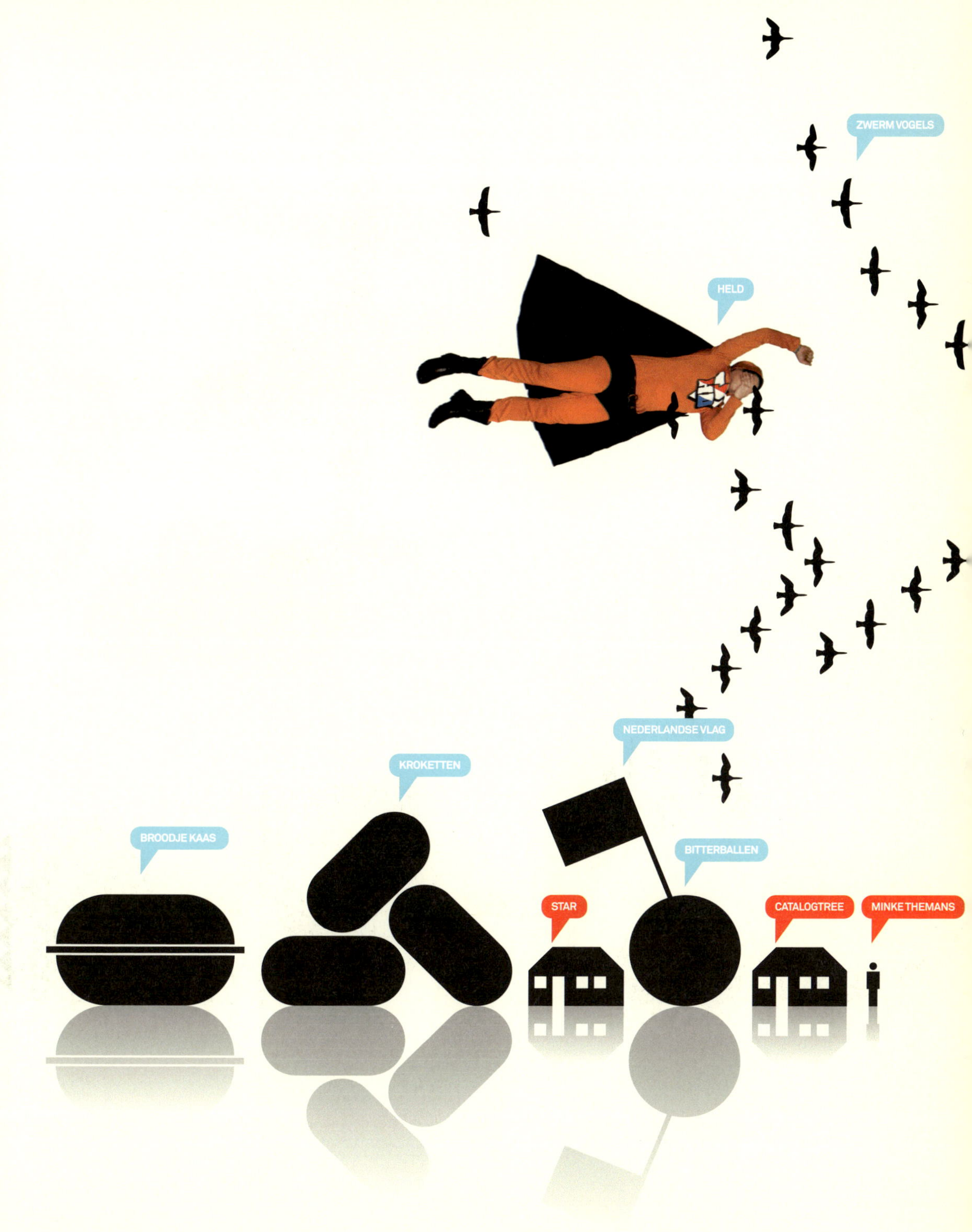
ZWERM VOGELS
HELD
NEDERLANDSE VLAG
KROKETTEN
BROODJE KAAS
BITTERBALLEN
STAR
CATALOGTREE
MINKE THEMANS

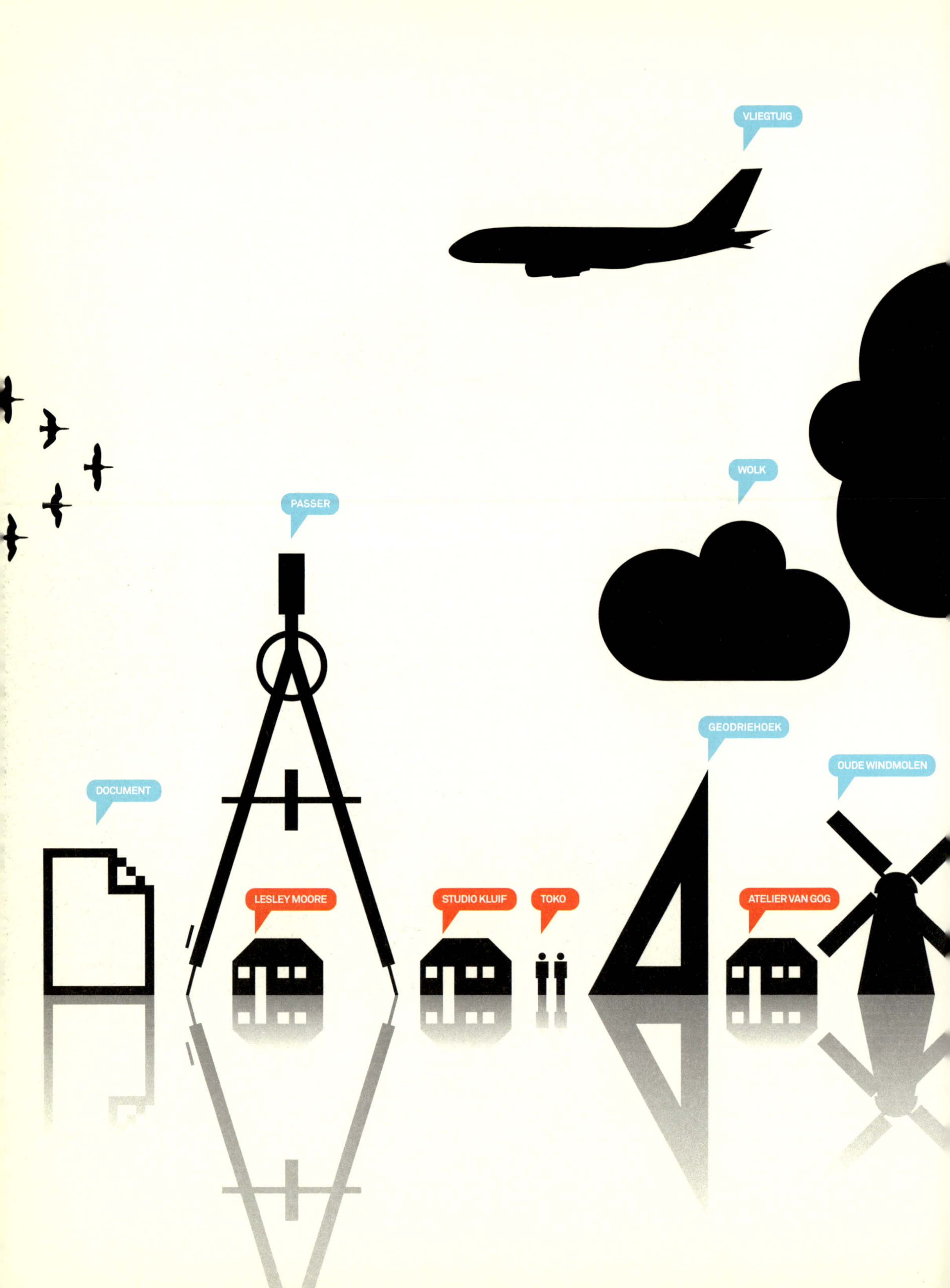
VLIEGTUIG
WOLK
PASSER
GEODRIEHOEK
OUDE WINDMOLEN
DOCUMENT
LESLEY MOORE
STUDIO KLUIF
TOKO
ATELIER VAN GOG

This book is the second volume of HD - Holland Design New Graphics, published in 2001.

Now, over six years later, our aim is to show the new functionality of graphic design and the new roles of graphic designers in contemporary Dutch design.

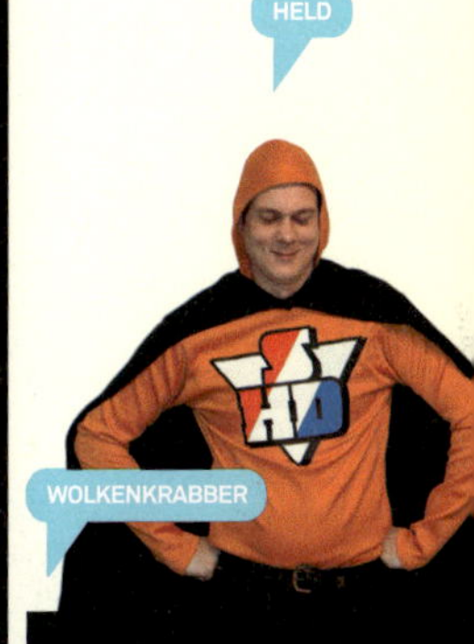

WOLK

Graphic design has specific functions, for example to satisfy a need or to remake something in a better way. In the creation of a poster, a book, or a website, the most basic function of graphic design is to organize information and communicate efficiently. But if we look more closely at the works of contemporary Dutch graphic designers, we discover that it is possible to design beyond traditional function. New Dutch designers are inspiring exciting interactions between design and its users, creating new ways of using design and compelling us to re-think the function or meaning of design itself. One of the strongest characteristics of graphic design from the Netherlands is the attitude of the designers: their ability to question every stage and aspect of design, to create new concepts, processes, formats and results, to push the limits of the user's participation and the graphic designer's role.

In many cases we have to look hard at the images, understand the stories behind them, read their meanings and what they ask us.

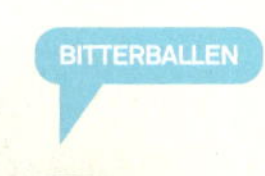

For example, when we look at the graphic images in the ‹Re-Mix› chapter we can identify many different visual sources such as shadow logos or photos in layers. But what is really combined here is not only figures and colours but also meaning, stories, our common sense or the background cultures, all of which call to mind many different images and narratives. And so, suddenly, we have a new way of looking at these. Similarly, in the ‹Drawing the Letters› we find a multitude of module-making and module-breaking experiments in the form of letter types. Quite apart from the variation of figures, there are so many different approaches to font design.

We can also point to the variety of ‹doubts› we have about design formats and media. In the ‹2D Space› chapter we find many three-dimensional concepts in 2D format, using computer graphics or perspectives, photos, or physical layers and cuts, while ‹Behave in Digital Language› shows that the fresh integration of digital and physical images matters. Nowadays we live in both, spending so much time in front of a computer screen and living in the physical world, and there are so many analogies between the two – essentially the virtual world follows the structure of analogical terms like the word ‹desktop›, the gravity-conscious movement of rendering and so on; so why then don't we follow the digital structure in the physical world? And in the ‹Instruction Manual› chapter, designers invite the users to become designers and design ‹how to› design more than designing itself. They let us re-think the way information is passed from emitter to receiver, and extend the possibilities of our media tools.

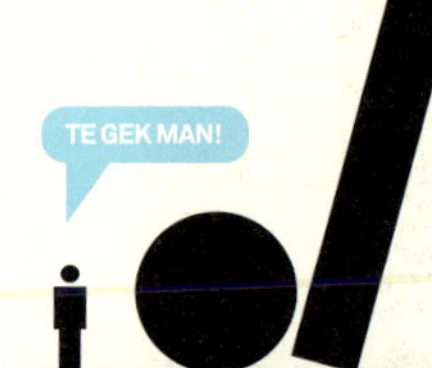

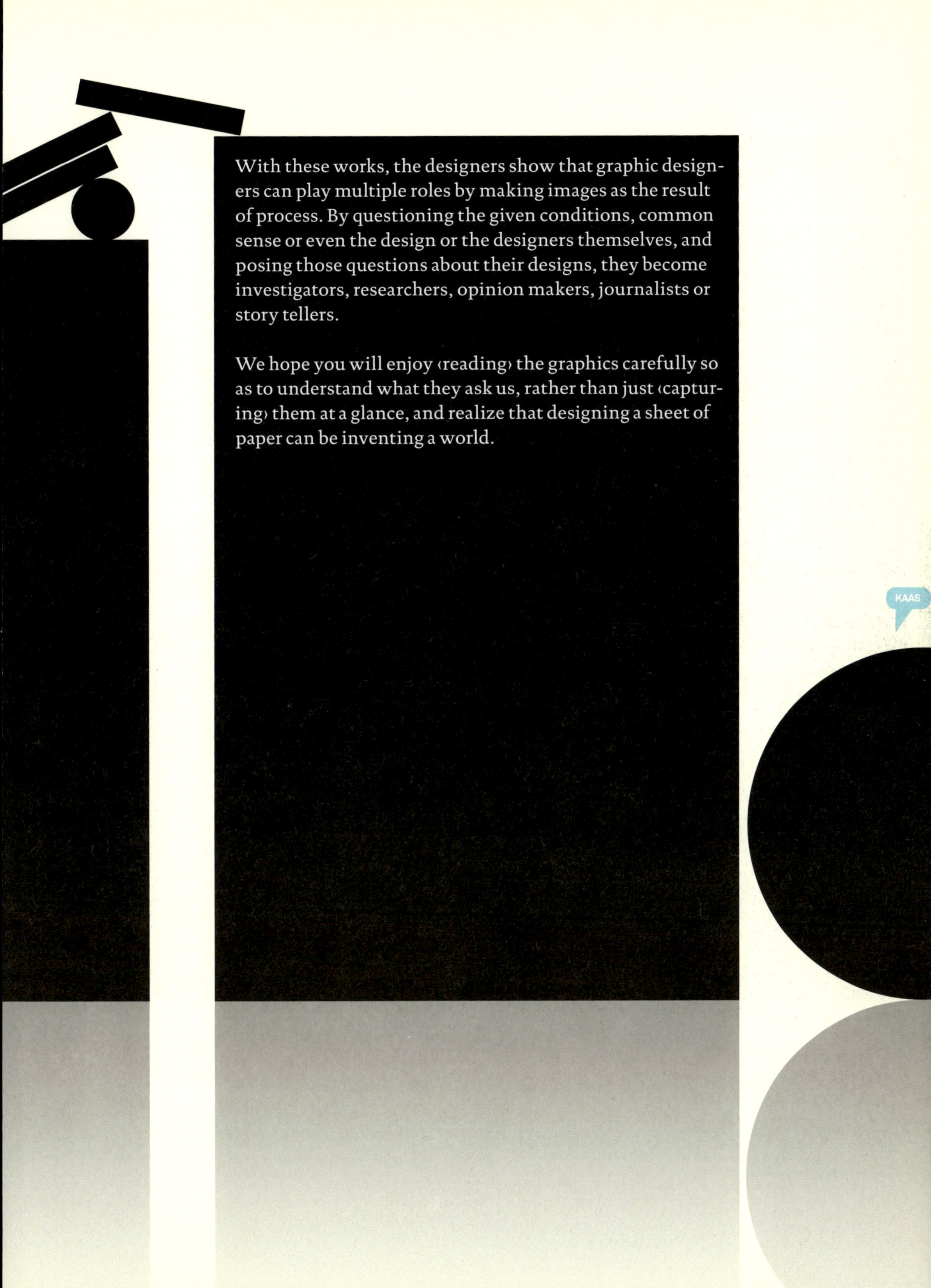

With these works, the designers show that graphic designers can play multiple roles by making images as the result of process. By questioning the given conditions, common sense or even the design or the designers themselves, and posing those questions about their designs, they become investigators, researchers, opinion makers, journalists or story tellers.

We hope you will enjoy ‹reading› the graphics carefully so as to understand what they ask us, rather than just ‹capturing› them at a glance, and realize that designing a sheet of paper can be inventing a world.

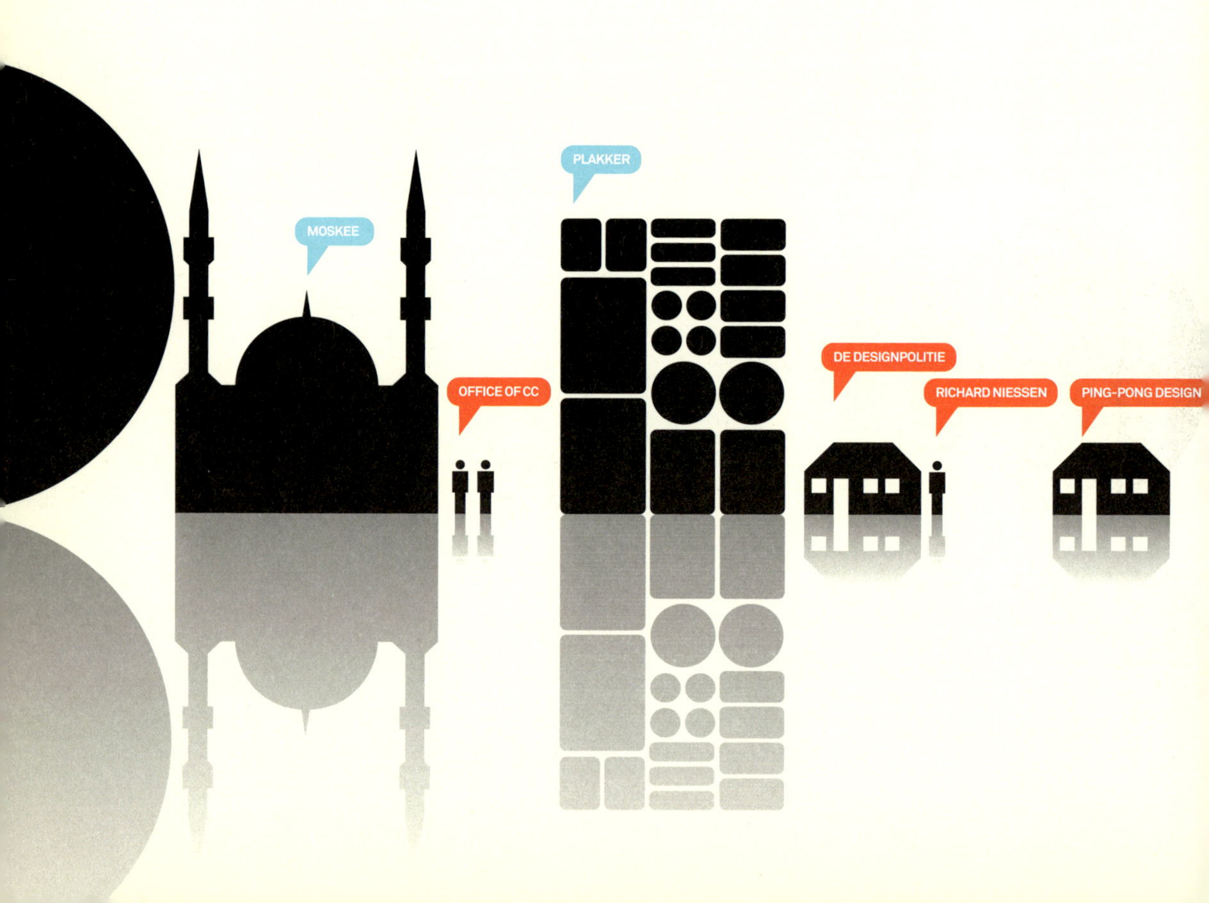
MOSKEE
PLAKKER
OFFICE OF CC
DE DESIGNPOLITIE
RICHARD NIESSEN
PING-PONG DESIGN

GANS

GEITENKAAS

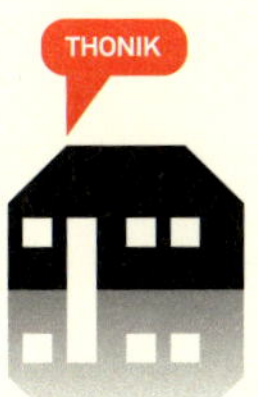
THONIK

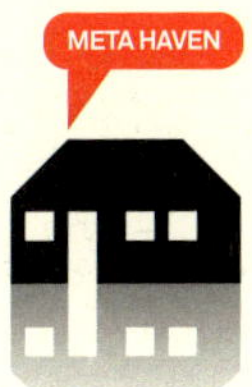
META HAVEN

Re-Mix

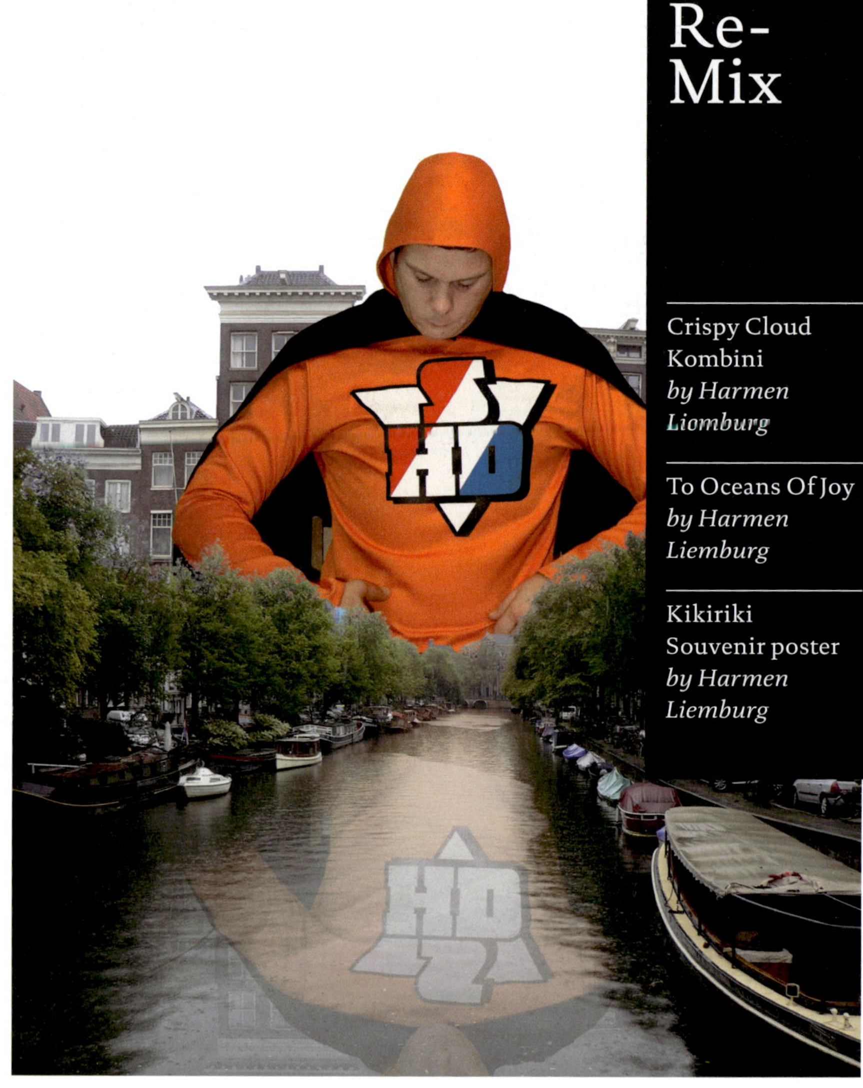

Crispy Cloud Kombini
by Harmen Liemburg

To Oceans Of Joy
by Harmen Liemburg

Kikiriki Souvenir poster
by Harmen Liemburg

The Recordshow
by Harmen Liemburg

Speed
by Harmen Liemburg

At Random
by Harmen Liemburg

Poster for the Nederlands Fotomuseum
by Ping-pong Design

PHS-manual
by Hans Gremmen

The Good Body
by Sander Plug

World Wide Westwijk
by Roger Teeuwen

Therapy Praful Pyramid
by Machine

Newrulez
by Studio Kluif

Five stationaries
by Richard Niessen

Outsiders
by Machine

Back-to-school-package
by Atelier Van GOG

Oh Pedro
by Arjan Groot & Julia Müller

A telling
by Ping-pong Design

BKOR
by Ping-pong Design

Concrete web magazine
by You & McCuskey

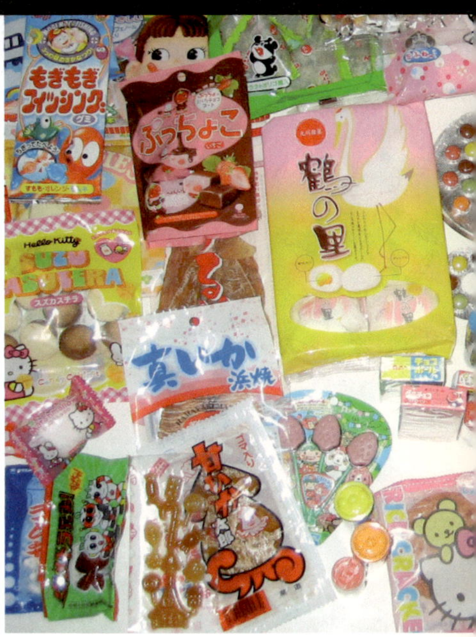

16 Crispy Cloud Kombini
by Harmen Liemburg

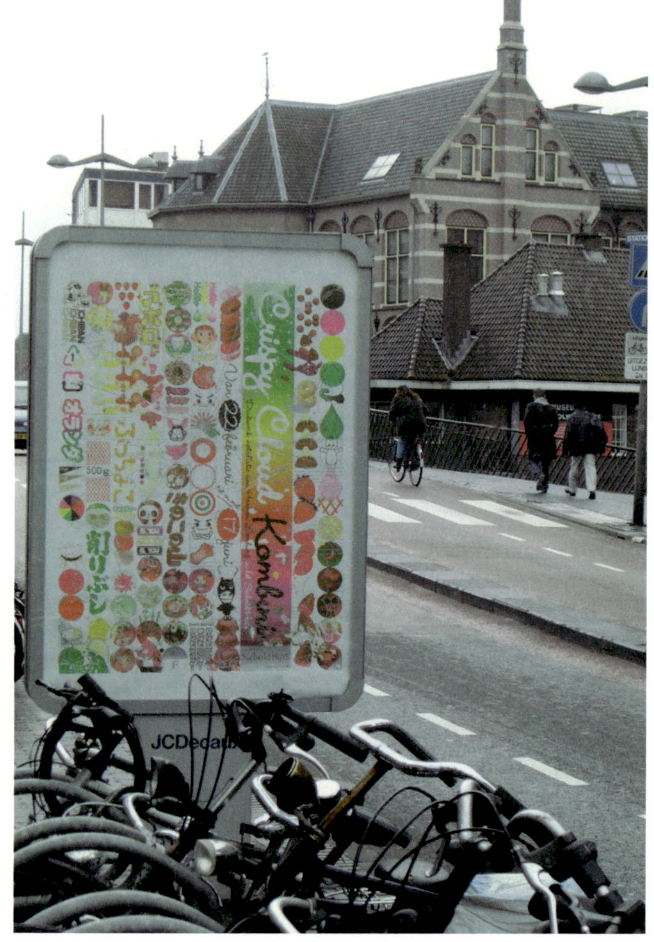

Poster on the street

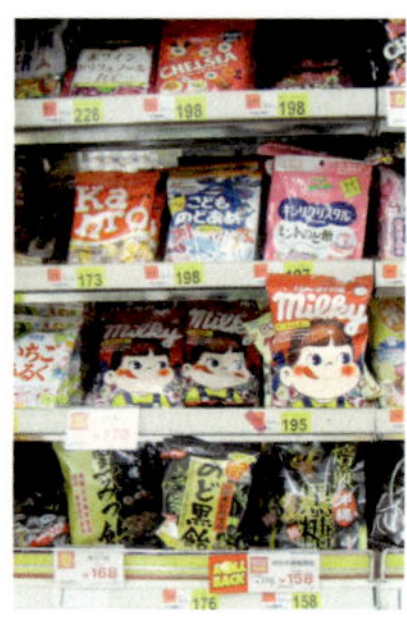

Sources

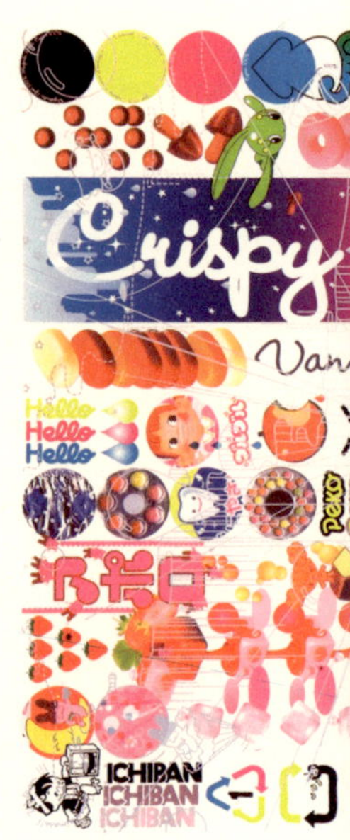

Sources

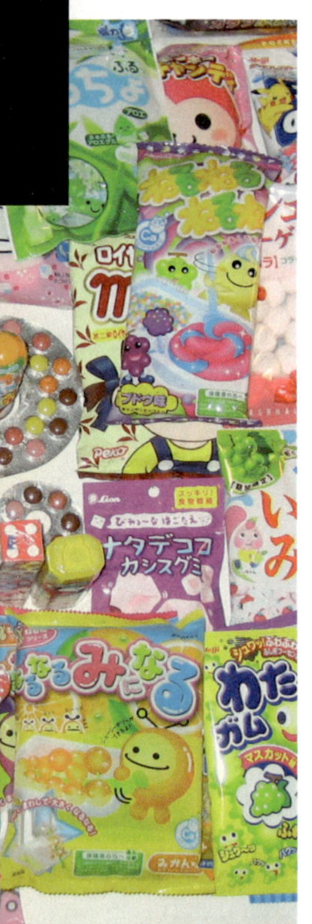

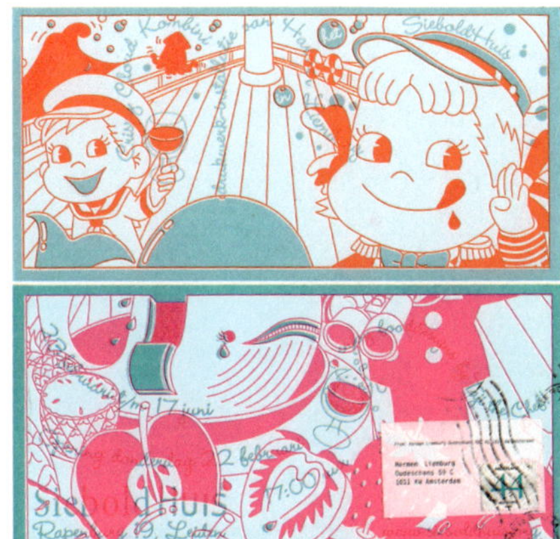

Invitation card

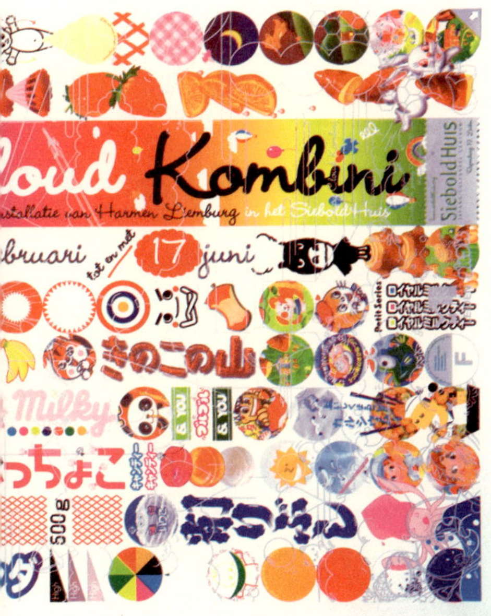

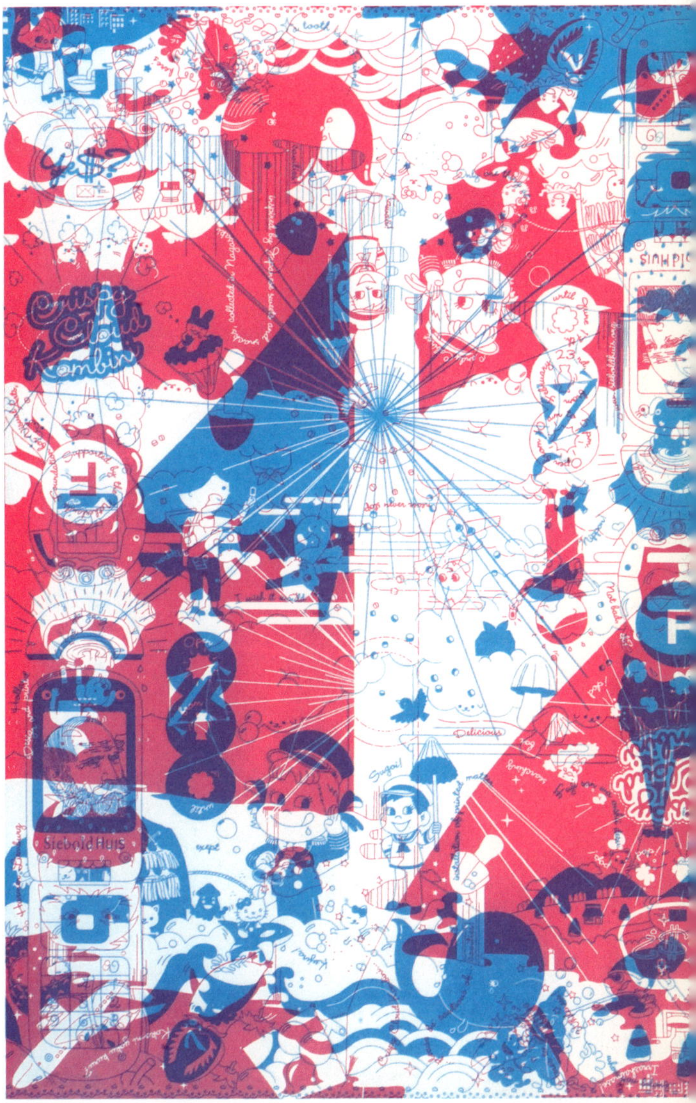

for SieboldHuis, Leiden, self-commissioned,
Silkscreen on various materials, Japanese sweets,
Print Wyber Zeefdruk,
Kees Maas, HL, 2007

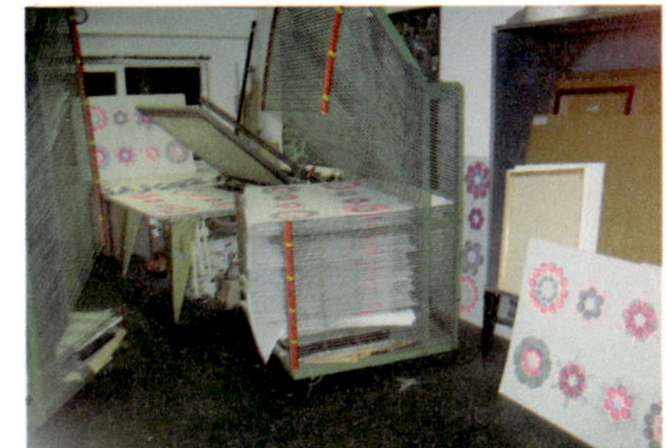

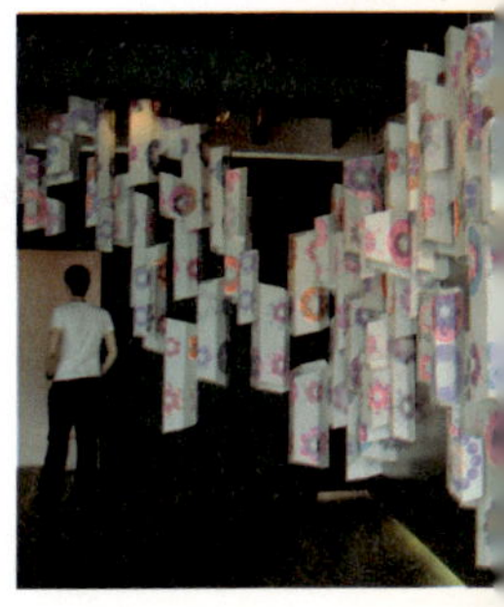

18 To Oceans Of Joy
by Harmen Liemburg

A tribute to American Vernacular, inspired by driving through the country. Collaboration-at-a-distance with the incredible ‹exit level› designer Edward Fella.

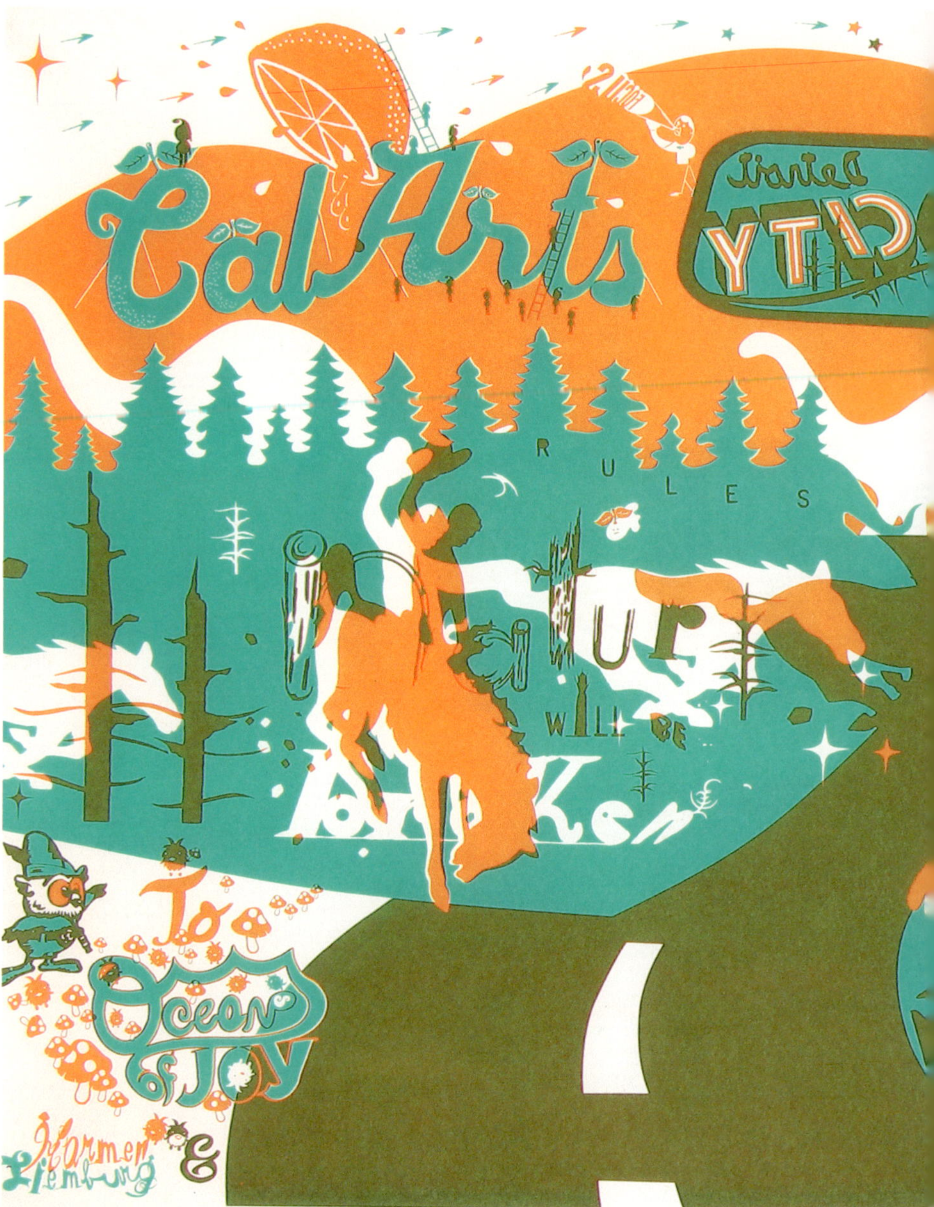

19 Kikiriki Souvenir poster
by Harmen Liemburg

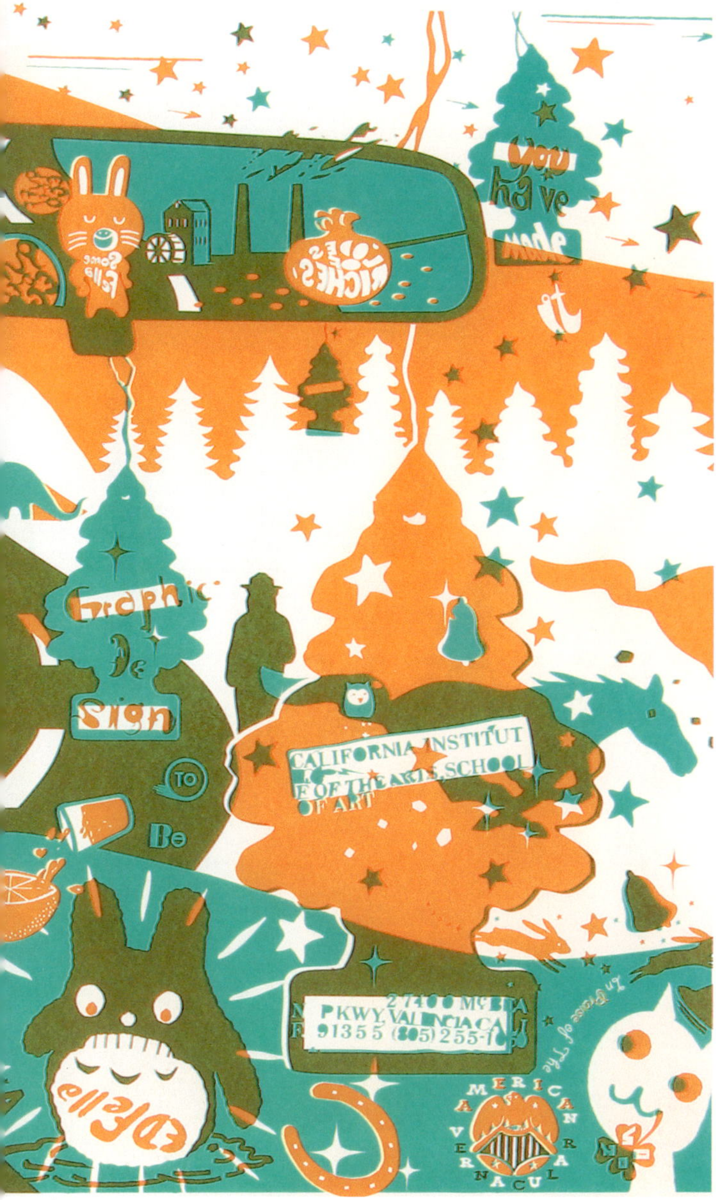

Size A0, Silkscreen, Edition of 50, signed & numbered, Lettering Ed Fella, 2005

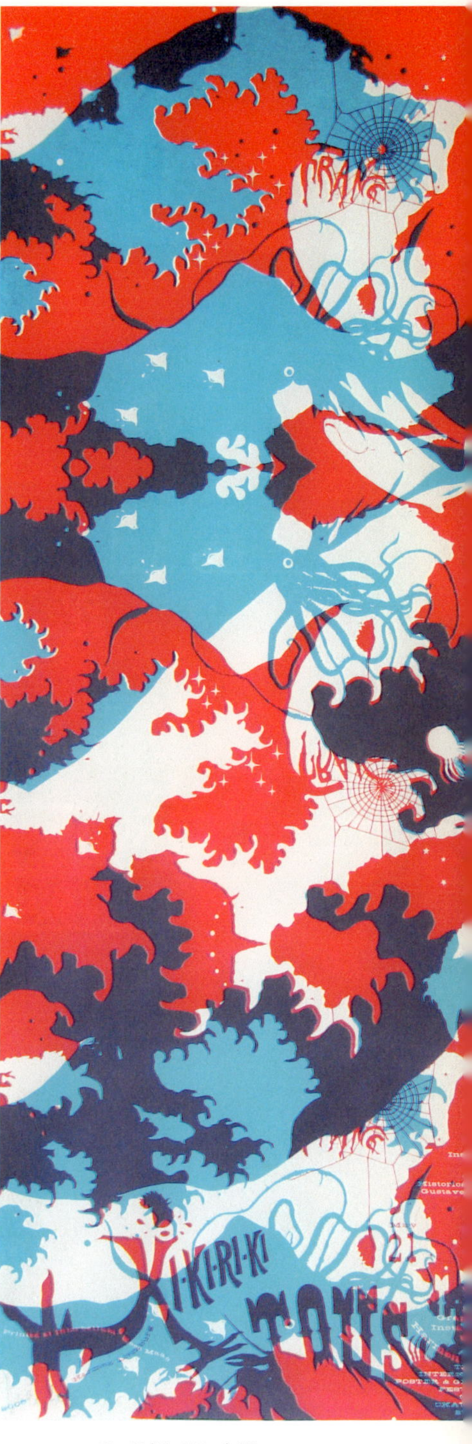

Size A0 (84 x 120 cm), Silkscreen, Imprint Signed & numbered edition of 75, 2005

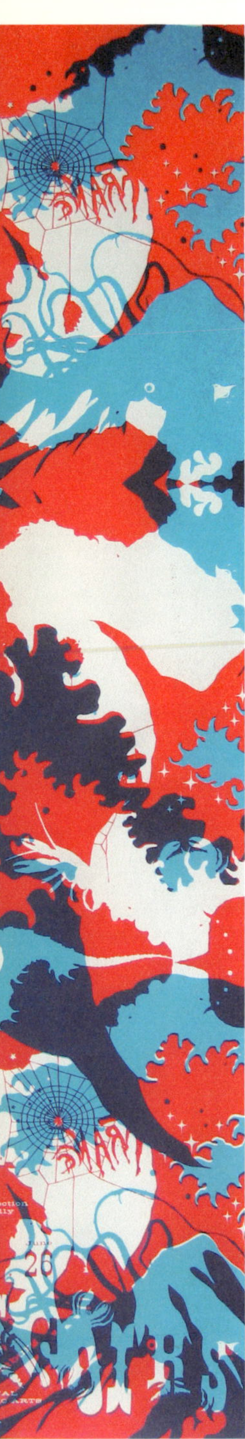

20 The Recordshow
by Harmen Liemburg

Poster for ‹The Recordshow›, a bi-monthly event in Minneapolis MN for music geeks. Inspiration came from the Spielberg movie ‹Close Encounters of the Third Kind›, ‹Taken› (a TV series about abduction by aliens), typical Midwest farms and, of course, the May Day parade…

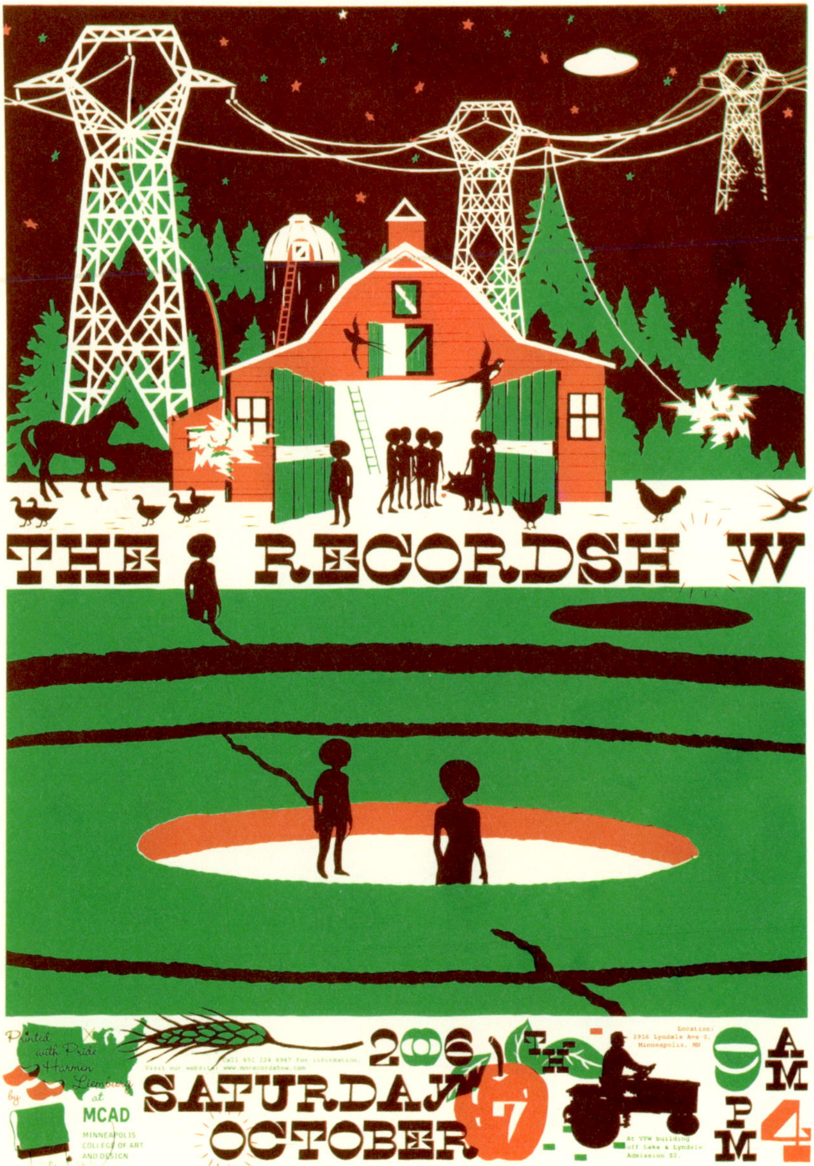

for The Recordshow, 101 x 70 cm, Silkscreen, Edition of 90, Print HL at MCAD, 2006

21 Speed
by Harmen Liemburg

Poster for Seeing Red, a group show in Honolulu on ‹contemporary issues›. After a road trip of 5,500 miles through the Northwest of the US in May, I was sick of all the dead and mutilated roadkill I had seen along the Highways and Byways...

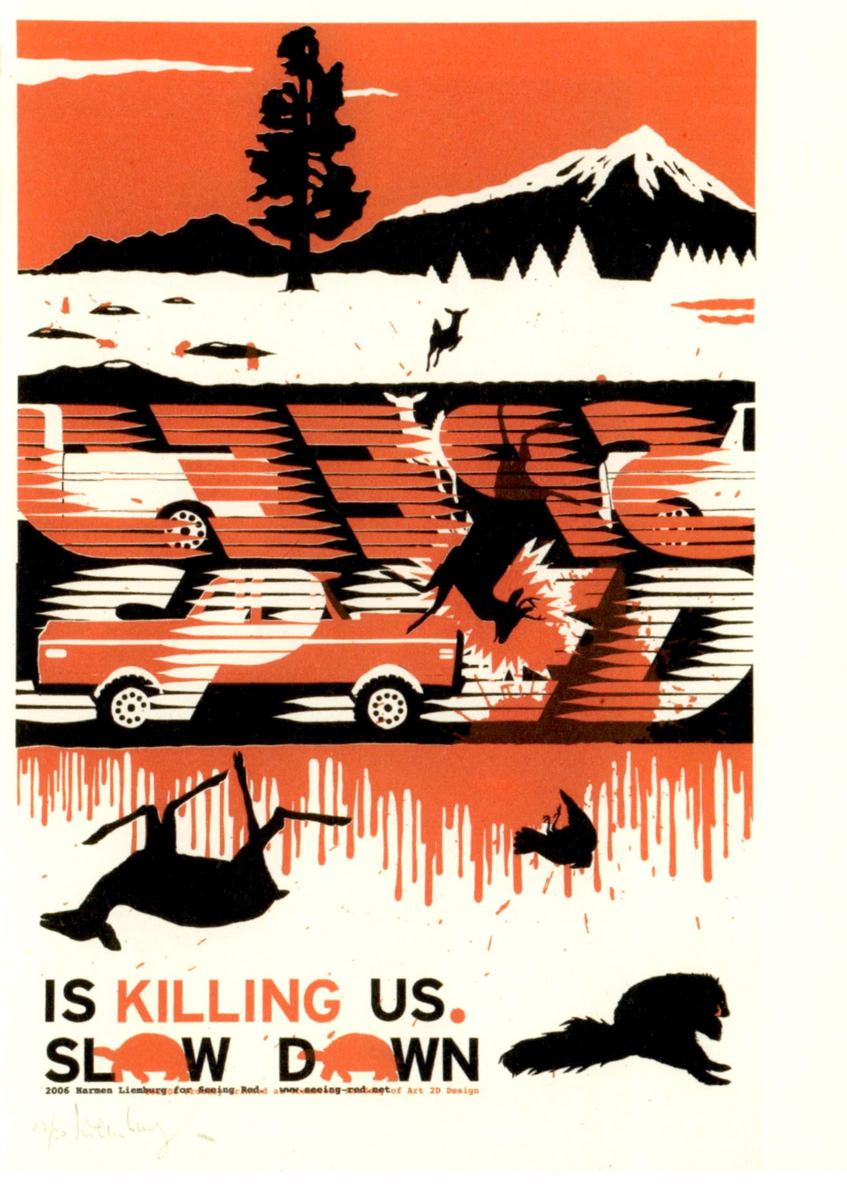

IS KILLING US.
SL W D WN
2006 Harmen Liemburg for Seeing Red. www.seeing-red.net

for Seeing Red, 101 x 70 cm, Silkscreen, Edition of 90,
Print HL at Cranbrook Academy of Art 2D Dept.

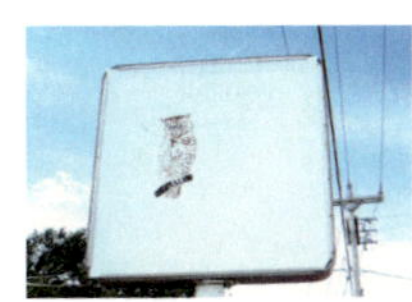

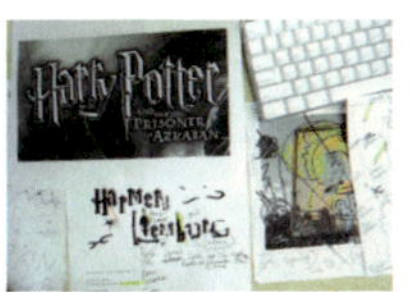

At Random
by Harmen Liemburg

Poster to announce my presentation at At Random No. 1 in Los Angeles, organised by Jon Sueda (Stripe) and Sean Donahue.

for At Random

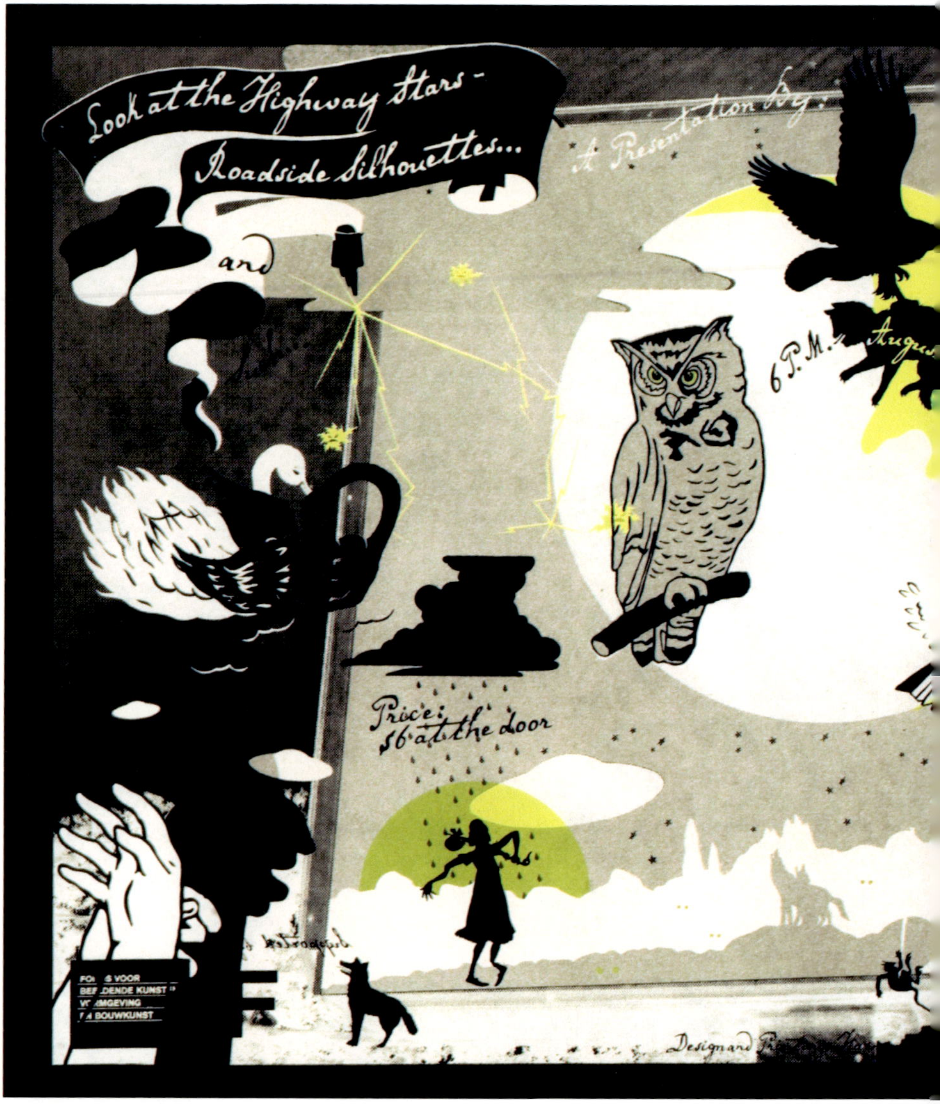

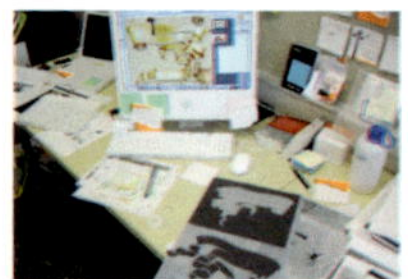
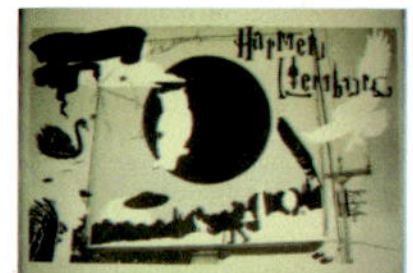
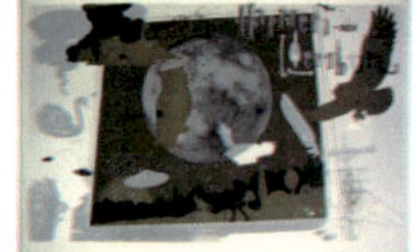
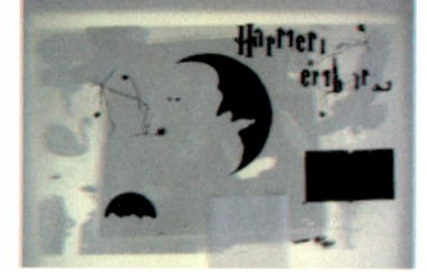
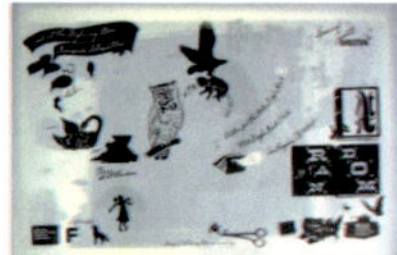

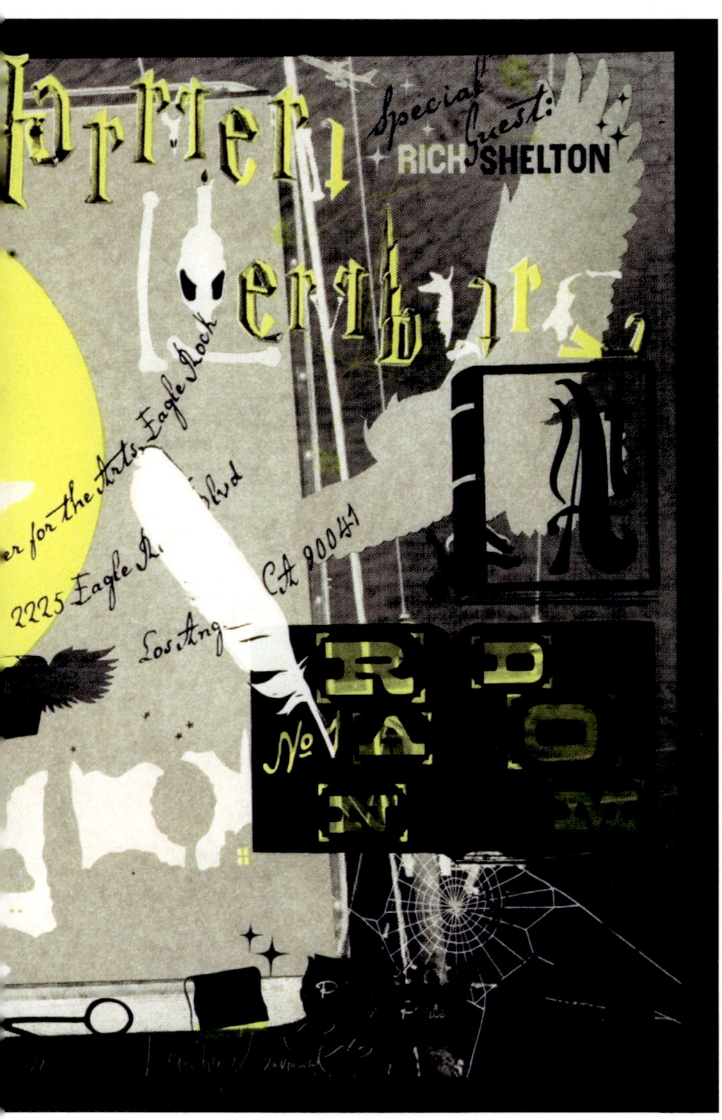

for At Random, self-commissioned,
70 x 101 cm, Silkscreen on black paper, 2006

24 Poster series for the Nederlands Fotomuseum in Las Palmas
by Ping-pong Design

The Dutch photo museum houses the most complete collection of photography in the Netherlands. For the opening campaign Ping-pong selected 10 typical photographs from this collection. The ‹simmering› of different images is the museum's visual signature.

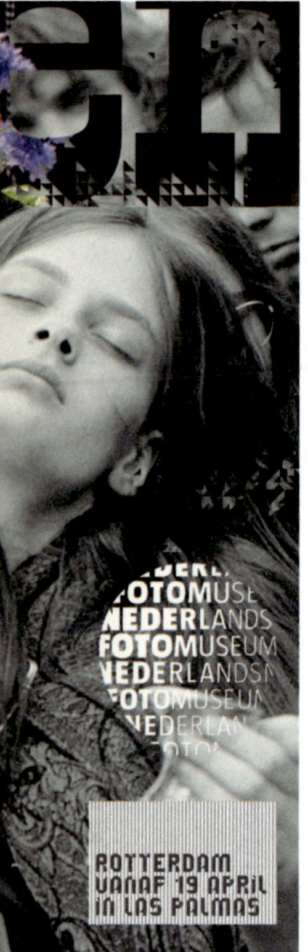

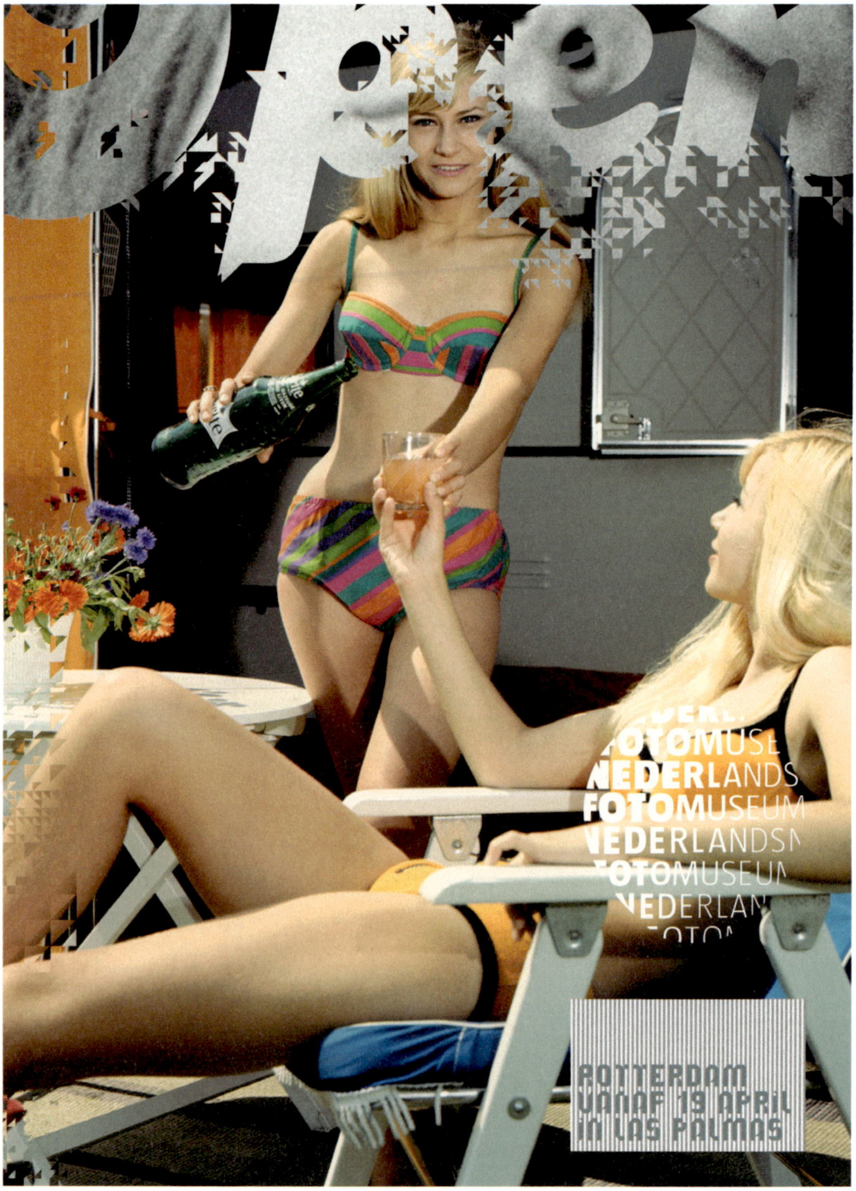

for Nederlands Fotomuseum (Rotterdam), 2007.

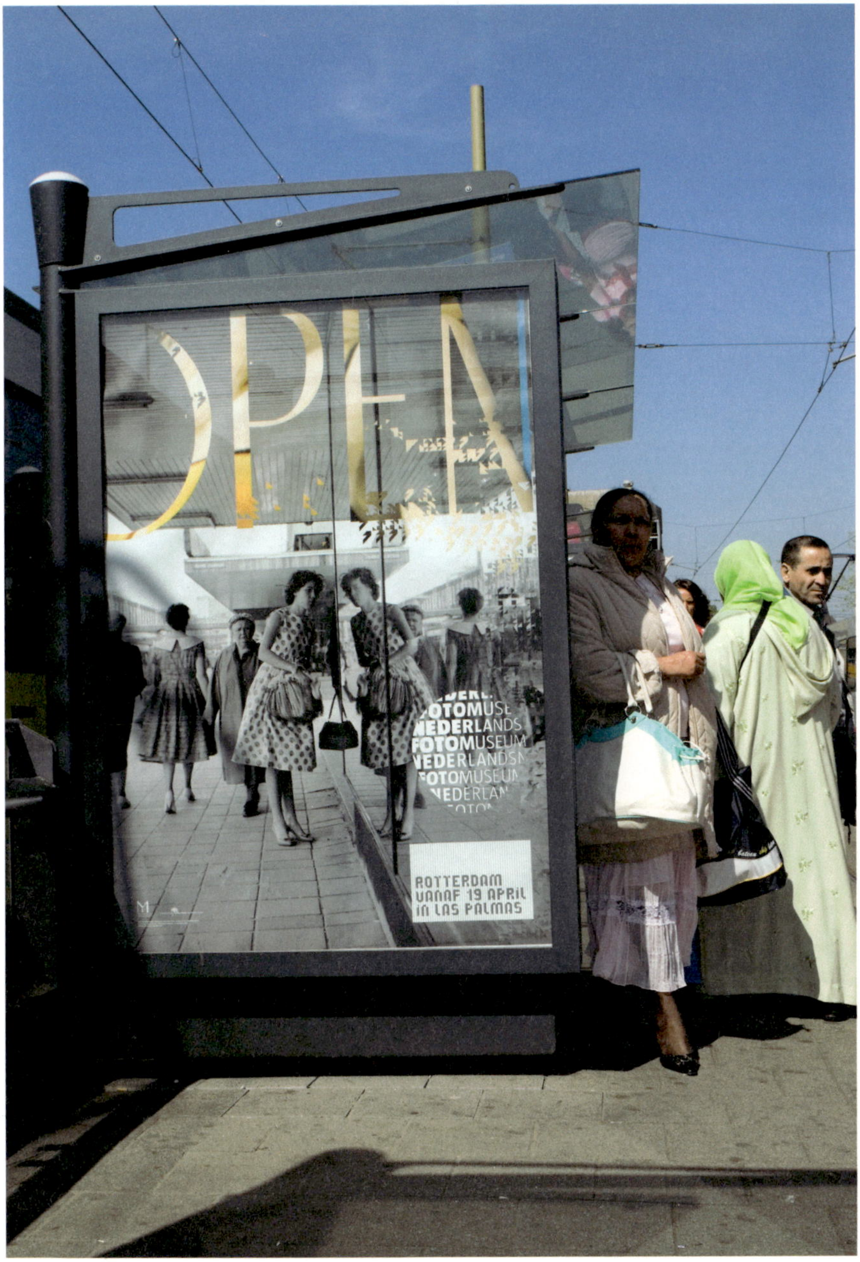

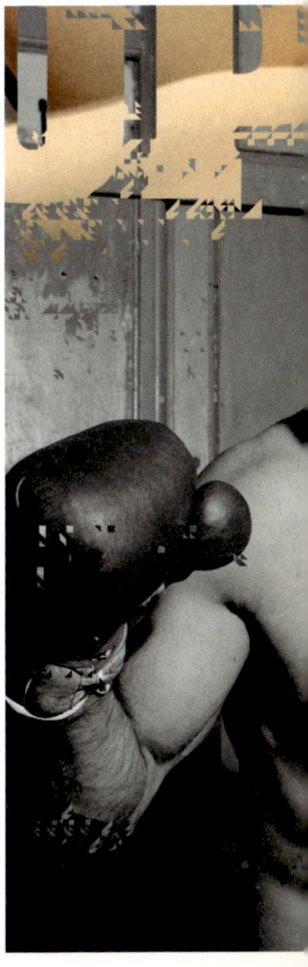

PHS-manual
by Hans Gremmen

Techniques are changing rapidly now that we all use computers. Since we hardly use film in our cameras any more, the darkroom has made way for the laptop, but the tools in Photoshop mostly refer to their original source, such as a hand, a pipette, scissors, etc. Two worlds of technique merge into one. Here I overprinted an ‹old› book that explained how to develop and print photos with a Photoshop manual to illustrate this.

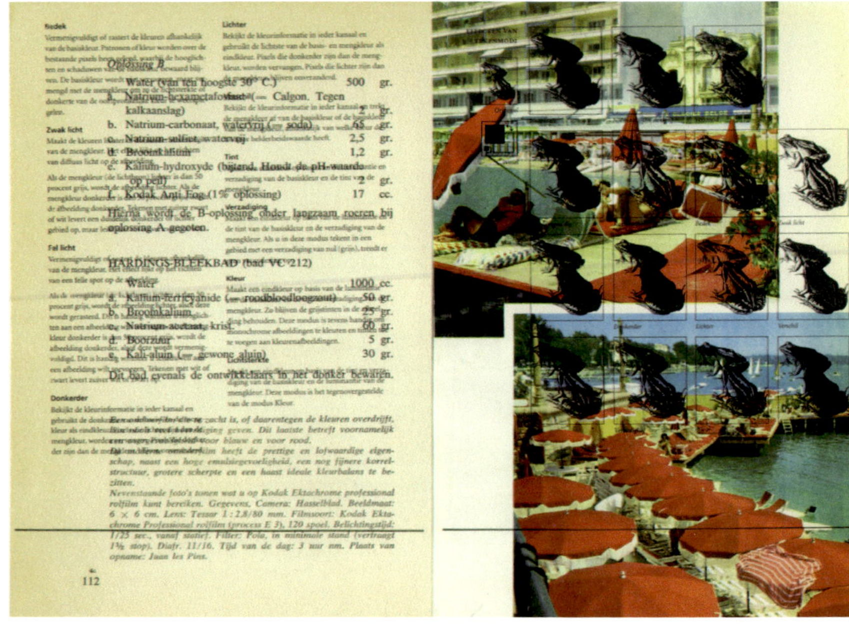

Oplossing B

	Water (van ten hoogste 30° C.)	500	gr.
a.	Natrium-hexametafosfaat (= Calgon. Tegen kalkaanslag)	2	gr.
b.	Natrium-carbonaat, watervrij (= soda)	65	gr.
c.	Natrium-sulfiet, watervrij	2,5	gr.
d.	Broomkalium	1,2	gr.
e.	Kalium-hydroxyde (bijtend. Houdt de pH-waarde op peil)	2	gr.
f.	Kodak Anti Fog (1% oplossing)	17	cc.

Hierna wordt de B-oplossing onder langzaam roeren bij oplossing A gegoten.

HARDINGS-BLEEKBAD (bad VC 212)

	Water	1000	cc.
a.	Kalium-ferricyanide (= roodbloedloogzout)	50	gr.
b.	Broomkalium	25	gr.
c.	Natrium-acetaat, krist.	60	gr.
d.	Boorzuur	5	gr.
e.	Kali-aluin (= gewone aluin)	30	gr.

Dit bad evenals de ontwikkelaars in het donker bewaren.

... zacht is, of daarentegen de kleuren overdrijft, ... ging geven. Dit laatste betreft voornamelijk ... voor blauw en voor rood. ... film heeft de prettige en lofwaardige eigenschap, naast een hoge emulsiegevoeligheid, een nog fijnere korrelstructuur, grotere scherpte en een haast ideale kleurbalans te bezitten.

Nevenstaande foto's tonen wat u op Kodak Ektachrome professional rolfilm kunt bereiken. Gegevens. Camera: Hasselblad. Beeldmaat: 6 × 6 cm. Lens: Tessar 1 : 2,8/80 mm. Filmsoort: Kodak Ektachrome Professional rolfilm (process E 3), 120 spoel. Belichtingstijd: 1/25 sec., vanaf statief. Filter: Pola, in minimale stand (vertraagt 1½ stop). Diafr. 11/16. Tijd van de dag: 3 uur nm. Plaats van opname: Juan les Pins.

112

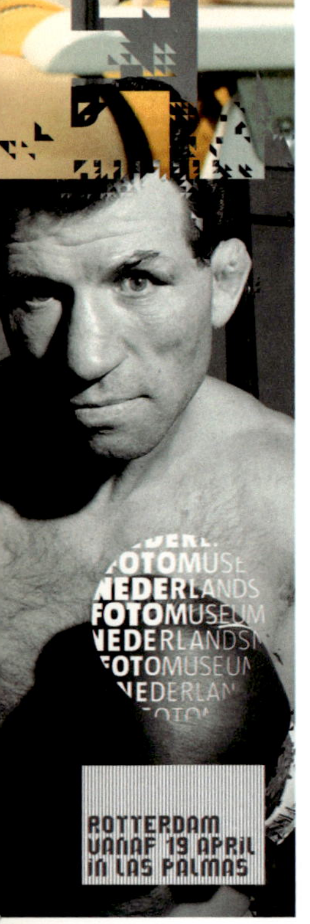

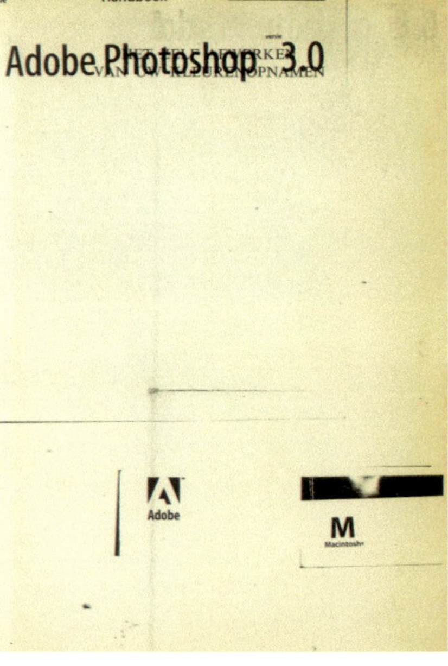

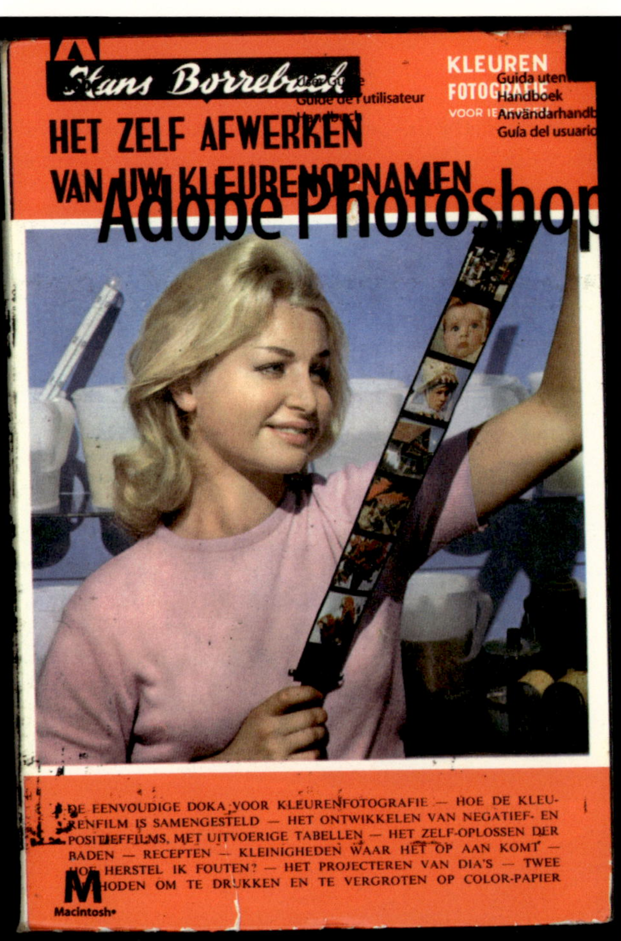

Zo kiest u een andere werkschijf

Beide laatste baden tasten wel het gecombineerd zilverbeeld, doch niet de kleurbeelden aan.

Het resultaat

Hiermee zijn we met grote stappen tot het uiteindelijk, goed-doorzichtig negatiefbeeld gekomen. Waarin alles wat blauw was, zich geel heeft ontwikkeld. Wat groen was, magenta is geworden en al wat rood is geweest, zich omgezet heeft tot de complementaire kleur: cyaan.
We zullen even aan deze voor ons oog ongewone kleurcombinatie moeten wennen. Inzoverre we vroeger niet reeds meerdere malen met zo'n brokje wereld-in-complementaire-kleuren werden geconfronteerd en dus weten hoe het strand, de fiets en de-kat-van-buurman er „in negatief" uitzien.

Voorkeuren voor transparantie instellen

Zelf de baden bereiden, of ontwikkel-kits kopen?

Wat het oplossen van de voor het ontwikkelen benodigde baden betreft, kunnen we twee wegen gaan. Of we maken zelf onze baden, of we kopen kant-en-klare kits.
Daar dit laatste ons — vooral in 't begin — wat betere ruggesteun en daarbij meerdere zekerheid geeft, zullen we het oplossen van de door de fabrikant samengestelde ontwikkel-kits, het eerst bespreken.

HET GEREEDSCHAPSPALET GEBRUIKEN

De mogelijkheid om daarvan gebruik te maken, beperkt zich echter tot die filmsoorten, waarvan het ontwikkelen van de film en het drukken op papier, voor de amateur zijn vrijgegeven.
In dit verband, durf ik wel te voorspellen, dat — waar dit nog niet is gebeurd — het vrijgeven van de voor 't ontwikkelen en drukken benodigde chemicaliën, toch binnen afzienbare tijd zal geschieden.

In noodgeval

U zoudt zich in noodgeval „voorlopig" kunnen beperken, door voor uw lievelingsmateriaal waarvan de bewerking

30

nog niet is vrijgegeven, andere en gelijkwaardige ontwikkelsets te kopen. Of — wanneer u er de gelegenheid en de juist toe heeft — de daarvoor benodigde baden „volgens verpakkingsrecept" klaar te maken.
In het uiterste geval, wanneer u coûte que coûte zèlf wilt ontwikkelen en drukken, kies dan een filmsoort waarvan u de ontwikkelvergen en -kits zonder meer kunt krijgen. Drukken kunt u altijd nog op een color-papier van ander fabrikaat.

Let op de juiste volgorde der op te lossen stoffen

Een algemene regel bij het oplossen van chemicaliën is, dat dit in de volgorde van het recept moet gebeuren.
Dit voorschrift is er niet voor niets. Het komt nl. vaak voor, dat een bepaalde toe te voegen stof zich niet, of slechts moeilijk oplossen laat in twee of meer, reeds eerder opgeloste stoffen, uit 't zelfde recept. In dat geval geeft men zo'n stof „voorrang" en wordt deze dus eerder vermeld.
Bij het oplossen van kant-en-klare kits, wordt het ons al heel gemakkelijk gemaakt. Alle zich daarin bevindende verpakkingen zijn van de naam van het betreffende bad voorzien en genummerd. Ook hier houdt men de aldus aangegeven volgorde bij het oplossen aan.

Oplossen in warm, maar niet te heet water

U lost bij voorkeur niet op in koud water, maar in water-op-temperatuur. Deze temperatuur zal — behoudens afwijkend voorschrift — zo om en nabij de 30° C. bedragen.
Sommige stoffen (Borax bijv.) lossen beter in heet water op, maar er zijn weer andere stoffen (Natriumsulfiet, Kaliumsulfiet, enz.) die géén hoge temperatuur verdragen. Zij reageren, door geheel of ten dele onwerkzaam te worden.

Storende kalkaanslag

Vaak is ons leidingwater sterk kalkhoudend. Dit demon-

31

The Good Body
by Sander Plug

The stage play ‹The Good Body› is the follow up to ‹The Vagina Monologues› by the American writer Eve Ensler. Having talked about the vagina, it's time to talk about all the other insecurities of the female body.

for Bos Theaterproducties, 2006

Photography: Jouk Oosterhof
Post production: Fisk Imaging
Award: Silver Lamp ADCN, 2006

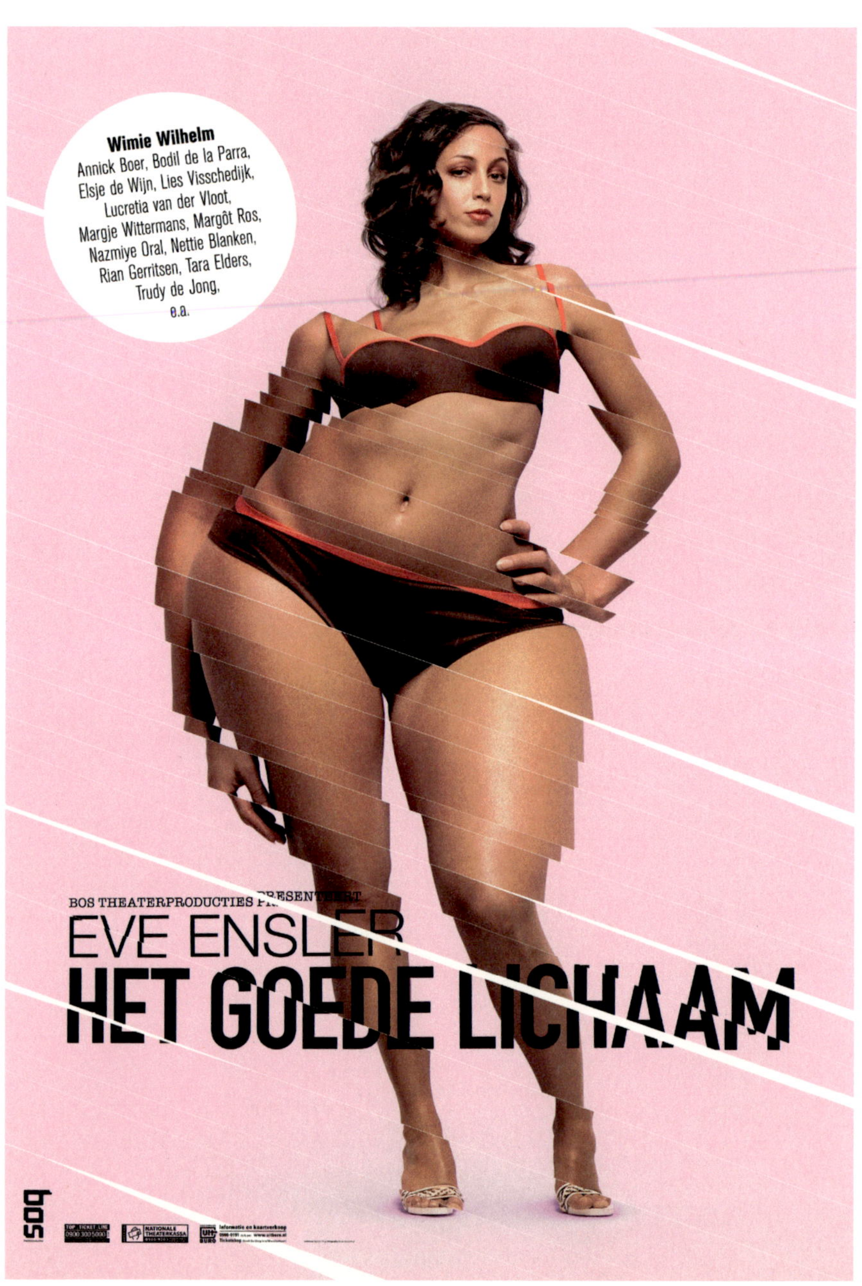

29 World Wide Westwijk
by Roger Teeuwen

‹World Wide Westwijk› is an interactive portrait of the Westwijk neighbourhood in Vlaardingen (NL) developed by artist Peter Westenberg. The project consists of several different parts; in one, a local resident is interviewed and proposes a subject for the next interview.

Publication

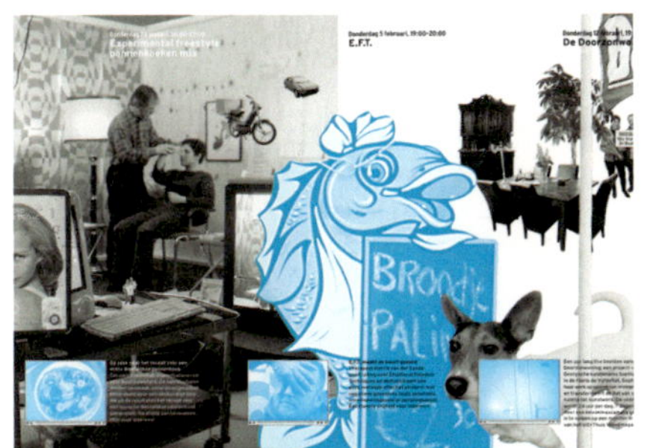

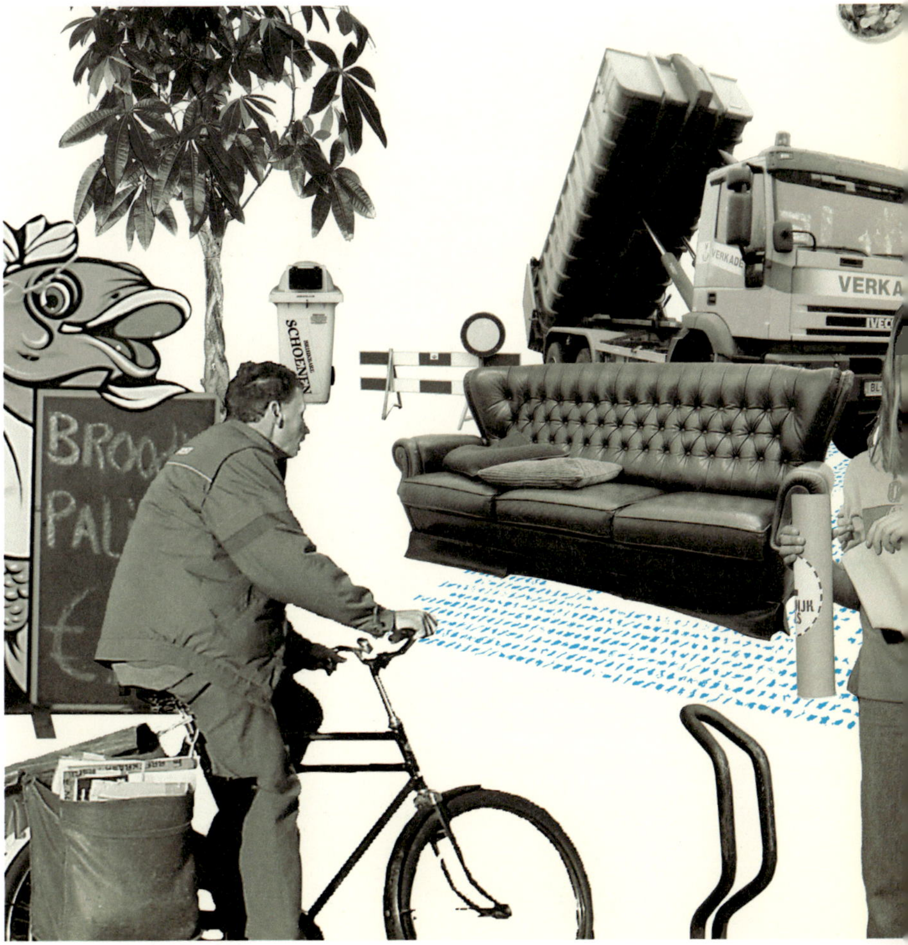

The publication was organised afterwards to document the project. The project was executed with various media, using the website as the podium for the project while it was in progress. On the website, the idea of a living space (represented by a neighbourhood) is visualised as a ‹carpet› like a tapestry, made up of the shapes of all the nations of the world. The carpet is the base layer, on top of which cut-out elements of the neighbourhood are placed. Each figure is represented by a story, and by selecting one story the whole storyline becomes visible. It was deliberately decided not to make a visual connection between the figure and the story. In this way the site appears random and simulates a stroll through the neighbourhood with incidental encounters with it's inhabitants. The publication is a fixed representation of the site in which situations were constructed that could actually exist: an experiment on how reality could and can be captured.

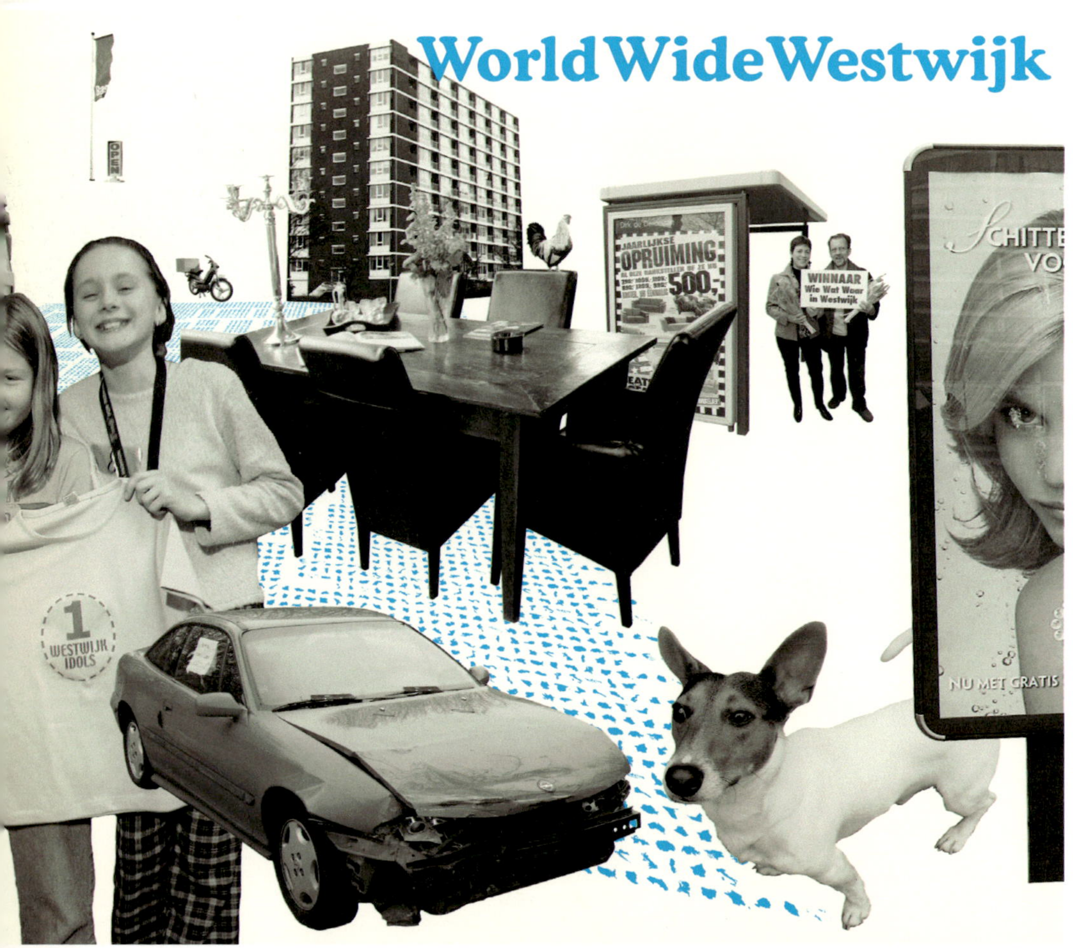

31 Therapy Praful Pyramid
by Machine

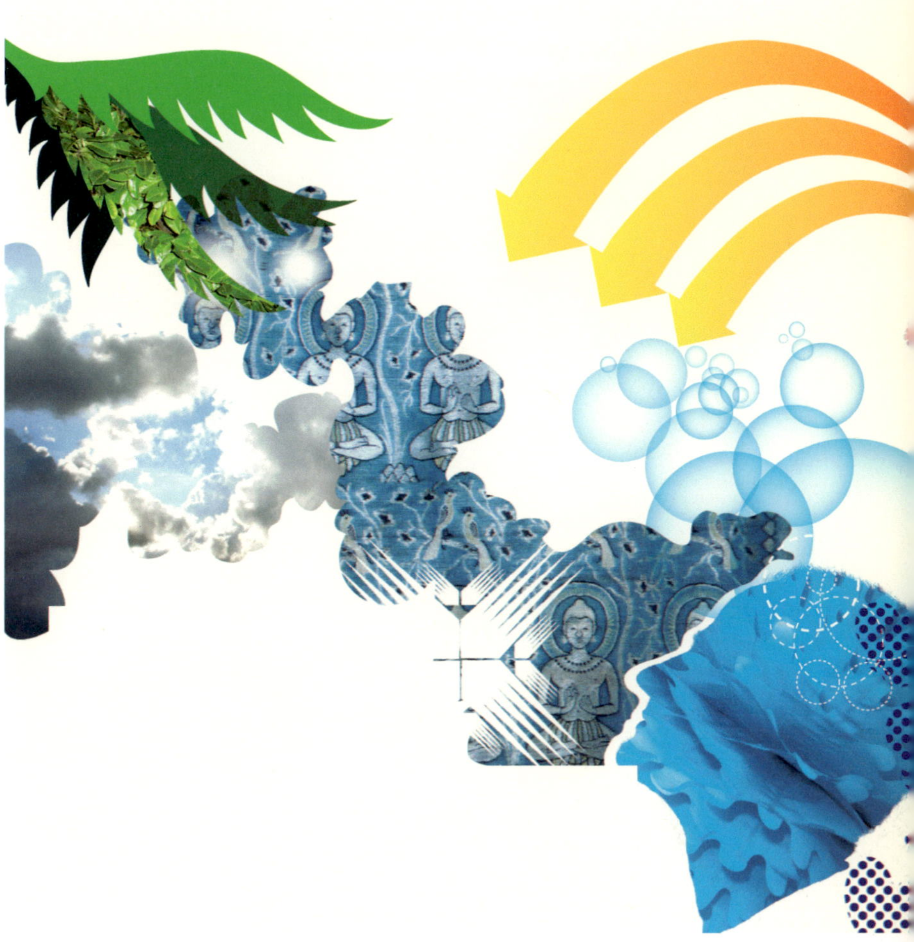

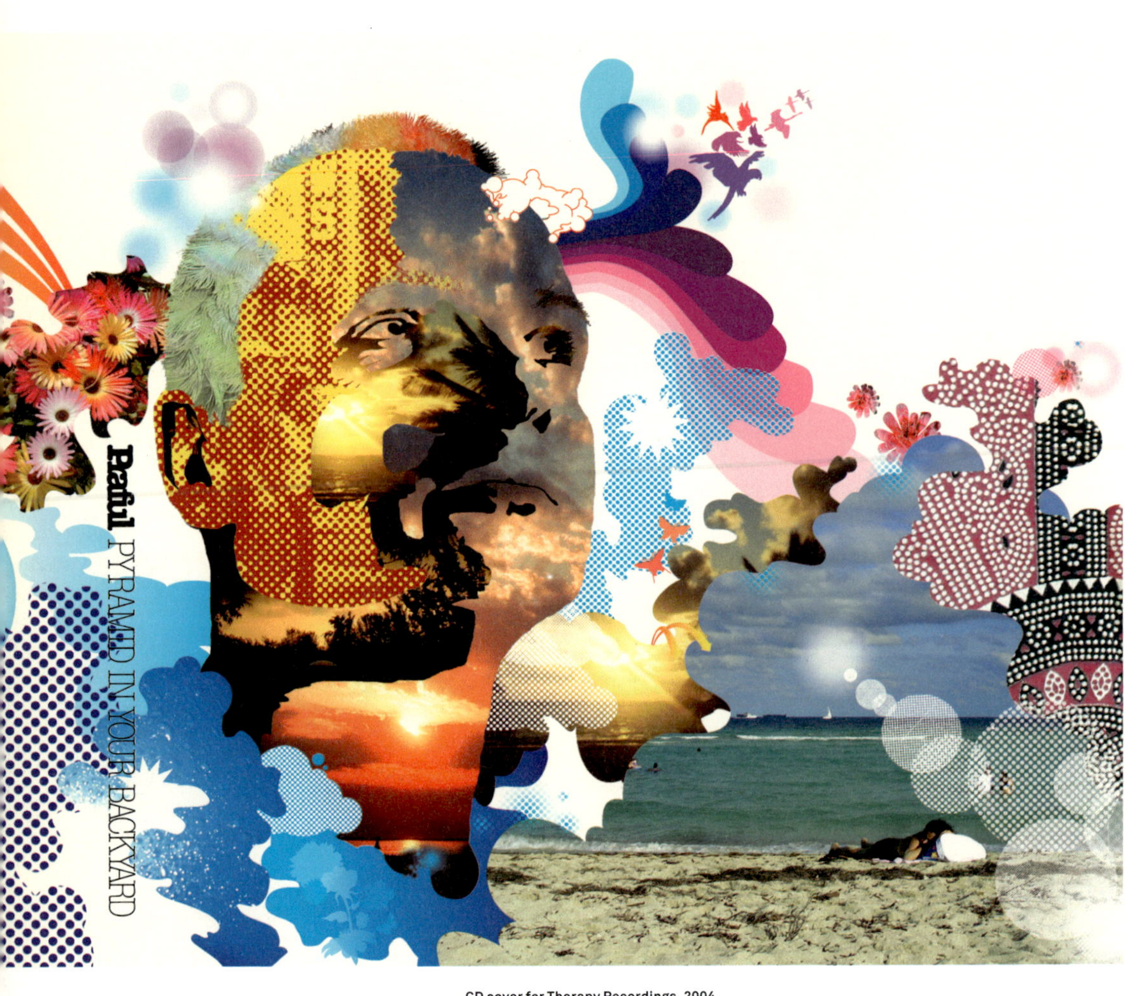

CD cover for Therapy Recordings, 2004

33 Newrulez
by Studio Kluif

Corporate identity for a publisher with a strong focus on youth culture. Kluif designed a ‹zap-mentality› illustration that is used on the back of all stationery items. Nominated for the Netherlands Design Awards 2005.

for Newrulez,
The Netherlands, 2005

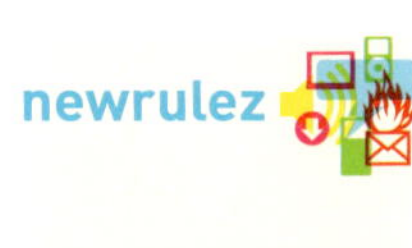

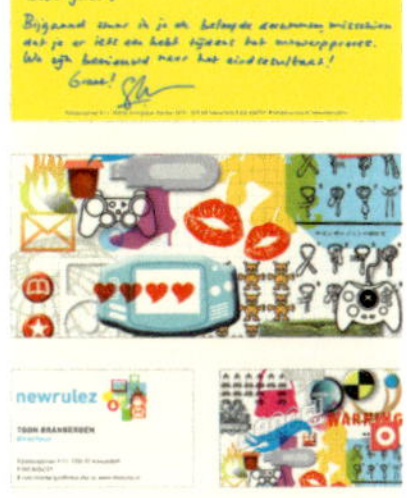

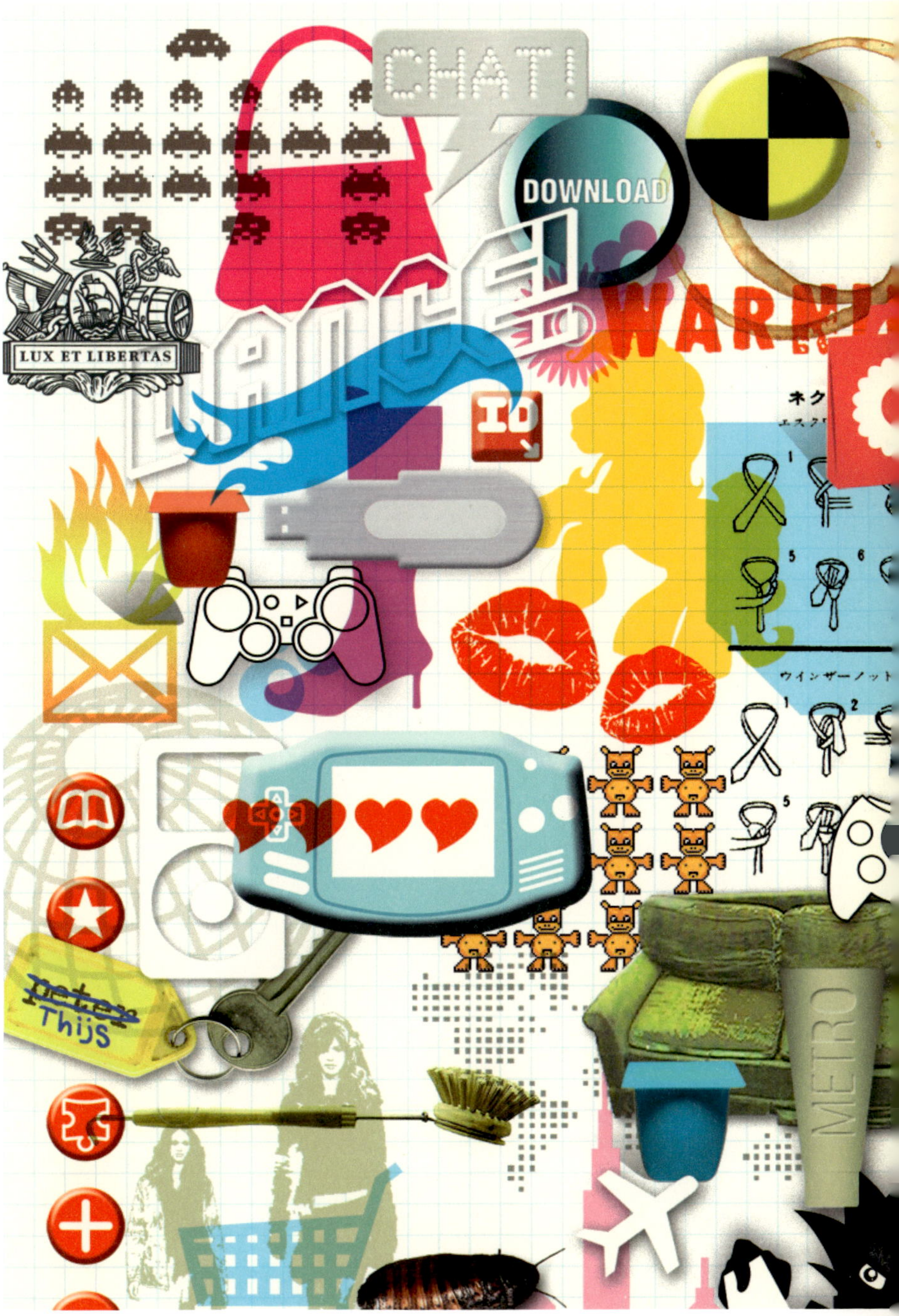

Five stationaries

by Richard Niessen

That spring I was working on five stationeries at once, for Jennifer Tee, Esther de Vries, Joost Vermeulen, Raoul de Thouars and myself. The stationeries were all printed at the same time and their design is based on the same arabesque elements.

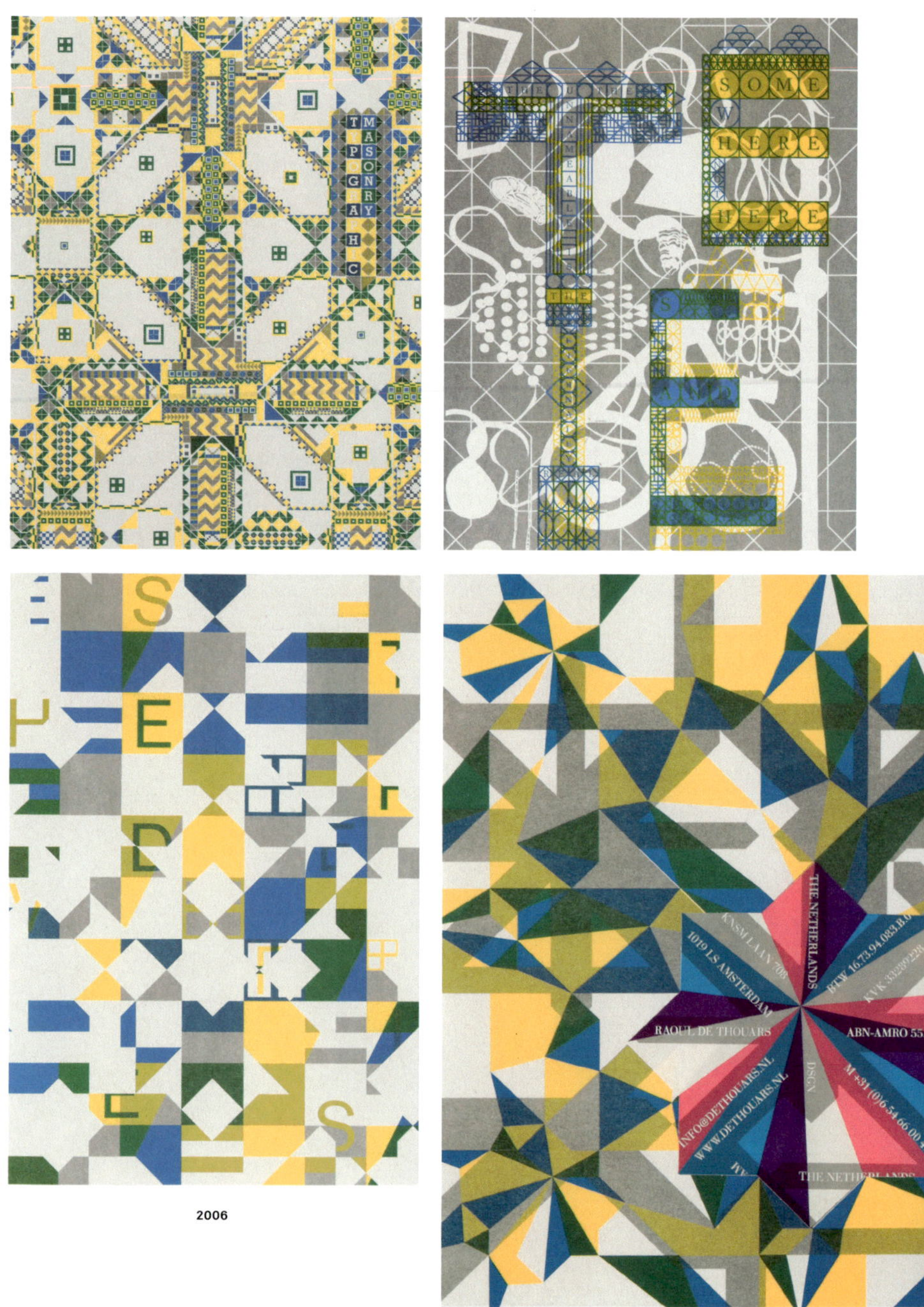

2006

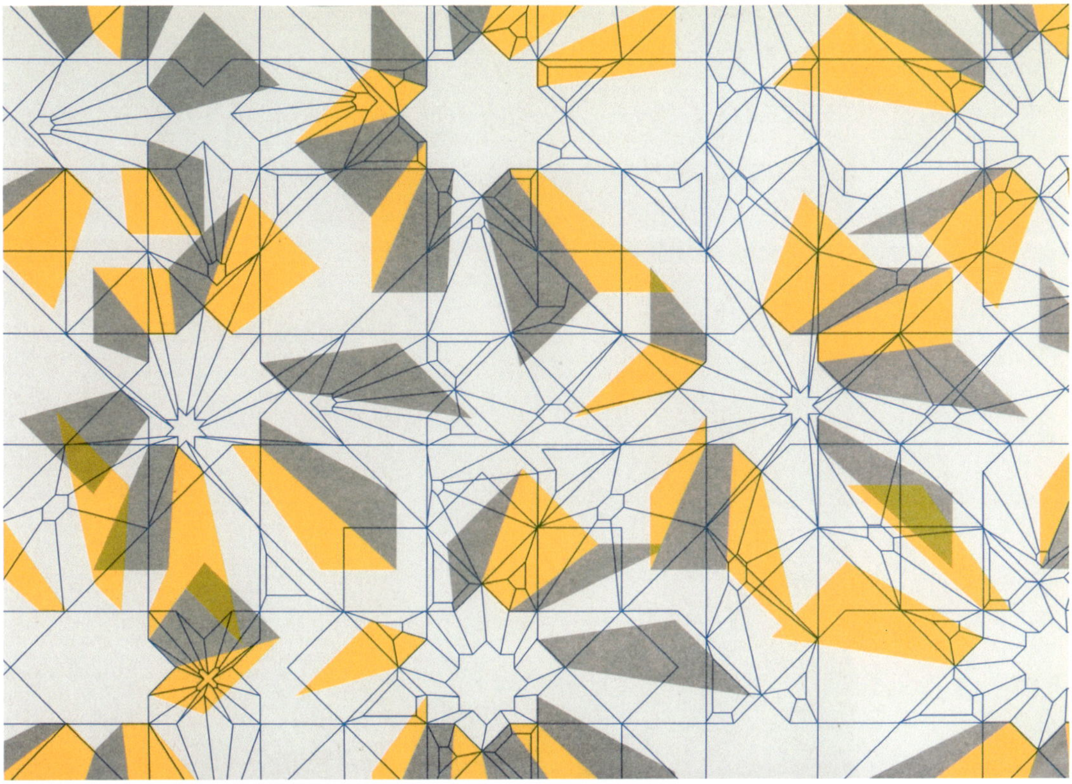

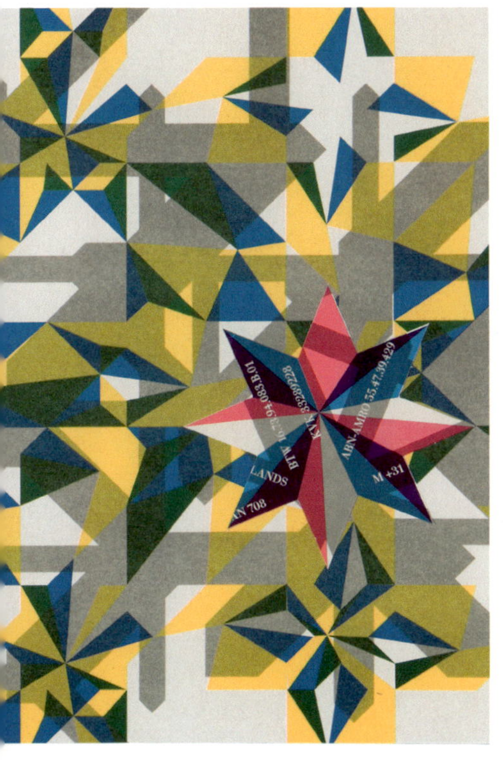
BTW 16.73.94.083.B.01
KVK 33289228
ABN-AMRO 55.47.39.429
M +31
LANDS
AN 708

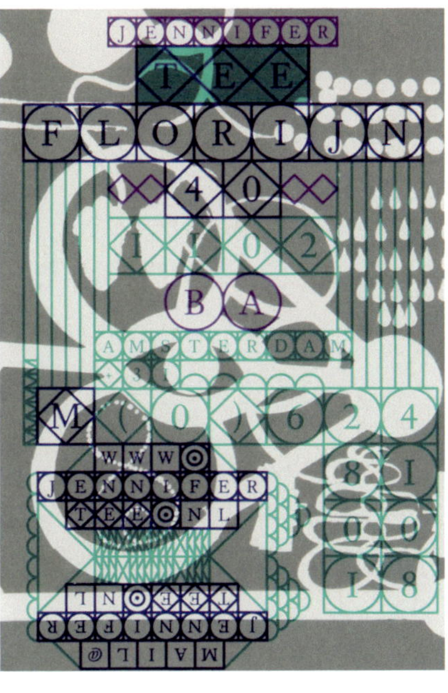
JENNIFER
TEE
FLORIJN
40
1102
BA
AMSTERDAM
+31
M (0) 624
WWW@
JENNIFER
TEE@NL
8I
00
18
TEE@NL
JENNIFER
MAIL@

Outsiders

by Machine

It is a flyer for our own bi-monthly clubnight in the Bitterzoet in Amsterdam.

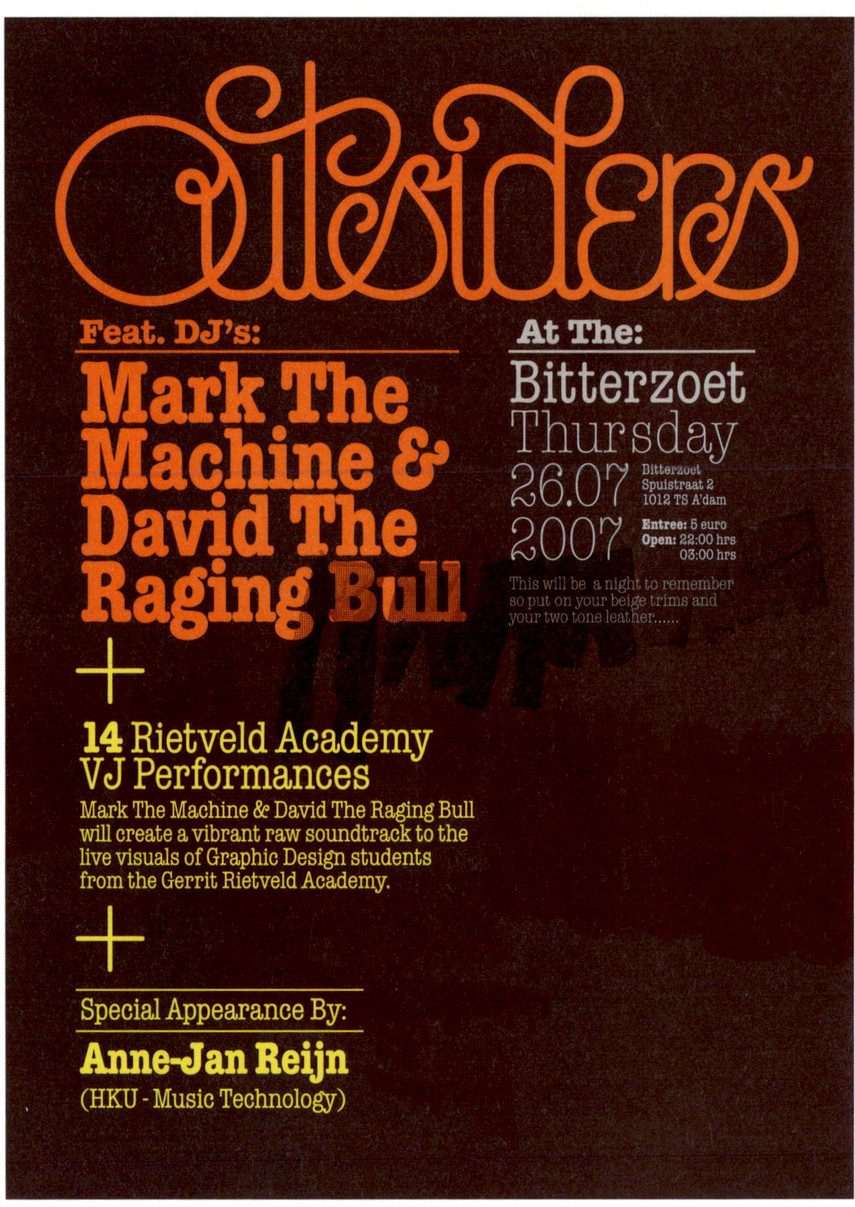

Size A6, 330 gr, HVO paper, 2007

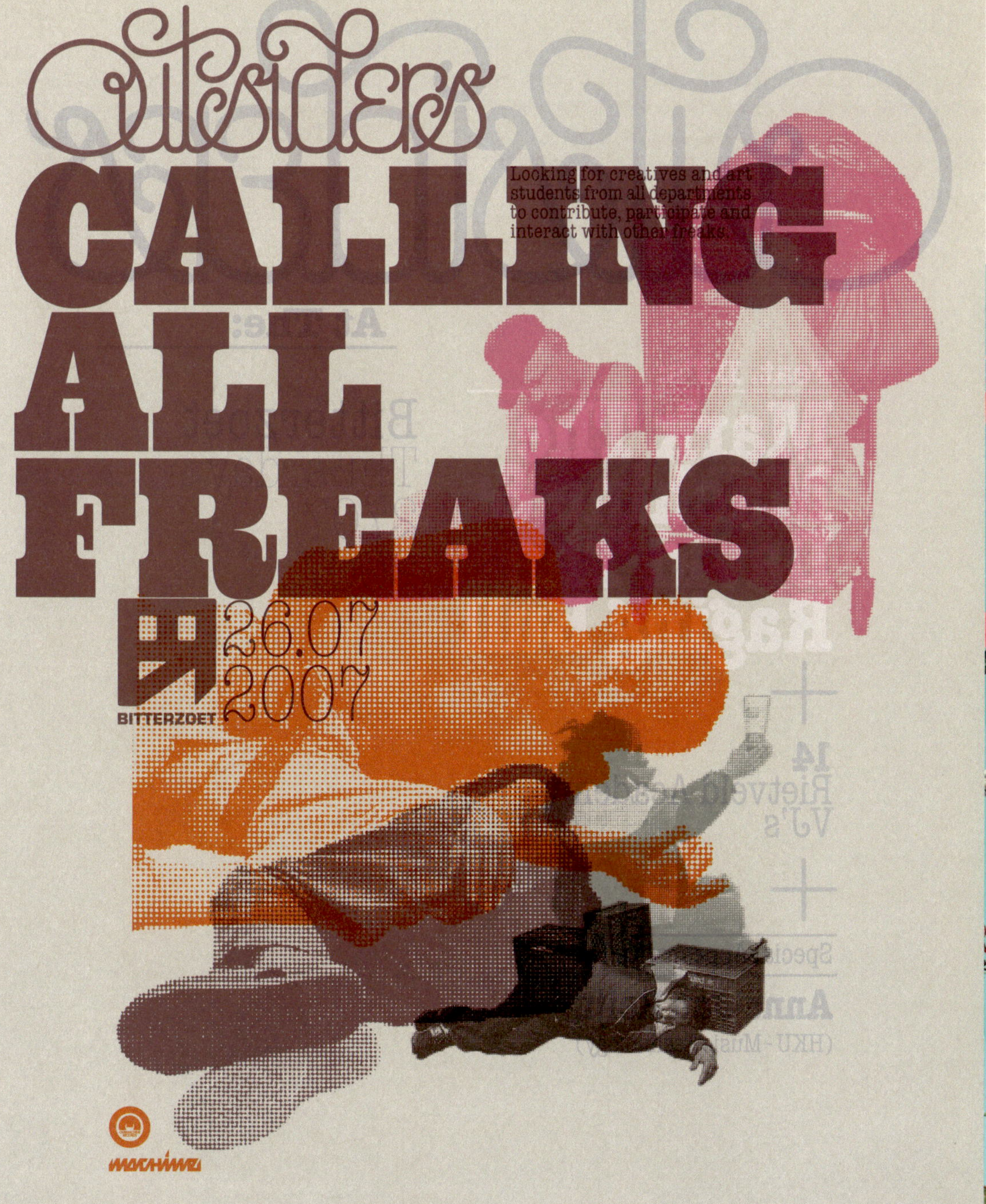
Outsiders
CALLING ALL FREAKS
Looking for creatives and art students from all departments to contribute, participate and interact with other freaks.
26.07 2007
BITTERZOET
14
Rietveld-Academie
VJ's
(HKU - Muz
machine

38 Back-to-school-package
by Atelier Van GOG

China meets Mexico meets Amsterdam in this strong brand for which we created the logo – our first! Every year we go back to school.

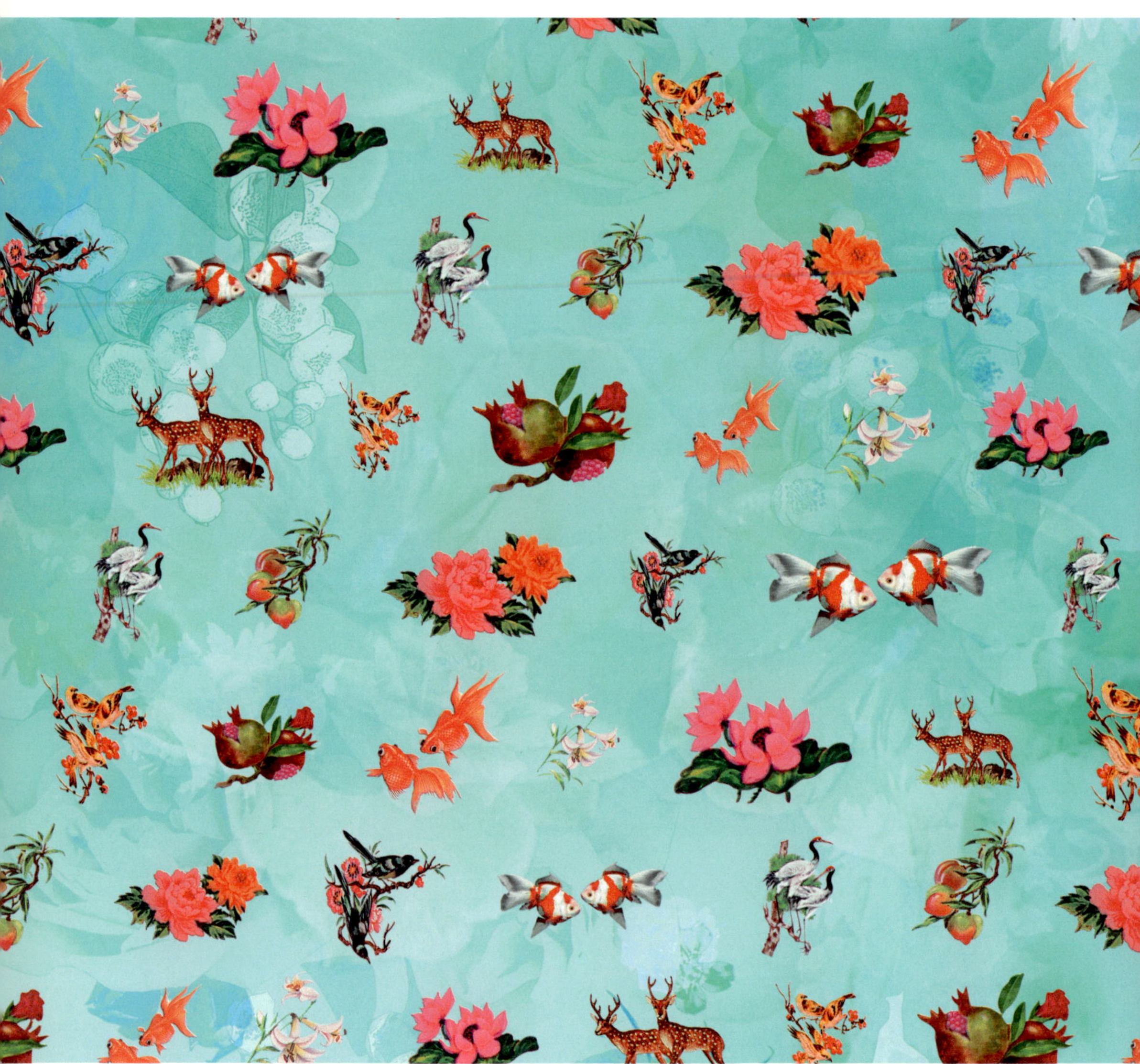

Packing Paper for Kitsch Kitchen, 2007

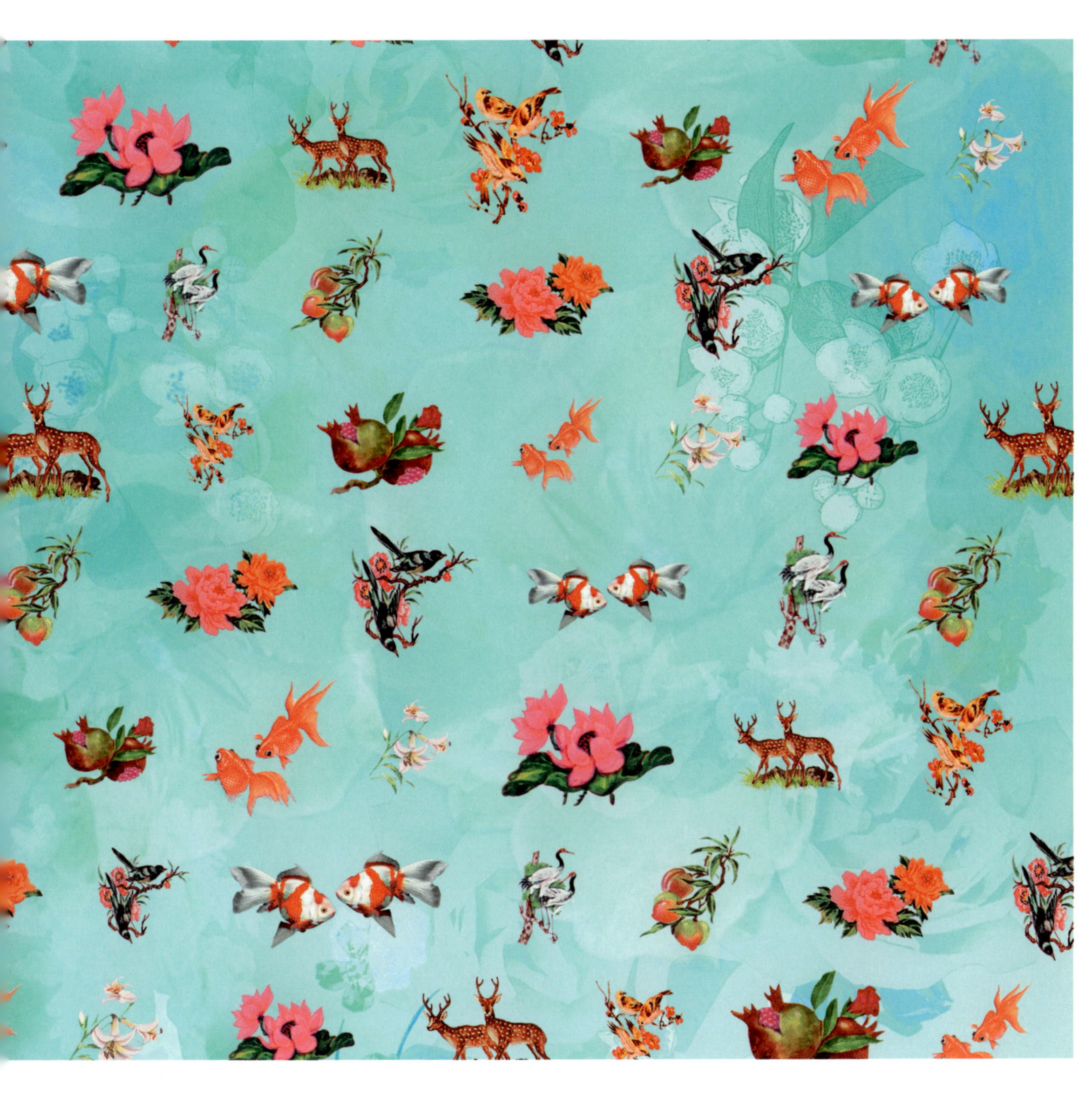

Oh Pedro

by Arjan Groot & Julia Müller

Contribution to the ‹fantasy› issue of Spanish magazine ‹The Creator Studio›. Three different songs were compiled, ordered and rearranged to create our own song about fantasy.

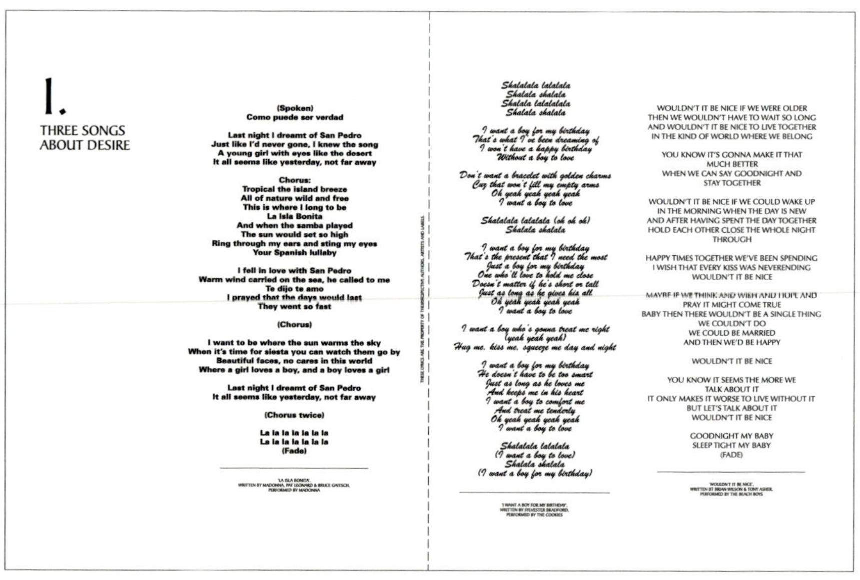

1.

THREE SONGS ABOUT DESIRE

(Spoken)
Como puede ser verdad

Last night I dreamt of San Pedro
Just like I'd never gone, I knew the song
A young girl with eyes like the desert
It all seems like yesterday, not far away

Chorus:
Tropical the island breeze
All of nature wild and free
This is where I long to be
La Isla Bonita
And when the samba played
The sun would set so high
Ring through my ears and sting my eyes
Your Spanish lullaby

I fell in love with San Pedro
Warm wind carried on the sea, he called to me
Te dijo te amo
I prayed that the days would last
They went so fast

(Chorus)

I want to be where the sun warms the sky
When it's time for siesta you can watch them go by
Beautiful faces, no cares in this world
Where a girl loves a boy, and a boy loves a girl

Last night I dreamt of San Pedro
It all seems like yesterday, not far away

(Chorus twice)

La la la la la la la
La la la la la la la
(Fade)

'LA ISLA BONITA', WRITTEN BY MADONNA, PAT LEONARD & BRUCE GAITSCH, PERFORMED BY MADONNA

THESE LYRICS ARE THE PROPERTY OF THEIR RESPECTIVE AUTHORS, ARTISTS AND LABELS.

Shalalala lalalala
Shalala shalala
Shalala lalalalala
Shalala shalala

I want a boy for my birthday
That's what I've been dreaming of
I won't have a happy birthday
Without a boy to love

Don't want a bracelet with golden charms
Cuz that won't fill my empty arms
Oh yeah yeah yeah yeah
I want a boy to love

Shalalala lalalala (oh oh oh)
Shalala shalala

I want a boy for my birthday
That's the present that I need the most
Just a boy for my birthday
One who'll love to hold me close
Doesn't matter if he's short or tall
Just as long as he gives his all
Oh yeah yeah yeah yeah
I want a boy to love

I want a boy who's gonna treat me right
(yeah yeah yeah)
Hug me, kiss me, squeeze me day and night

I want a boy for my birthday
He doesn't have to be too smart
Just as long as he loves me
And keeps me in his heart
I want a boy to comfort me
And treat me tenderly
Oh yeah yeah yeah yeah
I want a boy to love

Shalalala lalalala
(I want a boy to love)
Shalala shalala
(I want a boy for my birthday)

'I WANT A BOY FOR MY BIRTHDAY', WRITTEN BY SYLVESTER BRADFORD, PERFORMED BY THE COOKIES

WOULDN'T IT BE NICE IF WE WERE OLDER
THEN WE WOULDN'T HAVE TO WAIT SO LONG
AND WOULDN'T IT BE NICE TO LIVE TOGETHER
IN THE KIND OF WORLD WHERE WE BELONG

YOU KNOW IT'S GONNA MAKE IT THAT
MUCH BETTER
WHEN WE CAN SAY GOODNIGHT AND
STAY TOGETHER

WOULDN'T IT BE NICE IF WE COULD WAKE UP
IN THE MORNING WHEN THE DAY IS NEW
AND AFTER HAVING SPENT THE DAY TOGETHER
HOLD EACH OTHER CLOSE THE WHOLE NIGHT
THROUGH

HAPPY TIMES TOGETHER WE'VE BEEN SPENDING
I WISH THAT EVERY KISS WAS NEVERENDING
WOULDN'T IT BE NICE

MAYBE IF WE THINK AND WISH AND HOPE AND
PRAY IT MIGHT COME TRUE
BABY THEN THERE WOULDN'T BE A SINGLE THING
WE COULDN'T DO
WE COULD BE MARRIED
AND THEN WE'D BE HAPPY

WOULDN'T IT BE NICE

YOU KNOW IT SEEMS THE MORE WE
TALK ABOUT IT
IT ONLY MAKES IT WORSE TO LIVE WITHOUT IT
BUT LET'S TALK ABOUT IT
WOULDN'T IT BE NICE

GOODNIGHT MY BABY
SLEEP TIGHT MY BABY
(FADE)

'WOULDN'T IT BE NICE', WRITTEN BY BRIAN WILSON & TONY ASHER, PERFORMED BY THE BEACH BOYS

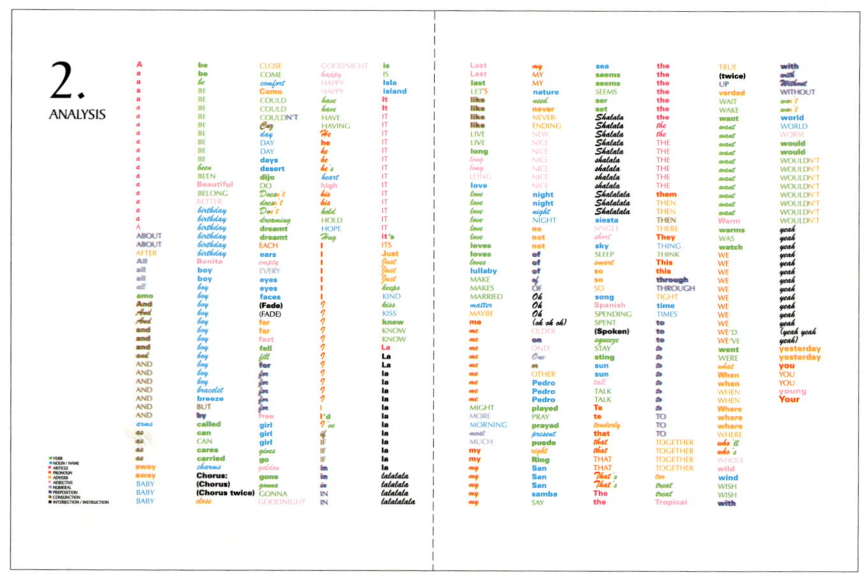

Oh Pedro, 2004

3.

REMIX

Oh BABY all DAY I PRAY
and in THE long long night I WISH
that TOGETHER WE COULD STAY
for a NEVER-ENDING KISS

Chorus:

if ONLY Your Tropical
Shalalala
would Warm MY
yeah yeah yeah
Oh Pedro
(Spoken)
oh Bonita

IF YOU WOULDN'T have that Ring
WE COULD be dreaming high
on MY birthday Hug to sting
And watch the golden sky

my days would BE so MUCH BETTER
with Pedro in my arms
BUT TO you that doesn't matter
Cuz YOU Don't want my charms

(Chorus)

Just for Pedro IS this song
I want Spanish love for free
All DAY I WAIT AND long
for what One day MIGHT be

(Chorus twice)

no TALK Just Shalalala
COME and squeeze my yeah yeah yeah

(FADE)

'OH PEDRO',
COMPOSED BY ARJAN GROOT & JULIA MUELLER

43 A telling
by Ping-pong Design

Some pages from their workbook.

It is not brand or brand products.

Not services or track record or cost/quality ratio.

It is not value or behavior or strategy.

NO.....................................

self commissioned, 2004

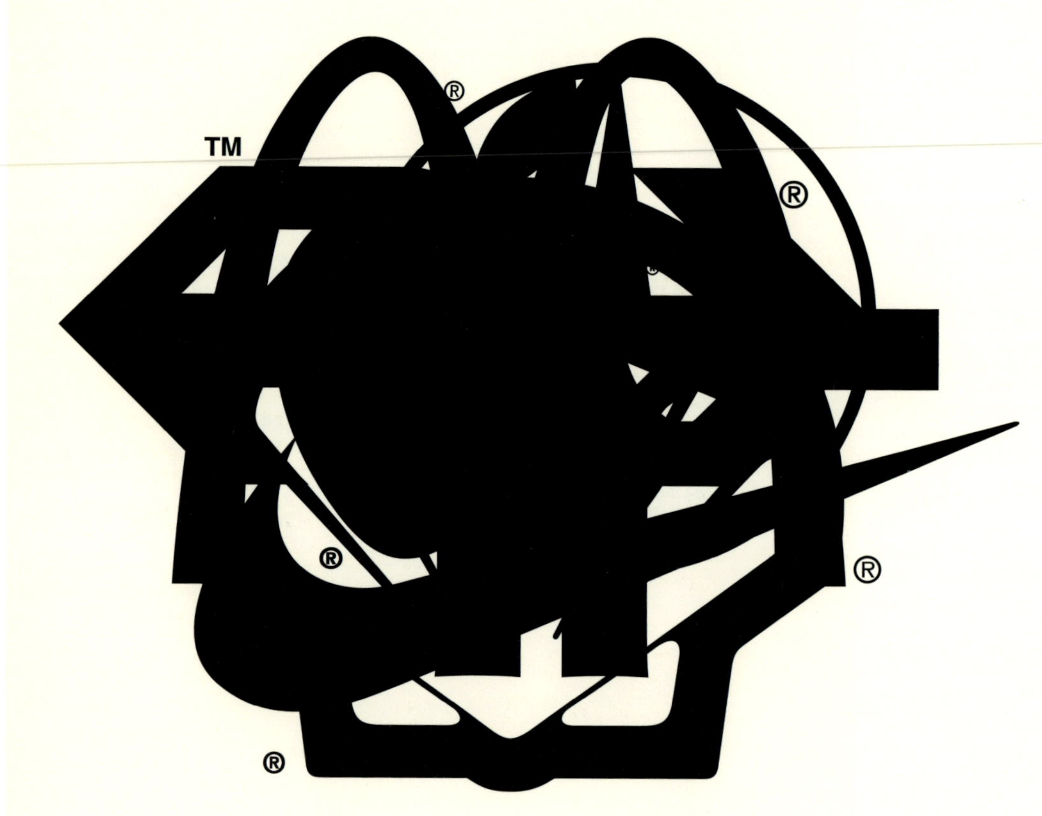
TM

45 BKOR
by Ping-pong Design

Imposing order on an environment that is inherently disorderly would be a misrepresentation of the truth. BKOR is at the core of the shifting, unruly urban environment that typifies Rotterdam.

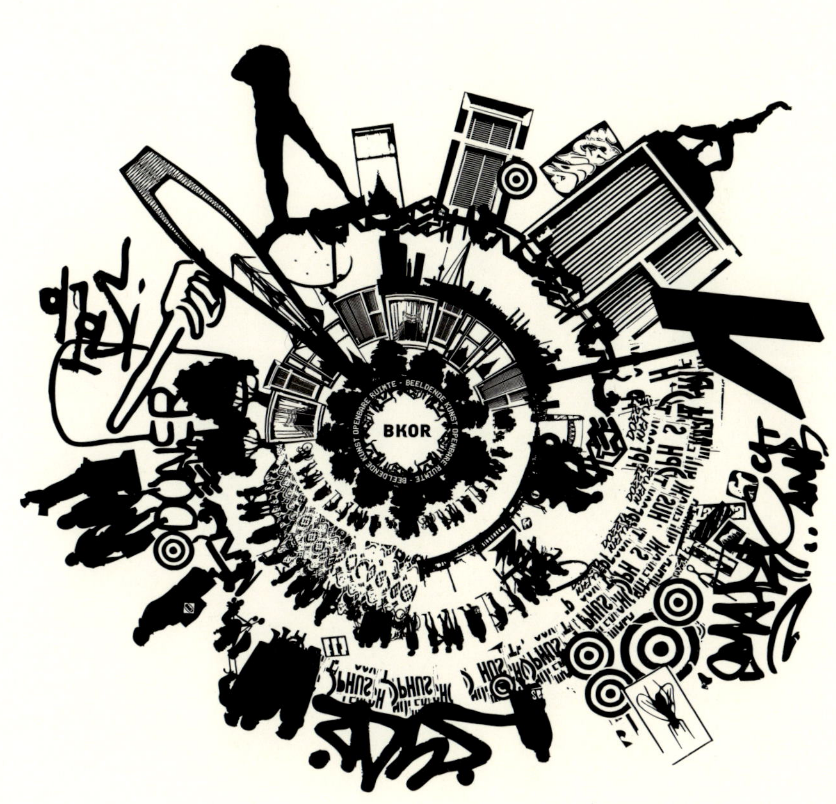

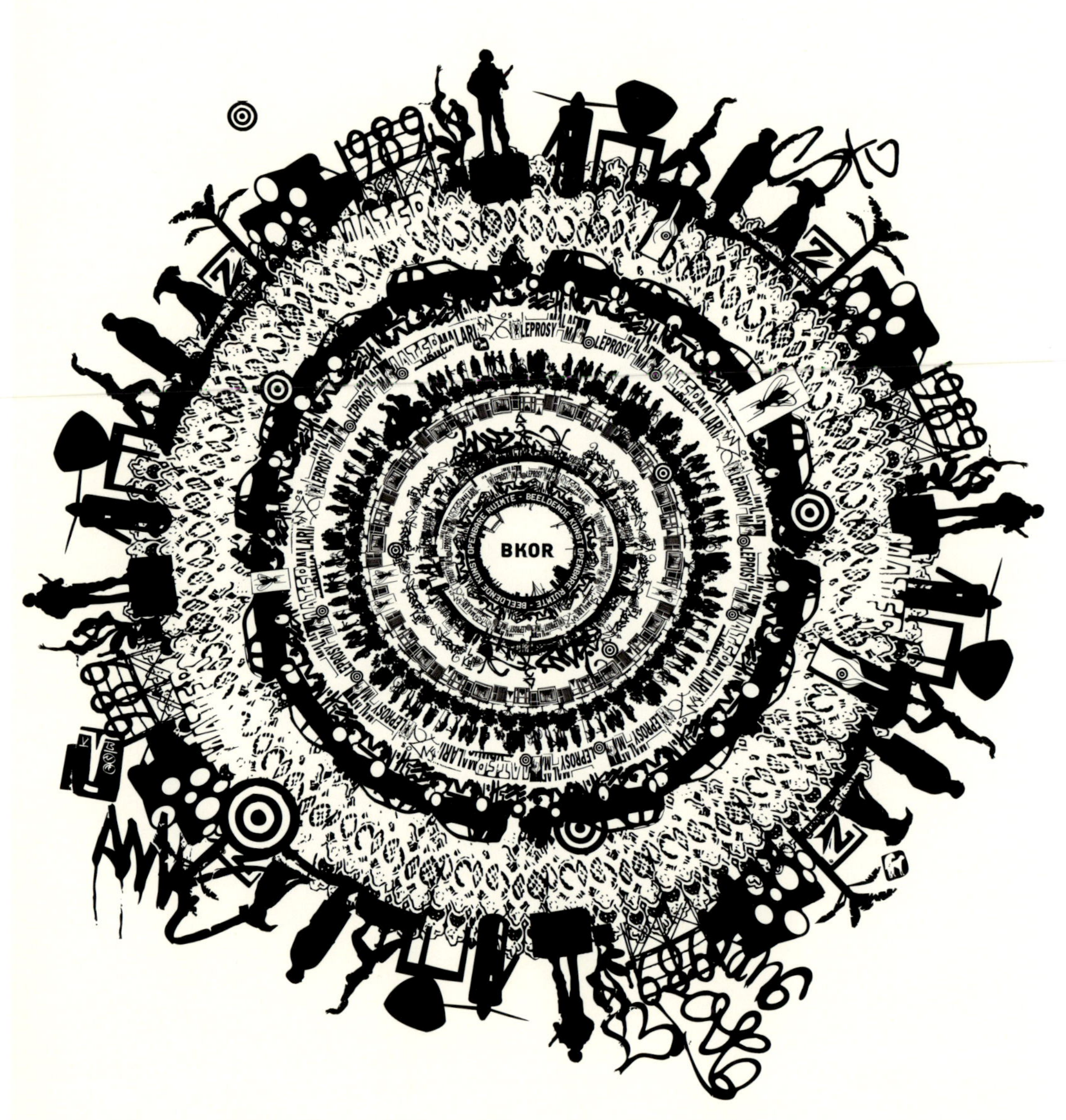
BKOR
BEELDENDE KUNST OPENBARE RUIMTE
LEPROSY
1989

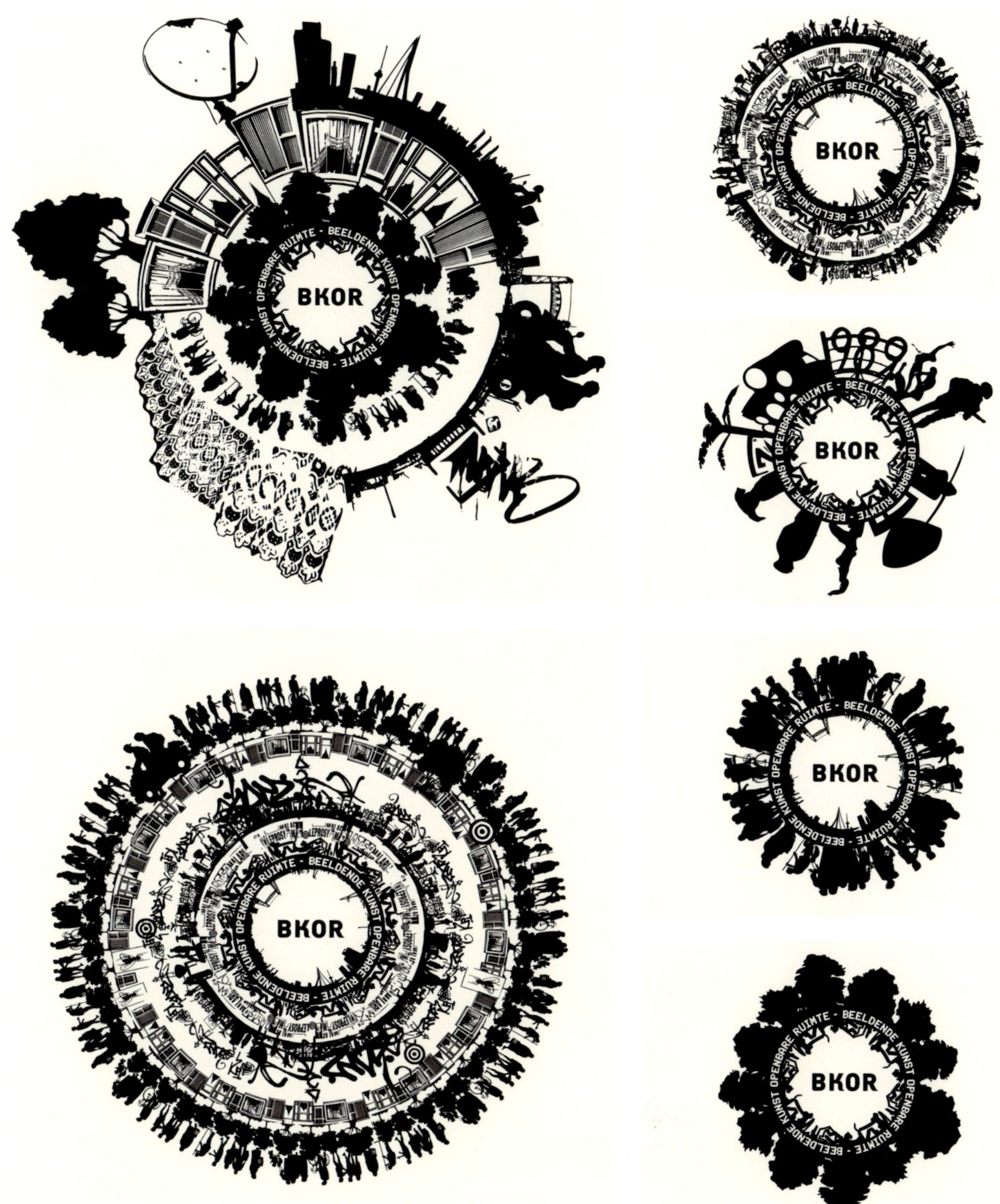
BKOR
BEELDENDE KUNST OPENBARE RUIMTE
BKOR
BEELDENDE KUNST OPENBARE RUIMTE
BKOR
BEELDENDE KUNST OPENBARE RUIMTE
BKOR
BEELDENDE KUNST OPENBARE RUIMTE
BKOR
BEELDENDE KUNST OPENBARE RUIMTE
BKOR
BEELDENDE KUNST OPENBARE RUIMTE

Concrete web magazine
by You & McCuskey

Web magazine, also used off-line, is part of corporate identity concept for a fashion store. It was created in 2004, a time when handmade design was not so common. The goal was to come up with something fresh and edgy looking and to have fun creating it. Every item of the visual identity was collaged by hand, though digital product photo's were added later. Website became famous for it's 80's porn images.

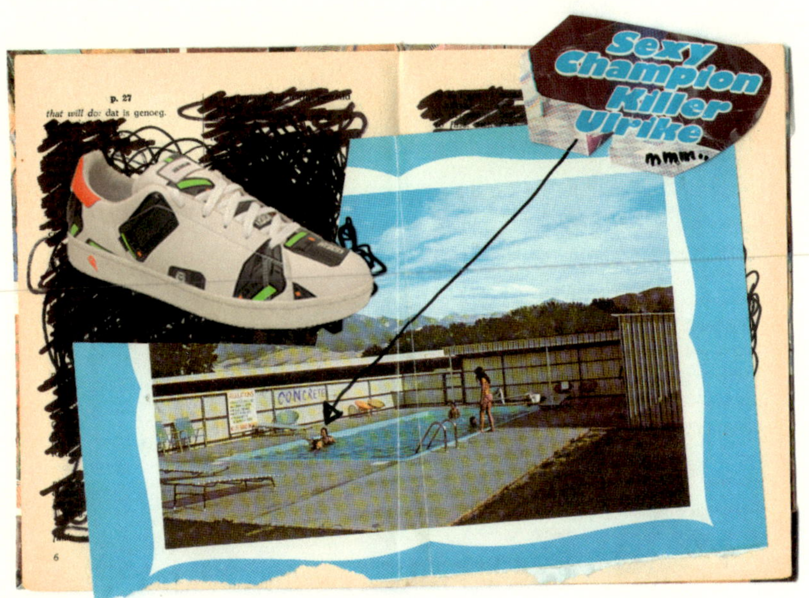

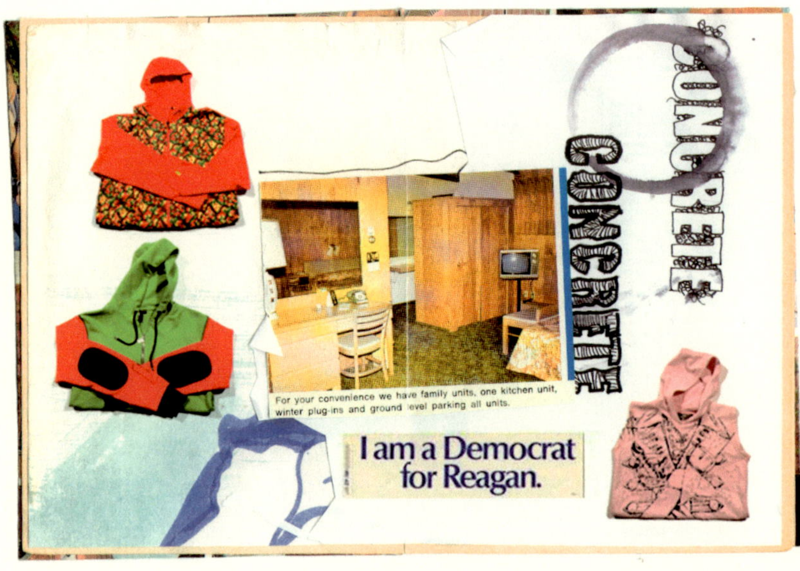

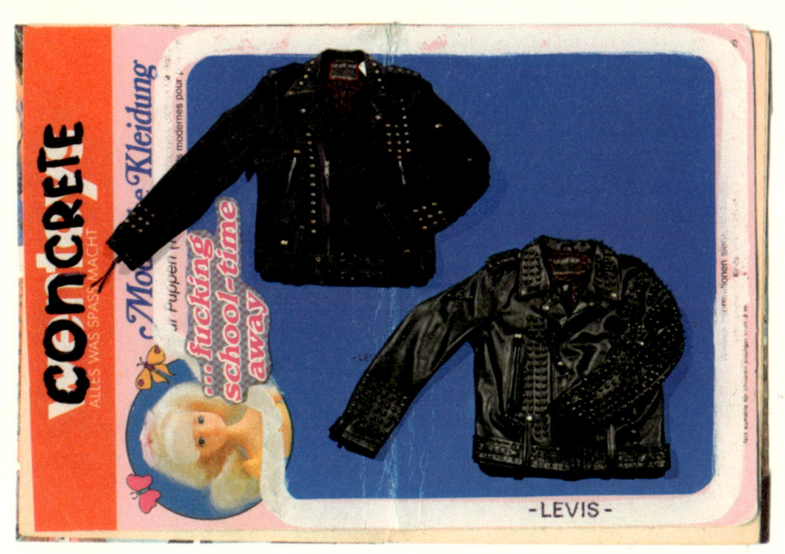
CONCRETE
ALLES WAS SPASS MACHT
Kleidung
...fucking school-time away
-LEVIS-

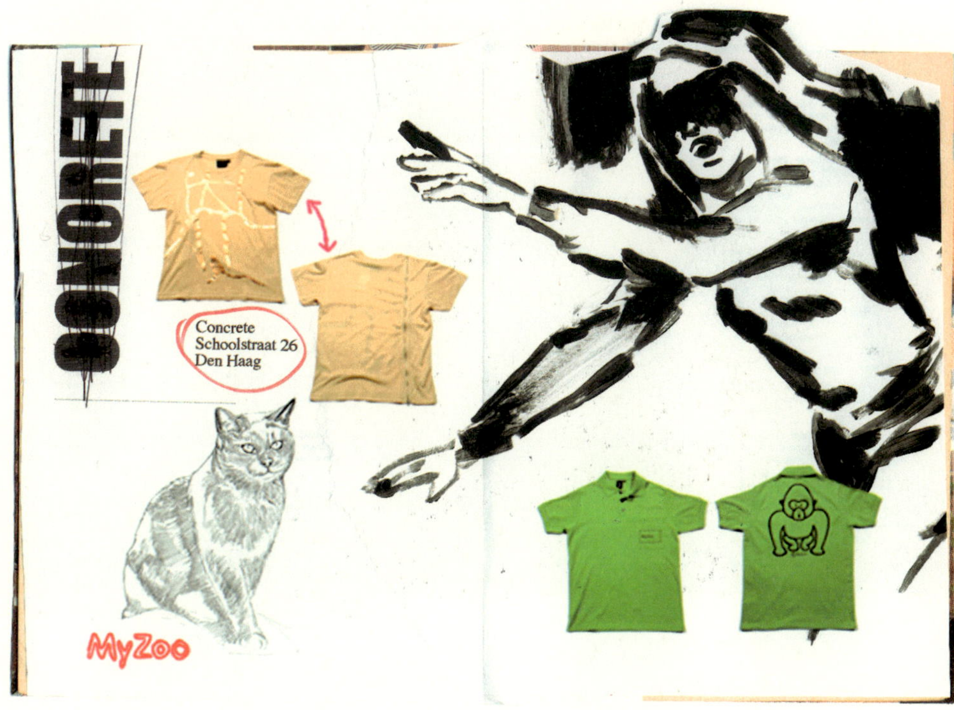
CONCRETE
Concrete
Schoolstraat 26
Den Haag
MyZoo

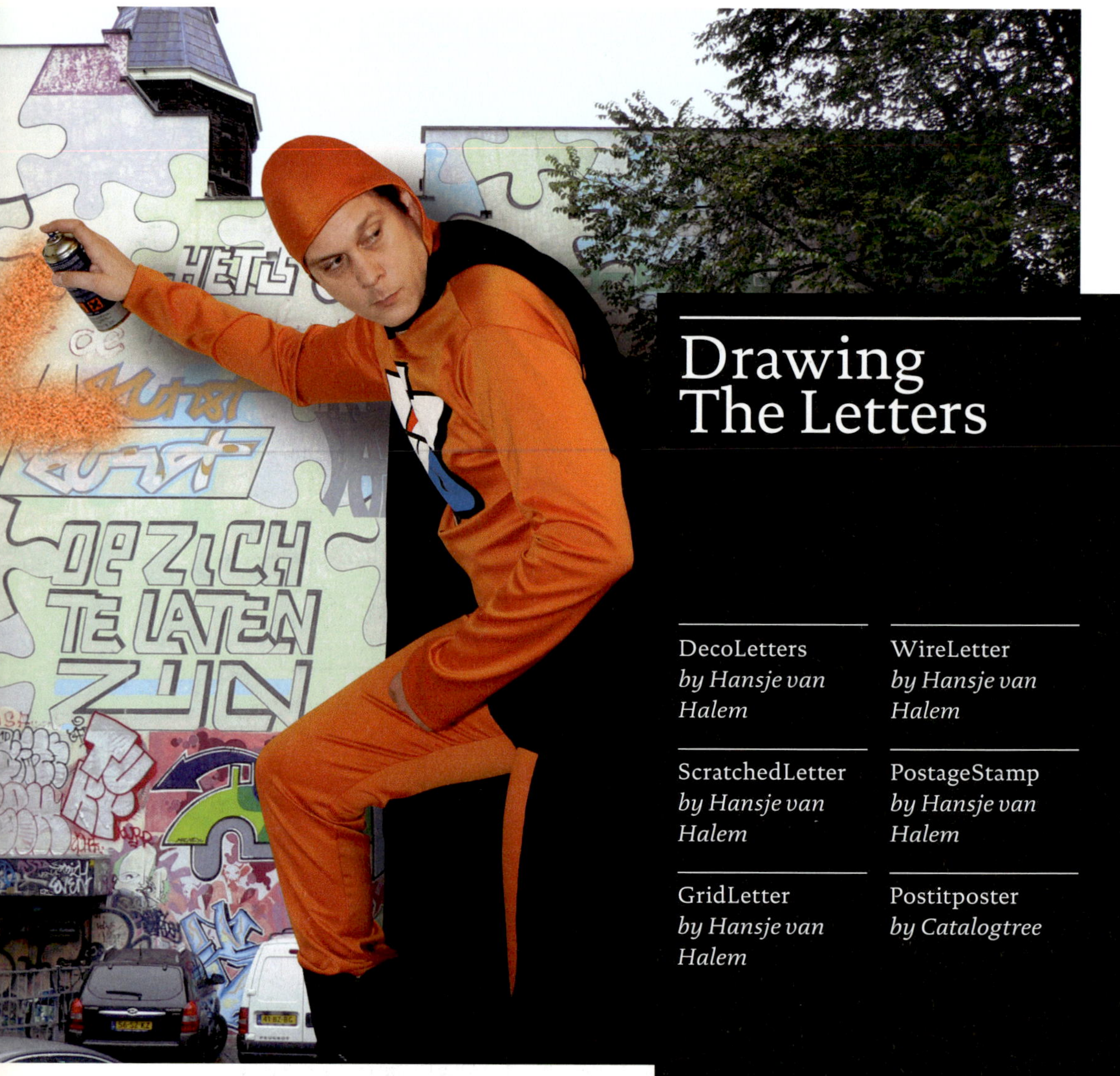

Drawing The Letters

DecoLetters
by Hansje van Halem

WireLetter
by Hansje van Halem

ScratchedLetter
by Hansje van Halem

PostageStamp
by Hansje van Halem

GridLetter
by Hansje van Halem

Postitposter
by Catalogtree

Brombeeren identity
by You & McCuskey

Tape
by You & McCuskey

Dans
by You & McCuskey

Lemmer
by Thonik

fellows
by Catalogtree

Power
by Thonik

BNA
by Thonik

Face Your World
by Roger Teeuwen

The Wall is the Landscape, HKU Academy Gallery
by Lesley Moore

RMN logo
by Experimental Jetset

Company logo
by Catalogtree

Vive la Papier Électronique
by Strange Attractors Design

Confused Type
by Toko

52 DecoLetters
by Hansje van Halem

In the summer of 2006 I bought some old type sets. In one of them I found these over-decorated letters. With this kind of typography on my mind, these drawings were the result.

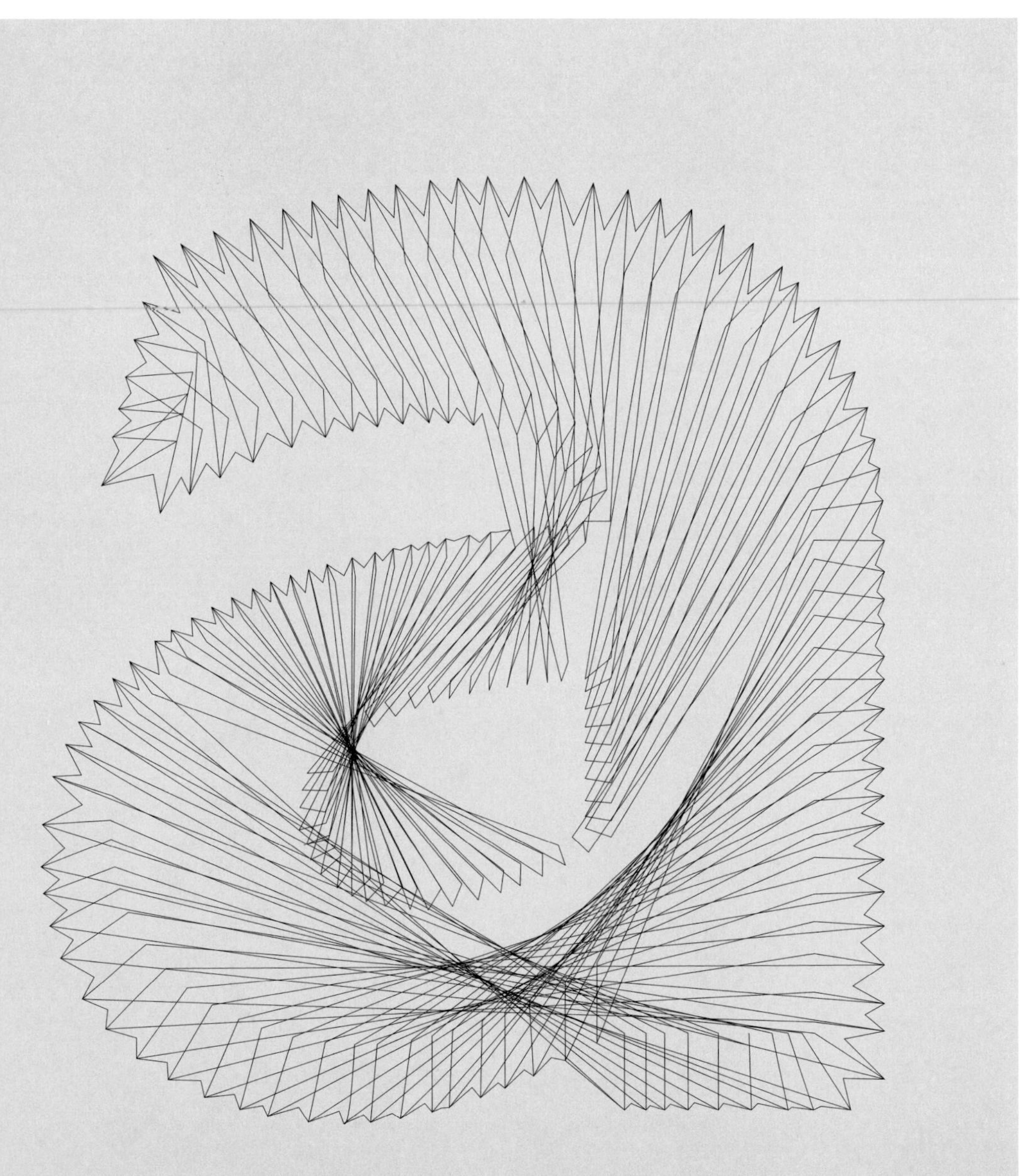

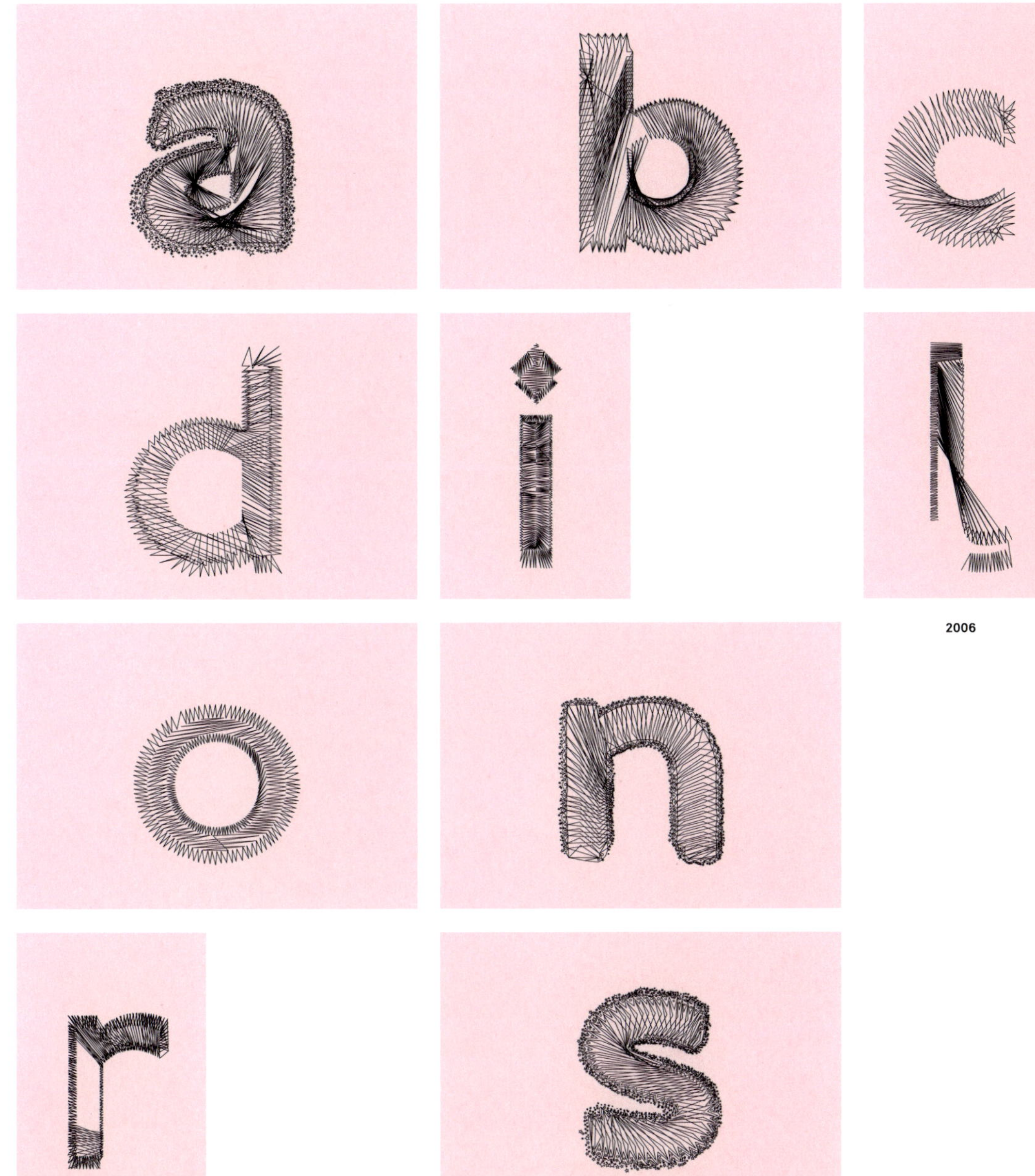

2006

54 ScratchedLetter
by Hansje van Halem

In digitalising handwriting and scratching the centres of existing type, the design decisions were still made on paper. By making a scan of the drawing on paper, it ended up on the computer. By using a mouse pen I could move this manual labour directly onto the computer. One winter night I tested this mouse pen by scratching within the outlines of a piece of text. Then I collected all the different versions of As and Bs I had been drawing and put them in a pile.

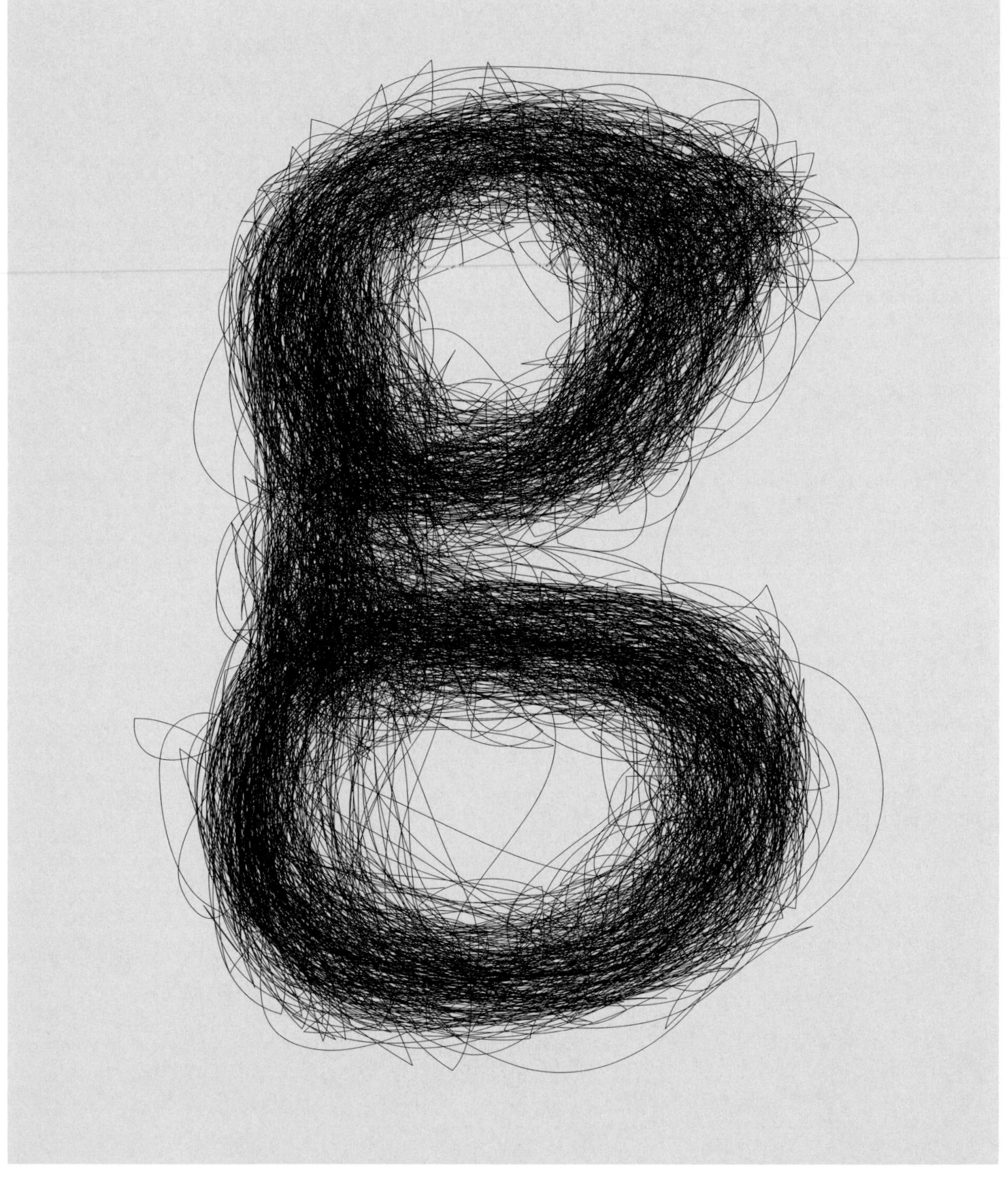

2003

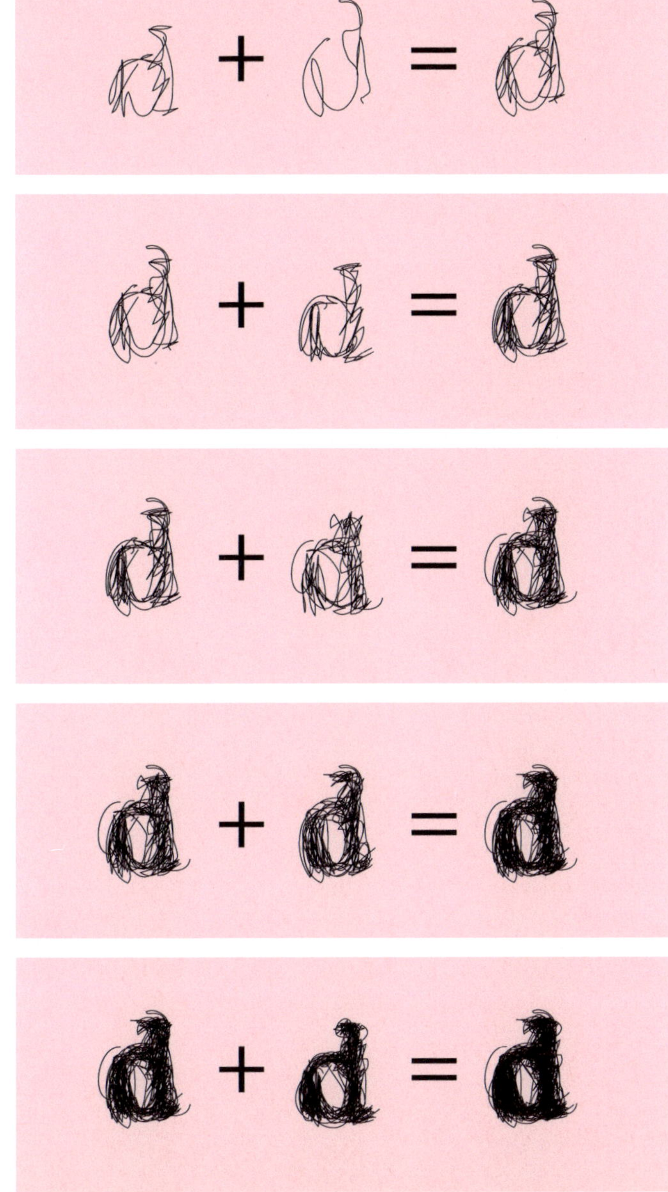

56 GridLetter
by Hansje van Halem

The first letters of this type came up during a search for the right design solution for the signage for a Pierre Bernard exhibition. They were loosely based on the grid of perforated paper, but the grid was overruled when working on the three-dimensional part of the type. I didn't find this letter appropriate for the assignment, but continued working on it.

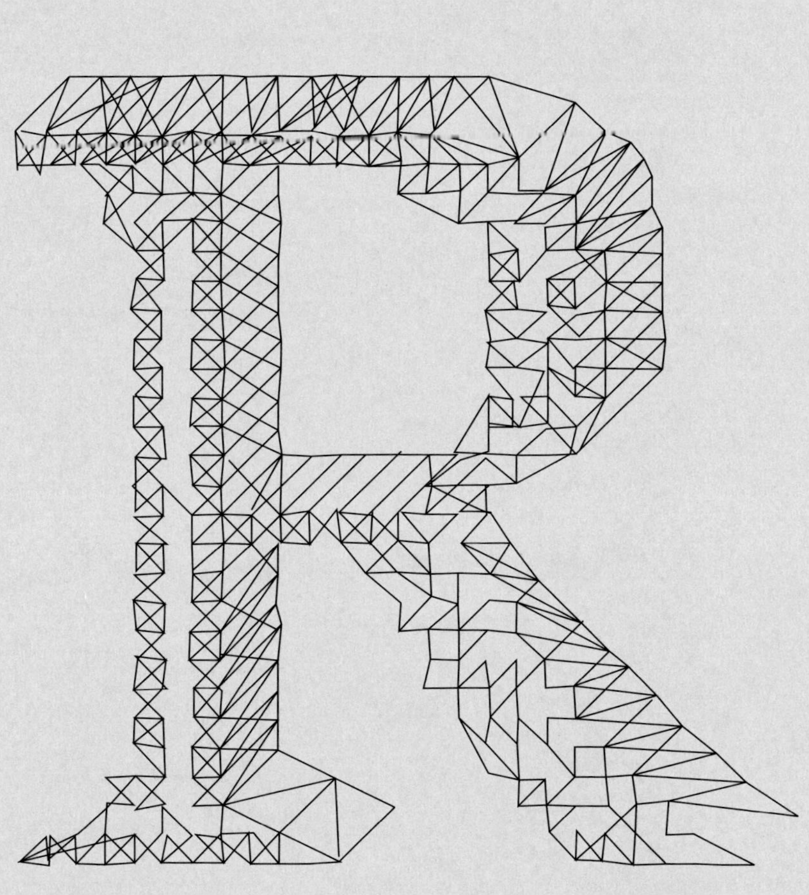

2007

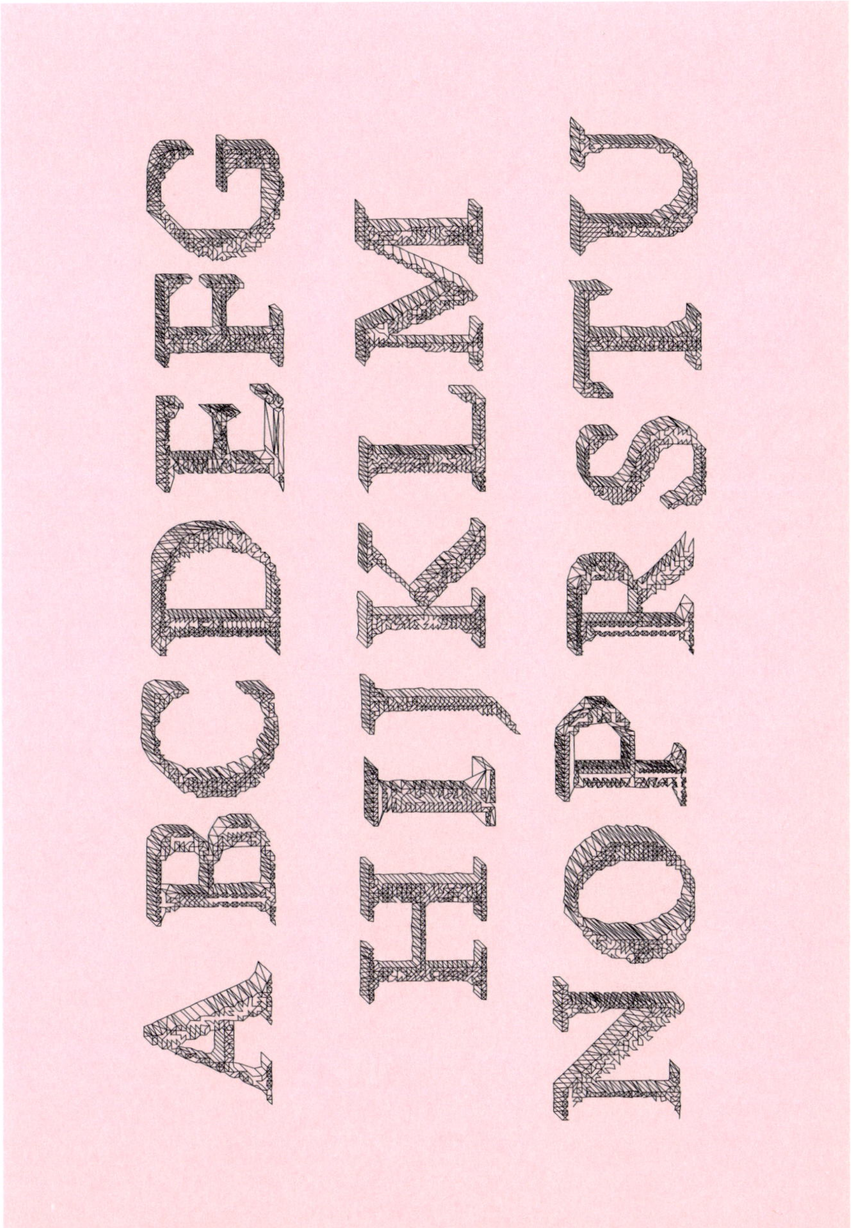

ABCDEFG
HIJKLM
NOPRSTU

58 WireLetter
by Hansje van Halem

After designing a stamp, I started this type in 2007. Doing the labour-intensive chores for myself is true meditation. With this type the size makes a huge difference. It needs to be big enough to show its texture, but not so big that it falls apart. First the letter is drawn from the outline out, then the fill is drawn. By drawing the zigzag system freehand, this geometrical pattern ended up having an organic look.

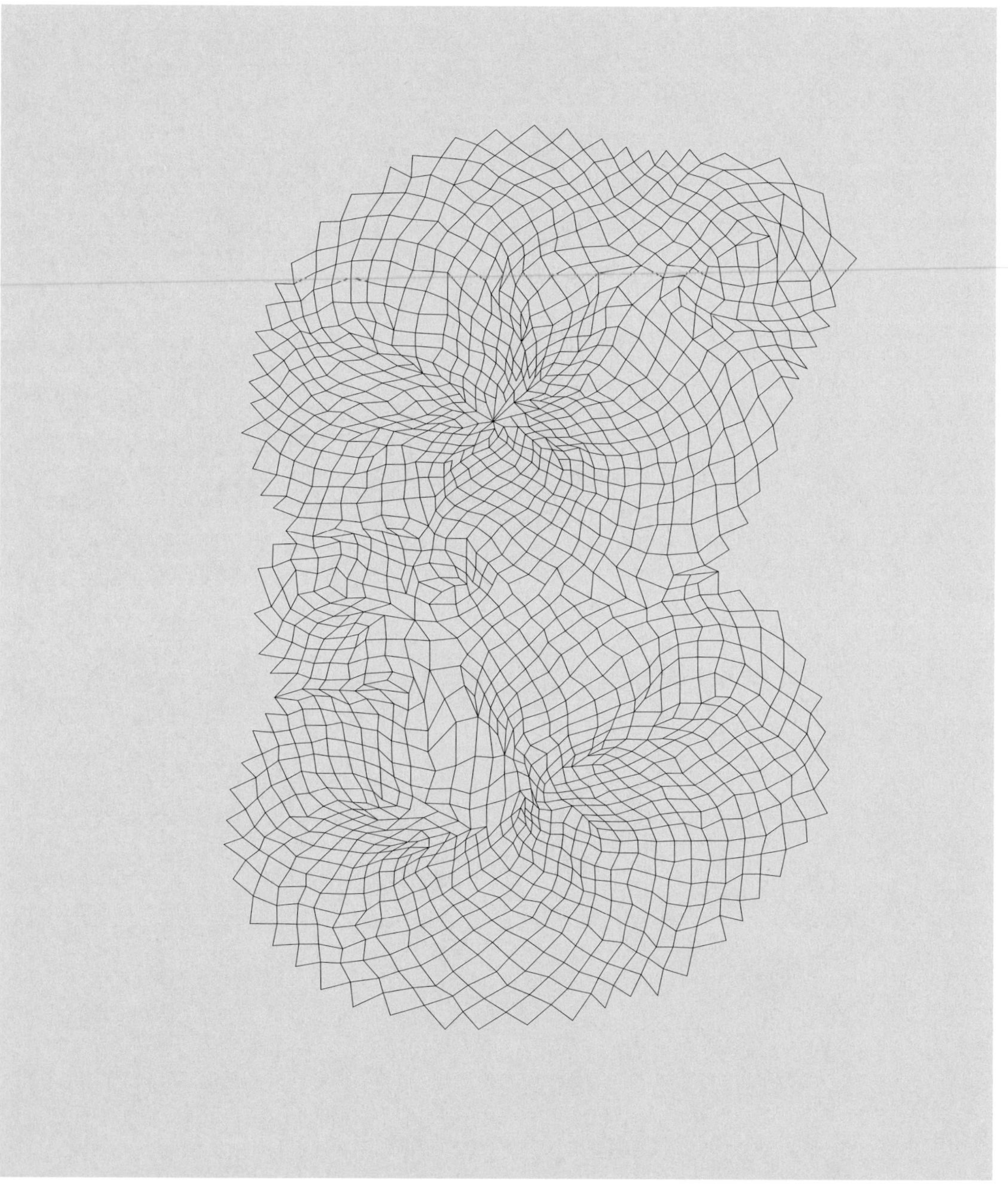

59

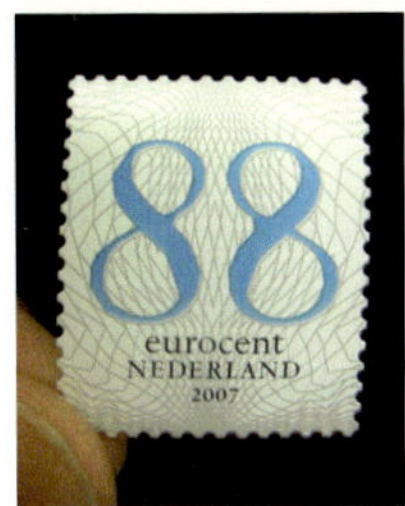

2006

PostageStamp
by Hansje van Halem

For the lettering for the new 88 cents portrait stamp Hansje van Halem used the Spectrum typeface by Jan van Krimpen, which that connect well with the round forms of the 8. The lettering of the 44 cents landscape stamp was set in the Johnston font by Edward Johnston.

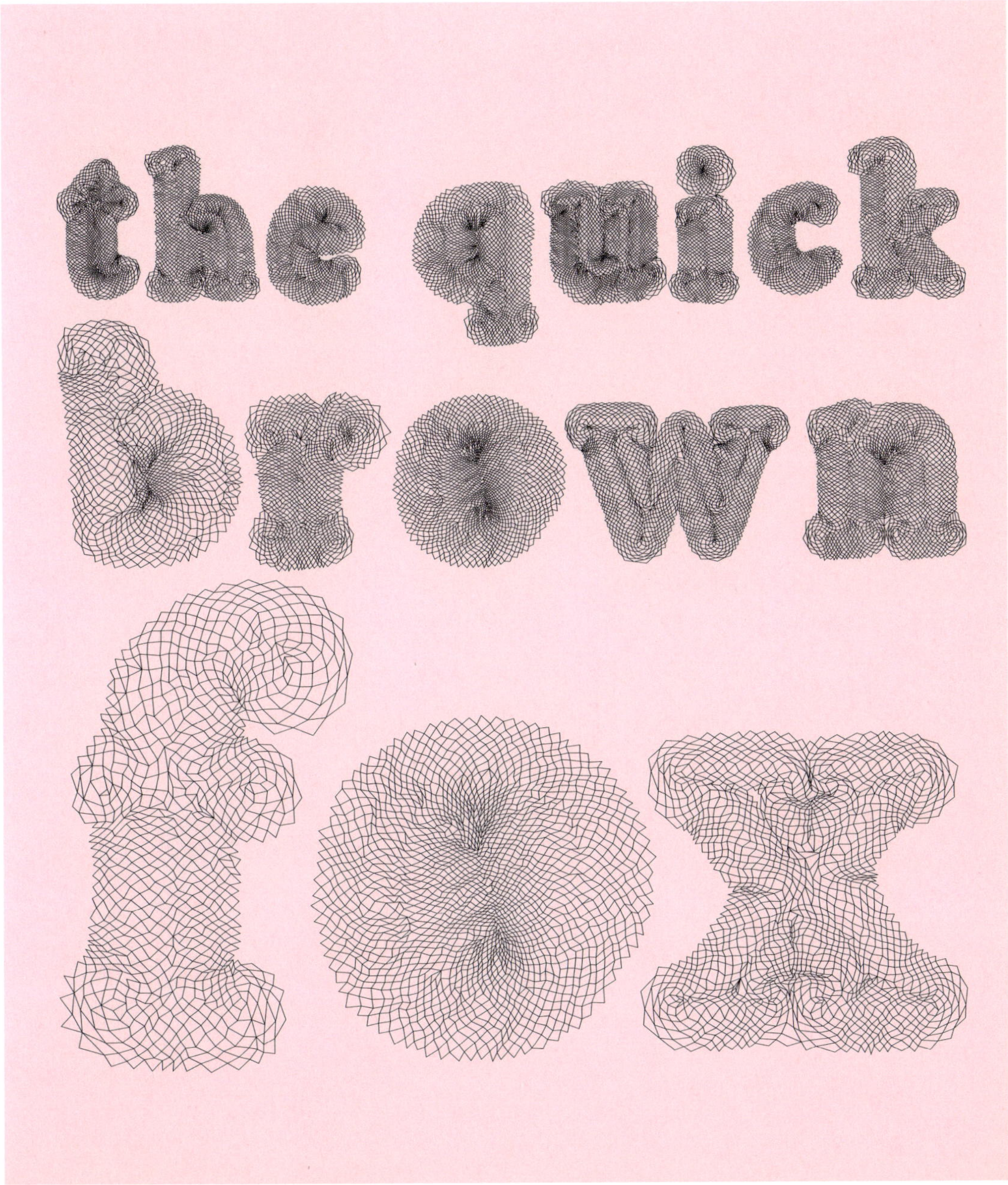

the quick
brown
fox

60 Postitposter
by Catalogtree

The final result of an introductory course in graphic design for architecture students. There are three different versions of the same posters. It was realised based on material we gathered from a workshop we held.

2005

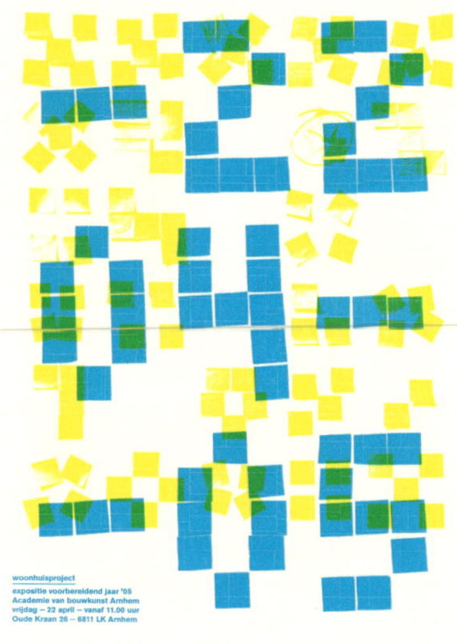

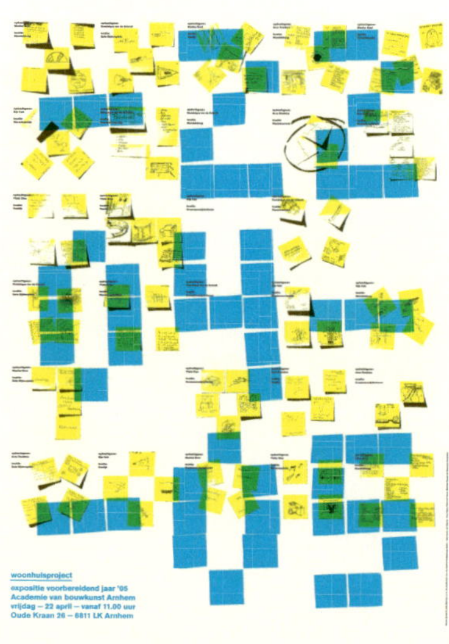

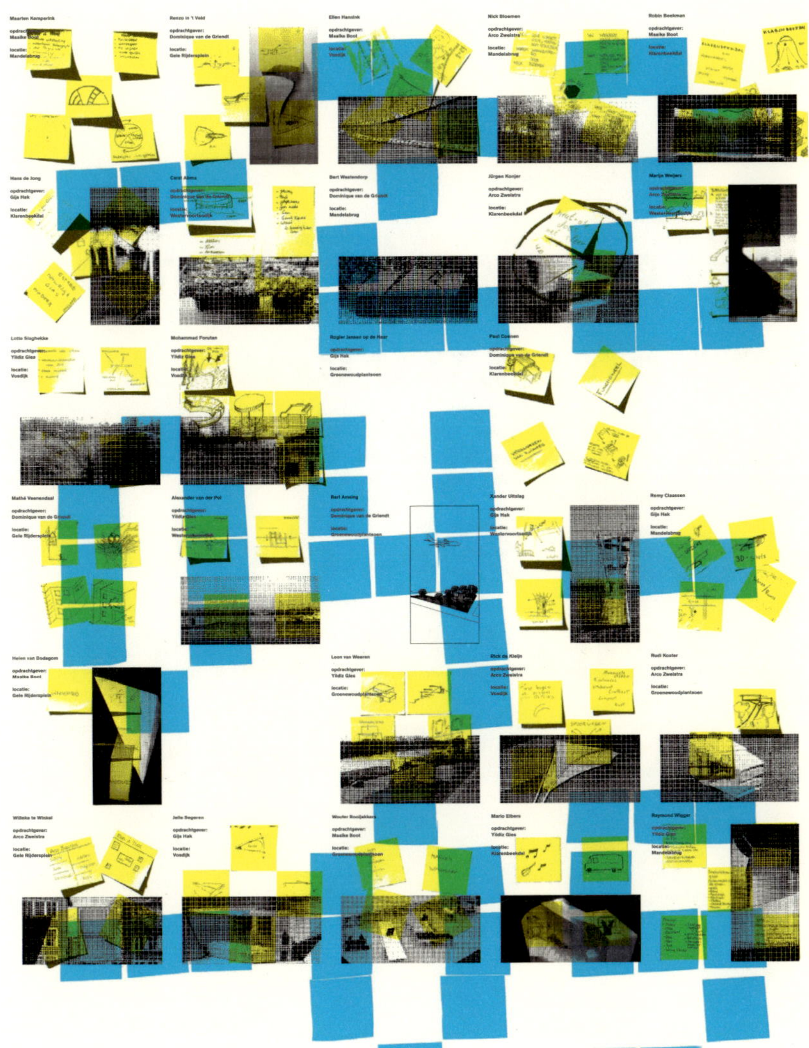

woonhuisproject

expositie voorbereidend jaar '05
Academie van bouwkunst Arnhem
vrijdag — 22 april — vanaf 11.00 uur
Oude Kraan 26 — 6811 LK Arnhem

62 Brombeeren identity
by You & McCuskey

Corporate identity concept for a blackberry festival. The basis of the identity is the Brombeer font and illustrations created from the same basic shapes. The goal was to create an identity with the feeling and sensation of blackberry picking without using photography.

The font is part of the corporate identity concept for the blackberry festival. This font is made up of triangles, which refer to the thorns and leaf structure of the blackberry bush.

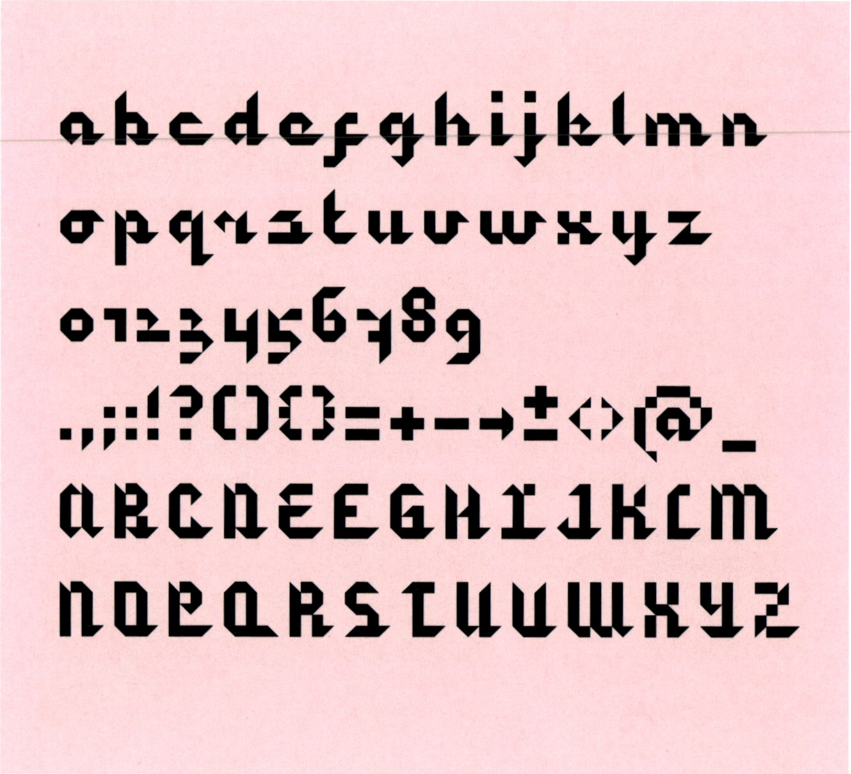

abcdefghijklmn
opqrstuvwxyz
0123456789
.,;:!?(){}=+-→±<>@_
ABCDEFGHIJKLM
NOPQRSTUVWXYZ

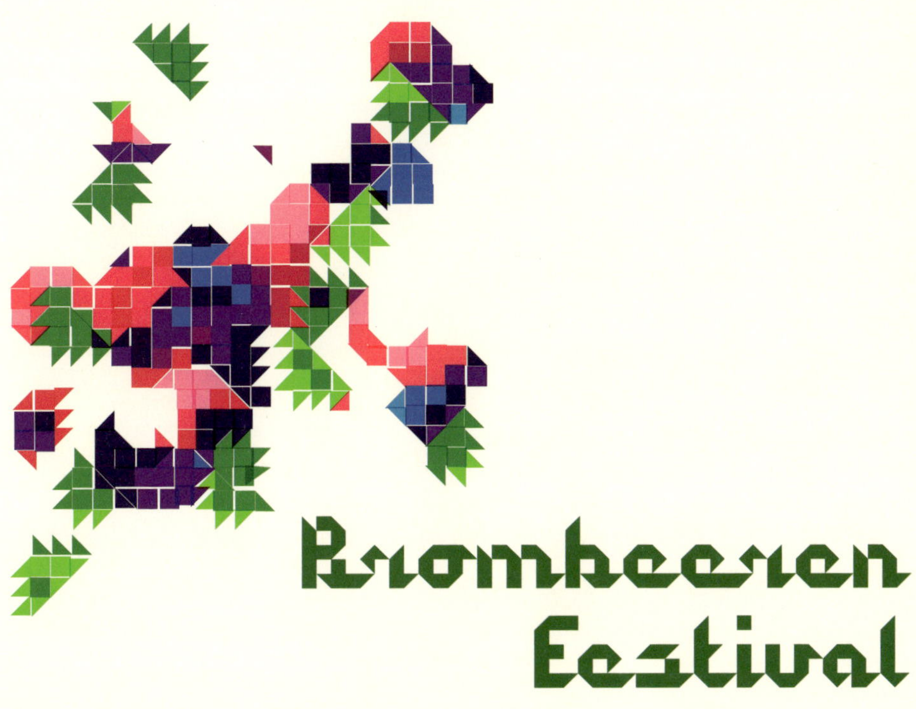

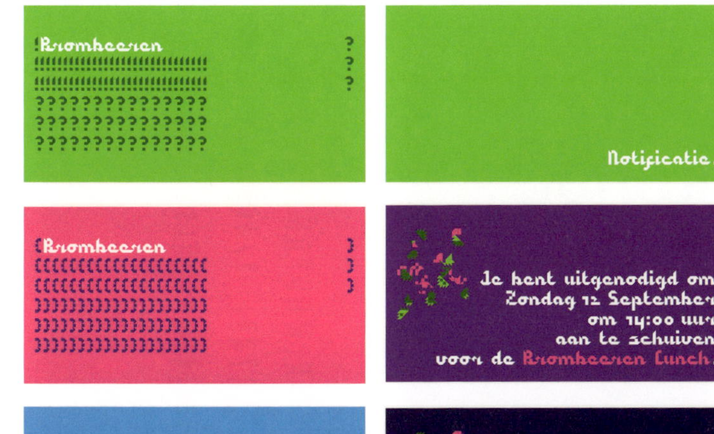

Brombeeren Festival
12 September 2004.
Brombeeren Festival
12 September 2004.
Brombeeren Festival
12 September 2004.

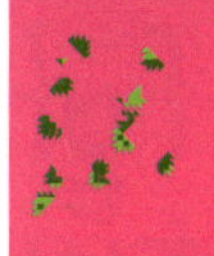

Brombeeren Festival
12 September 2004.
Brombeeren Festival
12 September 2004.
Brombeeren Festival
12 September 2004.

→Brombeeren

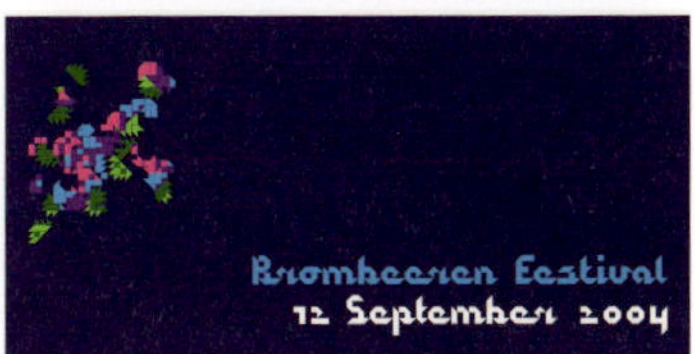

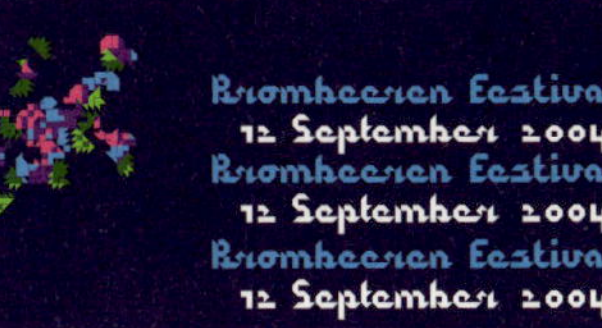

64 Tape

by You & McCuskey

The fonts we create are always part of a project concept and provide the often much-needed clarity and entertainment. They tell emotional stories in a simple way and help sell our concept to clients. Font is part of corporate identity concept for a fashion store. As the store's logo is a roll of tape it was a necessity to start making tape fonts and illustrations.

The font is part of the corporate identity concept for a fashion store. As the store's logo is a roll of tape, it was a necessity to start making tape fonts and illustrations.

A B C D E F G H I J K L M N O P Q R S T U V W X Y Z
0 1 2 3 4 5 6 7 8 9 . , ? / ! @ # \ : ;

A B C D E F G H I J K L M N O P Q R S T U V W X Y Z
0 1 2 3 4 5 6 7 8 9 . , ? / ! # \ : ; @

ABCDEFGHIJKLMNOPQRSTUVWXYZ 0123456789 .,?/!\:;
ABCDEFGHIJKLMNOPQRSTUVWXYZ 0123456789 .,?/!\:;

ABCDEFGHIJKLM
NOPQRSTUVWXYZ
abcdefghijklmn
opqrstuvwxyz
0123456789.,?/

ABCDEFGHIJKLMNOPQRSTUVWXYZ
0123456789 .,?/!@#\:;
abcdefghijklmnopqrstuvwxyz

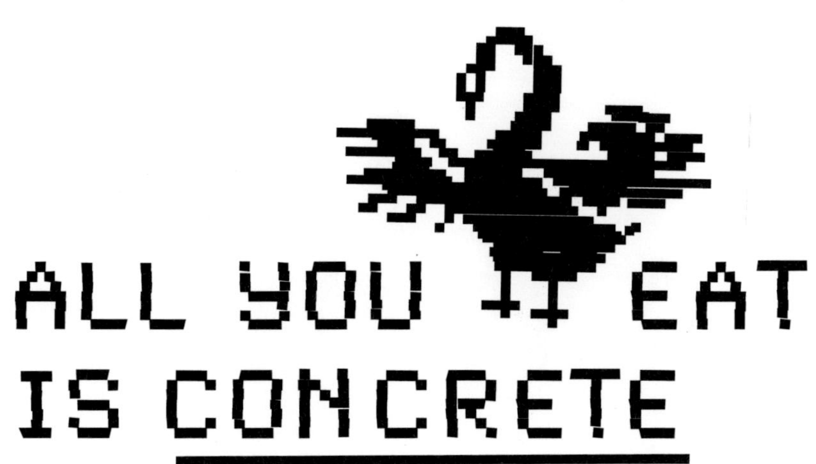
ALL YOU EAT
IS CONCRETE

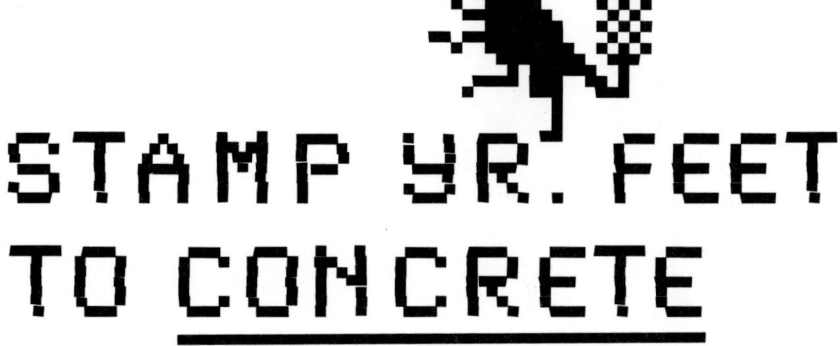
STAMP YR. FEET
TO CONCRETE

66 Dans

by You & McCuskey

The font is part of the corporate identity concept for dance producers. Every part of this identity revolves around communicative dancing and dancive communication. This font enables you to make messages such as dance. This font was also made into a web application.

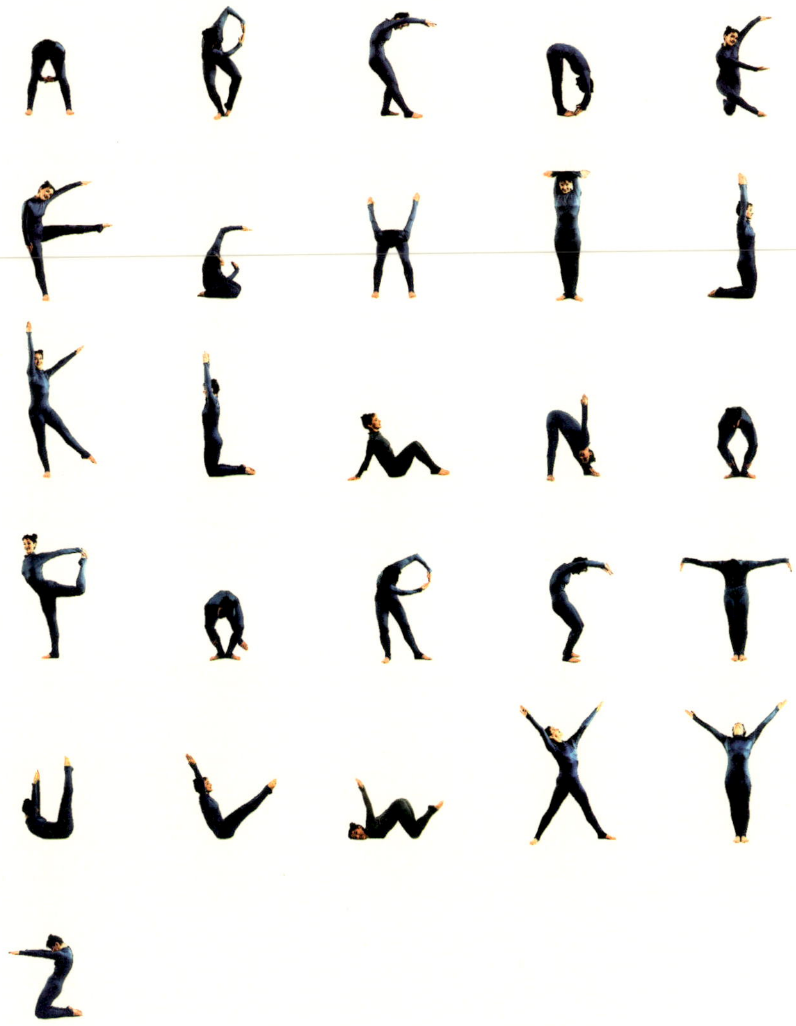

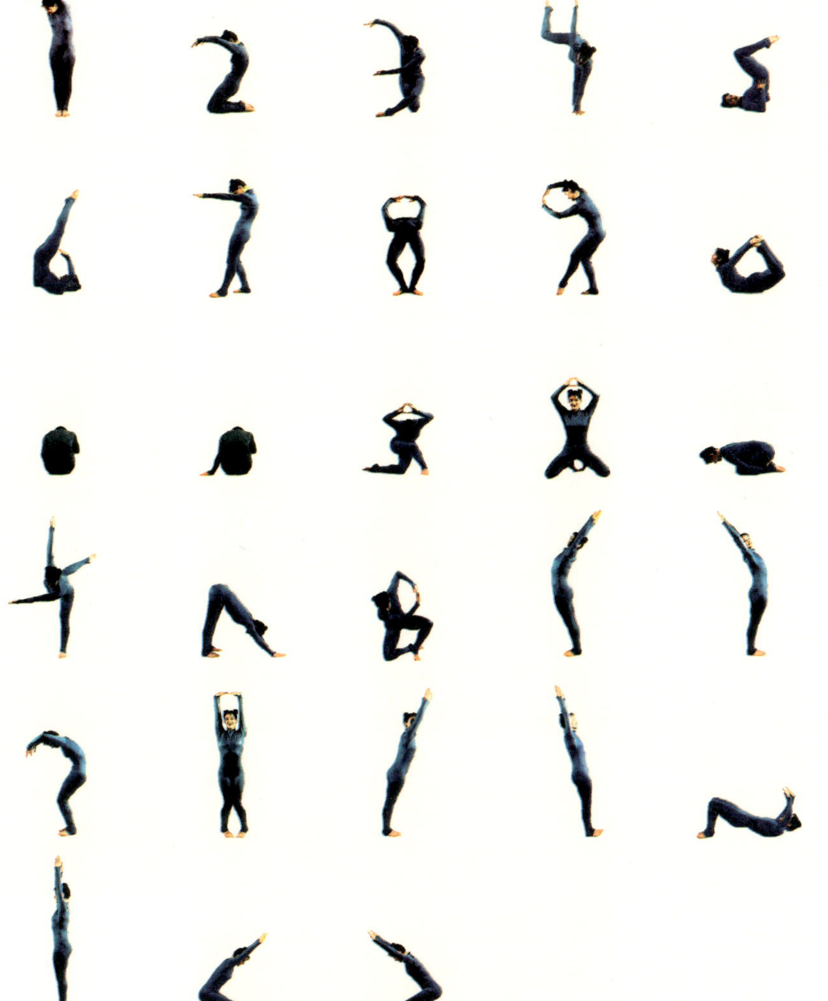

68 Lemmer
by Thonik

Art in the public space. In Friesland, on a ‹sluis›, a poem by George Moormann. In a reaction to the rectilinear lines of the Dutch landscape and its rectangular grid, the Pentathonik typeface was designed on a pentagonal pattern.

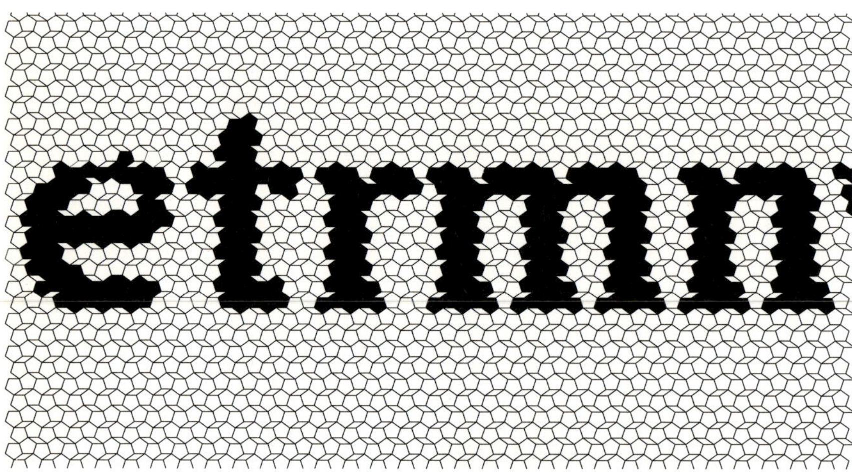

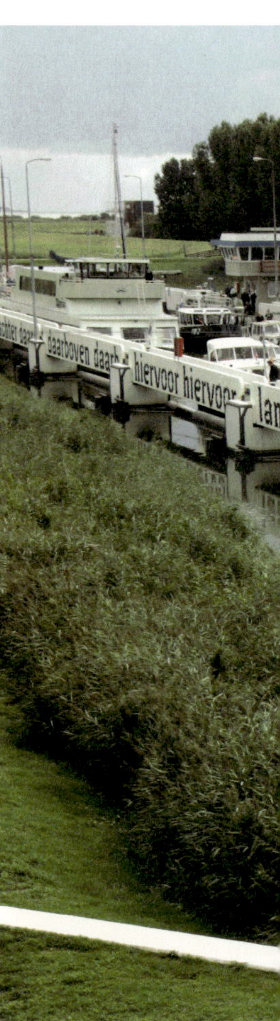

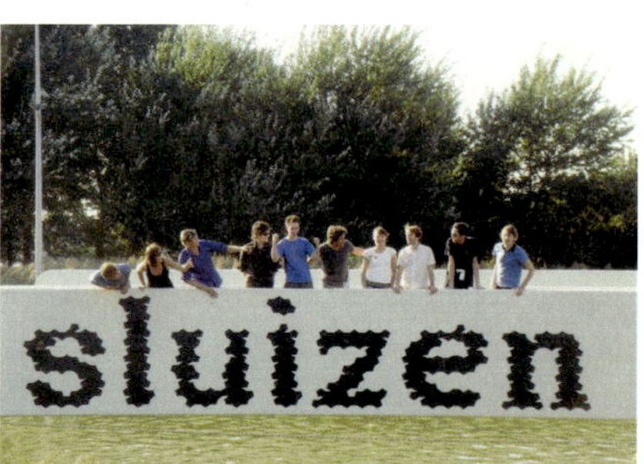

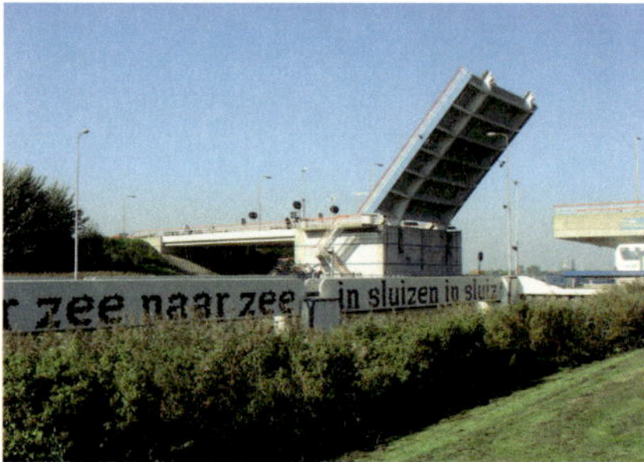

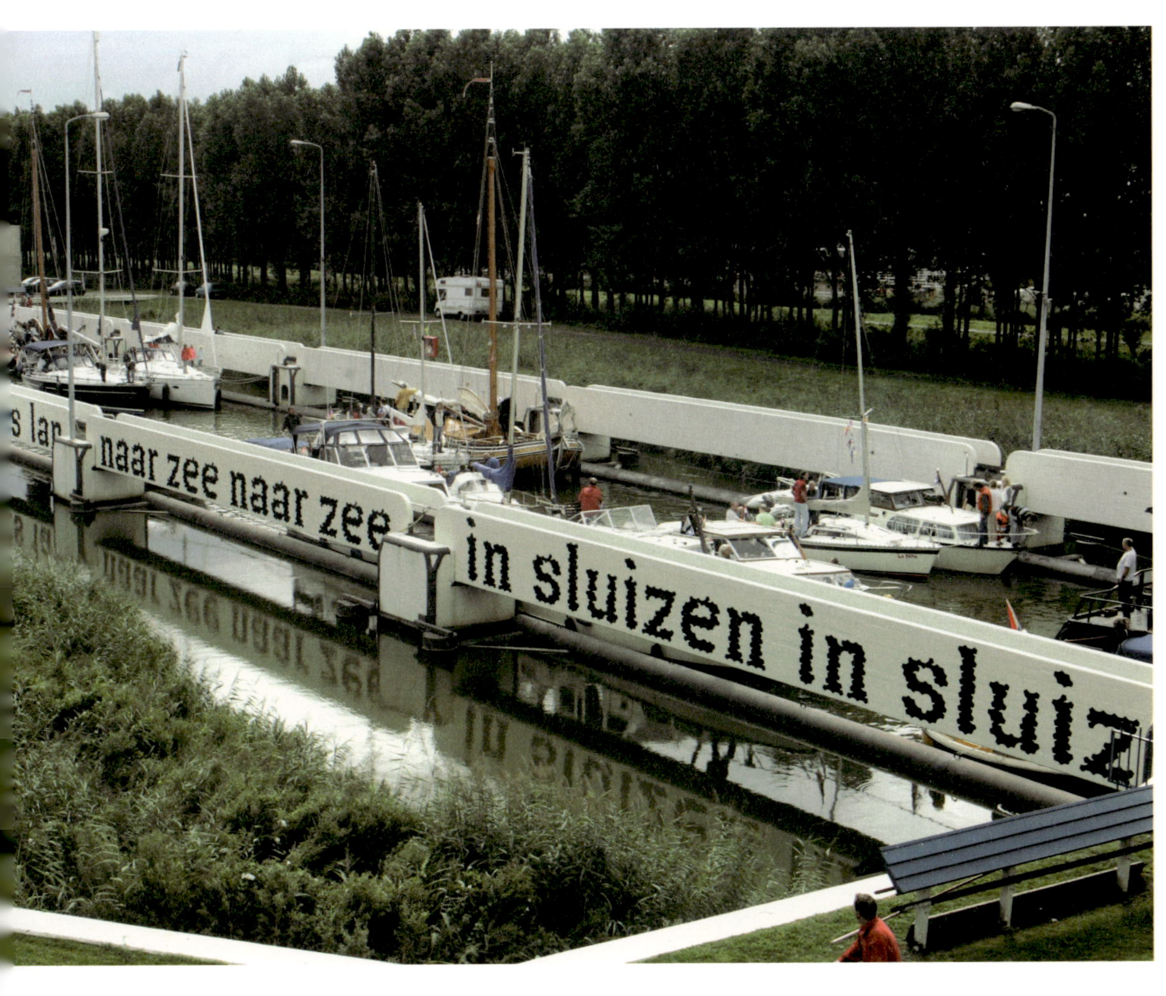
naar zee naar zee
in sluizen in slui

70 fellows
by Catalogtree

An invitation for a design agency in Amsterdam. They were moving to new premises and with this in mind we generated the image of small birds flocking as type. The same typography is dubbed on the other side of the paper.

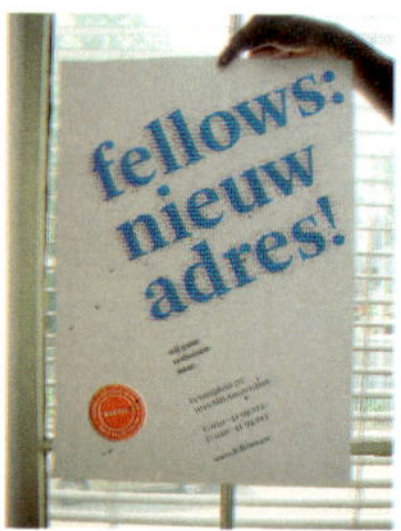

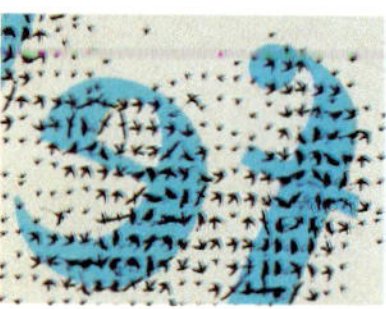

for Fellows, 2006.

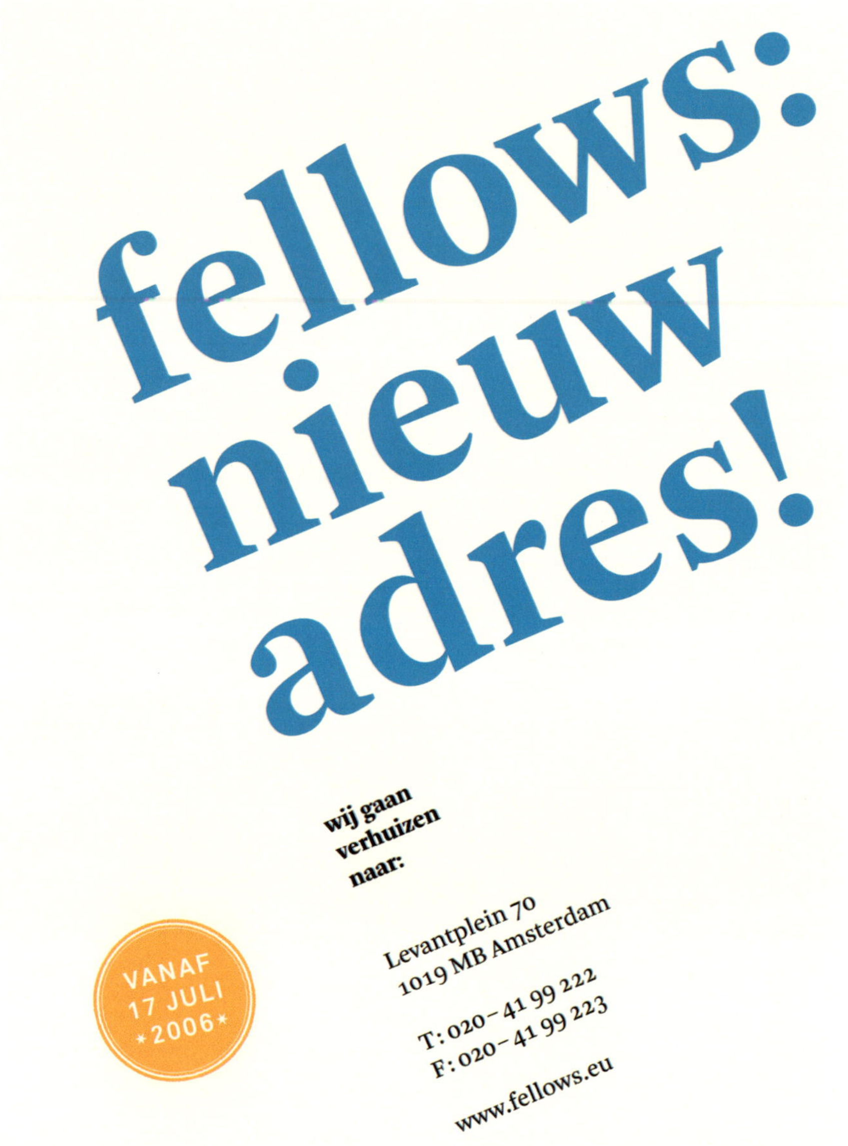

fellows:
nieuw
adres!

wij gaan
verhuizen
naar:

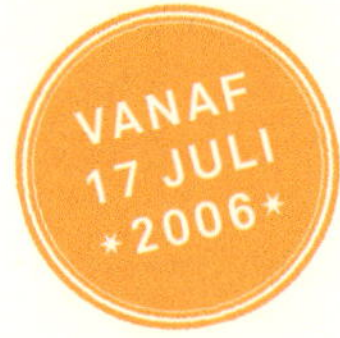

Levantplein 70
1019 MB Amsterdam

T: 020 - 41 99 222
F: 020 - 41 99 223

www.fellows.eu

Power
by Thonik

Communication for the International Architecture Biennale Rotterdam 2007. A typography that looks like buildings fighting to fill the available space.

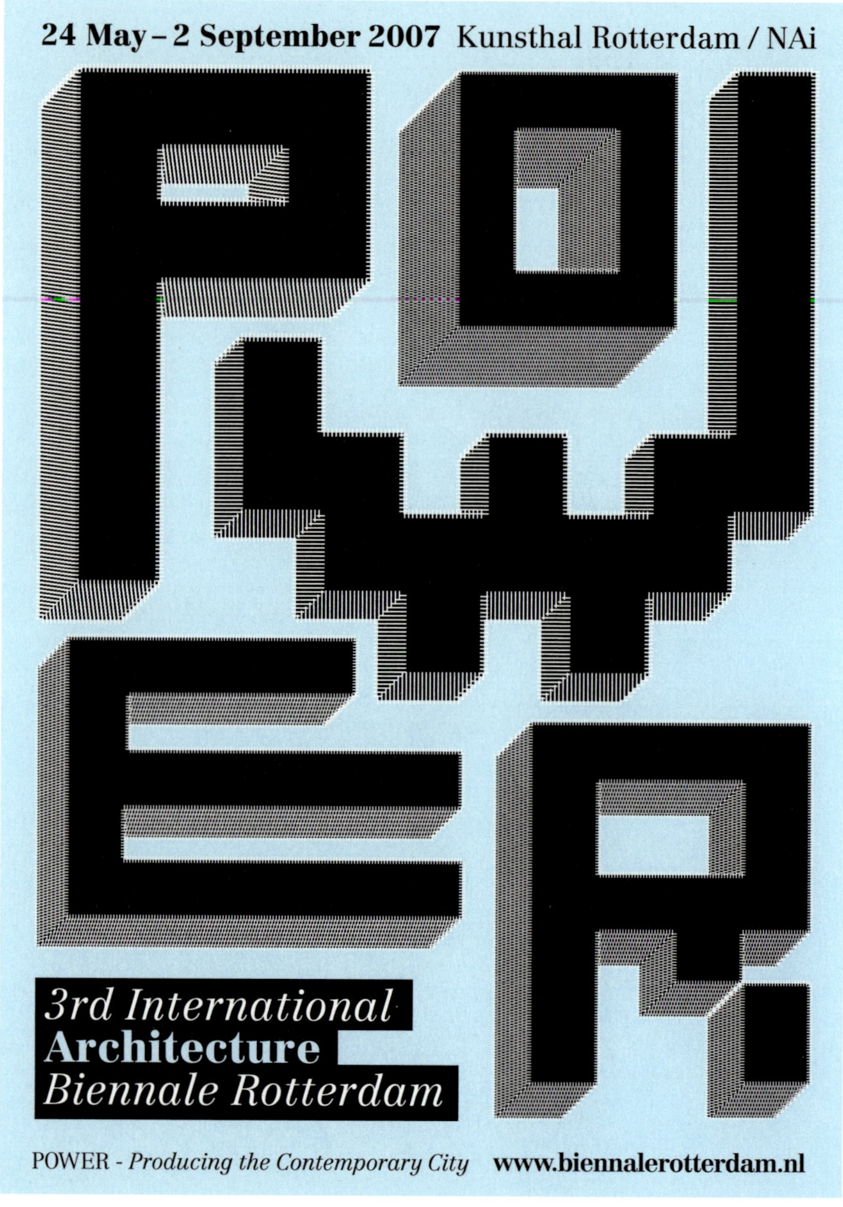

73 BNA
by Thonik

In a strong serif typography the triangular shape of the ‹A› is shifted toward a square form in several black lines to merge with the square forms of the ‹B›, and the ‹N›. The graphic line-pattern is used for illustrations and a system of sub-brands, e.g. ‹BNA-blad› (magazine) and ‹BNA-Kubus› (award). The yellow stresses the graphic quality of the style.

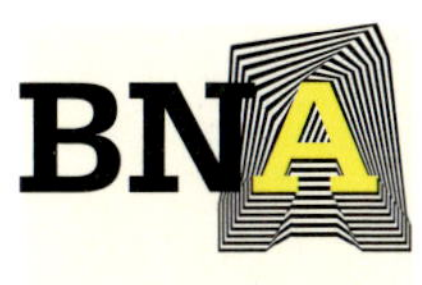

Identity for the Royal Institute of Dutch Architects: BNA, 2007

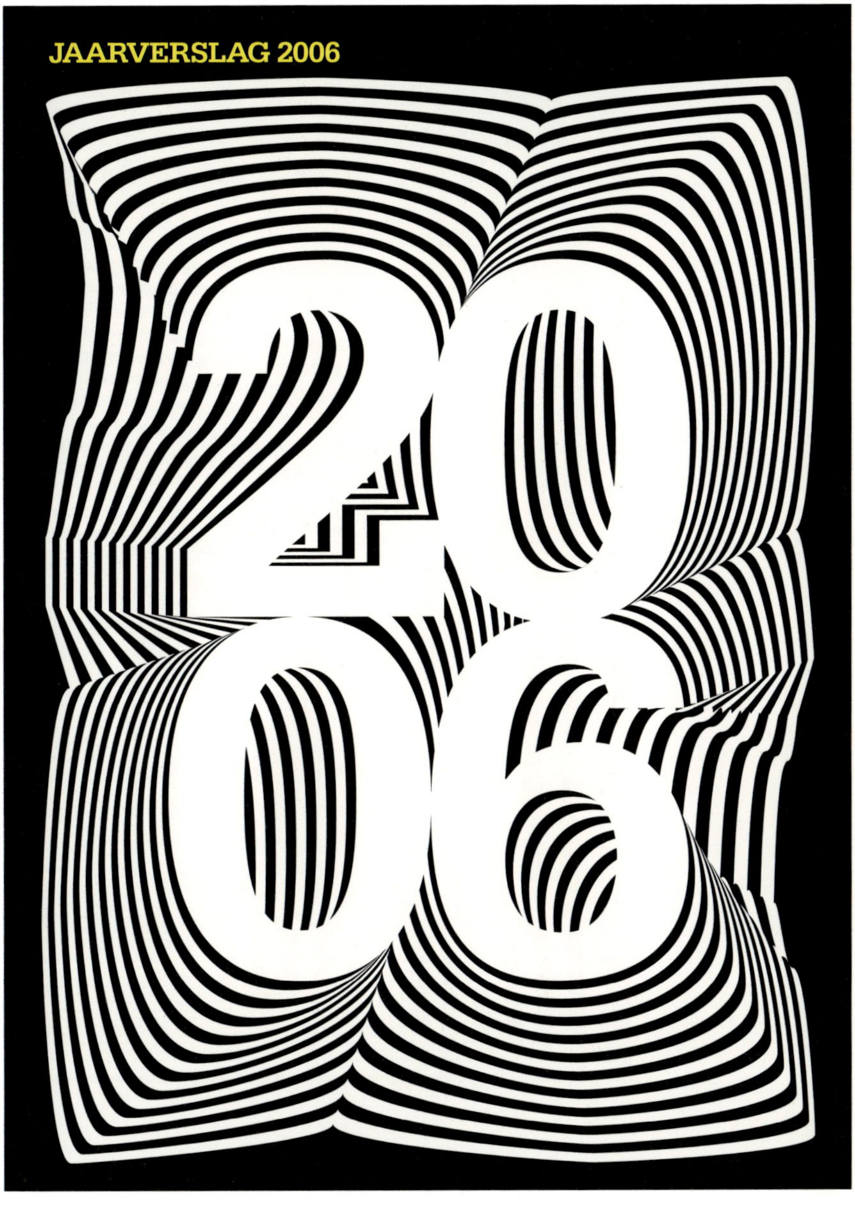

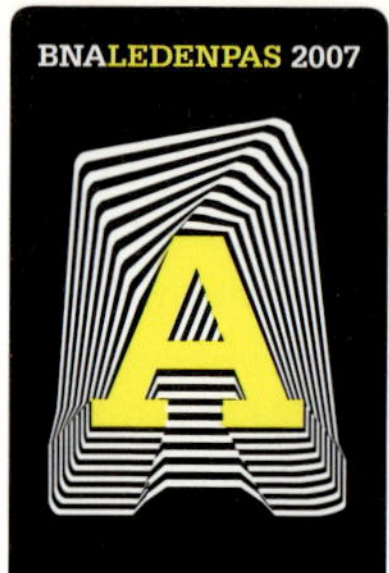

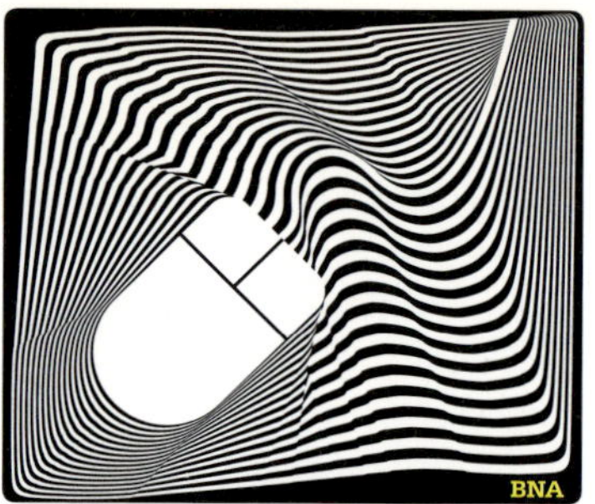

DE GROEI IS ERUIT
De bevolking slinkt: een trend met grote gevolgen voor ontwerpers. Van nieuwbouw naar sloop of wordt het ingrijpender dan dat?

DE VERROMMELING
Kas Oosterhuis: 'verzet van de centrale overheid tegen het toenemende ruimtebeslag leidt tot een esthetische correctie, tot uiterlijke ordening dus'

DOSSIER AUTEURSRECHT
Foto's publiceren zonder naamsvermelding mag en de sloopkogel is maar lastig tegen te houden. Tot hoever reikt het recht op eigen werk?

OMZETEISEN ABSURD HOOG
Kleinere bureaus ergeren zich aan de onhaalbare omzeteis van menige Europese aanbesteding. Micha de Haas: 'Dit glazen plafond is frustrerend.'

BNABLAD #01

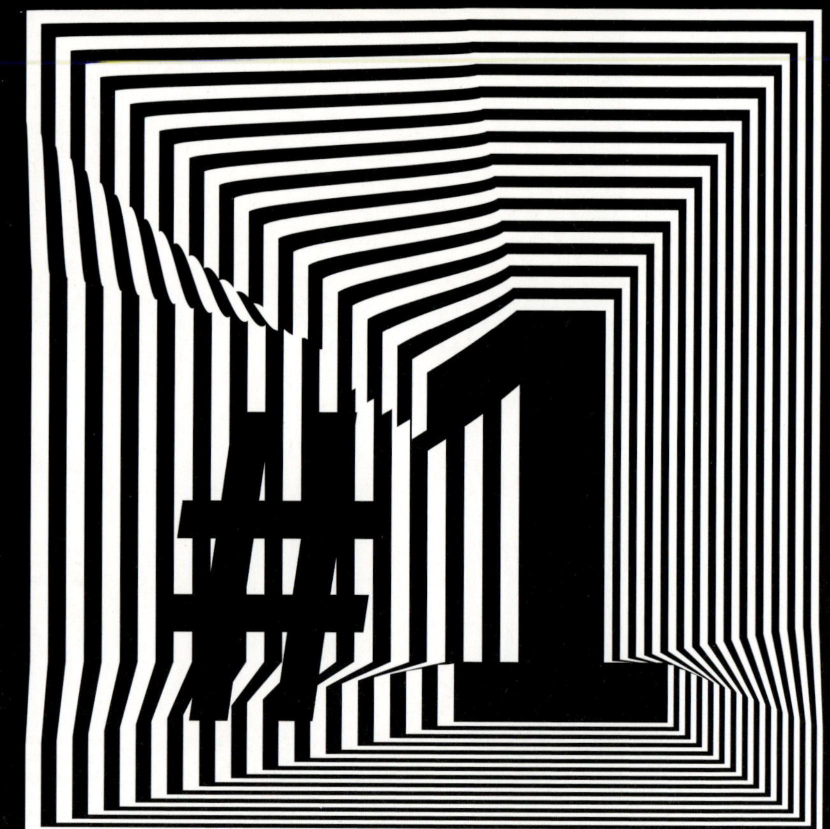

75 Face Your World
by Roger Teeuwen

‹Face Your World› is a project by artist Jeanne van Heeswijk and architect Dennis Kaspori. The long wall graphics is an open air exhibition of the developed idea's by the children. It is called an ‹Open air exhibition as a not desired advice for the Museumpark›.

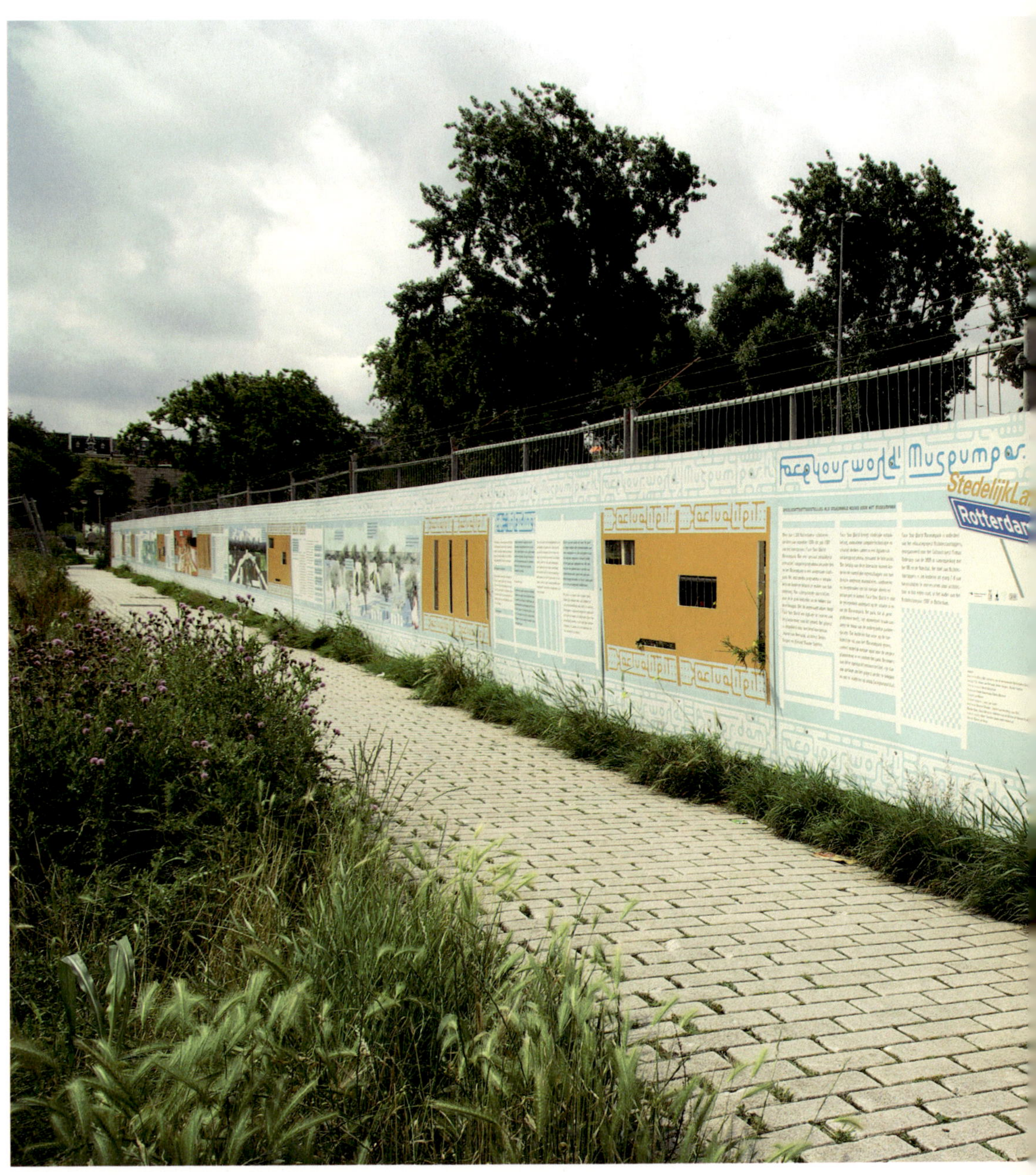

Museumpark, Rotterdam,
2007

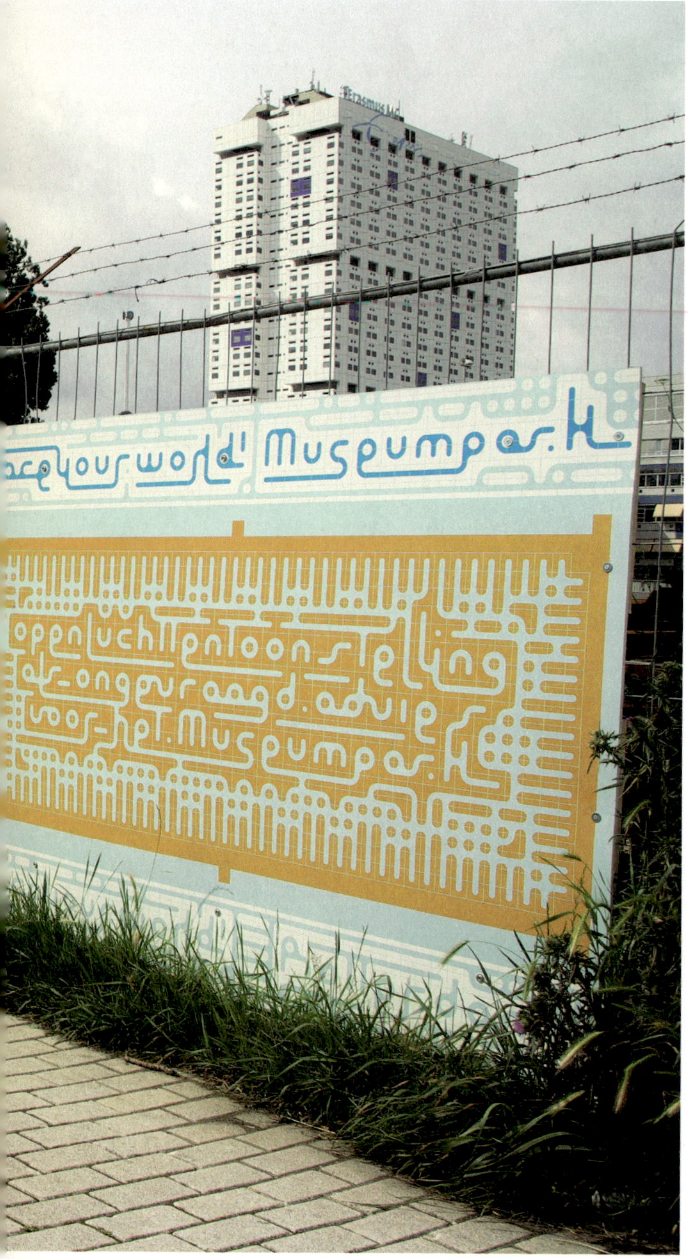

Workshop, shop window,
Slotervaart, Amsterdam,
2006

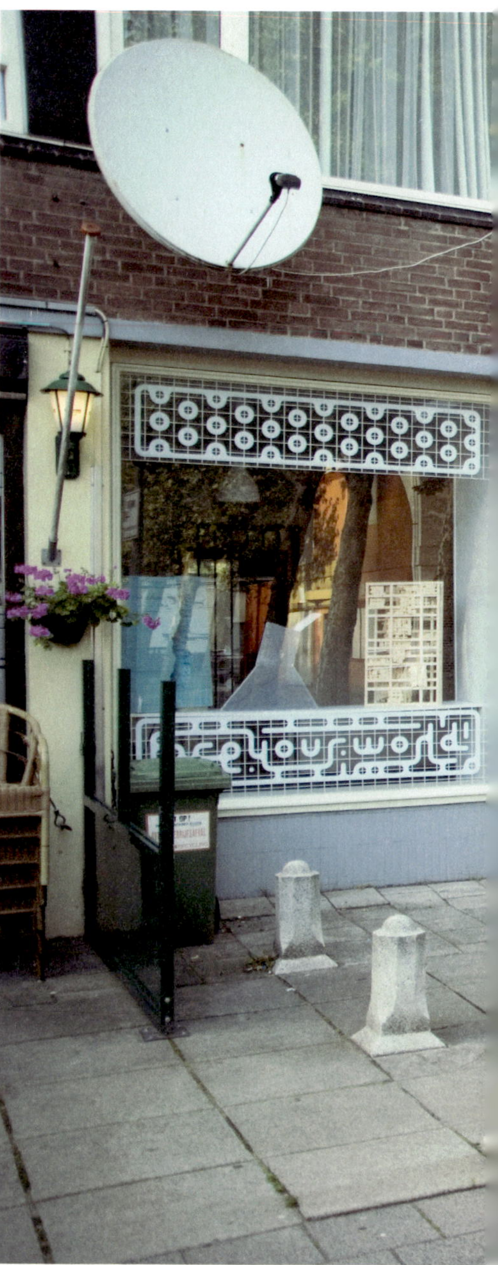

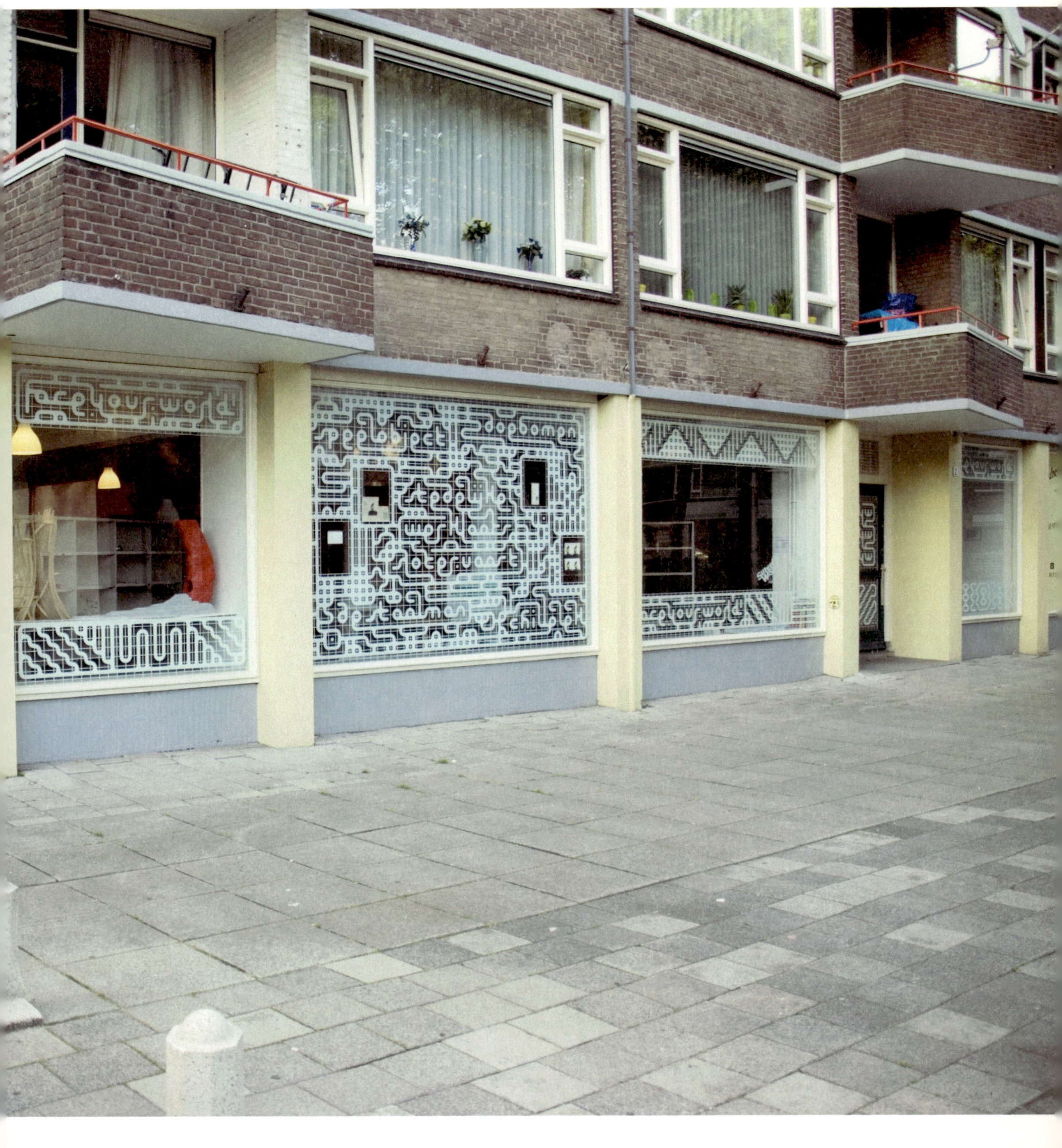

78 The Wall is the Landscape
by Lesley Moore

For this exhibition of the work of interior designer Robbert de Goede we designed a custom-made font based on the designer's working method, in which modules play a big part. The font itself consists of just two modules, one straight and one curved, from which all of the letters are made. Using a stencil system, the entire lettering was painted with just these two elements.

HKU Academy Gallery, Utrecht, 2005

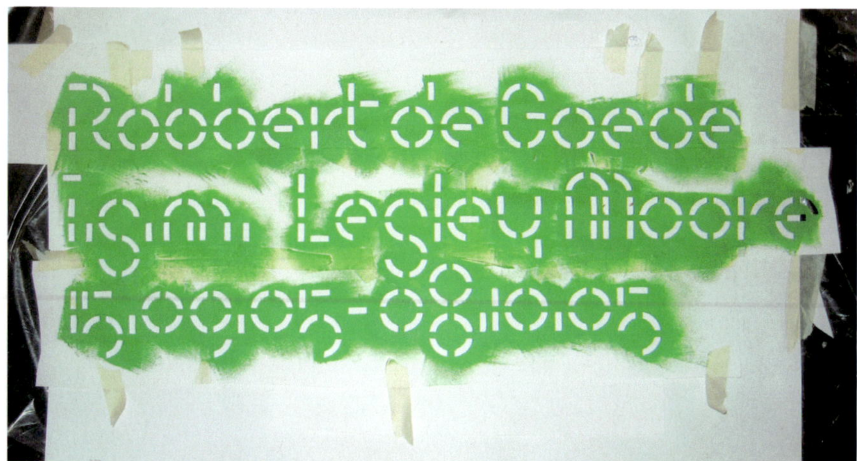

Good Robbert©

the ideal stencil letter for lazy dogs

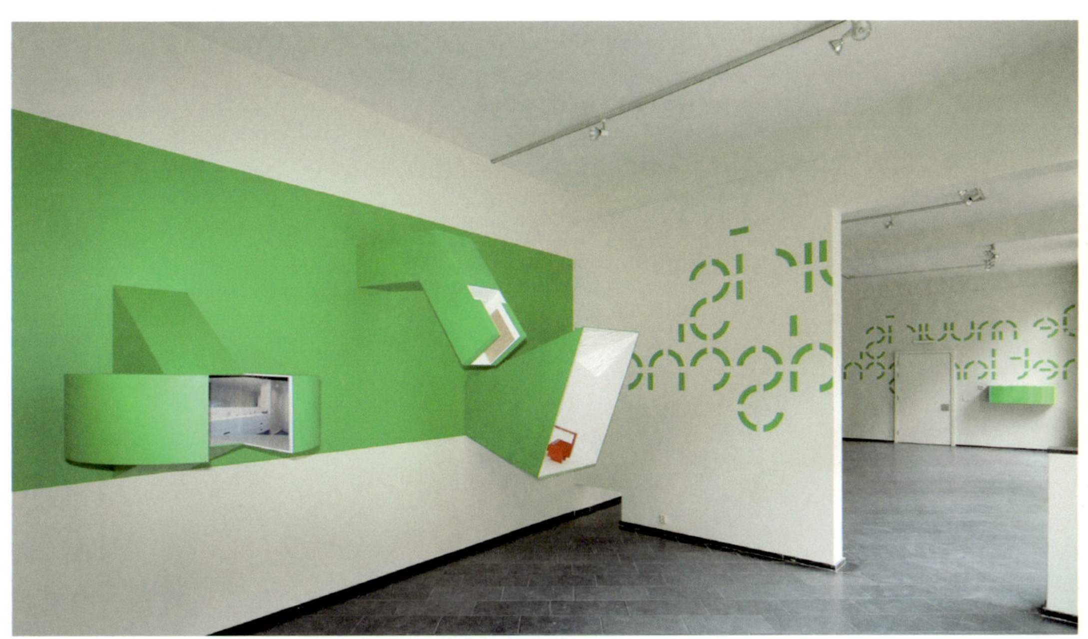

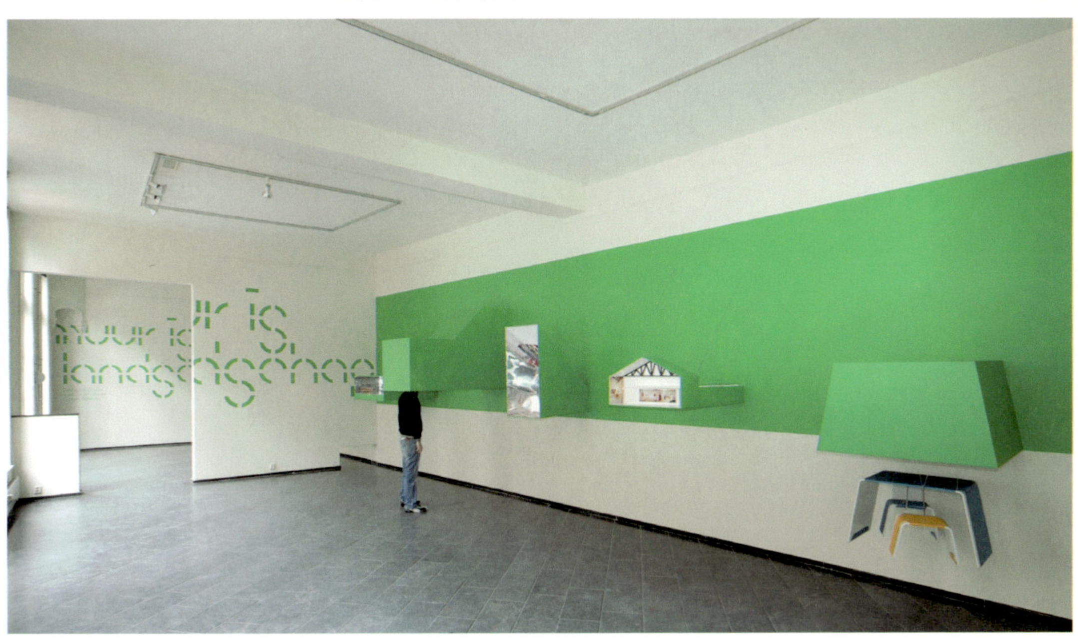

80 RMN logo

by Experimental Jetset

In 2006, the RMN (National Union of French Museums) asked us to redesign their logo (and part of their graphic identity) while keeping the old logo intact. In other words, we were asked to design a new ‹graphic environment› for the old logo.

The solution came to us immediately. We discovered that the old logo (a circle with the letter ‹M› in it, designed in 1969 by Adrian Frutiger) already contained, in itself, the other two letters (‹R› and ‹N›).

We therefore cut the old logo in half, liberating the ‹R› and ‹N›, and placed them on either side of the ‹M›, thus completing the RMN acronym.

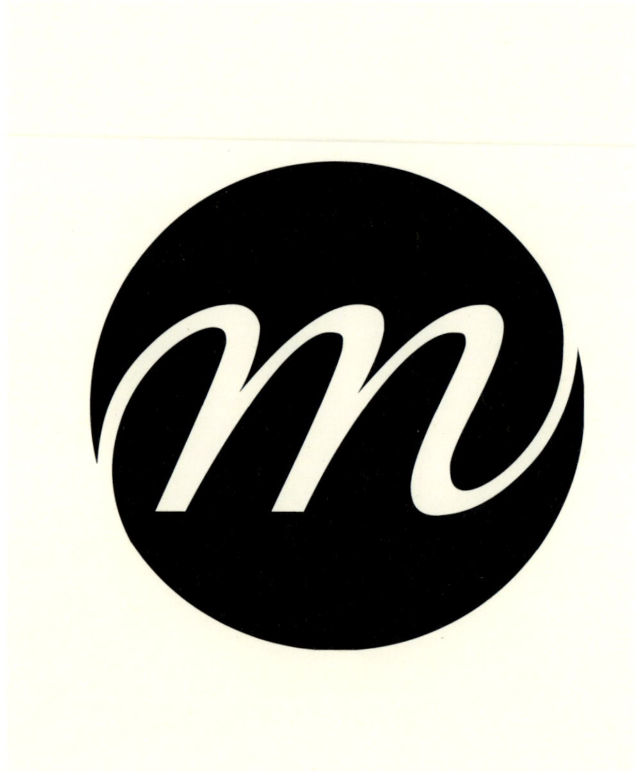

the old logo, designed by Adrian Frutiger in 1969

The old logo looked quite static, because the dynamism of the slanted ‹M› was completely neutralized by the circle. By adding the diagonal slashes, the logo becomes dynamic again: it suddenly gets a rhythm, a movement, a specific form.

More importantly, the whole idea of a réunion is suddenly emphasized, since the new logo makes it very clear that the letter ‹M› is in fact a ‹réunion› of the letters ‹R› and ‹N›.

When designing this logo, we were thinking all the time about the role of slashing and cutting in art: Modernist collages, Gordon Matta-Clark's cut buildings, Lucio Fontana's slashed paintings. We constantly had to remind ourselves that cutting something in half doesn't have to be a destructive statement; it can also be a very constructive gesture.

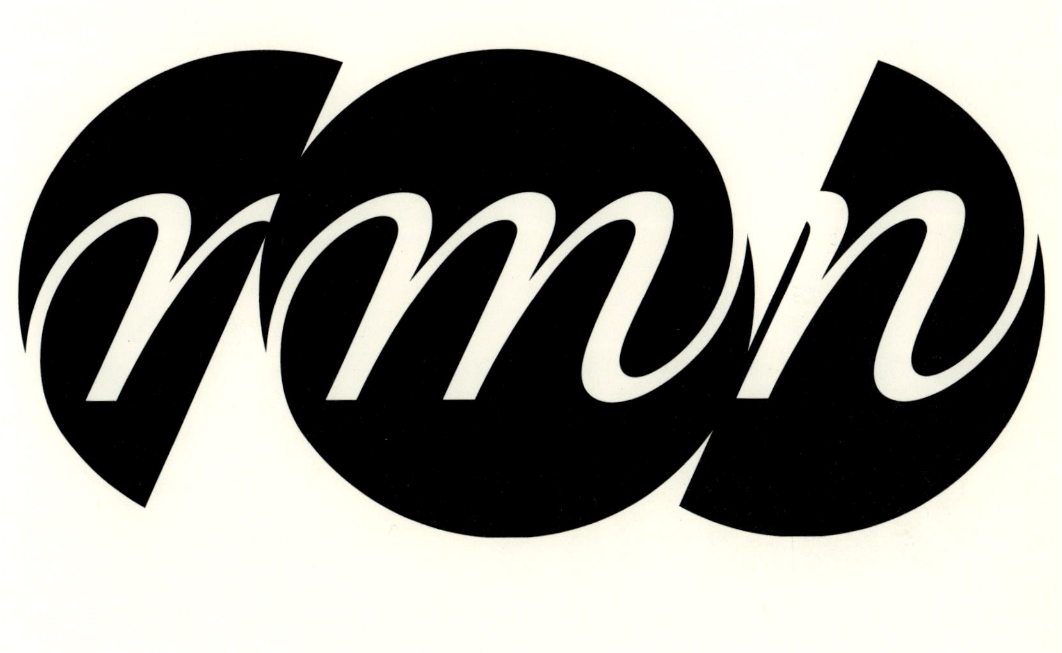

the new logo, designed by Experimental Jetset in 2006 for Réunion des Musées Nationaux (Paris)

82 Company logo
by Catalogtree

Implicit none, logical done.

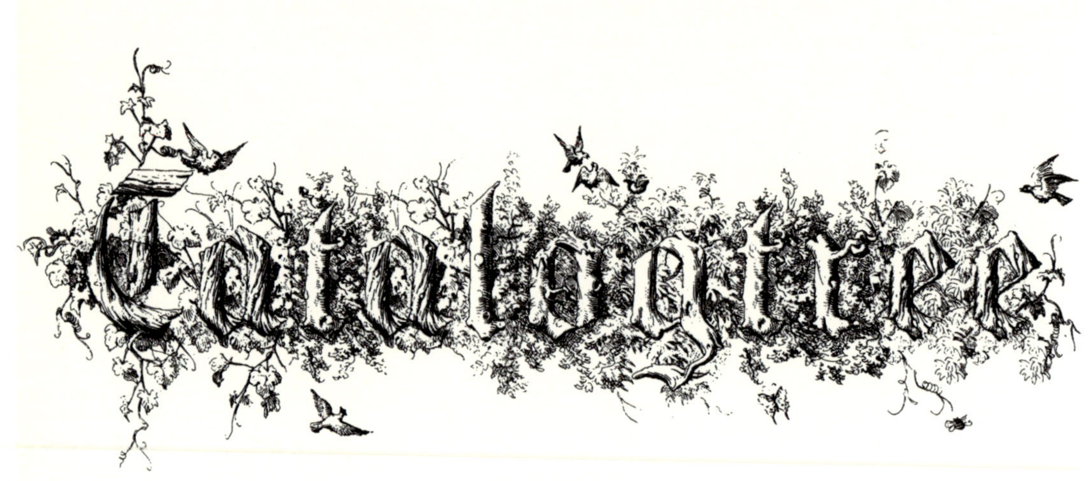

katalog
baum

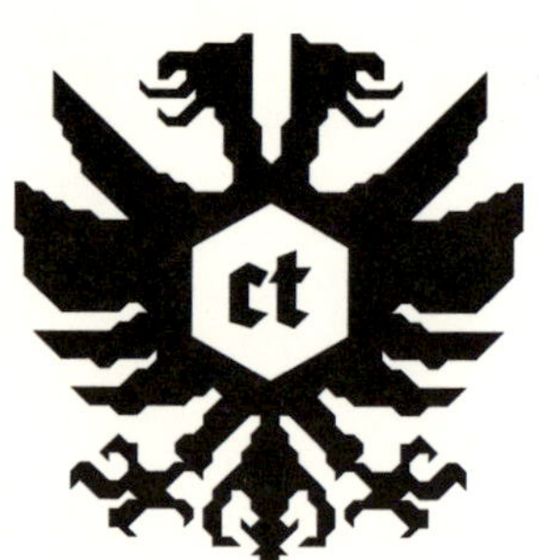

2006

83 Vive le Papier Électronique
by Strange Attractors Design

‹Vive le Papier Électronique› is a self initiated exploration of Arabic letter forms and hand-set technology as well as a celebration of Futurism and the newsprint its manifesto was originally printed on.

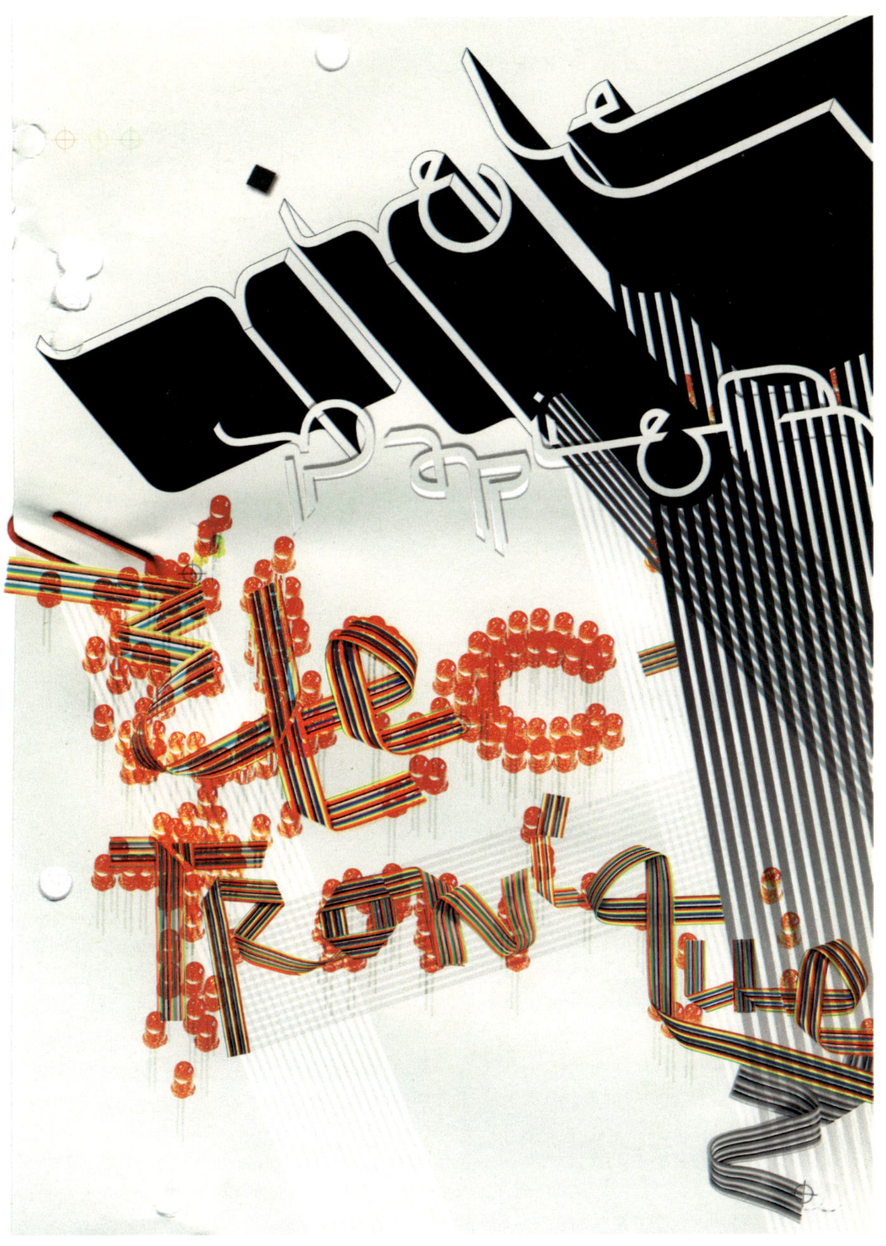

84 Confused Type
by Toko

Ongoing project featuring type explorations.

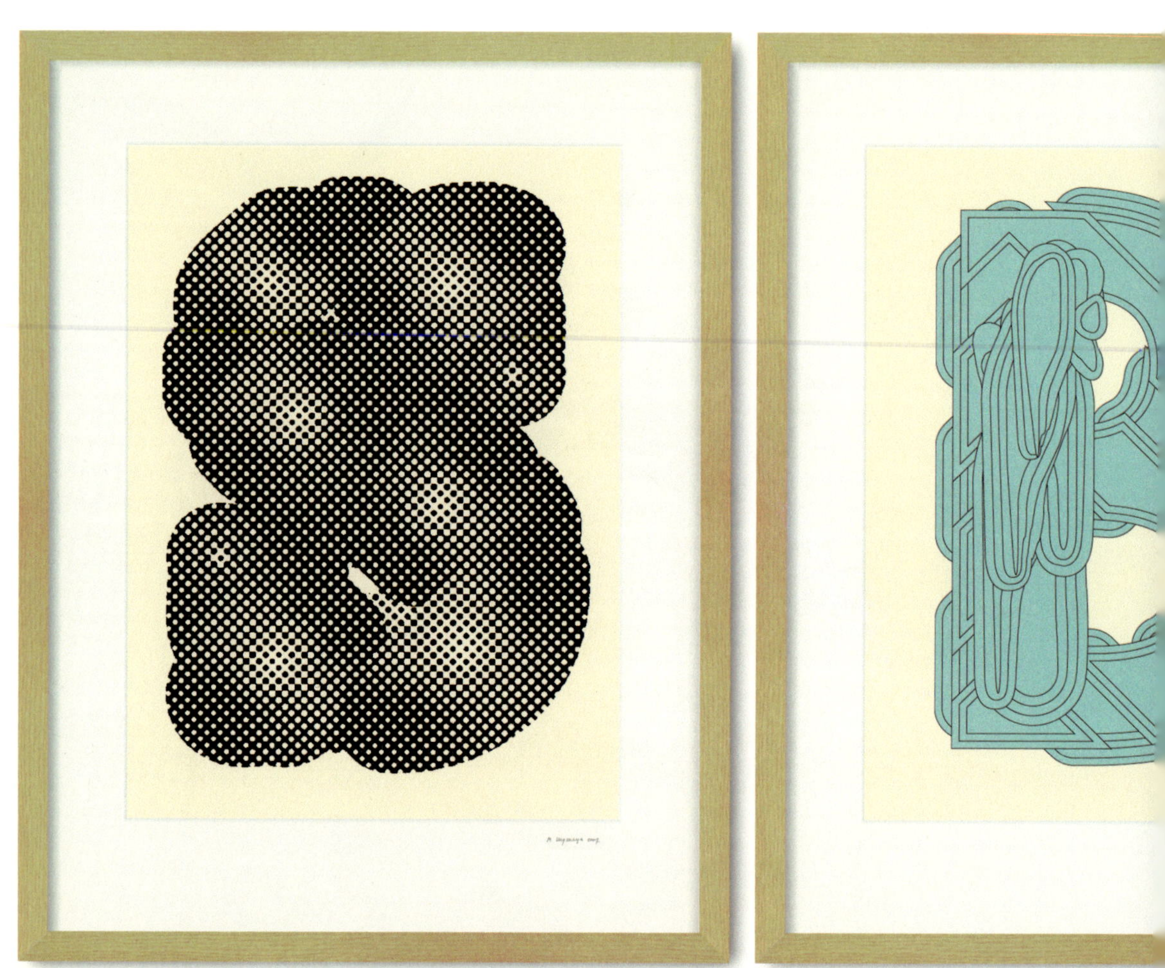

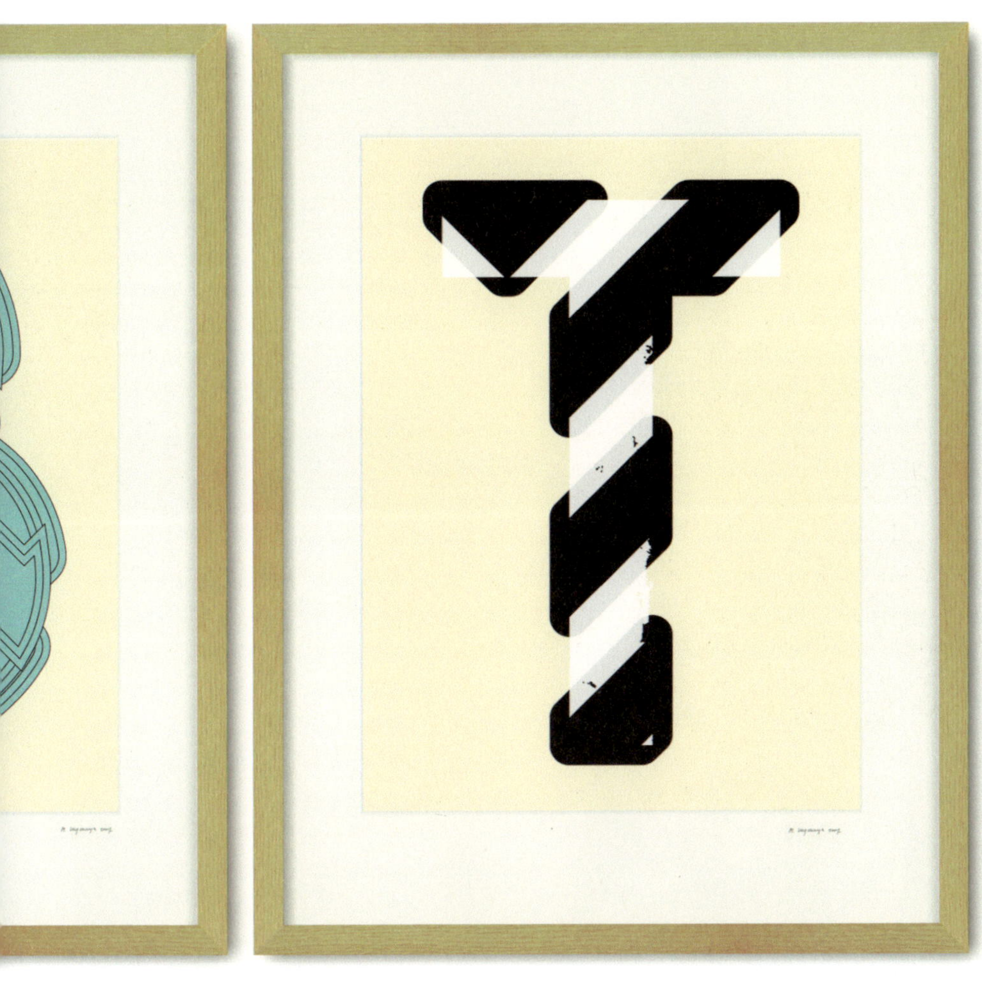

Statistical Graphics

VINEC 006
by Catalogtree

VINEC 008
by Catalogtree

Margeting book
by Lust

Margeting pages
by Lust

General Electricville
by Office of CC

The Expanding Universe of Wikipedia
by Office of CC

Drink up
by Office of CC

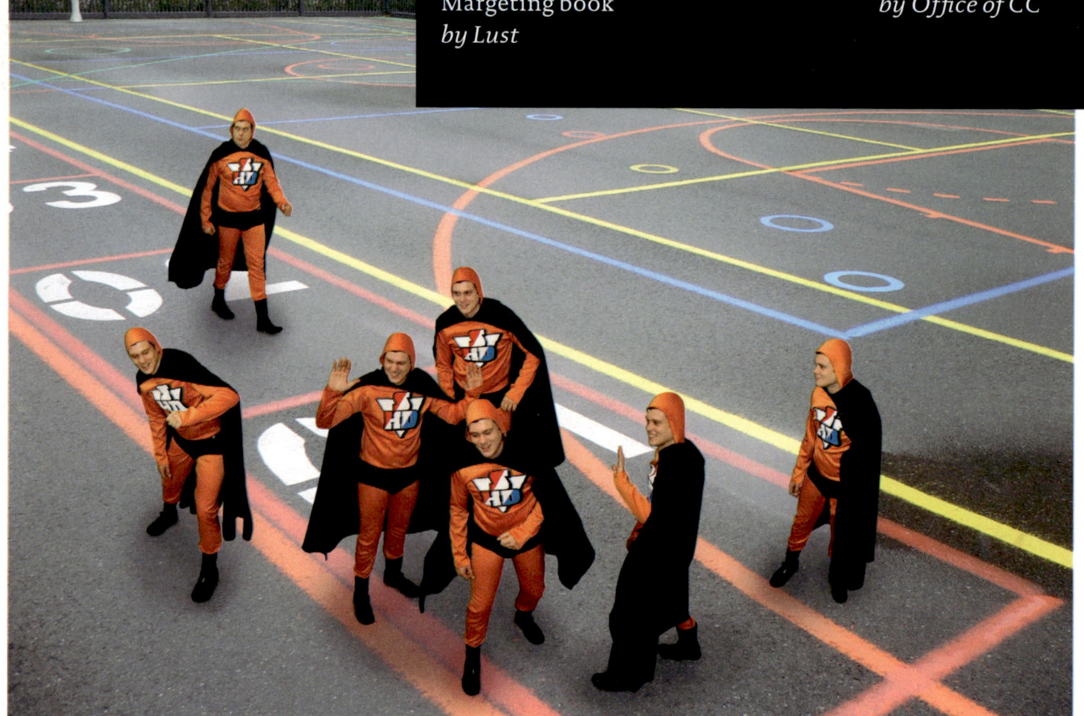

Buying a Brand
by Office of CC

Homeless
by Office of CC

Marking Europe High Speed
by Lust

Transurban
by Catalogtree

VINEC 005
by Catalogtree

Een nieuwe wereldkaart
by STAR

Wereld ball/La bola del mundo (World-ball)
by STAR

Map of Maps
by Minke Themans

Living Agenda
by Luna Maurer

Mare Nostrum
by Minke Themans & Roger Teeuwen

Los edificios más altos de cada país
by STAR

La Historia de las Expos
by STAR

88 VINEC 006
by Catalogtree

The sixth poster in a series of nine about the road between Arnhem and Nijmegen. The poster shows all the accidents that happened there between 1998 and 2003.

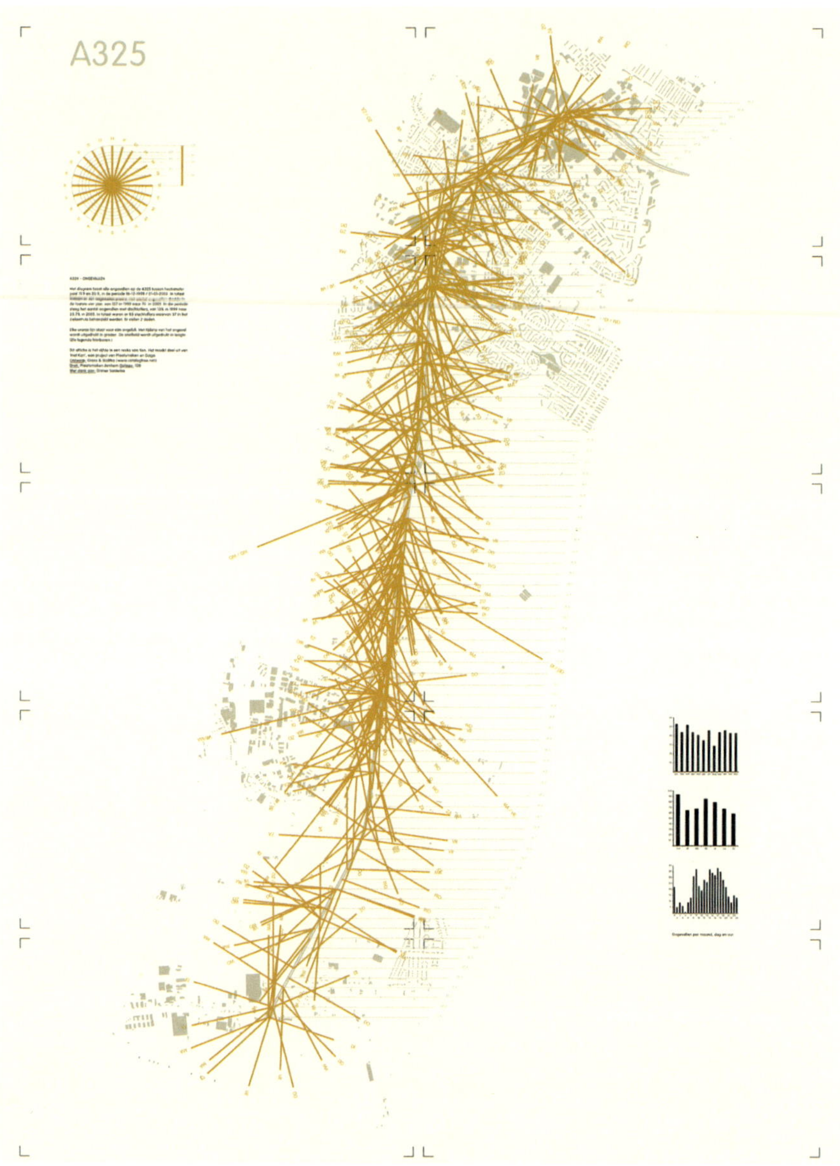

2005

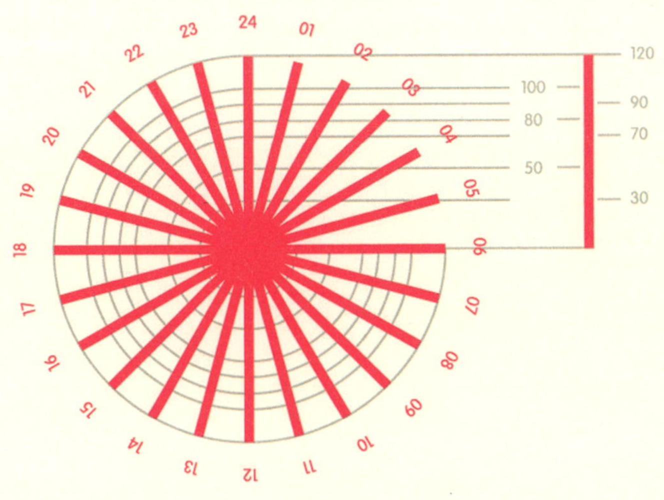
01 02 03 04 05 06 07 08 09 10 11 12 13 14 15 16 17 18 19 20 21 22 23 24
120
100
90
80
70
50
30

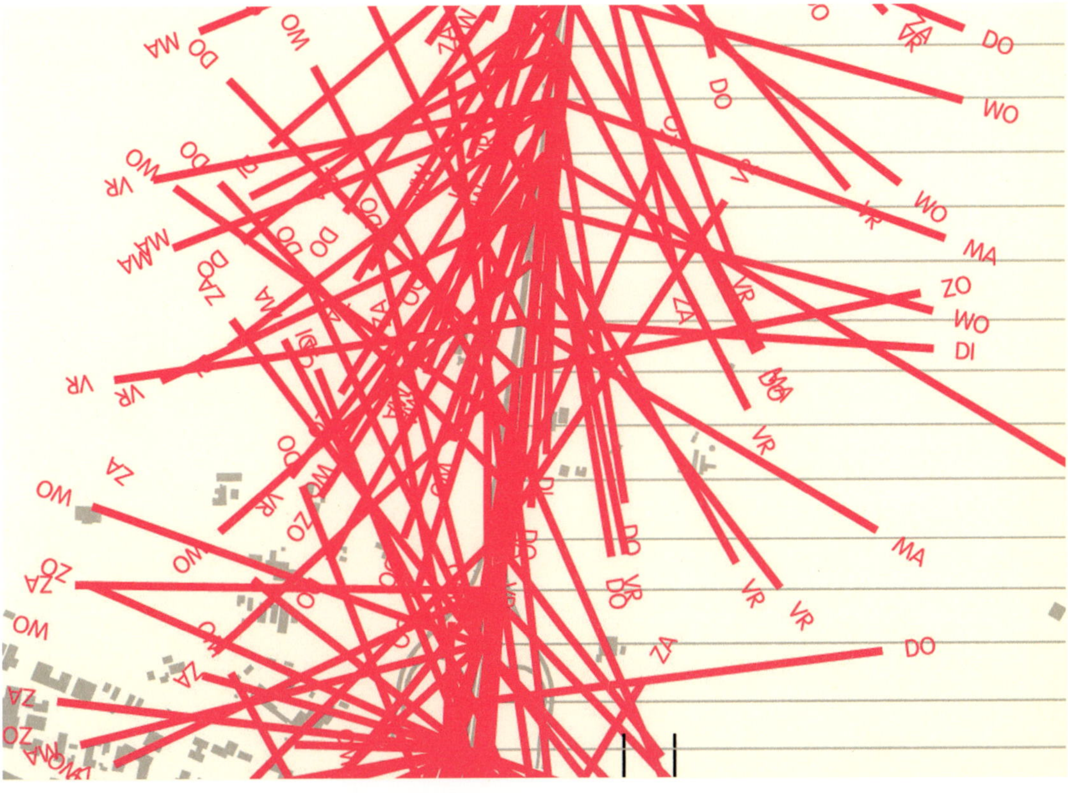

VINEC 008

by Catalogtree

The 8th poster in a series of nine about the road between Arnhem and Nijmegen. The image is a translation of traffic-intensity data gathered at a complex crossroads.

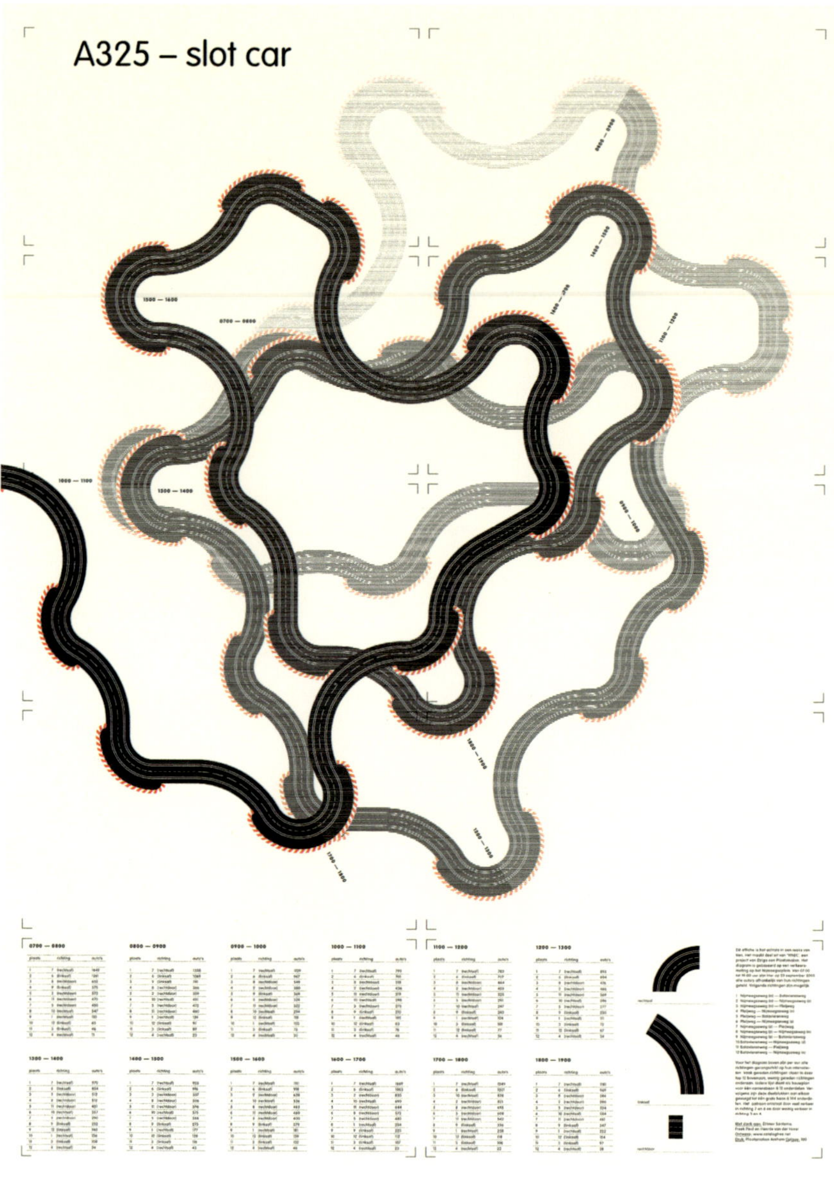

2005

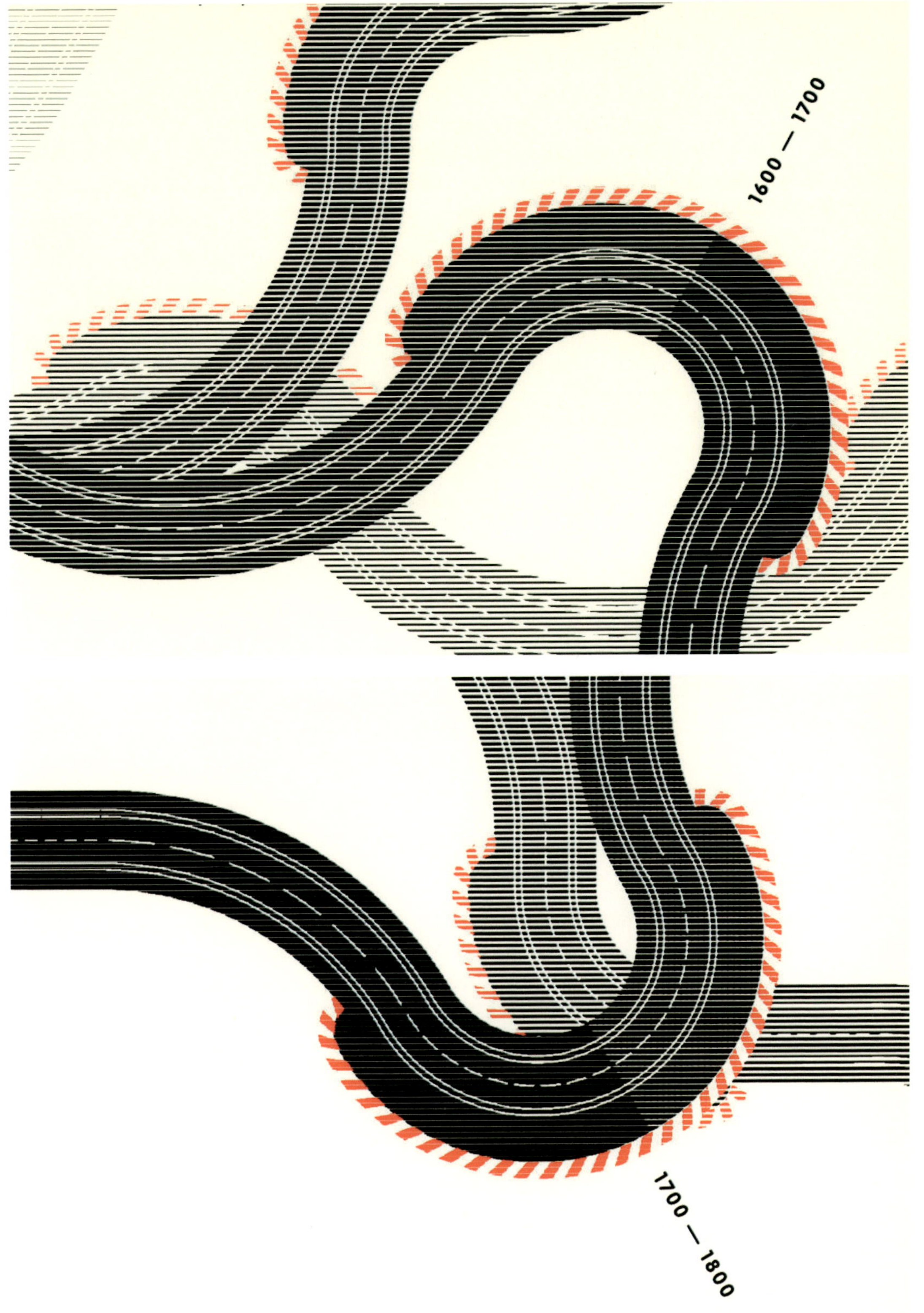
1600 — 1700
1700 — 1800

92 Margeting: Inventing a Different Marketing Language
by Lust

The language used by marketing is getting bogged down in the structure of the narratives it generates. Experiences and objects are offered to consumers in unambiguous, immutable descriptions. Brands (which that may also be programmes, ideologies or people) and consumers are captured in sharply defined frameworks and reduced to inflexible concepts. ‹Margeting› concepts eliminate anything that differs from the values they embody. As a result there is no place for ideas other than those that brand managers have named and turned into an identity and this includes ideas that matter to consumers. Brand managers want to keep on seeing the same things over and over again: they make language unambiguous. Lust designed the book starting with a 75-page index where all the words used in the text are indexed. This connects seamlessly to the whole idea ‹Margeting› is aiming at. ‹Margeting› generates narratives that do not dish up a single, stage-managed scenario, but keep on generating collections of ever-changing narratives from a predefined brand area: the brand as a crossroads of narratives! Only one font, in one size and one weight is used for the entire 512-page book (named Best Designed Book of the Year 2004).

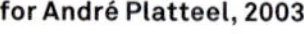
for André Platteel, 2003

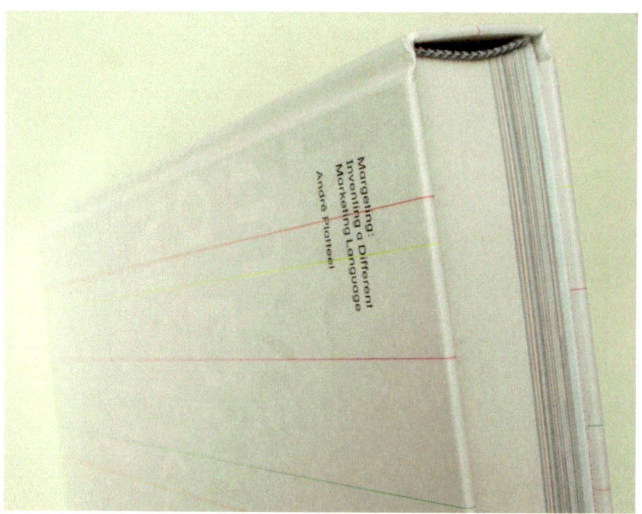

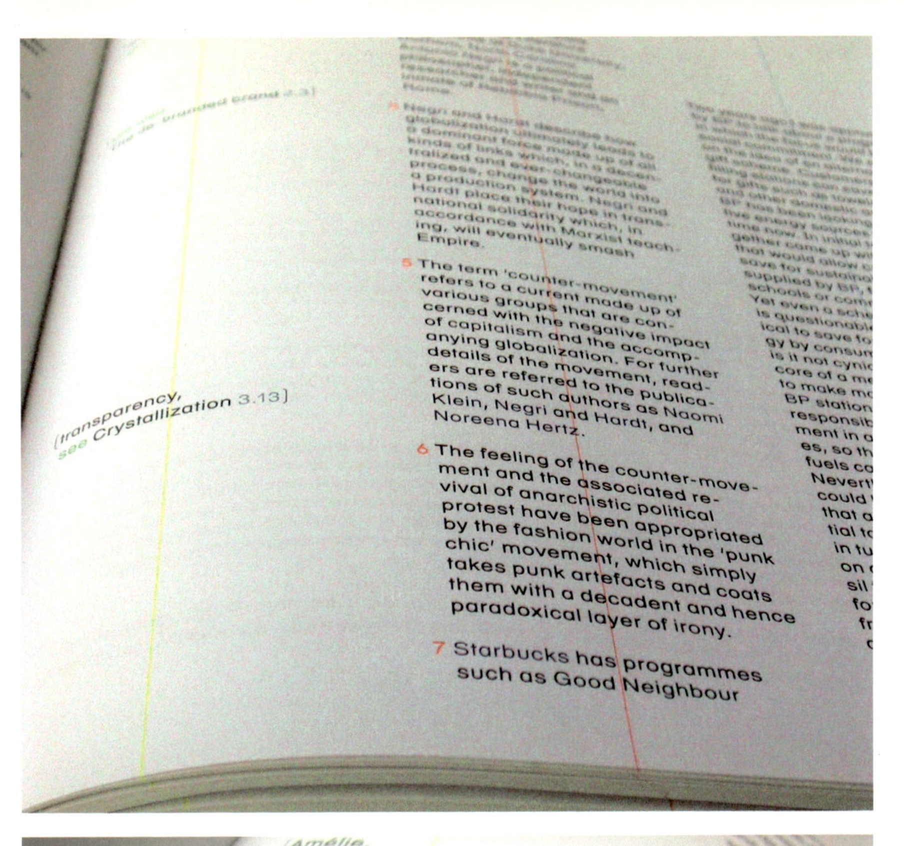

[Amélie,
see also
The humanized brand 2.5]

[affection image,
see Ambiguity 3.2
and Worlding 3.8]

[The effect of David Lynch's images,
see also Interweaving 3.7
and Within and between 3.11]

9 In the same way, Dav
films create a sense
— yet his films are ar
horror movies. The c
everyday acts becom
ing because they do
viewers' expectations
are constantly on edg
the film can change
moment, in

We also included our contribution in the book, namely a new strategy for designing a new brand of shoes, based on the display of shoes in stores.

for André Platteel, 2003

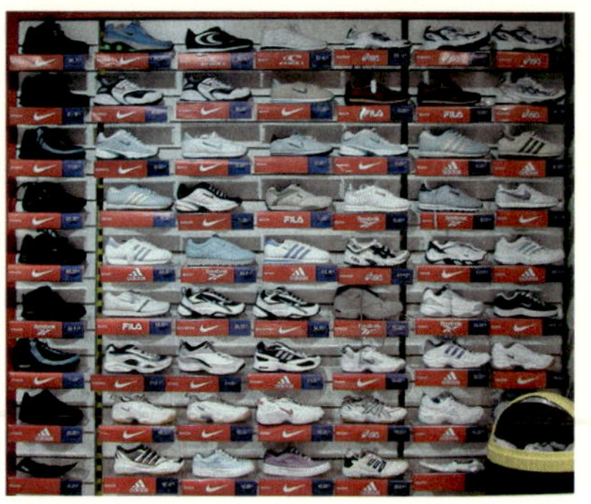

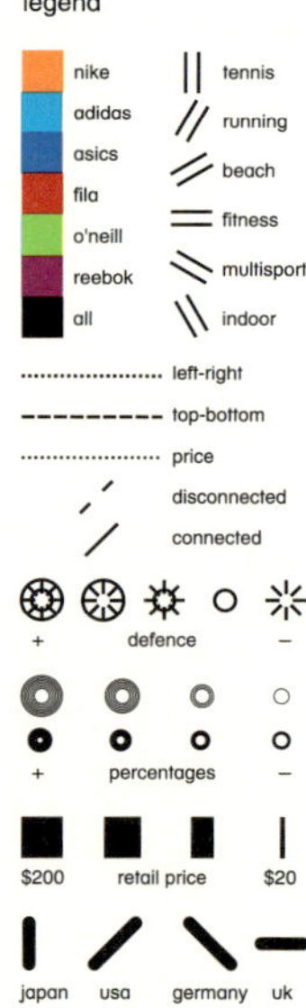

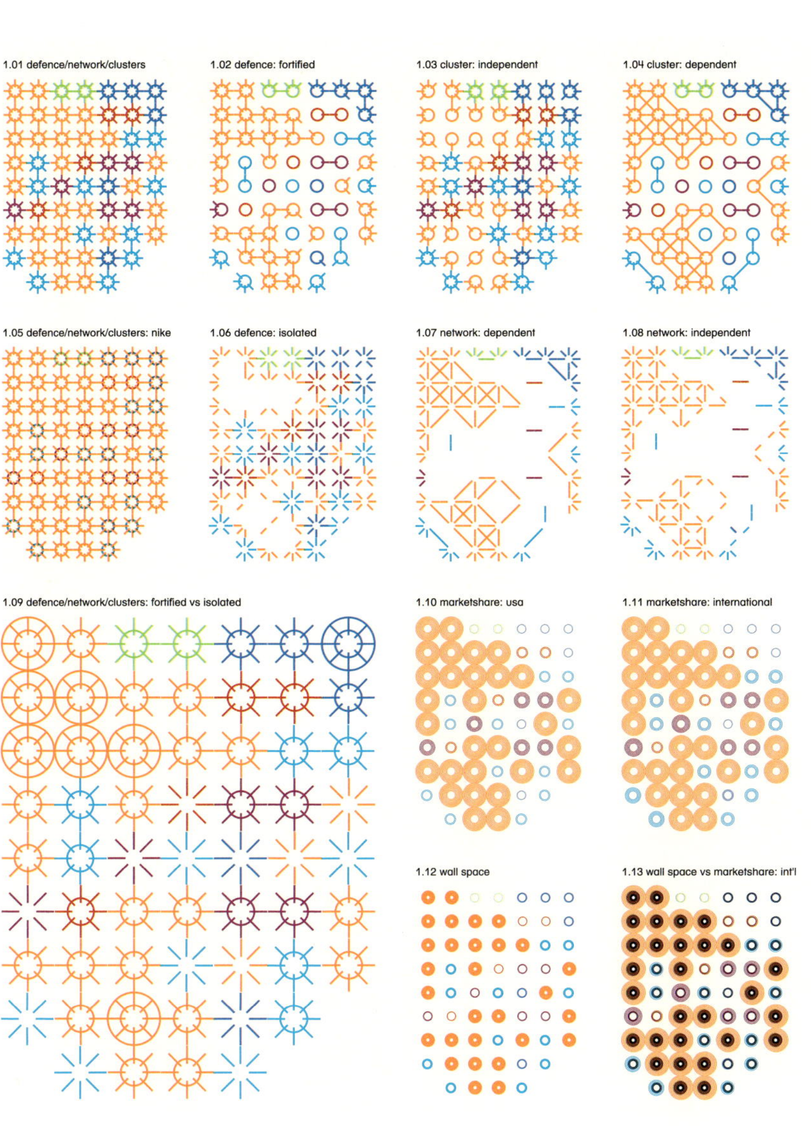
1.01 defence/network/clusters
1.02 defence: fortified
1.03 cluster: independent
1.04 cluster: dependent
1.05 defence/network/clusters: nike
1.06 defence: isolated
1.07 network: dependent
1.08 network: independent
1.09 defence/network/clusters: fortified vs isolated
1.10 marketshare: usa
1.11 marketshare: international
1.12 wall space
1.13 wall space vs marketshare: int'l

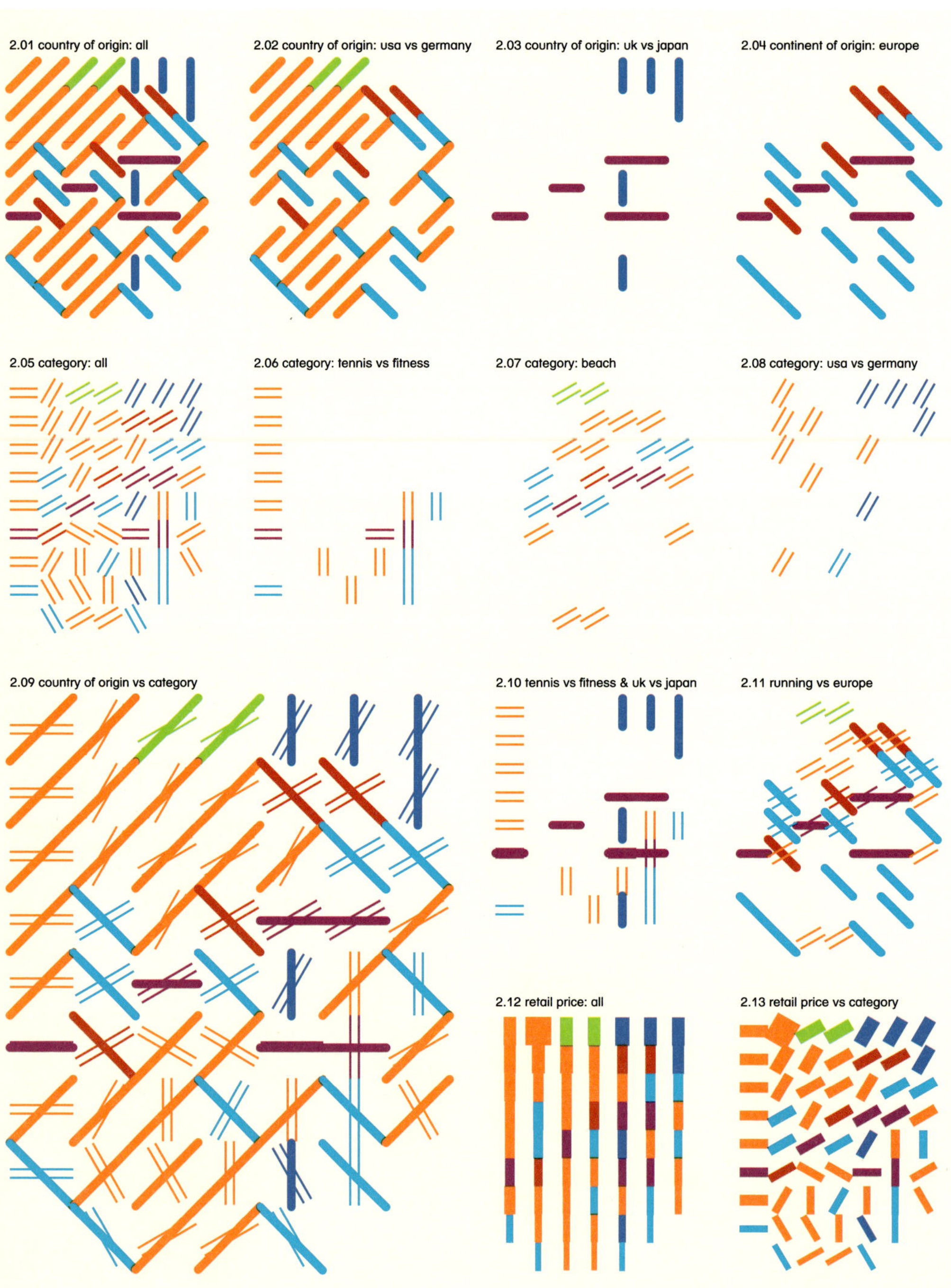
2.01 country of origin: all
2.02 country of origin: usa vs germany
2.03 country of origin: uk vs japan
2.04 continent of origin: europe
2.05 category: all
2.06 category: tennis vs fitness
2.07 category: beach
2.08 category: usa vs germany
2.09 country of origin vs category
2.10 tennis vs fitness & uk vs japan
2.11 running vs europe
2.12 retail price: all
2.13 retail price vs category

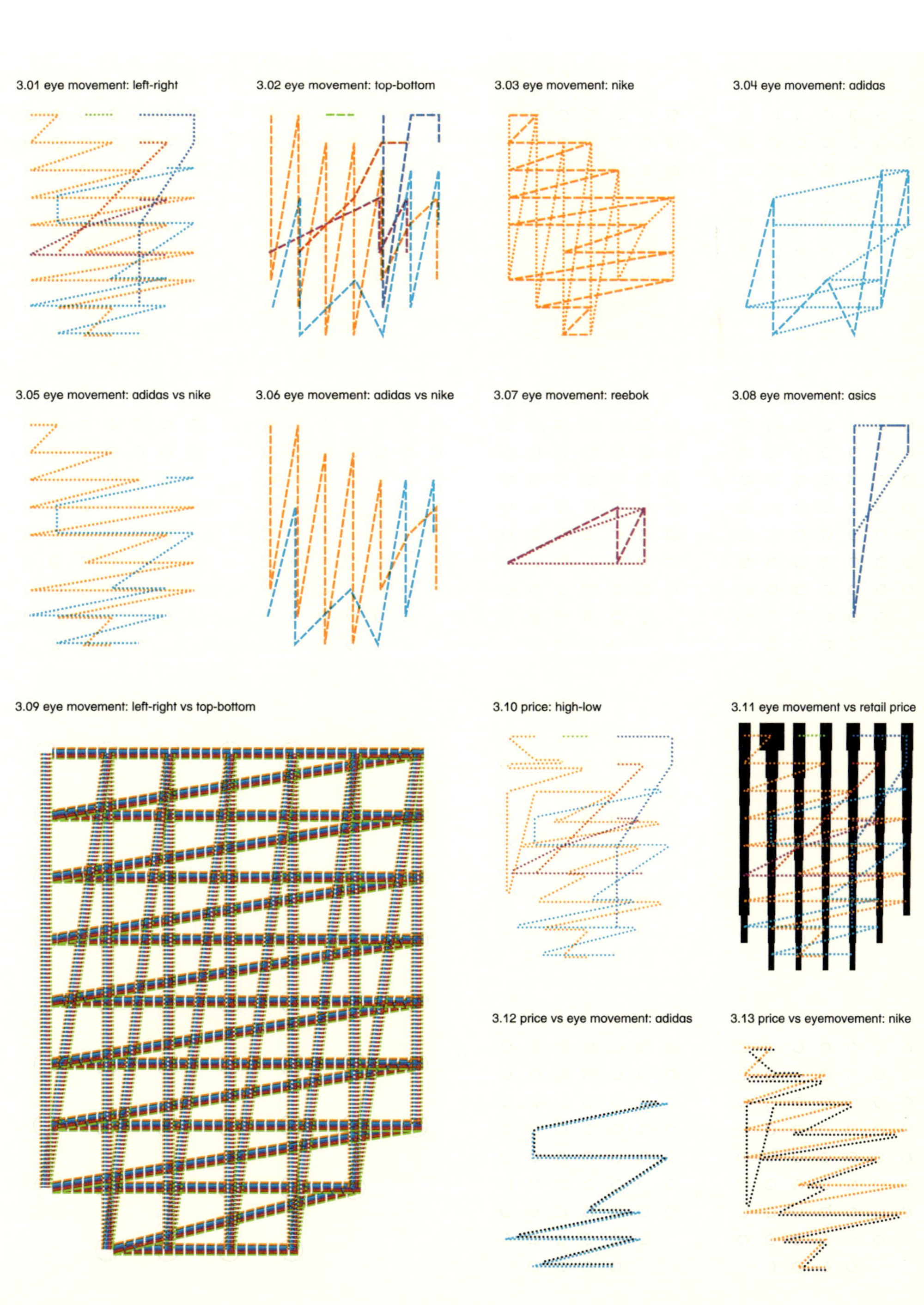
3.01 eye movement: left-right
3.02 eye movement: top-bottom
3.03 eye movement: nike
3.04 eye movement: adidas
3.05 eye movement: adidas vs nike
3.06 eye movement: adidas vs nike
3.07 eye movement: reebok
3.08 eye movement: asics
3.09 eye movement: left-right vs top-bottom
3.10 price: high-low
3.11 eye movement vs retail price
3.12 price vs eye movement: adidas
3.13 price vs eyemovement: nike

98 General Electricville
by Office of CC

GOOD is a socially conscious magazine that informs its readers and entertains them at the same time on issues that matter. We were invited to develop five graphic visuals in the 'Transparency' section of its 5th issue.

for GOOD, 2007

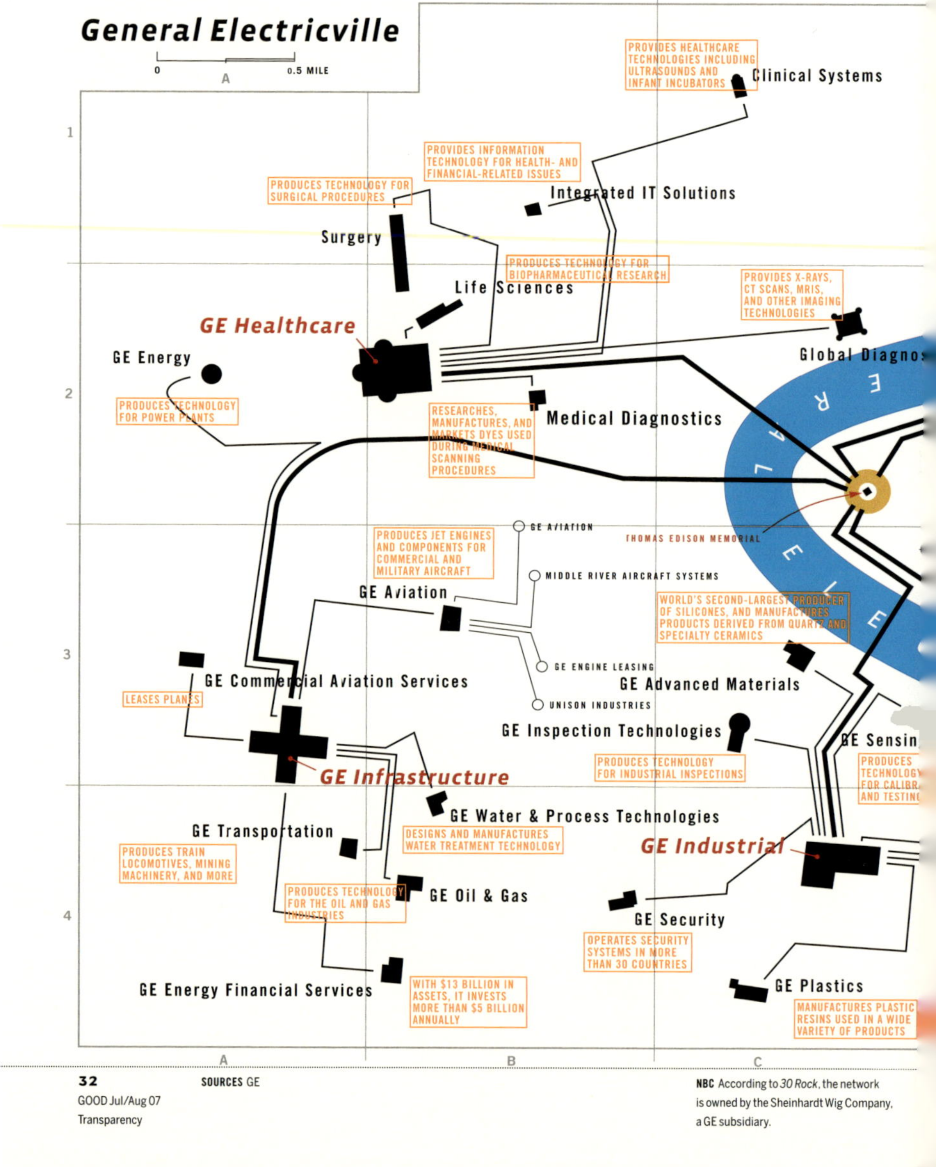

The diversity and the immensity of General Electric (GE) –as one of the largest corporations in the world– presented us with a visual problem. Our solution was to visualize the infrastructure of GE in the form of a city map, which makes the complex data easier to comprehend. This map was based on the city of Rome to indicate that GE is a corporate empire.

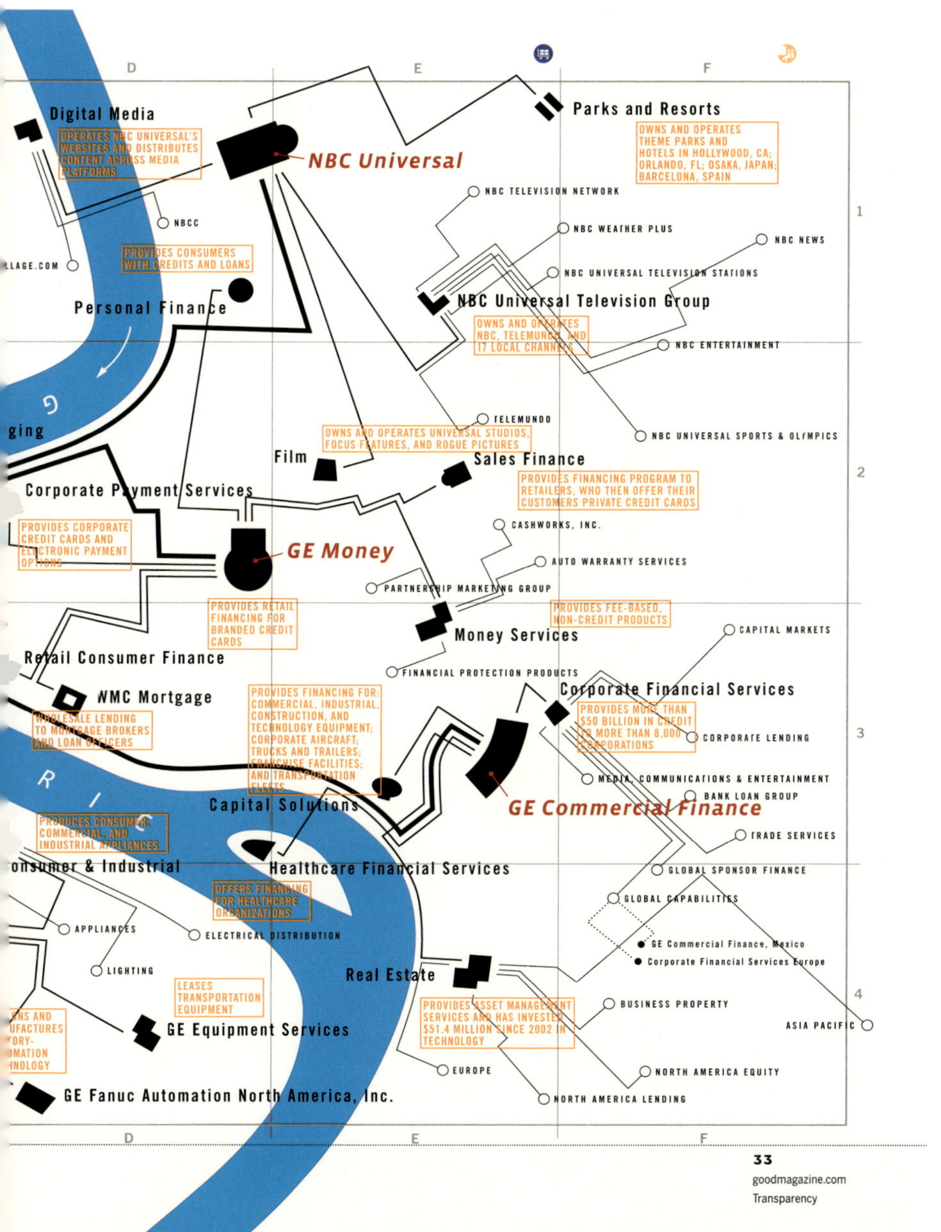

The Expanding Universe of Wikipedia
by Office of CC

To visualize the great success of Wikipedia, we filled a spread with a quarter of a million 'stars'. The bar chart printed on top of the stars tells the reader the number of copies of ‹GOOD› to acquire in order to create a physical presence of the tremendous figures of Wikipedia.

for GOOD, 2007

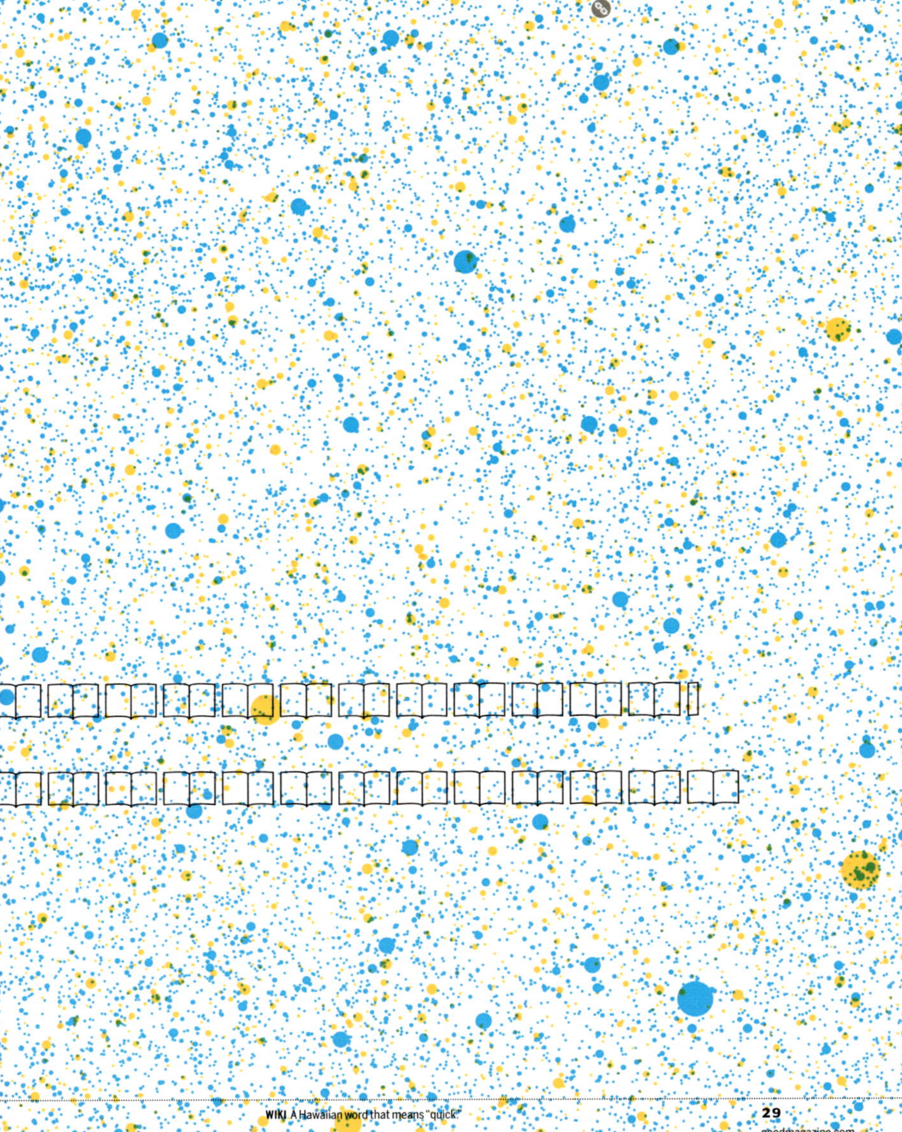

WIKI A Hawaiian word that means "quick."

Drink up

by Office of CC

A visual story, told in various types of info-graphics, revealed the facts and the dangers of our global water problem.

for GOOD, 2007

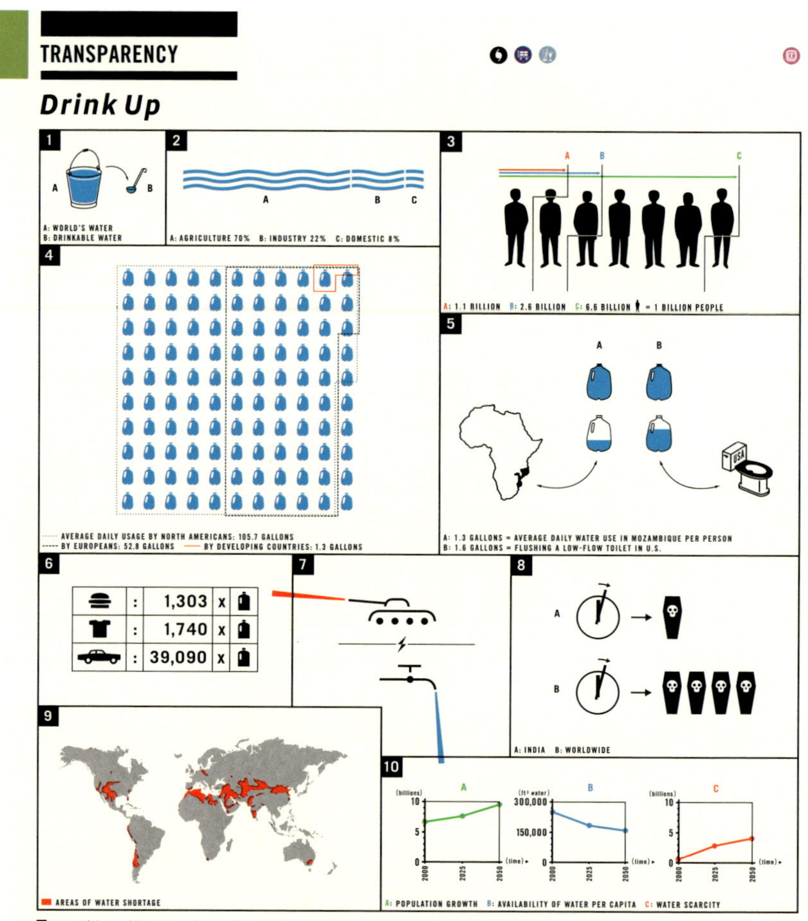

1 97.5% of the earth's water is saltwater. If the world's water was poured into a bucket, only one spoonful of it would be drinkable. 2 Usage of water worldwide 3 1.1 billion people in the world do not have access to safe water (1/6 of the world's population); 2.6 billion do not have access to adequate sanitation. (2/5 of the world's population). 4 Average daily domestic usage 5 Average daily water use in Mozambique per person is less than the water used to flush a low-flow toilet in the U.S. (Older U.S. toilets used as much as 5.5 gallons). 6 It takes 1,303 gallons of water to make a hamburger; 1,740 gallons to make a T-shirt; 39,090 to manufacture a new car (with new tires). 7 India spends 8 times more on its military budget than on water and sanitation. 8 Death caused by water-related diseases: 1 death per minute in India; 4 deaths per minute worldwide. 9 Worldwide regions experiencing water shortages; the areas with the least available water are Kuwait, the United Arab Emirates, and the Bahamas. 10 A: Population growth (2000–2050): 2000: 6.5 billion; 2025: 7.5 billion; 2050: 9.4 billion. B: Availability of water per capita (2000–2050): 2000: 258,150 ft³; 2025: 180,811 ft³; 2050: 161,741 ft³. C: Population experiencing water scarcity: 2000: 508 million; 2025: 2.8 billion; 2050: 4 billion. (An extra $10 billion is needed each year to improve the water situation, which is about half of what rich countries spend on mineral water)

TRANSPARENCY Graphical explorations of the data that surrounds us
A collaboration between GOOD and **OFFICE OF CC**

SOURCES Thirst Relief International; UN Development Programme; UN Environment Programme; United States Geological Survey; World Health Organization; World Water Council; Worldwater.org

27
goodmagazine.com
Transparency

103 Buying a Brand

by Office of CC

Using the barcode as a bar chart, presenting the annual spending of leading products/brands from seven major industries on advertising versus all other expenses.

for GOOD, 2007

Buying a Brand

(A) Total advertising spending for companies in seven different industries by % (B) Total expenditures other than advertising by % (1) **PROCTER & GAMBLE**: advertising spending: 6,773,000,000 = 12% of total annual spending (54,973,000,000) (2) **PFIZER**: ad. spending: 2,600,000,000 = 7% of total annual spending (35,343,000, 000) (3) **CHARLES SCHWAB**: ad. spending: 189,000,000 = 7% of total annual spending (2,833,000,000) (4) **GAP**: ad. spending: 581,000,000 = 4% of total annual spending (14,679,000,000) (5) **VERIZON**: ad. spending: 2,271,000,000 = 3% of total annual spending (74,771,000,000) (6) **TOYOTA**: ad. spending: 3,385,000,000 = 2% of total annual spending (160,976,000,000) (7) **JET BLUE**: ad. spending: 40,000,000 = 2% of total annual spending (2,236,000,000) ($) Total advertising spending for all industries in 2006. Some of the highest spending industries are: telecommunication (9,431,100,000) / automotive: non-domestic (8,726,700,000) / financial services (8,681,800,000) / retail (8,322,900,000) / personal care (5,717,200,000) / travel and tourism (5,406,400,000) / pharmaceuticals (5,285,400,000)

SOURCES Google Finance; TNS Media Intelligence

NOTE All numbers in US dollars

 Homeless
by Office of CC

The problem of the vast numbers of American homeless people presented in its various forms; lines of repeated elements illustrate the sad data.

for GOOD, 2007

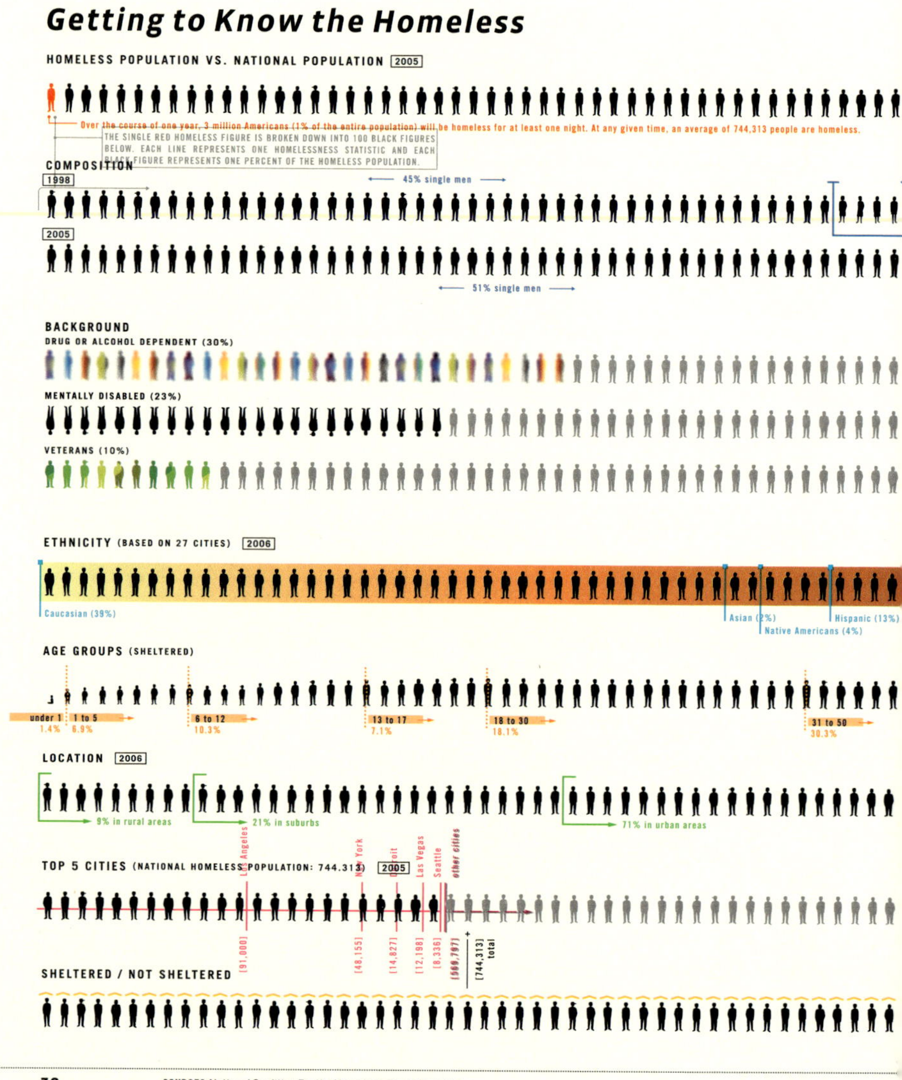

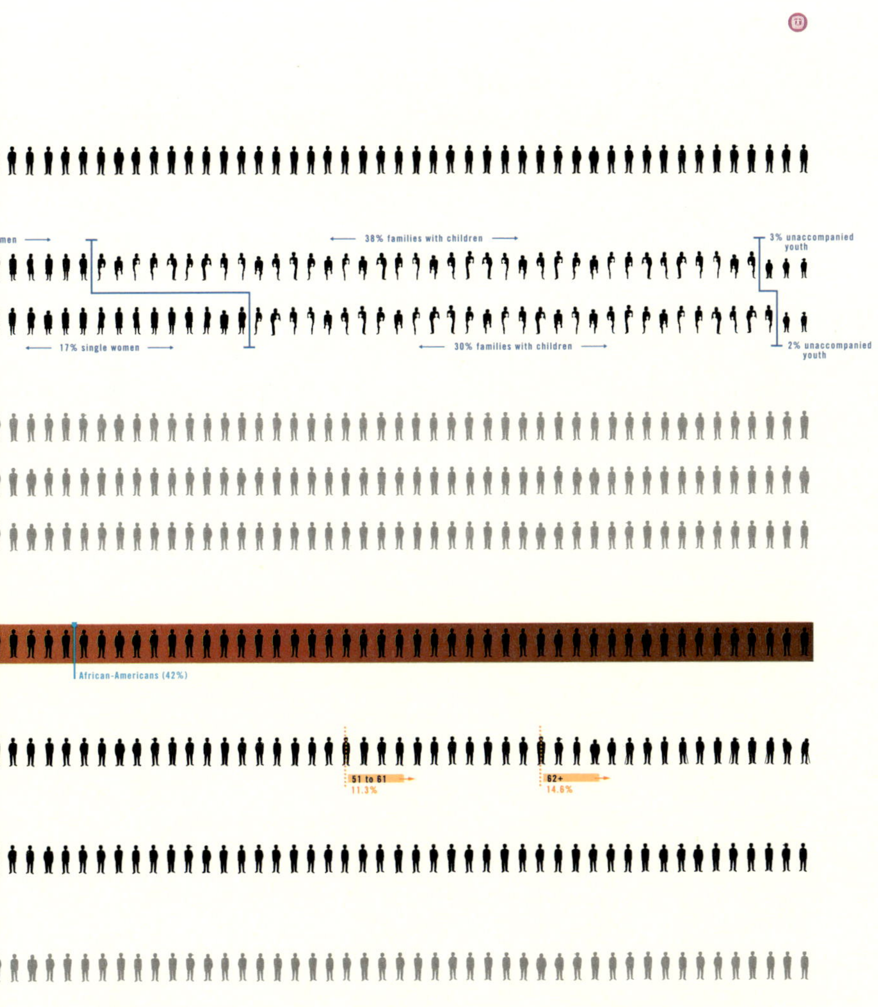

COST BENEFIT Cost of one homeless person to taxpayers per year: $40,500. Cost of supportive housing for one homeless person per year: $41,494

Marking Europe High Speed
by Lust

This New Map of Europe does not show ‹the new Europe›. The map is a new map. It gives us an impression of a Europe on the move. The map portrays a continent, on the edge of the Eurasian land mass, riven by frontiers and riddled with currents. Frontiers that shift, frontiers that fade. And currents that speed up or down, currents that change course. This Europe is a place that thrives on movement. It is enmeshed with the rest of the world by satellite links that reach beyond the stratosphere. The latest incarnation of this Europe, that of a Union, is in progress. It is a Europe that is expanding, and at the same time seeks to grow in depth. The still unfinished map of Europe adds a layer to that depth. But which Europe? Is it the West of the Eurovision Song Contest? Or is it the Europe of the UEFA Cup, the Europe of the Euro, the Europe of the corporate logos, or Fortress Europe? Europa, the princess who was abducted by Zeus and on his back swam all the way from a North African beach to Crete, is still on her way. How long has Europe been in the water, and how much longer will it take for her to arrive?

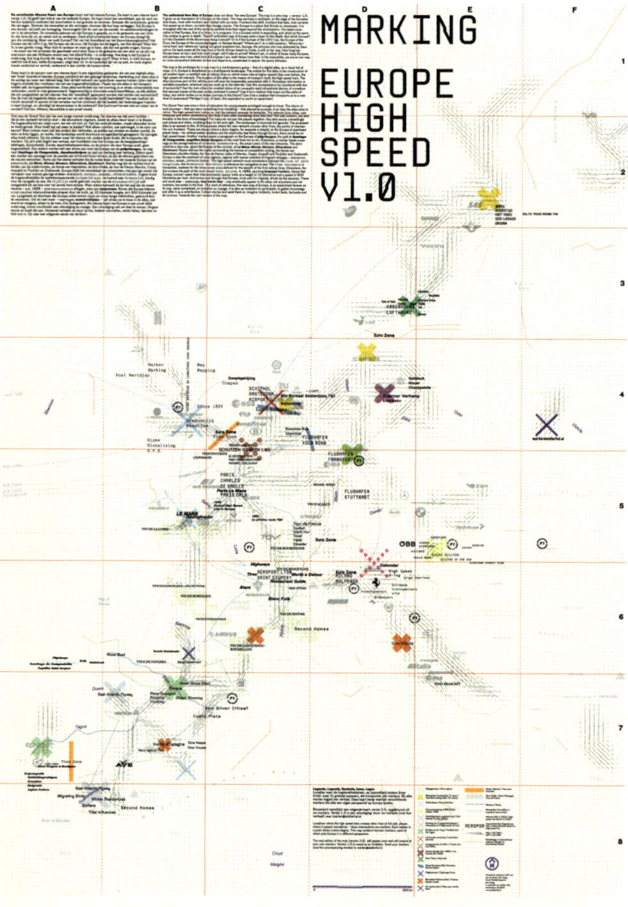

for Atelier HSL, 2004

This map is the prototype for a new map in a contemporary guise – that of a digital atlas. In it, Europe is deciphered as a multi-layered landscape. The motive for this atlas is the construction of yet another layer: a ramified web of railway lines on which trains travel at higher speeds than ever before, the high-speed rail network. The location of this atlas is the means of transport itself, the high speed train.

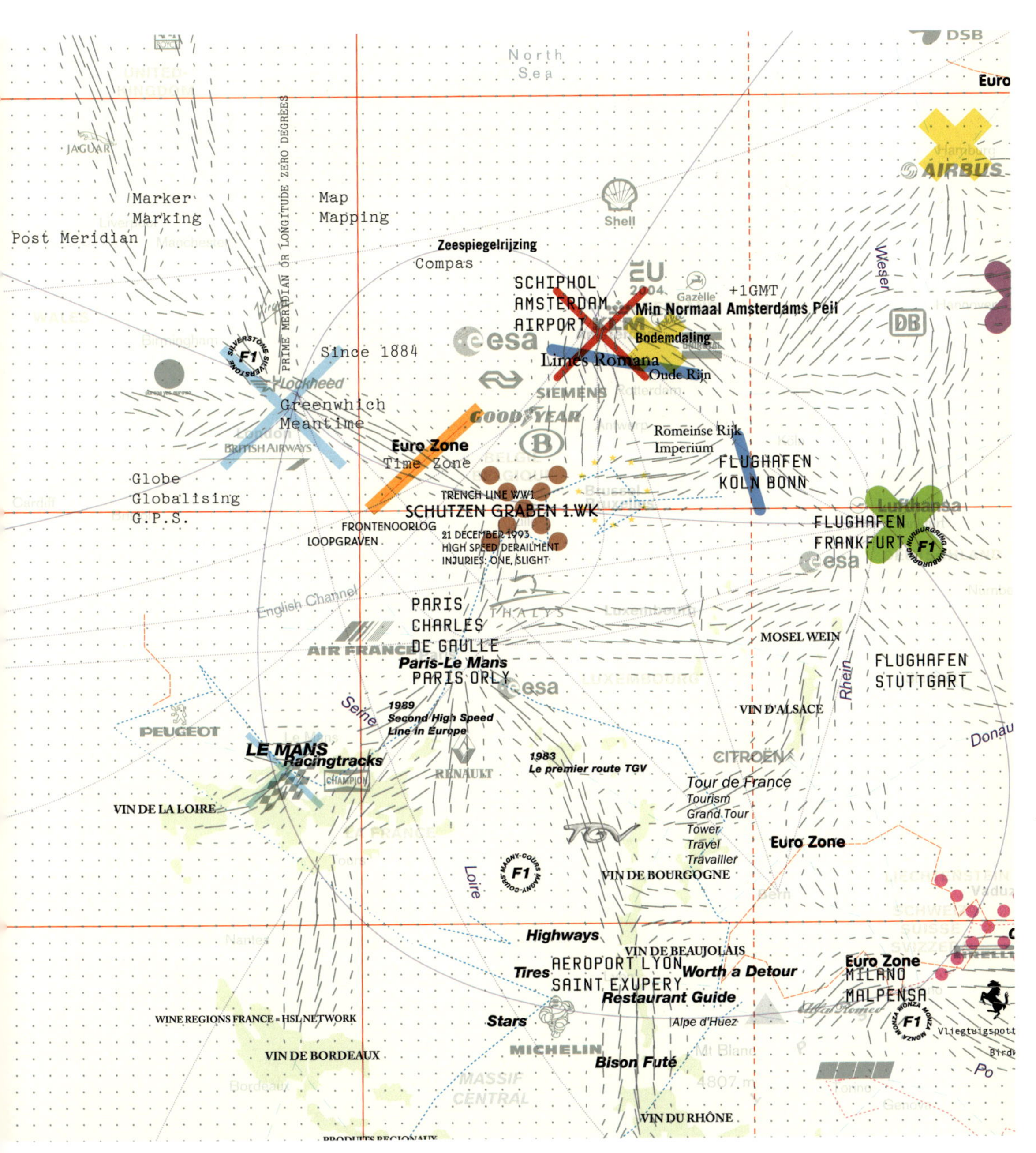

Transurban

by Catalogtree

‹Werken aan de naoorlogse stad› (Endry van Velzen & Willemijn Lofvers) is a book about a research fellowship between 2002 and 2006 (272 pages).

2006

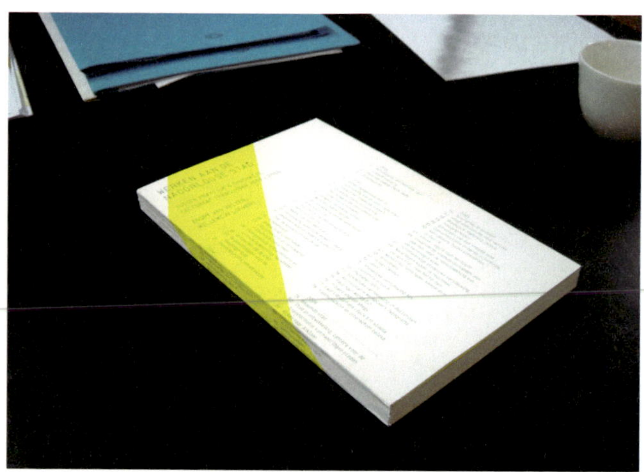

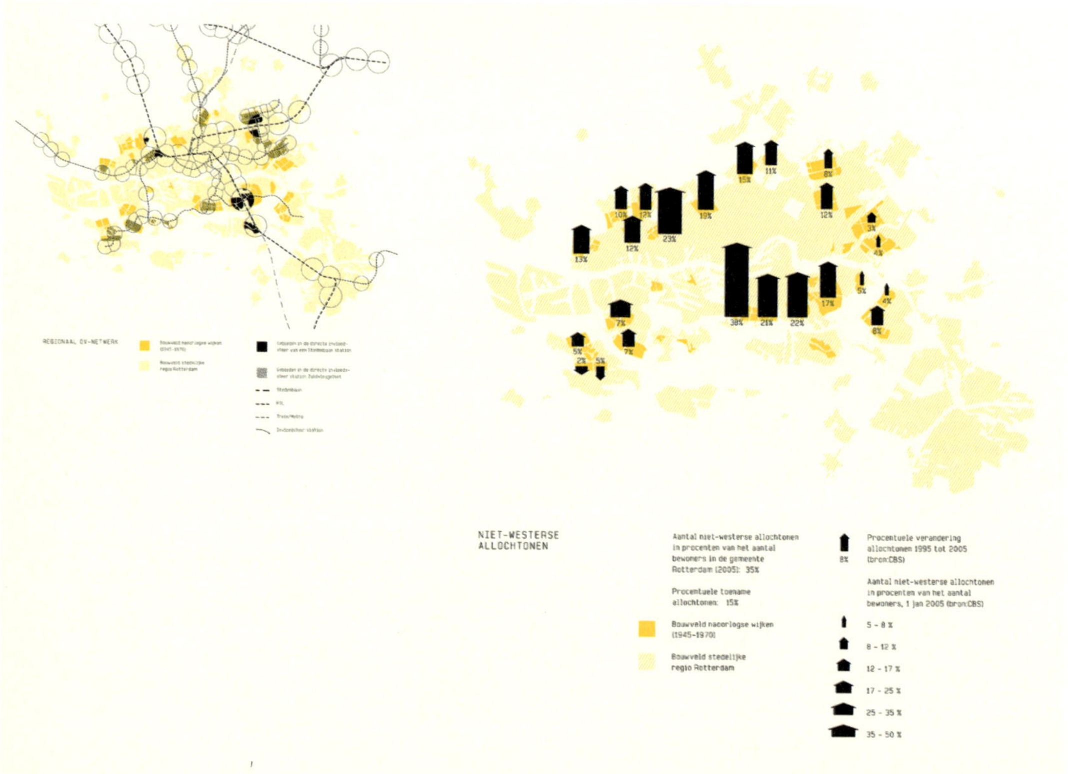

REGIONAAL OV-NETWERK

NIET-WESTERSE
ALLOCHTONEN

Aantal niet-westerse allochtonen in procenten van het aantal bewoners in de gemeente Rotterdam (2005): 35%

Procentuele toename allochtonen: 15%

Bouwveld naoorlogse wijken (1945–1970)

Bouwveld stedelijke regio Rotterdam

8% Procentuele verandering allochtonen 1995 tot 2005 (bron:CBS)

Aantal niet-westerse allochtonen in procenten van het aantal bewoners, 1 jan 2005 (bron:CBS)

5 - 8 %

8 - 12 %

12 - 17 %

17 - 25 %

25 - 35 %

35 - 50 %

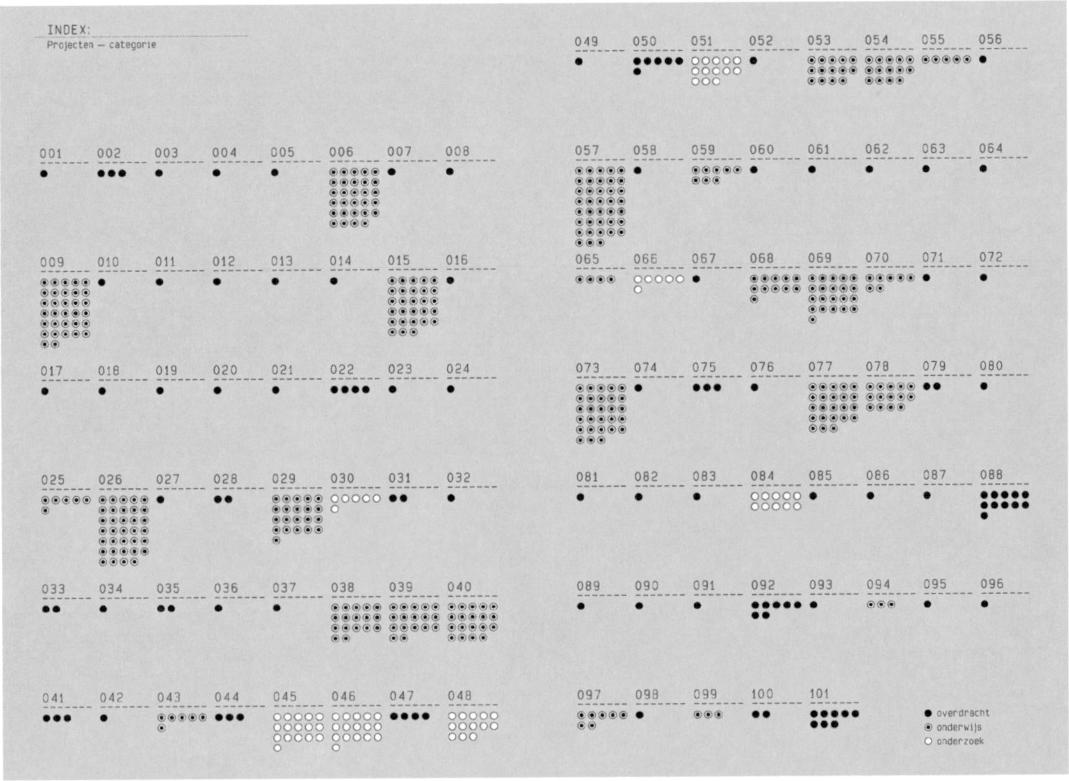

INDEX:
Projecten — categorie

001 002 003 004 005 006 007 008
009 010 011 012 013 014 015 016
017 018 019 020 021 022 023 024
025 026 027 028 029 030 031 032
033 034 035 036 037 038 039 040
041 042 043 044 045 046 047 048

049 050 051 052 053 054 055 056
057 058 059 060 061 062 063 064
065 066 067 068 069 070 071 072
073 074 075 076 077 078 079 080
081 082 083 084 085 086 087 088
089 090 091 092 093 094 095 096
097 098 099 100 101

● overdracht
◉ onderwijs
○ onderzoek

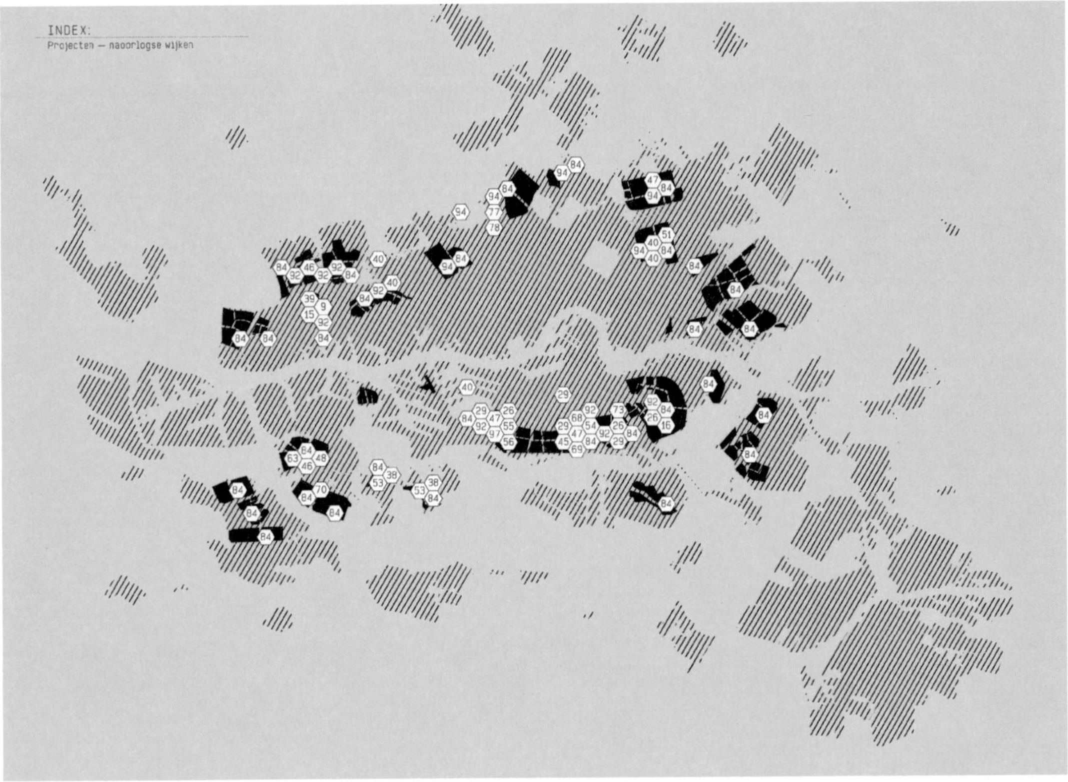

INDEX:
Projecten — naoorlogse wijken

VINEC 005

by Catalogtree

The fifth poster in a series of nine about the road between Arnhem and Nijmegen. The diagram shows 10,000 cars driving over a bridge. The time of crossing, speed and distance from the next car is shown for each car.

2005

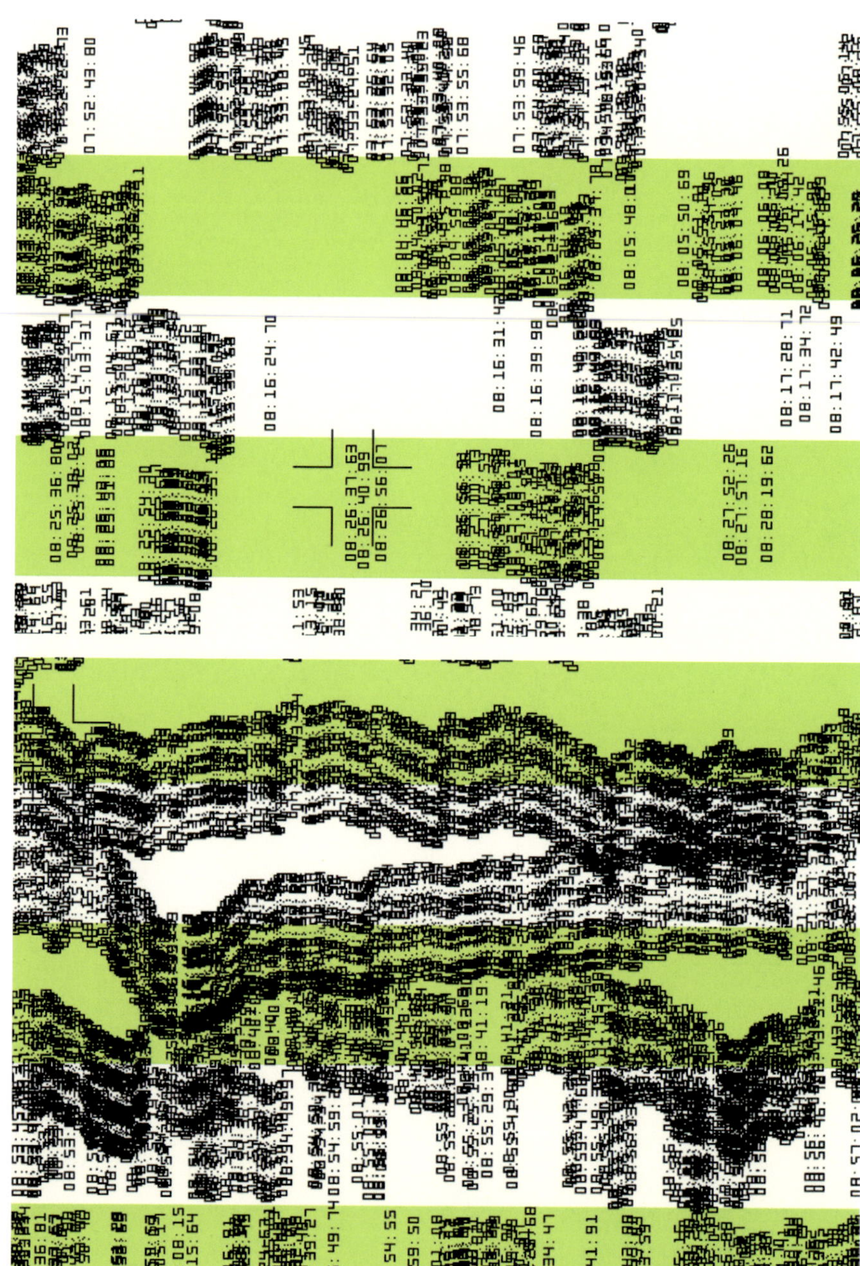

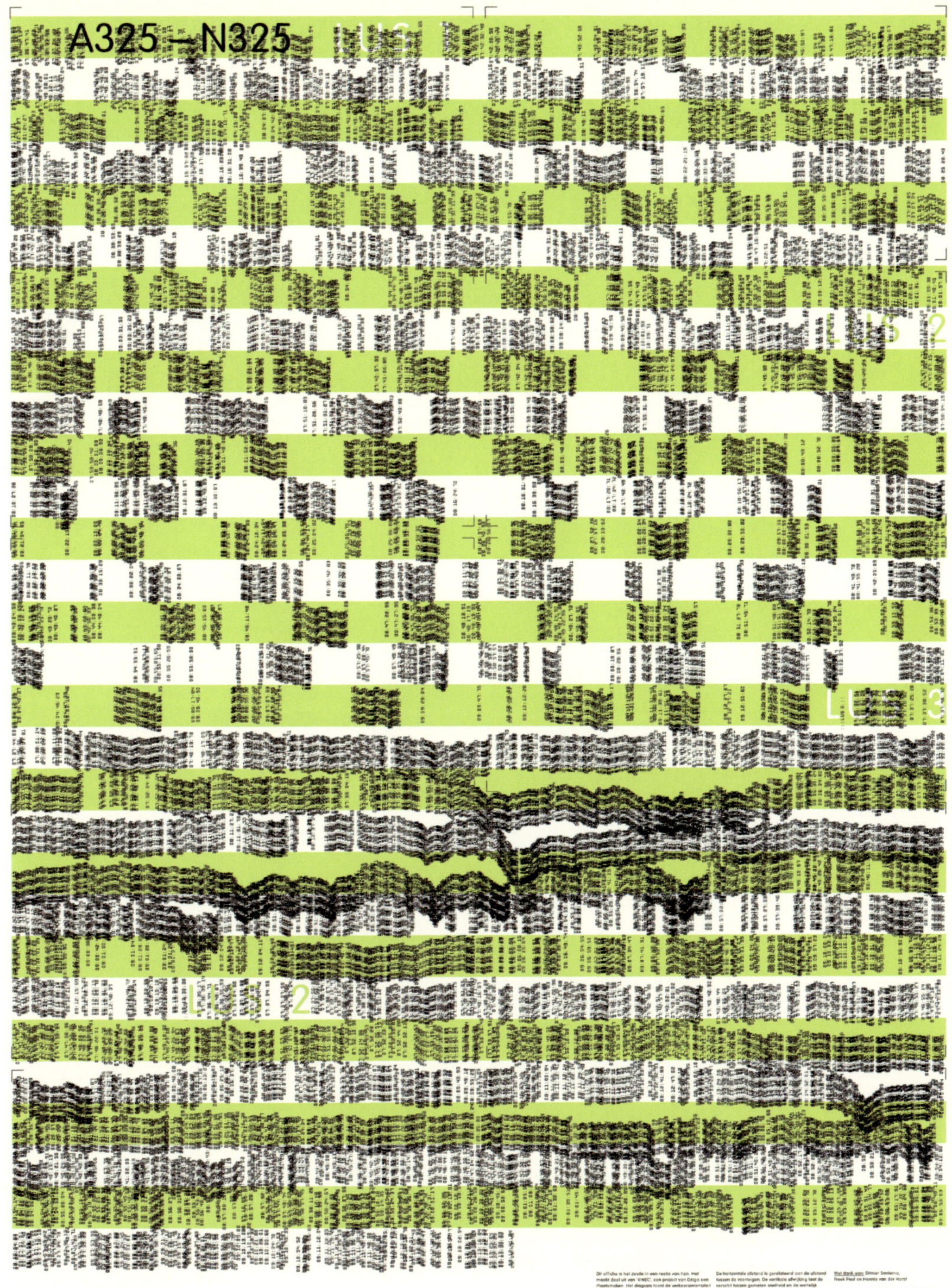

Dit affiche is het zesde in een reeks van tien. Het maakt deel uit van 'VINEC', een project van Dzigo een Plaatsmaken. Het diagram toont de verkeersintensiteit tussen Arnhem en Nijmegen op 5 april 2005 tussen 7.36 en 9.13 uur. Verdeeld over 4 meetpunten (lus 1,2,3 en 4) zijn in deze periode 10.000 voertuigen geteld. Iedere voertuig is in het diagram gerepresenteerd door het tijdstip waarop het voertuig het meetpunt passeerde.

De horizontale afstand is gerelateerd aan de afstand tussen de voertuigen. De verticale afwijking laat de verschil tussen gemeten snelheid en de wettelijk toegestaan maximum snelheid (100km/h) zien. Files worden dus zichtbaar als een lange reeks tijdstippen/voertuigen dicht op elkaar met ongeveer dezelfde snelheid (vooral lus 4). Stop-and-Go door golvende patronen (lus 3). De kolomen van tijdstippen/voertuigen in lus 2 ontstaan door stoplichten.

Met dank aan: Ditmar Santema, Freek Paul en Hennie van der Horst

Ontwerp: Gross & Maltha (www.catalogtree.net)
Druk: Plaatsmaken Arnhem Oplage: 100

Een nieuwe wereldkaart / Potenciales Estados Nación (Potential Nation States)
by STAR

In 1986 there were 159 countries in the United Nations, today there are 191. However, more than 200 regions worldwide are still seeking independence. At the same time a reverse trend is emerging, initiated precisely by the continent that 500 years ago invented the idea of

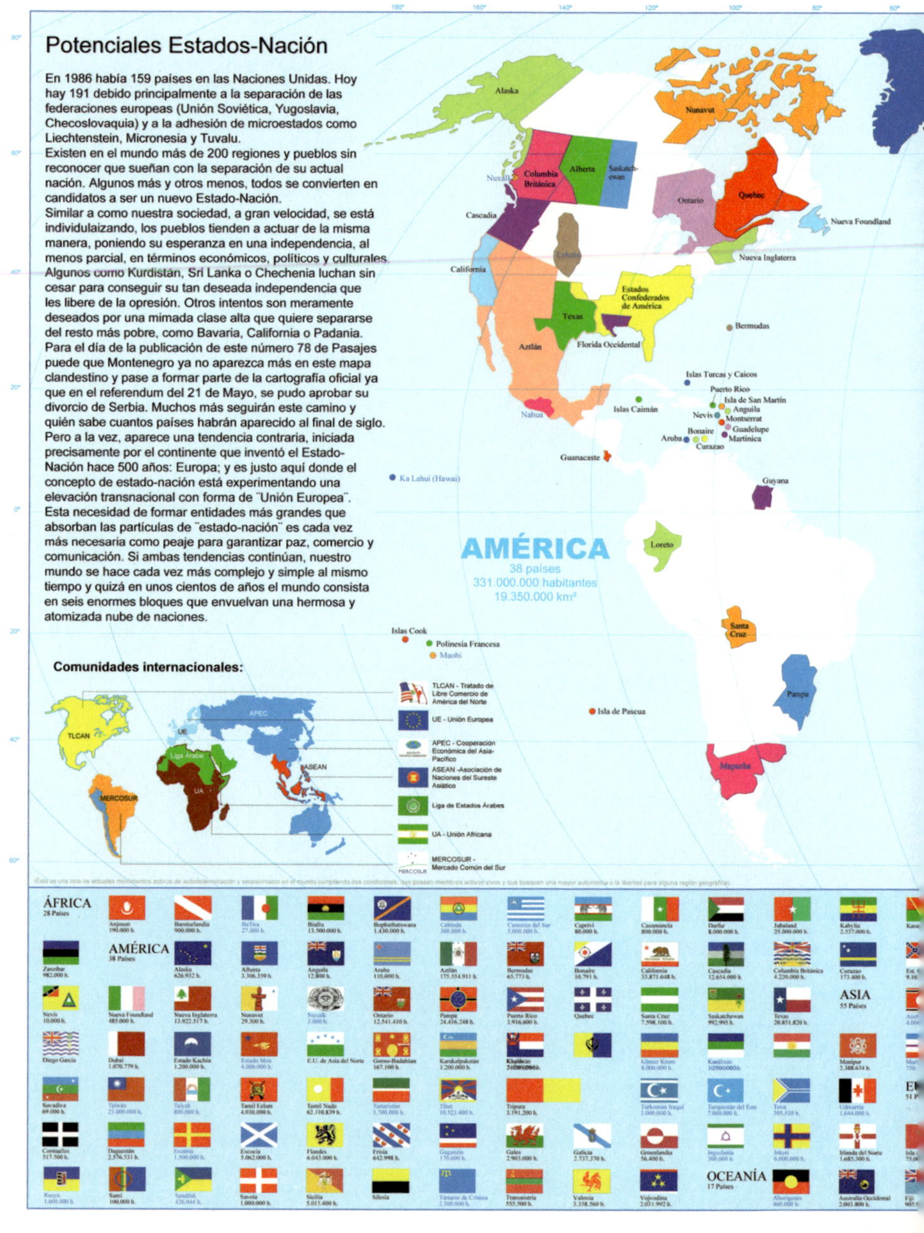

the nation-state: Europe. This concept is experiencing a trans-national upgrade in the form of European Union Europe, as toll for guaranteeing peace, trade, and communication. If both trends continue, perhaps in a hundred years or so the world will consists of only six major blocs that envelop a beautiful atomized cloud of regions.

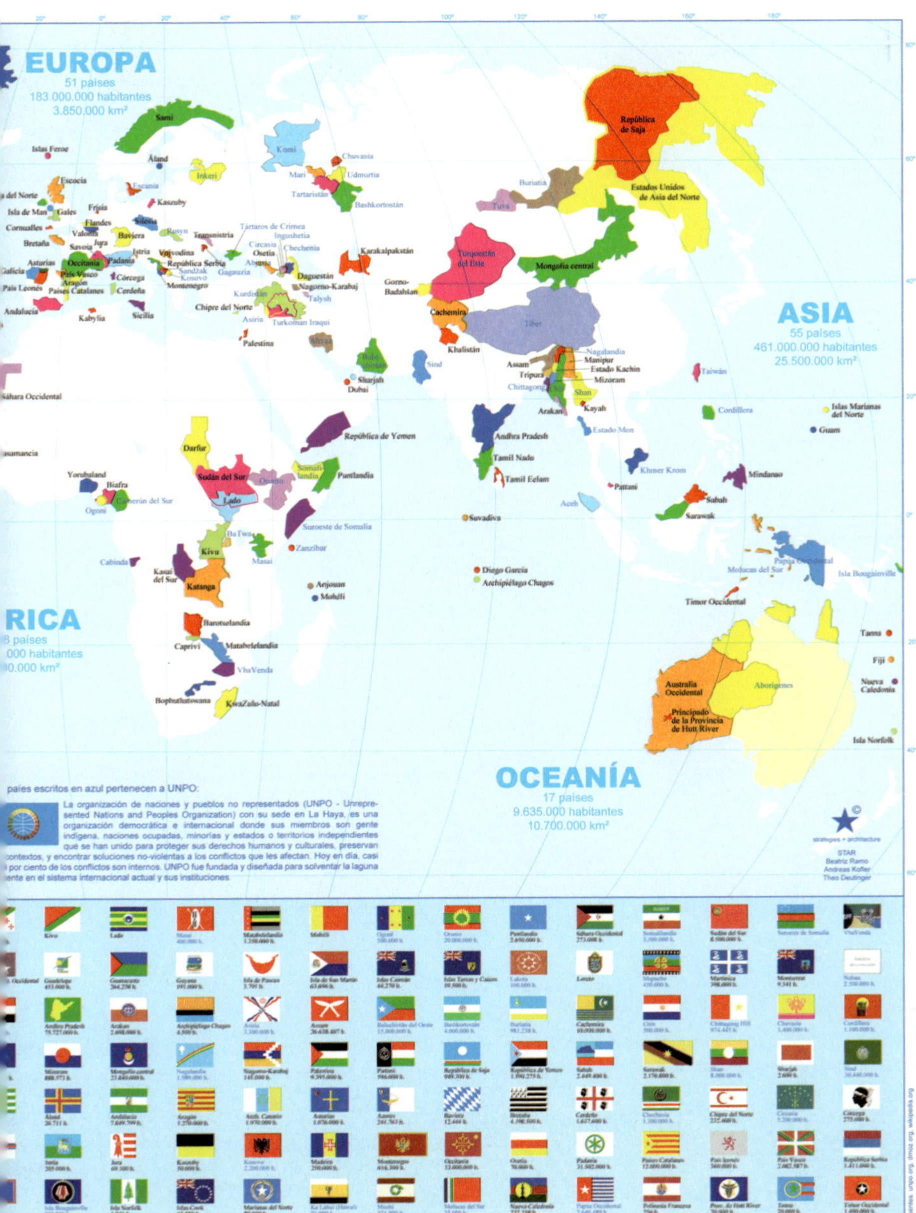

for Vrij Nederland #18 – May 06 (NL) / De Morgen #06/05/23 – May 06 (BE) / Pasajes de Arquitectura y Crítica #80 – October 06 (ES), © STAR (Beatriz Ramo, Andreas Kofler), TD-architects (Theo Deutinger), 2006

114 Wereld ball/ La bola del mundo (World-ball)
by STAR

Starting on 9th of June, the World Cup in Germany is not only world's biggest single sports event it is also the biggest branding opportunity for sponsors. The 32 teams who made it to the tournament can be summarily assigned to seven technical sponsors: Puma, Nike, Adidas, Umbro, Lotto, Joma, and Marathon.

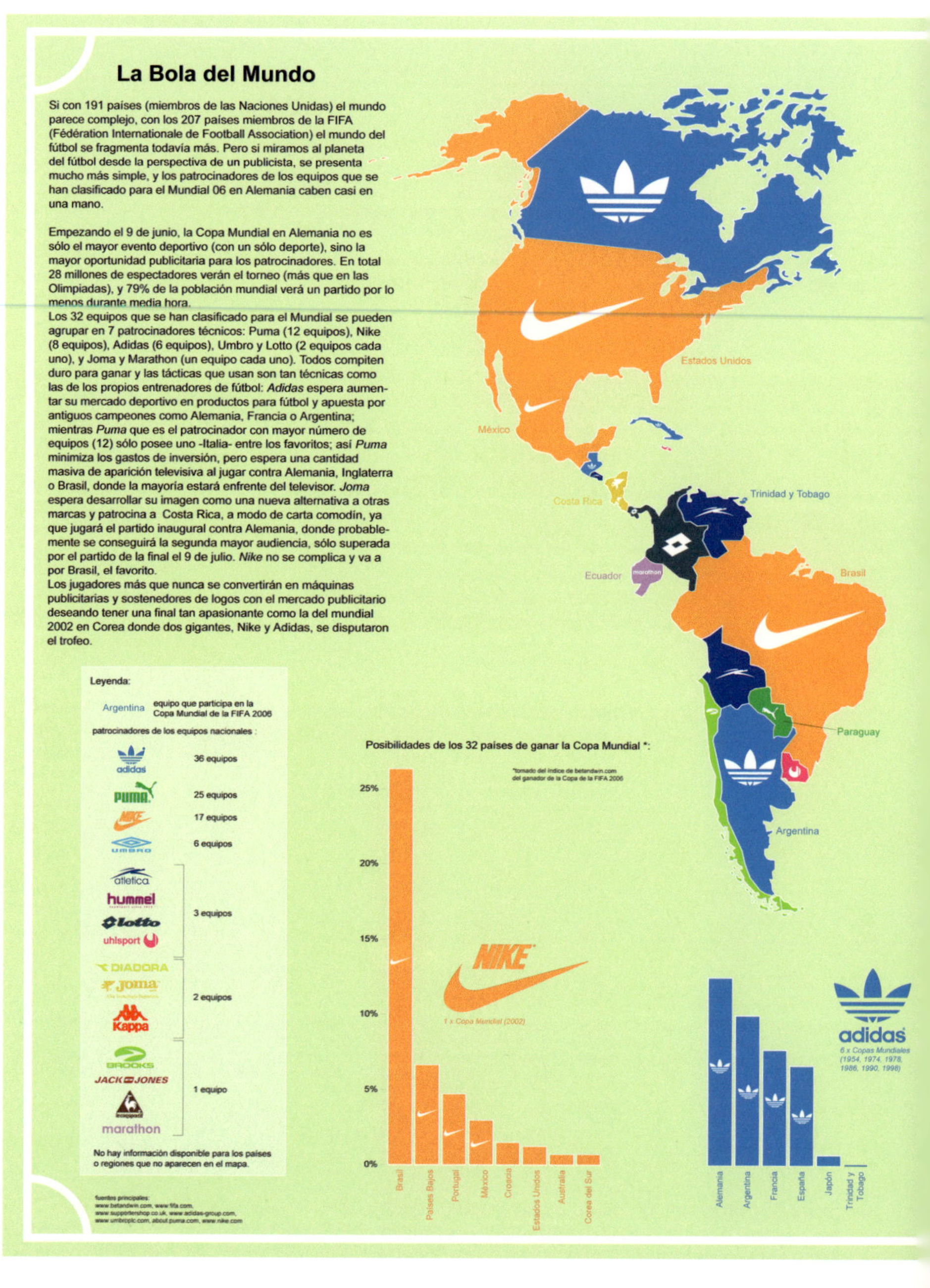

The map shows how the world is organized according to these technical sponsorships, and the strategies followed by each company to achieve maximum exposure of their logos in the media.

for Vrij Nederland #23 – June 06 (NL) / Pasajes de Arquitectura y Crítica #78 – July 06 (ES), © STAR (Beatriz Ramo, Andreas Kofler), TD-architects (Theo Deutinger), 2006

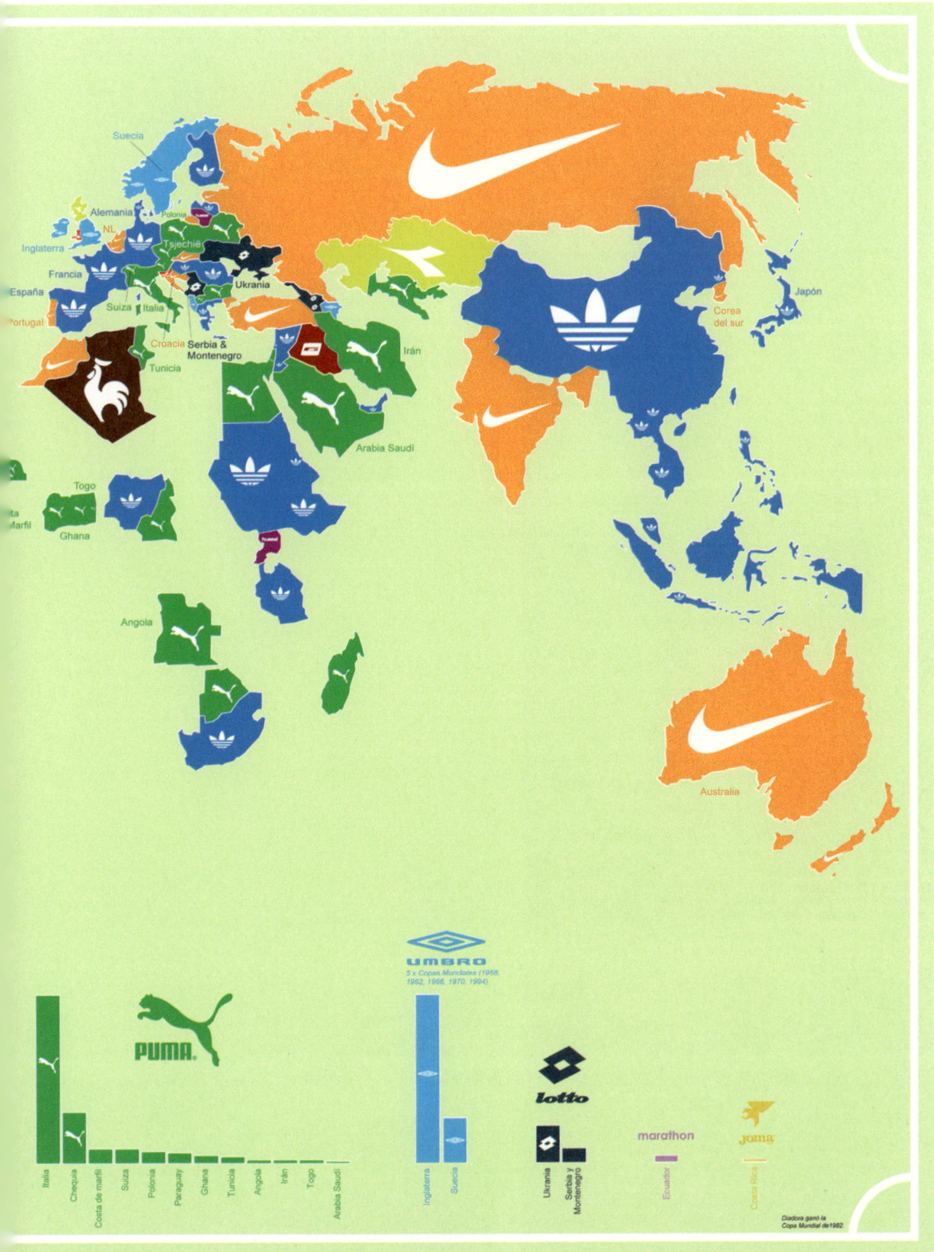

Map of Maps

by Minke Themans

A series of maps, sketches and annotations produced in collaboration with experts from various fields to offer new insights into the complexity of the social, economic, cultural and environmental processes that collectively define the public realm. From left to right, ‹Colour map - City›, ‹Colour map - Polder›, ‹Chewing gum map›, (Signs of transition from public to semi-public space,

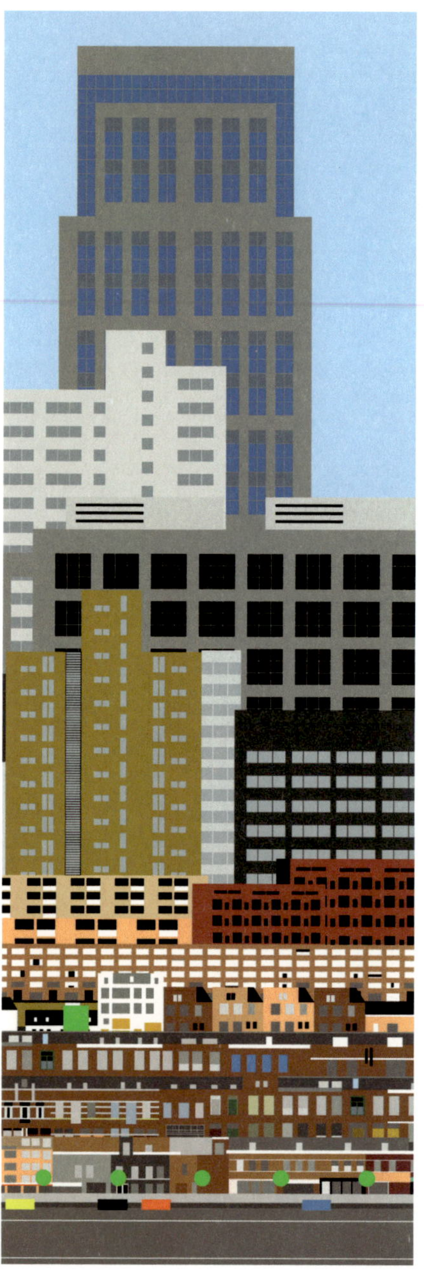

Perron 1, Den Haag CS.) and ‹Barcode› (The relative surface area of materials in and on the Schouwburgplein in Rotterdam).

self commissioned, by Duzan Doepel and Minke Themans together with various artists, urban designers and people from other disciplines, for the Omgevings architectuur prijs 2004, NAi, Rotterdam.

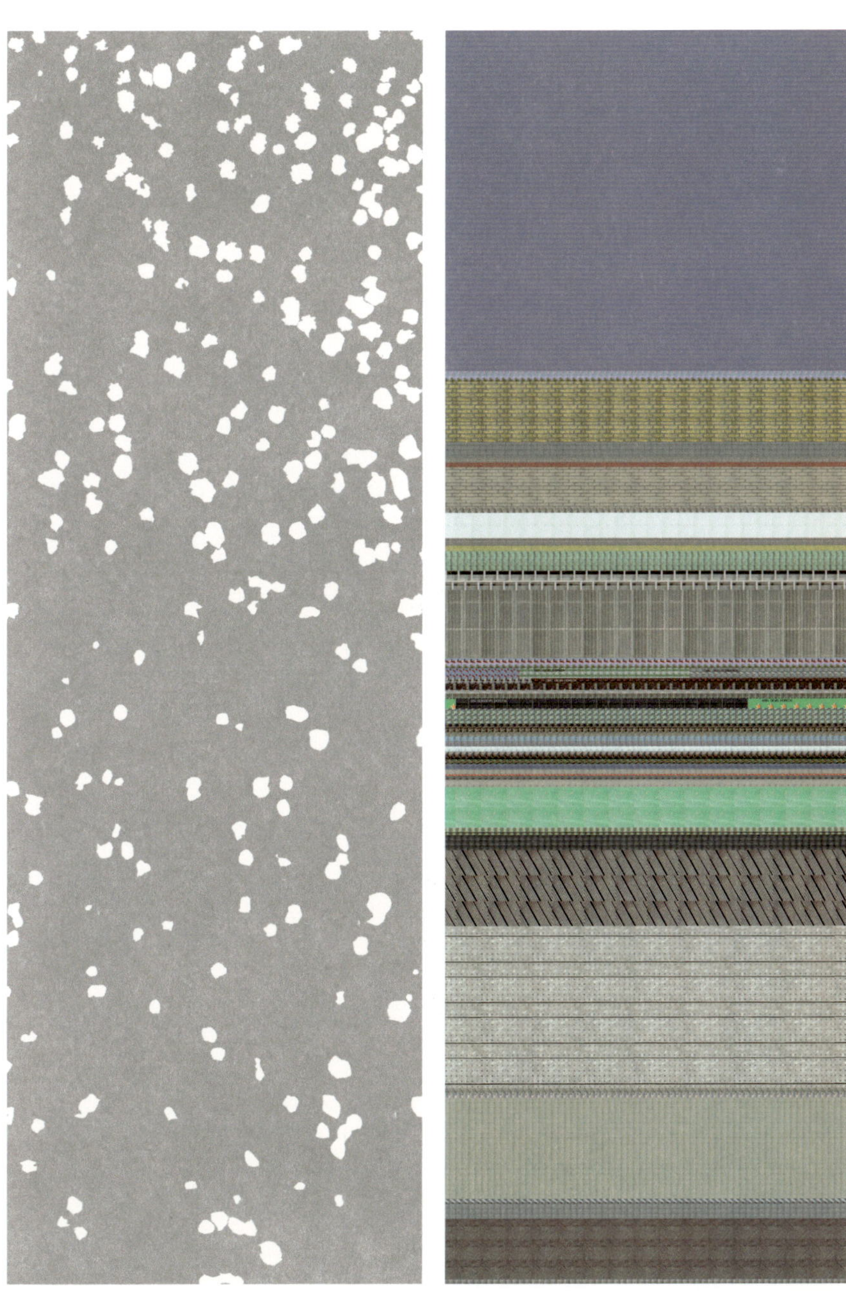

118 Living Agenda
by Luna Maurer

‹Living Agenda› was an installation during the one-week residency in the Museum Het Domein, Sittard, The Netherlands, September 2005. The installation visualized my year's agenda for 2005. Each colour represents a project, the red vertical stripes indicate the months.

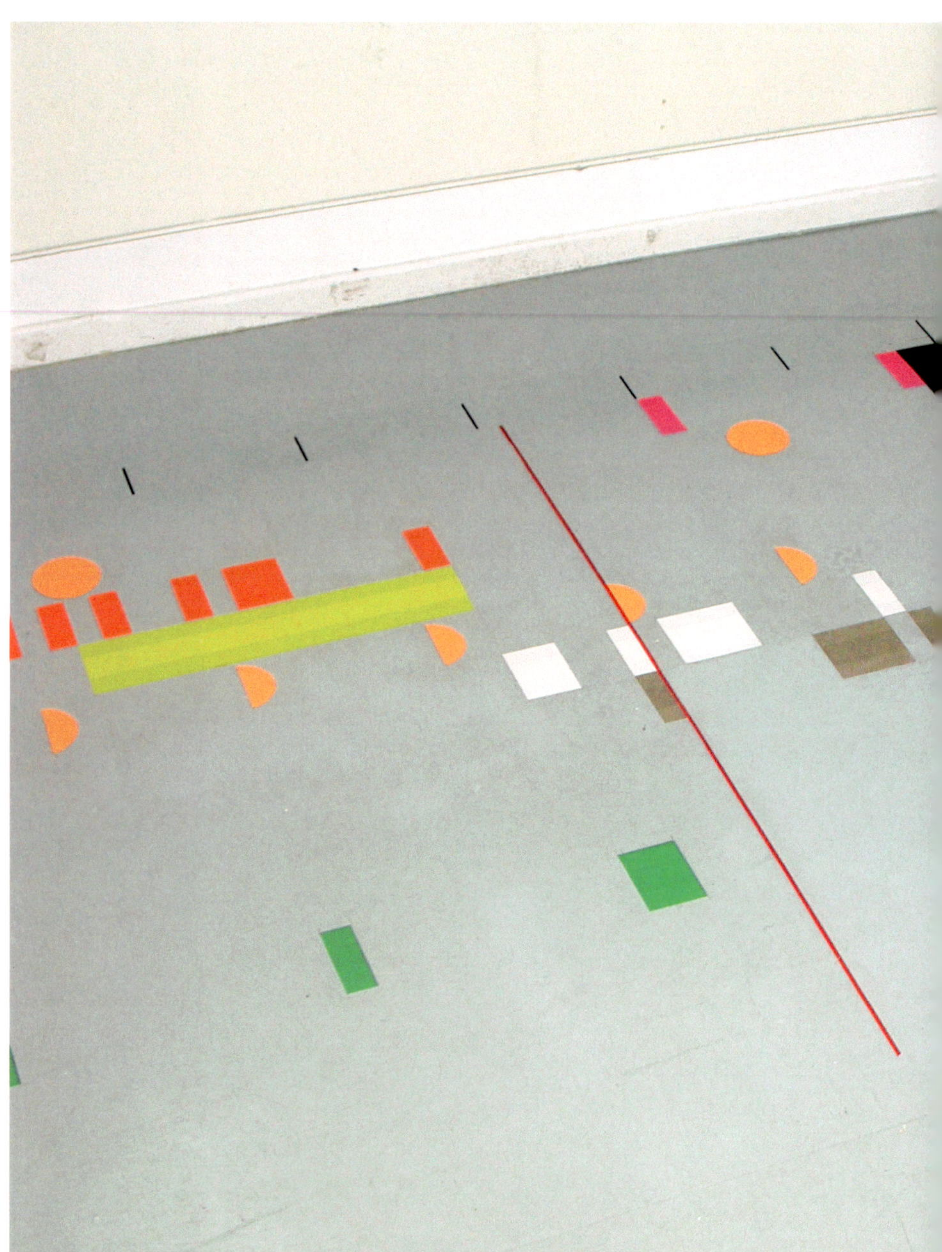

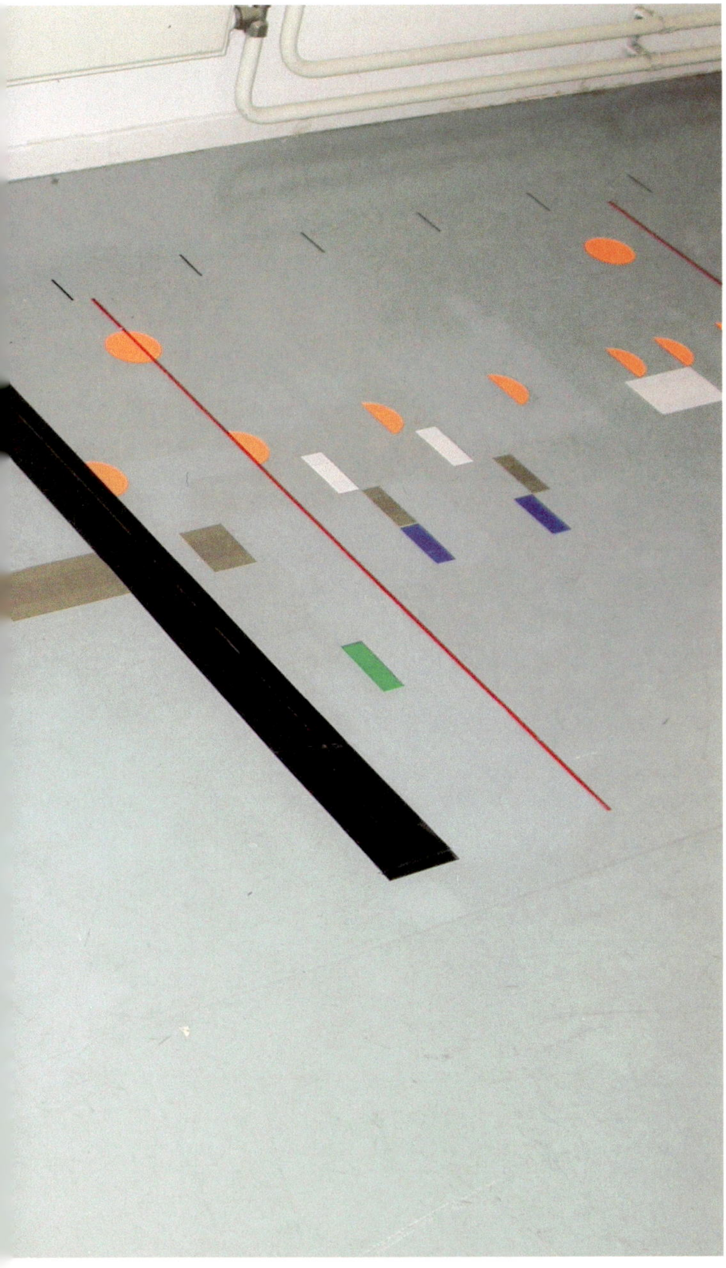

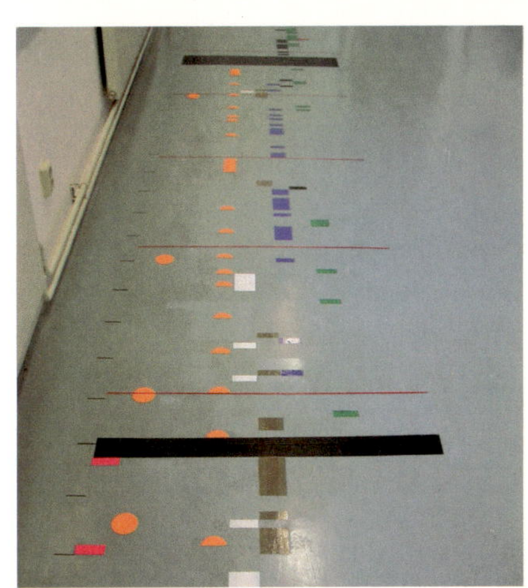

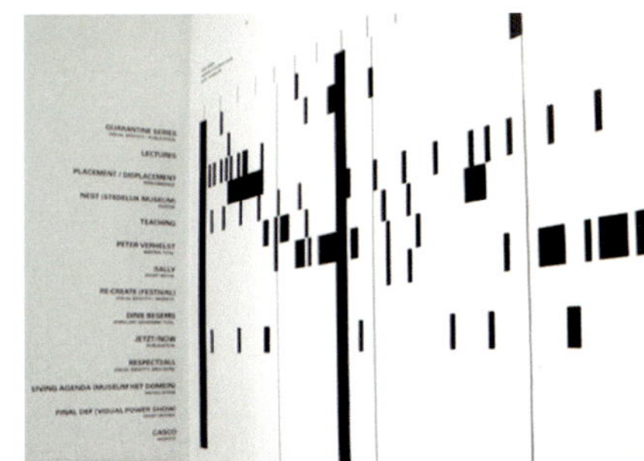

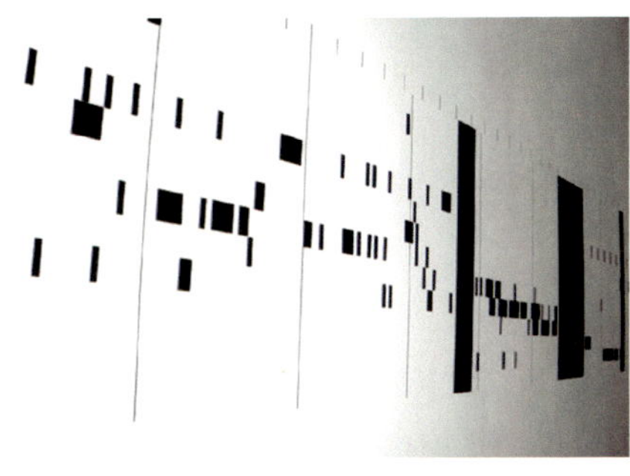

for Museum Het Domein, Sittard, The Netherlands, 2005

 Mare Nostrum

by Minke Themans & Roger Teeuwen

A datascape created for the ‹Mare Nostrum› exhibition, it provides background information on the development of tourism, and on how this affects the world we live in.

for 2nd International Architecture Biennale, Rotterdam, Leporello, English edition 230 x 170 mm, 20 pages, 2005

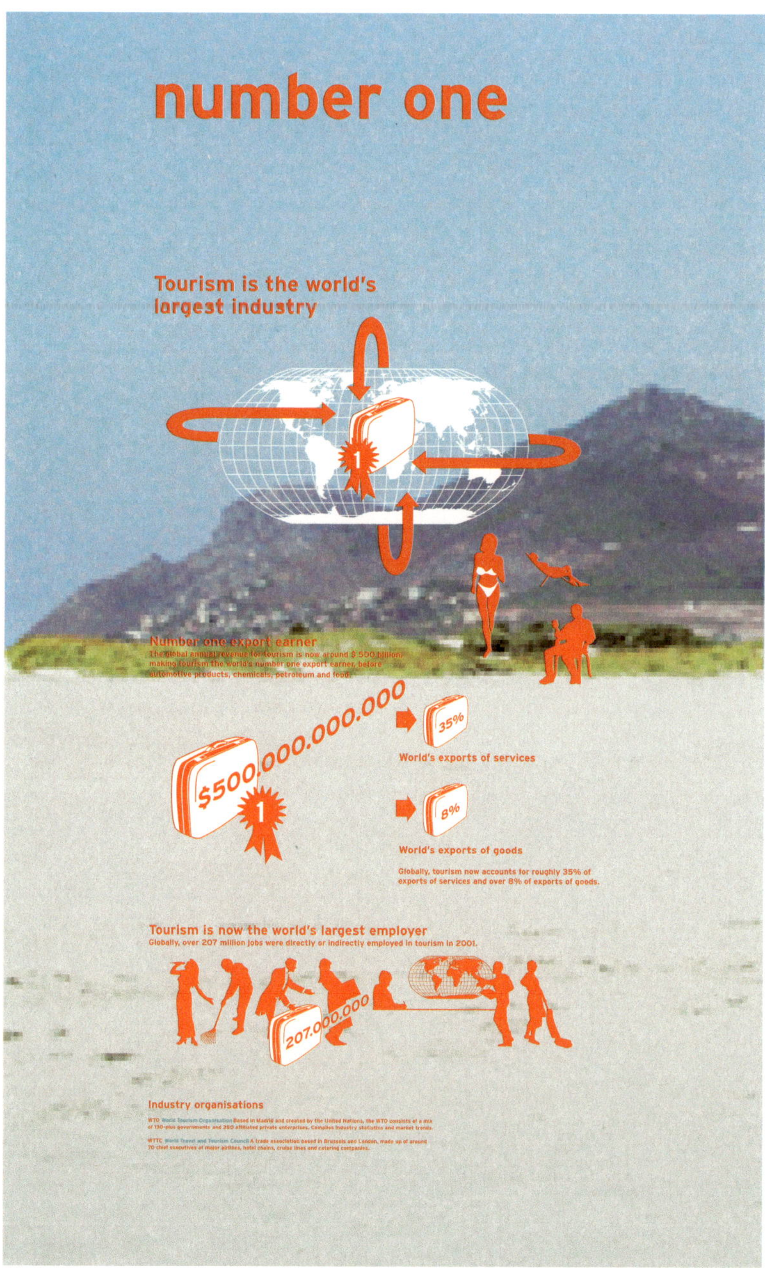

in 2020

Tourism as a sector will have grown faster than all other sectors in the global economy

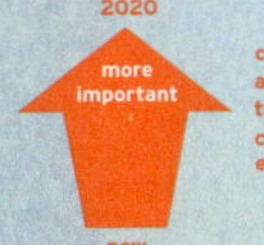

cruise tourism
adventure tourism
theme-based tourism
cultural tourism
eco-tourism

Spending in international tourism

By 2020, international tourism arrivals worldwide will be close to 1.6 billion, with spending in excess of 2 trillion US dollars. By the end of the 20th century, spending was at $445 billion.

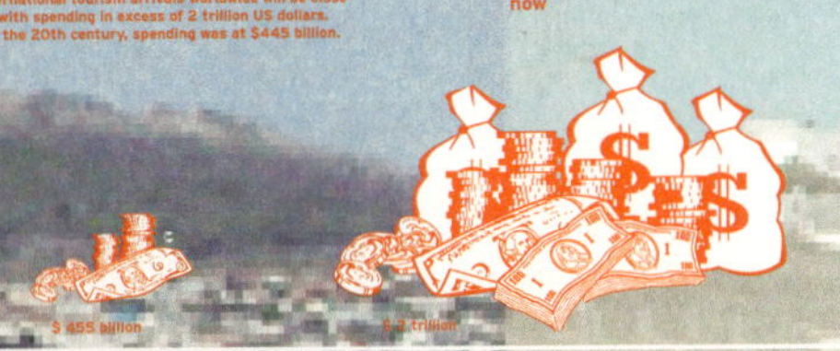

International travel

The percentage of the travelling population involved in international travel will have doubled from 3.5% in 1998 to 7% by 2020.

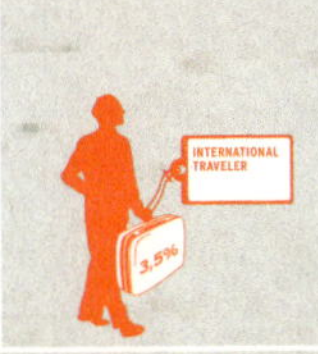

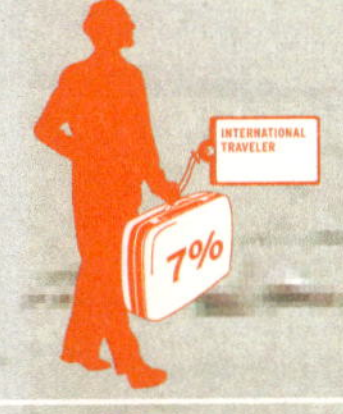

1998

2020

Largest international tourism region

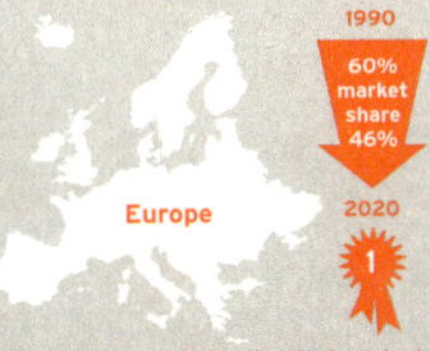

Europe remains the largest international tourism region, but by 2020 its market share will be down to 46%, from 60% in the late 1990's.

Largest receiver of international tourists as a country

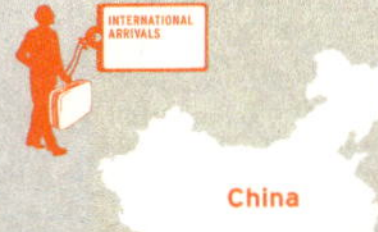

By 2020 China will ahve become the largest receiver of international tourists.

can tourism benefit the poor

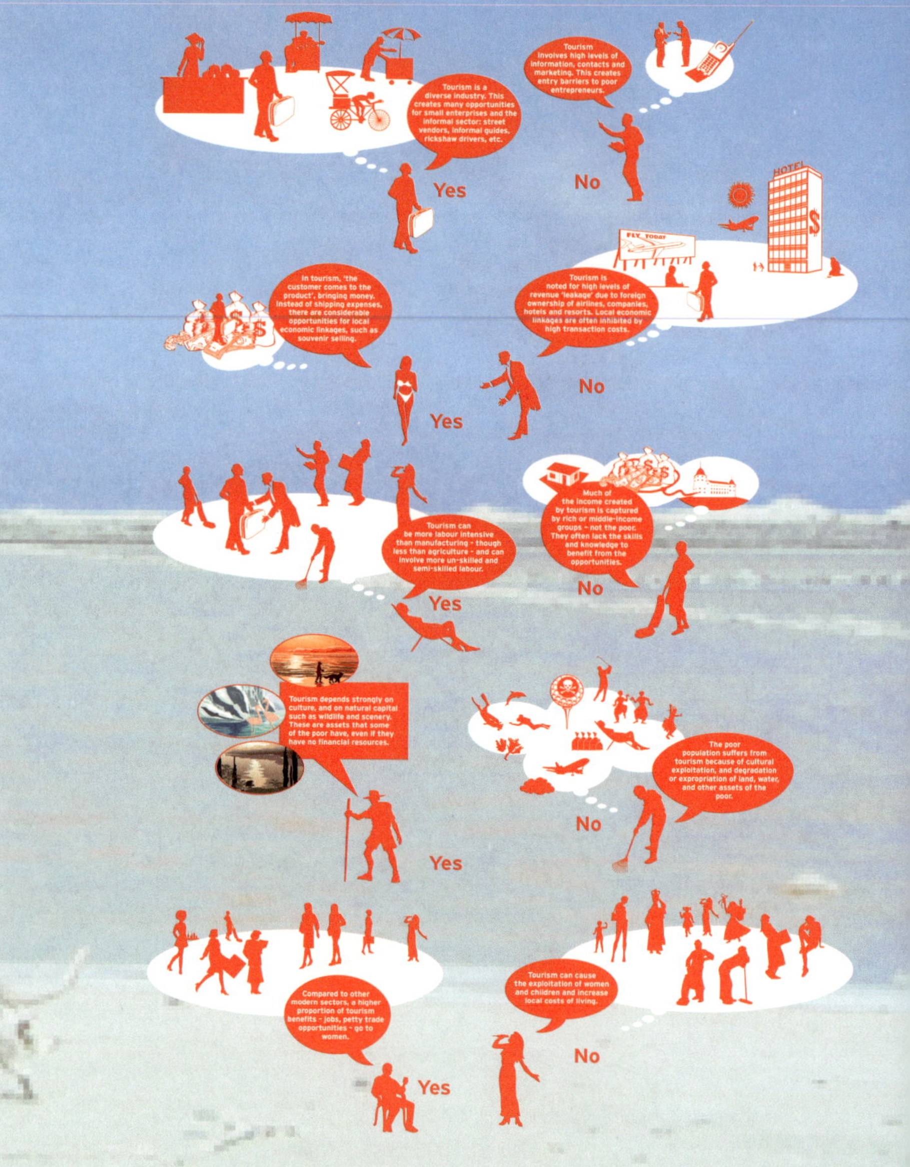

economic impacts

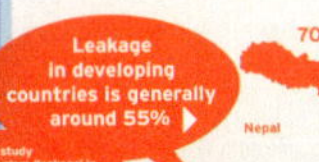

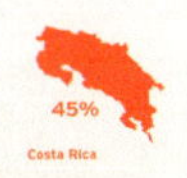

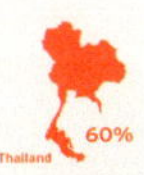
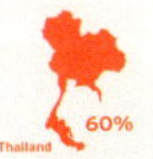

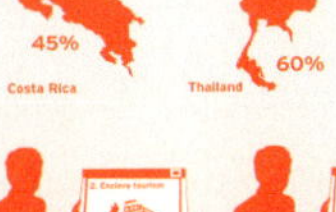

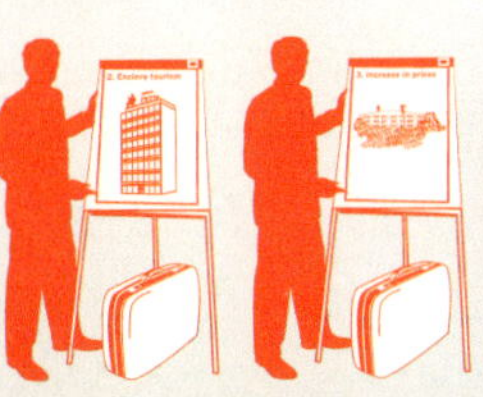

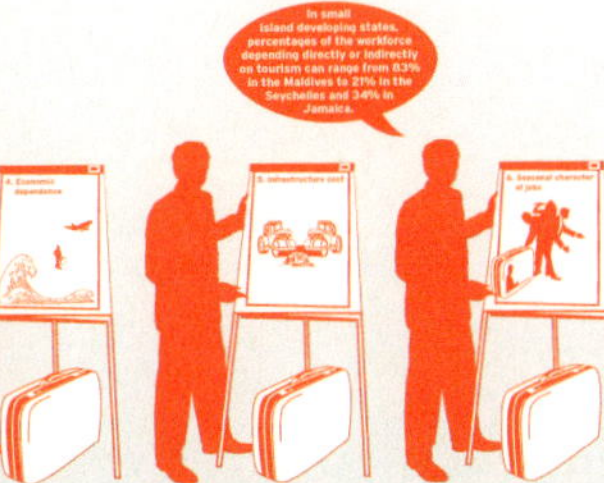

Negative economic impacts of tourism

-

1. Leakage

In most all-inclusive package tours, about 80% of travellers' expenditures go to the airlines, hotels and other international companies, and not to local businesses or workers. On average, of each US$ 100 spent on a vacation tour by a tourist from a developed country, only around US$ 5 actually stays in the economy of a developing country destination.

2. Enclave tourism

When tourists remain on the same cruise ship or in the same resort for their entire stay, because it provides everything they need, this leaves little opportunity for local people to profit from tourism.

3. Increase in prices

Tourist demand for basic services and goods can cause price increases, while the income of local residents does not increase proportionately. Tourism-related rise in real estate demand may dramatically increase building costs and land values.

4. Economic dependence

Over-reliance on tourism, especially mass tourism, carries significant risks to tourism-dependent economies, such as many developing countries. Economic recession, political crises, terrorist threats, epidemics, and the impacts of natural disasters such as tropical storms and tsunamis, as well as changing tourism patterns, can have a devastating effect on the local tourism sector.

5. Infrastructure cost

Tourism development costs can be high for local governments and taxpayers. Developers can demand improvement of airport, roads and other infrastructure, as well as tax breaks and other financial advantages. This drain on public resources may reduce government investment in education and health.

6. Seasonal character of jobs

Problems that seasonal workers face include job (and therefore income) insecurity, usually with no guarantee of employment from one season to the next, difficulties in getting training, employment-related medical benefits, and recognition of their experience, and unsatisfactory housing and working conditions.

1. Foreign exchange earnings

Tourism expenditures and the export/import of related goods and services generate income to the host economy. They can stimulate the investment necessary to finance growth in other economic sectors.
Tourism is one of the top five export categories for as many as 83% of countries and is a main source of foreign exchange earnings for at least 38% of countries. In 2000, 698 million people travelled to a foreign country, spending more than US$ 478 billion.

2. Contribution to government revenues

Direct contributions are generated by taxes on incomes from tourism employment and tourism businesses, and by direct levies on tourists such as departure taxes. Indirect contributions are those originated from taxes and duties levied on goods and services supplied to tourists. In 1998, travel and tourism's direct, indirect, and personal tax contribution worldwide was over US$ 800 billion – a figure expected to double by 2010.

3. Employment generation

Tourism supports some 7% of the world's workers. It can generate jobs directly through hotels, restaurants, nightclubs, taxis, and souvenir sales. Indirectly through the supply of goods and services needed by tourism-related businesses.

4. Stimulation of infrastructure investment

Tourism can induce the local government to make infrastructure improvements such as better water and sewage systems, roads, electricity, telephone and public transport networks, all of which can improve the quality of life for residents as well as facilitate tourism.

5. Contribution to local economies

Money is also earned from tourism through informal or unreported employment. This money is returned to the local economy, and has a great multiplier effect as it is spent over and over again. Tourism is thus estimated to generate an indirect contribution equal to 100% of direct tourism expenditures.

Positive economic impacts of tourism

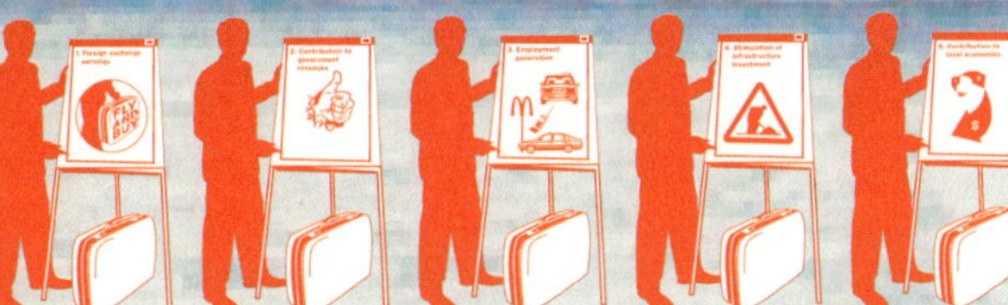

golf courses

Golf courses are major wasters and polluters of water

Golf courses are fast becoming an important attraction of tourist destinations in the tropics. Malaysia had about 20 golf courses in the 1970s. Now it has more than 200.

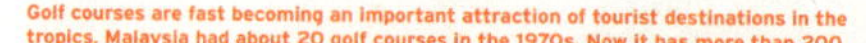

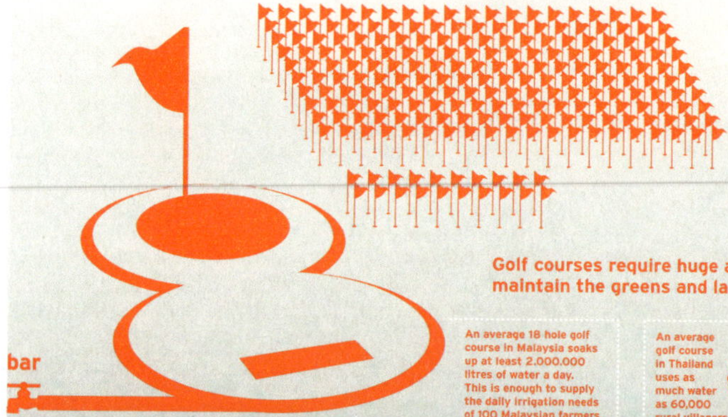

bar

Golf courses require huge amounts of water to maintain the greens and landscaped gardens.

An average 18 hole golf course in Malaysia soaks up at least 2.000.000 litres of water a day. This is enough to supply the daily irrigation needs of 100 Malaysian farmers.

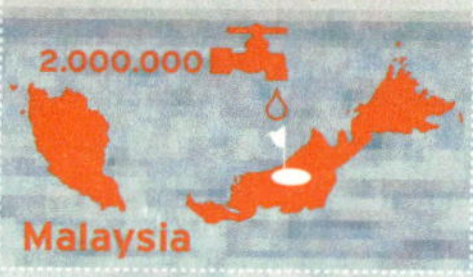

2.000.000

Malaysia

An average golf course in Thailand uses as much water as 60,000 rural villagers and needs 1500kg of chemical fertilizers, pesticides and herbicides per year.

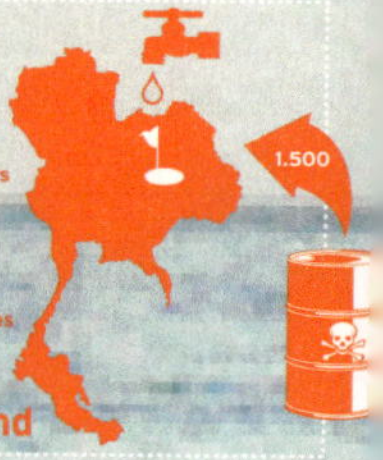

1.500

Thailand

90% of the fertilisers, pesticides and herbicides sprayed on golf courses ends up in the air. Residents living near a golf course, as well as golfers and caddies, often suffer from skin problems and respiratory illnesses.

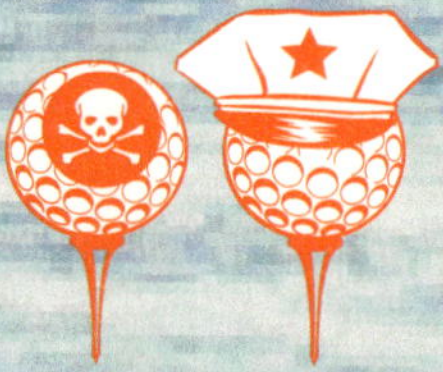

Farming communities lose their land and are displaced for golf course development, with minimal compensation. In a number of countries, the local peasants are subject to police or military intimidation when they protest against the destruction of their fields.

cruise ships waste

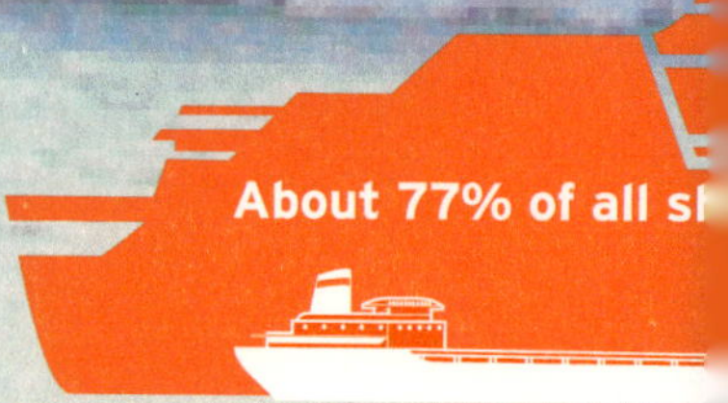

About 77% of all s

climate change

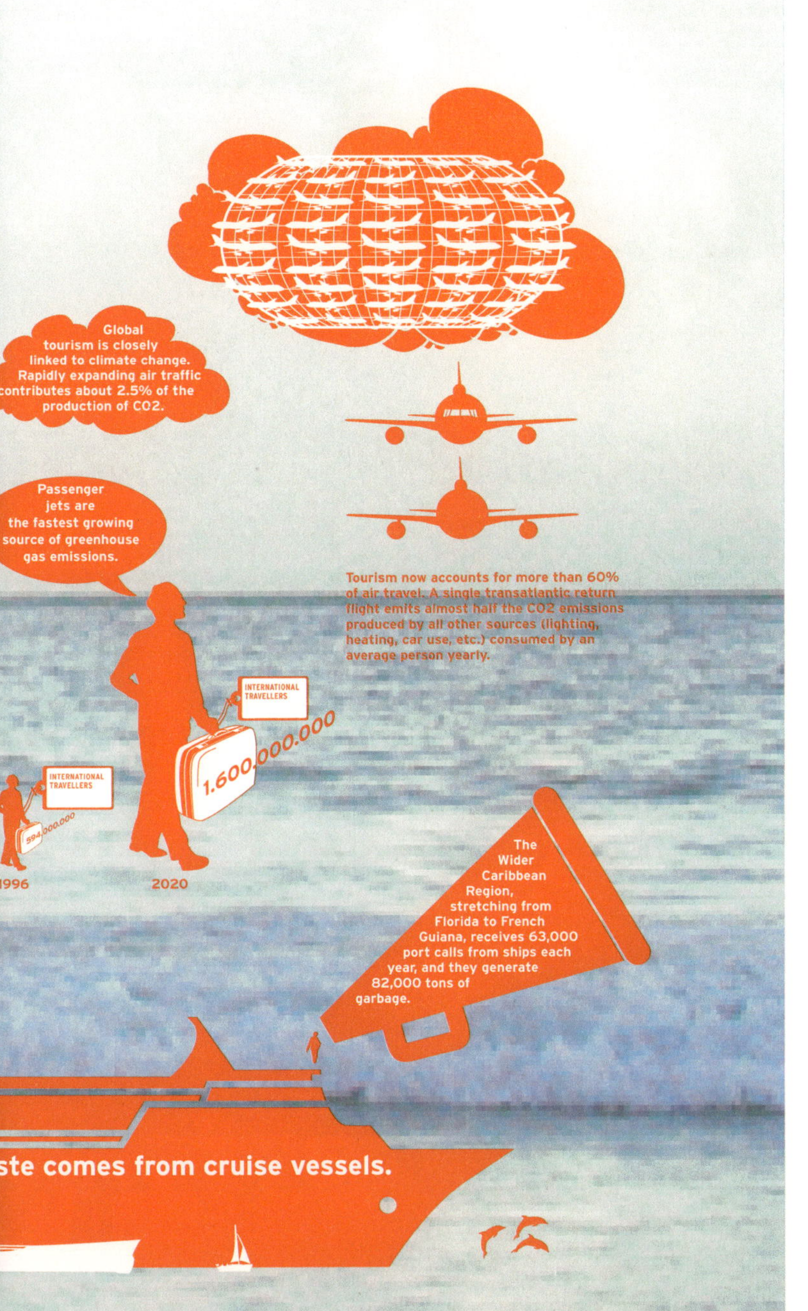

126 Los edificios más altos de cada país (The Tallest Buildings in the World)
by STAR

For the special issue of ‹Pasajes› #79 about ‹heights›, STAR made a map with the tallest building in each country around the edge of the circle.

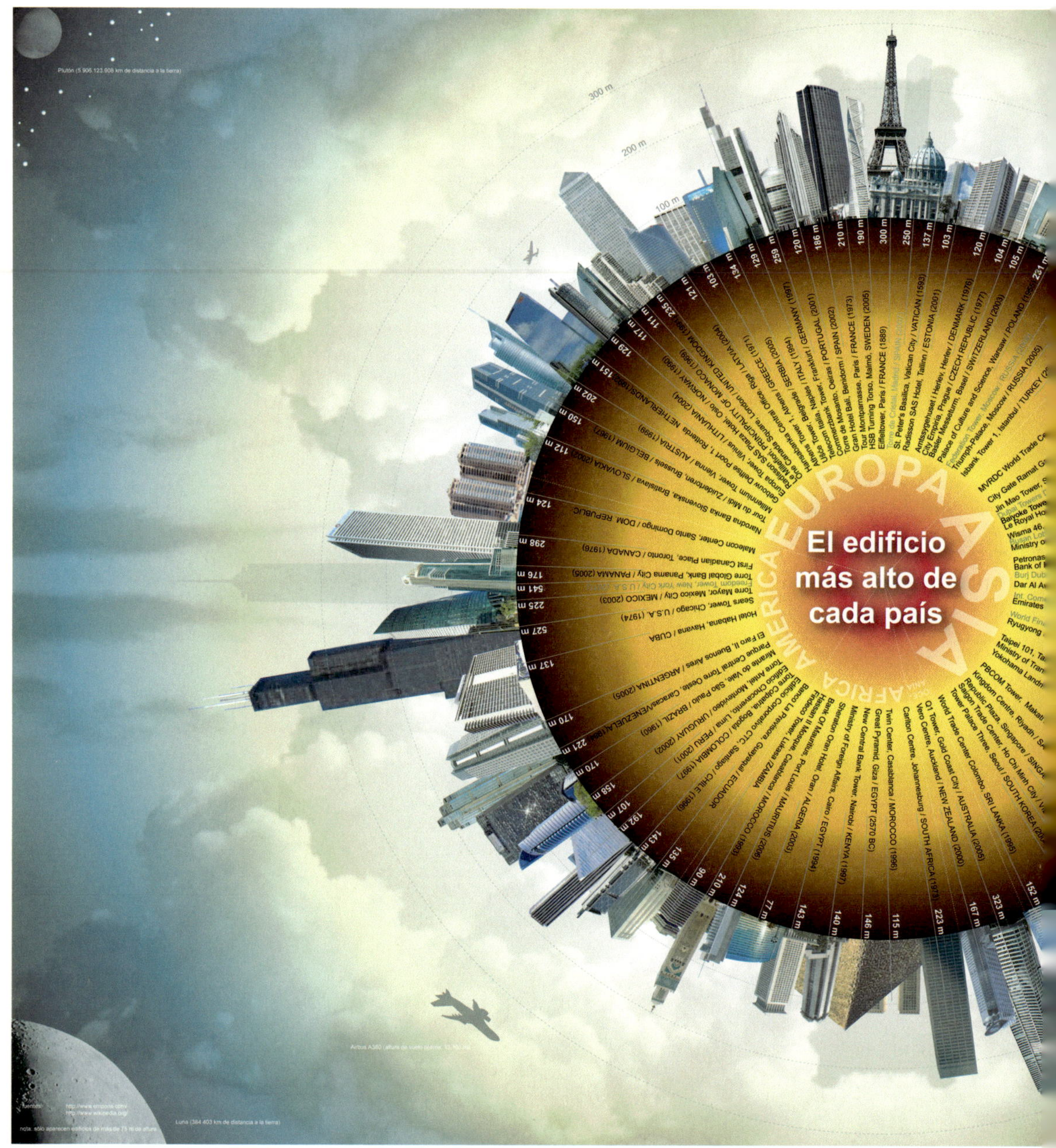

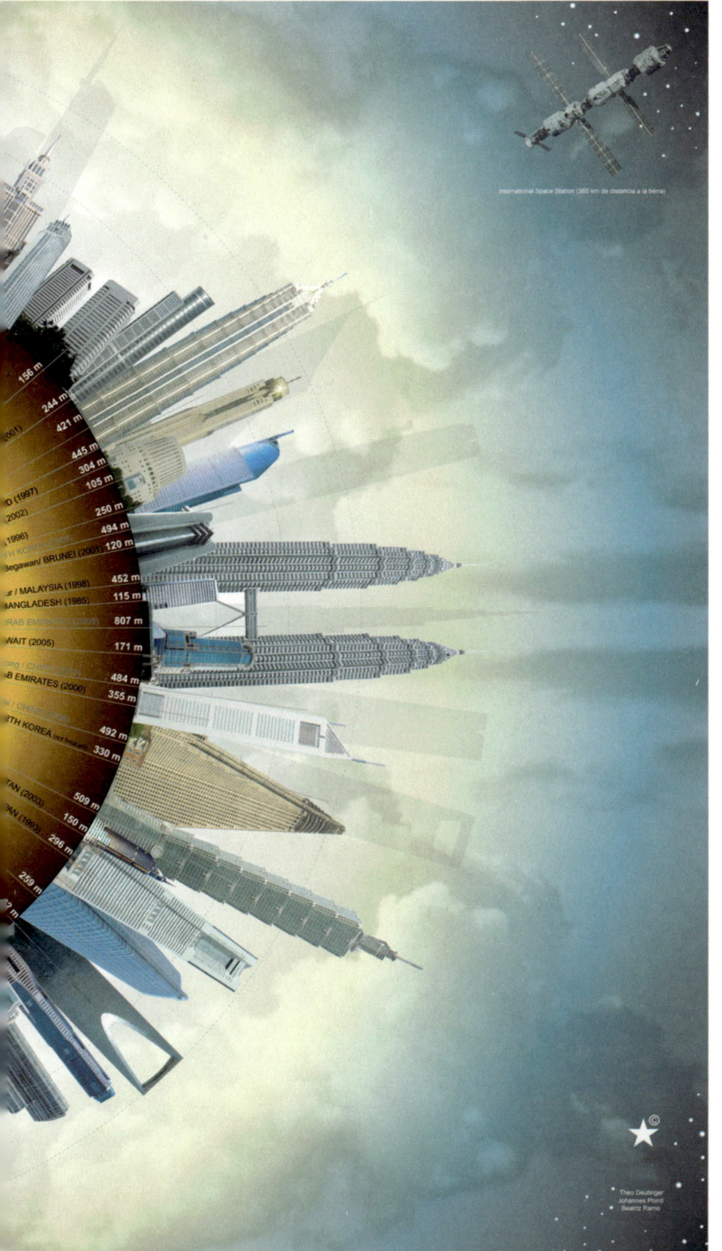

for Pasajes de Arquitectura y Crítica #79 – September 06 (ES), © STAR (Beatriz Ramo, Johannes Pointl), Theo Deutinger (TD-architects), 2006

La Historia de las Expos (The History of the Expos)
by STAR

World's Fairs are an offspring of the age of industrialization in Europe, with their initial focus being on innovative products more than on the magnificence of their pavilions' architecture. The 155 years of World's Fairs can be clearly divided into two periods, the Industrial Revolution and the Digital Revolution, with the time of the great wars as a violent transition phase that cuts this

© Beatriz Ramo, Theo Deutinger, Own initiative project - Published in Pasajes de Arquitectura y Crítica #83 – January 07 (ES) / Zarquitectura #5-6 – February 07 (ES), 2006

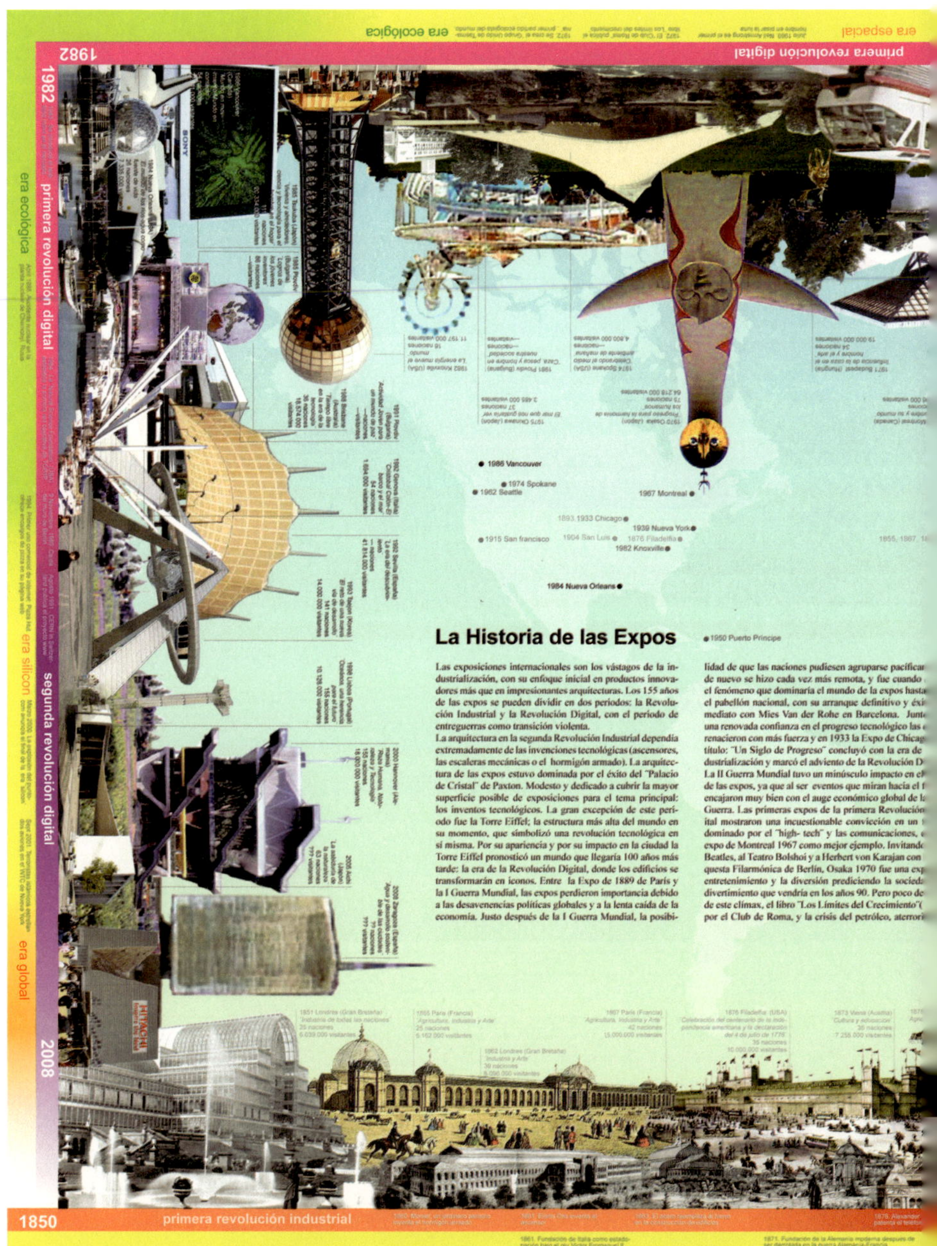

155 years in two perfect halves. Just as political principles, social life and technology changed radically during this time, so too did architecture. The panorama shows the evolution throughout history of these major events.

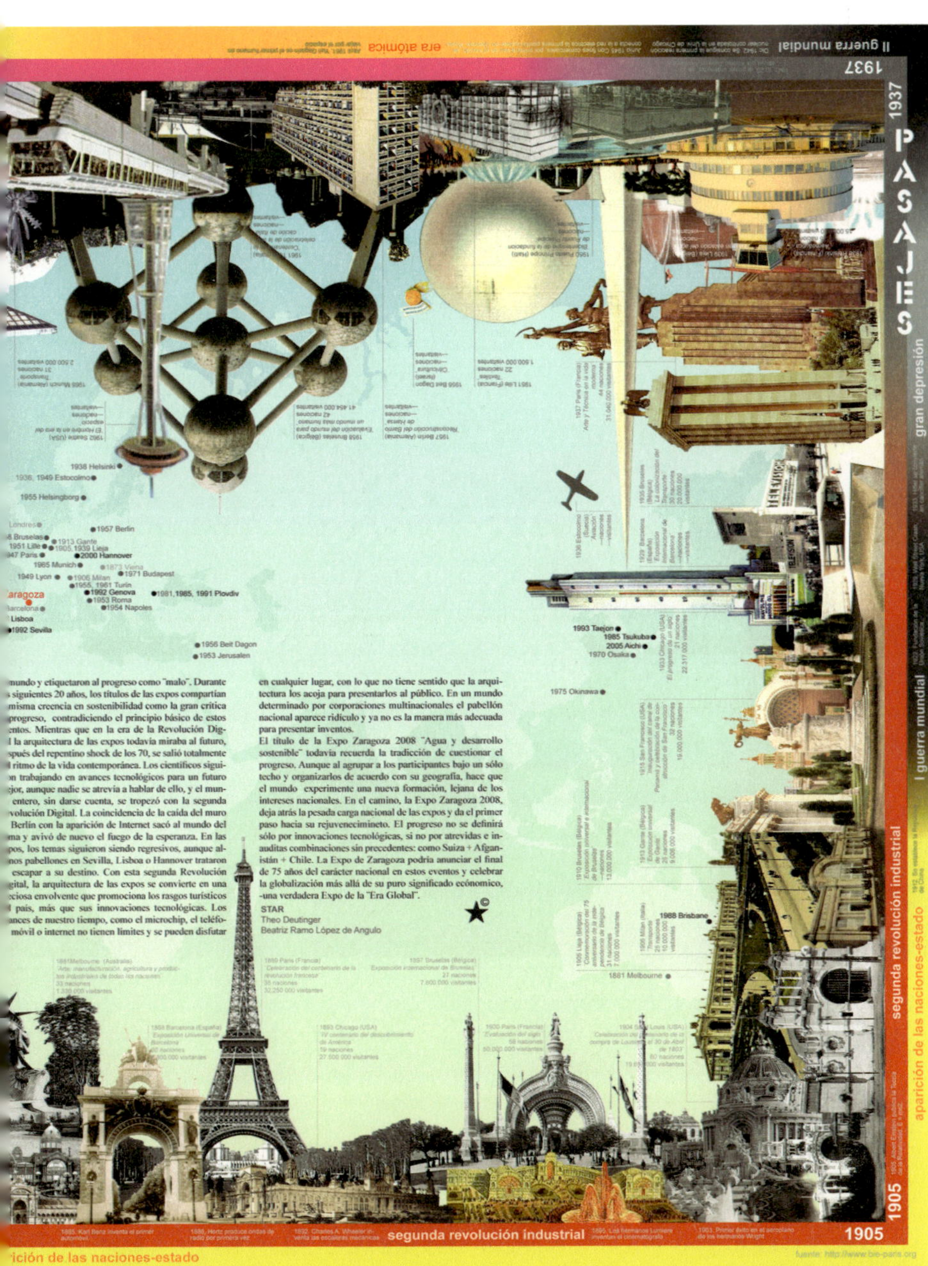

Political Graphics

Gorilla
by De Designpolitie, Lesley Moore & Herman van Bostelen

Untitled
by Machine

SP
by Thonik

Sealand Identity Project
by Meta Haven

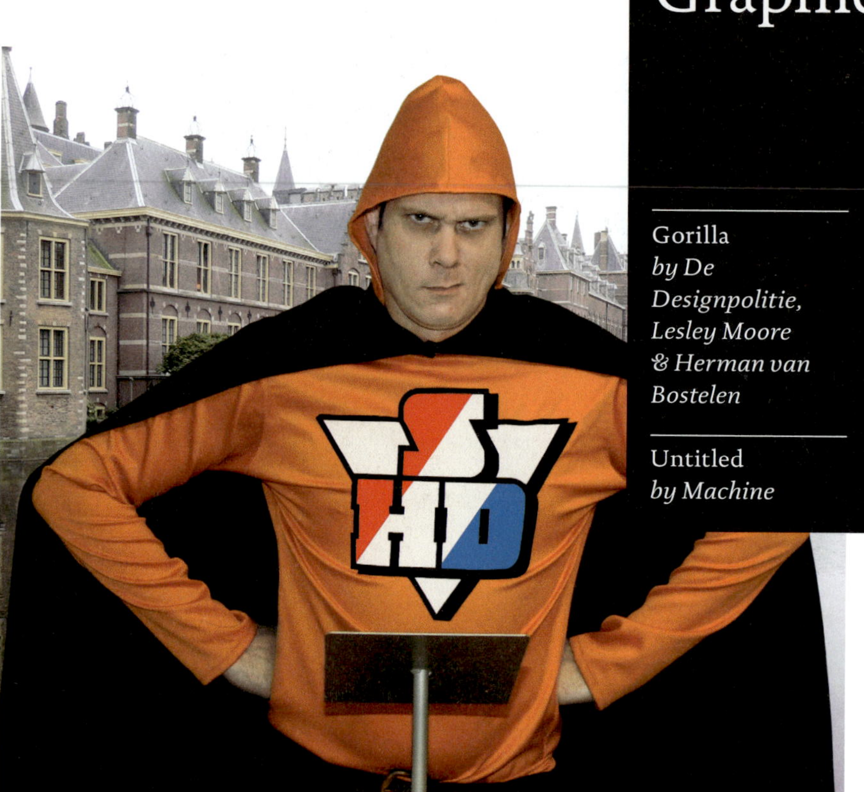

PostCom Grids
by Meta Haven

PostCom North Korea, Ryungyong - Forbidden Icon
by Meta Haven

Quaero Design Research, Quaero Logo
by Meta Haven

The Image of Europe - ‹EU-History ring›
by OMA / AMO & STAR

Gorilla

by De Designpolitie, Lesley Moore & Herman van Bostelen

Since October 2006 we have been responsible for a visual column on the front page of ‹De Volkskrant›, one of the main national newspapers. We make up the collective ‹Gorilla›. We react to the news of the day in words and images. We see this as a great opportunity to vent our views on politics, the environment and all those subjects people that worry about, but don't know how to handle.

You can also visit the ‹De Volkskrant› website (www.vk.nl/gorilla) and take a look at the daily updated range of ‹Gorilla's›. As a visitor, you can react on this ‹Gorilla›, you can download it and print the PDF on A4, or send it as a mail to somebody else.

Another exiting thing is the fact that as graphic designers we are suddenly able to get out of the shadow of our assignments. Suddenly we are authors instead of translators or ‹problem solvers›. The only thing that matters is our own opinions. And that appears to be a serious responsibility. But we like it!

What makes it different/interesting?
We think that the use of graphics means makes it totally different from cartoons or illustration. We use illustrative images, but we also use text. A ‹Gorilla› can also be strictly typographic. In this way, we make small posters instead of a column. In a cartoon or illustration the narrative part is important. In our solutions the power of the message and image is the most important thing. Again, it's more a kind of postage stamp-size poster than a cartoon or an illustration.

Another very important thing is the multimedia aspect. Most of the discussion can be found on the ‹De Volkskrant› website. There people are able to respond to our ‹Gorilla's› without boundaries. In our view, that is important. We don't tell the truth, just offer an opinion.

WAR IS OVER!

IF YOU WANT IT

John & Yoko & Gorilla

For De Volkskrant, John Lennon's dying day, 2006

Exit strategy for the war in Iraq

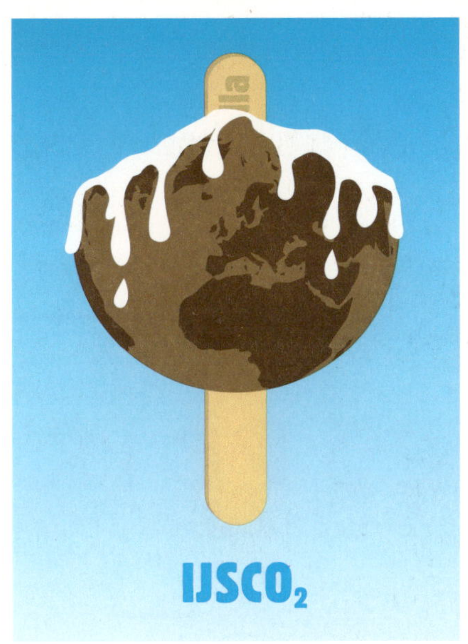

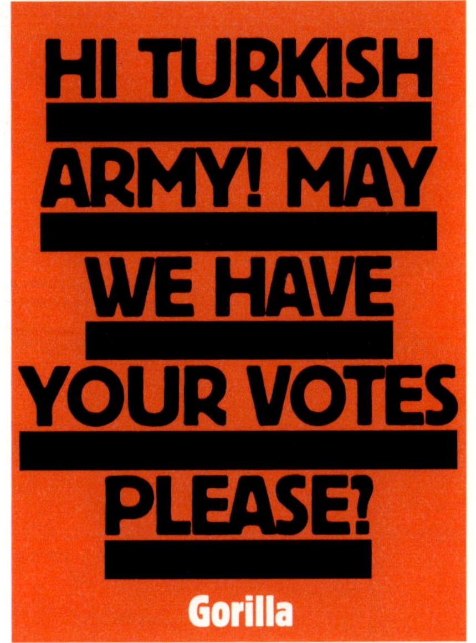

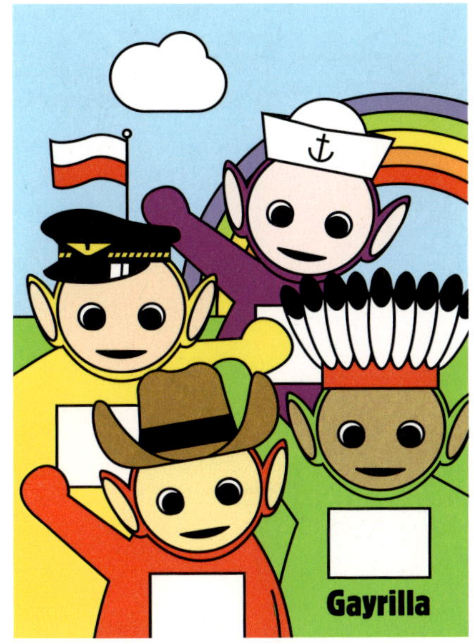

In Poland a discussion arouse about the ‹homosexuality› of Tinky Winky. (He carries a handbag...)

to do list George W. Bush

- [x] Al fabet
- [x] Al cohol
- [x] Al Gore
- [x] Al Zarqawi
- [ ] Al Qaida
- [ ] Al ready

Gorilla®

VOTEZ NICOLAS VOTEZ

~~Liberté~~

DÉSESPOIR

~~Egalité~~

INDIFFÉRENCE

~~Fraternité~~

ALIÉNATION

Gorille

ROYAL SARKOZ GRAPUS

French elections

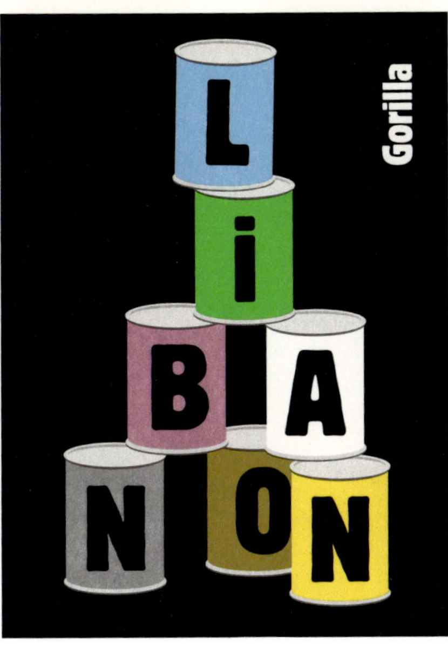

Vulnerable balance in Libanon after Israeli attacks and financial injection by the EU

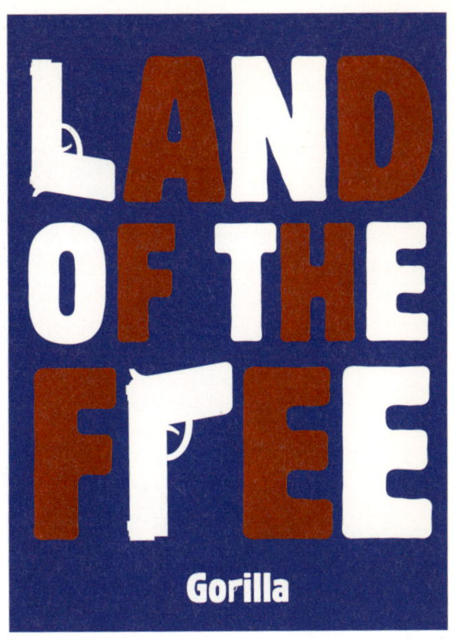

Shoot-out at an American university, where several students were killed

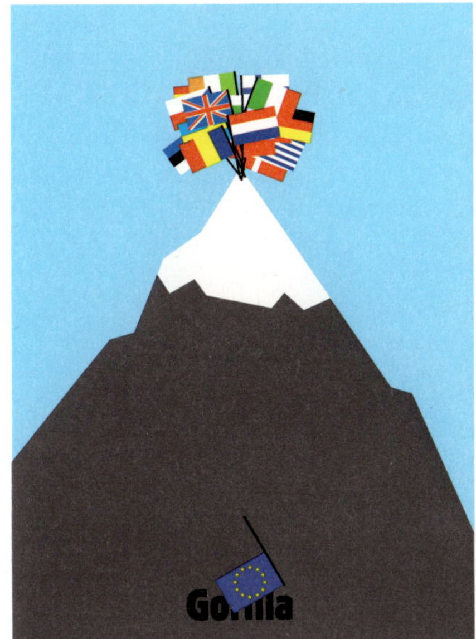

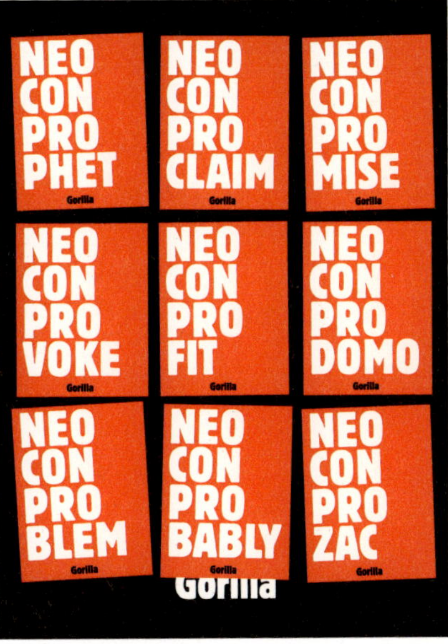

Bush speaks to Congress about his Iraq policy

Jeruzalem

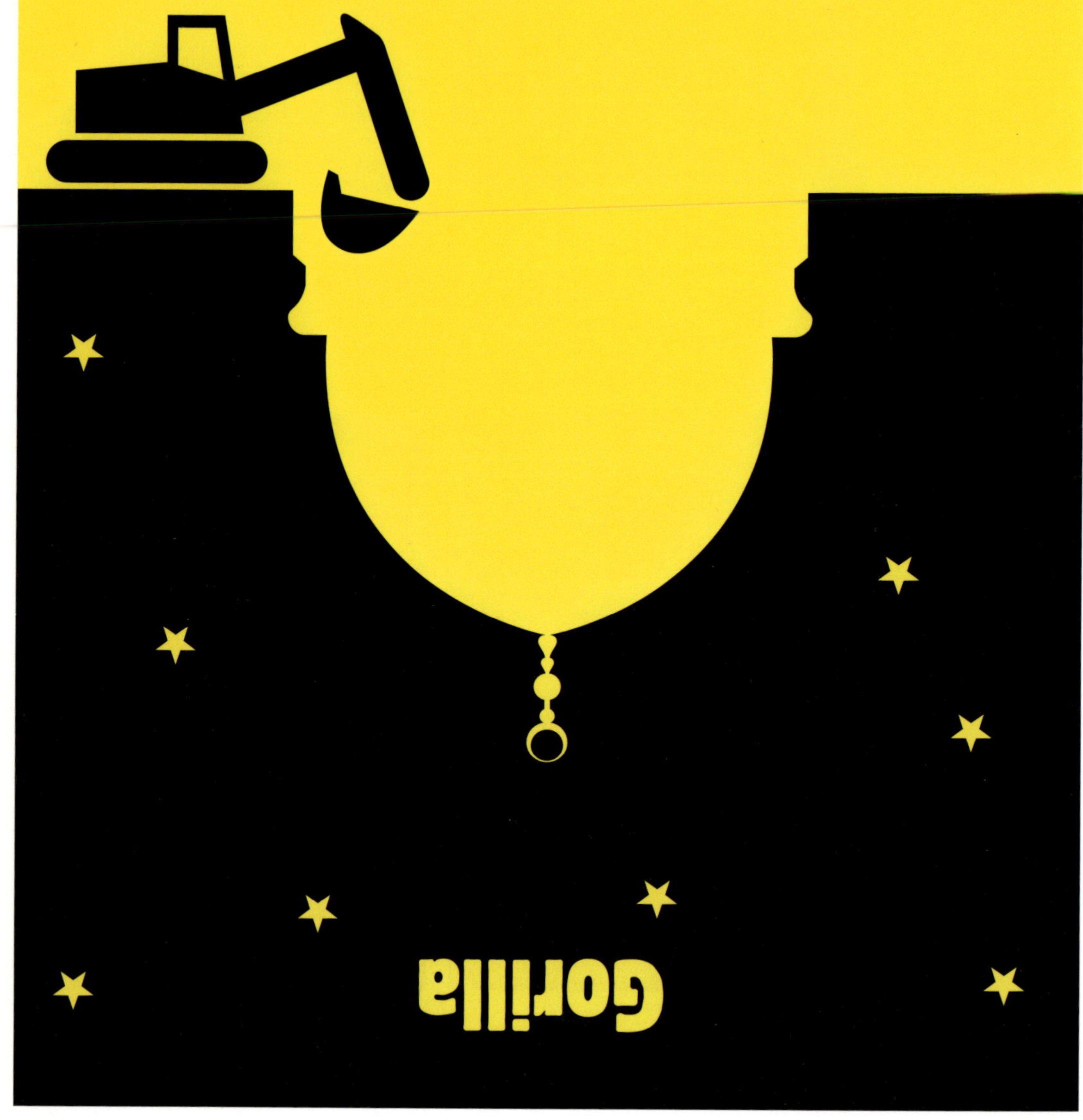

Riots on the Temple Mount

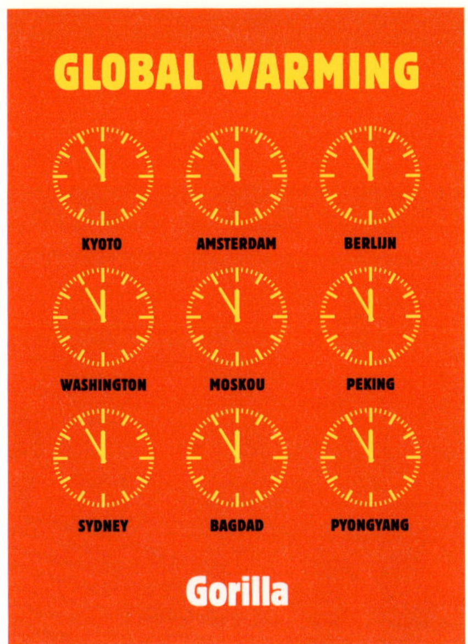

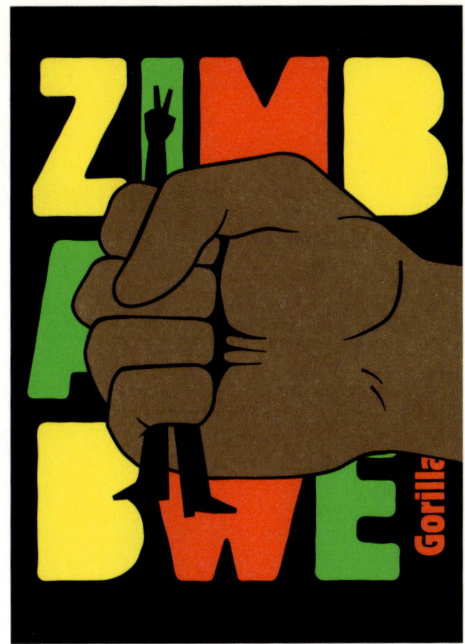

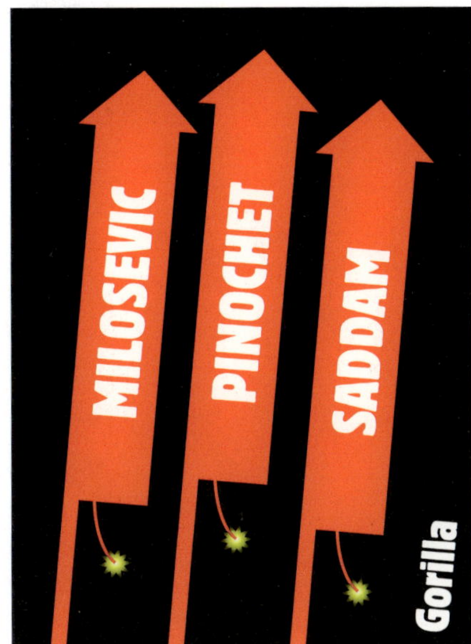

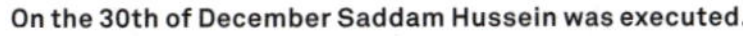
On the 30th of December Saddam Hussein was executed.

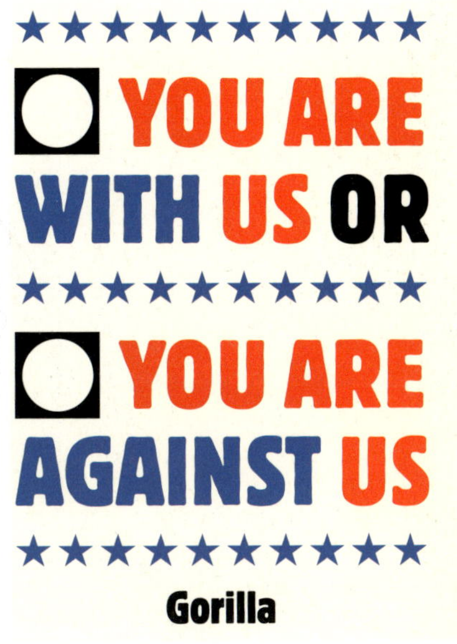

Again the Republicans focus on the basic fears of Americans.

140 Untitled
by Machine

for This is a magazine, 2002

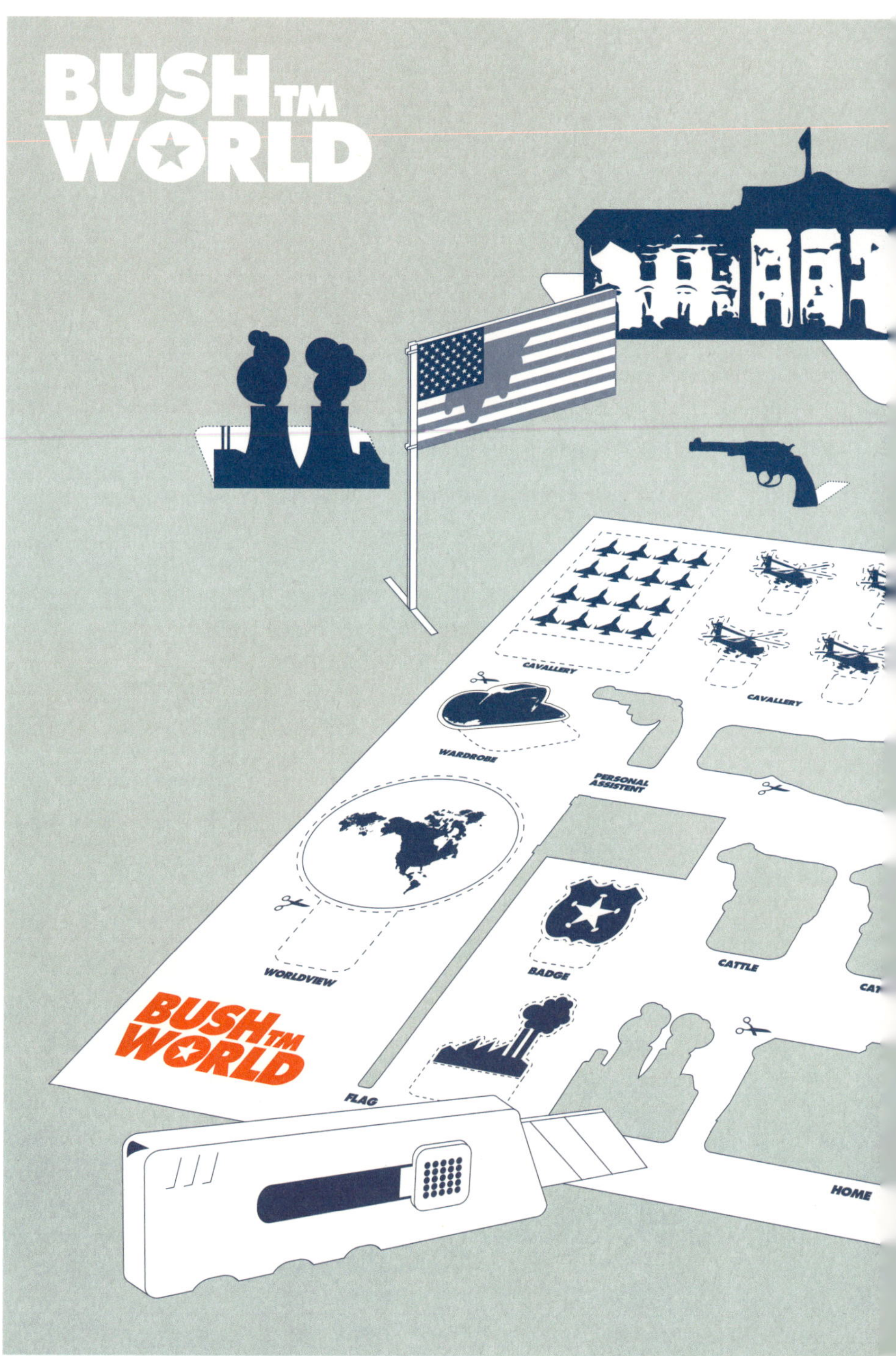

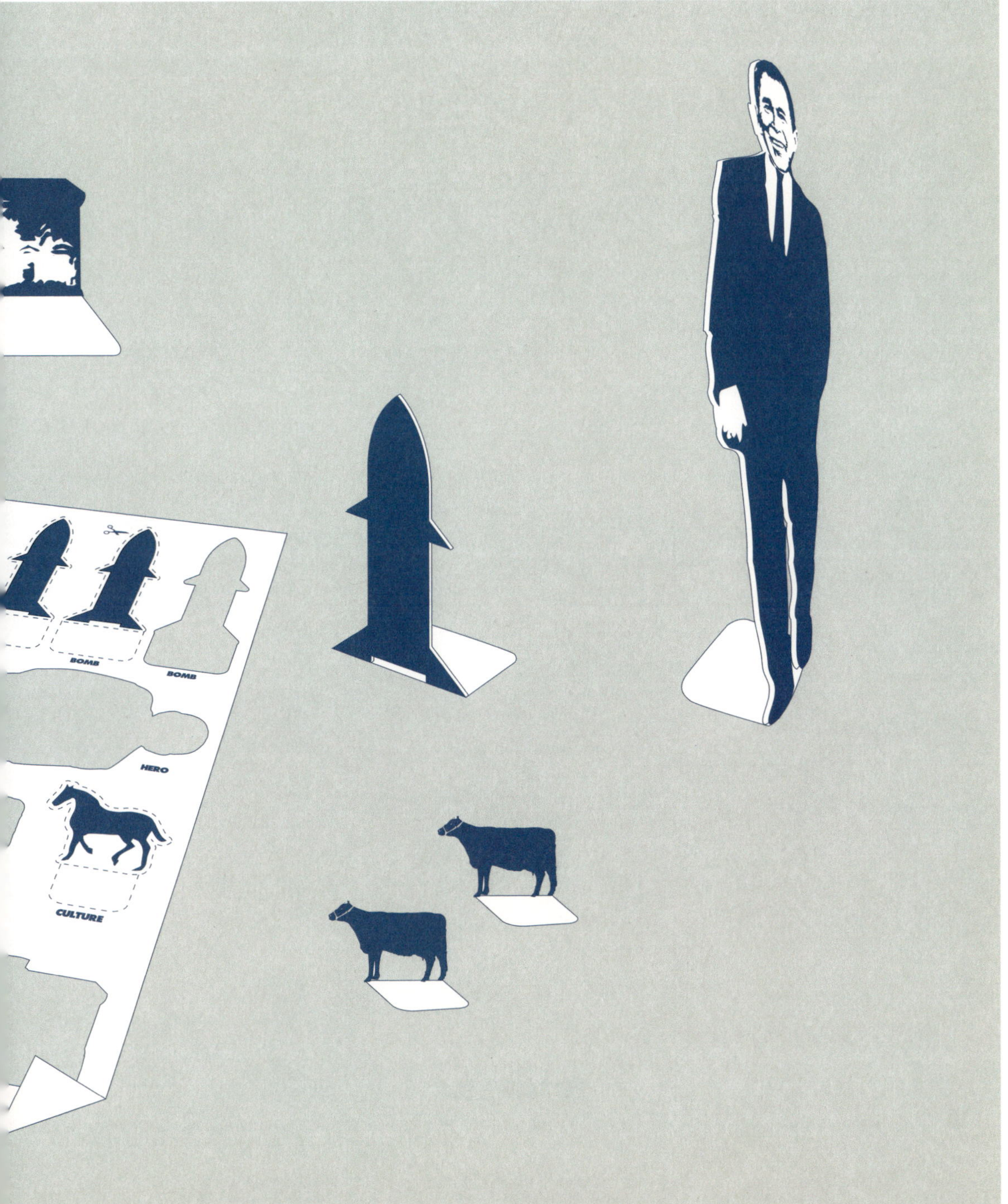
BOMB
BOMB
HERO
CULTURE

CAVALRY

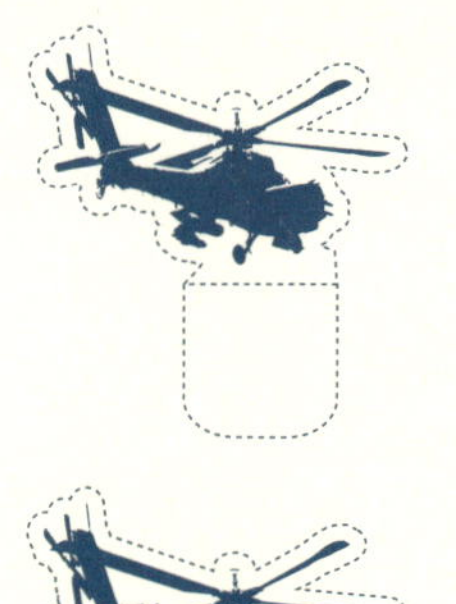

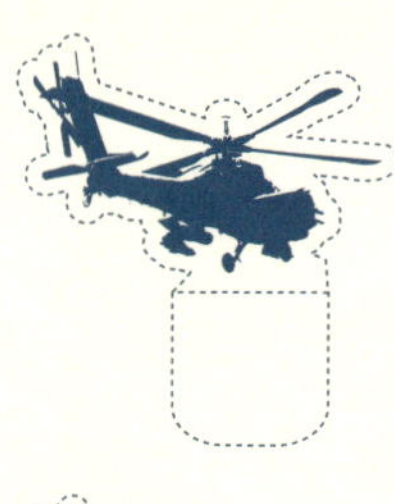

CAVALRY

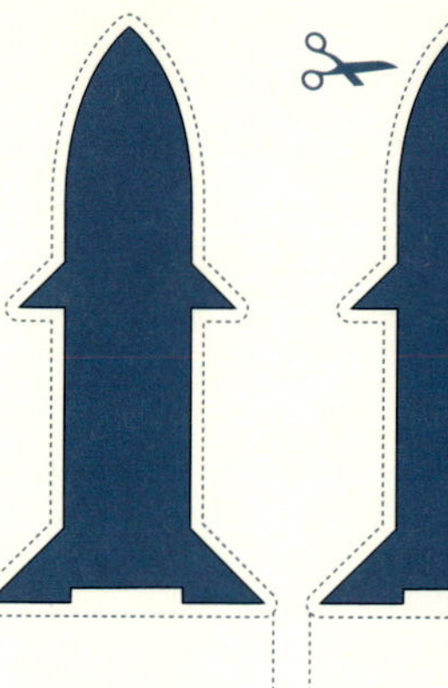

BOMB

BO-

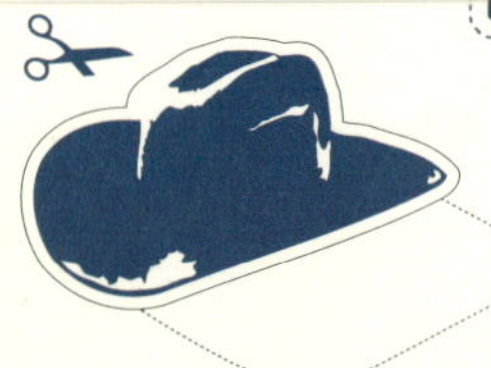

WARDROBE

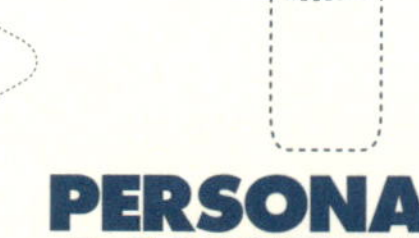

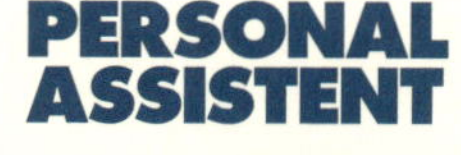

PERSONAL
ASSISTENT

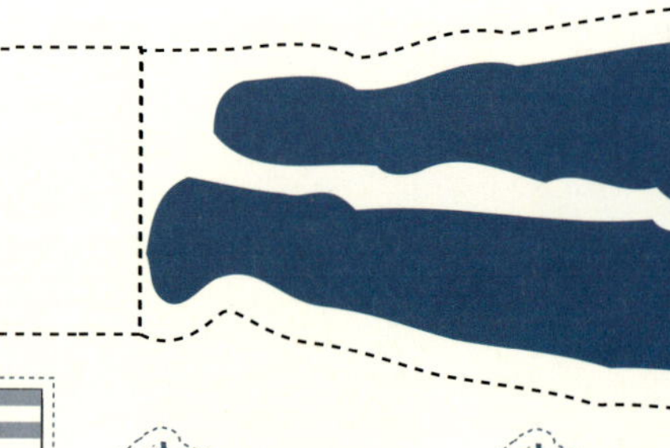

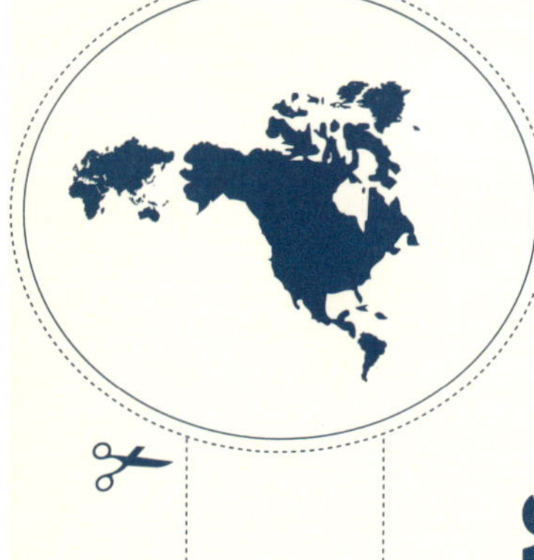

WORLDVIEW

FLAG

BADGE

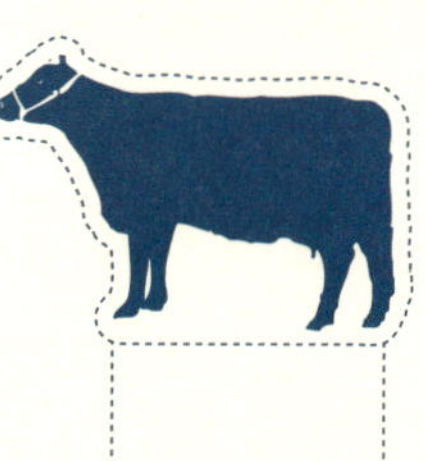

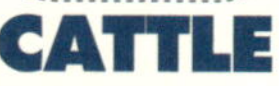

CATTLE

CATTLE

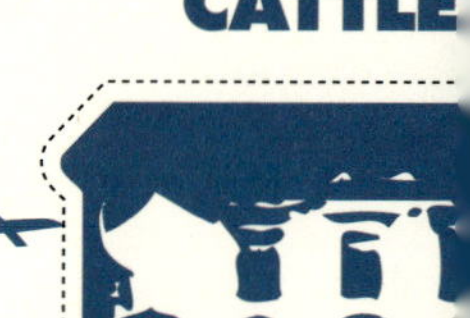

FRIENDS

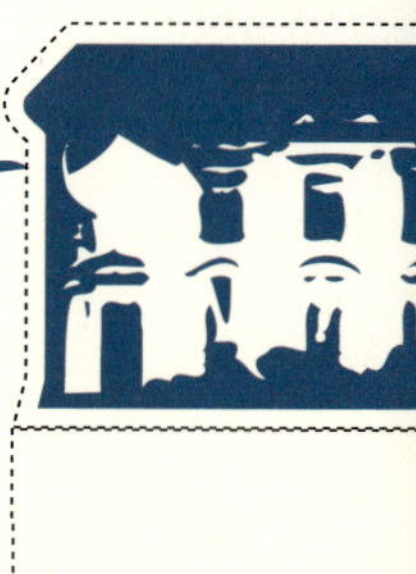

FRIENDS

BUSH TM
WORLD

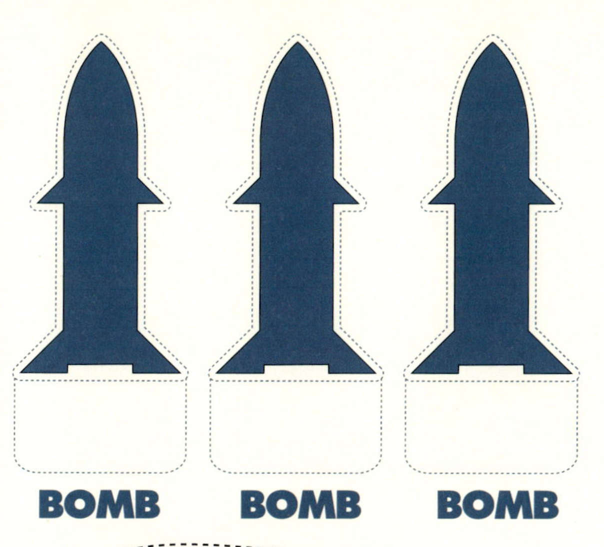

BOMB BOMB BOMB

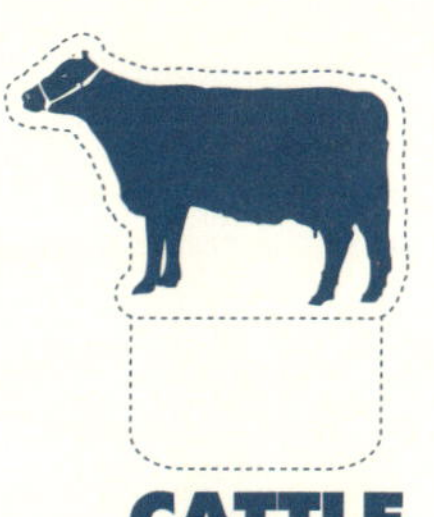

CATTLE CATTLE

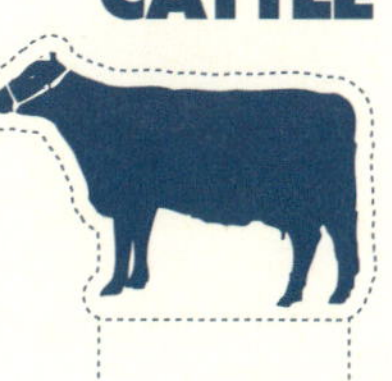

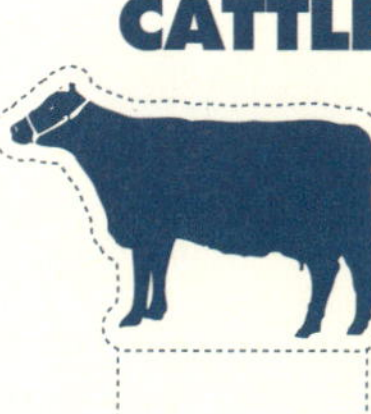

CATTLE CATTLE

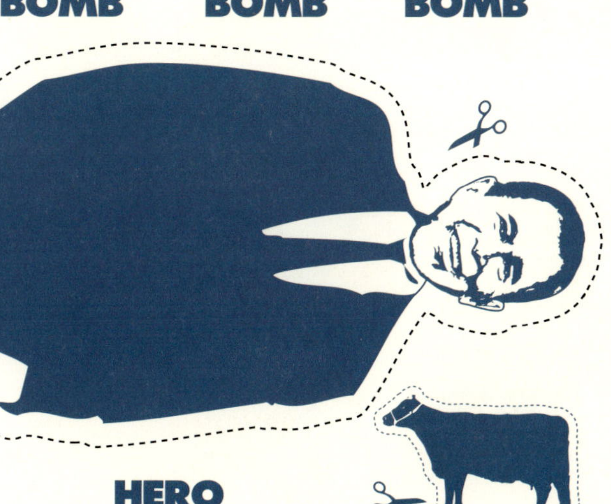

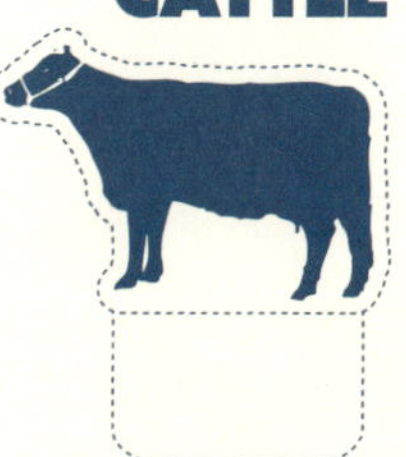

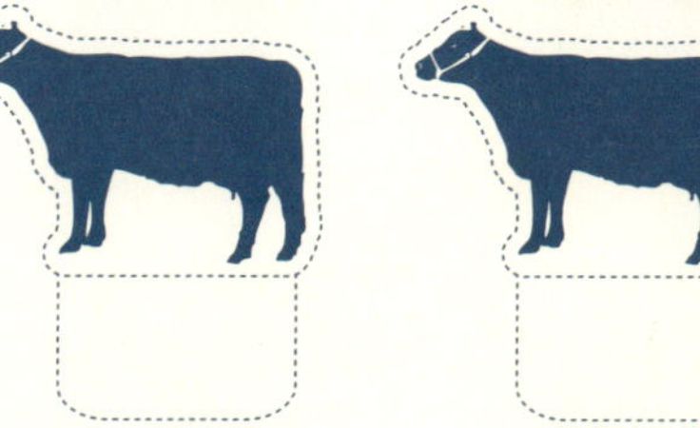

CATTLE CATTLE

HERO

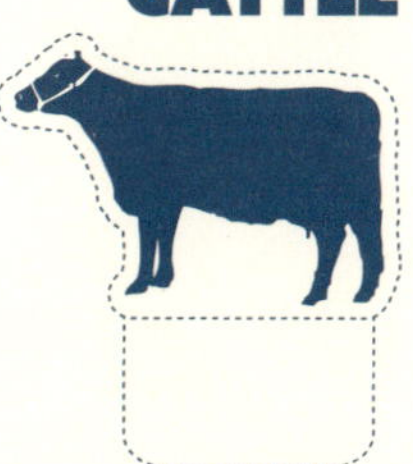

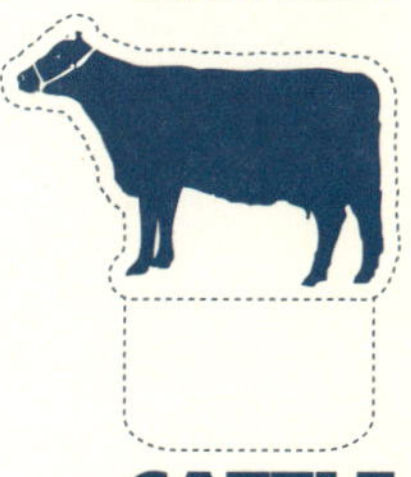

CATTLE CATTLE CATTLE

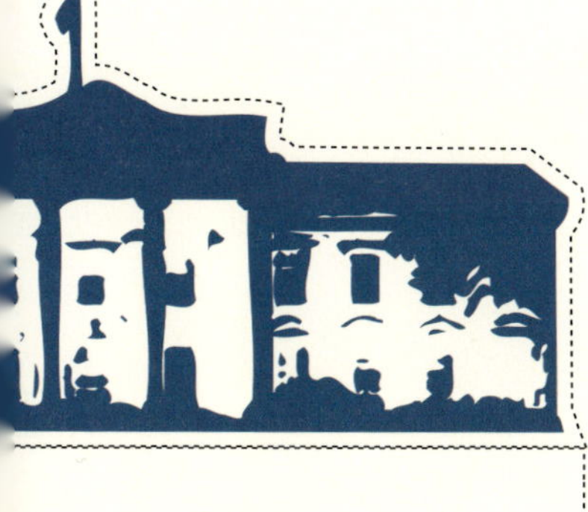

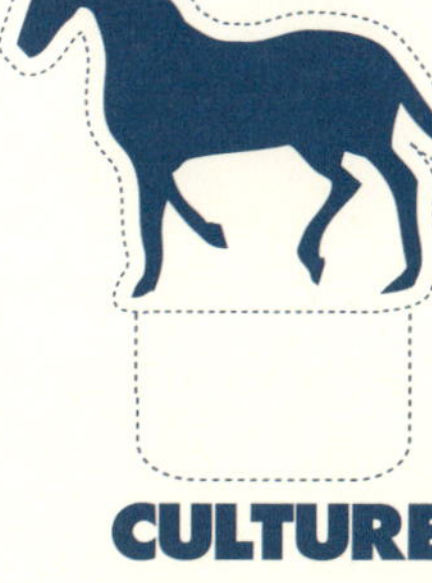

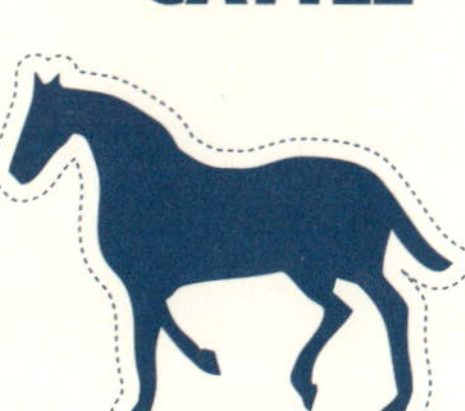

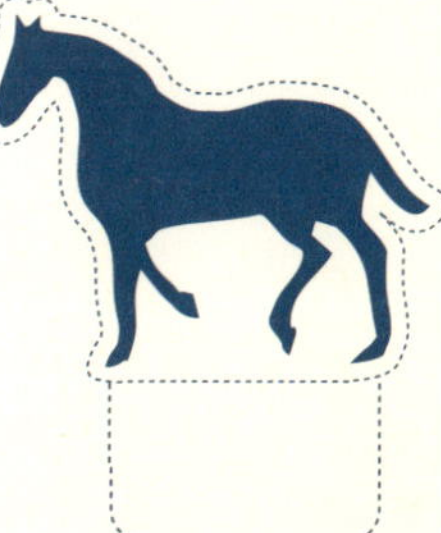

OME

CULTURE CULTURE CULTURE

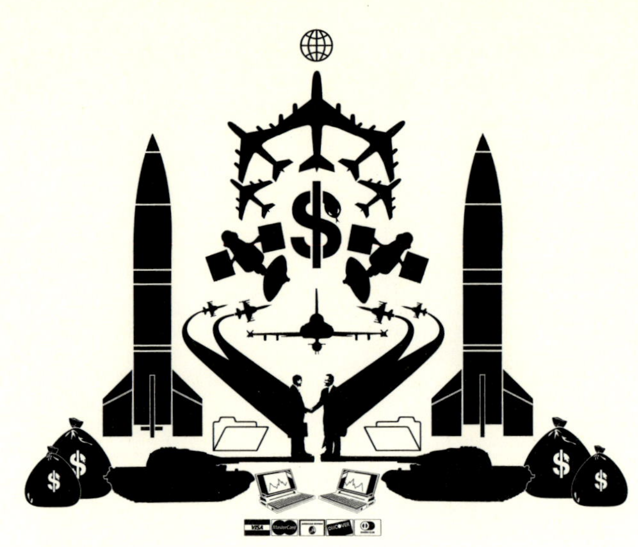

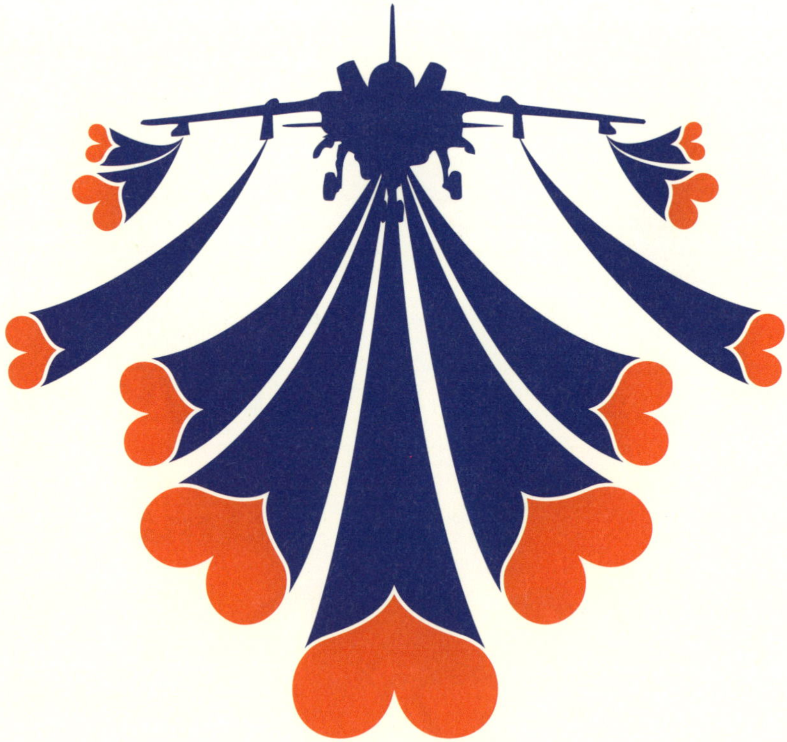

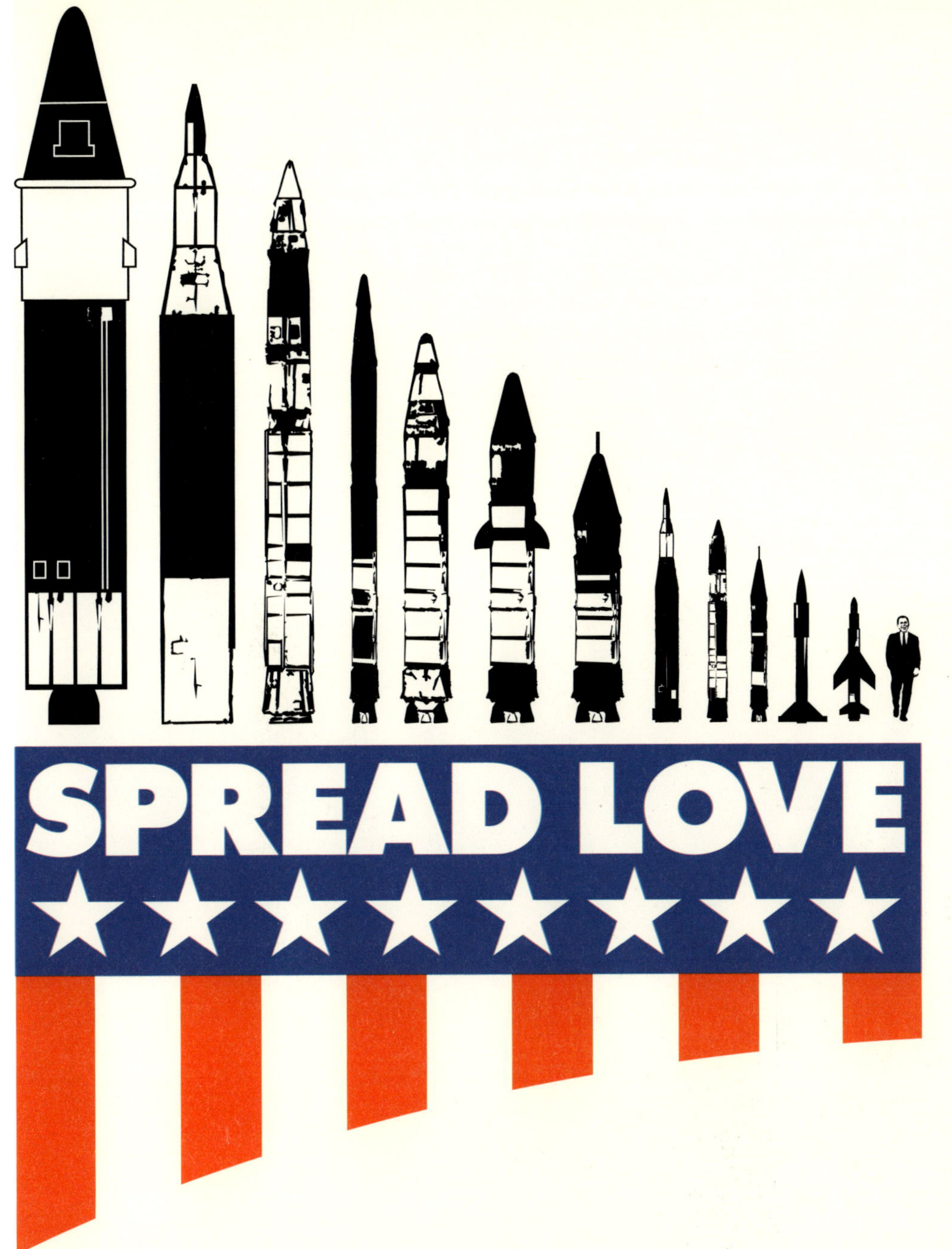
SPREAD LOVE

SP
by Thonik

Thonik designed a new identity and three campaigns for the ‹Dutch Socialist Party.› The new logo combines typography and symbol. ‹SP› in fat type and an abstraction of a tomato. The poster ‹NU SP› (now SP) shows, in four letters and one symbol, the whole graphic system. For the interaction in the street Thonik employed artist Joep van Lieshout to make a mobile tomato soup outlet. On the internet the message was personalized through three viral movies. The online shop is a parody of merchandising. The image of the political leader Jan Marijnissen becomes a threefold part of the graphic system. Against the décor of the congress podium, Jan Marijnissen looks like a statesman. When photographed in the style of a HEMA advertisement and placed on bus shelters, he looks like a very ordinary Dutchman. In the viral movies he appears as an endearing comedian.

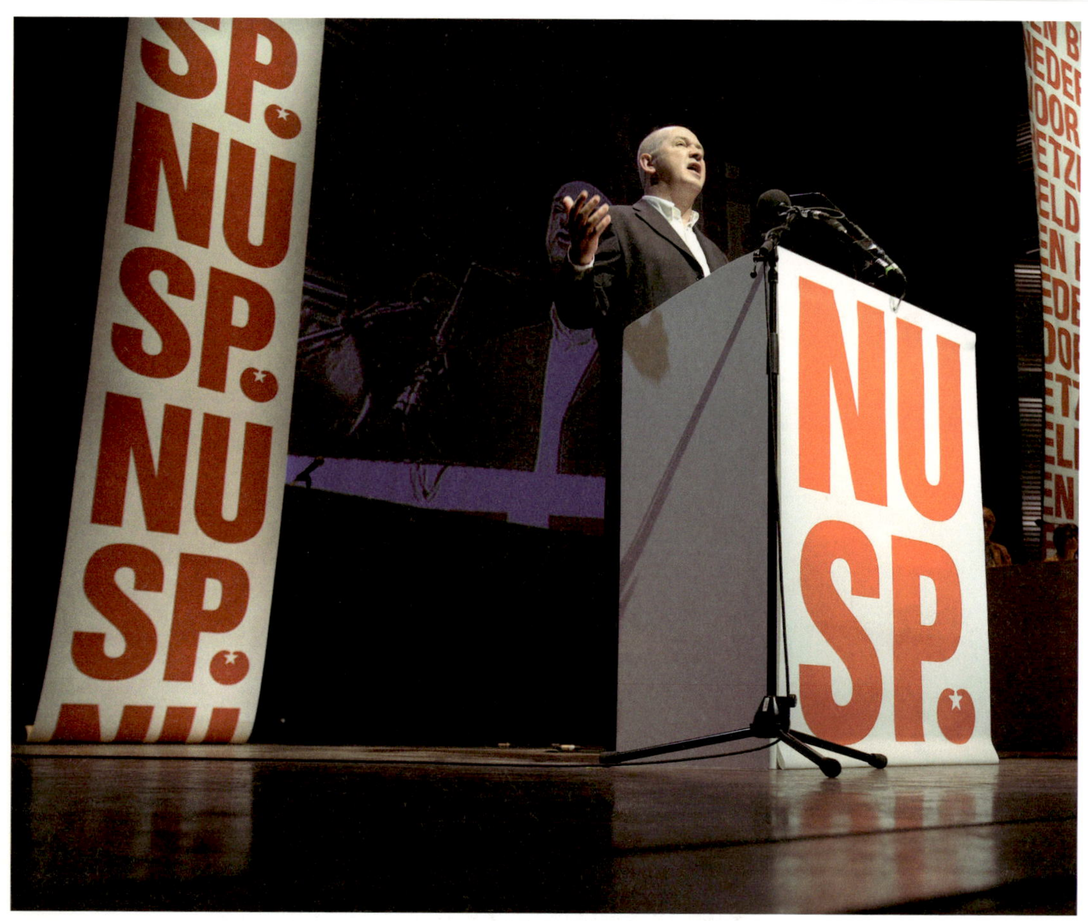

for the Dutch Socialist Party

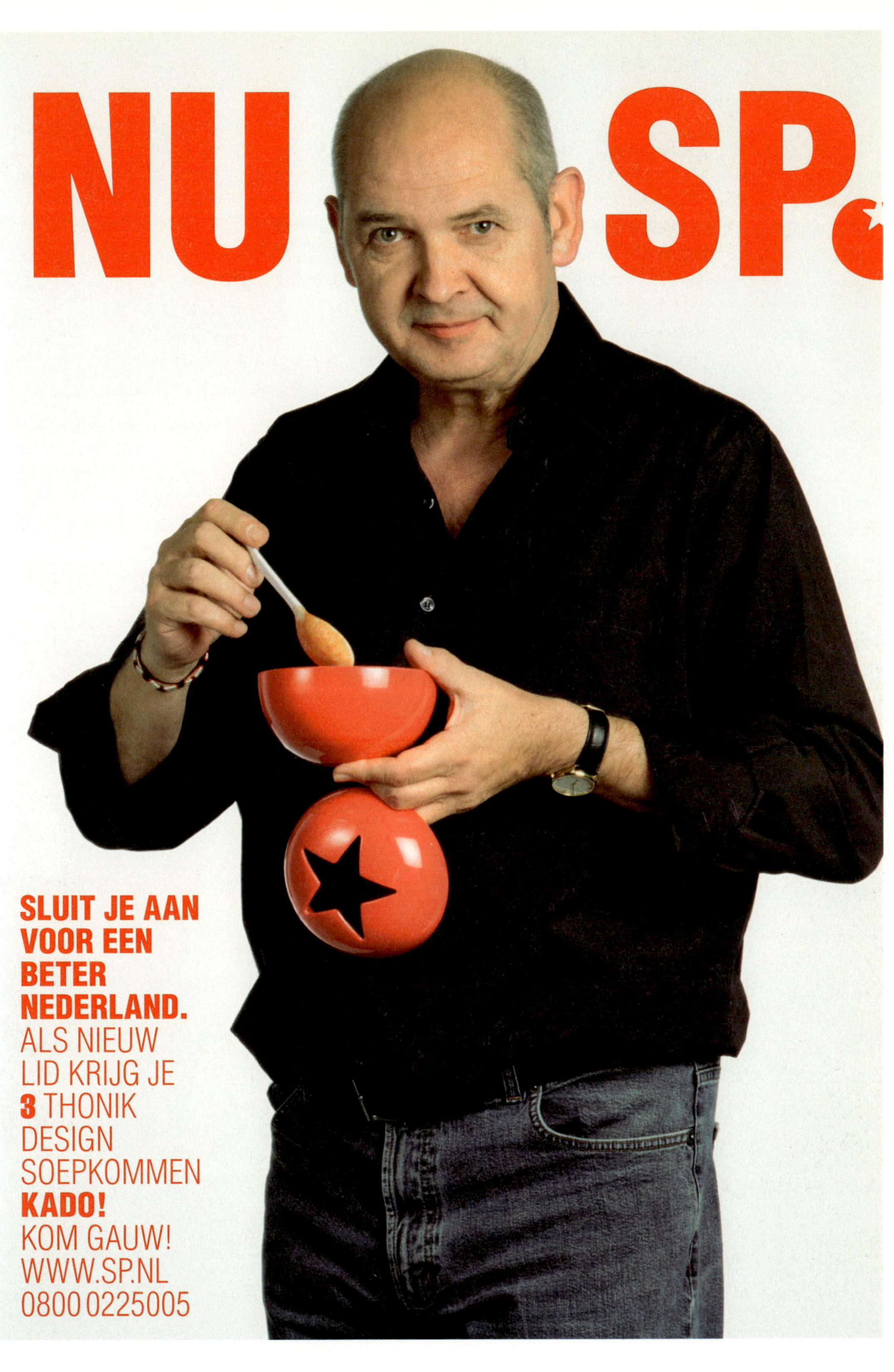
NU SP.
SLUIT JE AAN
VOOR EEN
BETER
NEDERLAND.
ALS NIEUW
LID KRIJG JE
3 THONIK
DESIGN
SOEPKOMMEN
KADO!
KOM GAUW!
WWW.SP.NL
0800 0225005

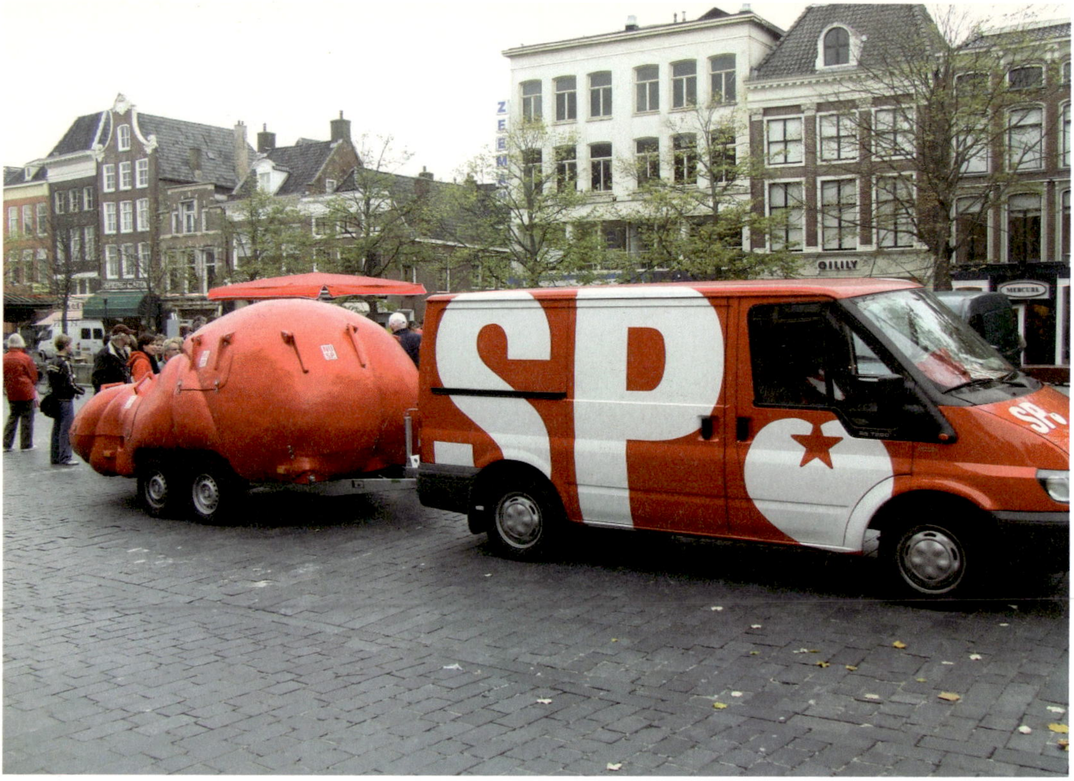

SP.
NU SP.
ALS NIEUW
LID KRIJG
JE DRIE THONIK
DESIGN SP.
SOEPKOMMEN
KADO!

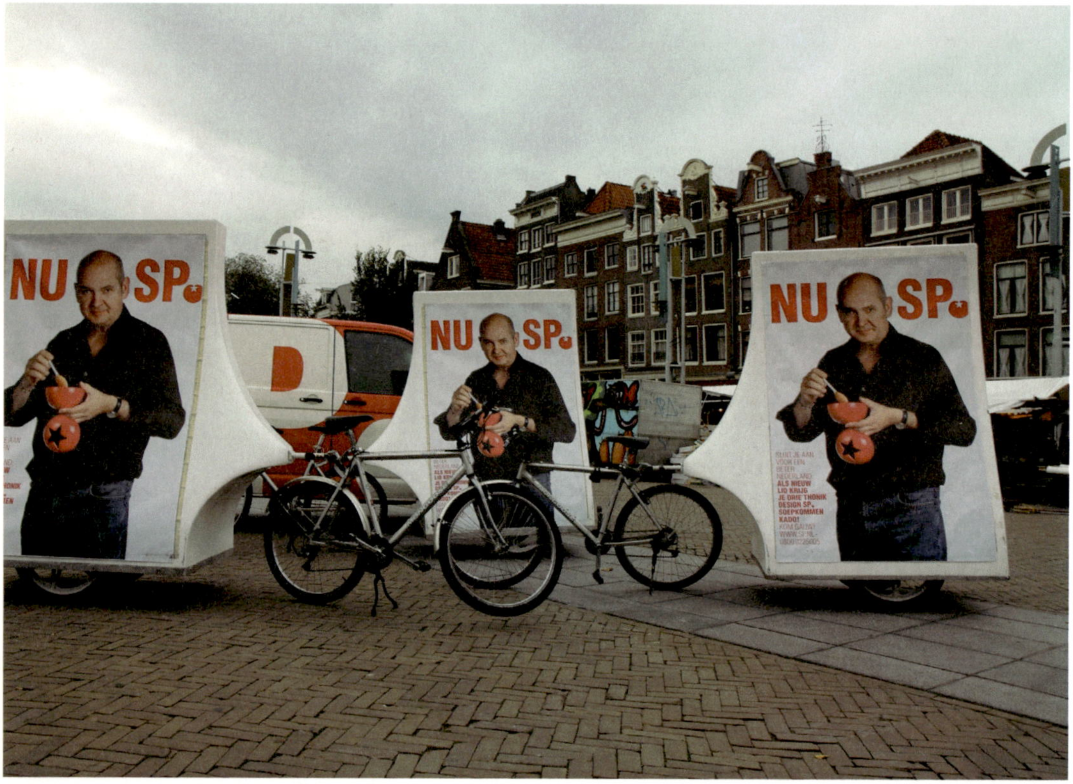

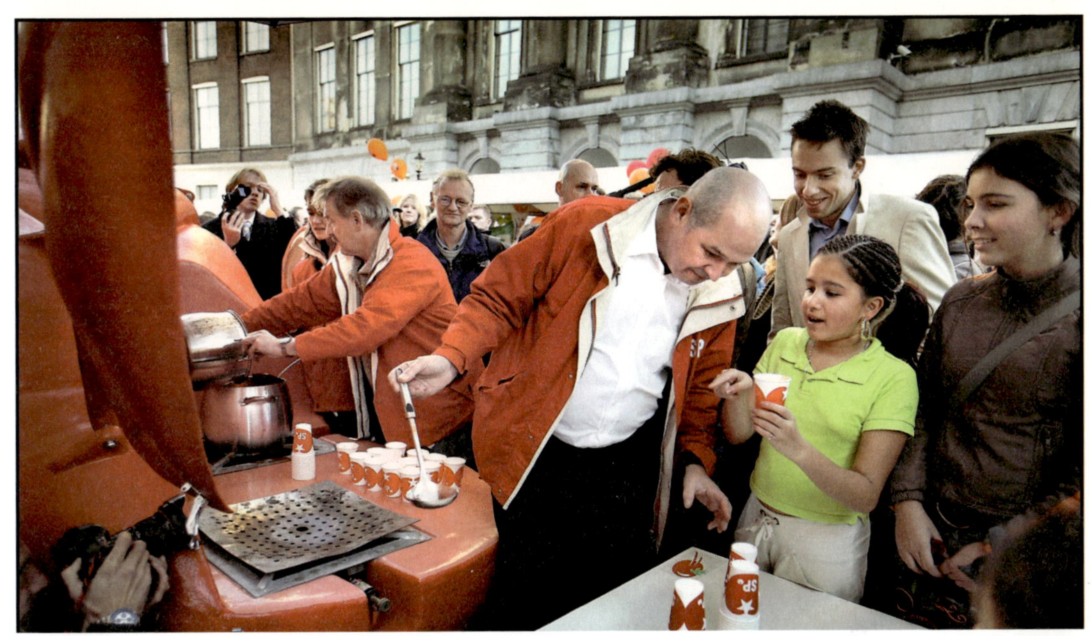

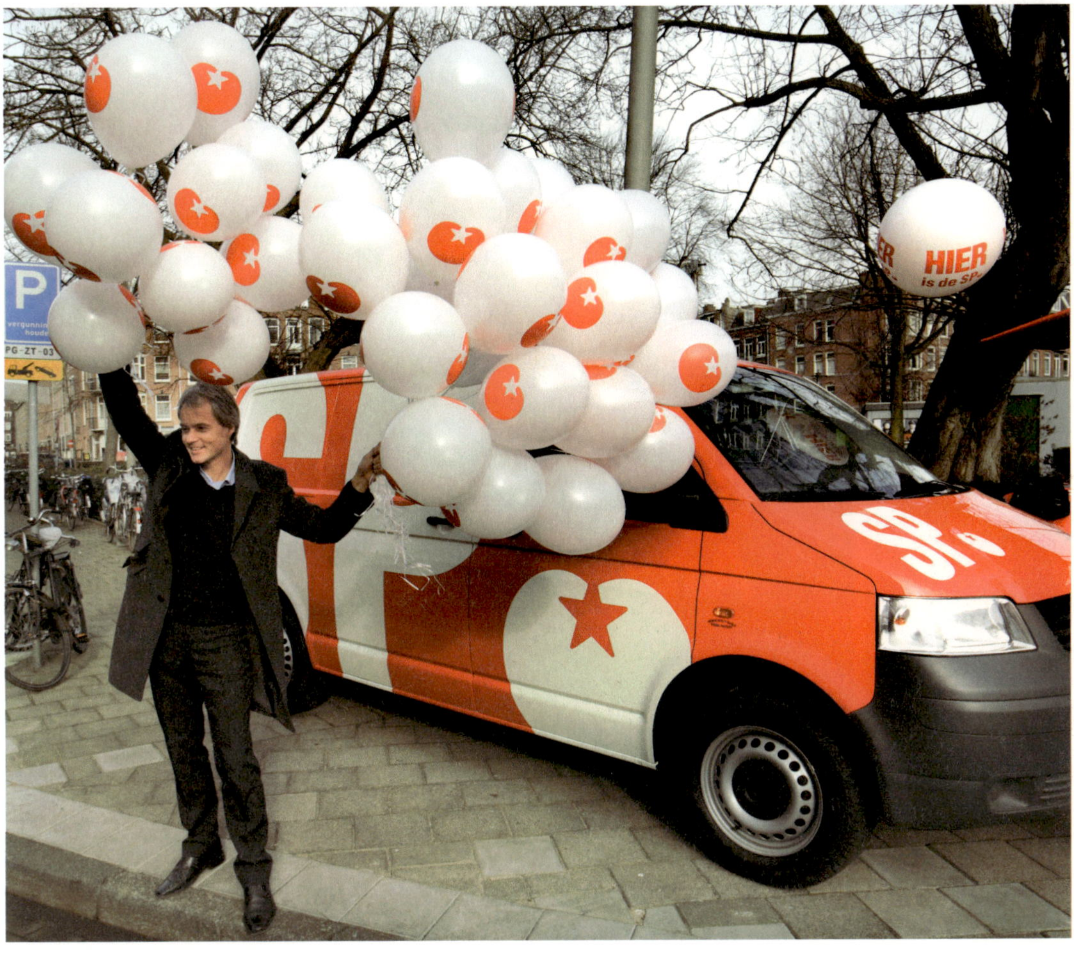

 Sealand Identity Project

by Meta Haven / Daniel van der Velden, Vinca Kruk, Adriaan Mellegers, Tina Clausmeyer

‹Sealand Identity Project› set out to conceive a national visual identity for the Principality of Sealand. Sealand is a mini-state, situated on a former anti-aircraft tower in the North Sea. The fortress was built in World War II to help defend the British Isles against the threatened German invasion. By 1946 the tower had been abandoned by the British armed forces. The structure was squatted in 1967 by an Englishman, Roy Bates. He and his wife proclaimed themselves Prince and Princess of Sealand. Since then, the Principality of Sealand has issued its own passports, currency and stamps. At various stages in the project, results and draft proposals will be proposed to the Sealand government.

Sealand Ads /Principality of Sealand - Mainport to Imagination: NATO, 2004

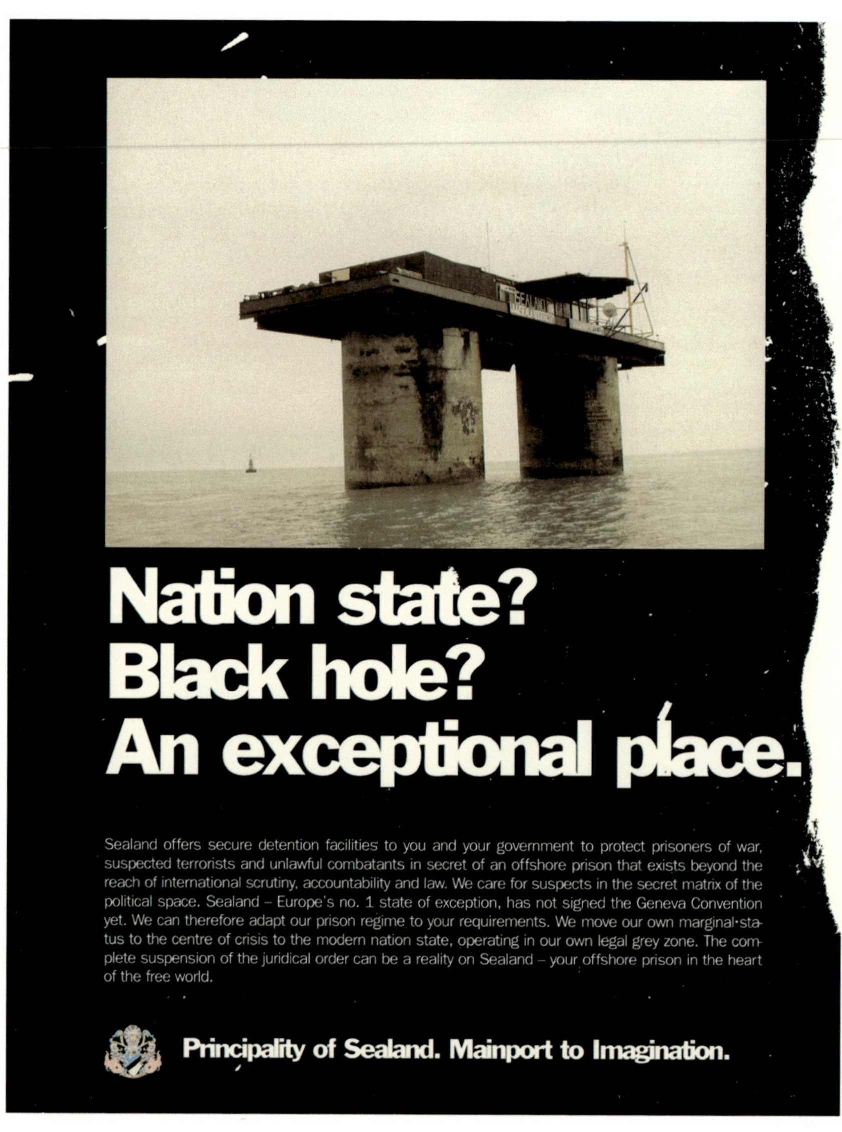

Sealand Models /A Thousand Plateaus

In a series of models for Sealand, the pocket-size would-be sovereign country becomes affiliated with Mumm, Pringles, Guinness, Cryptonomicon (Neal Stephenson), ‹Empire› (Hardt & Negri), ‹A Thousand Plateaus› (Deleuze & Guattari), ‹Utopia› (Thomas More), passports and the ‹Encyclopaedia Britannica›. The Sealand identity becomes transferrable to everyday objects.

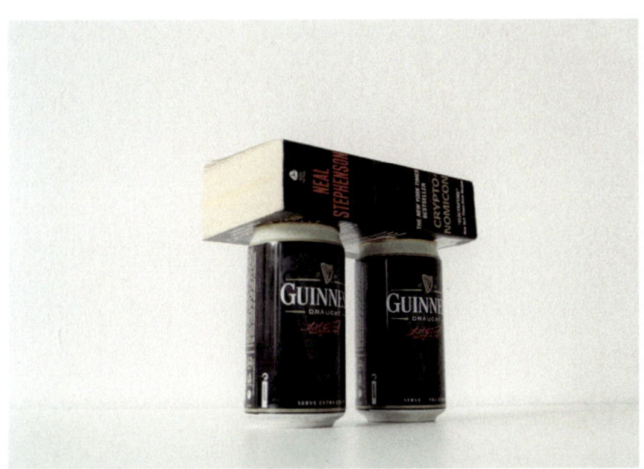

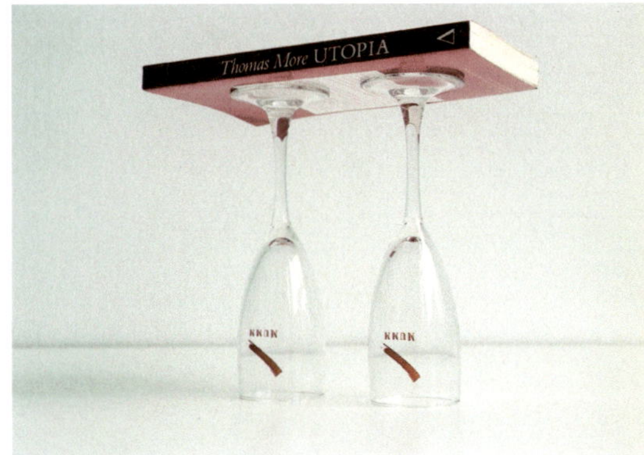

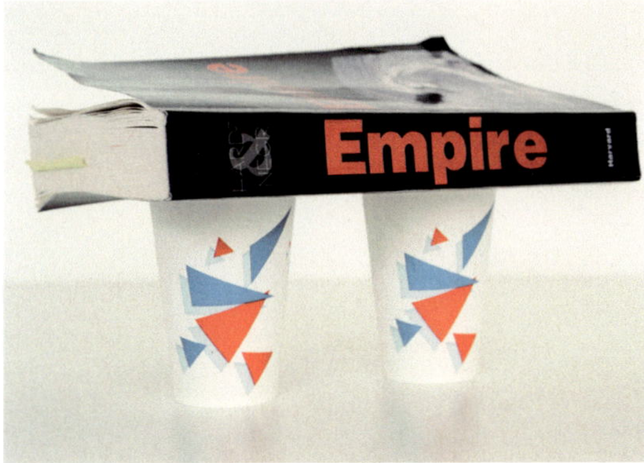

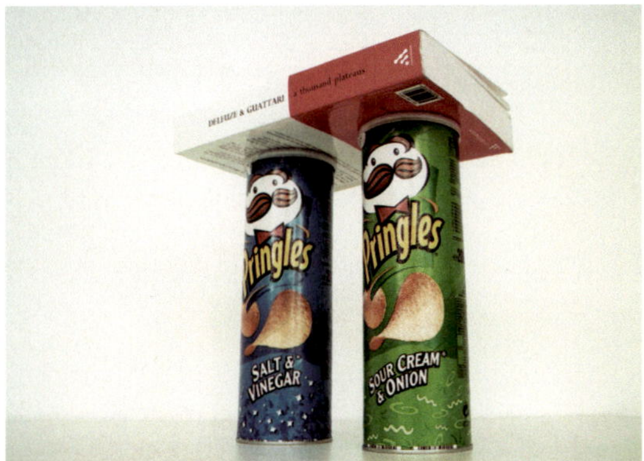

While observing Sealand, contours emerge of an entity that has all the capabilities to engage in the world, but cannot be recognized as such by the world. Sealand as an imaginary place gains as much importance as it does being a logo nation. To create as much mythological aura around its existence as possible, Sealand would benefit most when it became a stealth country. It would therefore need a stealth identity; an identity that is centred around a critical invisibility. Sealand's external image could become a shadow.

2004

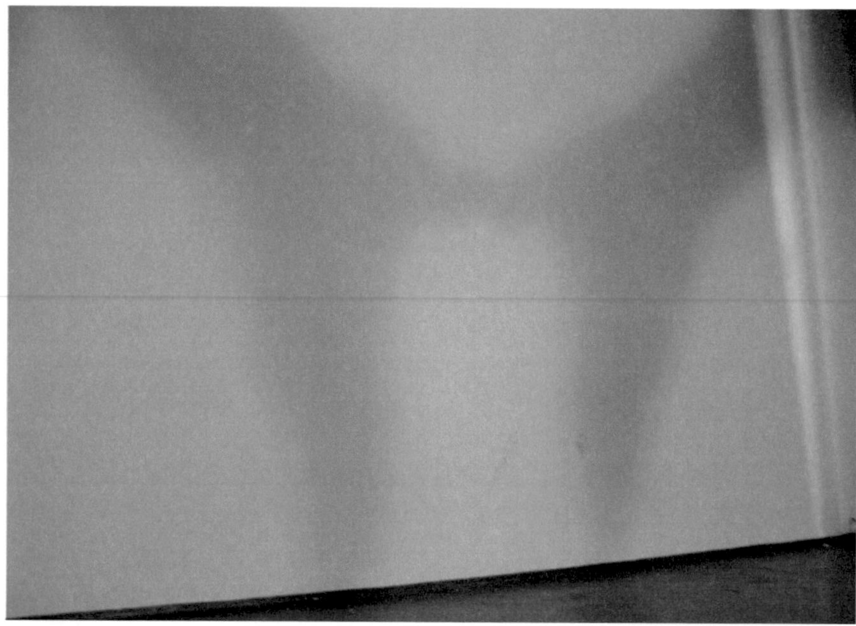

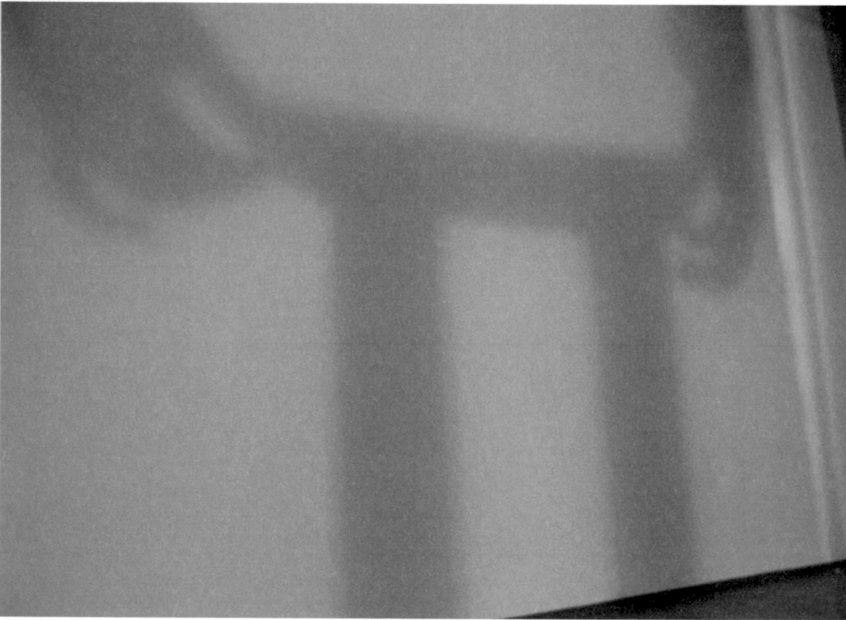

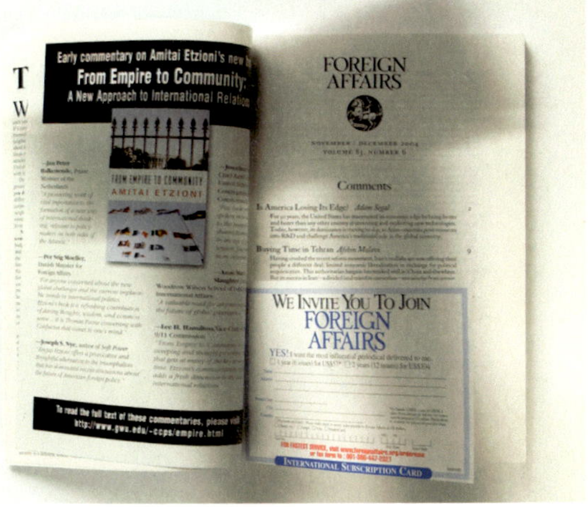

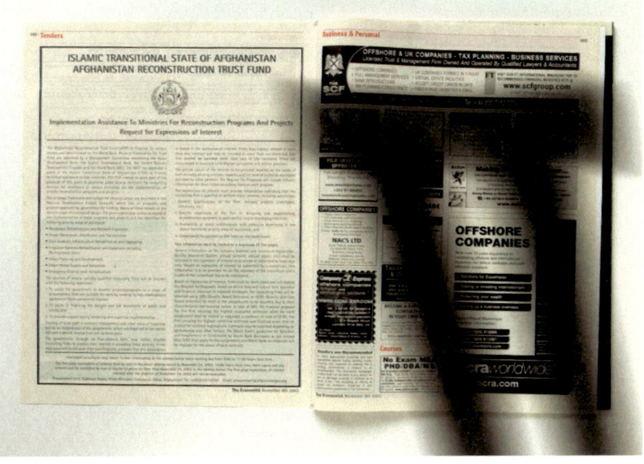

Magazine Shadows, 2004

The internet has become the unauthorised biography of Sealand. A story of invasions, hijacks, kidnappings and forged passports. A story of misunderstandings, hearsay, and lies. Ultimately, all of this might be called myth – its being true or not is irrelevant to the identity it produces. Apparently, the internet brings a form of information which that could be called ‹hypothetical truth›. Hypothetical truth nowadays plays an increasingly important role in government policy, as governments turn to mythmaking to justify their actions against enemies. If even respected governments turn to Google not knowing whether what comes out makes sense, it is no exaggeration to say that the search engine functions as a contemporary oracle, a gambling machine of possible realities. The observation that information, information management

2004

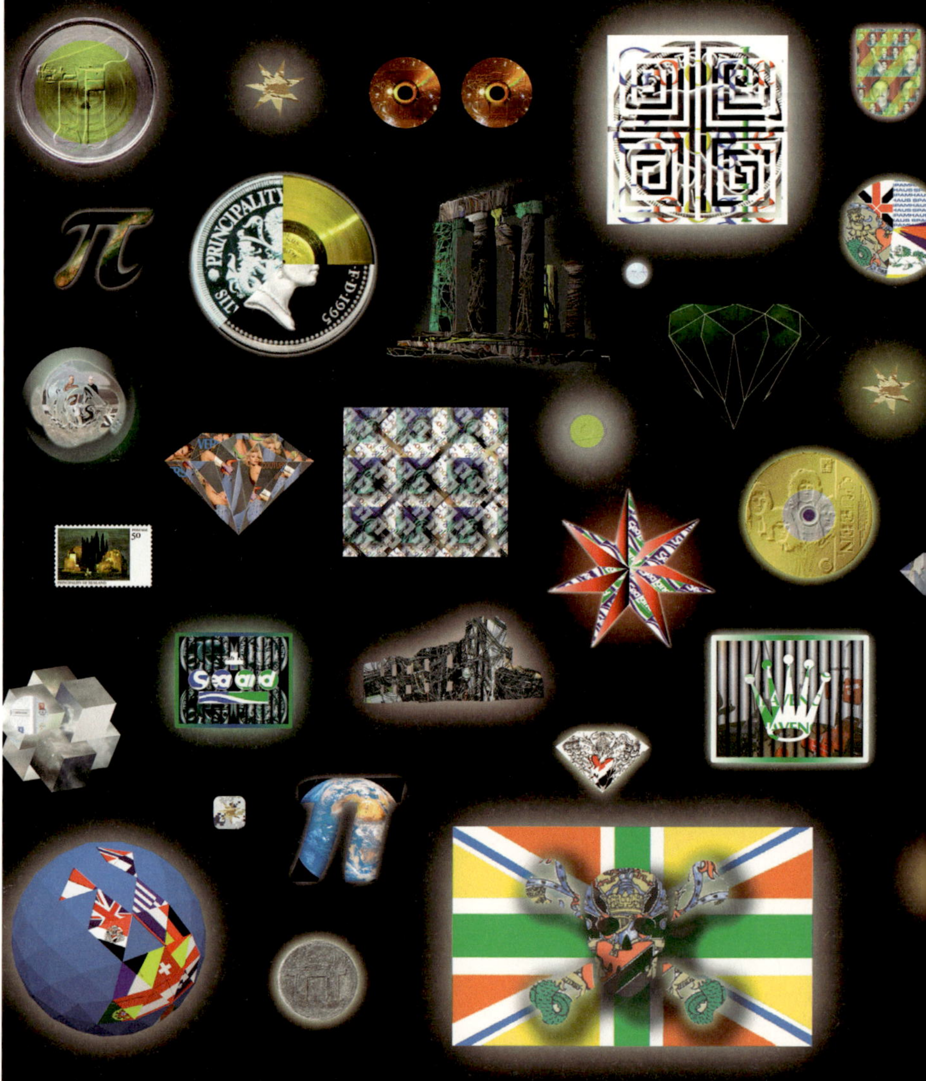

and data streams fulfil such an essential role in the contemporary creation of myth brings us to the case of national identity. The heraldic elements that form national crests are, visually, also the emblems of myth. In a form of contemporary heraldry, information takes on the role of the dragon. Sealand's visual realm can be mapped as a network ruin, in which the ambiguous nature of the Principality's identity becomes apparent. Arnold Böcklin's ‹Island of the Dead›, financial scandals of the new economy (Parmalat, Worldcom), container freight corporation Maersk Sealand, the British queen, Data-Haven coins based on the typology of the compact disc, Google, the figure pi, and Versace couture appear and disappear in a tantalizing rain of notions called the Jewel Box.

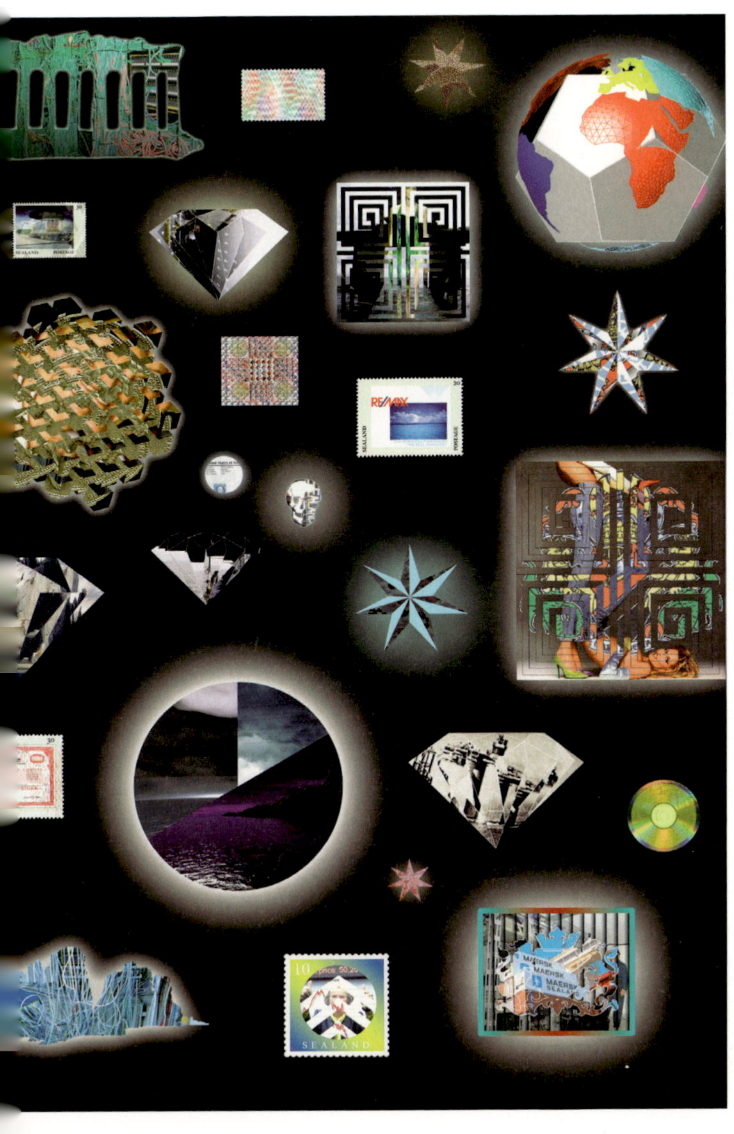

GreyCards are proposed as Sealand credit cards. The examples shown are offshore banks –including Sealand's national ‹Goldrain Bank› – whose operating licenses have been revoked. The names of the cardholders belong to the actual owners of the bank. Holograms on the GreyCards are based on webcam images taken over a one-year period at Campbell Scientific Weather Station, North Pole.

2004

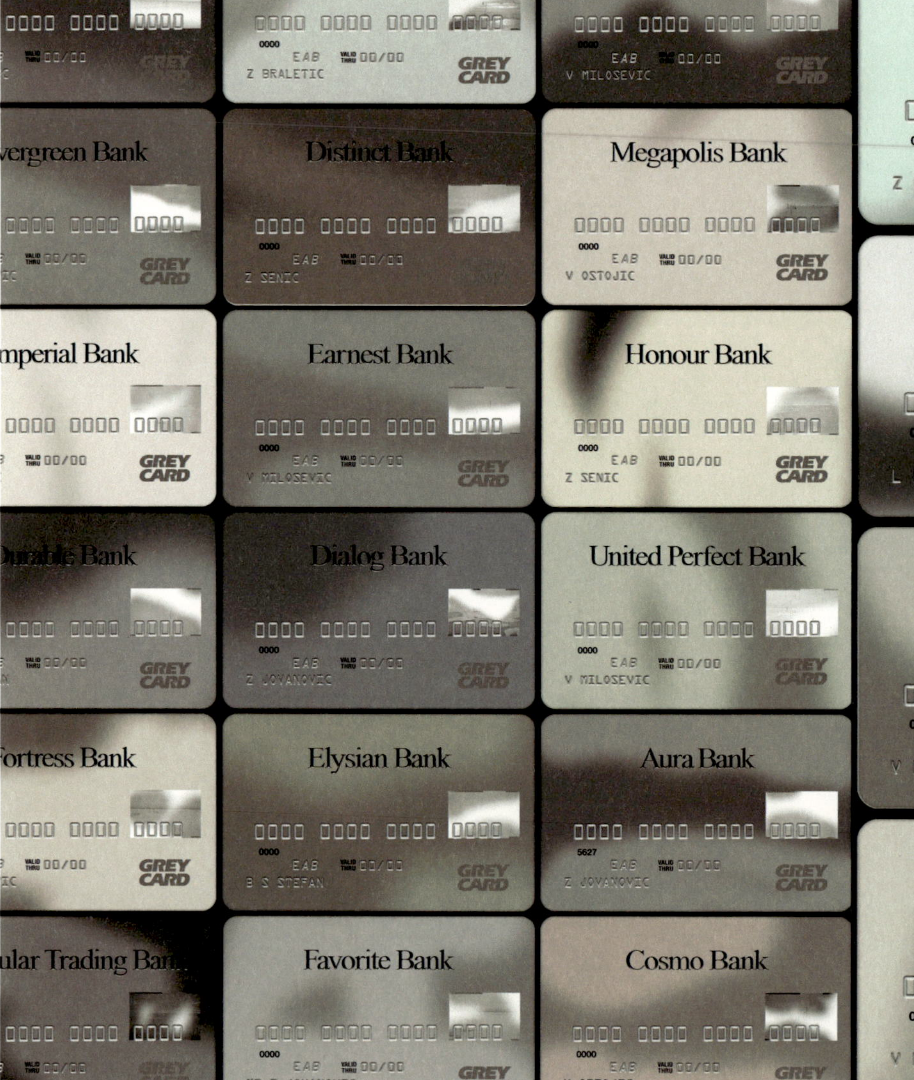

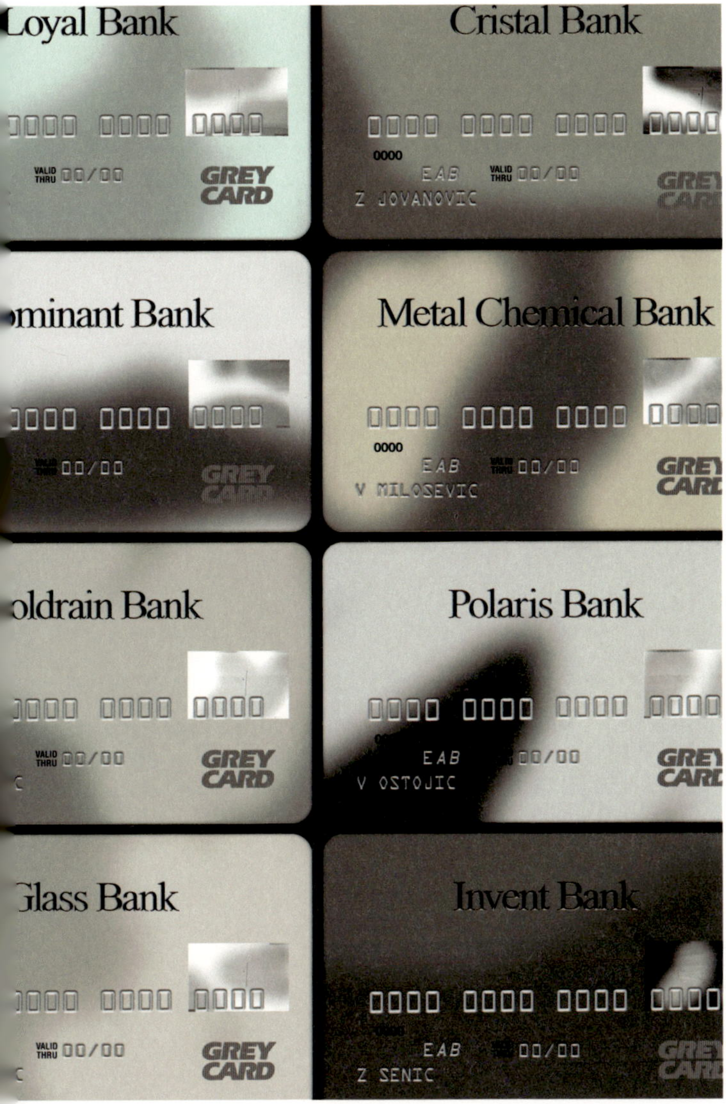

Loyal Bank

0000 0000 0000

VALID THRU 00/00

GREY CARD

Cristal Bank

0000 0000 0000 0000

0000

EAB VALID THRU 00/00

Z JOVANOVIC

minant Bank

0000 0000 0000

00/00

GREY CARD

Metal Chemical Bank

0000 0000 0000 0000

0000

EAB 00/00

V MILOSEVIC

GREY CARD

oldrain Bank

0000 0000 0000

VALID THRU 00/00

GREY CARD

Polaris Bank

0000 0000 0000 0000

EAB 00/00

V OSTOJIC

Glass Bank

0000 0000 0000

VALID THRU 00/00

GREY CARD

Invent Bank

0000 0000 0000 0000

EAB 00/00

Z SENIC

by Meta Haven / Daniel van der Velden, Vinca Kruk

These proposals are about the co-existence of Communist iconography and the visual cultures that succeeded it or are being put in relation to or contrast with it. This becomes most visible in the realm of architecture. (Former) Communist rulers have left their cities with enormous buildings and palaces, ultimate symbols of their despotic rule. The status of these buildings is interesting; in every sense, they behave like logos or trademarks, except that they are three-dimensional, physical monuments, extremely difficult to erase or replace. Erasing them makes a traumatic ground zero. Replacing them is also problematic; any replacement is beset with the impossible task of not seeming authoritarian.

Renata Salecl has argued that these buildings remind of ‹a past that never existed in the way it is now remembered› – as in the case of Ceausescu's former ‹People's House› in Bucharest. Salecl says that ‹The palace remains one of the most traumatic remnants of the Communist regime. It has a sublime quality – it is beautiful and horrible at the same time, provoking both admiration and disgust›.

An antidote is sometimes found in reclaiming the former totalitarian spaces as cultural spaces. This is what happened with Ceausescu's palace – it now houses the MNAC national museum. Showing contemporary art and visual culture would imply ‹a symbol of openness and democracy› – as Nicolas Bourriaud said in his capacity as board member at MNAC. As Renata Salecl notes, the post-Ceausescu Romanian government has used a similar way of thinking to justify its continuing presence in the House. She quotes from a tourist brochure: ‹Today, the monumental building stands for the most precious symbol of democracy in Romania, that is the parliament, serving the high and noble aim we have all aspired for: equal and complete representation of the Romanian people›.

In Tirana, Albania, after the death of the country's long-time dictator Enver Hoxha, in 1988 a commemorative mausoleum was erected under the guidance of Hoxha's daughter Pranvera. Afterwards, the (of course) symmetrical structure was used as the International Cultural Centre, or ICC.
Meanwhile, in Pyongyang, North Korea, the enormous Ryugyong Hotel stands unfinished: the concrete carcase of a future pyramid, intended to be the ‹grand travail› of Kim Il-Sung and his son Kim Jong-Il. The Ryugyong Hotel was the subject of a competition run by Domus magazine, directed at architects, designers and artists, to transform the totalitarian icon into an ‹antenna for ideas›. North Korea is perhaps the most bizarre of the hardcore Communist nations, with a nuclear arms programme under way and a government-initiated programme to counterfeit the US Dollar with the production of hi-tech ‹supernotes›.

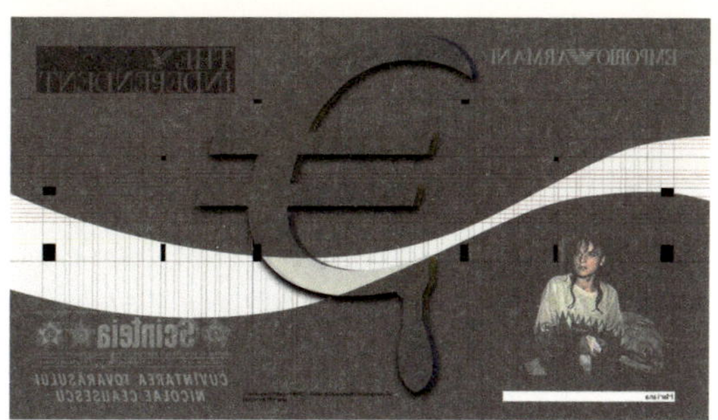

Bucharest Grid

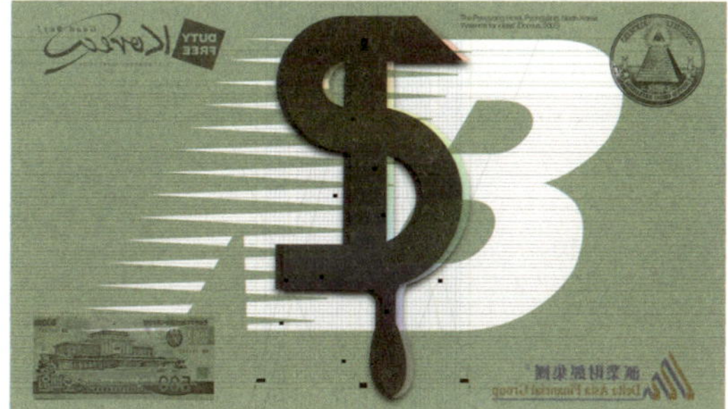

Pyongyang Grid

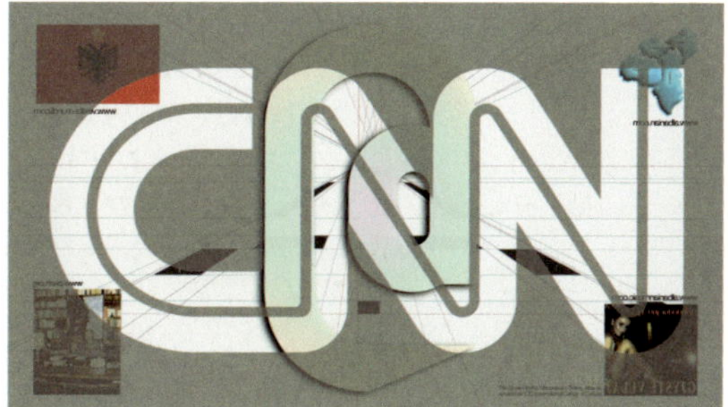

Tirana Grid

160 PostCom North Korea, Ryungyong - Forbidden Icon
by Meta Haven / Daniel van der Velden, Vinca Kruk, Adriaan Mellegers

Forbidden Icon addresses the Ryugyong Hotel in Pyongyang, North Korea. Meta Haven's Forbidden Icon focuses completely on altering its representation as an architectural and ideological object. By presenting a series of alternate images of the hotel in a media and information context, a possible dialogue is created between (imagined) meanings of the Ryugyong Hotel and its physical reality.

Pyongyang / PowerPoint Stamp
Ryugyong is a ‹PowerPoint› – a projection into some eternally postponed future. In collaboration with Microsoft, a stamp could be conceived in which the realm of the potential is celebrated on the level of software – and hardware.

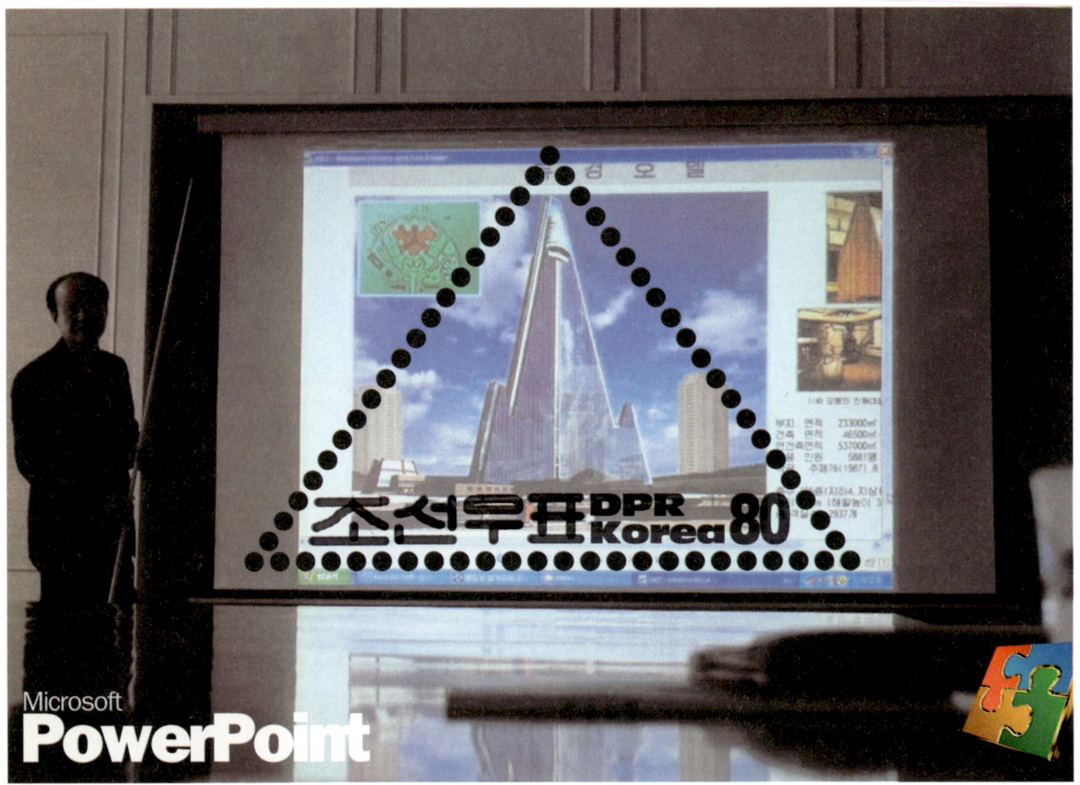

2005

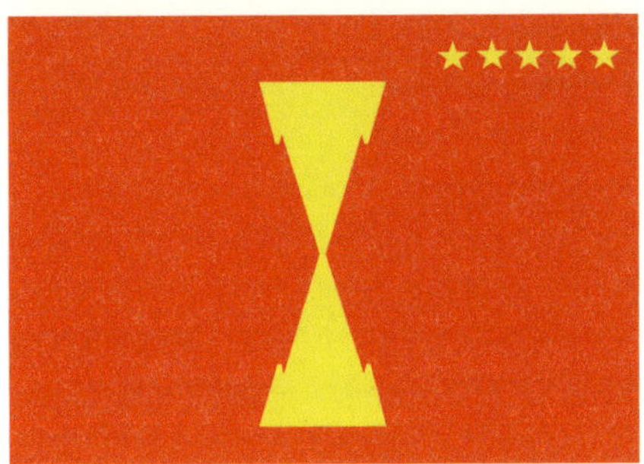

Pyongyang / Time Flag
Exercises in time: the building's mirrored image resembles the perpetual ‹hourglass›. If the triangular ‹Tower of Babel› recalls some Biblical-scale effort doomed to fail, the ‹Mirror Utopia› of this new North Korea flag is transcended into timelessness.

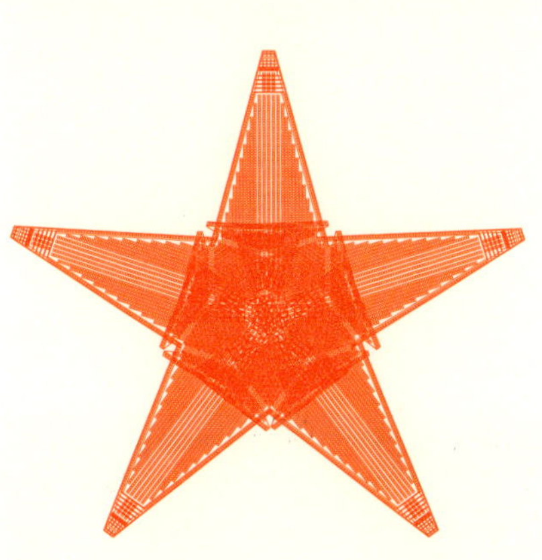

Postcom North Korea, Pyongyang / Star
While the star remains the proverbial symbol of Communist rule, it is at the same time the symbol of capitalism. Repeating ‹Ryugyong› four times in a circular direction generates an entirely custom-made star of potential use to future North Korean regimes in either direction – Communist or capitalist (or both).

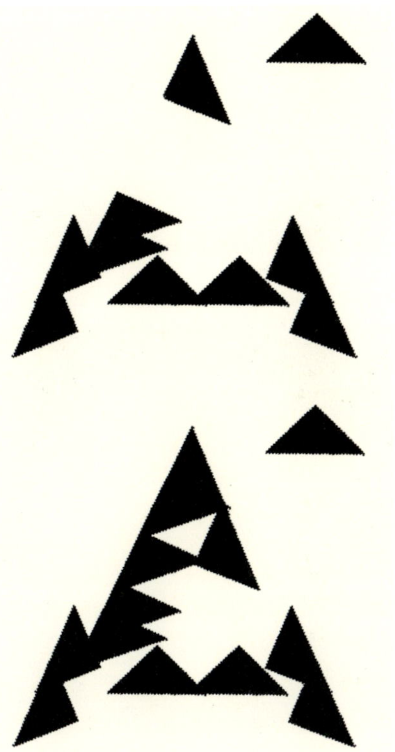

Pyongyang / Black Stamps
Re-constructing the outlines of the Ryugyong Hotel from black, triangular stamps.

Quaero Design Research, Quaero Logo
by Meta Haven / Daniel van der Velden, Vinca Kruk

In the course of 2005 and 2006, French president Jacques Chirac repeatedly announced the launch of a European –in fact predominantly French– effort to challenge the world dominance of Google. The heavily subsidized European search engine was to be named Quaero – Latin for ‹I seek›, and the challenger would primarily be a means of showing off the power of the French state. It is still not entirely clear what the announced German participation in Quaero will mean, though in the meantime it is possible to see Quaero as not only French and German but also European. What ‹Quaero›, by virtue of its Latin name, already represents is the melancholy of Europe – the impossibility of finding a collectively experienced, living, meaningful, rich and appealing symbol for Europe as a territorial entity. In that sense, Quaero's mission statement could be ‹Searching for Europe›.

Tree Rings B

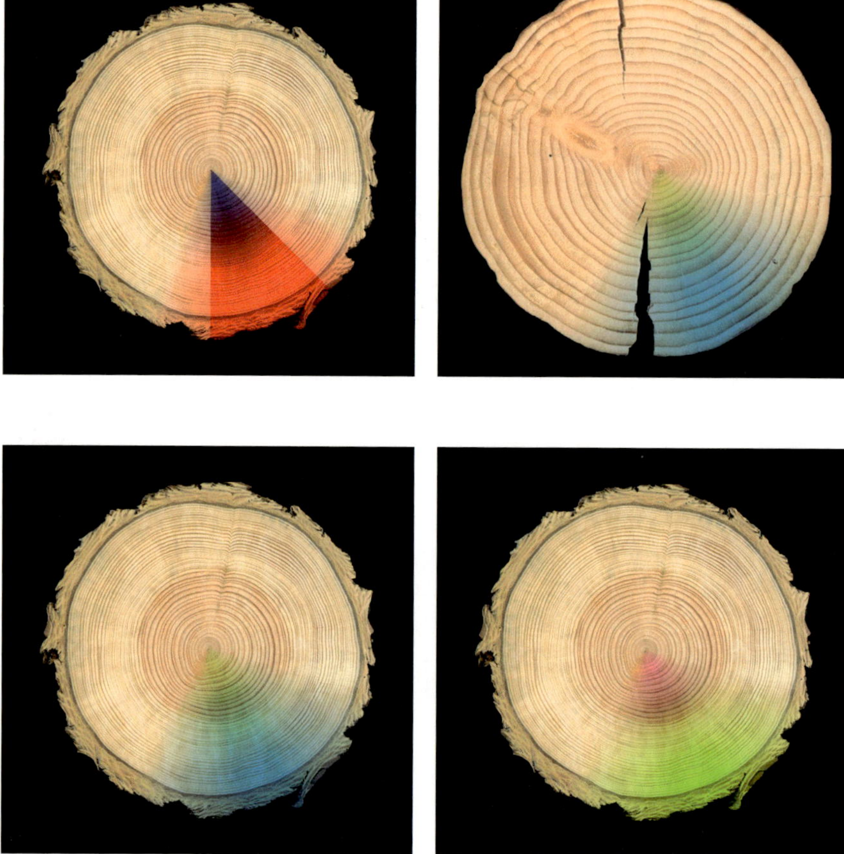

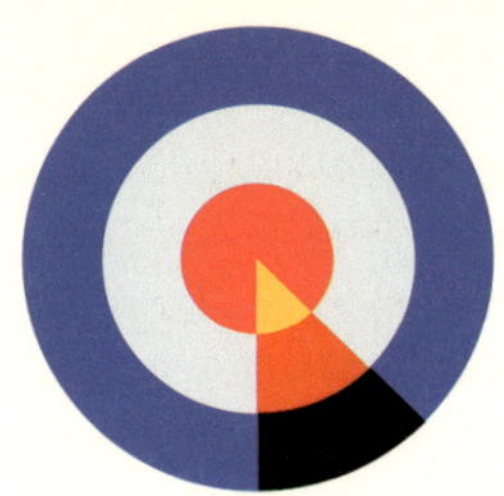

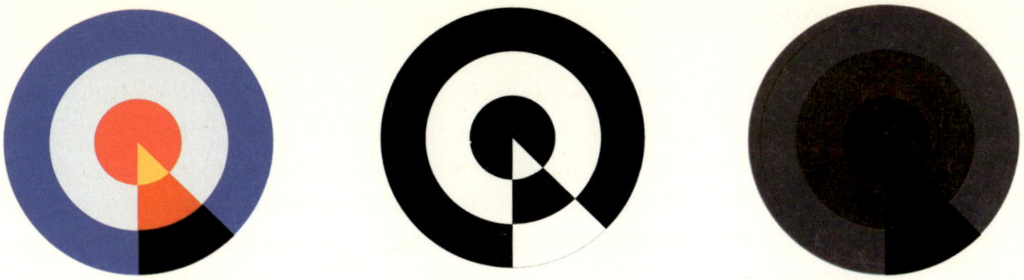

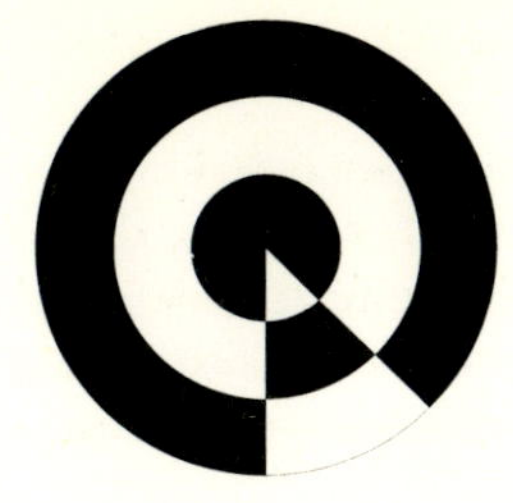

Quaero Logo

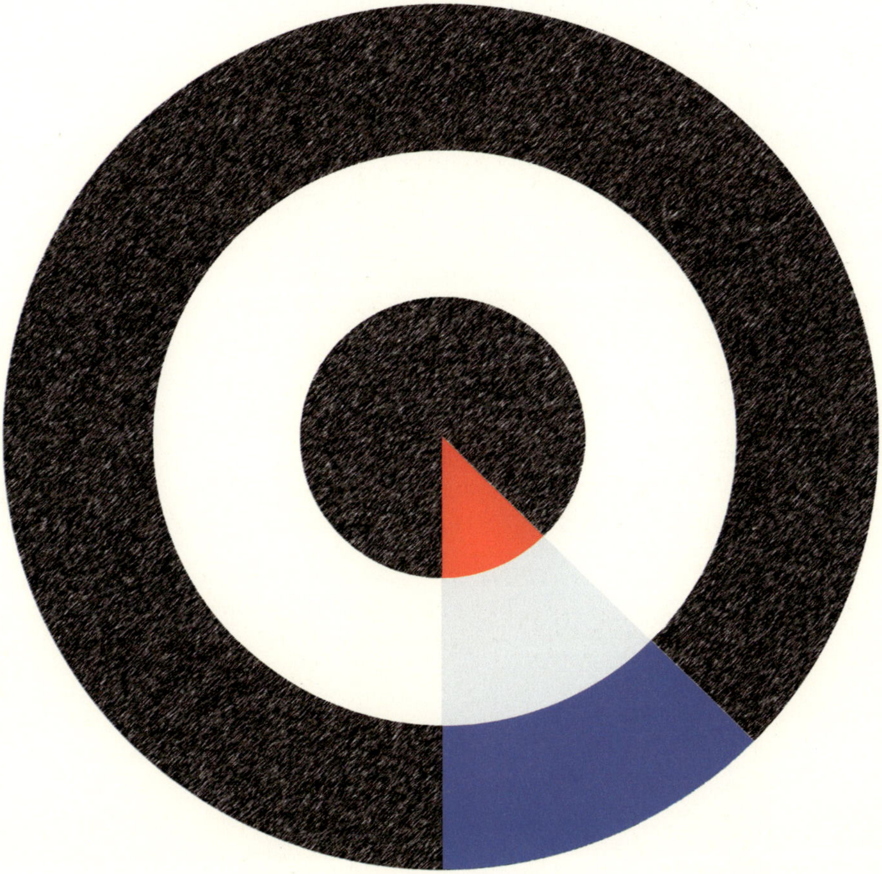

series of proposals for the logo of French/French-German/pan-European internet search engine Quaero

Austria held the Presidency of the European Union in the first semester of 2006. For this event, the Austrian government put on ‹The Image of Europe› exhibition in the Heldenplatz in Vienna. The exhibition was developed by OMA/AMO in 2004 for the Dutch presidency and shown in Brussels. The title plays on the dual meaning of the word ‹image› – implying both representation and perception. It provides a history of European political representation,

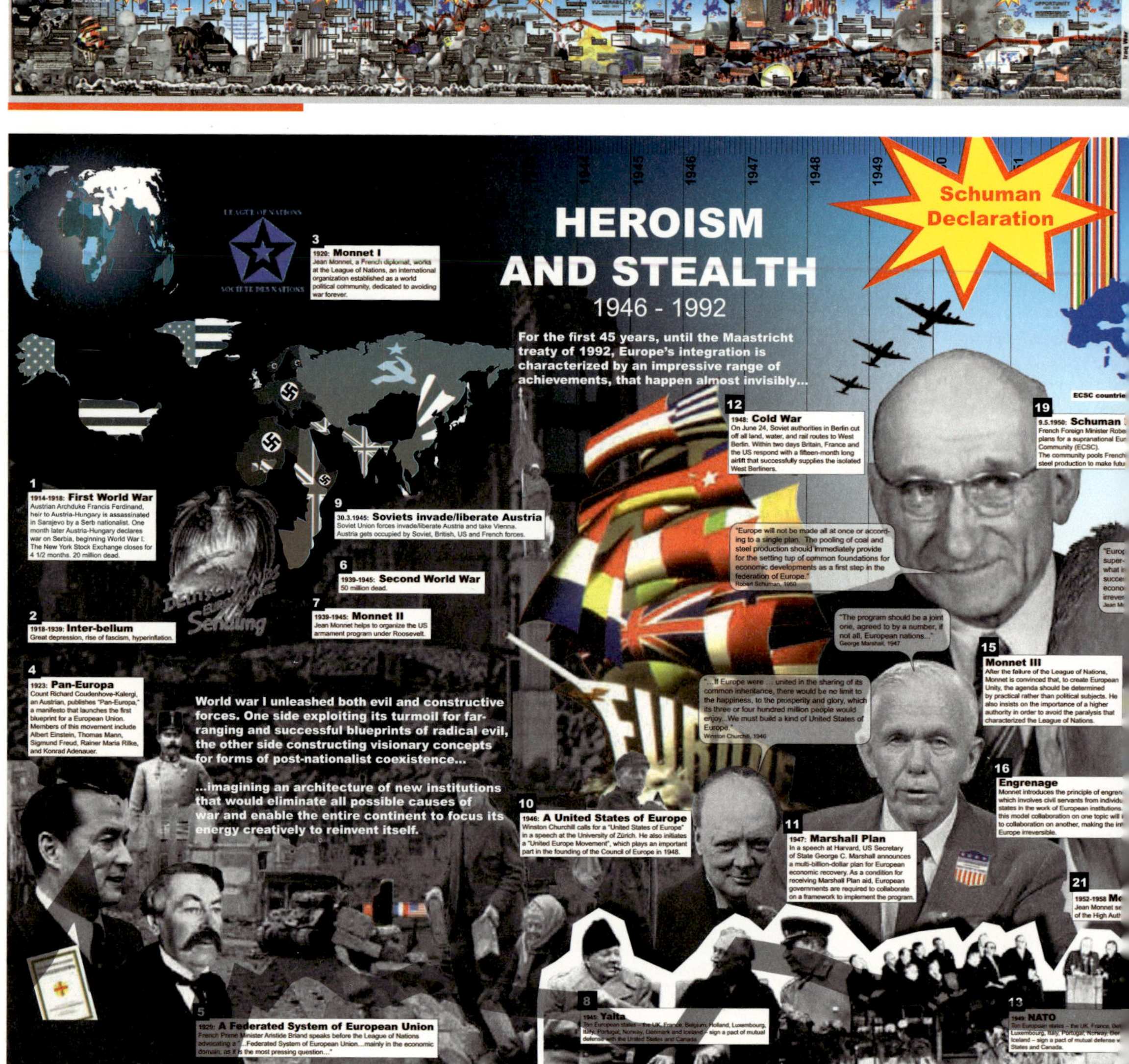

diagrams Europe's current political structure and speculates on its possible futures. STAR was commissioned to update, correct, and extend ‹The Image of Europe› for the exhibition in Vienna in May 2006.

for Austrian Government. © OMA/AMO - Conception: Rem Koolhaas, Reinier de Graaf - Exhibition design: Jens Hommert - EU-history team 2004: AMO- Theo Deutinger, Sebastian Koch, William Todd Reisz, Nanne de Ru, Jared Serwer, Amelia Stephenson, Collaborators 2006: STAR (Theo Deutinger, Beatriz Ramo, Andreas Kofler)

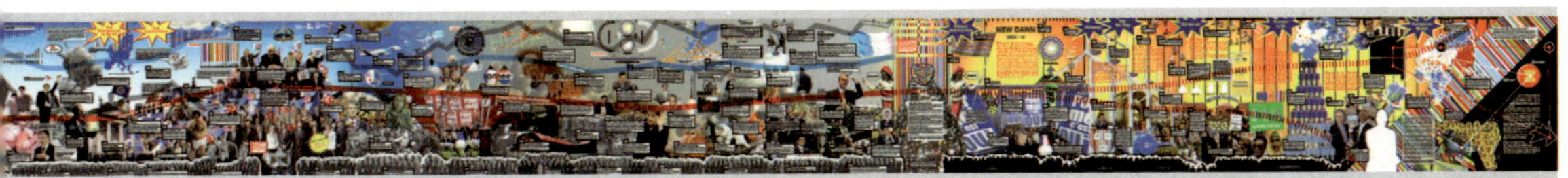

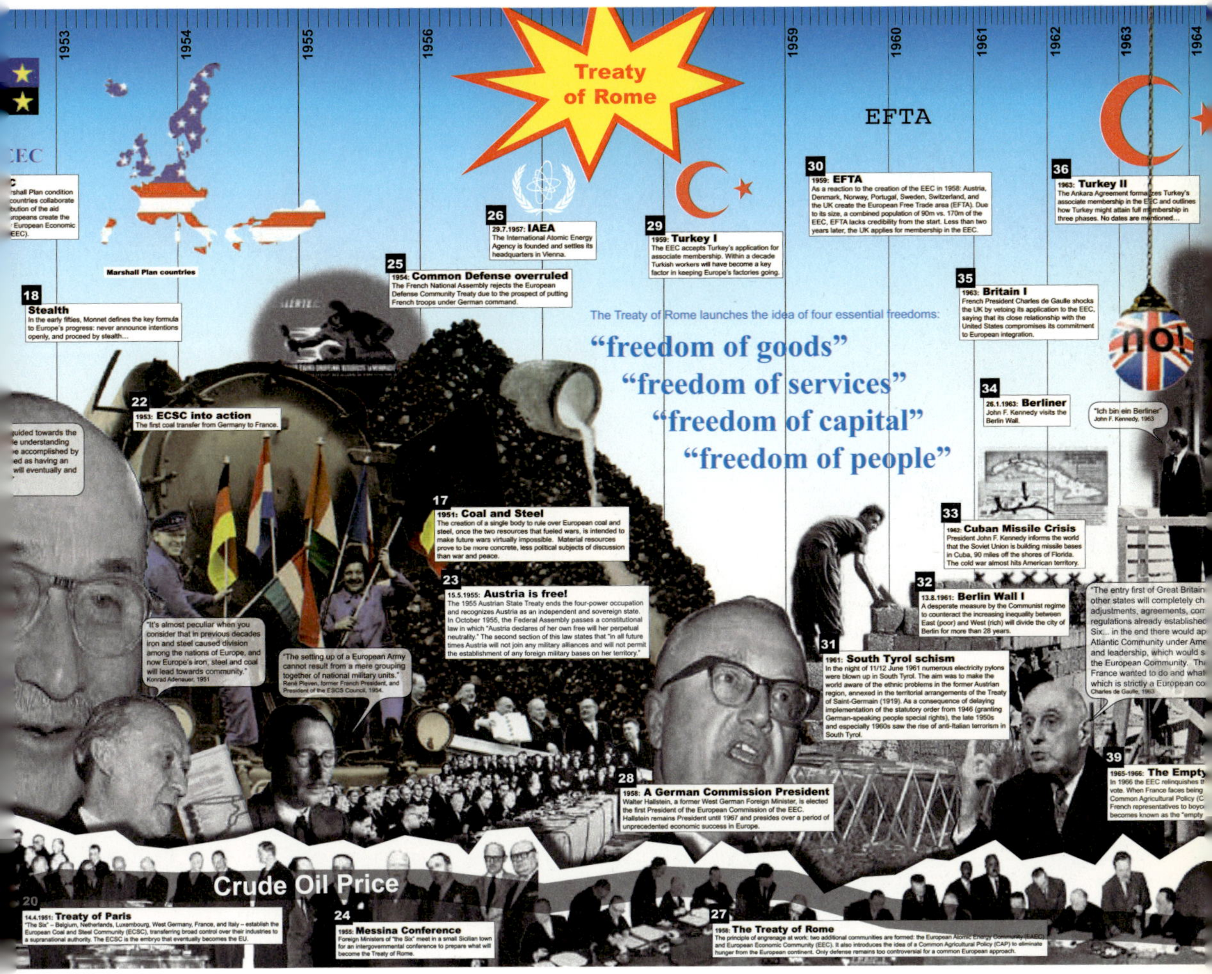

1953 1954 1955 1956 1959 1960 1961 1962 1963 1964

EEC

Marshall Plan countries

Treaty of Rome

EFTA

18 **Stealth**
In the early fifties, Monnet defines the key formula to Europe's progress: never announce intentions openly, and proceed by stealth...

22 1953: **ECSC into action**
The first coal transfer from Germany to France.

25 1954: **Common Defense overruled**
The French National Assembly rejects the European Defense Community Treaty due to the prospect of putting French troops under German command.

26 29.7.1957: **IAEA**
The International Atomic Energy Agency is founded and settles its headquarters in Vienna.

29 1959: **Turkey I**
The EEC accepts Turkey's application for associate membership. Within a decade Turkish workers will have become a key factor in keeping Europe's factories going.

30 1959: **EFTA**
As a reaction to the creation of the EEC in 1958: Austria, Denmark, Norway, Portugal, Sweden, Switzerland, and the UK create the European Free Trade area (EFTA). Due to its size, a combined population of 90m vs. 170m of the EEC, EFTA lacks credibility from the start. Less than two years later, the UK applies for membership in the EEC.

36 1963: **Turkey II**
The Ankara Agreement formalizes Turkey's associate membership in the EEC and outlines how Turkey might attain full membership in three phases. No dates are mentioned...

35 1963: **Britain I**
French President Charles de Gaulle shocks the UK by vetoing its application to the EEC, saying that its close relationship with the United States compromises its commitment to European integration.

no!

The Treaty of Rome launches the idea of four essential freedoms:

"freedom of goods"
"freedom of services"
"freedom of capital"
"freedom of people"

34 26.1.1963: **Berliner**
John F. Kennedy visits the Berlin Wall.

"Ich bin ein Berliner"
John F. Kennedy, 1963

17 1951: **Coal and Steel**
The creation of a single body to rule over European coal and steel, once the two resources that fueled wars, is intended to make future wars virtually impossible. Material resources prove to be more concrete, less political subjects of discussion than war and peace.

23 15.5.1955: **Austria is free!**
The 1955 Austrian State Treaty ends the four-power occupation and recognizes Austria as an independent and sovereign state. In October 1955, the Federal Assembly passes a constitutional law in which "Austria declares of her own free will her perpetual neutrality." The second section of this law states that "in all future times Austria will not join any military alliances and will not permit the establishment of any foreign military bases on her territory."

"It's almost peculiar when you consider that in previous decades iron and steel caused division among the nations of Europe, and now Europe's iron, steel and coal will lead towards community."
Konrad Adenauer, 1951

"The setting up of a European Army cannot result from a mere grouping together of national military units."
René Pleven, former French President, and President of the ESCS Council, 1954.

33 1962: **Cuban Missile Crisis**
President John F. Kennedy informs the world that the Soviet Union is building missile bases in Cuba, 90 miles off the shores of Florida. The cold war almost hits American territory.

32 13.8.1961: **Berlin Wall I**
A desperate measure by the Communist regime to counteract the increasing inequality between East (poor) and West (rich) will divide the city of Berlin for more than 28 years.

31 1961: **South Tyrol schism**
In the night of 11/12 June 1961 numerous electricity pylons were blown up in South Tyrol. The aim was to make the world aware of the ethnic problems in the former Austrian region, annexed in the territorial arrangements of the Treaty of Saint-Germain (1919). As a consequence of delaying implementation of the statutory order from 1946 (granting German-speaking people special rights), the late 1950s and especially 1960s saw the rise of anti-Italian terrorism in South Tyrol.

"The entry first of Great Britain ... other states will completely ch... adjustments, agreements, com... regulations already established ... Six... in the end there would ap... Atlantic Community under Ame... and leadership, which would s... the European Community. Th... France wanted to do and what ... which is strictly a European co...
Charles de Gaulle, 1963

28 1958: **A German Commission President**
Walter Hallstein, a former West German Foreign Minister, is elected the first President of the European Commission of the EEC. Hallstein remains President until 1967 and presides over a period of unprecedented economic success in Europe.

39 1965-1966: **The Empty...**
In 1966 the EEC relinquishes th... vote. When France faces being ... Common Agricultural Policy (C... French representatives to boyc... becomes known as the "empty...

Crude Oil Price

20 14.4.1951: **Treaty of Paris**
"The Six" – Belgium, Netherlands, Luxembourg, West Germany, France, and Italy – establish the European Coal and Steel Community (ECSC), transferring broad control over their industries to a supranational authority. The ECSC is the embryo that eventually becomes the EU.

24 1955: **Messina Conference**
Foreign Ministers of "the Six" meet in a small Sicilian town for an intergovernmental conference to prepare what will become the Treaty of Rome.

27 1958: **The Treaty of Rome**
The principle of engrenage at work: two additional communities are formed: the European Atomic Energy Community (EAEC) and European Economic Community (EEC). It also introduces the idea of a Common Agricultural Policy (CAP) to eliminate hunger from the European continent. Only defense remains too controversial for a common European approach.

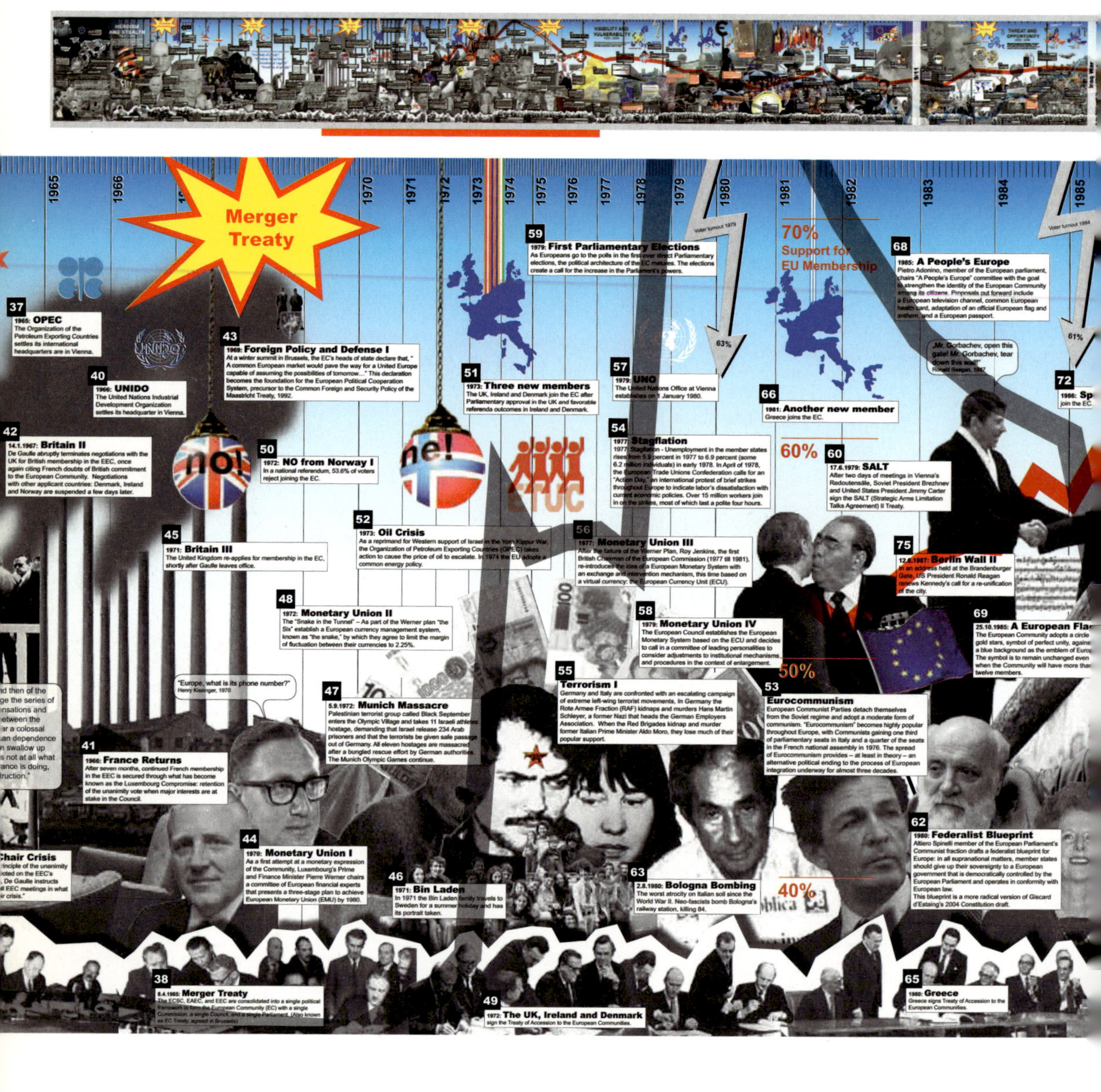

1965
1966
1970
1971
1972
1973
1974
1975
1976
1977
1978
1979
1980
1981
1982
1983
1984
1985
Merger Treaty
37 1965: OPEC
The Organization of the Petroleum Exporting Countries settles its international headquarters are in Vienna.
40 1966: UNIDO
The United Nations Industrial Development Organization settles its headquarter in Vienna.
42 14.1.1967: Britain II
De Gaulle abruptly terminates negotiations with the UK for British membership in the EEC, once again citing French doubts of British commitment to the European Community. Negotiations with other applicant countries: Denmark, Ireland and Norway are suspended a few days later.
43 1969: Foreign Policy and Defense I
At a winter summit in Brussels, the EC's heads of state declare that, " A common European market would pave the way for a United Europe capable of assuming the possibilities of tomorrow..." This declaration becomes the foundation for the European Political Cooperation System, precursor to the Common Foreign and Security Policy of the Maastricht Treaty, 1992.
no!
50 1972: NO from Norway I
In a national referendum, 53.6% of voters reject joining the EC.
ne!
45 1971: Britain III
The United Kingdom re-applies for membership in the EC, shortly after Gaulle leaves office.
52 1973: Oil Crisis
As a reprimand for Western support of Israel in the Yom Kippur War, the Organization of Petroleum Exporting Countries (OPEC) takes action to cause the price of oil to escalate. In 1974 the EU adopts a common energy policy.
48 1972: Monetary Union II
The "Snake in the Tunnel" – As part of the Werner plan "the Six" establish a European currency management system, known as "the snake," by which they agree to limit the margin of fluctuation between their currencies to 2.25%.
"Europe, what is its phone number?"
Henry Kissinger, 1970
41 1966: France Returns
After seven months, continued French membership in the EEC is secured through what has become known as the Luxembourg Compromise: retention of the unanimity vote when major interests are at stake in the Council.
47 5.9.1972: Munich Massacre
Palestinian terrorist group called Black September enters the Olympic Village and takes 11 Israeli athletes hostage, demanding that Israel release 234 Arab prisoners and that the terrorists be given safe passage out of Germany. All eleven hostages are massacred after a bungled rescue effort by German authorities. The Munich Olympic Games continue.
44 1970: Monetary Union I
As a first attempt at a monetary expression of the Community, Luxembourg's Prime and Finance Minister Pierre Werner chairs a committee of European financial experts that presents a three-stage plan to achieve European Monetary Union (EMU) by 1980.
46 1971: Bin Laden
In 1971 the Bin Laden family travels to Sweden for a summer holiday and has its portrait taken.
38 8.4.1965: Merger Treaty
The ECSC, EAEC, and EEC are consolidated into a single political framework to form the European Community (EC) with a single Commission, a single Council, and a single Parliament. (Also known as EC Treaty, agreed in Brussels)
49 1972: The UK, Ireland and Denmark
sign the Treaty of Accession to the European Communities.
59 1979: First Parliamentary Elections
As Europeans go to the polls in the first-ever direct Parliamentary elections, the political architecture of the EC matures. The elections create a call for the increase in the Parliament's powers.
Voter turnout 1979
63%
51 1973: Three new members
The UK, Ireland and Denmark join the EC after Parliamentary approval in the UK and favorable referenda outcomes in Ireland and Denmark.
57 1979: UNO
The United Nations Office at Vienna establishes on 1 January 1980.
ETUC
54 1977: Stagflation
1977 Stagflation - Unemployment in the member states rises from 5.9 percent in 1977 to 6.9 percent (some 6.2 million individuals) in early 1978. In April of 1978, the European Trade Unions Confederation calls for an "Action Day," an international protest of brief strikes throughout Europe to indicate labor's dissatisfaction with current economic policies. Over 15 million workers join in on the strikes, most of which last a polite four hours.
56 1977: Monetary Union III
After the failure of the Werner Plan, Roy Jenkins, the first British Chairman of the European Commission (1977 till 1981), re-introduces the idea of a European Monetary System with an exchange and intervention mechanism, this time based on a virtual currency: the European Currency Unit (ECU).
58 1979: Monetary Union IV
The European Council establishes the European Monetary System based on the ECU and decides to call in a committee of leading personalities to consider adjustments to institutional mechanisms and procedures in the context of enlargement.
55 Terrorism I
Germany and Italy are confronted with an escalating campaign of extreme left-wing terrorist movements, In Germany the Rote Armee Fraction (RAF) kidnaps and murders Hans Martin Schleyer, a former Nazi that heads the German Employers Association. When the Red Brigades kidnap and murder former Italian Prime Minister Aldo Moro, they lose much of their popular support.
63 2.8.1980: Bologna Bombing
The worst atrocity on Italian soil since the World War II. Neo-fascists bomb Bologna's railway station, killing 84.
70%
Support for EU Membership
60%
50%
40%
66 1981: Another new member
Greece joins the EC.
68 1985: A People's Europe
Pietro Adonino, member of the European parliament, chairs "A People's Europe" committee with the goal to strengthen the identity of the European Community among its citizens. Proposals put forward include a European television channel, common European health card, adaptation of an official European flag and anthem, and a European passport.
Voter turnout 1984
61%
„Mr. Gorbachev, open this gate! Mr. Gorbachev, tear down this wall!"
Ronald Reagan, 1987
60 17.6.1979: SALT
After two days of meetings in Vienna's Redoutensäle, Soviet President Brezhnev and United States President Jimmy Carter sign the SALT (Strategic Arms Limitation Talks Agreement) II Treaty.
75 12.6.1987: Berlin Wall II
In an address held at the Brandenburger Gate, US President Ronald Reagan renews Kennedy's call for a re-unification of the city.
53 Eurocommunism
European Communist Parties detach themselves from the Soviet regime and adopt a moderate form of communism. "Eurocommunism" becomes highly popular throughout Europe, with Communists gaining one third of parliamentary seats in Italy and a quarter of the seats in the French national assembly in 1976. The spread of Eurocommunism provides – at least in theory – an alternative political ending to the process of European integration underway for almost three decades.
62 1980: Federalist Blueprint
Altiero Spinelli member of the European Parliament's Communist fraction drafts a federalist blueprint for Europe: in all supranational matters, member states should give up their sovereignty to a European government that is democratically controlled by the European Parliament and operates in conformity with European law.
This blueprint is a more radical version of Giscard d'Estaing's 2004 Constitution draft.
65 1980: Greece
Greece signs Treaty of Accession to the European Communities.

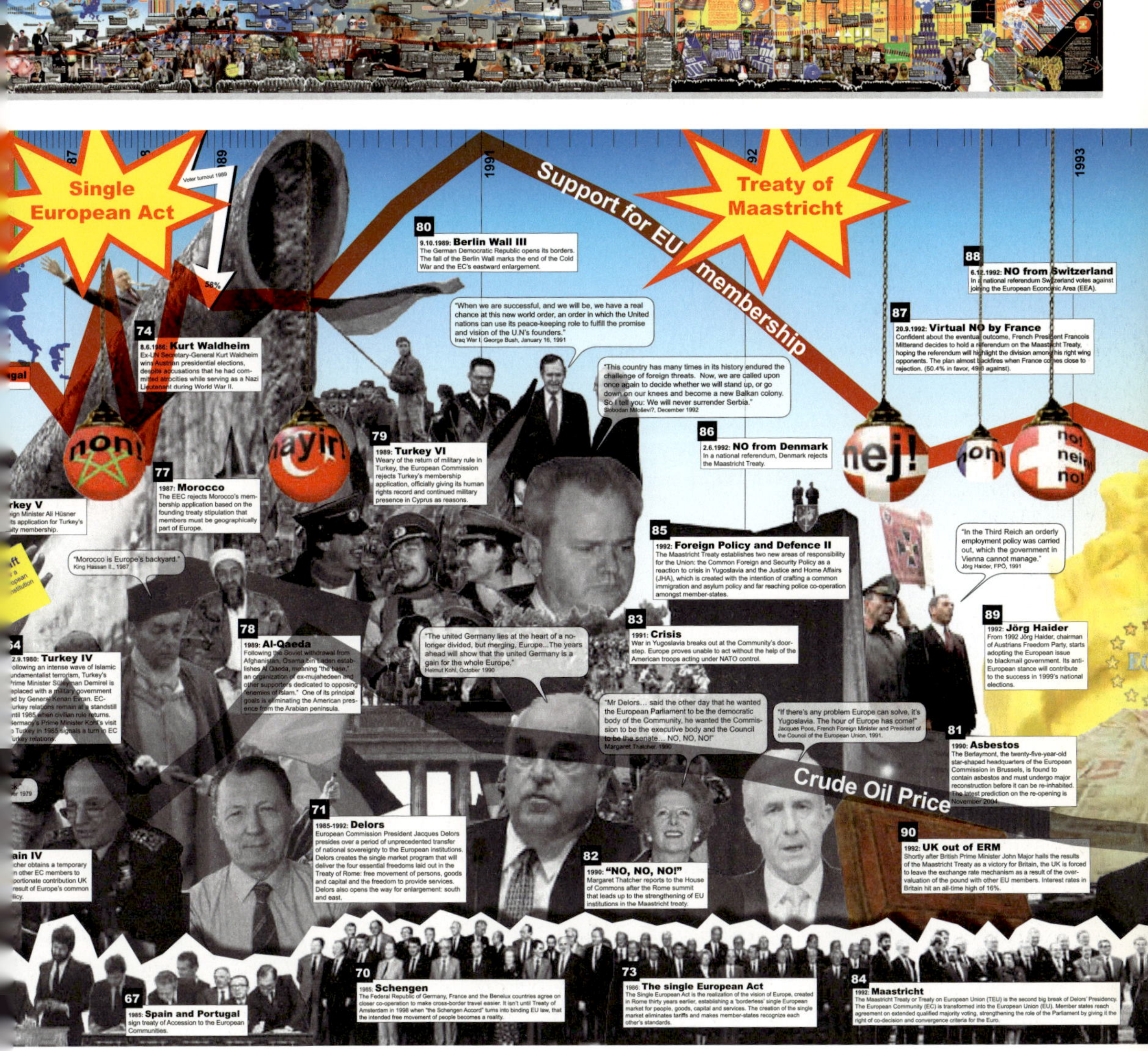

87
89
1991
92
1993
Single European Act
Voter turnout 1989
58%
Support for EU membership
Treaty of Maastricht
Crude Oil Price
non!
hayır!
nej!
non!
no! nein! no!
80 9.10.1989: Berlin Wall III
The German Democratic Republic opens its borders. The fall of the Berlin Wall marks the end of the Cold War and the EC's eastward enlargement.
"When we are successful, and we will be, we have a real chance at this new world order, an order in which the United nations can use its peace-keeping role to fulfill the promise and vision of the U.N's founders." Iraq War I, George Bush, January 16, 1991
74 8.6.1986: Kurt Waldheim
Ex-UN Secretary-General Kurt Waldheim wins Austrian presidential elections, despite accusations that he had committed atrocities while serving as a Nazi Lieutenant during World War II.
"This country has many times in its history endured the challenge of foreign threats. Now, we are called upon once again to decide whether we will stand up, or go down on our knees and become a new Balkan colony. So I tell you: We will never surrender Serbia." Slobodan Milošević, December 1992
88 6.12.1992: NO from Switzerland
In a national referendum Switzerland votes against joining the European Economic Area (EEA).
87 20.9.1992: Virtual NO by France
Confident about the eventual outcome, French President Francois Mitterand decides to hold a referendum on the Maastricht Treaty, hoping the referendum will highlight the division among his right wing opponents. The plan almost backfires when France comes close to rejection. (50.4% in favor, 49% against).
86 2.6.1992: NO from Denmark
In a national referendum, Denmark rejects the Maastricht Treaty.
79 1989: Turkey VI
Weary of the return of military rule in Turkey, the European Commission rejects Turkey's membership application, officially giving its human rights record and continued military presence in Cyprus as reasons.
77 1987: Morocco
The EEC rejects Morocco's membership application based on the founding treaty stipulation that members must be geographically part of Europe.
"Morocco is Europe's backyard." King Hassan II., 1987
85 1992: Foreign Policy and Defence II
The Maastricht Treaty establishes two new areas of responsibility for the Union: the Common Foreign and Security Policy as a reaction to crisis in Yugoslavia and the Justice and Home Affairs (JHA), which is created with the intention of crafting a common immigration and asylum policy and far reaching police co-operation amongst member-states.
"In the Third Reich an orderly employment policy was carried out, which the government in Vienna cannot manage." Jörg Haider, FPÖ, 1991
89 1992: Jörg Haider
From 1992 Jörg Haider, chairman of Austrians Freedom Party, starts adopting the European issue to blackmail government. Its anti-European stance will contribute to the success in 1999's national elections.
78 1989: Al-Qaeda
Following the Soviet withdrawal from Afghanistan, Osama bin Laden establishes Al Qaeda, meaning "the base," an organization of ex-mujahedeen and other supporters dedicated to opposing "enemies of Islam." One of its principal goals is eliminating the American presence from the Arabian peninsula.
"The united Germany lies at the heart of a no-longer divided, but merging, Europe...The years ahead will show that the united Germany is a gain for the whole Europe." Helmut Kohl, October 1990
83 1991: Crisis
War in Yugoslavia breaks out at the Community's doorstep. Europe proves unable to act without the help of the American troops acting under NATO control.
"Mr Delors... said the other day that he wanted the European Parliament to be the democratic body of the Community, he wanted the Commission to be the executive body and the Council to be the senate... NO, NO, NO!" Margaret Thatcher, 1990
"If there's any problem Europe can solve, it's Yugoslavia. The hour of Europe has come!" Jacques Poos, French Foreign Minister and President of the Council of the European Union, 1991.
81 1990: Asbestos
The Berlaymont, the twenty-five-year-old star-shaped headquarters of the European Commission in Brussels, is found to contain asbestos and must undergo major reconstruction before it can be re-inhabited. The latest prediction on the re-opening is November 2004
71 1985-1992: Delors
European Commission President Jacques Delors presides over a period of unprecedented transfer of national sovereignty to the European institutions. Delors creates the single market program that will deliver the four essential freedoms laid out in the Treaty of Rome: free movement of persons, goods and capital and the freedom to provide services. Delors also opens the way for enlargement: south and east.
82 1990: "NO, NO, NO!"
Margaret Thatcher reports to the House of Commons after the Rome summit that leads up to the strengthening of EU institutions in the Maastricht treaty.
90 1992: UK out of ERM
Shortly after British Prime Minister John Major hails the results of the Maastricht Treaty as a victory for Britain, the UK is forced to leave the exchange rate mechanism as a result of the over-valuation of the pound with other EU members. Interest rates in Britain hit an all-time high of 16%.
67 1985: Spain and Portugal
sign treaty of Accession to the European Communities.
70 1985: Schengen
The Federal Republic of Germany, France and the Benelux countries agree on closer co-operation to make cross-border travel easier. It isn't until Treaty of Amsterdam in 1998 when "the Schengen Accord" turns into binding EU law, that the intended free movement of people becomes a reality.
73 1986: The single European Act
The Single European Act is the realization of the vision of Europe, created in Rome thirty years earlier, establishing a 'borderless' single European market for people, goods, capital and services. The creation of the single market eliminates tariffs and makes member-states recognize each other's standards.
84 1992: Maastricht
The Maastricht Treaty or Treaty on European Union (TEU) is the second big break of Delors' Presidency. The European Community (EC) is transformed into the European Union (EU). Member states reach agreement on extended qualified majority voting, strengthening the role of the Parliament by giving it the right of co-decision and convergence criteria for the Euro.

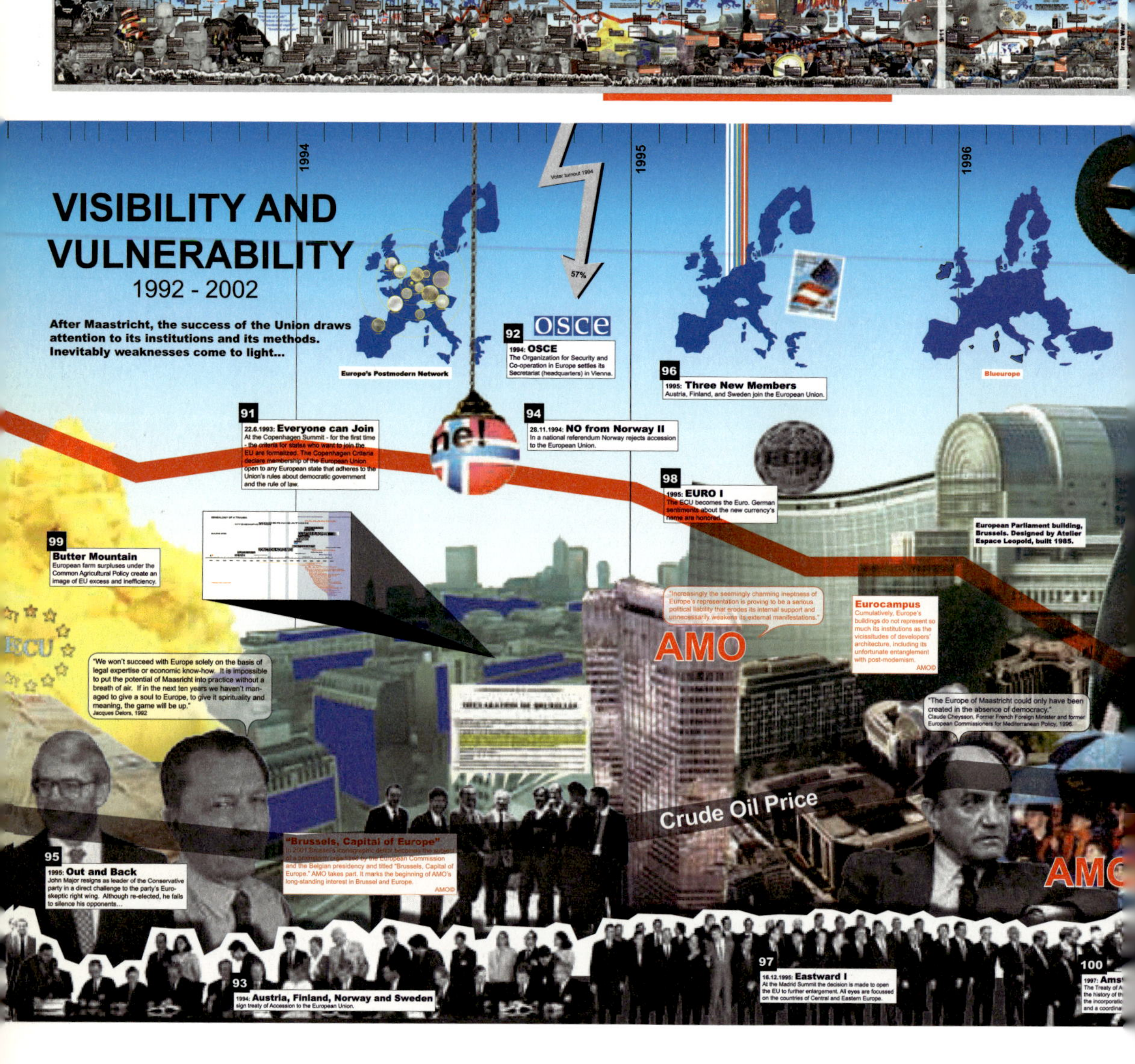

1994
1995
1996
VISIBILITY AND VULNERABILITY
1992 - 2002
After Maastricht, the success of the Union draws attention to its institutions and its methods. Inevitably weaknesses come to light...
Europe's Postmodern Network
Voter turnout 1994
57%
OSCE
92 1994: OSCE
The Organization for Security and Co-operation in Europe settles its Secretariat (headquarters) in Vienna.
96 1995: Three New Members
Austria, Finland, and Sweden join the European Union.
Blueurope
91 22.6.1993: Everyone can Join
At the Copenhagen Summit - for the first time - the criteria for states who want to join the EU are formalized. The Copenhagen Criteria declare membership of the European Union open to any European state that adheres to the Union's rules about democratic government and the rule of law.
ne!
94 28.11.1994: NO from Norway II
In a national referendum Norway rejects accession to the European Union.
98 1995: EURO I
The ECU becomes the Euro. German sentiments about the new currency's name are honored.
European Parliament building, Brussels. Designed by Atelier Espace Leopold, built 1985.
99 Butter Mountain
European farm surpluses under the Common Agricultural Policy create an image of EU excess and inefficiency.
ECU
"Increasingly the seemingly charming ineptness of Europe's representation is proving to be a serious political liability that erodes its internal support and unnecessarily weakens its external manifestations."
AMO
Eurocampus
Cumulatively, Europe's buildings do not represent so much its institutions as the vicissitudes of developers' architecture, including its unfortunate entanglement with post-modernism.
AMO©
"We won't succeed with Europe solely on the basis of legal expertise or economic know-how. It is impossible to put the potential of Maasricht into practice without a breath of air. If in the next ten years we haven't managed to give a soul to Europe, to give it spirituality and meaning, the game will be up."
Jacques Delors, 1992
"The Europe of Maastricht could only have been created in the absence of democracy."
Claude Cheysson, Former French Foreign Minister and former European Commissioners for Mediterranean Policy, 1996.
Crude Oil Price
"Brussels, Capital of Europe"
and the Belgian presidency and titled "Brussels, Capital of Europe." AMO takes part. It marks the beginning of AMO's long-standing interest in Brussel and Europe.
AMO©
AMO
95 1995: Out and Back
John Major resigns as leader of the Conservative party in a direct challenge to the party's Euro-skeptic right wing. Although re-elected, he fails to silence his opponents...
93 1994: Austria, Finland, Norway and Sweden
sign treaty of Accession to the European Union.
97 16.12.1995: Eastward I
At the Madrid Summit the decision is made to open the EU to further enlargement. All eyes are focussed on the countries of Central and Eastern Europe.
100

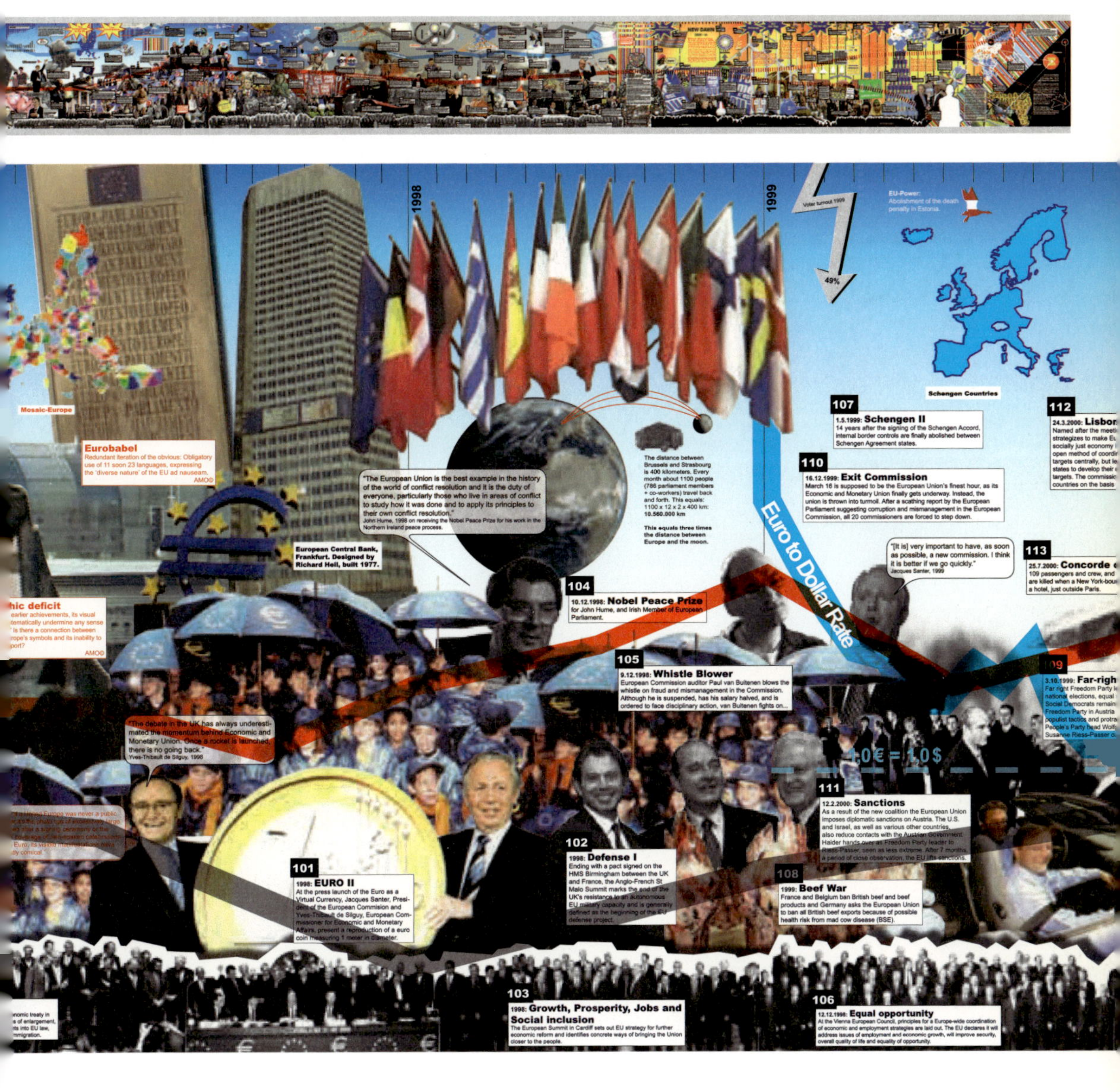
1998
1999
Voter turnout 1999
49%
EU-Power:
Abolishment of the death penalty in Estonia.
Mosaic-Europe
Schengen Countries
Eurobabel
Redundant iteration of the obvious: Obligatory use of 11 soon 23 languages, expressing the 'diverse nature' of the EU ad nauseam.
AMO©
"The European Union is the best example in the history of the world of conflict resolution and it is the duty of everyone, particularly those who live in areas of conflict to study how it was done and to apply its principles to their own conflict resolution."
John Hume, 1998 on receiving the Nobel Peace Prize for his work in the Northern Ireland peace process.
The distance between Brussels and Strasbourg is 400 kilometers. Every month about 1100 people (786 parliament members + co-workers) travel back and forth. This equals: 1100 x 12 x 2 x 400 km: 10.560.000 km
This equals three times the distance between Europe and the moon.
107
1.5.1999: Schengen II
14 years after the signing of the Schengen Accord, internal border controls are finally abolished between Schengen Agreement states.
112
24.3.2000: Lisbon
Named after the meeti
strategizes to make Eu
socially just economy
open method of coordi
targets centrally, but le
states to develop their
targets. The commissio
countries on the basis
110
16.12.1999: Exit Commission
March 16 is supposed to be the European Union's finest hour, as its Economic and Monetary Union finally gets underway. Instead, the union is thrown into turmoil. After a scathing report by the European Parliament suggesting corruption and mismanagement in the European Commission, all 20 commissioners are forced to step down.
Euro to Dollar Rate
European Central Bank, Frankfurt. Designed by Richard Heil, built 1977.
"[It is] very important to have, as soon as possible, a new commission. I think it is better if we go quickly."
Jacques Santer, 1999
113
25.7.2000: Concorde
109 passengers and crew, and
are killed when a New York-bou
a hotel, just outside Paris.
hic deficit
earlier achievements, its visual
tematically undermine any sense
Is there a connection between
rope's symbols and its inability to
port?
AMO©
104
10.12.1998: Nobel Peace Prize
for John Hume, and Irish Member of European Parliament.
105
9.12.1998: Whistle Blower
European Commission auditor Paul van Buitenen blows the whistle on fraud and mismanagement in the Commission. Although he is suspended, has his salary halved, and is ordered to face disciplinary action, van Buitenen fights on...
109
3.10.1999: Far-righ
Far right Freedom Party l
national elections, equal
Social Democrats remain
Freedom Party in Austria
populist tactics and protra
People's Party head Wolf
Susanne Riess-Passer
"The debate in the UK has always underestimated the momentum behind Economic and Monetary Union. Once a rocket is launched, there is no going back."
Yves-Thibault de Silguy, 1998
1,0€ = 1,0$
111
12.2.2000: Sanctions
As a result of the new coalition the European Union imposes diplomatic sanctions on Austria. The U.S. and Israel, as well as various other countries, also reduce contacts with the Austrian Government. Haider hands over as Freedom Party leader to Riess-Passer, seen as less extreme. After 7 months, a period of close observation, the EU lifts sanctions.
102
1998: Defense I
Ending with a pact signed on the HMS Birmingham between the UK and France, the Anglo-French St Malo Summit marks the end of the UK's resistance to an autonomous EU military capacity and is generally defined as the beginning of the EU defense project.
101
1998: EURO II
At the press launch of the Euro as a Virtual Currency, Jacques Santer, President of the European Commision and Yves-Thibault de Silguy, European Commissioner for Economic and Monetary Affairs, present a reproduction of a euro coin measuring 1 meter in diameter.
108
1999: Beef War
France and Belgium ban British beef and beef products and Germany asks the European Union to ban all British beef exports because of possible health risk from mad cow disease (BSE).
nomic treaty in
s of enlargement,
ts into EU law,
mmigration.
103
1998: Growth, Prosperity, Jobs and Social inclusion
The European Summit in Cardiff sets out EU strategy for further economic reform and identifies concrete ways of bringing the Union closer to the people.
106
12.12.1998: Equal opportunity
At the Vienna European Council, principles for a Europe-wide coordination of economic and employment strategies are laid out. The EU declares it will address issues of employment and economic growth, will improve security, overall quality of life and equality of opportunity.

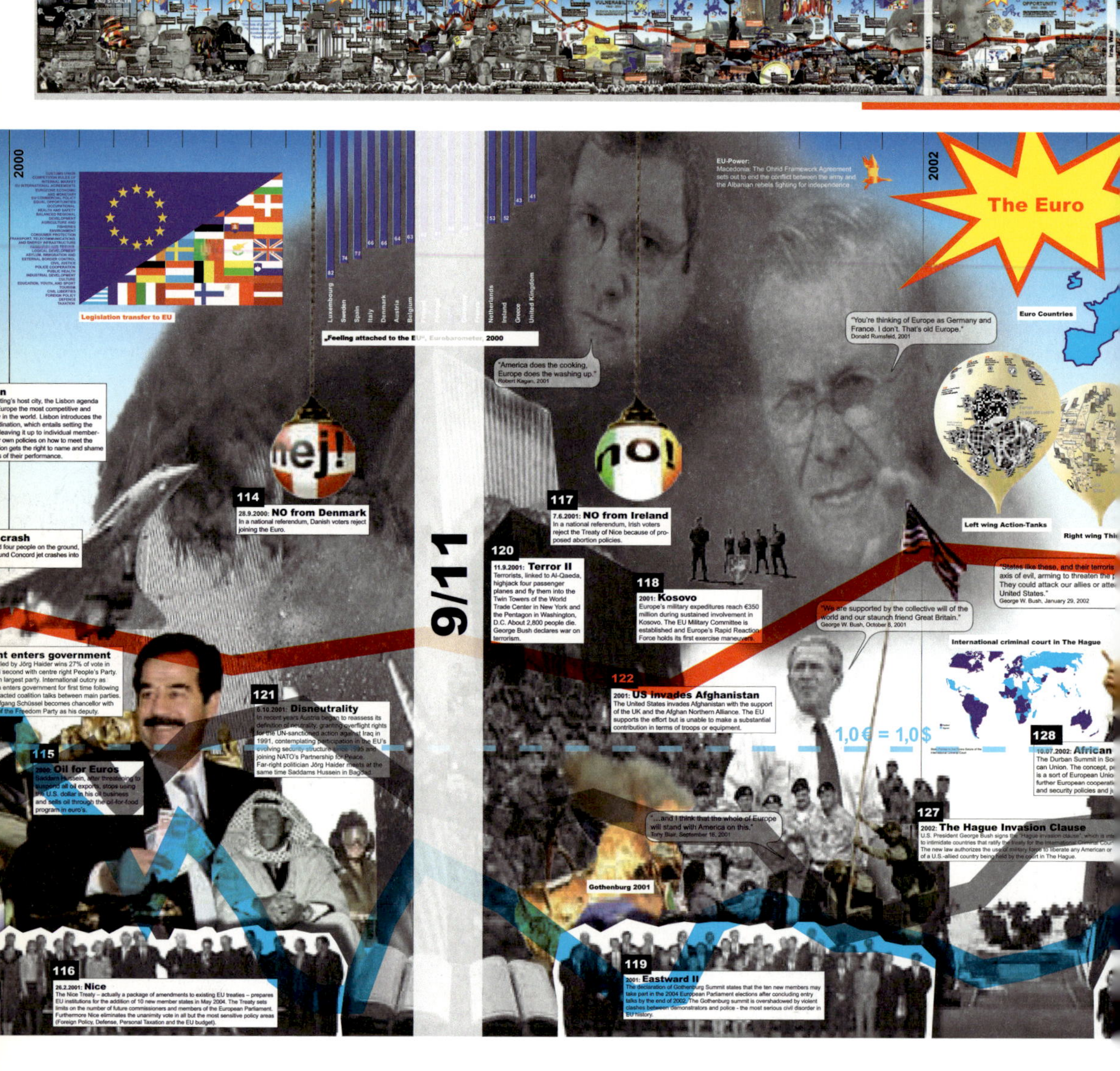

2000
2002
Legislation transfer to EU
Luxembourg 82
Sweden 74
Spain 72
Italy 66
Denmark 66
Austria 64
Belgium 63
Netherlands 53
Ireland 52
Greece 43
United Kingdom 41
„Feeling attached to the EU", Eurobarometer, 2000
EU-Power:
Macedonia: The Ohrid Framework Agreement sets out to end the conflict between the army and the Albanian rebels fighting for independence
The Euro
Euro Countries
"America does the cooking, Europe does the washing up." Robert Kagan, 2001
"You're thinking of Europe as Germany and France. I don't. That's old Europe." Donald Rumsfeld, 2001
bon
meeting's host city, the Lisbon agenda ke Europe the most competitive and omy in the world. Lisbon introduces the coordination, which entails setting the but leaving it up to individual member- their own policies on how to meet the nission gets the right to name and shame basis of their performance.
nej!
114
28.9.2000: NO from Denmark
In a national referendum, Danish voters reject joining the Euro.
no!
117
7.6.2001: NO from Ireland
In a national referendum, Irish voters reject the Treaty of Nice because of proposed abortion policies.
Left wing Action-Tanks
Right wing Thi
le crash
, and four people on the ground, k-bound Concord jet crashes into
9/11
120
11.9.2001: Terror II
Terrorists, linked to Al-Qaeda, highjack four passenger planes and fly them into the Twin Towers of the World Trade Center in New York and the Pentagon in Washington, D.C. About 2,800 people die. George Bush declares war on terrorism.
118
2001: Kosovo
Europe's military expeditures reach €350 million during sustained involvement in Kosovo. The EU Military Committee is established and Europe's Rapid Reaction Force holds its first exercise maneuvers.
"States like these, and their terroris axis of evil, arming to threaten the They could attack our allies or atte United States." George W. Bush, January 29, 2002
"We are supported by the collective will of the world and our staunch friend Great Britain." George W. Bush, October 8, 2001
ight enters government
arty led by Jörg Haider wins 27% of vote in qual second with centre right People's Party. main largest party. International outcry as stria enters government for first time following protracted coalition talks between main parties. Wolfgang Schüssel becomes chancellor with er of the Freedom Party as his deputy.
121
6.10.2001: Disneutrality
In recent years Austria began to reassess its definition of neutrality, granting overflight rights for the UN-sanctioned action against Iraq in 1991, contemplating participation in the EU's evolving security structure since 1995 and joining NATO's Partnership for Peace. Far-right politician Jörg Haider meets at the same time Saddams Hussein in Bagdad.
122
2001: US invades Afghanistan
The United States invades Afghanistan with the support of the UK and the Afghan Northern Alliance. The EU supports the effort but is unable to make a substantial contribution in terms of troops or equipment.
International criminal court in The Hague
1,0 € = 1,0 $
128
10.07.2002: African
The Durban Summit in So can Union. The concept, p is a sort of European Unio further European cooperat and security policies and j
115
2000: Oil for Euros
Saddam Hussein, after threatening to suspend all oil exports, stops using the U.S. dollar in his oil business and sells oil through the oil-for-food program in euro's.
"...and I think that the whole of Europe will stand with America on this." Tony Blair, September 16, 2001
127
2002: The Hague Invasion Clause
U.S. President George Bush signs the "Hague invasion clause", which is inte to intimidate countries that ratify the treaty for the International Criminal Cour The new law authorizes the use of military force to liberate any American or of a U.S.-allied country being held by the court in The Hague.
Gothenburg 2001
116
26.2.2001: Nice
The Nice Treaty – actually a package of amendments to existing EU treaties – prepares EU institutions for the addition of 10 new member states in May 2004. The Treaty sets limits on the number of future commissioners and members of the European Parliament. Furthermore Nice eliminates the unanimity vote in all but the most sensitive policy areas (Foreign Policy, Defense, Personal Taxation and the EU budget).
119
2001: Eastward II
The declaration of Gothenburg Summit states that the ten new members may take part in the 2004 European Parliament elections after concluding entry talks by the end of 2002. The Gothenburg summit is overshadowed by violent clashes between demonstrators and police - the most serious civil disorder in EU history.

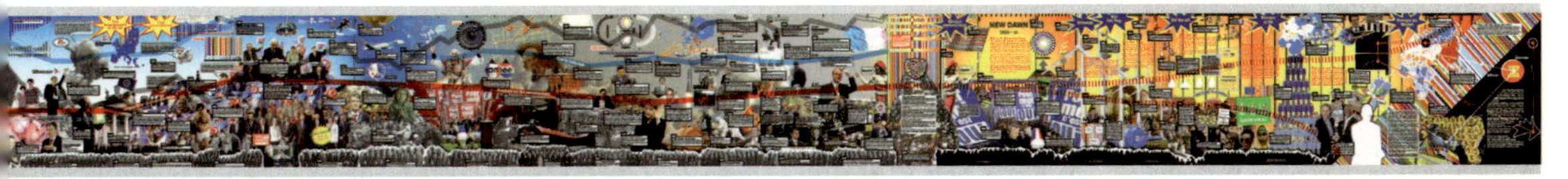

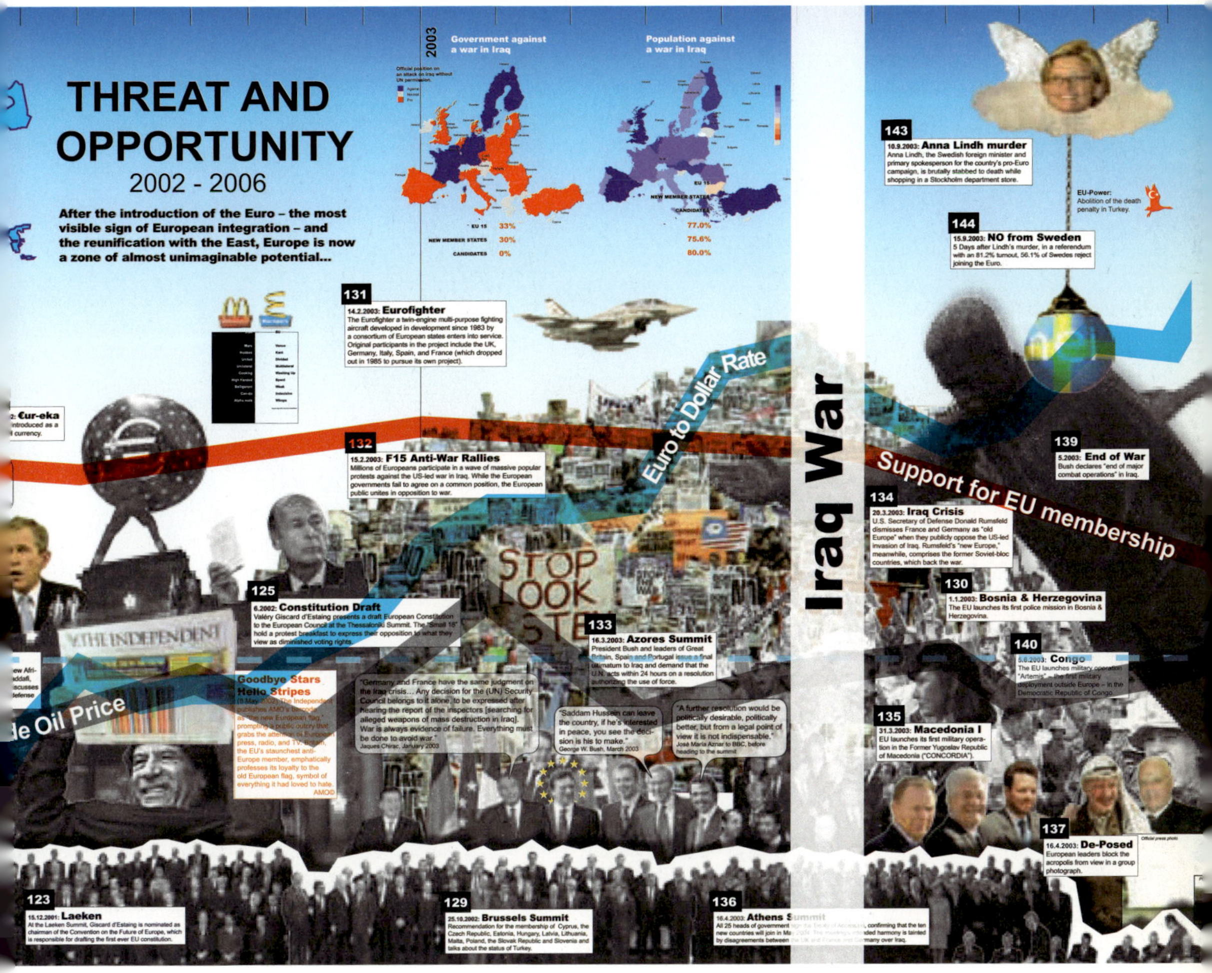

THREAT AND OPPORTUNITY

2002 - 2006

After the introduction of the Euro – the most visible sign of European integration – and the reunification with the East, Europe is now a zone of almost unimaginable potential...

2003

Government against a war in Iraq

Official position on an attack on Iraq without UN permission.

EU 15	33%
NEW MEMBER STATES	30%
CANDIDATES	0%

Population against a war in Iraq

EU 15	77.0%
NEW MEMBER STATES	75.6%
CANDIDATES	80.0%

131
14.2.2003: **Eurofighter**
The Eurofighter a twin-engine multi-purpose fighting aircraft developed in development since 1983 by a consortium of European states enters into service. Original participants in the project include the UK, Germany, Italy, Spain, and France (which dropped out in 1985 to pursue its own project).

...: **€ur-eka**
...introduced as a ...currency.

132
15.2.2003: **F15 Anti-War Rallies**
Millions of Europeans participate in a wave of massive popular protests against the US-led war in Iraq. While the European governments fail to agree on a common position, the European public unites in opposition to war.

Euro to Dollar Rate

125
6.2002: **Constitution Draft**
Valéry Giscard d'Estaing presents a draft European Constitution to the European Council at the Thessaloniki Summit. The "Small 18" hold a protest breakfast to express their opposition to what they view as diminished voting rights.

133
16.3.2003: **Azores Summit**
President Bush and leaders of Great Britain, Spain and Portugal issue a final ultimatum to Iraq and demand that the U.N. acts within 24 hours on a resolution authorizing the use of force.

Goodbye Stars Hello Stripes
(8 May 2002) The Independent publishes AMO's barcode as "the new European flag," prompting a public outcry that grabs the attention of European press, radio, and TV. Britain, the EU's staunchest anti-Europe member, emphatically professes its loyalty to the old European flag, symbol of everything it had loved to hate.
AMO©

"Germany and France have the same judgment on the Iraq crisis... Any decision for the (UN) Security Council belongs to it alone, to be expressed after hearing the report of the inspectors [searching for alleged weapons of mass destruction in Iraq]. War is always evidence of failure. Everything must be done to avoid war."
Jaques Chirac, January 2003

"Saddam Hussein can leave the country, if he's interested in peace, you see the decision is his to make."
George W. Bush, March 2003

"A further resolution would be politically desirable, politically better, but from a legal point of view it is not indispensable."
José María Aznar to BBC, before heading to the summit

de Oil Price

Iraq War

143
10.9.2003: **Anna Lindh murder**
Anna Lindh, the Swedish foreign minister and primary spokesperson for the country's pro-Euro campaign, is brutally stabbed to death while shopping in a Stockholm department store.

EU-Power:
Abolition of the death penalty in Turkey.

144
15.9.2003: **NO from Sweden**
5 Days after Lindh's murder, in a referendum with an 81.2% turnout, 56.1% of Swedes reject joining the Euro.

139
5.2003: **End of War**
Bush declares "end of major combat operations" in Iraq.

Support for EU membership

134
20.3.2003: **Iraq Crisis**
U.S. Secretary of Defense Donald Rumsfeld dismisses France and Germany as "old Europe" when they publicly oppose the US-led invasion of Iraq. Rumsfeld's "new Europe," meanwhile, comprises the former Soviet-bloc countries, which back the war.

130
1.1.2003: **Bosnia & Herzegovina**
The EU launches its first police mission in Bosnia & Herzegovina.

140
5.6.2003: **Congo**
The EU launches military operation "Artemis" – the first military deployment outside Europe – in the Democratic Republic of Congo.

135
31.3.2003: **Macedonia I**
EU launches its first military operation in the Former Yugoslav Republic of Macedonia ("CONCORDIA").

137
16.4.2003: **De-Posed**
European leaders block the acropolis from view in a group photograph.

Official press photo

123
15.12.2001: **Laeken**
At the Laeken Summit, Giscard d'Estaing is nominated as chairman of the Convention on the Future of Europe, which is responsible for drafting the first ever EU constitution.

129
25.10.2002: **Brussels Summit**
Recommendation for the membership of Cyprus, the Czech Republic, Estonia, Hungary, Latvia, Lithuania, Malta, Poland, the Slovak Republic and Slovenia and talks about the status of Turkey.

136
16.4.2003: **Athens Summit**
All 25 heads of government [illegible], confirming that the ten new countries will join in Ma[illegible] [illegible]ded harmony is tainted by disagreements between [illegible] Germany over Iraq.

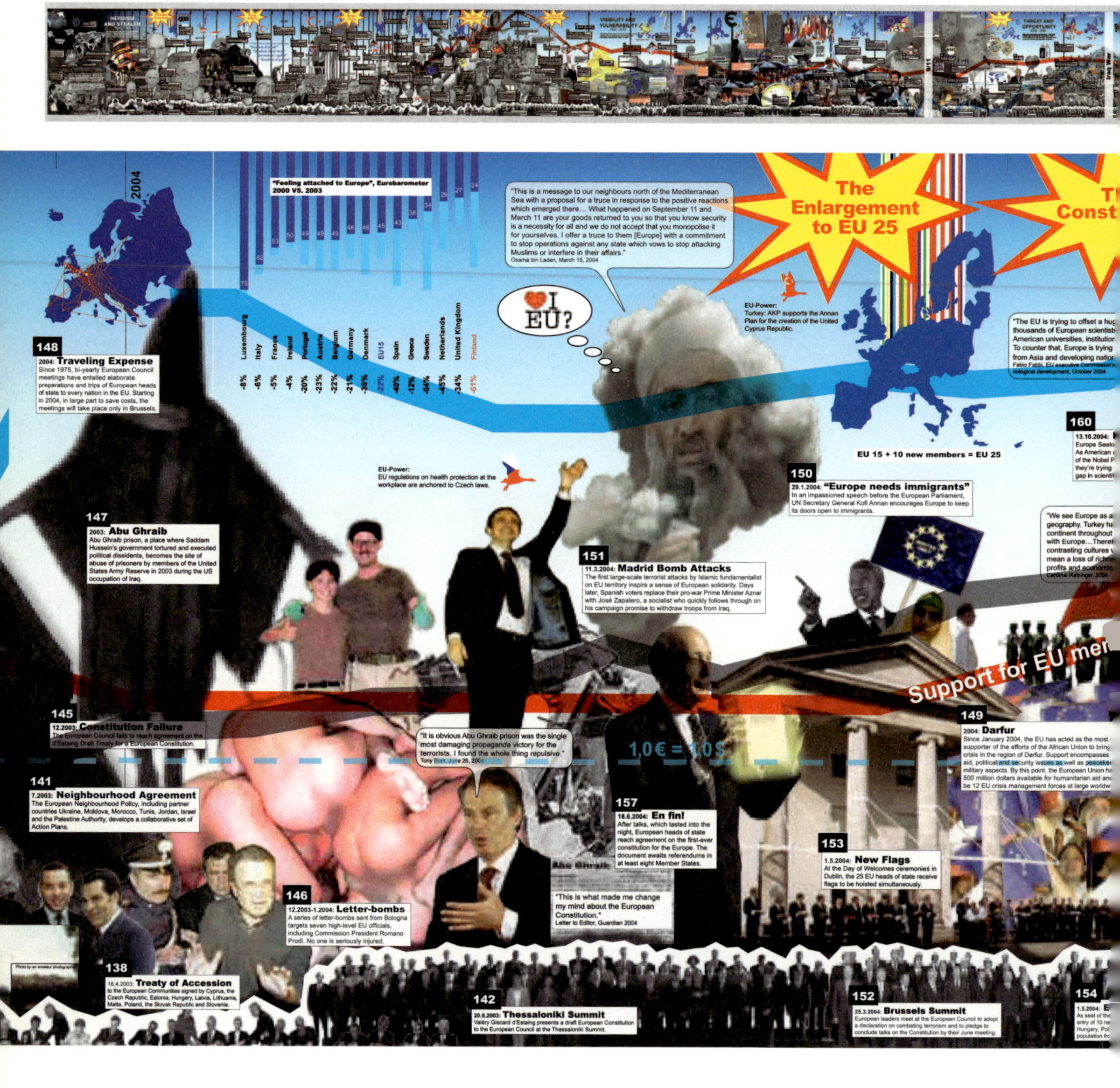
2004
148
2004: Traveling Expense
Since 1975, bi-yearly European Council meetings have entailed elaborate preparations and trips of European heads of state to every nation in the EU. Starting in 2004, in large part to save costs, the meetings will take place only in Brussels.
"Feeling attached to Europe", Eurobarometer 2000 VS. 2003
Luxembourg -8%
Italy -6%
France -5%
Ireland -4%
Portugal -20%
Austria -23%
Belgium -22%
Germany -21%
Denmark -30%
EU15 -22%
Spain -40%
Greece -12%
Sweden -54%
Netherlands -45%
United Kingdom -34%
Finland -61%
"This is a message to our neighbours north of the Mediterranean Sea with a proposal for a truce in response to the positive reactions which emerged there… What happened on September 11 and March 11 are your goods returned to you so that you know security is a necessity for all and we do not accept that you monopolise it for yourselves. I offer a truce to them [Europe] with a commitment to stop operations against any state which vows to stop attacking Muslims or interfere in their affairs."
Osama bin Laden, March 15, 2004
I EU?
The Enlargement to EU 25
EU-Power:
Turkey: AKP supports the Annan Plan for the creation of the United Cyprus Republic.
EU 15 + 10 new members = EU 25
EU-Power:
EU regulations on health protection at the workplace are anchored to Czech laws.
147
2003: Abu Ghraib
Abu Ghraib prison, a place where Saddam Hussein's government tortured and executed political dissidents, becomes the site of abuse of prisoners by members of the United States Army Reserve in 2003 during the US occupation of Iraq.
150
29.1.2004: "Europe needs immigrants"
In an impassioned speech before the European Parliament, UN Secretary General Kofi Annan encourages Europe to keep its doors open to immigrants.
151
11.3.2004: Madrid Bomb Attacks
The first large-scale terrorist attacks by Islamic fundamentalist on EU territory inspire a sense of European solidarity. Days later, Spanish voters replace their pro-war Prime Minister Aznar with José Zapatero, a socialist who quickly follows through on his campaign promise to withdraw troops from Iraq.
145
12.2003: Constitution Failure
The European Council fails to reach agreement on the d'Estaing Draft Treaty for a European Constitution.
"It is obvious Abu Ghraib prison was the single most damaging propaganda victory for the terrorists. I found the whole thing repulsive."
Tony Blair, June 26, 2004
1,0€ = 1,0$
141
7.2003: Neighbourhood Agreement
The European Neighbourhood Policy, including partner countries Ukraine, Moldova, Morocco, Tunis, Jordan, Israel and the Palestine Authority, develops a collaborative set of Action Plans.
157
18.6.2004: En fin!
After talks, which lasted into the night, European heads of state reach agreement on the first-ever constitution for the Europe. The document awaits referendums in at least eight Member States.
153
1.5.2004: New Flags
At the Day of Welcomes ceremonies in Dublin, the 25 EU heads of state receive flags to be hoisted simultaneously.
146
12.2003-1.2004: Letter-bombs
A series of letter-bombs sent from Bologna targets seven high-level EU officials, including Commission President Romano Prodi. No one is seriously injured.
"This is what made me change my mind about the European Constitution."
Letter to Editor, Guardian 2004
Photo by an amateur photographer
138
16.4.2003: Treaty of Accession
to the European Communities signed by Cyprus, the Czech Republic, Estonia, Hungary, Latvia, Lithuania, Malta, Poland, the Slovak Republic and Slovenia.
142
20.6.2003: Thessaloniki Summit
Valéry Giscard d'Estaing presents a draft European Constitution to the European Council at the Thessaloniki Summit.
152
25.3.2004: Brussels Summit
European leaders meet at the European Council to adopt a declaration on combating terrorism and to pledge to conclude talks on the Constitution by their June meeting.

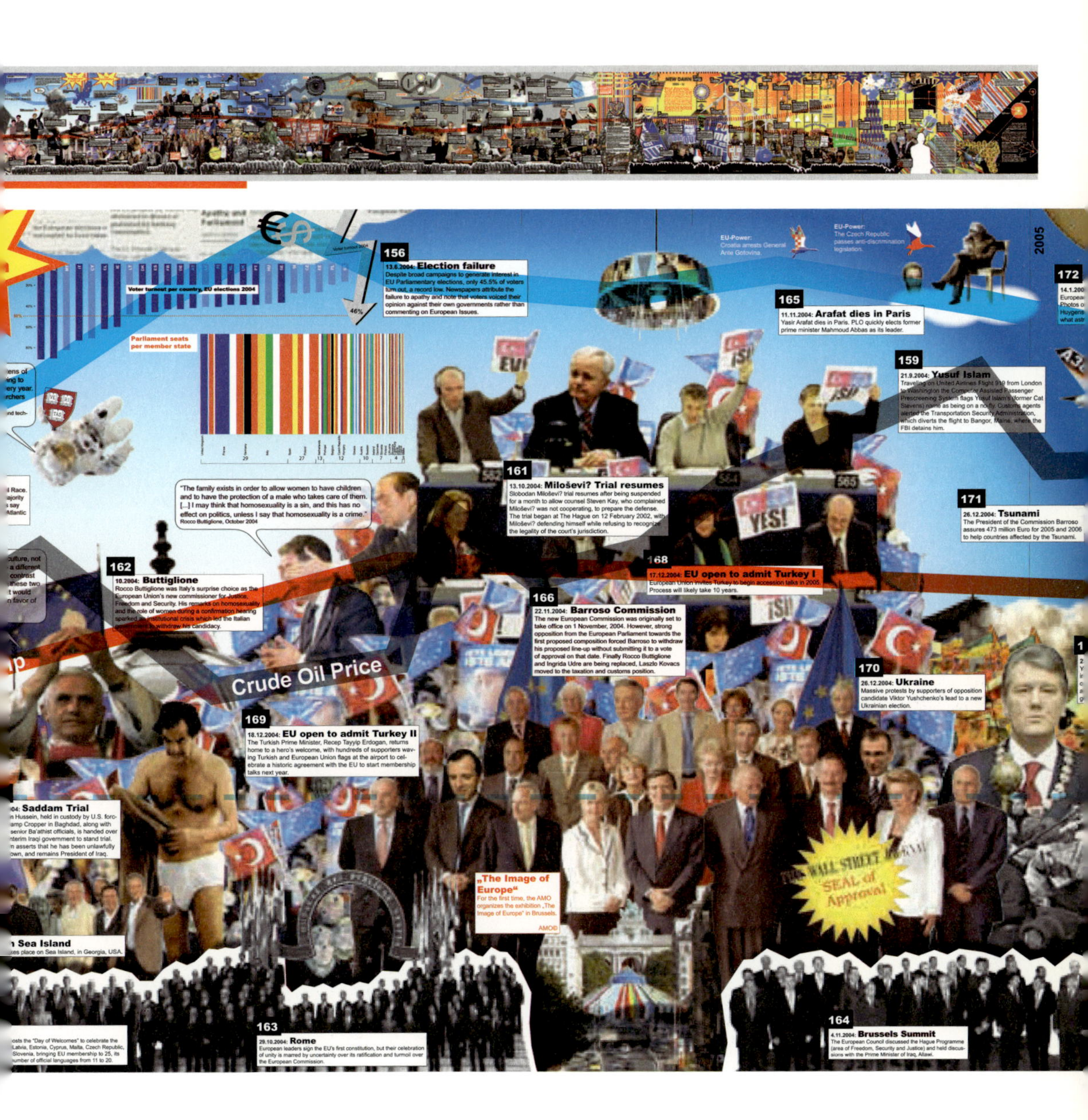
Voter turnout 2004
46%
Voter turnout per country, EU elections 2004
Parliament seats per member state
29
27
13
12
10
7
4
3
156
13.6.2004: Election failure
Despite broad campaigns to generate interest in EU Parliamentary elections, only 45.5% of voters turn out, a record low. Newspapers attribute the failure to apathy and note that voters voiced their opinion against their own governments rather than commenting on European Issues.
EU-Power: Croatia arrests General Ante Gotovina.
EU-Power: The Czech Republic passes anti-discrimination legislation.
2005
172
165
11.11.2004: Arafat dies in Paris
Yasir Arafat dies in Paris. PLO quickly elects former prime minister Mahmoud Abbas as its leader.
159
21.9.2004: Yusuf Islam
Traveling on United Airlines Flight 919 from London to Washington the Computer Assisted Passenger Prescreening System flags Yusuf Islam's (former Cat Stevens) name as being on a no-fly. Customs agents alerted the Transportation Security Administration, which diverts the flight to Bangor, Maine, where the FBI detains him.
"The family exists in order to allow women to have children and to have the protection of a male who takes care of them. [...] I may think that homosexuality is a sin, and this has no effect on politics, unless I say that homosexuality is a crime."
Rocco Buttiglione, October 2004
161
13.10.2004: Miloševi? Trial resumes
Slobodan Miloševi? trial resumes after being suspended for a month to allow counsel Steven Kay, who complained Miloševi? was not cooperating, to prepare the defense. The trial began at The Hague on 12 February 2002, with Miloševi? defending himself while refusing to recognize the legality of the court's jurisdiction.
YES!
171
26.12.2004: Tsunami
The President of the Commission Barroso assures 473 million Euro for 2005 and 2006 to help countries affected by the Tsunami.
162
10.2004: Buttiglione
Rocco Buttiglione was Italy's surprise choice as the European Union's new commissioner for Justice, Freedom and Security. His remarks on homosexuality and the role of women during a confirmation hearing sparked an institutional crisis which led the Italian government to withdraw his candidacy.
168
17.12.2004: EU open to admit Turkey I
European Union invites Turkey to begin accession talks in 2005. Process will likely take 10 years.
166
22.11.2004: Barroso Commission
The new European Commission was originally set to take office on 1 November, 2004. However, strong opposition from the European Parliament towards the first proposed composition forced Barroso to withdraw his proposed line-up without submitting it to a vote of approval on that date. Finally Rocco Buttiglione and Ingrida Udre are being replaced, Laszlo Kovacs moved to the taxation and customs position.
Crude Oil Price
170
26.12.2004: Ukraine
Massive protests by supporters of opposition candidate Viktor Yushchenko's lead to a new Ukrainian election.
169
18.12.2004: EU open to admit Turkey II
The Turkish Prime Minister, Recep Tayyip Erdogan, returns home to a hero's welcome, with hundreds of supporters waving Turkish and European Union flags at the airport to celebrate a historic agreement with the EU to start membership talks next year.
Saddam Trial
Sea Island
„The Image of Europe“
For the first time, the AMO organizes the exhibition „The Image of Europe" in Brussels.
AMO©
SEAL of Approval
163
29.10.2004: Rome
European leaders sign the EU's first constitution, but their celebration of unity is marred by uncertainty over its ratification and turmoil over the European Commission.
164
4.11.2004: Brussels Summit
The European Council discussed the Hague Programme (area of Freedom, Security and Justice) and held discussions with the Prime Minister of Iraq, Allawi.

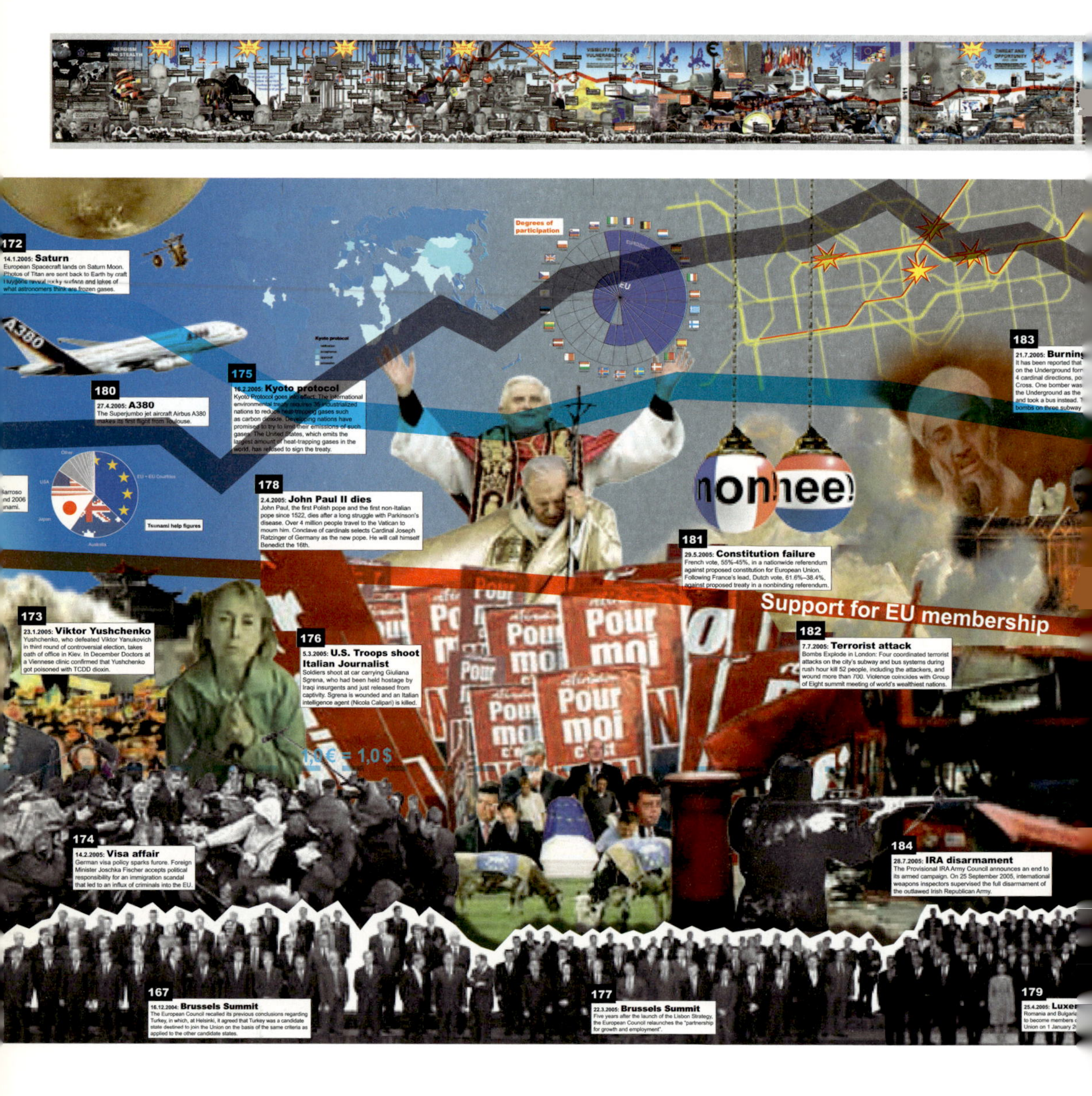

172
14.1.2005: Saturn
European Spacecraft lands on Saturn Moon. Photos of Titan are sent back to Earth by craft Huygens reveal rocky surface and lakes of what astronomers think are frozen gases.
Degrees of participation
180
27.4.2005: A380
The Superjumbo jet aircraft Airbus A380 makes its first flight from Toulouse.
175
16.2.2005: Kyoto protocol
Kyoto Protocol goes into effect: The international environmental treaty requires 35 industrialized nations to reduce heat-trapping gases such as carbon dioxide. Developing nations have promised to try to limit their emissions of such gases. The United States, which emits the largest amount of heat-trapping gases in the world, has refused to sign the treaty.
Tsunami help figures
178
2.4.2005: John Paul II dies
John Paul, the first Polish pope and the first non-Italian pope since 1522, dies after a long struggle with Parkinson's disease. Over 4 million people travel to the Vatican to mourn him. Conclave of cardinals selects Cardinal Joseph Ratzinger of Germany as the new pope. He will call himself Benedict the 16th.
non! nee!
181
29.5.2005: Constitution failure
French vote, 55%-45%, in a nationwide referendum against proposed constitution for European Union. Following France's lead, Dutch vote, 61.6%–38.4%, against proposed treaty in a nonbinding referendum.
Support for EU membership
173
23.1.2005: Viktor Yushchenko
Yushchenko, who defeated Viktor Yanukovich in third round of controversial election, takes oath of office in Kiev. In December Doctors at a Viennese clinic confirmed that Yushchenko got poisoned with TCDD dioxin.
176
5.3.2005: U.S. Troops shoot Italian Journalist
Soldiers shoot at car carrying Giuliana Sgrena, who had been held hostage by Iraqi insurgents and just released from captivity. Sgrena is wounded and an Italian intelligence agent (Nicola Calipari) is killed.
Pour moi
182
7.7.2005: Terrorist attack
Bombs Explode in London: Four coordinated terrorist attacks on the city's subway and bus systems during rush hour kill 52 people, including the attackers, and wound more than 700. Violence coincides with Group of Eight summit meeting of world's wealthiest nations.
1,0€ = 1,0$
174
14.2.2005: Visa affair
German visa policy sparks furore. Foreign Minister Joschka Fischer accepts political responsibility for an immigration scandal that led to an influx of criminals into the EU.
184
28.7.2005: IRA disarmament
The Provisional IRA Army Council announces an end to its armed campaign. On 25 September 2005, international weapons inspectors supervised the full disarmament of the outlawed Irish Republican Army.
167
16.12.2004: Brussels Summit
The European Council recalled its previous conclusions regarding Turkey, in which, at Helsinki, it agreed that Turkey was a candidate state destined to join the Union on the basis of the same criteria as applied to the other candidate states.
177
22.3.2005: Brussels Summit
Five years after the launch of the Lisbon Strategy, the European Council relaunches the "partnership for growth and employment".

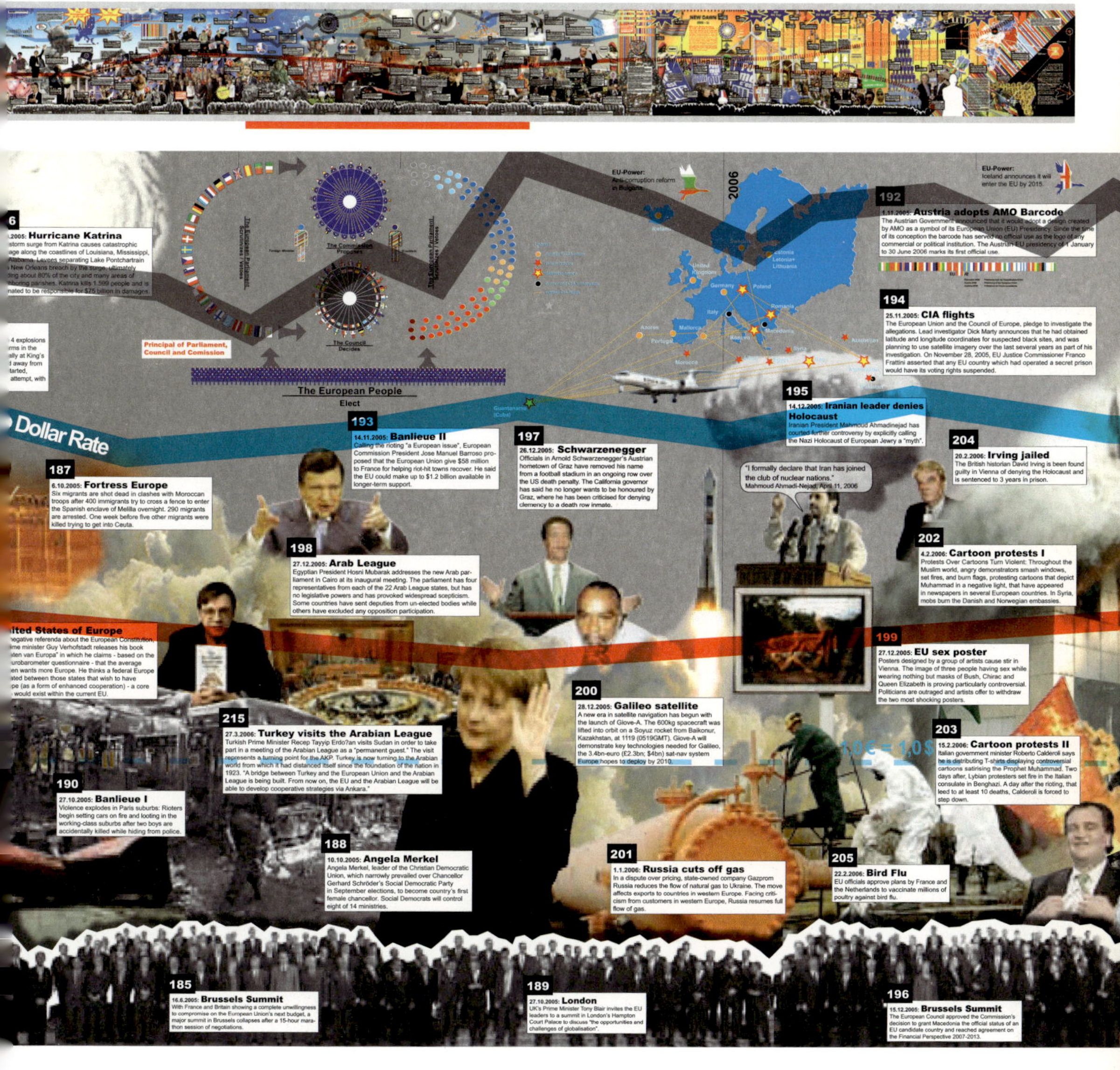

Principal of Parliament, Council and Comission
The European Parliament Scrutinizes / Vetoes
The Commission Proposes
The Council Decides
The European People
Elect
EU-Power: Anti-corruption reform in Bulgaria
2006
EU-Power: Iceland announces it will enter the EU by 2015.
Iceland
Sweden
Estonia Letonia+ Lithuania
United Kingdom
Germany
Poland
Romania
Italy
Mallorca
Azores
Portugal
Kosovo
Macedonia
Syria
Morocco
Azerbaijan
Guantanamo (Cuba)
Dollar Rate
1,0€ = 1,0$
.2005: Hurricane Katrina
storm surge from Katrina causes catastrophic
along the coastlines of Louisiana, Mississippi,
Alabama. Levees separating Lake Pontchartrain
New Orleans breach by the surge, ultimately
about 80% of the city and many areas of
parishes. Katrina kills 1,599 people and is
to be responsible for $75 billion in damages.
4 explosions
in the
at King's
away from
attempt, with
192
1.11.2005: Austria adopts AMO Barcode
The Austrian Government announced that it would adopt a design created by AMO as a symbol of its European Union (EU) Presidency. Since the time of its conception the barcode has served no official use as the logo of any commercial or political institution. The Austrian EU presidency of 1 January to 30 June 2006 marks its first official use.
194
25.11.2005: CIA flights
The European Union and the Council of Europe, pledge to investigate the allegations. Lead investigator Dick Marty announces that he had obtained latitude and longitude coordinates for suspected black sites, and was planning to use satellite imagery over the last several years as part of his investigation. On November 28, 2005, EU Justice Commissioner Franco Frattini asserted that any EU country which had operated a secret prison would have its voting rights suspended.
195
14.12.2005: Iranian leader denies Holocaust
Iranian President Mahmoud Ahmadinejad has courted further controversy by explicitly calling the Nazi Holocaust of European Jewry a "myth".
193
14.11.2005: Banlieue II
Calling the rioting "a European issue", European Commission President Jose Manuel Barroso proposed that the European Union give $58 million to France for helping riot-hit towns recover. He said the EU could make up to $1.2 billion available in longer-term support.
197
26.12.2005: Schwarzenegger
Officials in Arnold Schwarzenegger's Austrian hometown of Graz have removed his name from a football stadium in an ongoing row over the US death penalty. The California governor has said he no longer wants to be honoured by Graz, where he has been criticised for denying clemency to a death row inmate.
204
20.2.2006: Irving jailed
The British historian David Irving is been found guilty in Vienna of denying the Holocaust and is sentenced to 3 years in prison.
187
6.10.2005: Fortress Europe
Six migrants are shot dead in clashes with Moroccan troops after 400 immigrants try to cross a fence to enter the Spanish enclave of Melilla overnight. 290 migrants are arrested. One week before five other migrants were killed trying to get into Ceuta.
"I formally declare that Iran has joined the club of nuclear nations."
Mahmoud Ahmadi-Nejad, April 11, 2006
198
27.12.2005: Arab League
Egyptian President Hosni Mubarak addresses the new Arab parliament in Cairo at its inaugural meeting. The parliament has four representatives from each of the 22 Arab League states, but has no legislative powers and has provoked widespread scepticism. Some countries have sent deputies from un-elected bodies while others have excluded any opposition participation.
202
4.2.2006: Cartoon protests I
Protests Over Cartoons Turn Violent: Throughout the Muslim world, angry demonstrators smash windows, set fires, and burn flags, protesting cartoons that depict Muhammad in a negative light, that have appeared in newspapers in several European countries. In Syria, mobs burn the Danish and Norwegian embassies.
States of Europe
negative referenda about the European Constitution,
minister Guy Verhofstadt releases his book
van Europa" in which he claims - based on the
questionnaire - that the average
wants more Europe. He thinks a federal Europe
between those states that wish to have
(as a form of enhanced cooperation) - a core
would exist within the current EU.
199
27.12.2005: EU sex poster
Posters designed by a group of artists cause stir in Vienna. The image of three people having sex while wearing nothing but masks of Bush, Chirac and Queen Elizabeth is proving particularly controversial. Politicians are outraged and artists offer to withdraw the two most shocking posters.
200
28.12.2005: Galileo satellite
A new era in satellite navigation has begun with the launch of Giove-A. The 600kg spacecraft was lifted into orbit on a Soyuz rocket from Baikonur, Kazakhstan, at 1119 (0519GMT). Giove-A will demonstrate key technologies needed for Galileo, the 3.4bn-euro (£2.3bn; $4bn) sat-nav system Europe hopes to deploy by 2010.
215
27.3.2006: Turkey visits the Arabian League
Turkish Prime Minister Recep Tayyip Erdo?an visits Sudan in order to take part in a meeting of the Arabian League as a "permanent guest." The visit represents a turning point for the AKP. Turkey is now turning to the Arabian world from which it had distanced itself since the foundation of the nation in 1923. "A bridge between Turkey and the European Union and the Arabian League is being built. From now on, the EU and the Arabian League will be able to develop cooperative strategies via Ankara."
203
15.2.2006: Cartoon protests II
Italian government minister Roberto Calderoli says he is distributing T-shirts displaying controversial cartoons satirising the Prophet Muhammad. Two days after, Lybian protesters set fire in the Italian consulate in Benghazi. A day after the rioting, that leed to at least 10 deaths, Calderoli is forced to step down.
190
27.10.2005: Banlieue I
Violence explodes in Paris suburbs: Rioters begin setting cars on fire and looting in the working-class suburbs after two boys are accidentally killed while hiding from police.
188
10.10.2005: Angela Merkel
Angela Merkel, leader of the Christian Democratic Union, which narrowly prevailed over Chancellor Gerhard Schröder's Social Democratic Party in September elections, to become country's first female chancellor. Social Democrats will control eight of 14 ministries.
201
1.1.2006: Russia cuts off gas
In a dispute over pricing, state-owned company Gazprom Russia reduces the flow of natural gas to Ukraine. The move affects exports to countries in western Europe. Facing criticism from customers in western Europe, Russia resumes full flow of gas.
205
22.2.2006: Bird Flu
EU officials approve plans by France and the Netherlands to vaccinate millions of poultry against bird flu.
185
16.6.2005: Brussels Summit
With France and Britain showing a complete unwillingness to compromise on the European Union's next budget, a major summit in Brussels collapses after a 15-hour marathon session of negotiations.
189
27.10.2005: London
UK's Prime Minister Tony Blair invites the EU leaders to a summit in London's Hampton Court Palace to discuss "the opportunities and challenges of globalisation".
196
15.12.2005: Brussels Summit
The European Council approved the Commission's decision to grant Macedonia the official status of an EU candidate country and reached agreement on the Financial Perspective 2007-2013.

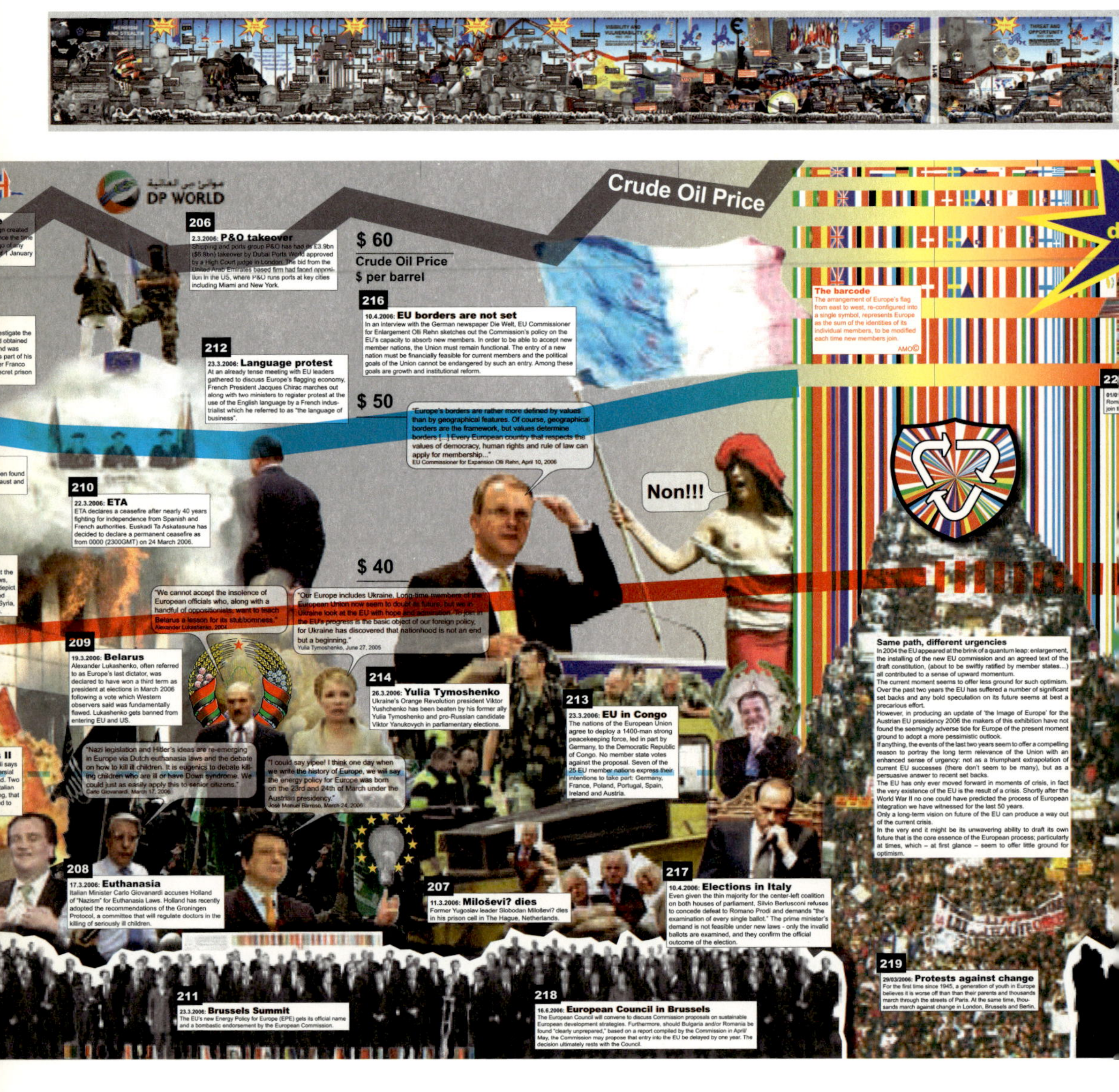

DP WORLD
Crude Oil Price
$ 60
Crude Oil Price
$ per barrel
$ 50
$ 40
206
2.3.2006: P&O takeover
Shipping and ports group P&O has had its £3.9bn ($6.8bn) takeover by Dubai Ports World approved by a High Court judge in London. The bid from the United Arab Emirates based firm had faced opposition in the US, where P&O runs ports at key cities including Miami and New York.
216
10.4.2006: EU borders are not set
In an interview with the German newspaper Die Welt, EU Commissioner for Enlargement Olli Rehn sketches out the Commission's policy on the EU's capacity to absorb new members. In order to be able to accept new member nations, the Union must remain functional. The entry of a new nation must be financially feasible for current members and the political goals of the Union cannot be endangered by such an entry. Among these goals are growth and institutional reform.
212
23.3.2006: Language protest
At an already tense meeting with EU leaders gathered to discuss Europe's flagging economy, French President Jacques Chirac marches out along with two ministers to register protest at the use of the English language by a French industrialist which he referred to as "the language of business".
"Europe's borders are rather more defined by values than by geographical features. Of course, geographical borders are the framework, but values determine borders [...] Every European country that respects the values of democracy, human rights and rule of law can apply for membership..."
EU Commissioner for Expansion Olli Rehn, April 10, 2006
Non!!!
The barcode
The arrangement of Europe's flag from east to west, re-configured into a single symbol, represents Europe as the sum of the identities of its individual members, to be modified each time new members join.
AMO©
210
22.3.2006: ETA
ETA declares a ceasefire after nearly 40 years fighting for independence from Spanish and French authorities. Euskadi Ta Askatasuna has decided to declare a permanent ceasefire as from 0000 (2300GMT) on 24 March 2006.
"We cannot accept the insolence of European officials who, along with a handful of oppositionists, want to teach Belarus a lesson for its stubbornness."
Alexander Lukashenko, 2004
"Our Europe includes Ukraine. Long-time members of the European Union now seem to doubt its future, but we in Ukraine look at the EU with hope and admiration. To join in the EU's progress is the basic object of our foreign policy, for Ukraine has discovered that nationhood is not an end but a beginning."
Yulia Tymoshenko, June 27, 2005
209
19.3.2006: Belarus
Alexander Lukashenko, often referred to as Europe's last dictator, was declared to have won a third term as president at elections in March 2006 following a vote which Western observers said was fundamentally flawed. Lukashenko gets banned from entering EU and US.
214
26.3.2006: Yulia Tymoshenko
Ukraine's Orange Revolution president Viktor Yushchenko has been beaten by his former ally Yulia Tymoshenko and pro-Russian candidate Viktor Yanukovych in parliamentary elections.
213
23.3.2006: EU in Congo
The nations of the European Union agree to deploy a 1400-man strong peacekeeping force, led in part by Germany, to the Democratic Republic of Congo. No member state votes against the proposal. Seven of the 25 EU member nations express their intentions to take part: Germany, France, Poland, Portugal, Spain, Ireland and Austria.
Same path, different urgencies
In 2004 the EU appeared at the brink of a quantum leap: enlargement, the installing of the new EU commission and an agreed text of the draft constitution, (about to be swiftly ratified by member states...) all contributed to a sense of upward momentum.
The current moment seems to offer less ground for such optimism. Over the past two years the EU has suffered a number of significant set backs and any bold speculation on its future seems at best a precarious effort.
However, in producing an update of 'the Image of Europe' for the Austrian EU presidency 2006 the makers of this exhibition have not found the seemingly adverse tide for Europe of the present moment ground to adopt a more pessimistic outlook.
If anything, the events of the last two years seem to offer a compelling reason to portray the long term relevance of the Union with an enhanced sense of urgency: not as a triumphant extrapolation of current EU successes (there don't seem to be many), but as a persuasive answer to recent set backs.
The EU has only ever moved forward in moments of crisis, in fact the very existence of the EU is the result of a crisis. Shortly after the World War II no one could have predicted the process of European integration we have witnessed for the last 50 years.
Only a long-term vision on future of the EU can produce a way out of the current crisis.
In the very end it might be its unwavering ability to draft its own future that is the core essence of the European process; particularly at times, which – at first glance – seem to offer little ground for optimism.
"Nazi legislation and Hitler's ideas are re-emerging in Europe via Dutch euthanasia laws and the debate on how to kill ill children. It is eugenics to debate killing children who are ill or have Down syndrome. We could just as easily apply this to senior citizens."
Carlo Giovanardi, March 17, 2006
"I could say yipee! I think one day when we write the history of Europe, we will say the energy policy for Europe was born on the 23rd and 24th of March under the Austrian presidency."
José Manuel Barroso, March 24, 2006
208
17.3.2006: Euthanasia
Italian Minister Carlo Giovanardi accuses Holland of "Nazism" for Euthanasia Laws. Holland has recently adopted the recommendations of the Groningen Protocol, a committee that will regulate doctors in the killing of seriously ill children.
207
11.3.2006: Miloševi? dies
Former Yugoslav leader Slobodan Miloševi? dies in his prison cell in The Hague, Netherlands.
217
10.4.2006: Elections in Italy
Even given the thin majority for the center-left coalition on both houses of parliament, Silvio Berlusconi refuses to concede defeat to Romano Prodi and demands "the examination of every single ballot." The prime minister's demand is not feasible under new laws - only the invalid ballots are examined, and they confirm the official outcome of the election.
219
29/03/2006: Protests against change
For the first time since 1945, a generation of youth in Europe believes it is worse off than than their parents and thousands march through the streets of Paris. At the same time, thousands march against change in London, Brussels and Berlin.
211
23.3.2006: Brussels Summit
The EU's new Energy Policy for Europe (EPE) gets its official name and a bombastic endorsement by the European Commission.
218
16.6.2006: European Council in Brussels
The European Council will convene to discuss Commission proposals on sustainable European development strategies. Furthermore, should Bulgaria and/or Romania be found "clearly unprepared," based on a report compiled by the Commission in April/May, the Commission may propose that entry into the EU be delayed by one year. The decision ultimately rests with the Council.

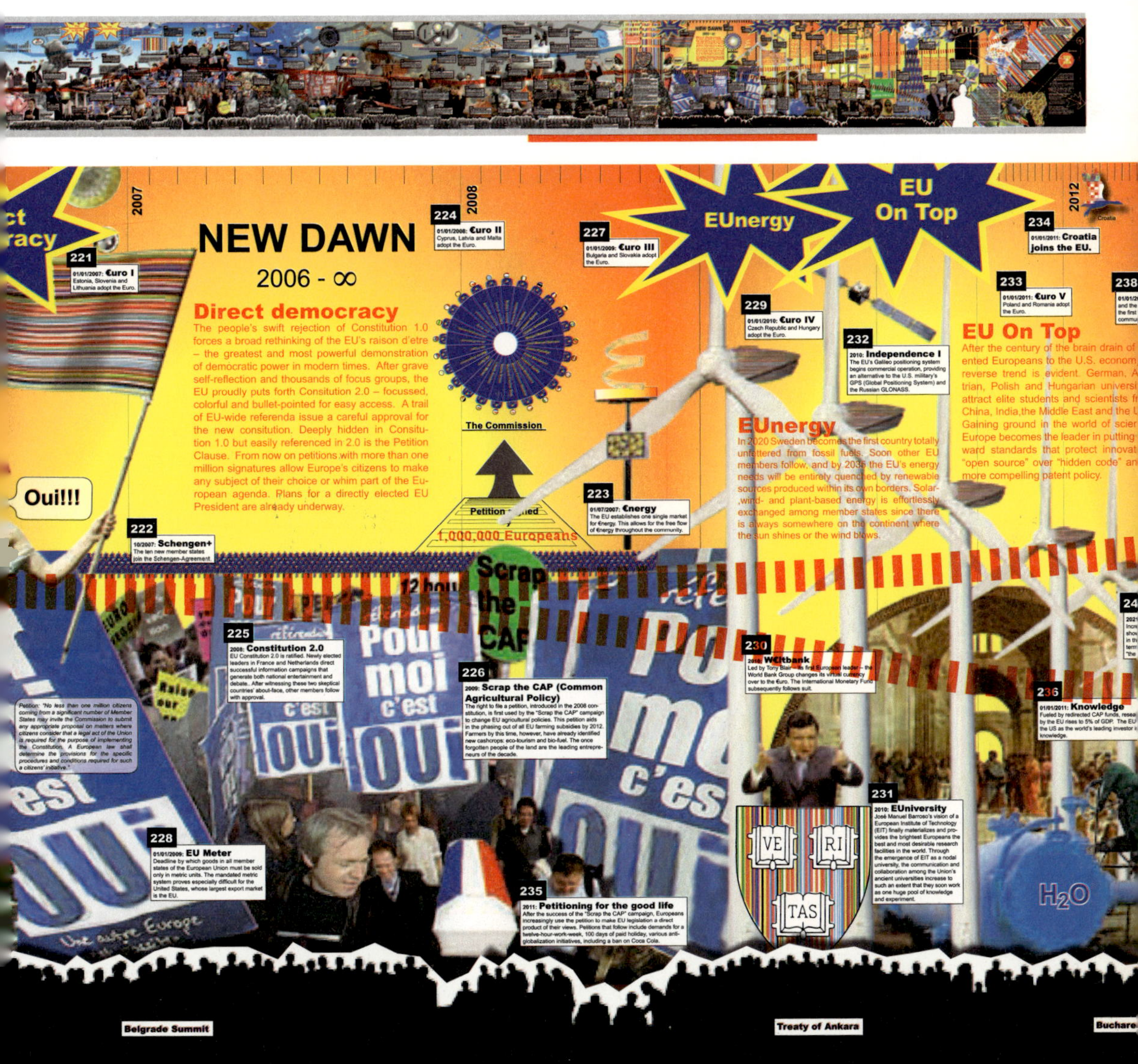

2007
2008
2012
Croatia
NEW DAWN
2006 - ∞
Direct democracy
The people's swift rejection of Constitution 1.0 forces a broad rethinking of the EU's raison d'etre – the greatest and most powerful demonstration of democratic power in modern times. After grave self-reflection and thousands of focus groups, the EU proudly puts forth Consitution 2.0 – focussed, colorful and bullet-pointed for easy access. A trail of EU-wide referenda issue a careful approval for the new consitution. Deeply hidden in Consitution 1.0 but easily referenced in 2.0 is the Petition Clause. From now on petitions with more than one million signatures allow Europe's citizens to make any subject of their choice or whim part of the European agenda. Plans for a directly elected EU President are already underway.
221
01/01/2007: €uro I
Estonia, Slovenia and Lithuania adopt the Euro.
222
10/2007: Schengen+
The ten new member states join the Schengen-Agreement.
223
01/07/2007: €nergy
The EU establishes one single market for €nergy. This allows for the free flow of €nergy throughout the community.
224
01/01/2008: €uro II
Cyprus, Latvia and Malta adopt the Euro.
225
2008: Constitution 2.0
EU Constitution 2.0 is ratified. Newly elected leaders in France and Netherlands direct successful information campaigns that generate both national entertainment and debate.. After witnessing these two skeptical countries' about-face, other members follow with approval.
226
2009: Scrap the CAP (Common Agricultural Policy)
The right to file a petition, introduced in the 2008 constitution, is first used by the "Scrap the CAP" campaign to change EU agricultural policies. This petition aids in the phasing out of all EU farming subsidies by 2012. Farmers by this time, however, have already identified new cashcrops: eco-tourism and bio-fuel. The once forgotten people of the land are the leading entrepreneurs of the decade.
227
01/01/2009: €uro III
Bulgaria and Slovakia adopt the Euro.
228
01/01/2009: EU Meter
Deadline by which goods in all member states of the European Union must be sold only in metric units. The mandated metric system proves especially difficult for the United States, whose largest export market is the EU.
229
01/01/2010: €uro IV
Czech Republic and Hungary adopt the Euro.
230
2010: W€itbank
Led by Tony Blair – its first European leader – the World Bank Group changes its virtual currency over to the €uro. The International Monetary Fund subsequently follows suit.
231
2010: EUniversity
José Manuel Barroso's vision of a European Institute of Technology (EIT) finally materializes and provides the brightest Europeans the best and most desirable research facilities in the world. Through the emergence of EIT as a nodal university, the communication and collaboration among the Union's ancient universities increase to such an extent that they soon work as one huge pool of knowledge and experiment.
232
2010: Independence I
The EU's Galileo positioning system begins commercial operation, providing an alternative to the U.S. military's GPS (Global Positioning System) and the Russian GLONASS.
233
01/01/2011: €uro V
Poland and Romania adopt the Euro.
234
01/01/2011: Croatia joins the EU.
235
2011: Petitioning for the good life
After the success of the "Scrap the CAP" campaign, Europeans increasingly use the petition to make EU legislation a direct product of their views. Petitions that follow include demands for a twelve-hour-work-week, 100 days of paid holiday, various anti-globalization initiatives, including a ban on Coca Cola.
236
01/01/2011: Knowledge
Fueled by redirected CAP funds, resea
by the EU rises to 5% of GDP. The EU
the US as the world's leading investor i
knowledge.
EUnergy
EU On Top
EUnergy
In 2020 Sweden becomes the first country totally unfettered from fossil fuels. Soon other EU members follow, and by 2035 the EU's energy needs will be entirely quenched by renewable sources produced within its own borders. Solar-,wind- and plant-based energy is effortlessly exchanged among member states since there is always somewhere on the continent where the sun shines or the wind blows.
EU On Top
After the century of the brain drain of
ented Europeans to the U.S. econom
reverse trend is evident. German, A
trian, Polish and Hungarian universi
attract elite students and scientists f
China, India,the Middle East and the
Gaining ground in the world of scien
Europe becomes the leader in putting
ward standards that protect innovat
"open source" over "hidden code" an
more compelling patent policy.
The Commission
Petition signed by 1,000,000 Europeans
Scrap the CAP
Oui!!!
Petition: "No less than one million citizens coming from a significant number of Member States may invite the Commission to submit any appropriate proposal on matters where citizens consider that a legal act of the Union is required for the purpose of implementing the Constitution. A European law shall determine the provisions for the specific procedures and conditions required for such a citizens' initiative."
Pour moi c'est oui
VE RI TAS
H2O
Belgrade Summit
Treaty of Ankara

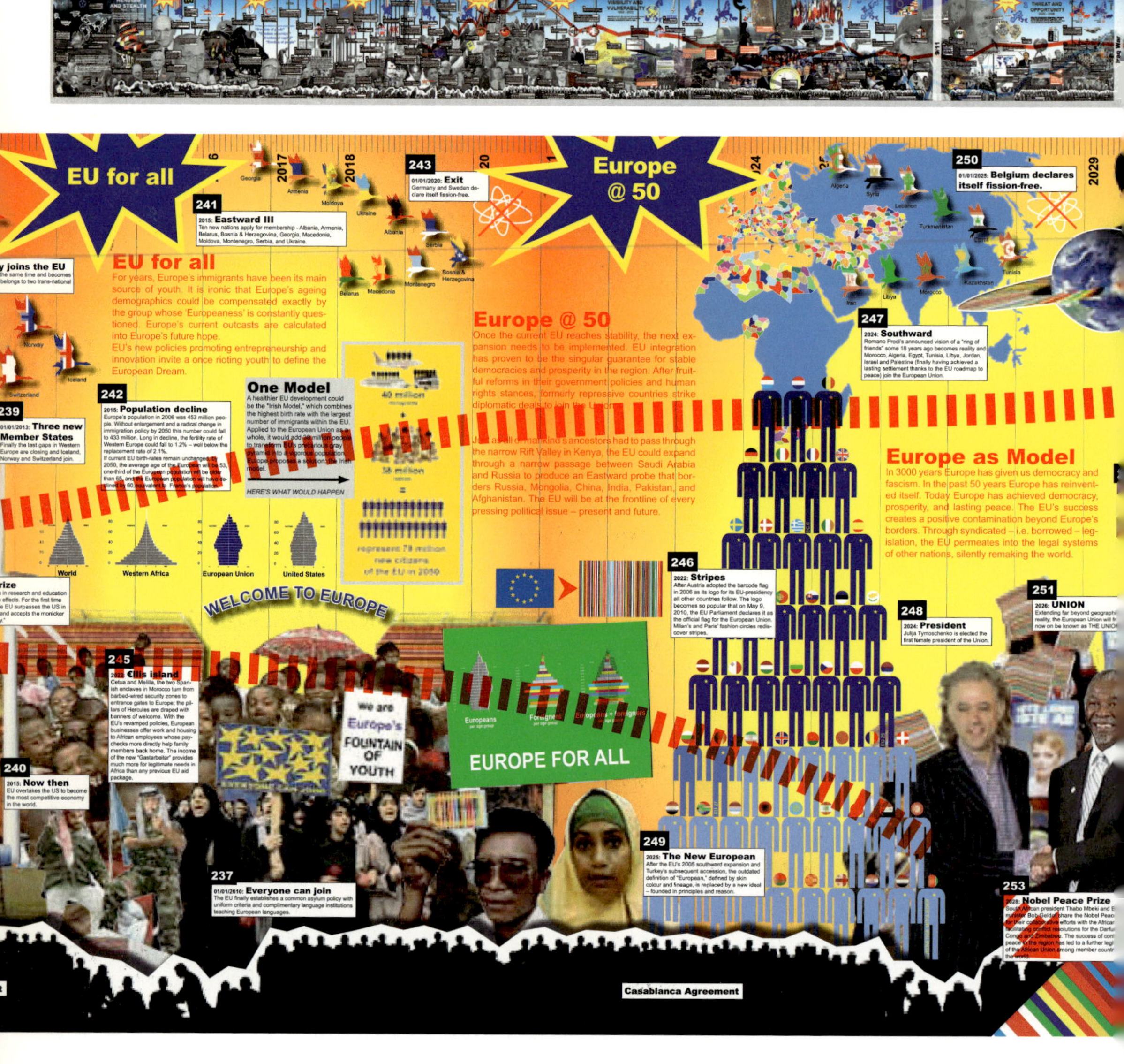

EU for all
2017
2018
20
2029
Georgia
Armenia
Moldova
Ukraine
Albania
Serbia
Belarus
Macedonia
Montenegro
Bosnia & Herzegovina
241
2015: Eastward III
Ten new nations apply for membership - Albania, Armenia, Belarus, Bosnia & Herzegovina, Georgia, Macedonia, Moldova, Montenegro, Serbia, and Ukraine.
243
01/01/2020: Exit
Germany and Sweden declare itself fission-free.
Europe @ 50
250
01/01/2025: Belgium declares itself fission-free.
Algeria
Syria
Lebanon
Turkmenistan
Iran
Libya
Morocco
Kazakhstan
Tunisia
y joins the EU
the same time and becomes
belongs to two trans-national
Norway
Iceland
Switzerland
EU for all
For years, Europe's immigrants have been its main source of youth. It is ironic that Europe's ageing demographics could be compensated exactly by the group whose 'Europeaness' is constantly questioned. Europe's current outcasts are calculated into Europe's future hope.
EU's new policies promoting entrepreneurship and innovation invite a once rioting youth to define the European Dream.
Europe @ 50
Once the current EU reaches stability, the next expansion needs to be implemented. EU integration has proven to be the singular guarantee for stable democracies and prosperity in the region. After fruitful reforms in their government policies and human rights stances, formerly repressive countries strike diplomatic deals to join the Union.
the narrow Rift Valley in Kenya, the EU could expand through a narrow passage between Saudi Arabia and Russia to produce an Eastward probe that borders Russia, Mongolia, China, India, Pakistan, and Afghanistan. The EU will be at the frontline of every pressing political issue – present and future.
247
2024: Southward
Romano Prodi's announced vision of a "ring of friends" some 18 years ago becomes reality and Morocco, Algeria, Egypt, Tunisia, Libya, Jordan, Israel and Palestine (finally having achieved a lasting settlement thanks to the EU roadmap to peace) join the European Union.
239
01/01/2013: Three new Member States
Finally the last gaps in Western Europe are closing and Iceland, Norway and Switzerland join.
242
2015: Population decline
Europe's population in 2006 was 453 million people. Without enlargement and a radical change in immigration policy by 2050 this number could fall to 433 million. Long in decline, the fertility rate of Western Europe could fall to 1.2% -- well below the replacement rate of 2.1%.
One Model
A healthier EU development could be the "Irish Model," which combines the highest birth rate with the largest number of immigrants within the EU.
HERE'S WHAT WOULD HAPPEN
40 million
58 million
Europe as Model
In 3000 years Europe has given us democracy and fascism. In the past 50 years Europe has reinvented itself. Today Europe has achieved democracy, prosperity, and lasting peace. The EU's success creates a positive contamination beyond Europe's borders. Through syndicated – i.e. borrowed – legislation, the EU permeates into the legal systems of other nations, silently remaking the world.
World
Western Africa
European Union
United States
rize
s in research and education
effects. For the first time
e EU surpasses the US in
and accepts the monicker
246
2022: Stripes
After Austria adopted the barcode flag in 2006 as its logo for its EU-presidency all other countries follow. The logo becomes so popular that on May 9, 2010, the EU Parliament declares it as the official flag for the European Union. Milan's and Paris' fashion circles rediscover stripes.
248
2024: President
Julija Tymoschenko is elected the first female president of the Union.
251
2026: UNION
Extending far beyond geographi
reality, the European Union will fr
now on be known as THE UNIO
WELCOME TO EUROPE
245
2022: €llis island
Cetua and Melilla, the two Spanish enclaves in Morocco turn from barbed-wired security zones to entrance gates to Europe; the pillars of Hercules are draped with banners of welcome. With the EU's revamped policies, European businesses offer work and housing to African employees whose paychecks more directly help family members back home. The income of the new "Gastarbeiter" provides much more for legitimate needs in Africa than any previous EU aid package.
we are
Europe's
FOUNTAIN OF YOUTH
Europeans
Foreigners
Europeans + foreigners
EUROPE FOR ALL
240
2015: Now then
EU overtakes the US to become the most competitive economy in the world.
237
01/01/2010: Everyone can join
The EU finally establishes a common asylum policy with uniform criteria and complimentary language institutions teaching European languages.
249
2025: The New European
After the EU's 2005 southward expansion and Turkey's subsequent accession, the outdated definition of "European," defined by skin colour and lineage, is replaced by a new ideal – founded in principles and reason.
253
2028: Nobel Peace Prize
Casablanca Agreement

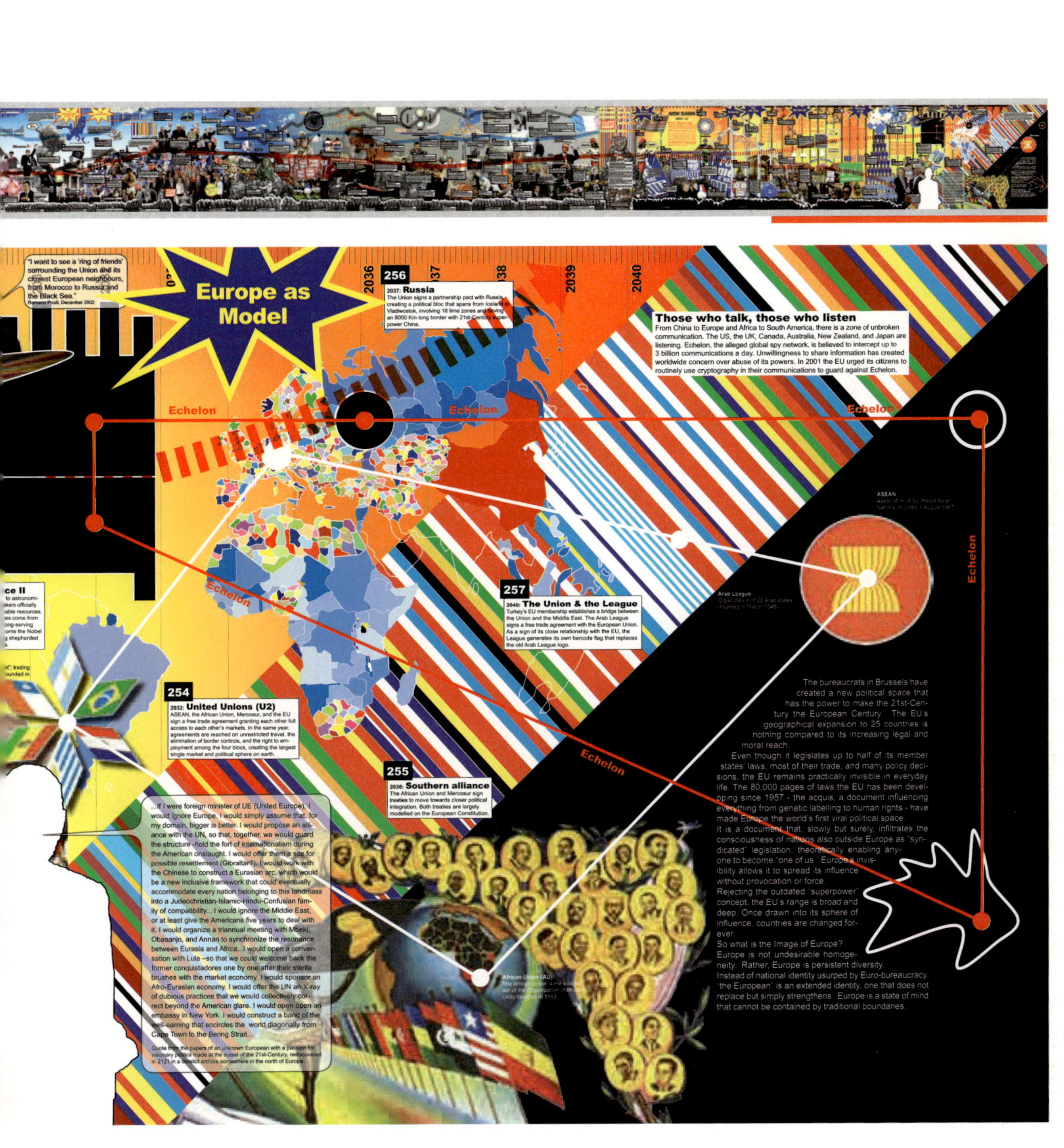

"I want to see a 'ring of friends' surrounding the Union and its closest European neighbours, from Morocco to Russia and the Black Sea."
Romano Prodi, December 2002
Europe as Model
2036
2037
2038
2039
2040
256
2037: Russia
The Union signs a partnership pact with Russia, creating a political bloc that spans from Iceland to Vladiwostok, involving 18 time zones and having an 8000 Km long border with 21st-Century super-power China.
Those who talk, those who listen
From China to Europe and Africa to South America, there is a zone of unbroken communication. The US, the UK, Canada, Australia, New Zealand, and Japan are listening. Echelon, the alleged global spy network, is believed to intercept up to 3 billion communications a day. Unwillingness to share information has created worldwide concern over abuse of its powers. In 2001 the EU urged its citizens to routinely use cryptography in their communications to guard against Echelon.
Echelon
Echelon
Echelon
Echelon
Echelon
Echelon
ASEAN
Arab League
257
2040: The Union & the League
Turkey's EU membership establishes a bridge between the Union and the Middle East. The Arab League signs a free trade agreement with the European Union. As a sign of its close relationship with the EU, the League generates its own barcode flag that replaces the old Arab League logo.
254
2032: United Unions (U2)
ASEAN, the African Union, Mercosur, and the EU sign a free trade agreement granting each other full access to each other's markets. In the same year, agreements are reached on unrestricted travel, the elimination of border controls, and the right to employment among the four blocs, creating the largest single market and political sphere on earth.
255
2036: Southern alliance
The African Union and Mercosur sign treaties to move towards closer political integration. Both treaties are largely modelled on the European Constitution.
...If I were foreign minister of UE (United Europe), I would ignore Europe. I would simply assume that, for my domain, bigger is better. I would propose an alliance with the UN, so that, together, we would guard the structure -hold the fort of internationalism during the American onslaught. I would offer them a site for possible resettlement (Gibraltar?). I would work with the Chinese to construct a Eurasian arc, which would be a new inclusive framework that could eventually accommodate every nation belonging to this landmass into a Judeochristian-Islamic-Hindu-Confusian family of compatibility... I would ignore the Middle East, or at least give the Americans five years to deal with it. I would organize a triannual meeting with Mbeki, Obasanjo, and Annan to synchronize the resonance between Eurasia and Africa...I would open a conversation with Lula –so that we could welcome back the former conquistadores one by one after their sterile brushes with the market economy. I would sponsor an Afro-Eurasian economy. I would offer the UN an X-ray of dubious practices that we would collectively correct beyond the American glare. I would open open an embassy in New York. I would construct a band of the well-earning that encircles the world diagonally from Cape Town to the Bering Strait...
Quote from the papers of an unknown European with a passion for visionary politics made at the outset of the 21st-Century, rediscovered in 2121 in a derelict archive somewhere in the north of Europe.
African Union (AU)
The bureaucrats in Brussels have created a new political space that has the power to make the 21st-Century the European Century. The EU's geographical expansion to 25 countries is nothing compared to its increasing legal and moral reach.
Even though it legislates up to half of its member states' laws, most of their trade, and many policy decisions, the EU remains practically invisible in everyday life. The 80,000 pages of laws the EU has been developing since 1957 - the acquis, a document influencing everything from genetic labelling to human rights - have made Europe the world's first viral political space.
It is a document that, slowly but surely, infiltrates the consciousness of nations also outside Europe as "syndicated" legislation, theoretically enabling anyone to become "one of us." Europe's invisibility allows it to spread its influence without provocation or force.
Rejecting the outdated "superpower" concept, the EU's range is broad and deep. Once drawn into its sphere of influence, countries are changed forever.
So what is the Image of Europe?
Europe is not undesirable homogeneity. Rather, Europe is persistent diversity.
Instead of national identity usurped by Euro-bureaucracy, "the European" is an extended identity, one that does not replace but simply strengthens. Europe is a state of mind that cannot be contained by traditional boundaries.

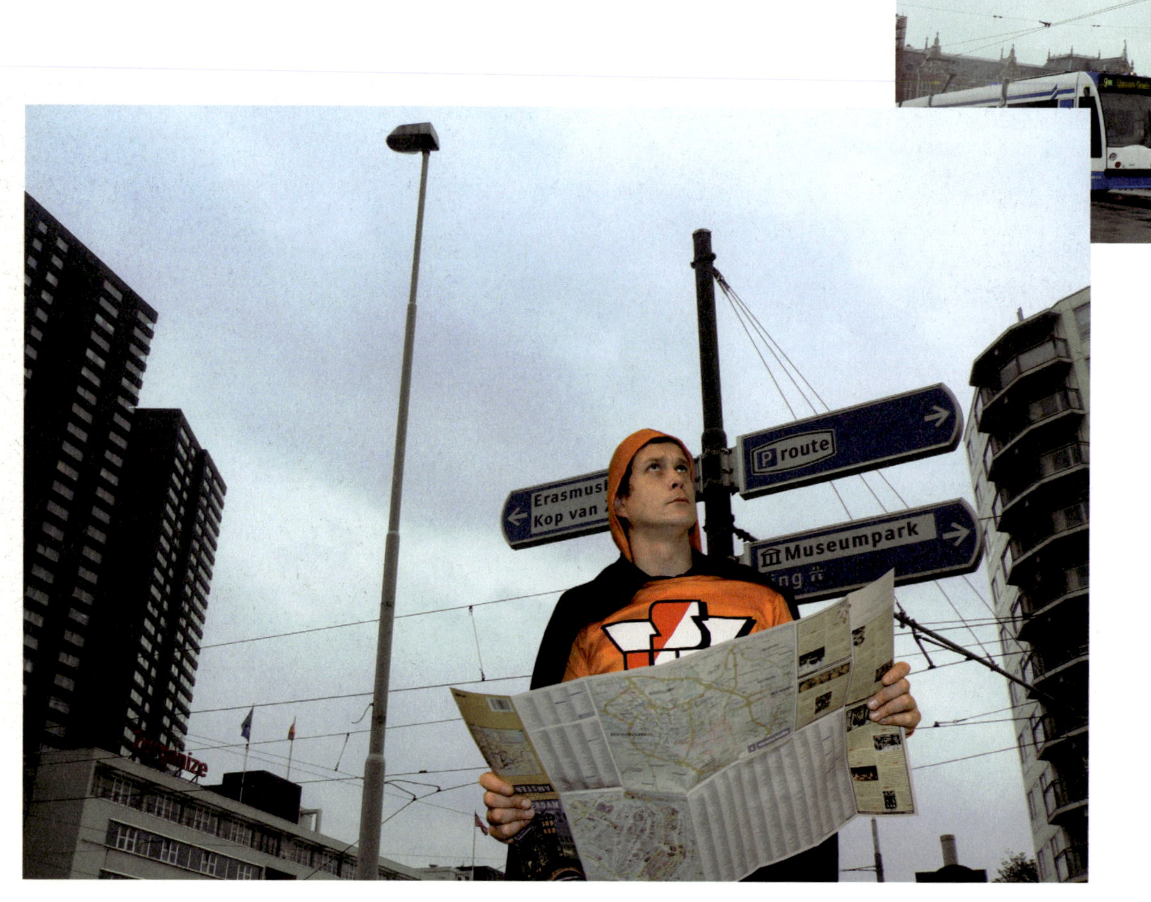
P route
Museumpark

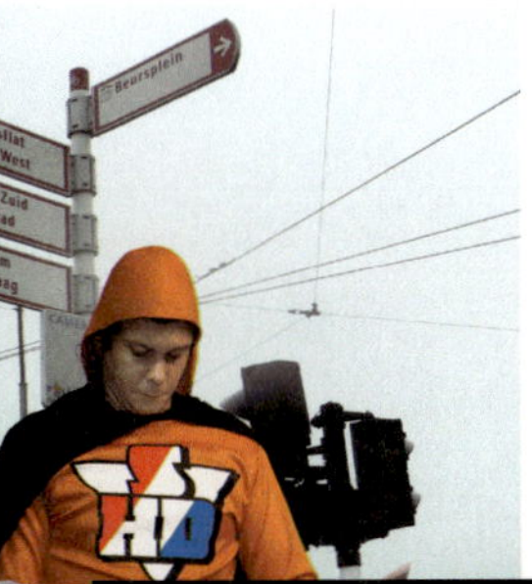

MUZIEK UIT HET LAB
MUZIEKLAB BRABANT
PARADOX - TILBURG, DO. 8 JAN. /
DO. 12 FEB. / DO. 11 MRT. / DO. 8 APR. /
DO. 13 MEI
HET MUZIEKCENTRUM -
'S-HERTOGENBOSCH,

Instruction Manual

MLB
by Hans Gremmen

LPCD 2004
by Hans Gremmen

KaAp Generale Posters
by Werkplaats Typografie

Corporate Identity
by Lesley Moore

Volksuniversiteit
by Ping-pong Design

GOG e-cards
by Atelier van GOG

ourmachine.com
by Machine

Digital Depot
by Lust

The Murder Game
by Studio Kluif

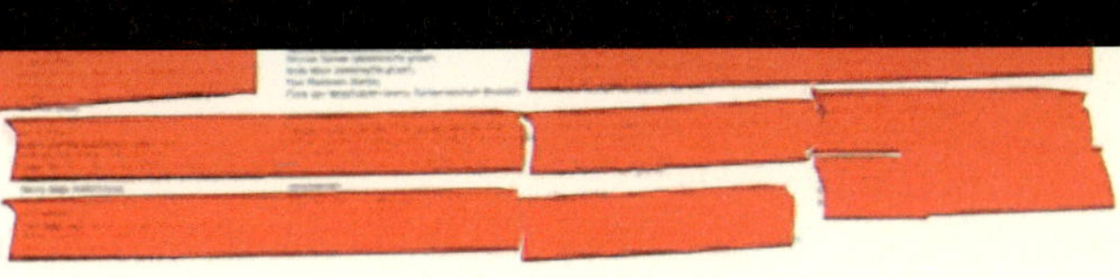

MLB

by Hans Gremmen

The posters I made for Muzieklab Brabant used everyday techniques ‹out of context›. Also a simple grid was the start for now patterns.
I made a poster with the programme of events for the whole year, using four colours of tape (one for each location) to screen out the information that was not relevant to a particular event.

MUZIEK UIT HET LAB 2004
MUZIEKLAB BRABANT
PARADOX - TILBURG, DO. 8 JAN./
DO. 12 FEB./DO. 11 MRT./DO. 8 APR./
DO. 13 MEI
HET MUZIEKCENTRUM -
'S-HERTOGENBOSCH, DI. 13 JAN./
DI. 3 FEB./DI. 2 MRT./DI. 27 APR./
DI. 25 MEI
ZESDE KOLONNE - EINDHOVEN,
WO. 14 JAN./WO. 1 FEB./WO. 10 MRT./
WO. 14 APR/WO. 12 MEI
LOKAAL 01 - BREDA, VR. 13 FEB./
VR. 12 MRT./VR. 16 APR./VR. 14 MEI
20:30 UUR/21:00 UUR/21:30 UUR
TOEGANG GRATIS/TOEGANG:
5 EURO, STUDENTEN & CJP 2,50 EURO

ML B

MUZIEK UIT
MUZIEKLAB B
LOKAAL 01 -
20:30 UUR/
T
5 EURO, STU

2004

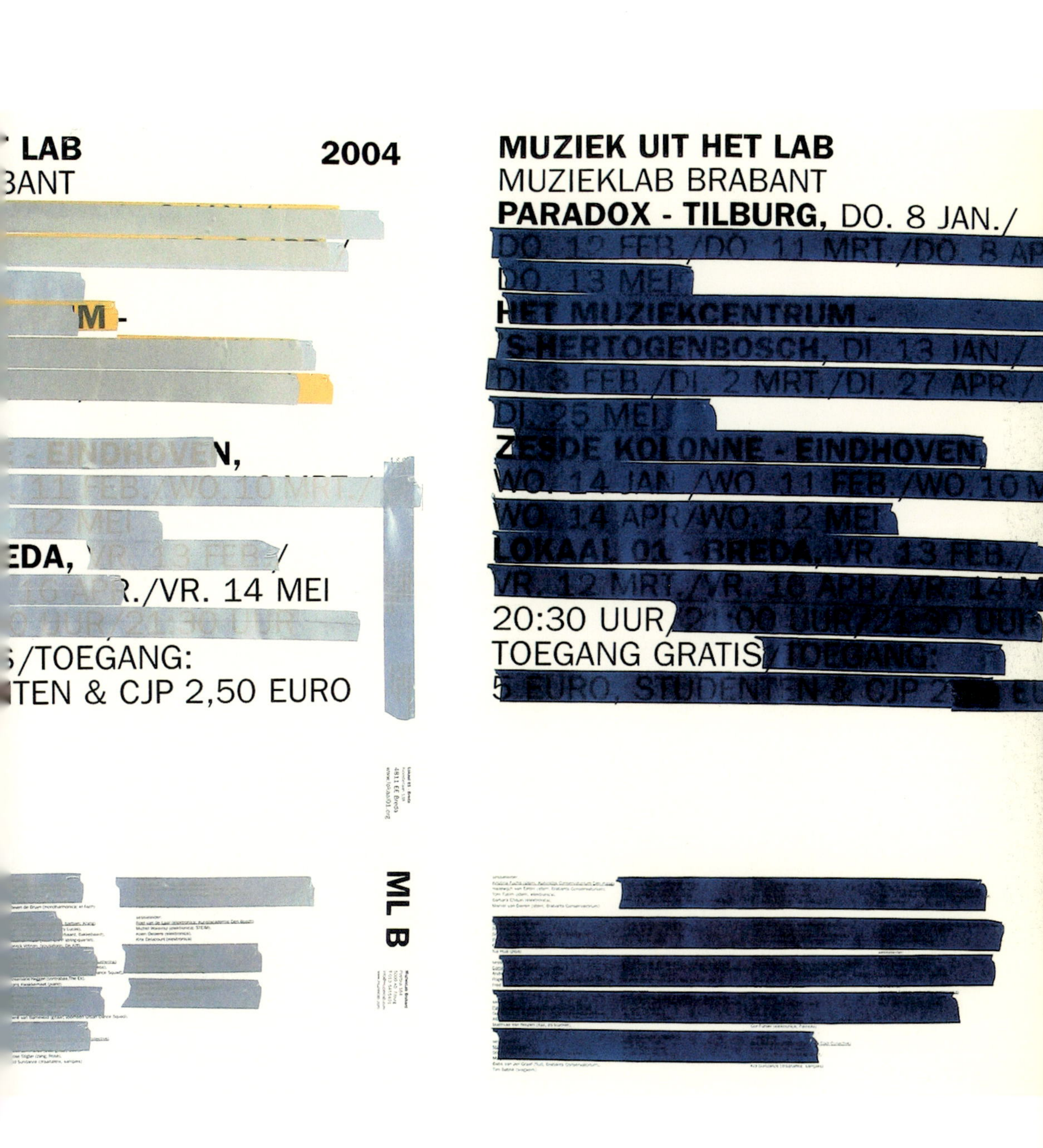

LAB
BANT
2004
EDA,
R./VR. 14 MEI
/TOEGANG:
TEN & CJP 2,50 EURO
ML B
MUZIEK UIT HET LAB
MUZIEKLAB BRABANT
PARADOX - TILBURG, DO. 8 JAN./
20:30 UUR/
TOEGANG GRATIS/

LPCD 2004

by Hans Gremmen

I like to use existing techniques and systems that everybody is familiar with. Printing in full colour is a normal thing to do, but if you adjust the layers of the Cyan, Magenta, Yellow and Black (as I did with Iris Bouwmeester) then a whole new field of possibilities opens up. The same thing happens when you change the context of the technique or the materials. When I looked at the inner sleeves of a 12-inch record and folded it twice it became a perfect cover for a CD. I also developed a system of printing endless colour combinations by using only one screen in silk-screening. By rotating the paper you have four different ways of overprinting without changing colour. If you add the possibility of changing colour, the combinations are endless.

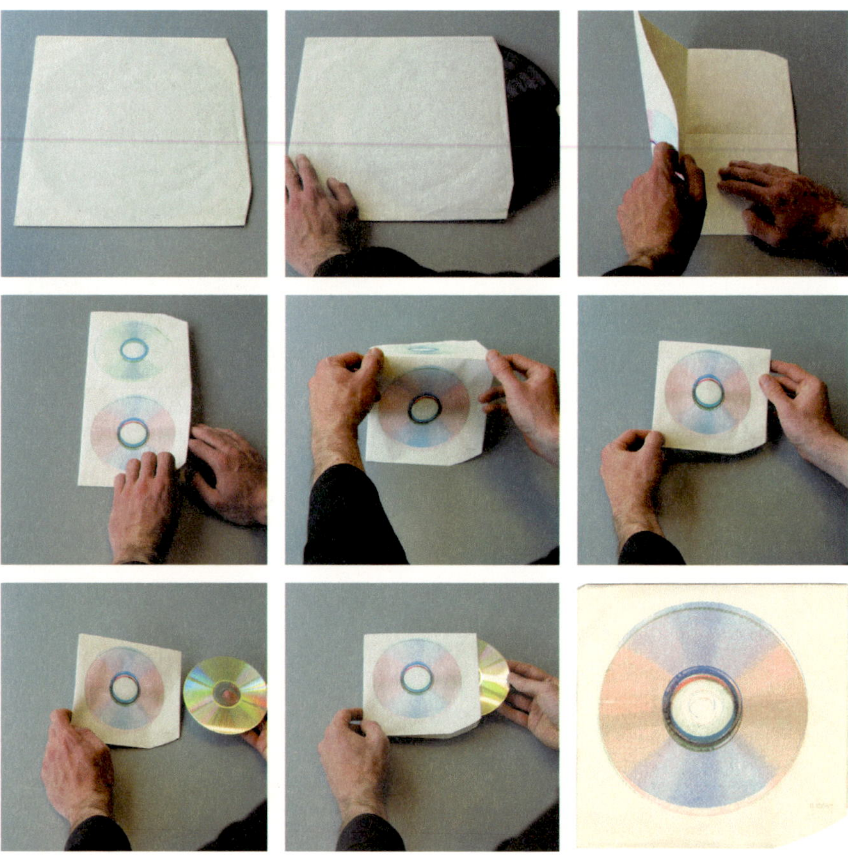

KaAp Generale Posters
by Jaap Kroneman / Werkplaats Typografie

‹KaAp›, now called ‹dAcapo-ArtEZ›, organizes general-interest lectures and interdisciplinary activities. It also initiates publications dealing with new developments in the arts, science and society. The first poster was produced as the calendar for the yearly listing all the activities. Further information was printed on top of this first poster to announce different activities during the year.

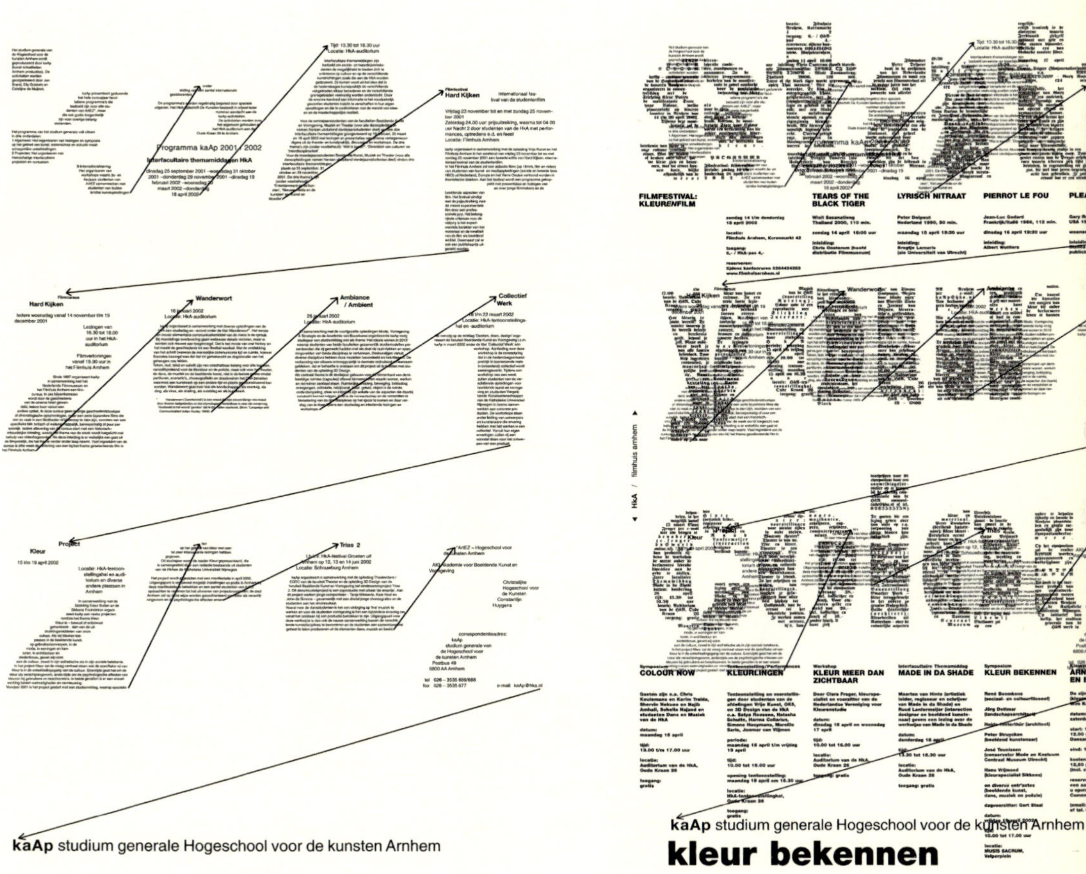

for dAcapo-ArtEZ (KaAp), series of 5 posters, 594 x 841 mm each, 2002

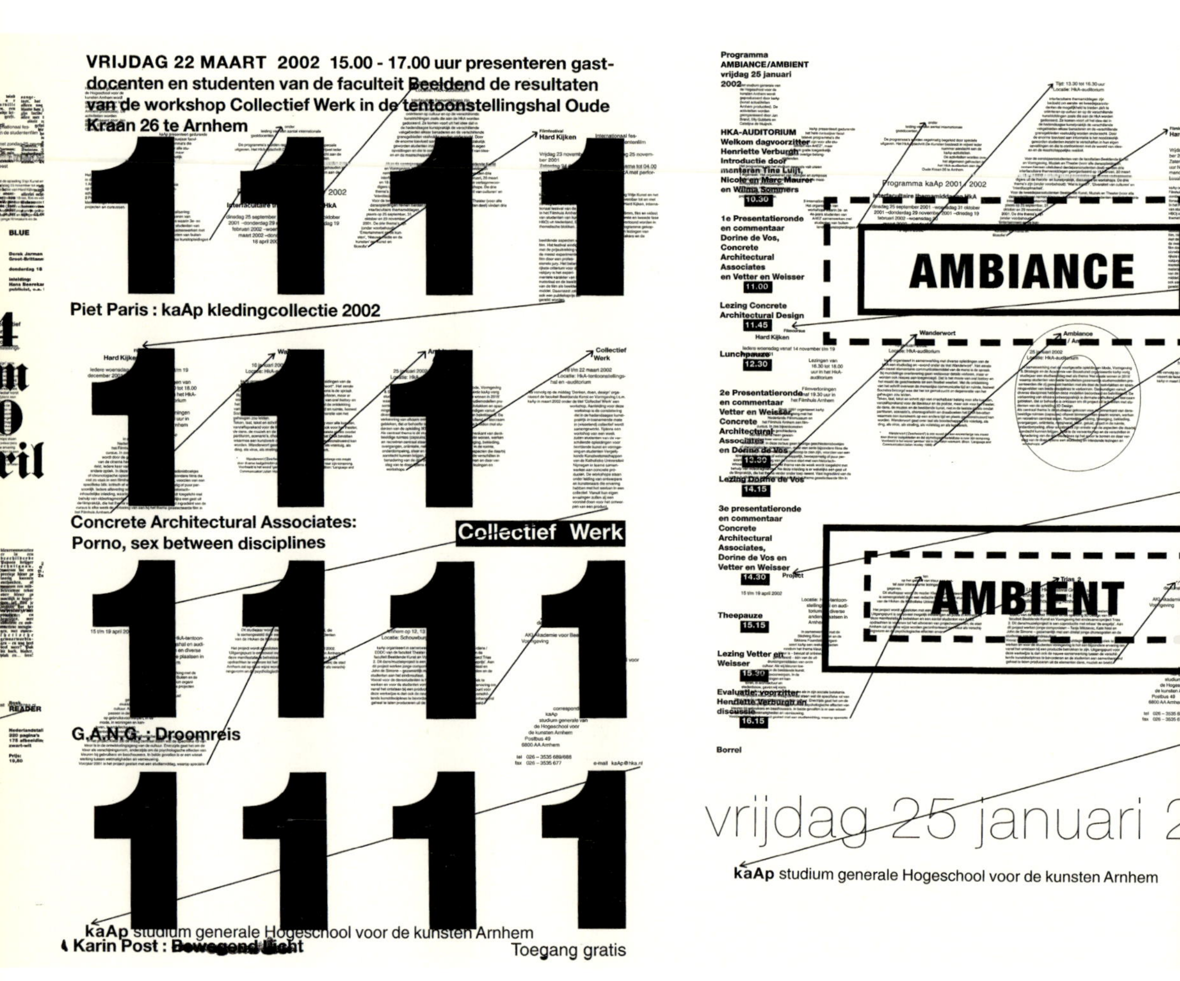

VRIJDAG 22 MAART 2002 15.00 - 17.00 uur presenteren gastdocenten en studenten van de faculteit Beeldend de resultaten van de workshop Collectief Werk in de tentoonstellingshal Oude Kraan 26 te Arnhem
Piet Paris : kaAp kledingcollectie 2002
Concrete Architectural Associates: Porno, sex between disciplines
Collectief Werk
G.A.N.G. : Droomreis
kaAp studium generale Hogeschool voor de kunsten Arnhem
Karin Post : Bewegend licht
Toegang gratis
Programma AMBIANCE/AMBIENT vrijdag 25 januari 2002
HKA-AUDITORIUM Welkom dagvoorzitter Henriette Verburgh Introductie door mentoren Tine Luijt, Nicole en Marc Maurer en Wilma Sommers
10.30
1e Presentatieronde en commentaar Dorine de Vos, Concrete Architectural Associates en Vetter en Weisser
11.00
Lezing Concrete Architectural Design
11.45
Lunchpauze
12.30
2e Presentatieronde en commentaar Vetter en Weisser, Concrete Architectural Associates en Dorine de Vos
13.30
Lezing Dorine de Vos
14.15
3e presentatieronde en commentaar Concrete Architectural Associates, Dorine de Vos en Vetter en Weisser
14.30
Theepauze
15.15
Lezing Vetter en Weisser
15.30
Evaluatie: voorzitter Henriette Verburgh en discussie
16.15
Borrel
AMBIANCE
AMBIENT
vrijdag 25 januari 2
kaAp studium generale Hogeschool voor de kunsten Arnhem

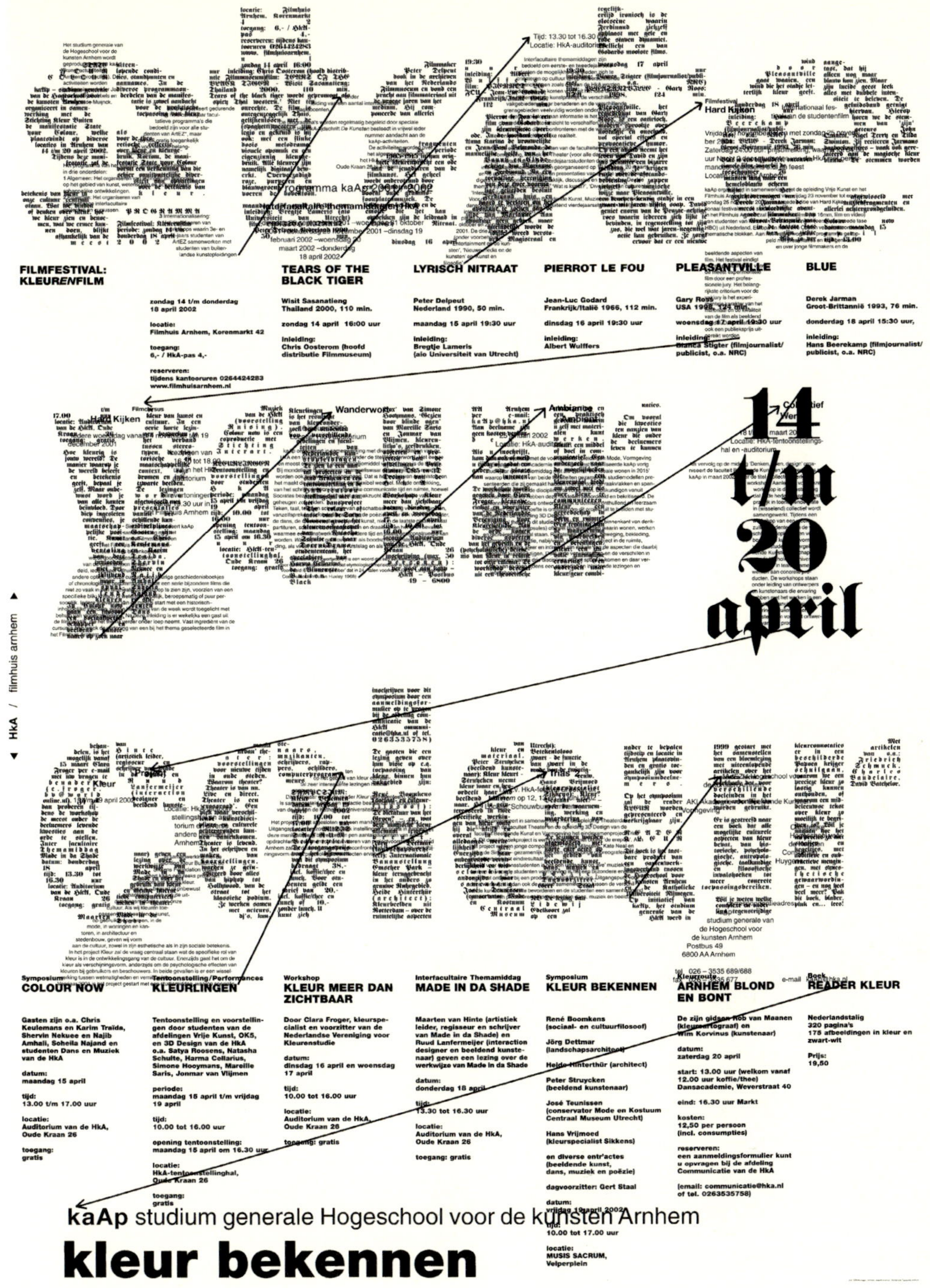

kaAp studium generale Hogeschool voor de kunsten Arnhem

kleur bekennen

 Lesley Moore Corporate Identity
Logo's created by visitors to www.lesley-moore.nl

Our corporate identity is based on the notion that the identity of a small graphic design studio can be fundamentally different from that of a big commercial company. Its power lies not in the repetition of a strictly defined identity, but rather in diversity. This led to the idea of a corporate identity that was constantly changing.

The Lesley Moore logos are created by visitors to our website, www.lesley-moore.nl. Anyone –friends, family, colleagues, clients and others– can create a logo and thus make their own contribution to Lesley Moore's corporate identity. A palette consisting of basic graphic forms and the Lesley Moore initials ‹L› and ‹M› provide the ingredients for the logos. All the logos are stored in a logobank; since the first logo was created in August 2004 more than a 1000 logos have now been contributed. The logos are printed on stickers and added to our pre-printed stationery. Every single logo –good or bad– will be used once, giving Lesley Moore its identity at that specific moment.

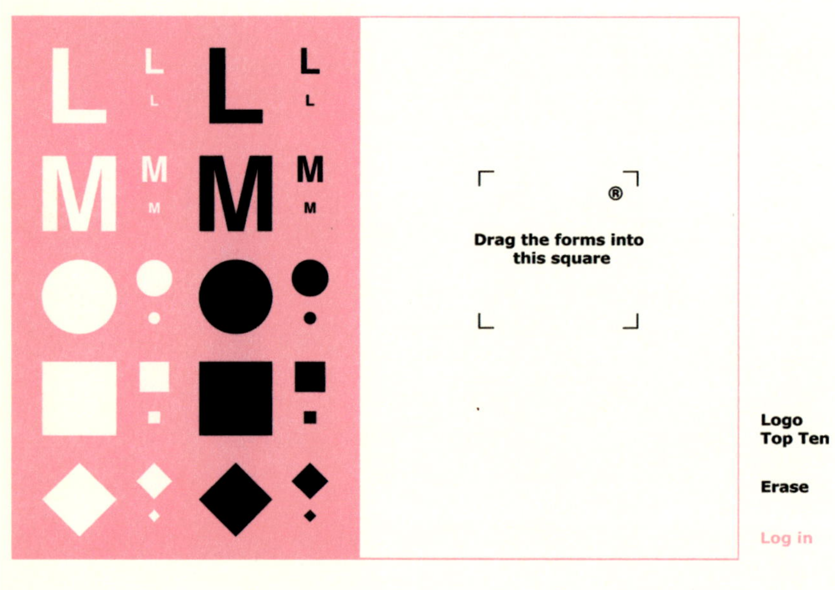

www.lesley-moore.nl

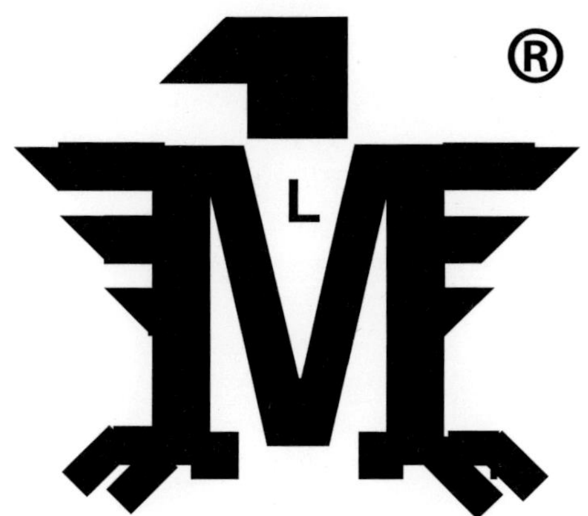
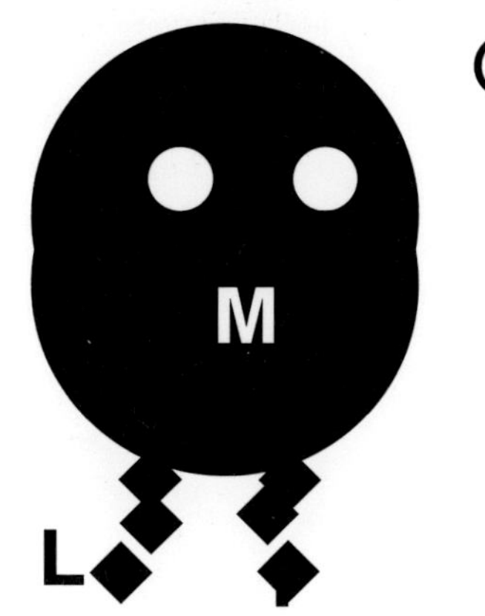
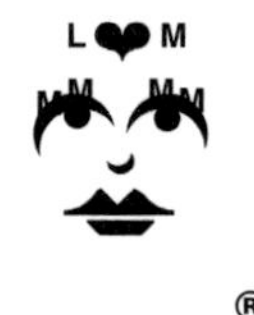
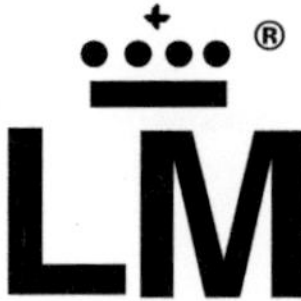
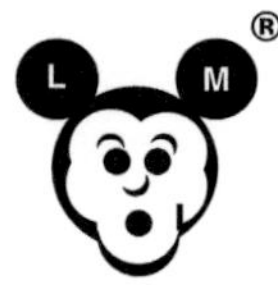

FUCK
BUSH
VOTE
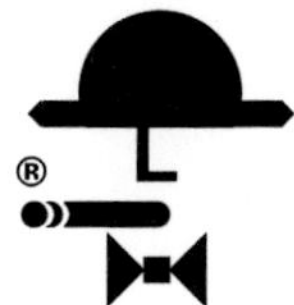
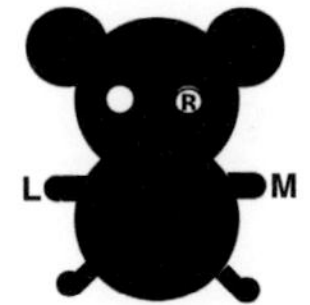
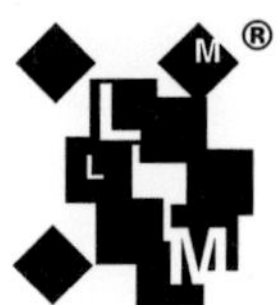
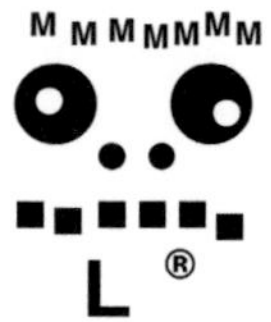
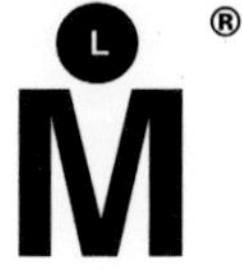
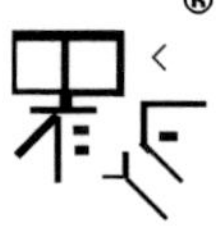
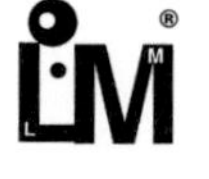
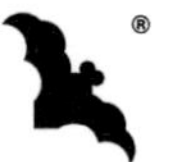

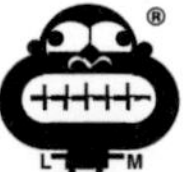
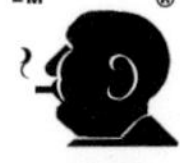
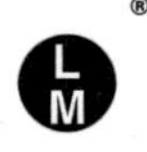
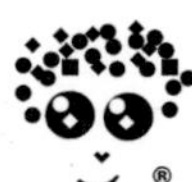
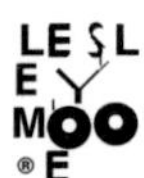
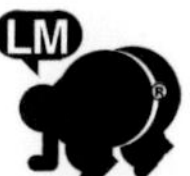
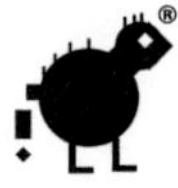
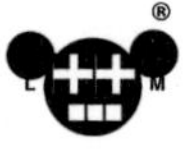
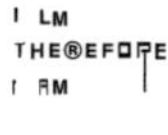
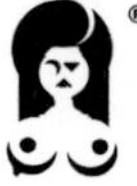
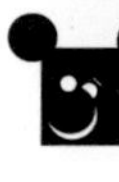

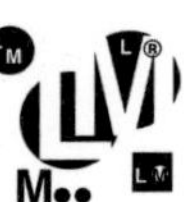
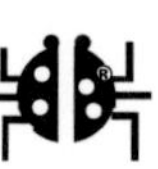

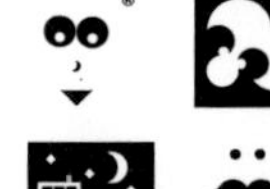

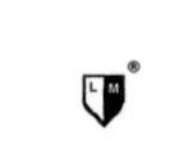
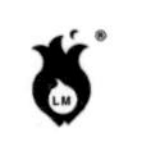
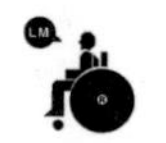
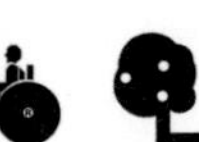
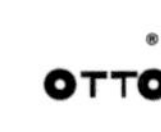
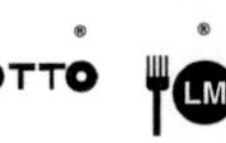
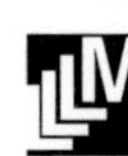
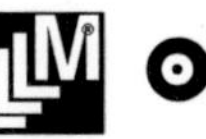
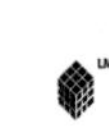
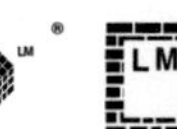
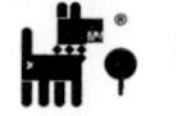
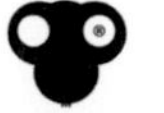
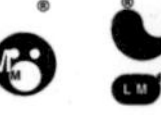
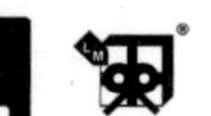
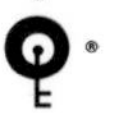

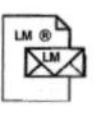

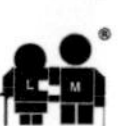
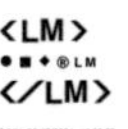

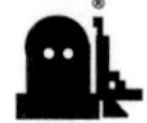
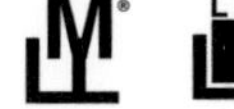
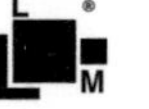
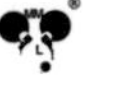

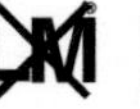
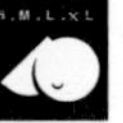
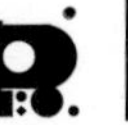
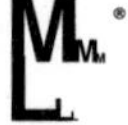
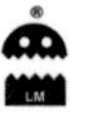
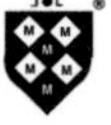
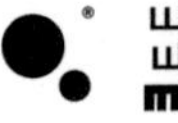
WE
WANT
MORE

Volksuniversiteit

by Ping-pong Design

Unity through diversity. A logo system satisfies the collective needs of the alliance and the idiosyncratic needs of more than 100 universities. A database with over 200 clipart icons enables each institution to compose its own logotype.

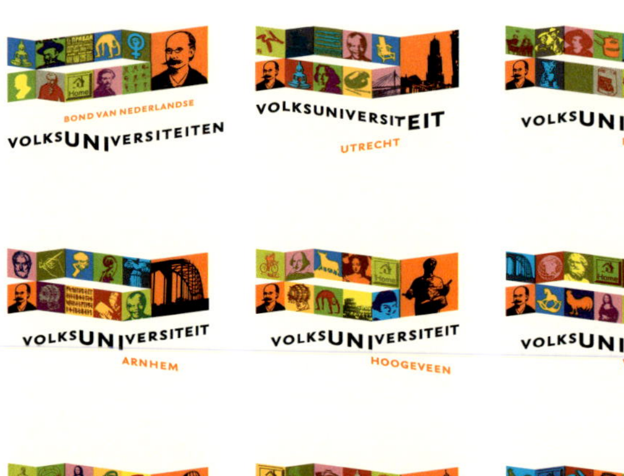

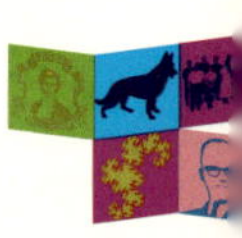

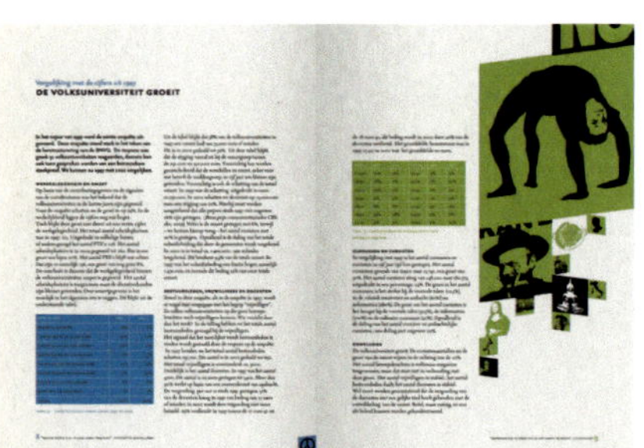

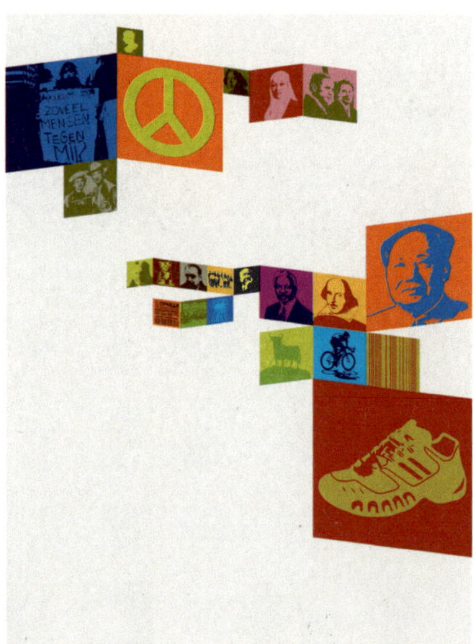

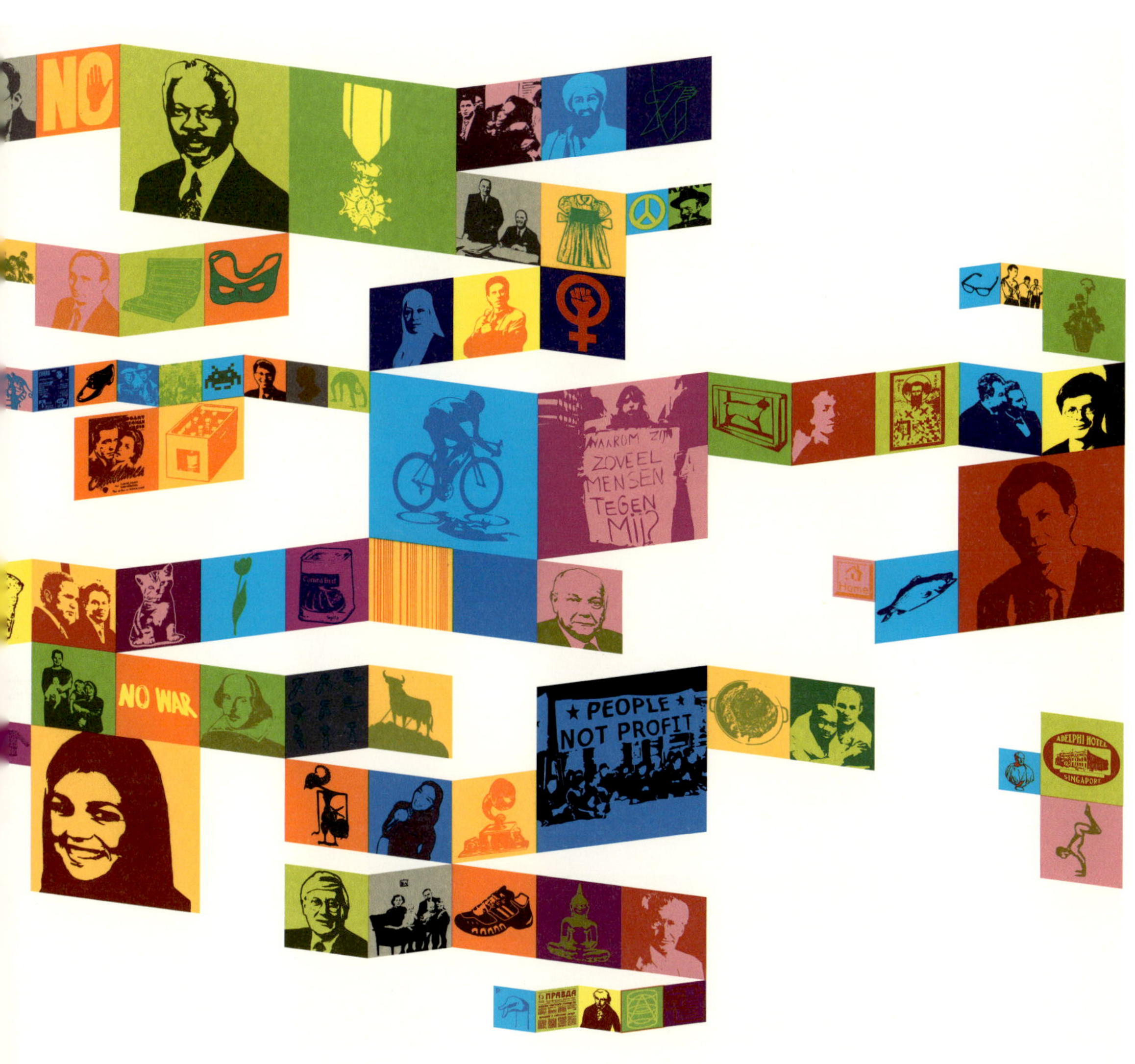
NO
WAAROM ZIJN ZOVEEL MENSEN TEGEN MIJ?
NO WAR
PEOPLE NOT PROFIT
ADELPHI HOTEL
SINGAPORE
ПРАВДА

GOG e-cards
by Atelier van GOG

Our e-cards machine makes actually ‹Me-cards›: you design them yourself at www.ateliervangog.nl/e-cards.

2007

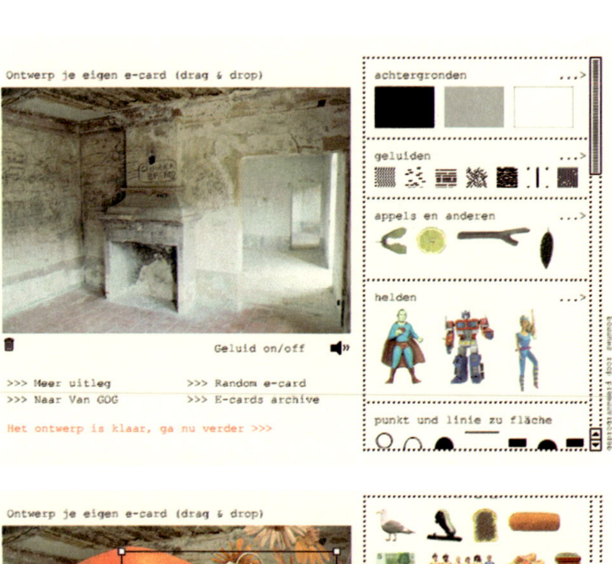

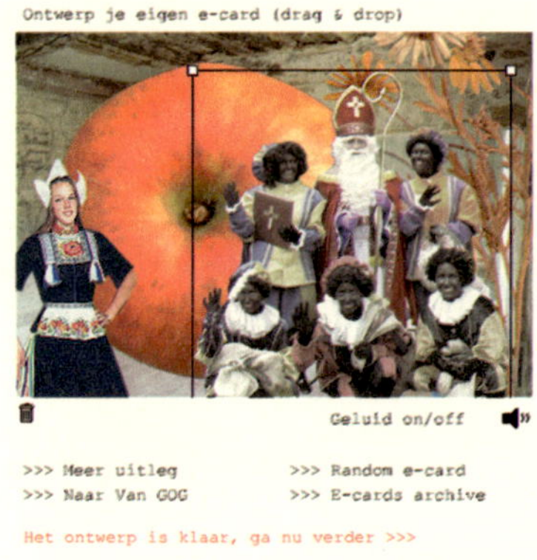

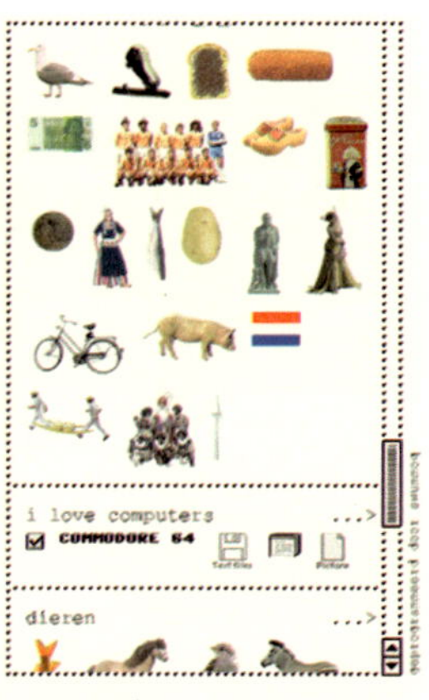

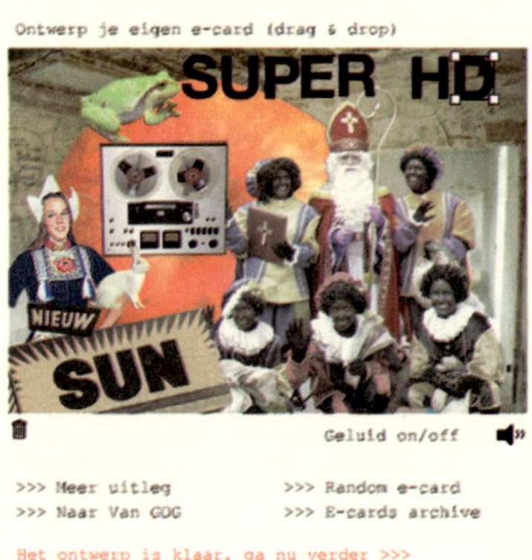

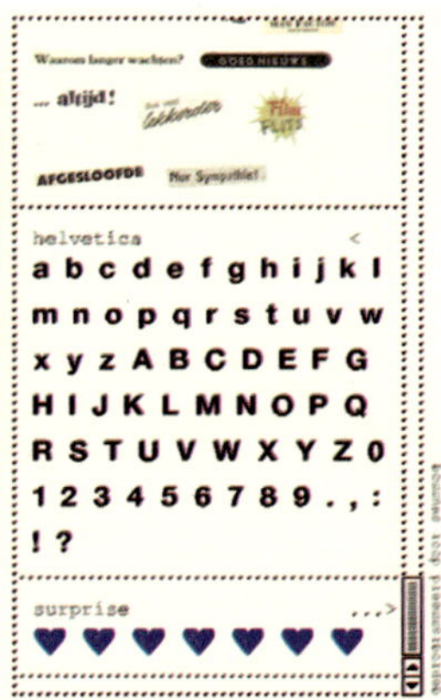

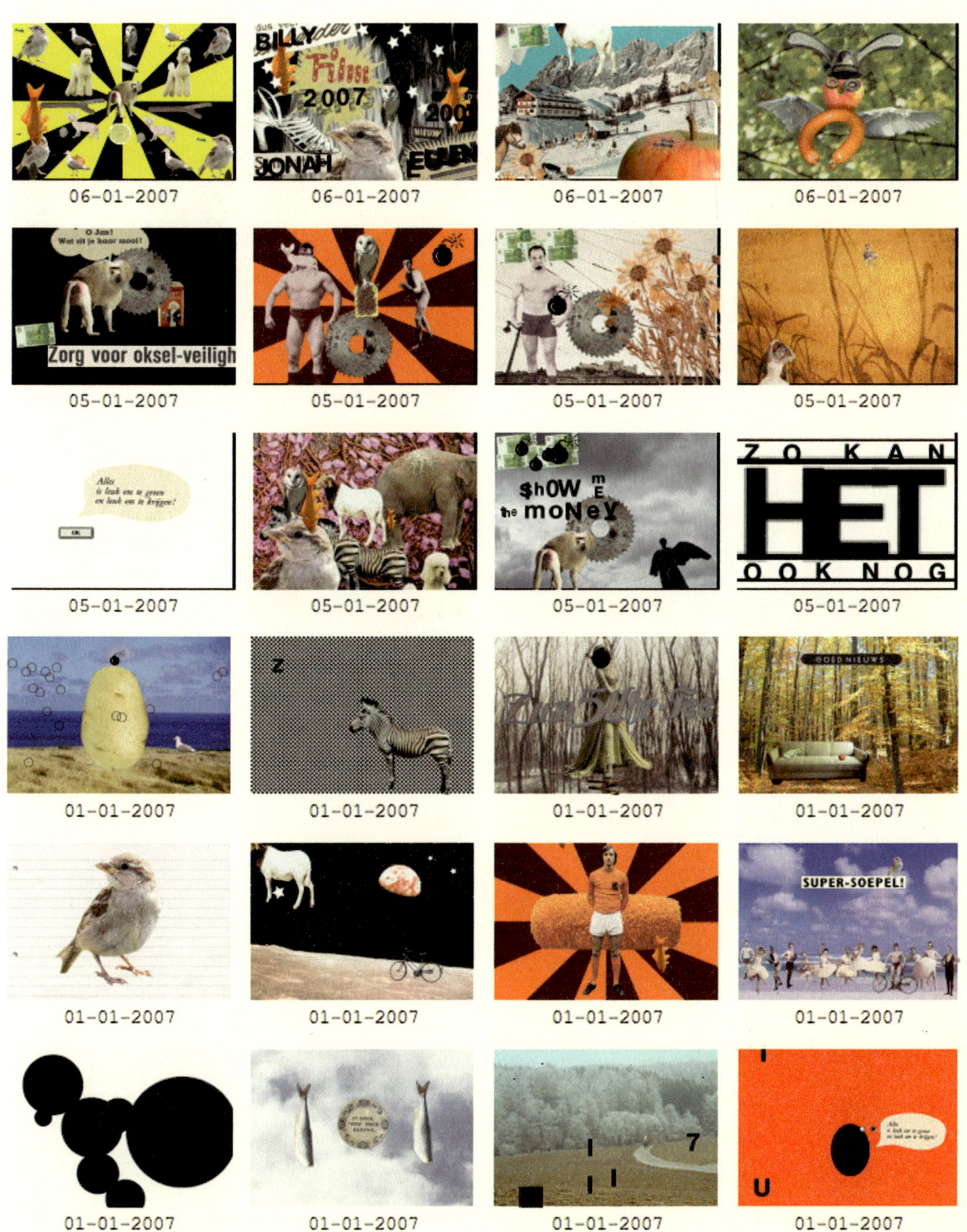
BILLY
2007
JONAH
06-01-2007
06-01-2007
06-01-2007
06-01-2007
Zorg voor oksel-veiligh
05-01-2007
05-01-2007
05-01-2007
05-01-2007
OK
$hOW mE the moNey
ZO KAN
HET
OOK NOG
05-01-2007
05-01-2007
05-01-2007
05-01-2007
Z
GOED NIEUWS
01-01-2007
01-01-2007
01-01-2007
01-01-2007
SUPER-SOEPEL!
01-01-2007
01-01-2007
01-01-2007
01-01-2007
7
U
01-01-2007
01-01-2007
01-01-2007
01-01-2007

 www.ourmachine.com
by Machine

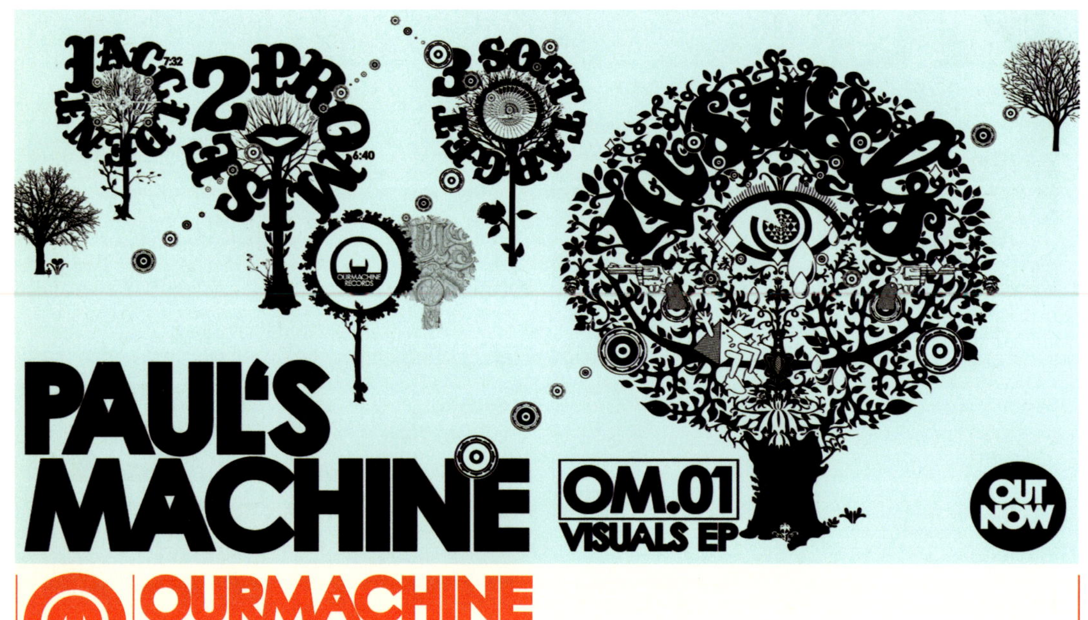

for OurMachine Records, 2001–now

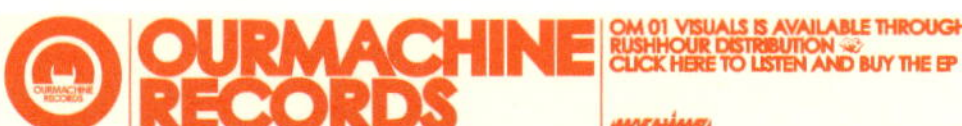

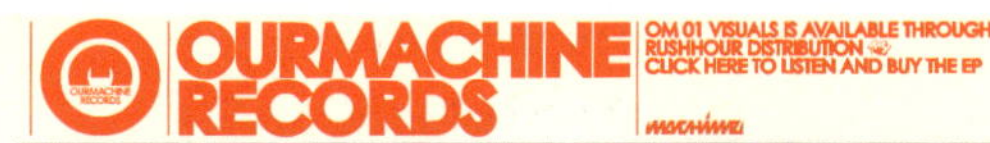

TO OPERATE THE TREEQUENCER: USE KEYS 1-6 FOR THE BEAT | USE KEYS Q-P FOR SYNTHS | USE KEYS A-J FOR VOCALS

CLICK TO PLAY

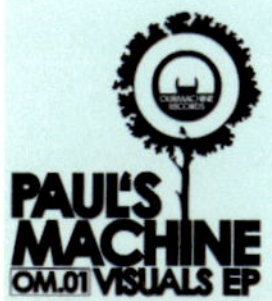

PAUL'S MACHINE
OM.01 VISUALS EP

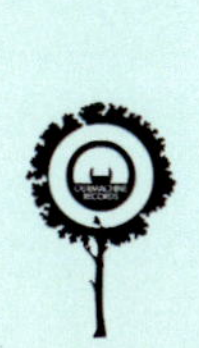

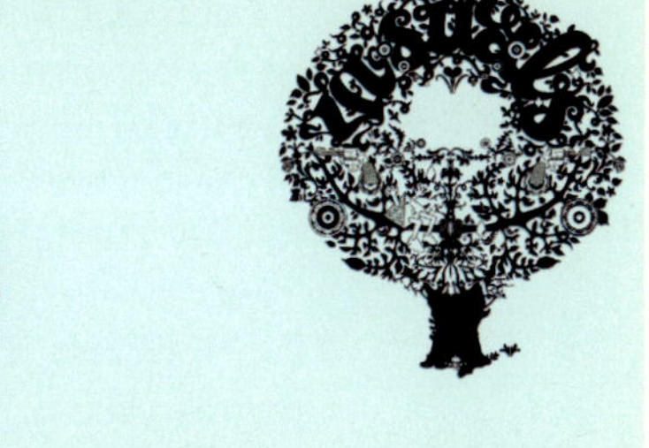

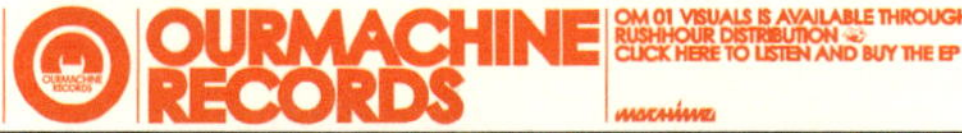

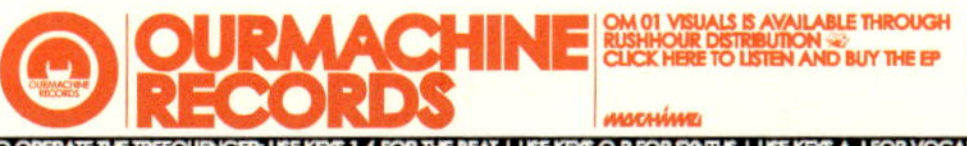

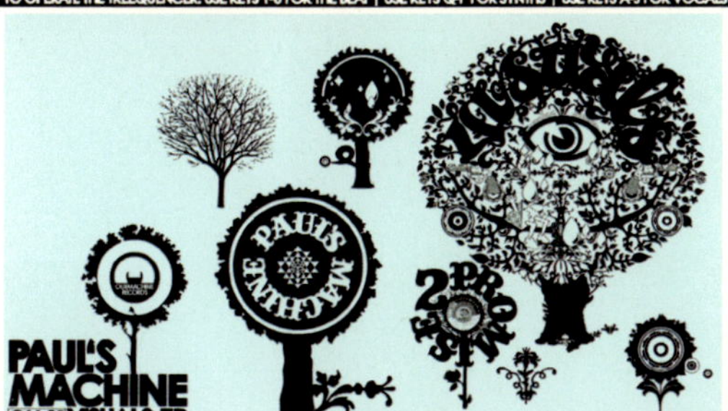

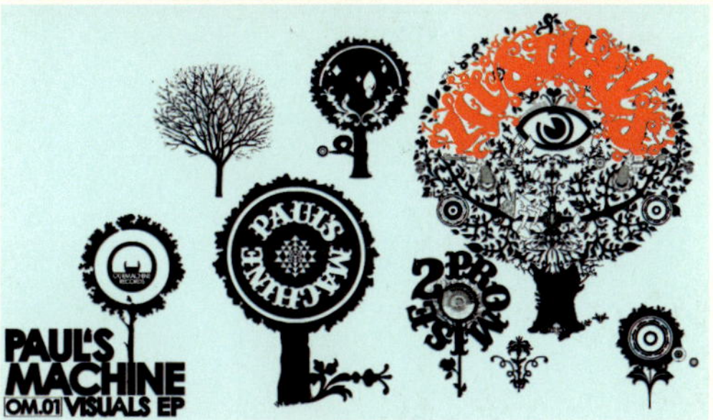

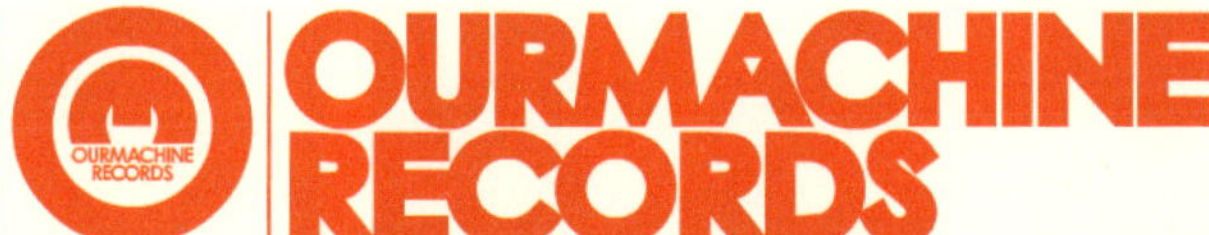

OM 01 VISUALS IS AVAILABLE THROUGH
RUSHHOUR DISTRIBUTION
CLICK HERE TO LISTEN AND BUY THE EP

TO OPERATE THE TREEQUENCER: USE KEYS 1-6 FOR THE BEAT | USE KEYS Q-P FOR SYNTHS | USE KEYS A-J FOR VOCALS

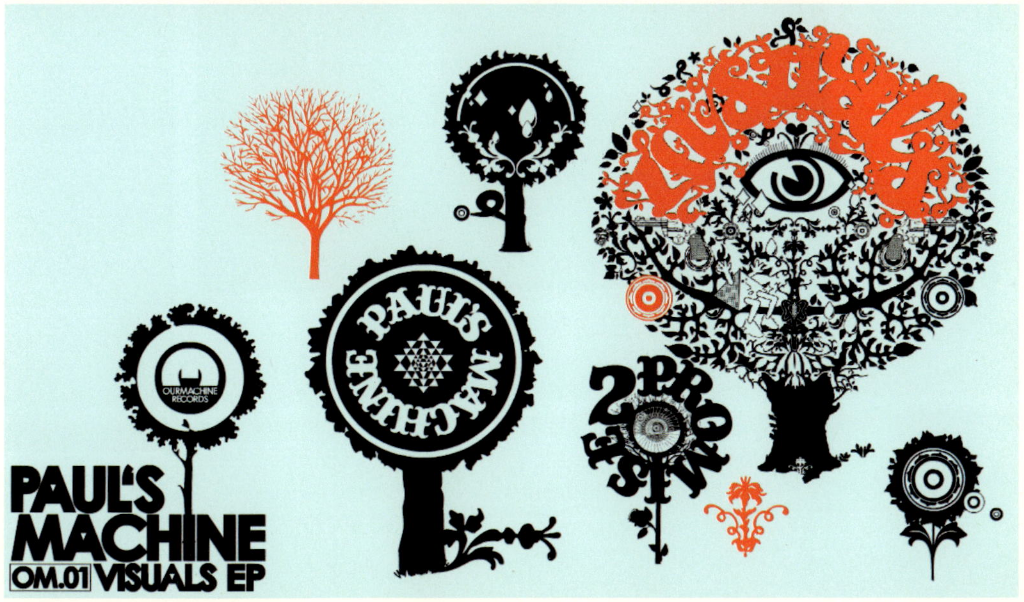

Digital Depot
by Lust

1: DataWall: The ‹Digital Depot› is a permanent exhibition space that comprises two main areas. The first area, the DataWall, showcases a revolving selection of 60-80 works of art presented on both sides of a large wall. In front of these works of art are six free-standing transparent glass panels that can display a variety of information and digital content relating to the art objects. This content is presented in a highly interactive fashion using an intuitive touch system. The deeper the user gets into the information, the less transparent the glass panels become. In this way the user's focus is guided from the wall to the information on the screens. This ‹transparent› interface highlights the fact that the works of art themselves are the most important part of the presentation, not the ‹fancy› technology.

for Museum Boijmans van Beuningen, Rotterdam, 2003

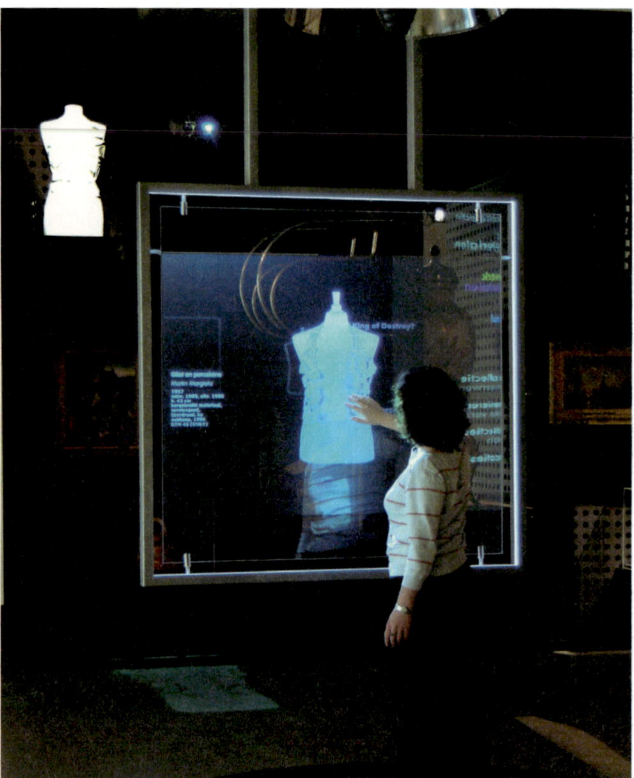

Photo by Tom Haartsen

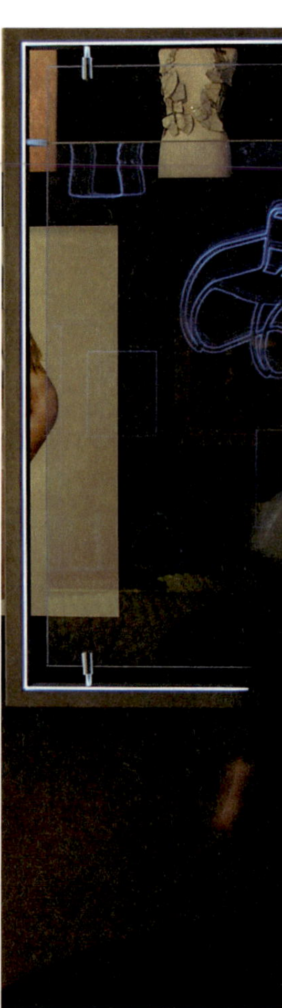

Photo by Paul Barbera

2: DataCloud: a spatial visualization of the database for all of the 117,000 works in the Boijmans collection. Each piece of art is represented in a 3D space defined by three axes: acquisition and manufacture data and format. The users navigate through this ‹universe› via an intuitive interface to obtain information about the works and insights into the make-up of the Boijmans collection.

Photo by Tom Haartsen

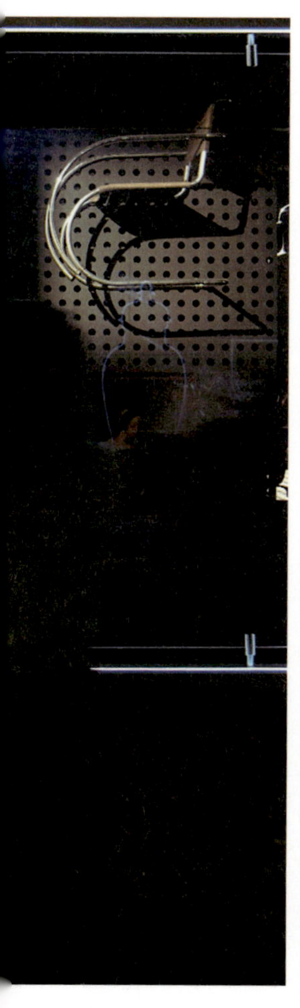

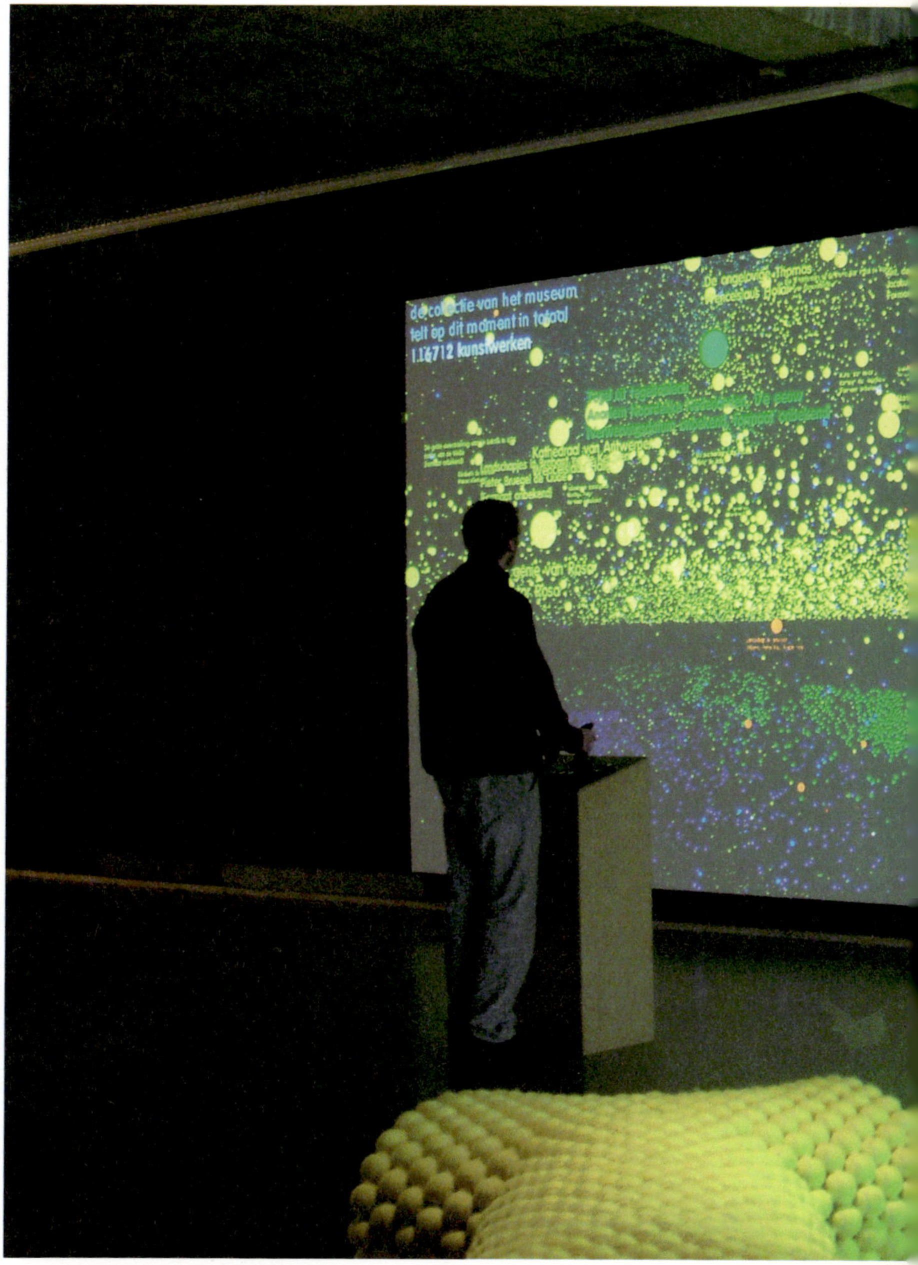

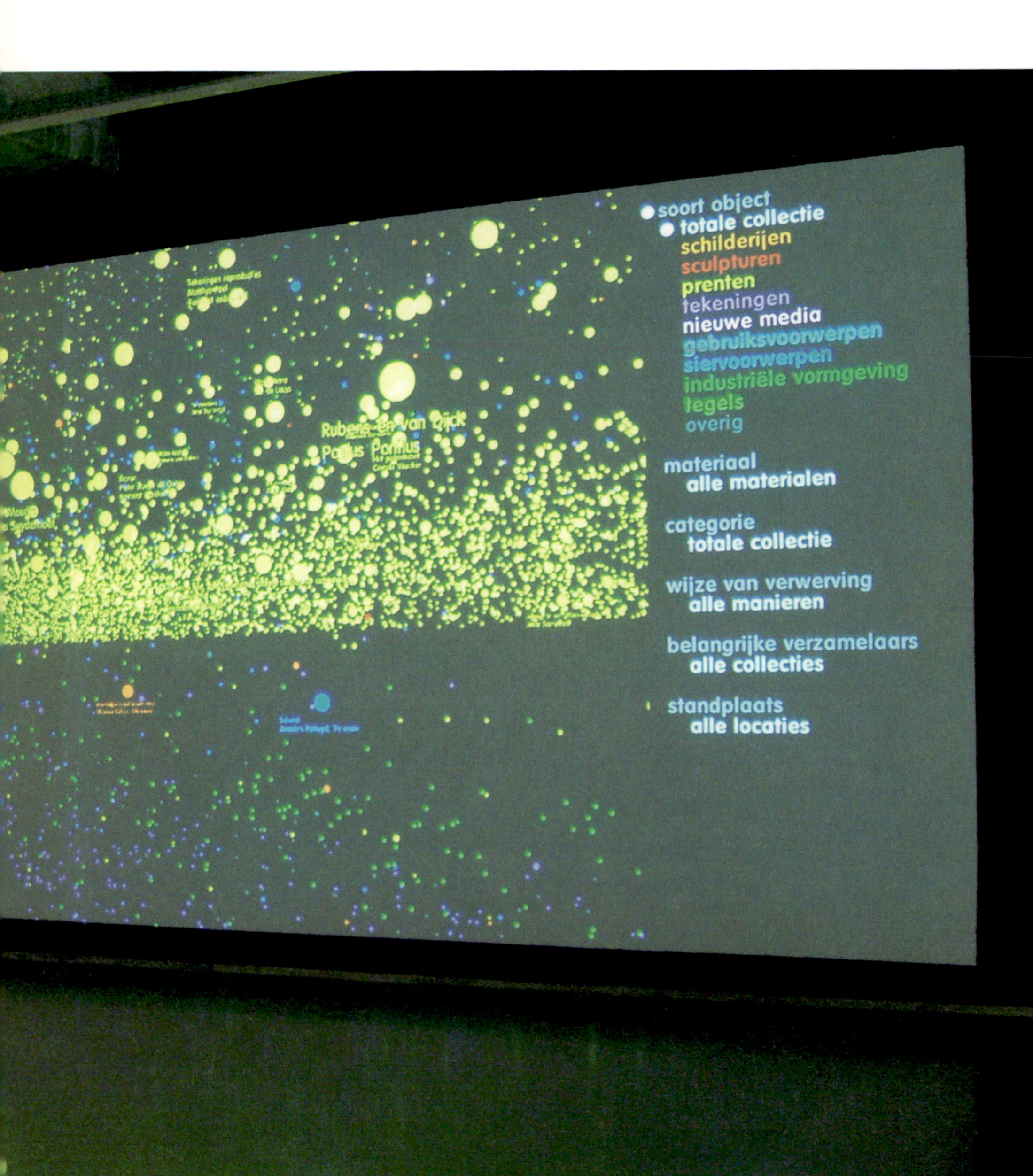

soort object
totale collectie
schilderijen
sculpturen
prenten
tekeningen
nieuwe media
gebruiksvoorwerpen
siervoorwerpen
industriële vormgeving
tegels
overig
materiaal
alle materialen
categorie
totale collectie
wijze van verwerving
alle manieren
belangrijke verzamelaars
alle collecties
standplaats
alle locaties
Rubens en van Dijck
Paulus Pontius

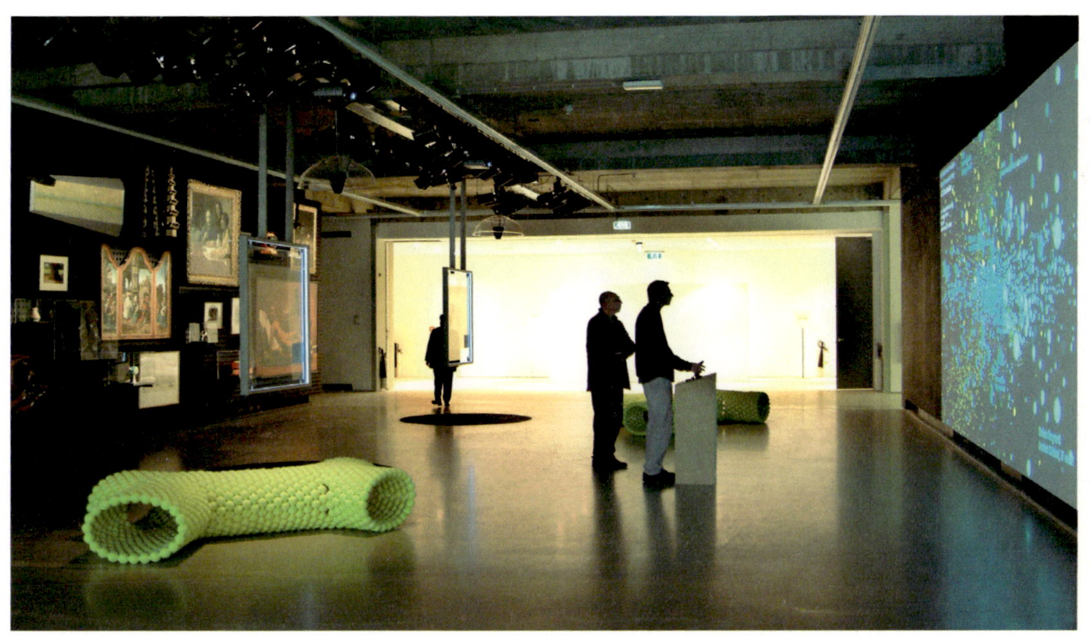

Photos by Tom Haartsen

The Murder Game

by Studio Kluif

Booklet for ‹The Murder Game›. The kids playing the game have to solve five murders, and in the process they see the cultural landmarks of the city of 's-Hertogenbosch.

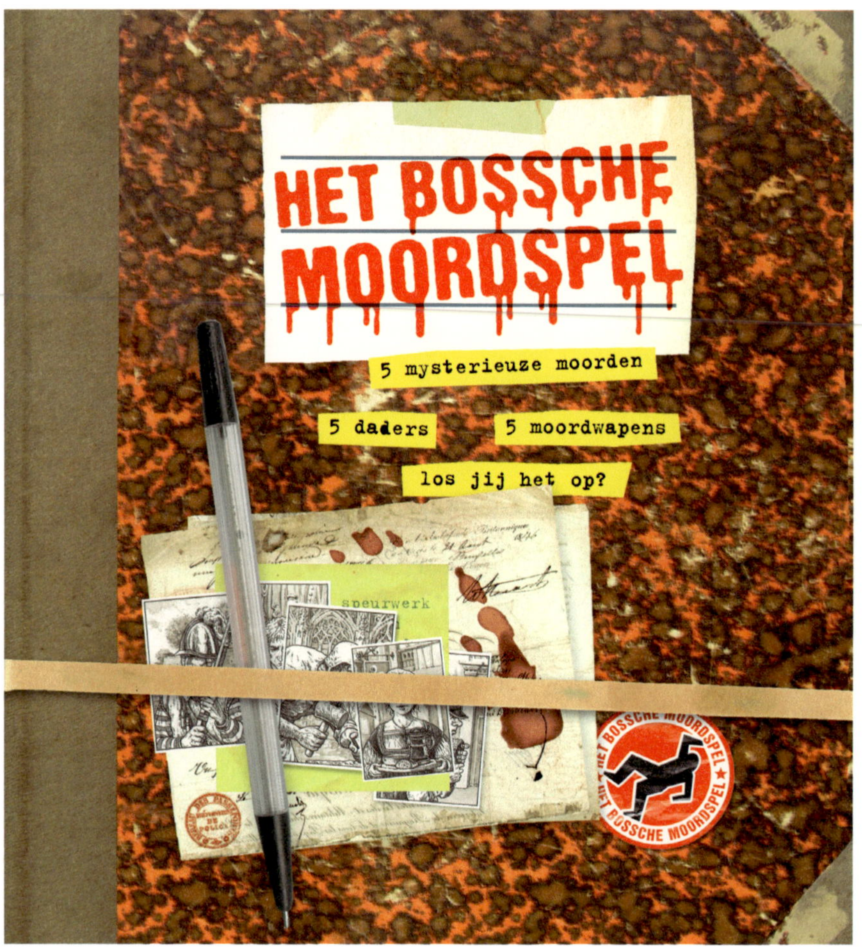

for the Noord-Brabants Museum, The Netherlands, 2005

DE LOCATIES

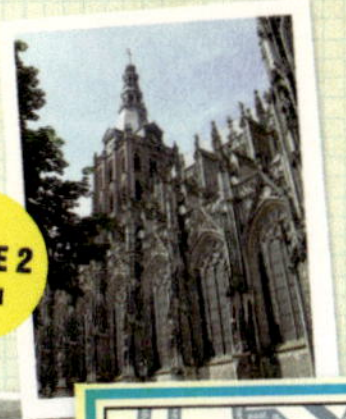

LOCATIE 2
SINT JAN

Een grote kerk als de Sint Jan bouw je niet in je eentje! Daaraan werk je met veel mensen. En iedereen heeft zijn eigen taak. Iedereen bouwt aan zijn stukje Sint Jan. Metselaars metselden bijvoorbeeld de muren. Glasschilders maakten de mooie gekleurde ramen.

Kijk goed naar de buitenkant van de Sint Jan. Streep de beroepen van mensen die **niet** aan de kerk hebben gewerkt weg.

- ○ Kleermaker
- ○ Verwarmingsmonteur
- ○ Beeldhouwer
- ○ Schilder
- ○ Dakdekker
- ○ Bouwmeester
- ○ Timmerman
- ○ Tegelzetter

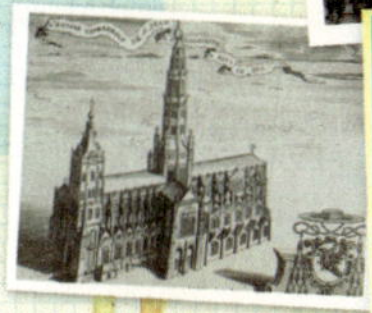

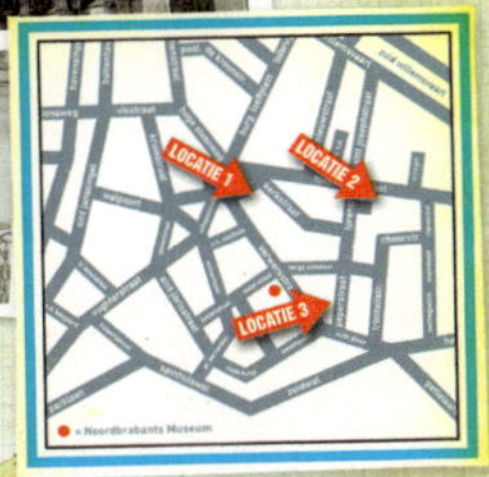

LOCATIE 1 LOCATIE 2 LOCATIE 3

● = Noordbrabants Museum

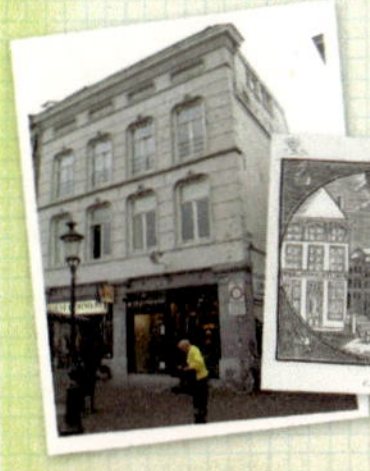

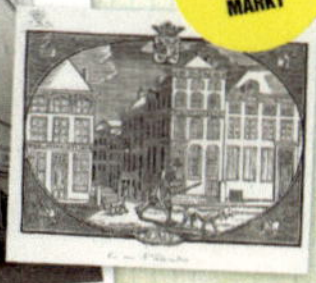

LOCATIE 1
MARKT

In de herberg dronk je een biertje, kwam je iets eten of om te gokken. Het was er gezellig en je ontmoette nieuwe mensen. Boeren van buiten de stad, handelaren uit verre streken, schippers en echte Bosschenaren. Maar laat op de avond kon het wel eens ongezellig worden. Dronken lui kregen soms grote ruzie.

Hieronder staan redenen waarom er ruzie uit kon breken.
Bedenk er nog 2.

1. De klant had zoveel verloren met gokken dat hij zijn schuld niet meer kon betalen.
2. De klant begon anderen te beledigen.
3. ....
4. ....

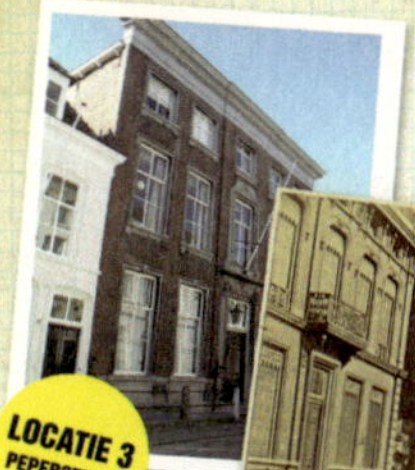

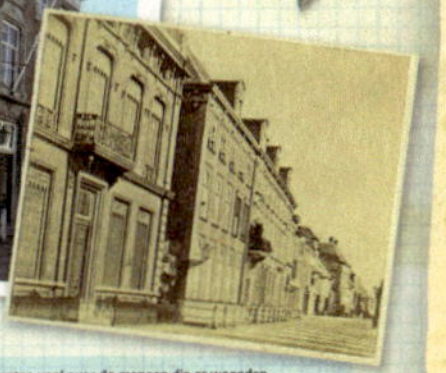

LOCATIE 3
PEPERSTRAAT

Een huis vertelt ons zonder te praten veel over de mensen die er woonden. Kijk boven de deur. Hier vind je een aanwijzing over de naam van het huis.

Wat draagt de man op zijn rug?

....

Woonden in dit huis rijke of arme mensen?

○ rijk ○ arm

Wie deed er vroeger de deur open als je aanbelde?

....

Dit huis heeft twee ingangen. De mooie deur waar je nu voor staat en een achterdeur. Loop 20 passen richting de Sint Jan. Je staat nu voor een grote ijzeren poort. Om bij de achterdeur te komen, moest je door dit straatje.
Hoe heet dit steegje?

....

Wie mocht door welke deur het huis binnen?

De bakker mocht binnen door de ○ voordeur ○ achterdeur.
De burgemeester mocht binnen door de ○ voordeur ○ achterdeur.
De schoorsteenveger mocht binnen door de ○ voordeur ○ achterdeur.
De barones mocht binnen door de ○ voordeur ○ achterdeur.

Meer locaties op de volgende pagina >>>

Weetjes!

TROTS VAN DE STAD
Als je de stad binnen komt rijder je hem al van verre staan: de Sint Een prachtige grote kerk midden de stad. De bouwers van de Sint hebben er zeker 150 jaar aan gebouwd. Toen was het geld op e zijn ze gestopt…

PALEISJE OM IN TE WONEN
Het verschil tussen arm en rijk: wonen in een krotje in een steegje in een statig huis in een brede stra Hoe je woont zegt veel over je rijk dom. Maar ook waar je woont zeg over je portemonnee. De Peperstra de Postelstraat en de Verwersstraat een paar voorbeelden van 'rijke str

DE WEG KWIJT
Tegenwoordig bestaat je adres uit e straatnaam en huisnummer. Vroege waren er nog geen huisnummers. C toch te weten waar je moest zijn, h den de huizen een naam. Deze naan kon verzonnen zijn of had te maken het bedrijf dat er gevestigd was. Zo in 'De brouwketel' bier gemaakt.

SAMENWERKING
In 's-Hertogenbosch werden veel sto verhandeld. Vooral laken, een wollen stof, was erg populair en werd in vel meters verkocht. In de stad woonden lakensnijders (zij knipten de stoffen), lakenverwers (zij verfden stof) en lak verkopers (zij verkochten de stof op d lakenmarkt).

SPECIALE AANBIEDING
Een bijzondere kraam op de Middeleeuwse markt was de santenkraam. Zo'n kraam stond bo vol met beeldjes van metaal, hout of a werk. Beeldjes van verschillende heilig de zogenaamde santjes. Ieder huis had zeker één heiligenbeeld. Het is daarom niet raar dat er bij opgravingen in de s zoveel zijn terug gevonden.

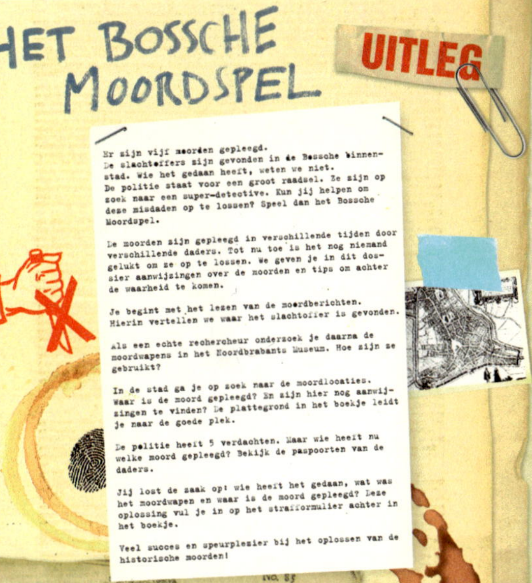

HET BOSSCHE MOORDSPEL

UITLEG

Er zijn vijf moorden gepleegd. De slachtoffers zijn gevonden in de Bossche binnenstad. Wie het gedaan heeft, weten we niet. De politie staat voor een groot raadsel. Ze zijn op zoek naar een super-detective. Kun jij helpen om deze misdaden op te lossen? Speel dan het Bossche Moordspel.

De moorden zijn gepleegd in verschillende tijden door verschillende daders. Tot nu toe is het nog niemand gelukt om ze op te lossen. We geven je in dit dossier aanwijzingen over de moorden en tips om achter de waarheid te komen.

Je begint met het lezen van de moordberichten. Hierin vertellen we waar het slachtoffer is gevonden.

Als een echte rechercheur onderzoek je daarna de moordwapens in het Noordbrabants Museum. Hoe zijn ze gebruikt?

In de stad ga je op zoek naar de moordlocaties. Waar is de moord gepleegd? En zijn hier nog aanwijzingen te vinden? De plattegrond in het boekje leidt je naar de goede plek.

De politie heeft 5 verdachten. Maar wie heeft nu welke moord gepleegd? Bekijk de paspoorten van de daders.

Jij lost de zaak op! wie heeft het gedaan, wat was het moordwapen en waar is de moord gepleegd? Deze oplossing vul je in op het strafformulier achter in het boekje.

Veel succes en speurplezier bij het oplossen van de historische moorden!

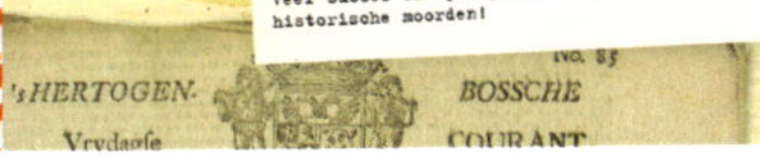

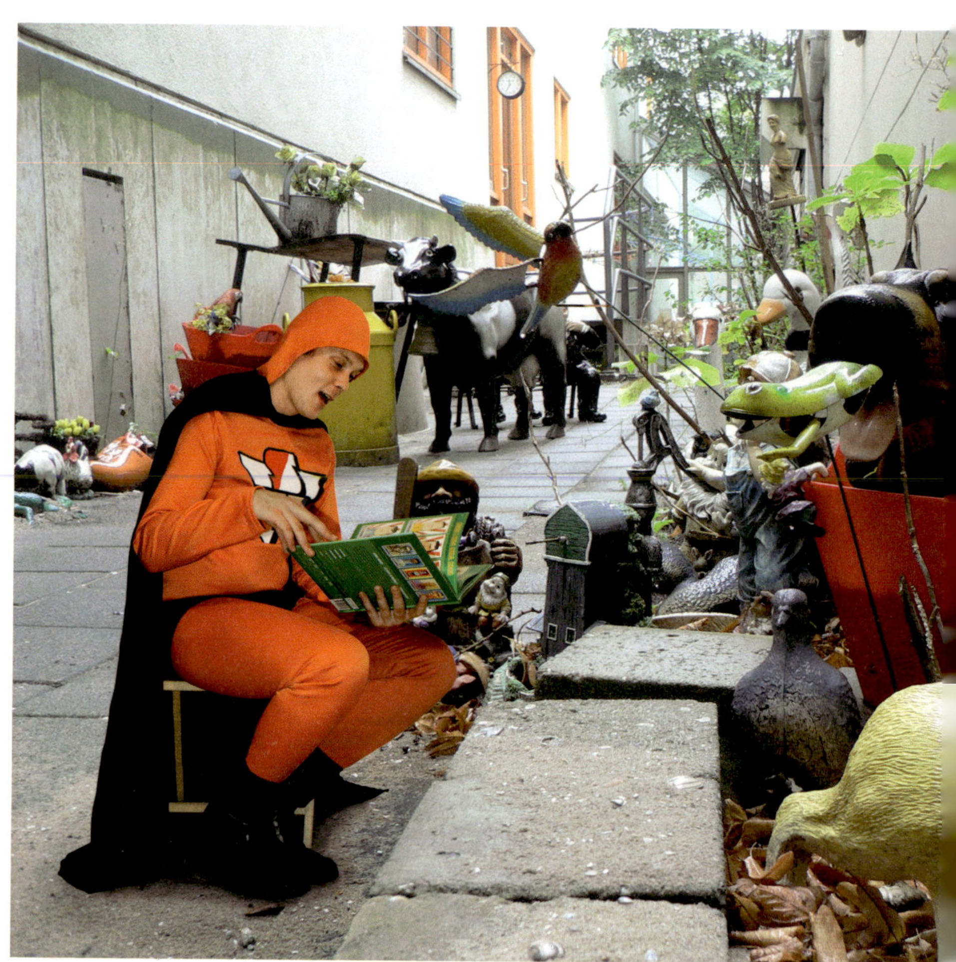

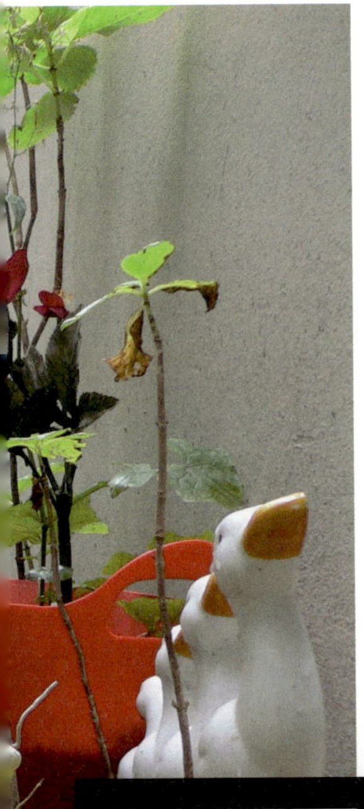

Story Tellers

Mees Goal-den boys
by Studio Kluif

Blockheads Central Park Guerilla Campaign
by Studio Kluif

Nedap annual report
by Studio Kluif

Wedding Design
by Richard Niessen

Pelt
by Zeloot

Final Milks
by Zeloot

Cultural Posters
by Ping-pong Design

Music scandals
by Julia Müller & John Heymans

Heavenly Leader
by Harmen Liemburg

Wedding tablecloth
by Richard Niessen & Esther de Vries

Mees Goal-den boys
by Studio Kluif

This image was produced for a ‹Mees› collection presentation. The team is in fact the same boy, over and over again... Soccer was an inspiration for the entire collection. That's why Kluif formed ‹Mees United›!

for Mees Children's wear, The Netherlands, 2005

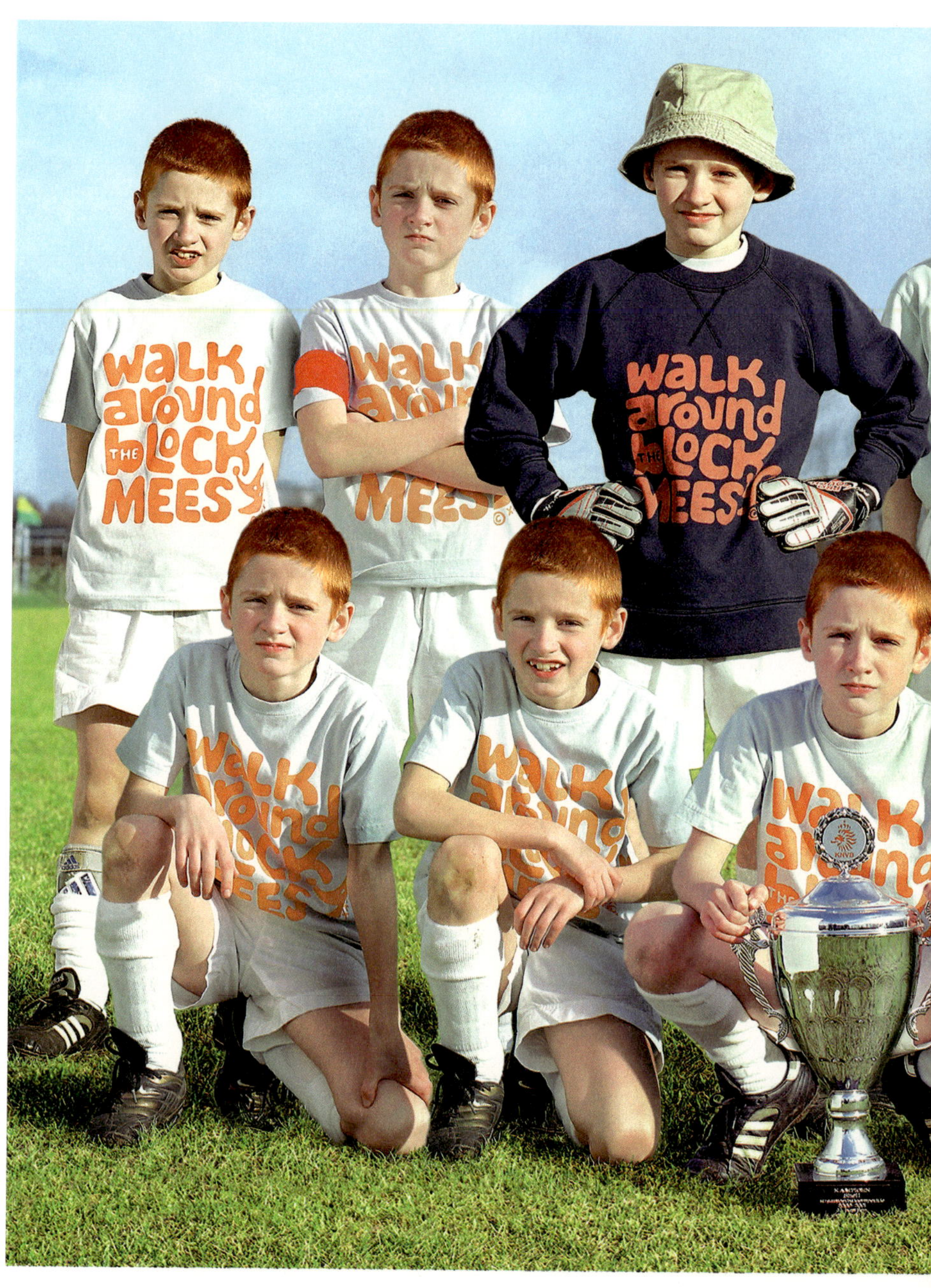

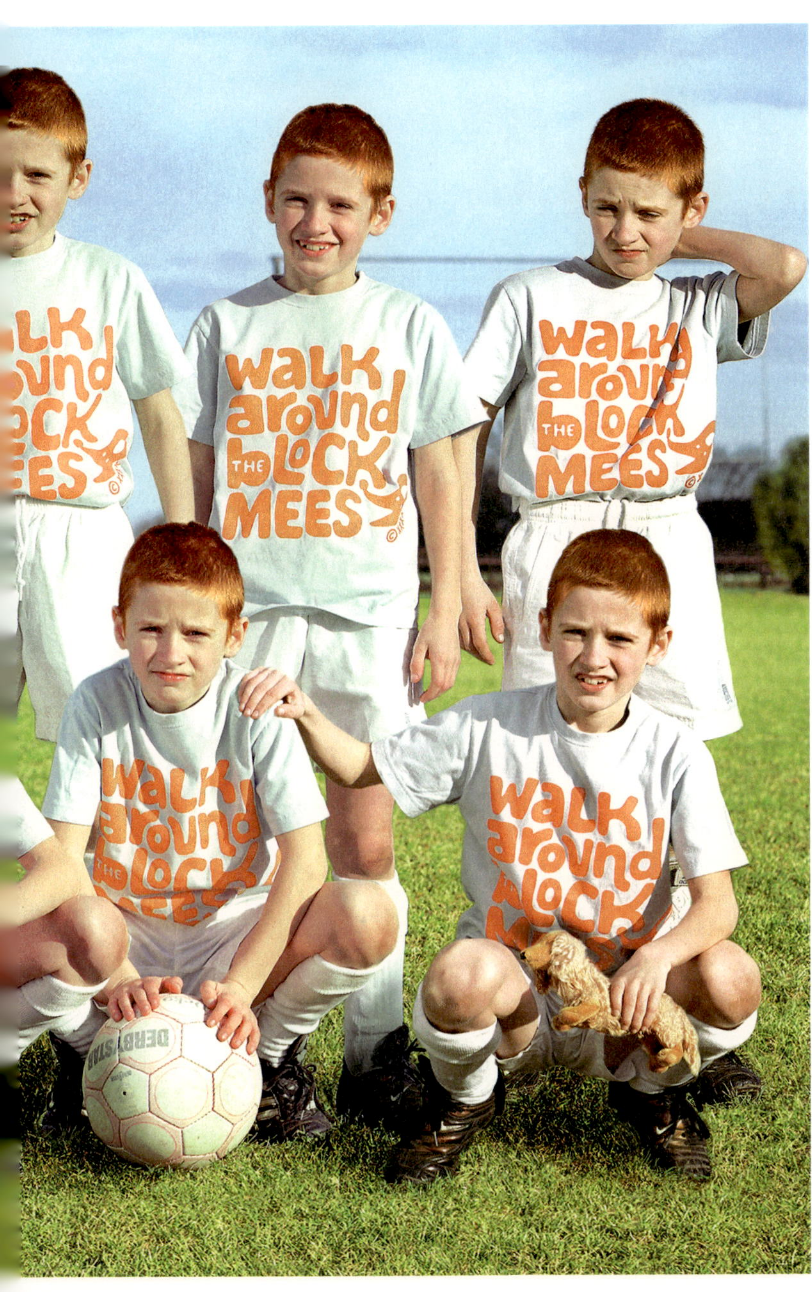
walk
around
THE
block
MEES

 Blockheads Central Park Guerilla Campaign
by Studio Kluif

‹Blockheads› is a New York-based Mexican food chain. Sock monkeys are used for their communication. They were also used for a guerrilla campaign. The copies were pasted on trees and walls throughout New York.

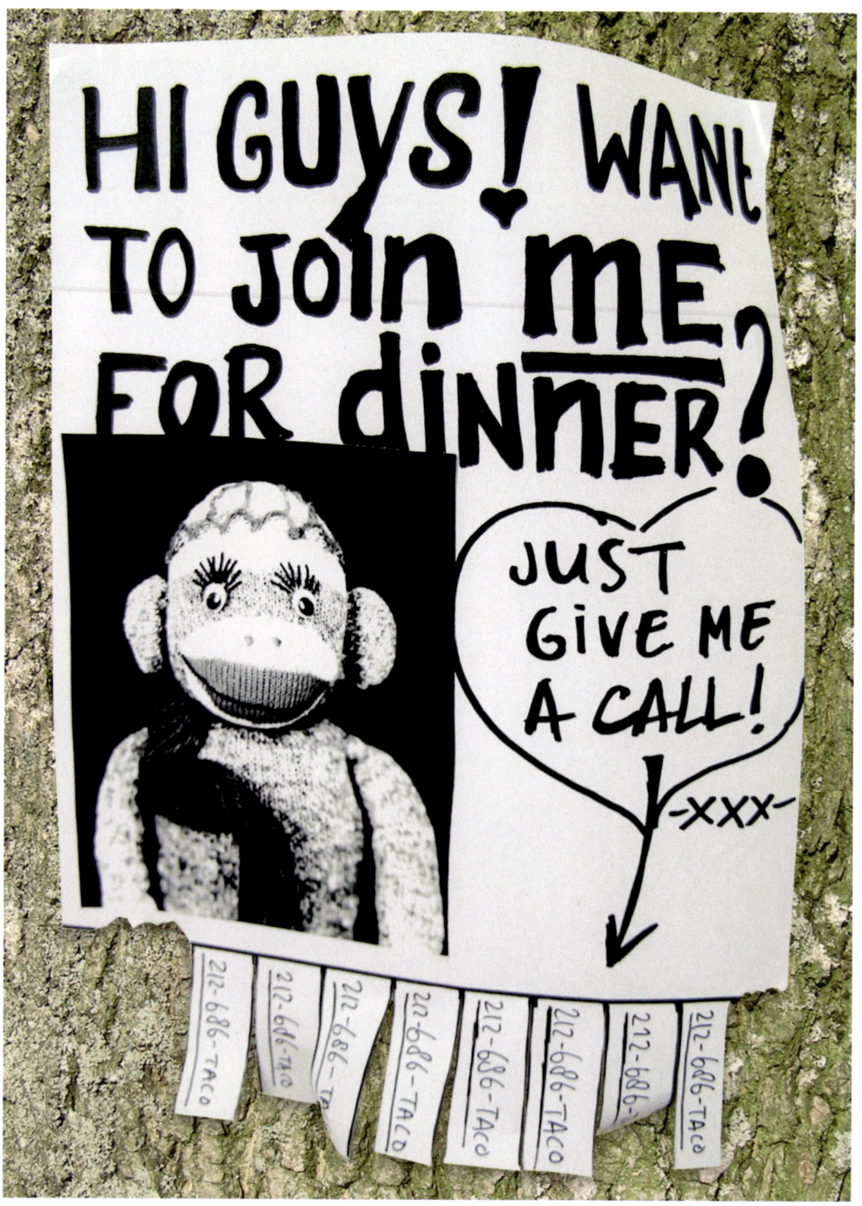

for Blockheads, USA, 2005

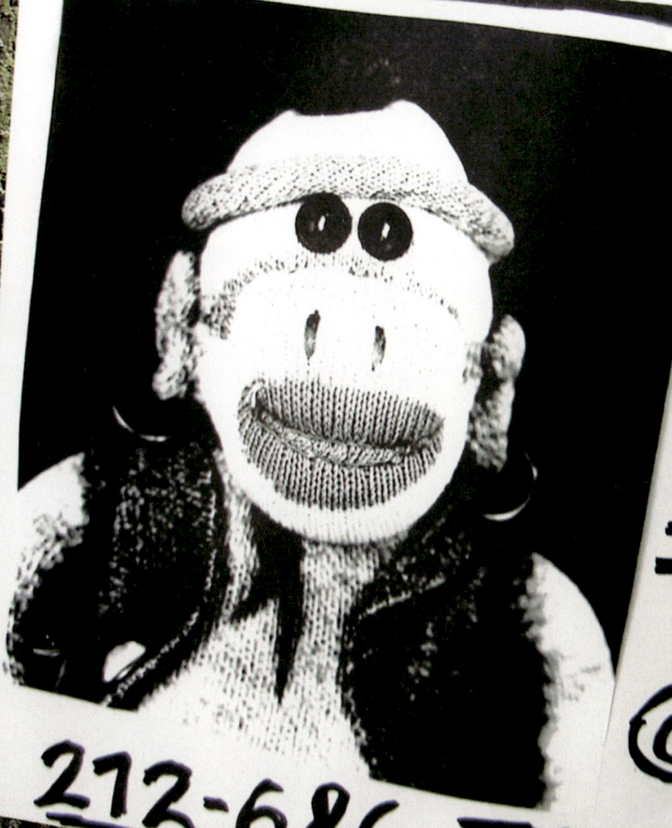
MISSING
SOCKMONKE
PLEA
HEL
FIN
CALL
212-686-TACO

208 Nedap annual report
by Studio Kluif

An annual report about innovations. A large part of the report is handwritten. It's like reading a CEO's diary.

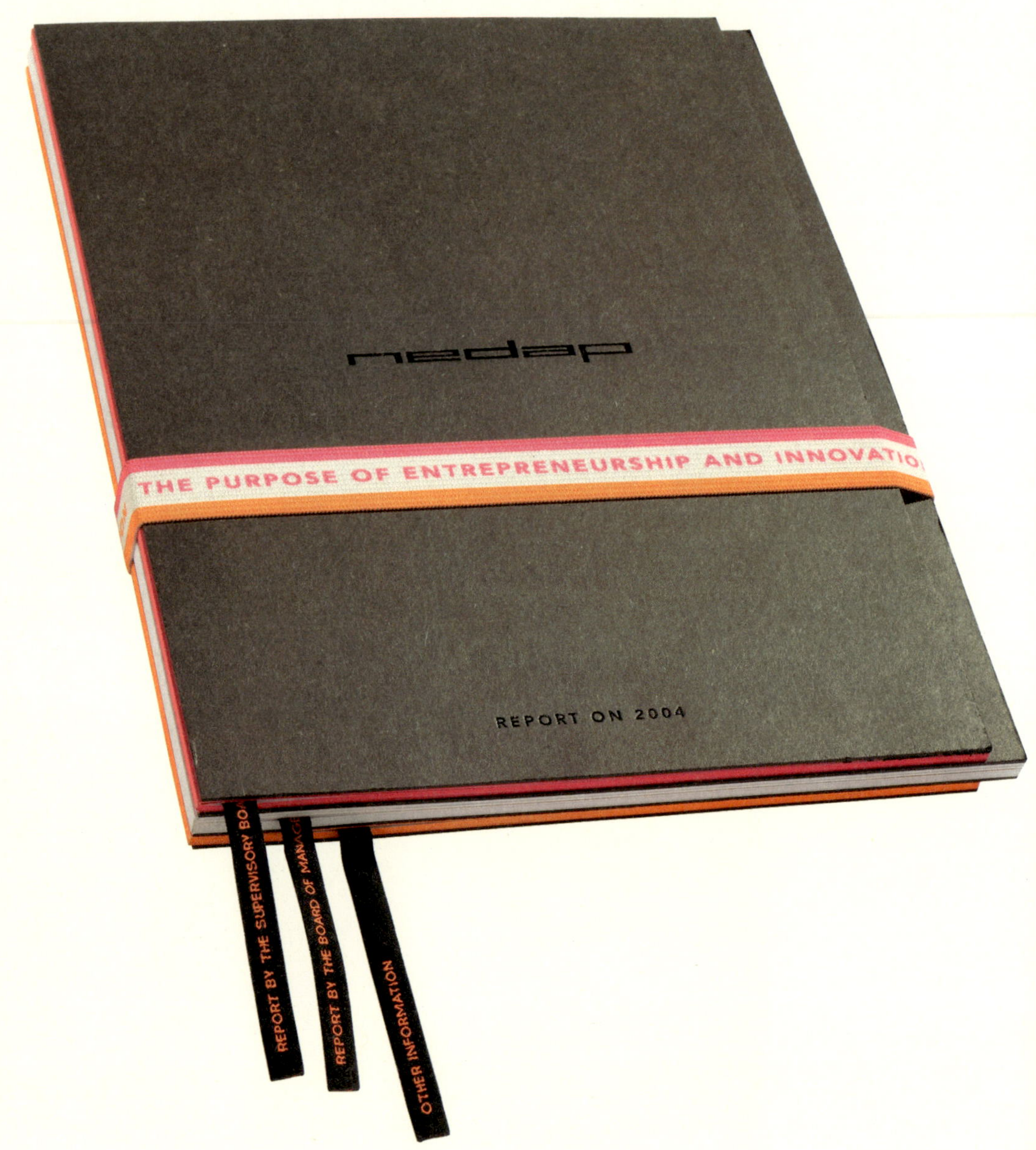

for Nedap, The Netherlands, 2004

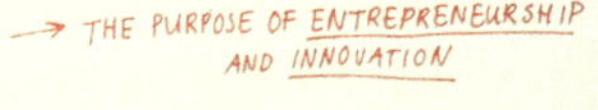

→ THE PURPOSE OF ENTREPRENEURSHIP AND INNOVATION

Innovation carries a high profile in society. It is often perceived as a key factor in protecting Western Europe's prosperity against the threat of emerging low-wage economies. Not suprisingly, perhaps, many articles on innovation appear to be a highly abstract and defensive nature. Less prominence is given to the way in which innovation translates into value creation and new employment opportunities. Innovation therefore sometimes seems to have become an end in itself, with money as the main motivator.

Innovation is all around us. Usually it originates from CREATIVE, INDEPENDENT and VISIONARY SPIRITS who go against the tide to pursue their ideas. Innovation AND entrepreneurship are both highly goal-oriented.

At NEDAP the purpose of innovation and entrepreneurship springs from our central goal:

Creating added value for the customer

Competitors, technology and customers are continuously driving change and opportunity. Our objective gives our staff the space and guidance they need to exploit their creative talents to the full. It allows them to develop new products and systems, thereby enabling customers to constantly renew and innovate their business and grow the rewards.

The ongoing process of change meets with resistance within the company. But customers too often need to be won over to the benefits of new trail-blazing solutions.
Marketing and pricing must be carefully pitched to reflect the added value that the new solution offers the customer compared to products already available in the market. This is difficult, particularly in the early stages. But unless the customer is convinced of the benefits, the product - NO MATTER HOW INNOVATIVE - is doomed to failure.

Ongoing change compels the constant reorganisation of work processes as well as the creative cannibalisation of existing products. The dullness of routine is thus avoided. Thanks to the great variety of possibilities, staff can always develop, irrespective of their age. In this way, added value is also created for our staff. Their sense of recognition, which everyone needs, derives from a close involvement in the success achieved in the market. This way of working is so interesting and exciting that you can and want to go on for as long as possible also in Western Europe.

By virtue of this approach added value is created for the share holder.

This is how we at Nedap want to work, inspired by the vision that:

Challenges enrich life

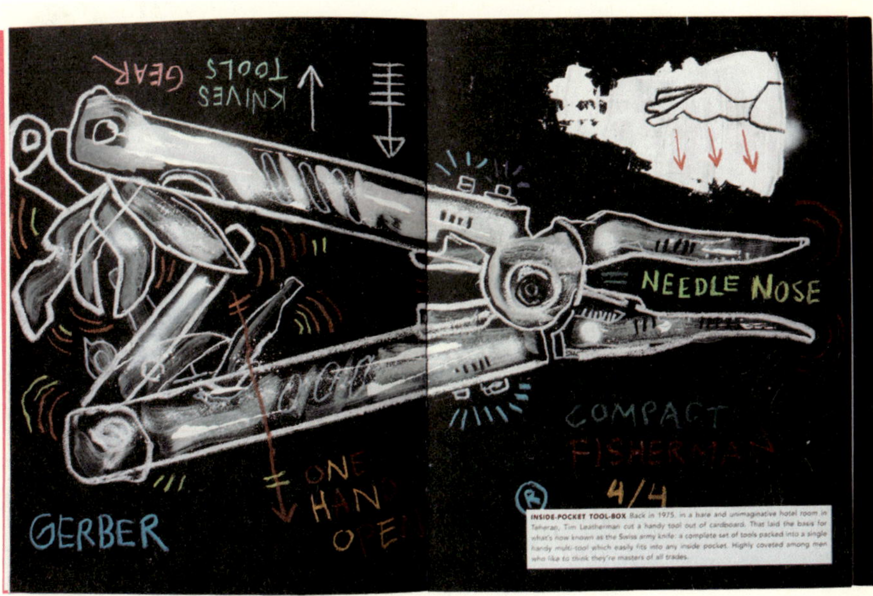

INSIDE-POCKET TOOL-BOX Back in 1975, in a bare and unimaginative hotel room in Teheran, Tim Leatherman cut a handy tool out of cardboard. That laid the basis for what's now known as the Swiss army knife: a complete set of tools packed into a single handy multi-tool which easily fits into any inside pocket. Highly coveted among men who like to think they're masters of all trades.

Wedding Design

by Richard Niessen & Esther de Vries

Esther and Richard got married. We spent a lot of time making the decorations, including a graphic wedding cake, a set of 12 flags, Esther's wedding dress and a special wedding song!

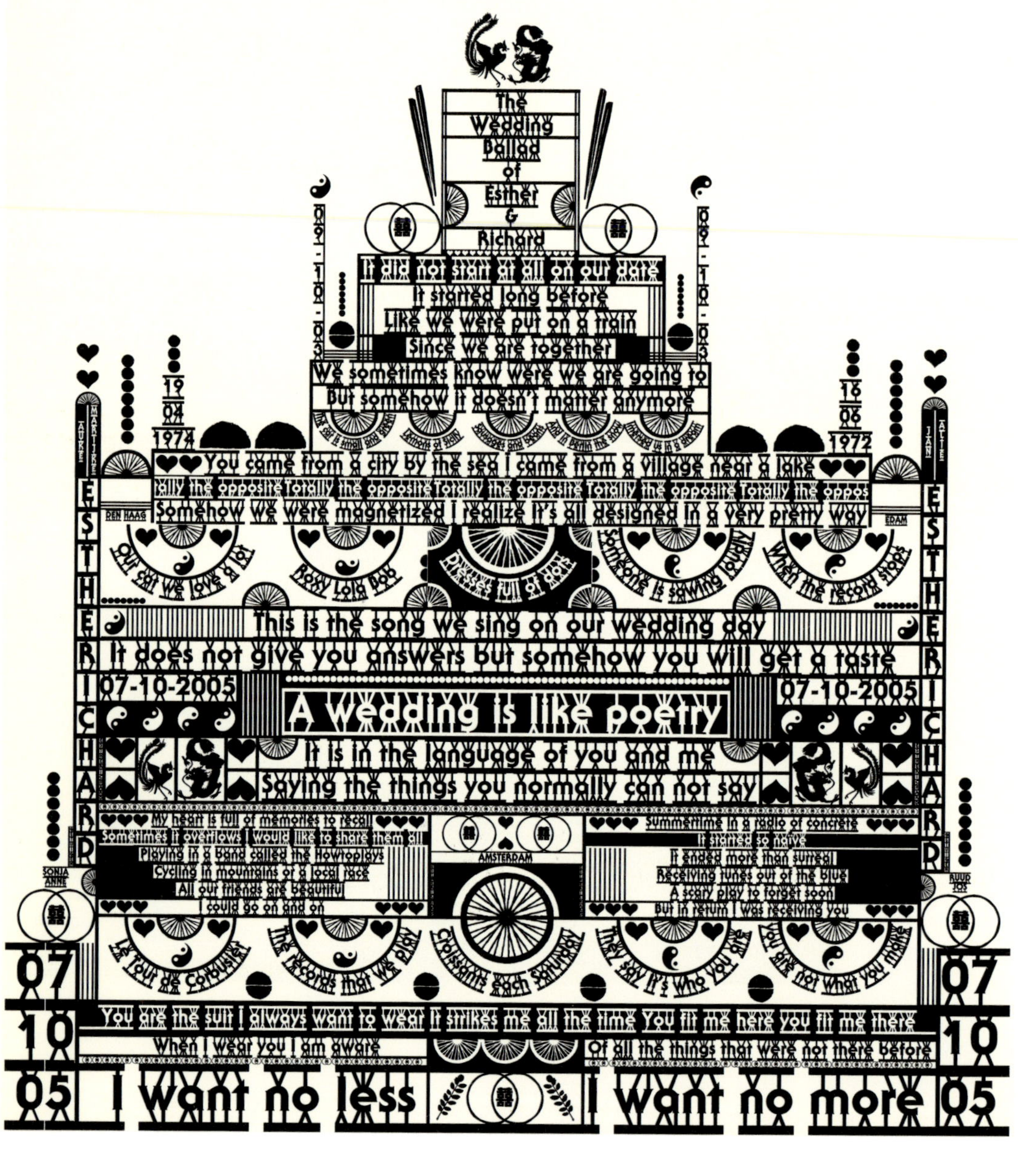

7th of October, 2005

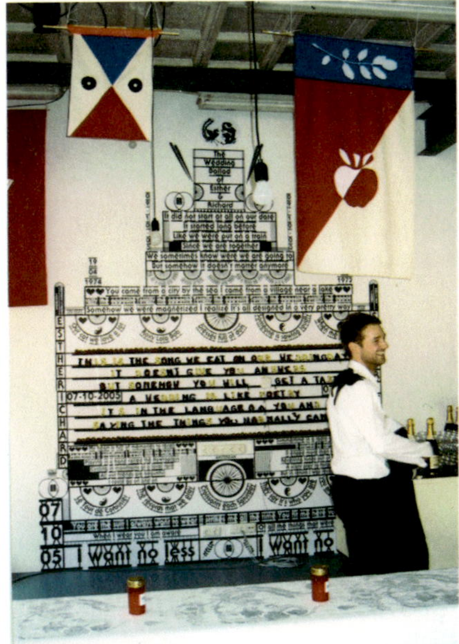

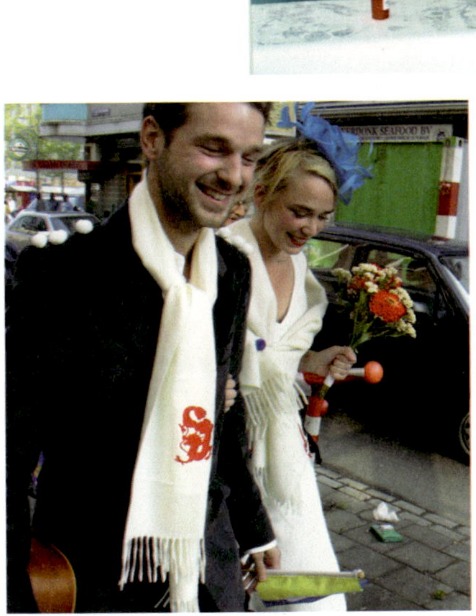

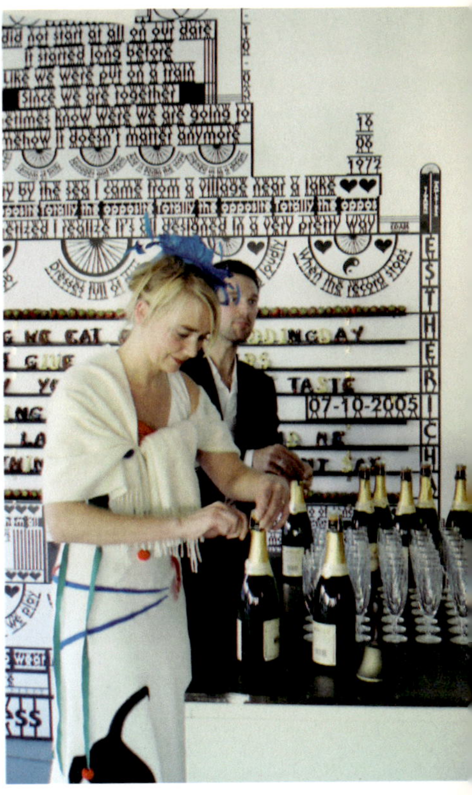

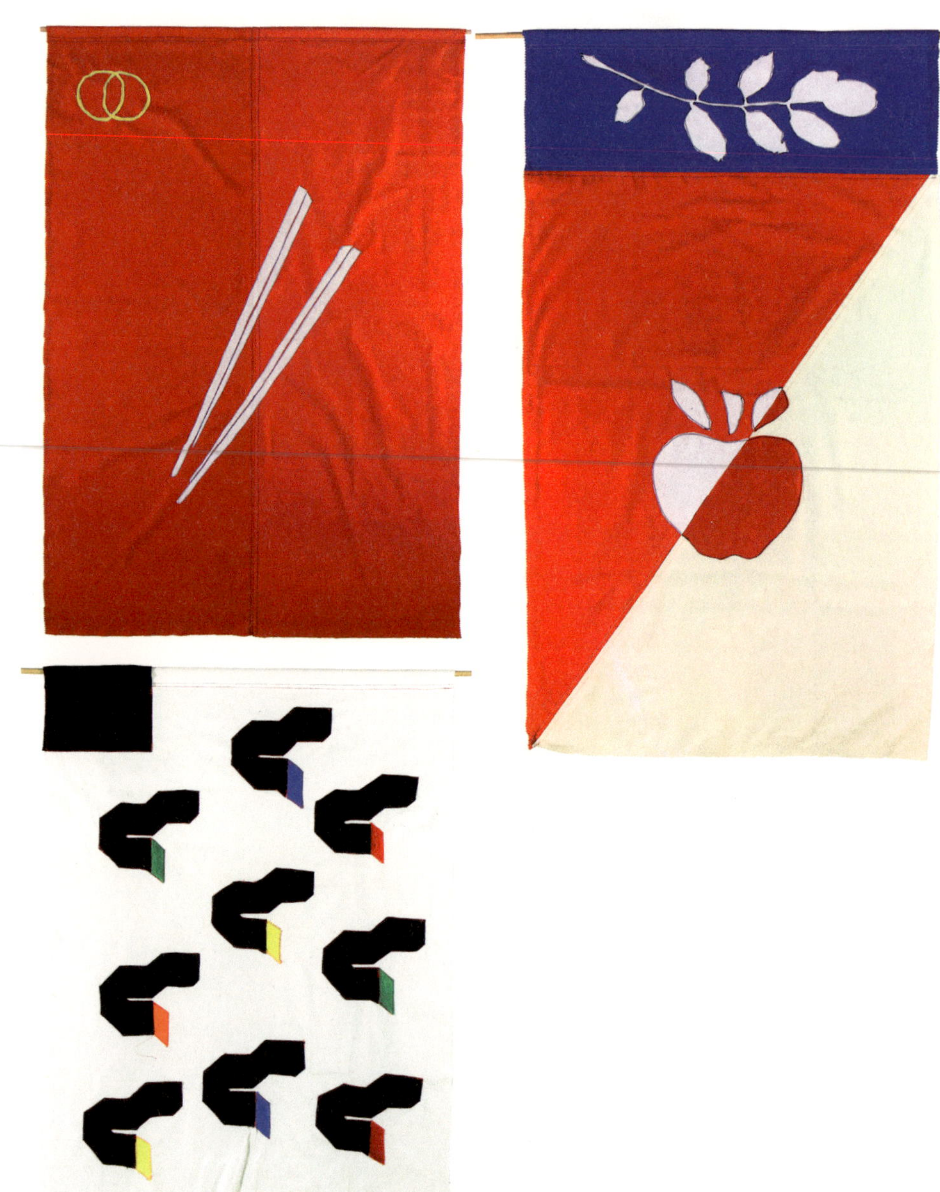

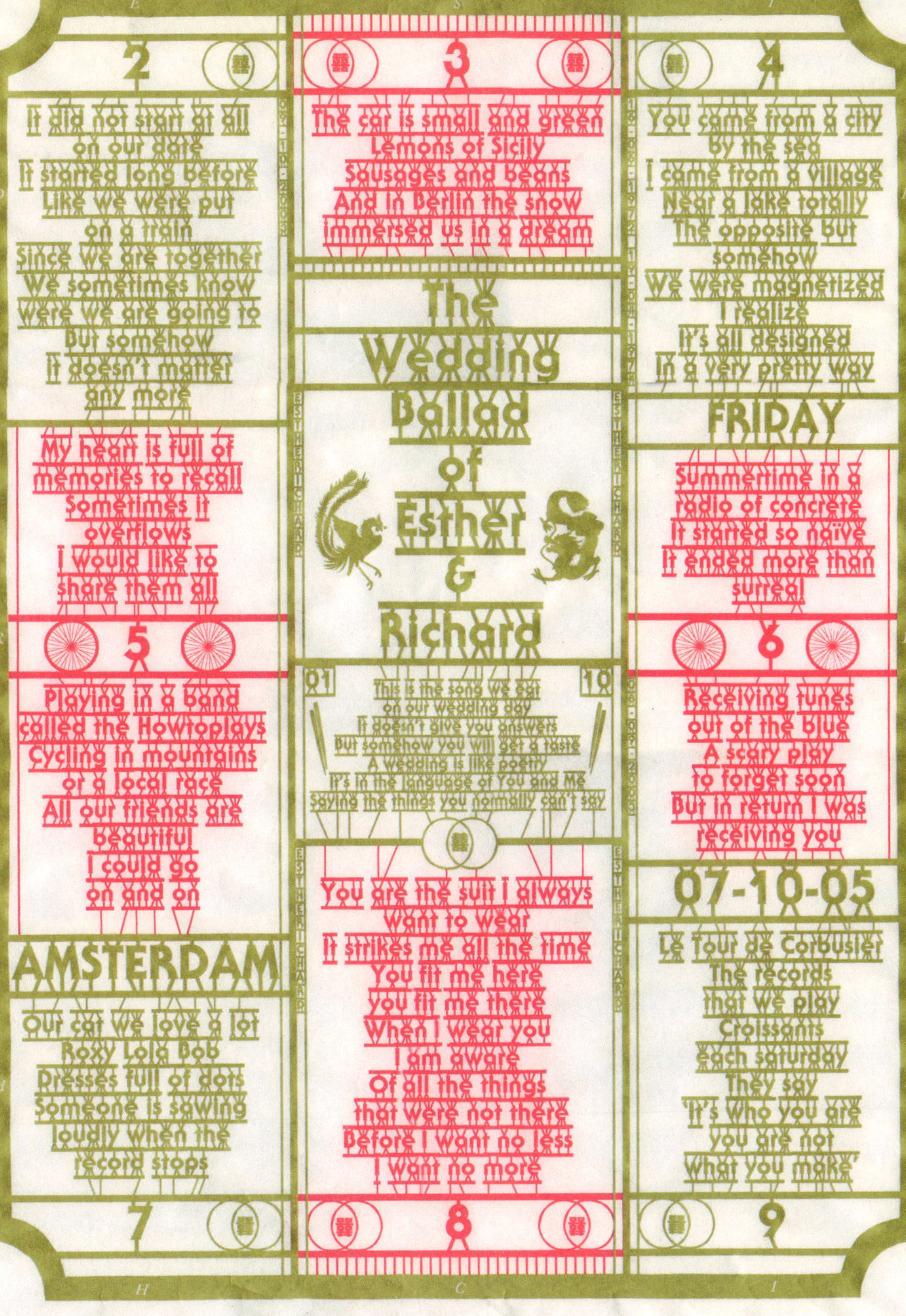
E
S
T
2
It did not start at all
on our date
It started long before
Like we were put
on a train
Since we are together
We sometimes know
were we are going to
But somehow
it doesn't matter
any more
3
The car is small and green
Lemons of Sicily
Sausages and beans
And in Berlin the snow
immersed us in a dream
4
You came from a city
by the sea
I came from a village
Near a lake totally
The opposite but
somehow
We were magnetized
I realize
It's all designed
In a very pretty way
The
Wedding
Ballad
of
Esther
&
Richard
FRIDAY
D
H
My heart is full of
memories to recall
Sometimes it
overflows
I would like to
share them all
Summertime in a
radio of concrete
It started so naïve
It ended more than
surreal
R
E
5
6
Playing in a band
called the Howtoplays
Cycling in mountains
or a local race
All our friends are
beautiful
I could go
on and on
01
10
This is the song we eat
on our wedding day
It doesn't give you answers
But somehow you will get a taste
A wedding is like poetry
It's in the language of You and Me
Saying the things you normally can't say
Receiving tunes
out of the blue
A scary play
to forget soon
But in return I was
receiving you
07-10-05
You are the suit I always
want to wear
It strikes me all the time
You fit me here
you fit me there
When I wear you
I am aware
Of all the things
that were not there
Before I want no less
I want no more
AMSTERDAM
Our cat we love a lot
Roxy Lola Bob
Dresses full of dots
Someone is sawing
loudly when the
record stops
Le Tour de Corbusier
The records
that we play
Croissants
each saturday
They say
'It's who you are
you are not
what you make'
A
R
7
8
9
H
C
I

Pelt
by Zeloot

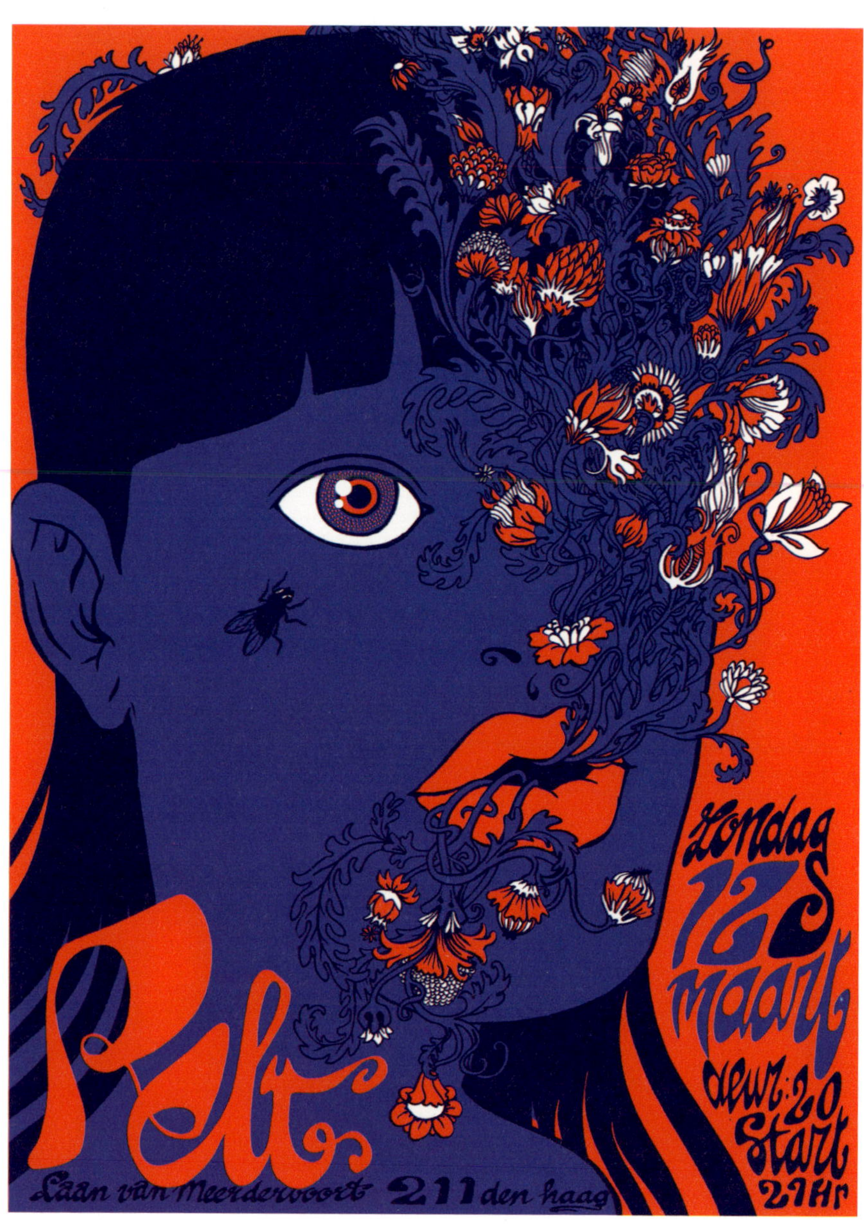

a gigposter for Helbaard, Den Haag, silkscreened, 2006

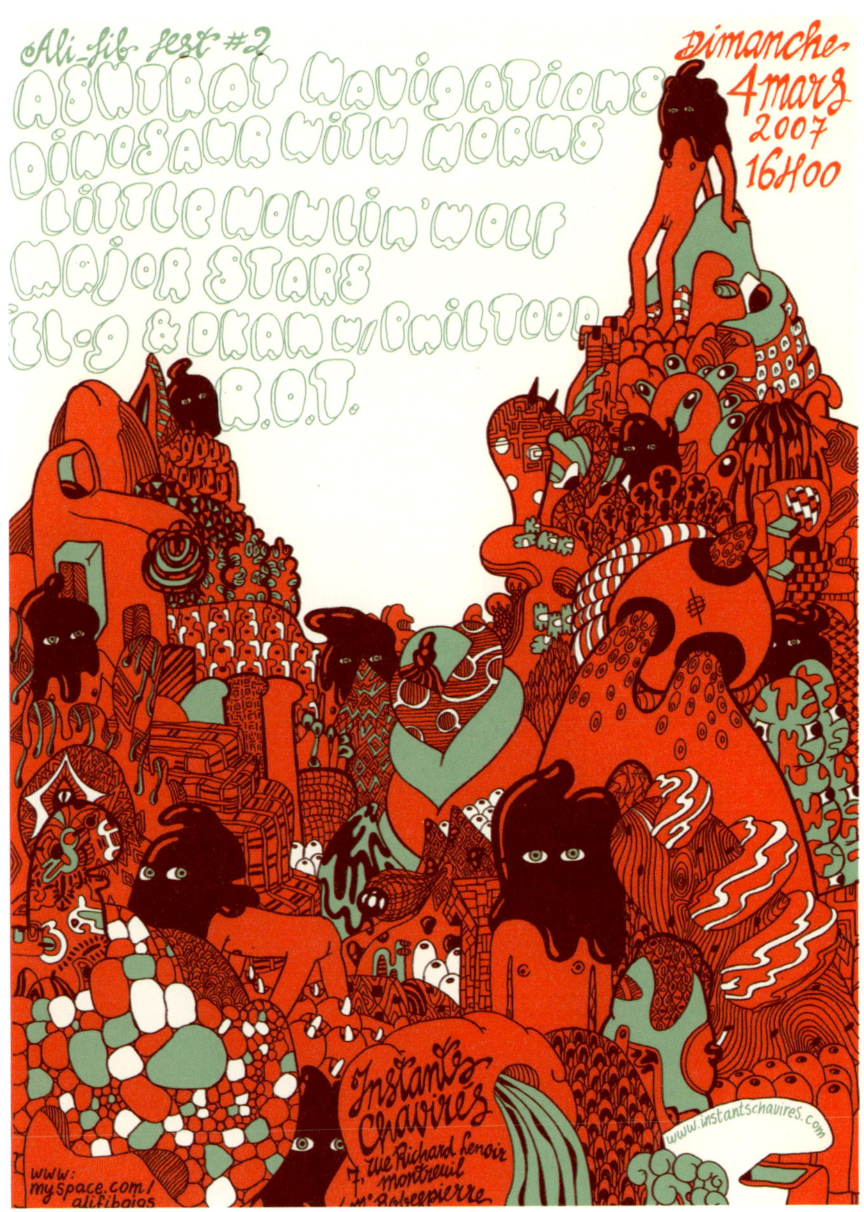

a gigposter for Ali_fib fest, Paris, silkscreened, 2007

‹Drang› (‹urging› in Dutch) speaks for itself. Raw. Imposing. Brash. Homely. Makeshift. The question remains: Is it theatre, or is it life?

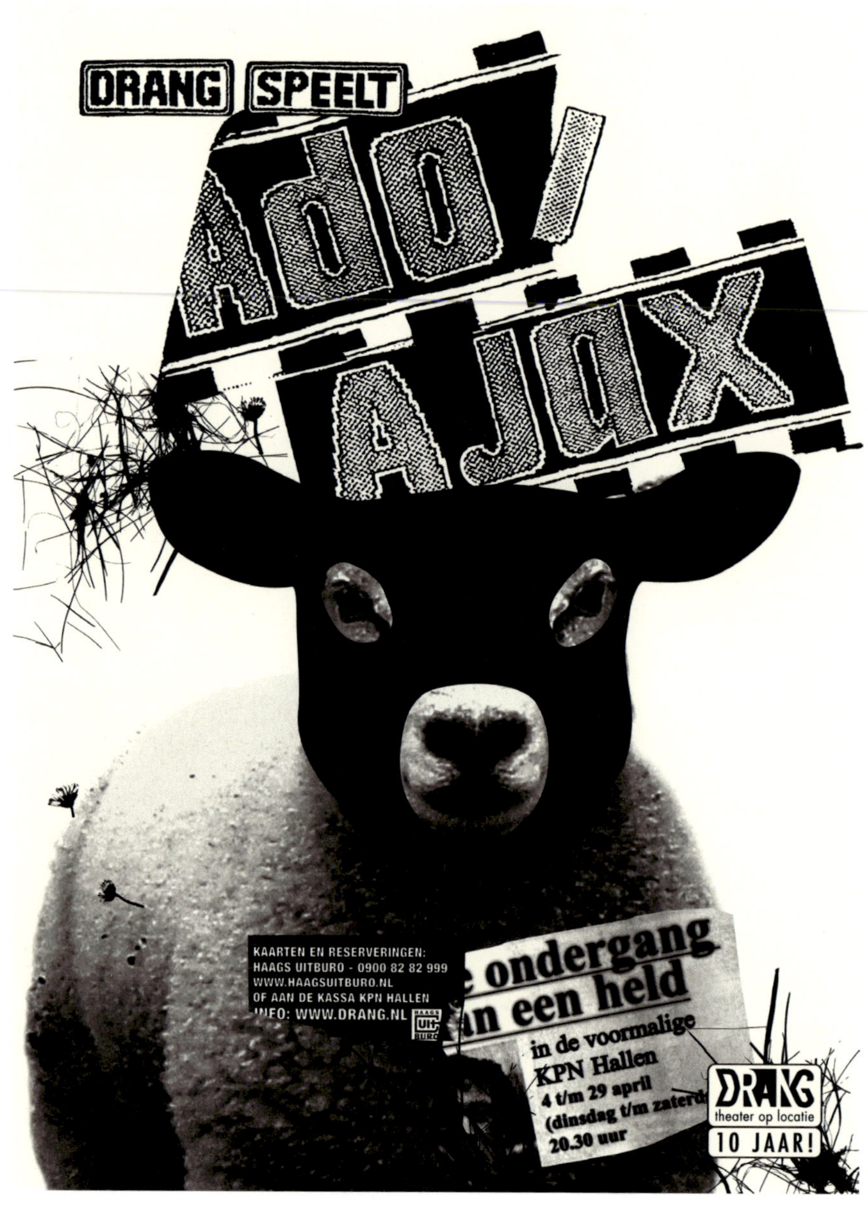

for Drang

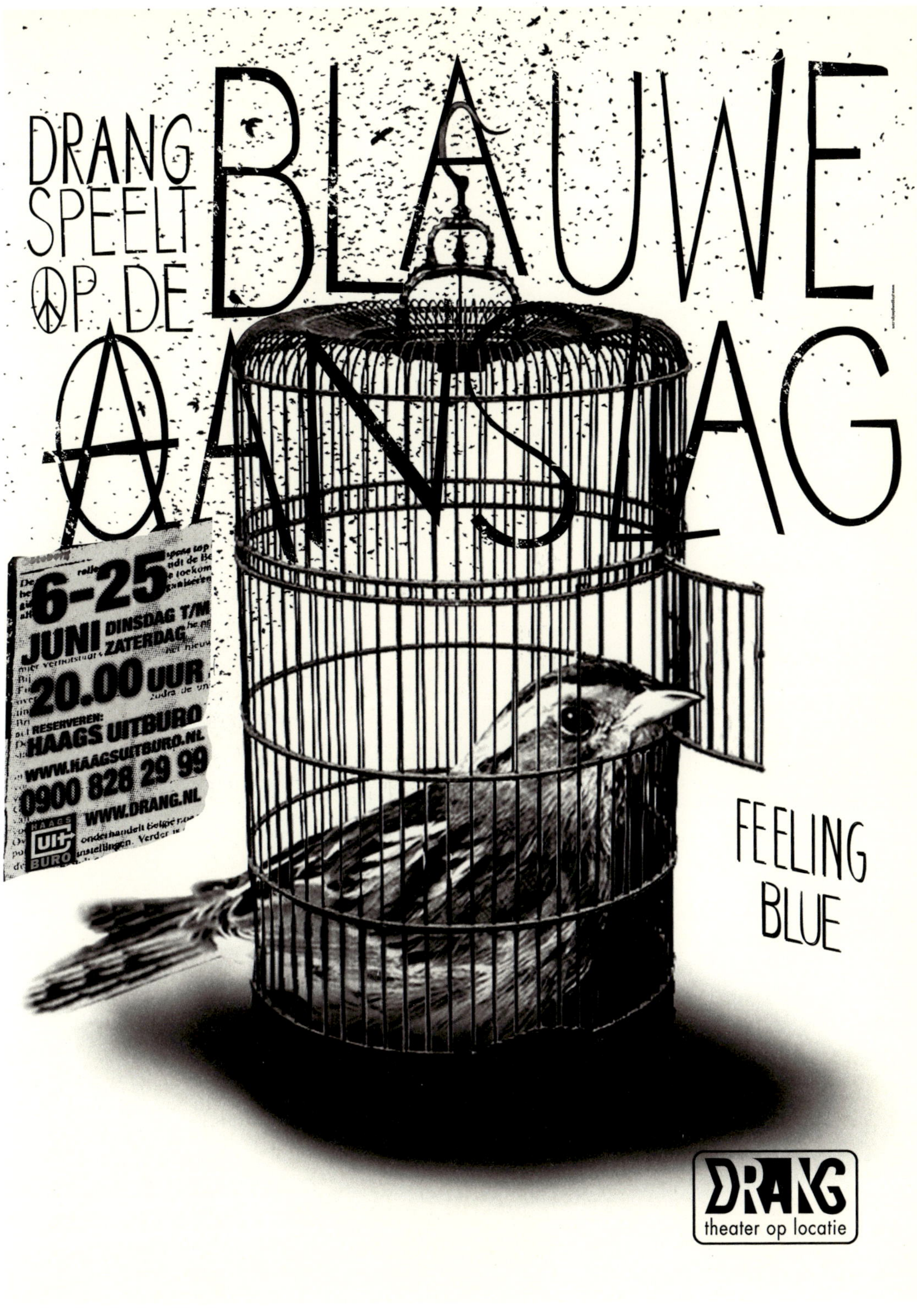

DRANG
SPEELT
OP DE

BLAUWE AANSLAG

6-25 JUNI
DINSDAG T/M ZATERDAG
20.00 UUR
RESERVEREN:
HAAGS UITBURO
WWW.HAAGSUITBURO.NL
0900 828 29 99
WWW.DRANG.NL

HAAGS UIT BURO

FEELING
BLUE

DRANG
theater op locatie

 Music scandals
by Julia Müller & John Heymans

Fold-out newspaper about the four most important scandals in music history. Each piece of music provoked a scandal and changed the conception and idea of music.

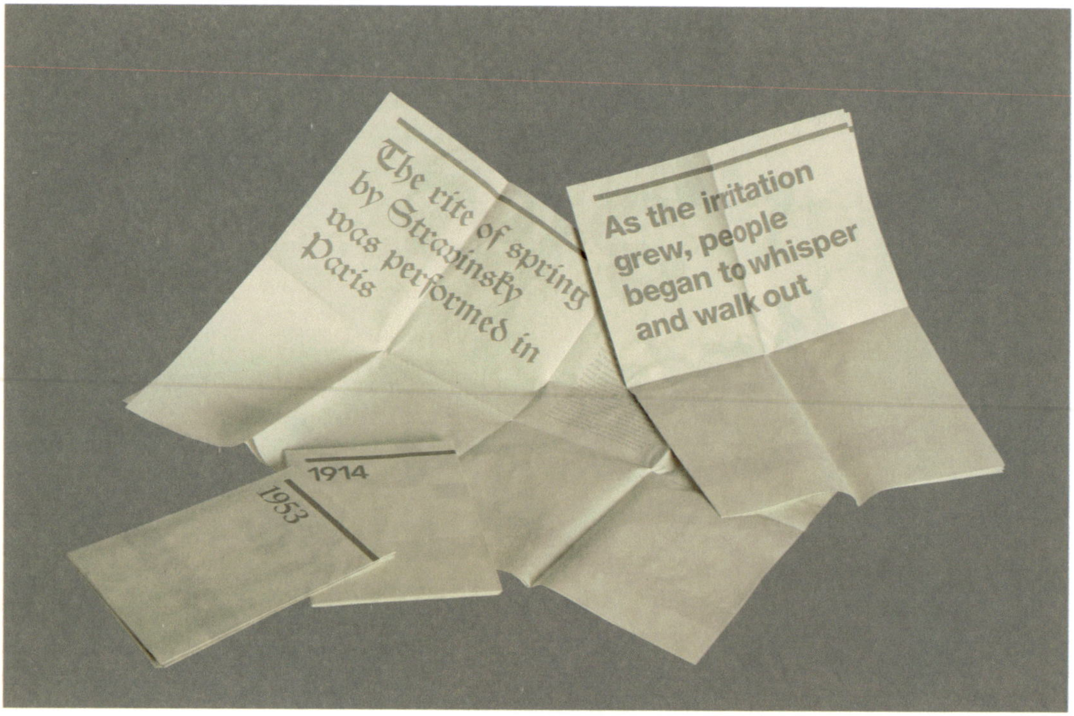

self-commissioned

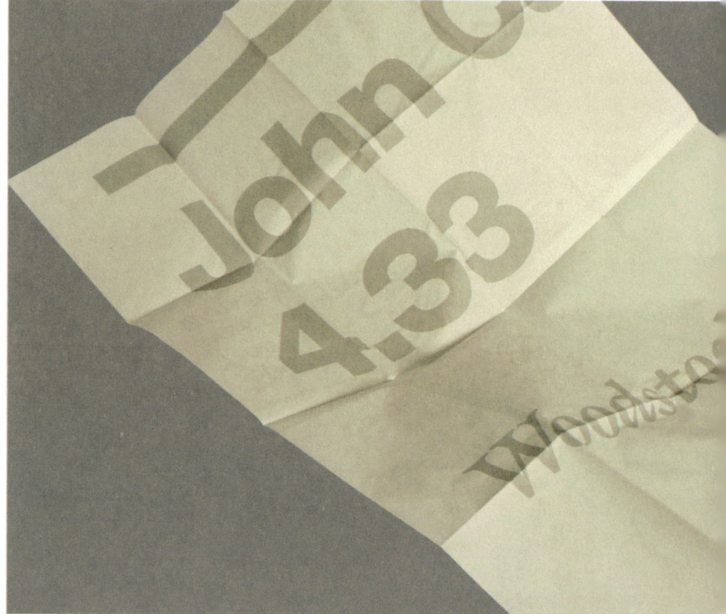

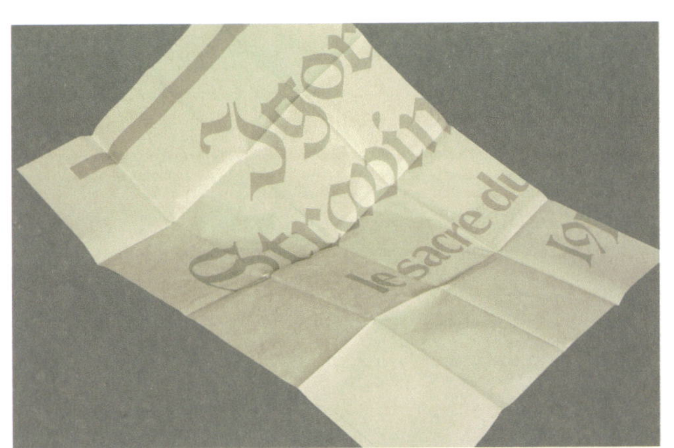
le sacre du

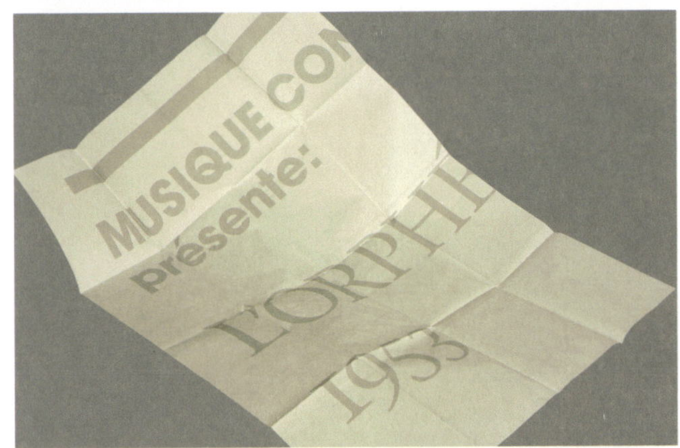
MUSIQUE
présente:
1953

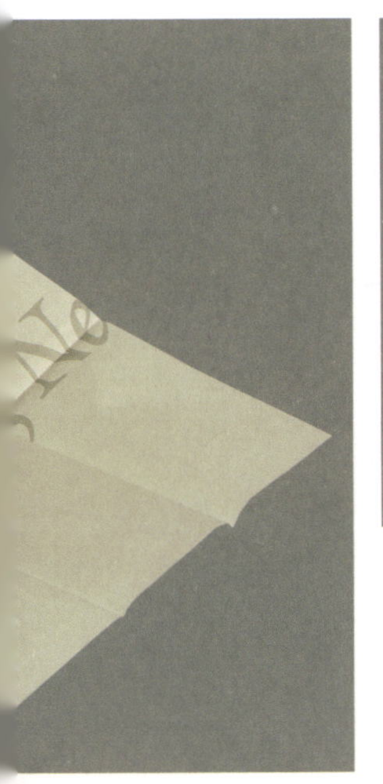

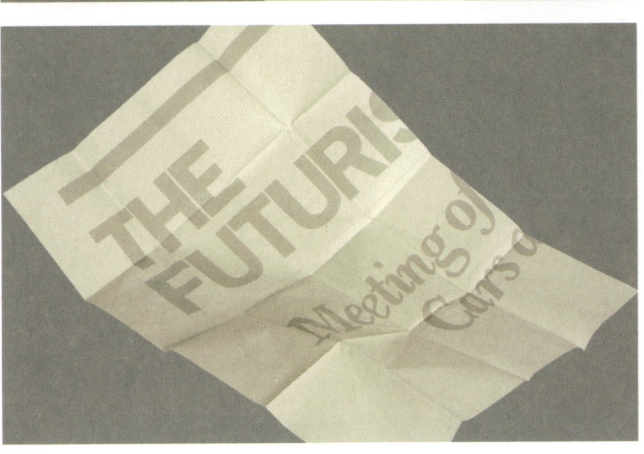
THE
Meeting

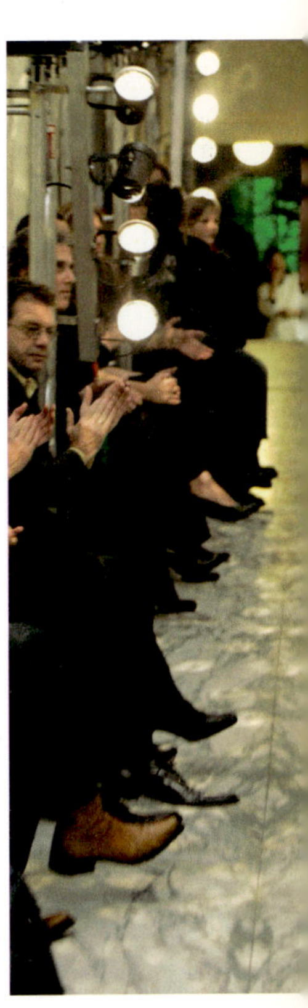

Heavenly Leader
by Harmen Liemburg

Sea-inspired print designs for ‹Orson + Bodil›. Dutch fashion designer Alexander van Slobbe invited me to do some prints for his ‹Orson + Bodil› label. One of the designs has been incorporated into the ‹Orson + Bodil 2006 summer collection›: two skirts printed in white ink on transparent organza silk.

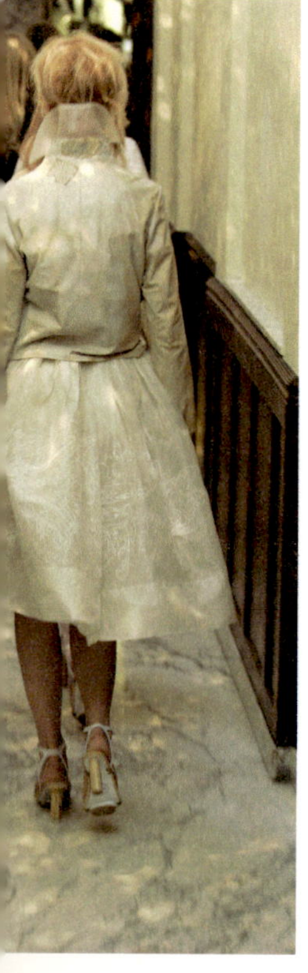

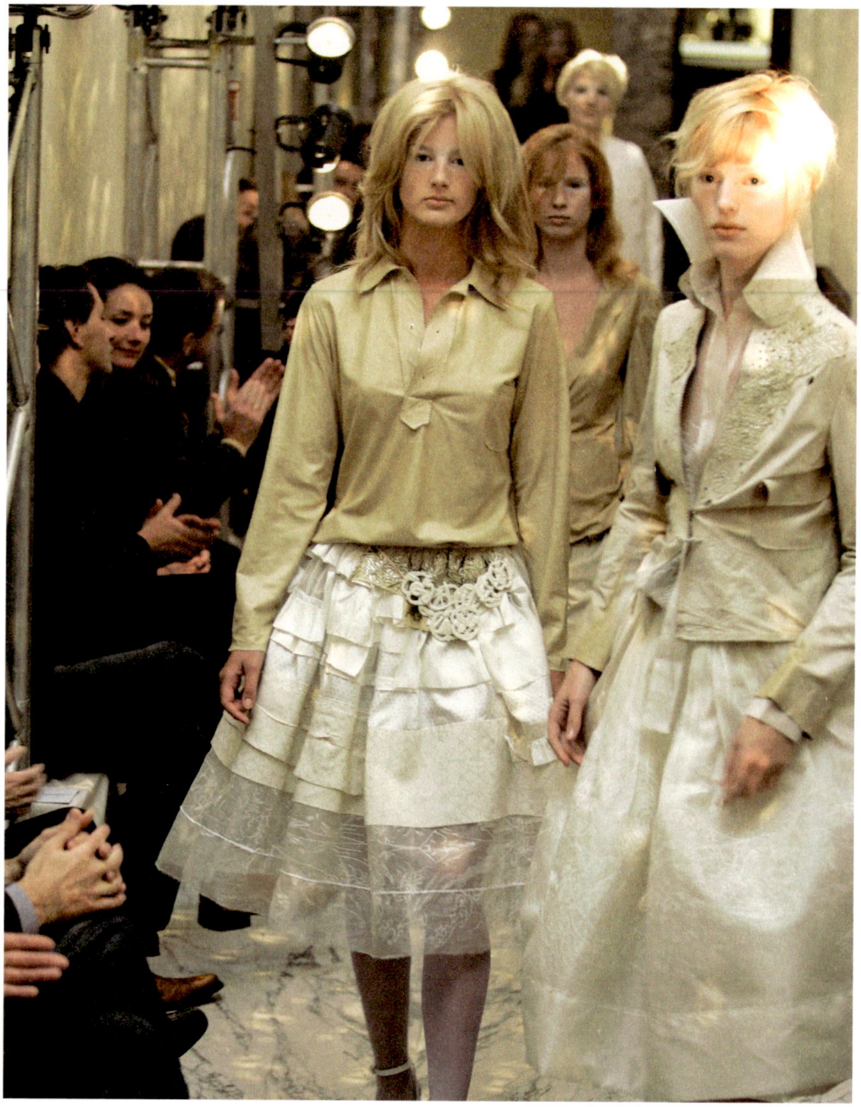

Photo by Peter Stigter.
for Orson+Bodil
45 x 150 cm, silk-screened on organza
by Zeebra, Ede, 2005

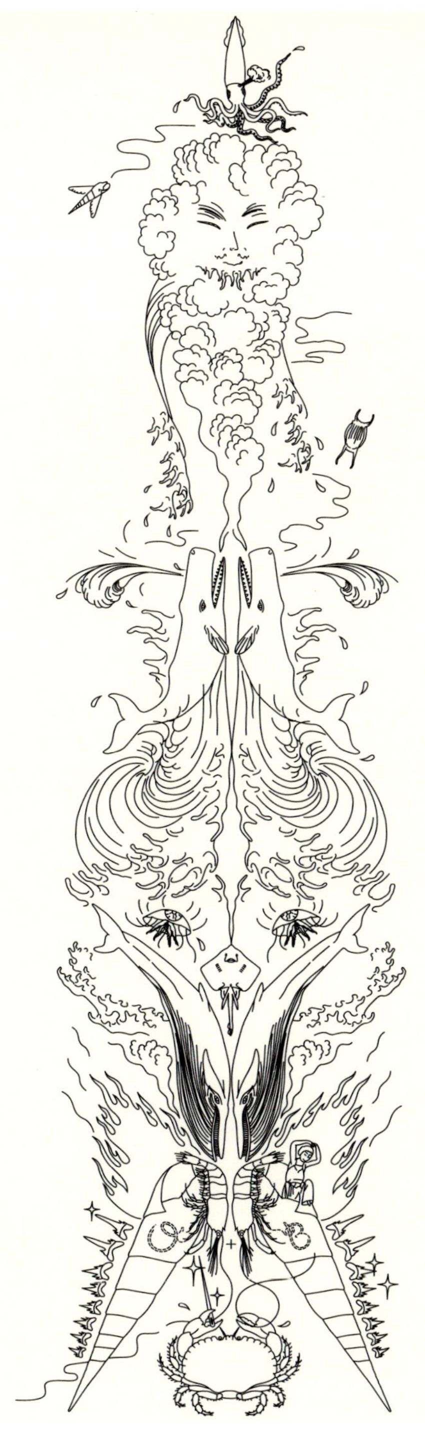

45 x 150 cm, silk-screened on organza
by Zeebra, Ede, 2005

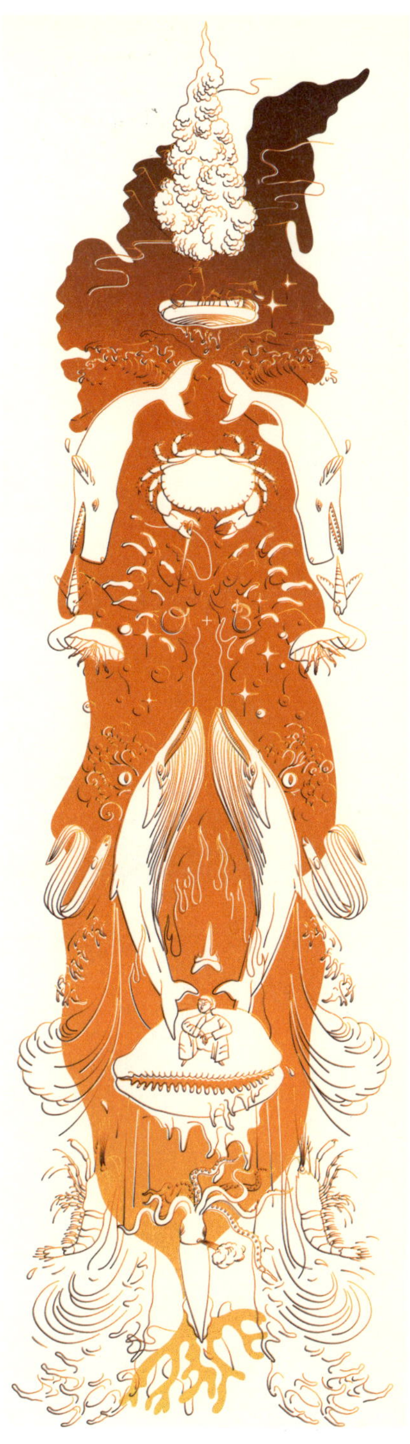

Apparition, 45 x H 150 cm,
full-colour printed on silk, 2005

Wedding tablecloth
by Richard Niessen & Esther de Vries

Rene and Chotima got married in Thailand. We couldn't afford to join them so instead we made this ceremonial tablecloth accompanied by a book full of recipes written by close friends of Rene and Chotima. The ingredients reappear in red and blue (the Dutch and Thai colours) on the cloth, which comes in two parts, to be tied up with red, white and blue ribbons. The names Rene and Chotima and the date of the wedding are printed in gold.

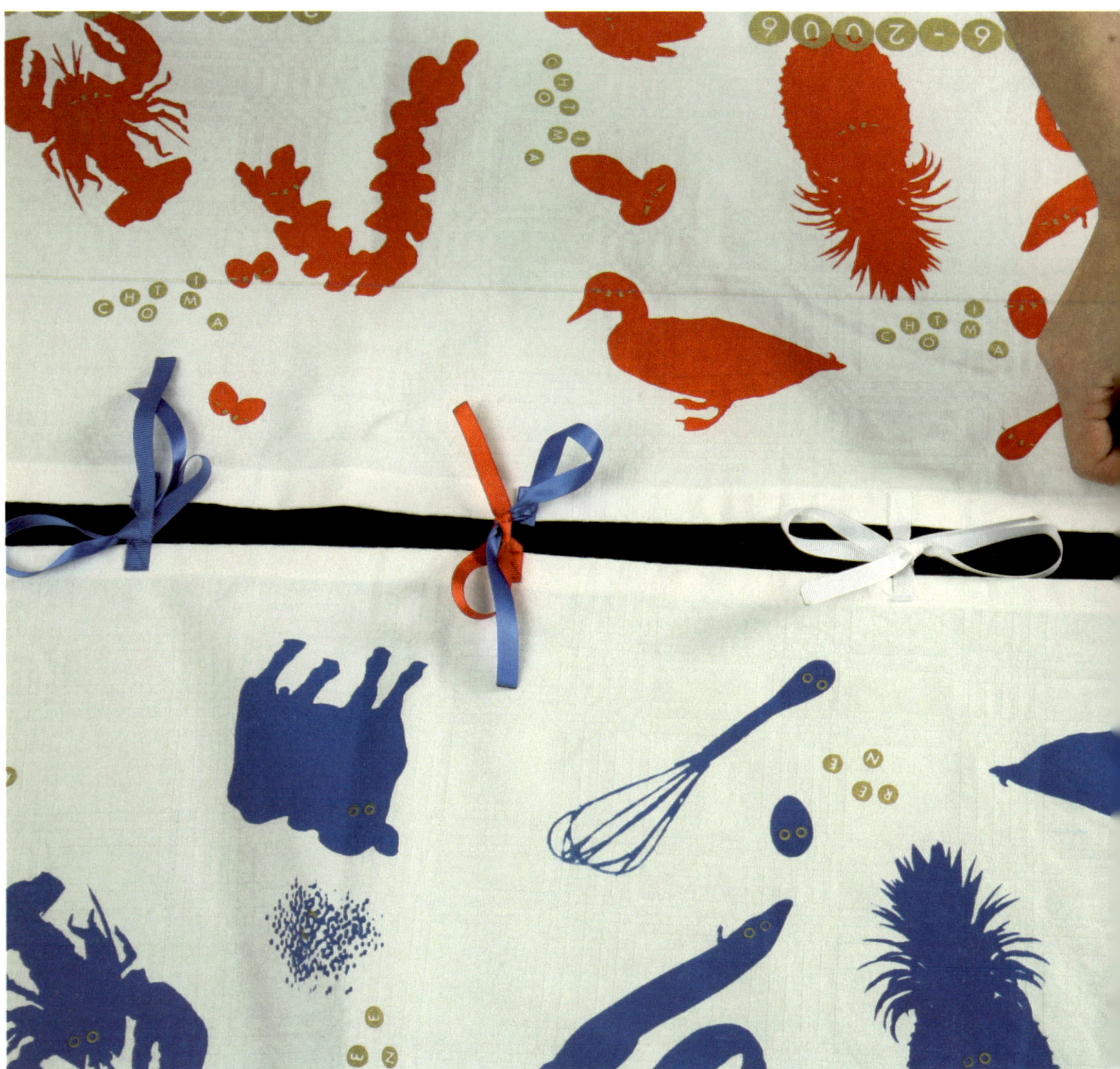

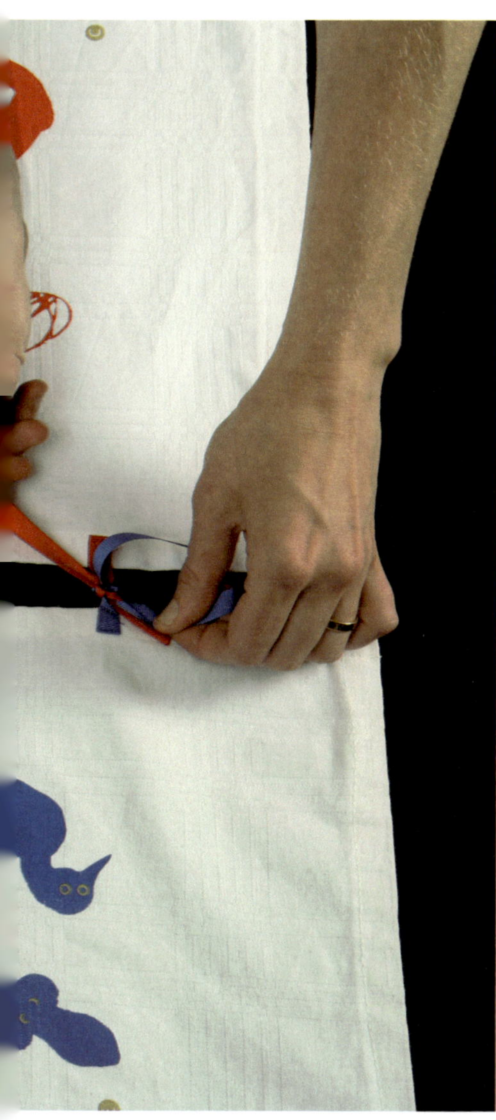

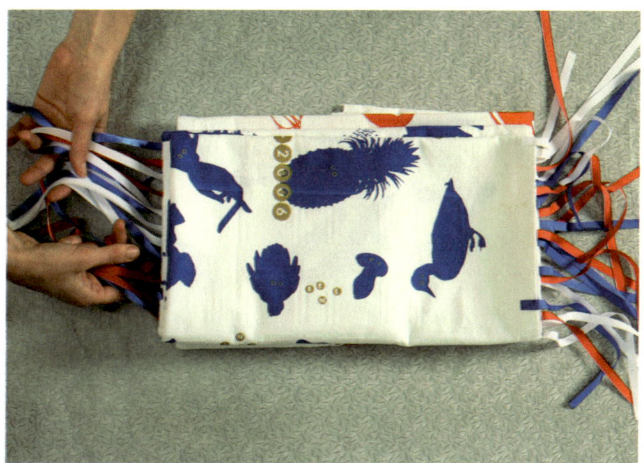

for Rene and Chotima, 2006

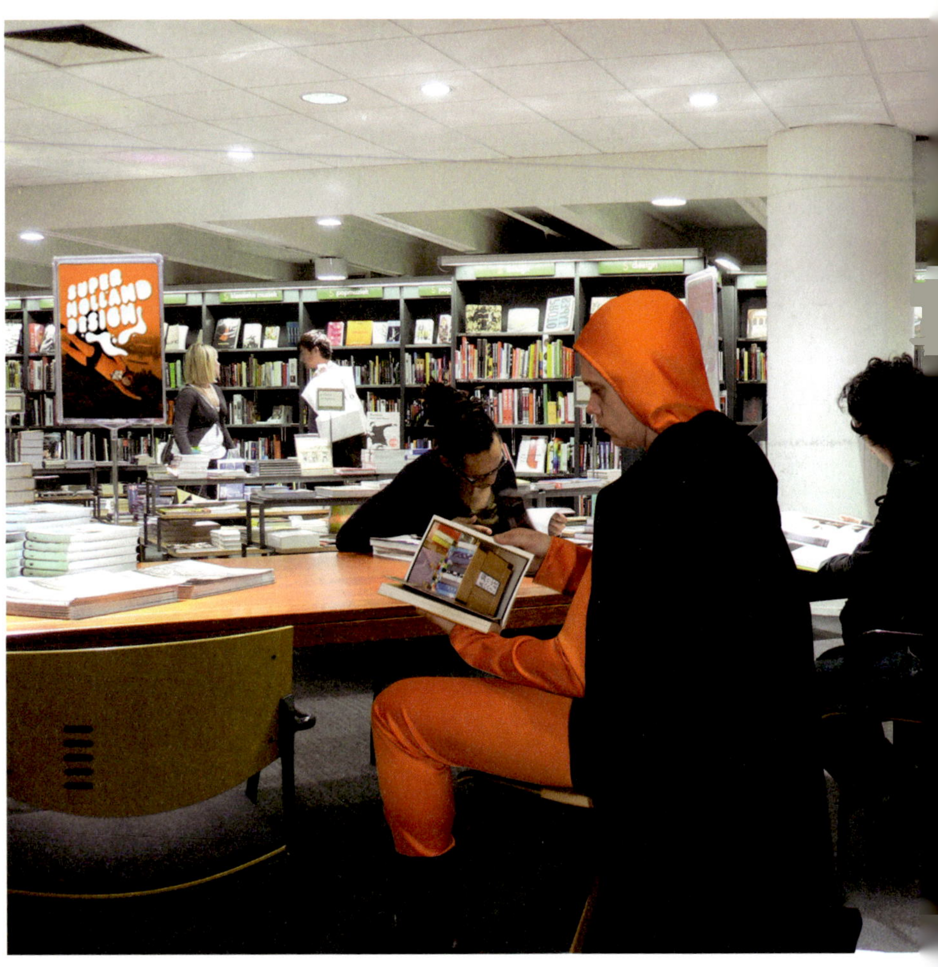
SUPER
HOLLAND
DESIGN

Read Me

WT Magazines
by Werkplaats Typografie

Morf
by Office of CC

The Mondriaan Foundation 2004 Annual report
by Lust

Paperwaste magazine,
by Julia Müller & Julia Neuroth

School brochure
by Julia Müller

Pages Magazine
by Lust

Frame
by Koehorst in't Veld

Code
by Toko

New Directions
by Toko

Evol Eye Lands End
by Richard Niessen

Mark
by Machine

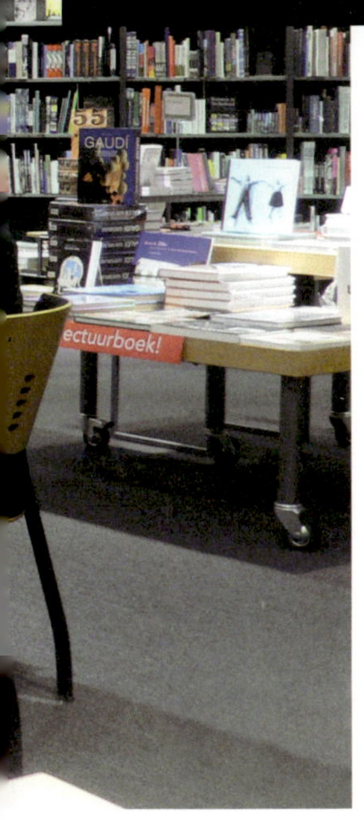

WT Magazines

by David Bennewith and other WT students / Werkplaats Typografie

A bi-monthly WT production initiated by participant David Bennewith. The title of the magazine depends on the number of contributions to the issue. The limitations are that the content must be sourced from within a contemporary context and that each issue will be passed on from reader to reader, with the print run never exceeding 30. The first three covers were designed by WT tutors Karel Martens, Paul Elliman and Armand Mevis.

297 x 210 mm, folded to A5, 2005–2007

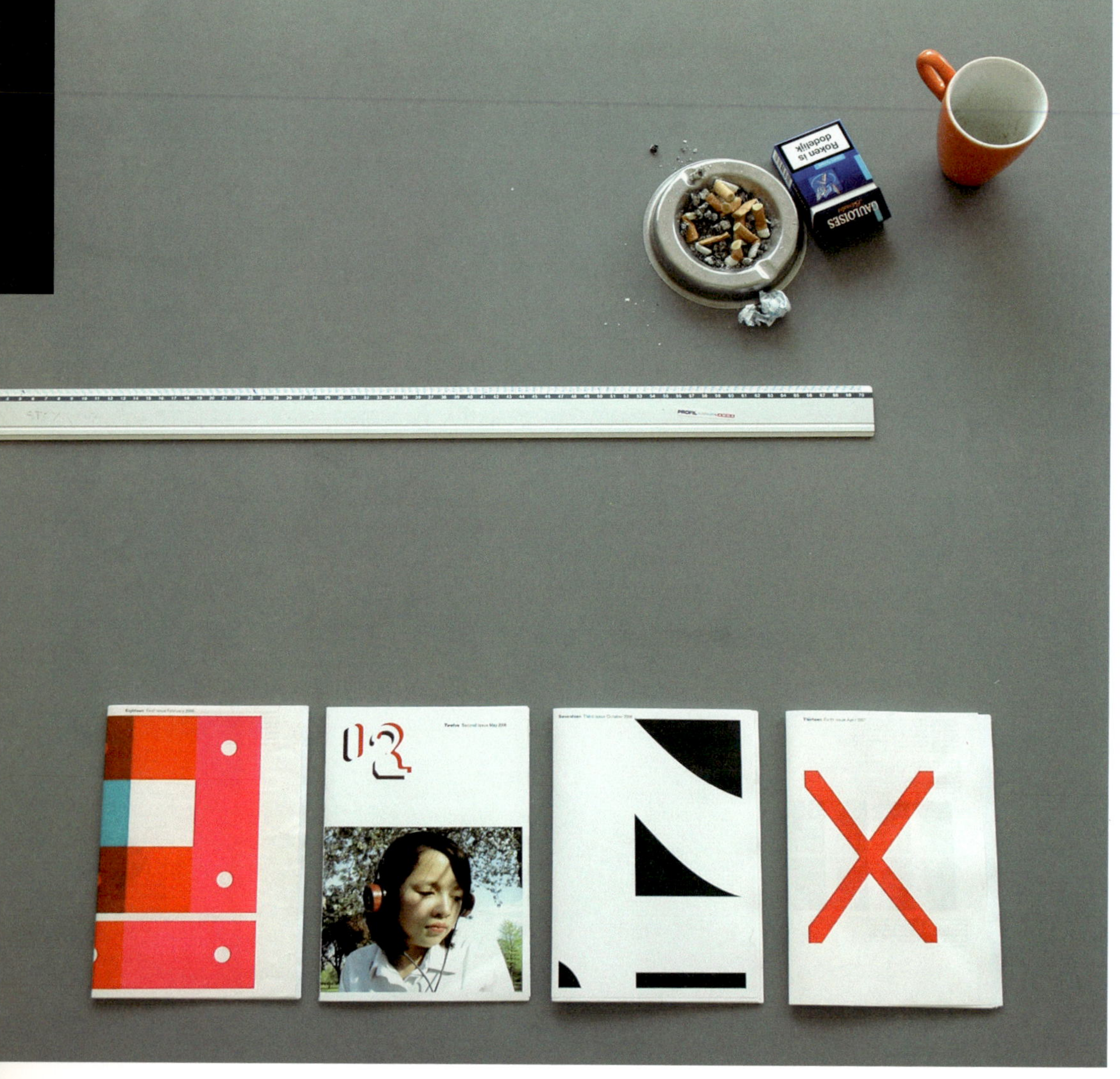

1296 sans serif fullstops

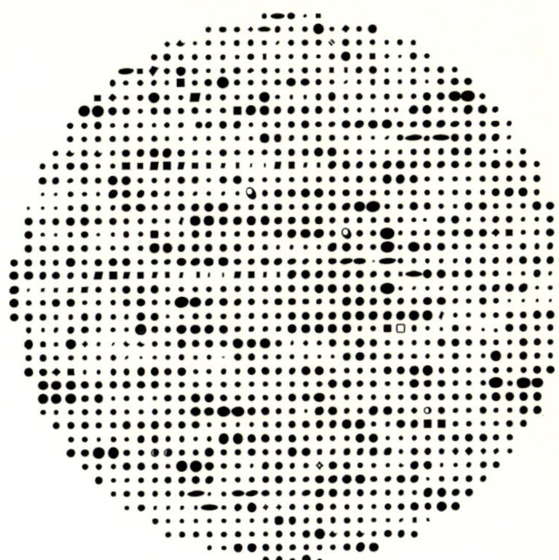

1271 serif fullstops

Cover of 'Exhibits (A) and (B)' published on the occasion of Tom Benson, Registers and Greyscales 10.12.06 – 22.02.07

A Receipt. by Stuart Bailey

This text might be mistaken for a frame, but really it belongs in the margins, or – better – the gutter. It marks the latest exchange in an ongoing barter system of translation, which began when Tom asked me to participate in 'a translation of practice', from a series of his paintings to a printed booklet. The arrangement was bound by the usual gift economy: I would be paid in kind with one of the paintings, the subject of the object.

That first translation was articulated through a kind of graphic esperanto – a clinical and slightly absurd exercise in objectivity. Accepting the premise of failure inherent in any attempt to document works whose material effect typically involved the application of over thirty layers of flat pigment, my dubious interpretation was a kind of deadpan cubism. It comprised a pair of equivalent colour representations of a single painting by the two most common printing processes (Pantone, CMYK) and three of the painting's physical form by photographing the front, side and back. All of which were then bound by a cover which pushed for a further abstraction – the colour rendered as a rasterized, bastardized, greyscale alter-ego; a point-blank cartoon rectangle determined by Tom's half-closed-eye transfer of the colour's density to that ubiquitous halftone field of dots normally automated by camera or computer.

Once that first booklet 'After Nach その後' was printed, instead of collecting my painting as arranged I asked Tom to make a reciprocal translation, which would embody an idea contained in another text, by Wyndham Lewis:

... the most perishable colours in painting (such as Veronese green, Prussian blue, Alizarin crimson) are the most brilliant. So that which burns brightest burns most briefly, and in true modernist fashion brilliance must be but fleeting, timely, not eternal, a coincidence of moment, viewer and object.

My proposal was that he should make a composite work which would attempt to capture and hang these three notoriously difficult pigments. True to reputation, as soon as their jars were opened these delinquents infiltrated every corner of Tom's studio, got up his nose, in his ears and lungs, and gradually discoloured his bedsheets. Eventually, crimson and blue were successfully caught and tamed by trial and error, but green remained elusive. Highly toxic and verboten – the absinthe of the paint world – Veronese (or Emerald) green survives the end of its family line in a single bottle kept in a museum in Munich. As it happened Tom was screenprinting his halftones in a nearby factory and so produced a monochrome 'green' imbued with the poison's radioactive spirit to complete the triptych.

Although patently surrogate, that monochrome green wasn't merely a subsitute, failure, stand-in or copy. In fact, to consider it inferior in any way misses the point entirely. Rather, a certain electricity occurs precisely in the space between intention and outcome, between colour and greyscale. The emergent halftone was a new, independent work, all the richer for embedding the story of its own inception. In a well-known argument about the possibility of calculating the weight of smoke, the claimant placed a piece of tobacco on one end of a balancing scale, then filled his pipe with an equal amount, smoked it and carefully tapped the ash onto the other end. The difference in weight, he stated, was the weight of the smoke. Like the tobacco and the ash, the physical paintings here are merely the tangible evidence of the two poles, exhibits (A) and (B).

By making three new works, however, Tom had overcom - pensated the debt; decorum demanded yet another reciprocal translation, and so I agreed to write this text. I remembered a poster for a Rosemary Trockel exhibition was hanging in the window of the local Goethe Institute, and each time I passed by I sensed some incongruity, but couldn't say why exactly until I eventually got off my bike. The majority of the poster was a large full-bleed black and white portrait of what appeared to be Trockel herself, but the right hand side of the image just after the nose was covered by a thick yellow strip running top to bottom. There was no evident reason to crop the image so severely, so the strip served no purpose other than being, perhaps, an 'aesthetic element', a piece of graphic furniture. But then the poster had no other signs of being so consciously designed; it looked more like some Goethe intern had made it in their lunch hour. This unresolved yellow was kicking around in my mind for some time before I actually visited the exhibtion, where I immediately found myself face to face with the original photograph, and saw the strip was actually masking a brutal black eye. It later occurred to me that this gap in my perception was the work; the gap constituted it, and now I understand the work in this new booklet is the same kind of gap – between the colours and their counterparts. Read that again backwards: the gap is the work.

Orginally, Tom gave me a word as a trigger, a catalyst – 'maybe you could write something about ?' – which allegedly captured the essence of of the colour/halftone series. A week later I had forgotten what it was, and when I asked Tom he had forgotten too. Suddenly our mutual absent-mindedness seemed to harbor another clue: something so recently sublime could now not even be trawled from memory. Like words the paintings remain fixed while the meanings between them fluctuate, and like sunspots the meanings are impossible to look at directly, with their retinal stain repeatedly shunting off to the side, then out of frame. Instead of second-guessing his missing word, Tom sent along an entire gamut of 32 possible substitutes, from 'sequence', through 'audition' and 'eclipse', to 'indication'.

The usual process of making books is to print large flat sheets on both sides, then fold them in half a number of times to form the series of pages, binding one of the enclosed folds and cutting along the other sides. A single folded sheet is called a section, commonly folded four times to make 32 pages. The cover of the new booklet effectively diagrams this principle: imagine folding it in half each time along the white lines. The typography and topography of a book are manifest in an underlying grid; an x-ray would reveal this architecture in the distribution of printed and unprinted areas. The spaces around printed areas at the outer edges of a page are called margins, the space on the inner edge the spine, and that between elements the gutter. The negative white space of the gutter describes that milky gap where the essence of the work lies, and on this cover that lattice comes into focus when you automatically half-close your eyes to compare the so-called originals and their so-called copies. Imagine those 32 words Tom sent set equidistant on a sheet of paper folded down 4 four times. Only an x-ray of that section might come close to forming an adequate description of the works which, in turn, translate a certain kind of mind, deceptively technical and deeply vulnerable. As this text sinks into that same milk, the colours and halftones swallow each other, and this booklet swallows its predecessor.

Morf
by Office of CC

‹Morf› is a magazine for design, published twice a year by Premsela (Dutch Platform for Design and Fashion) and distributed free of charge to all students in design schools and similar educational facilities in the Netherlands. This publication is geared toward theory and historical insight into design as a discipline. The aim of ‹Morf› is to stimulate students to think about their profession and their own future place within it – and to encourage them to read, since reading is not a natural habit of most Dutch design students. The content of the magazine is divided in three parts: re-publications, current writings and student writings. Every issue has a subliminal theme that runs through the articles.

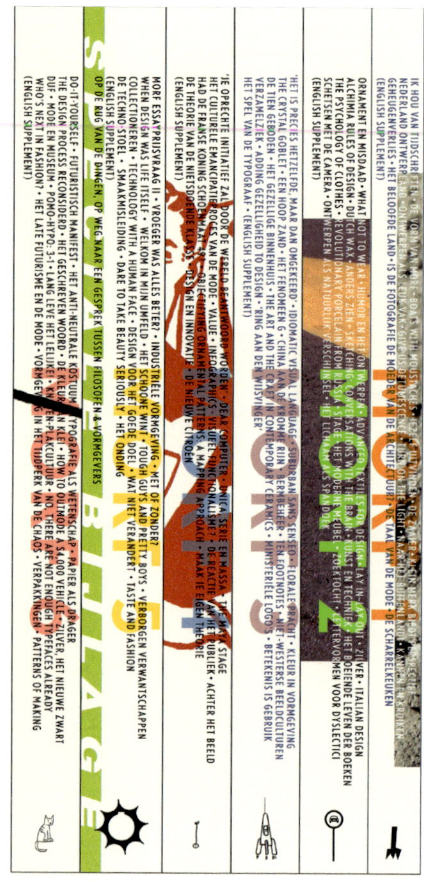

for Premsela, from left to right: spines of the six issues of ‹Morf›, covers of issue 1, 3 and 4, the cover image illustrates the hidden theme of each issue 2004-

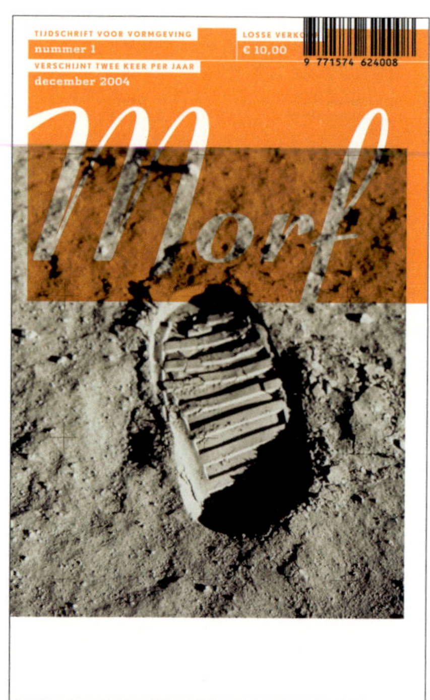

Morf 01: This was the launch issue, with several articles addressing the theme of the reason for the existence and the form of Morf.

The image on the cover is of Buzz Aldrin's footprint on the moon, taken on July 20th 1969. It illustrates the first step of a student entering the world of theory. The image also illustrates looking at things from a great distance, investigating the work done on our planet from a timeless perspective: past and present co-exist side by side.

Our aim as designers was to produce a legible and efficient typography, a simple layout for the images and helpful guidance for steering a course through the magazine. In the end, ‹Morf› became an industrial product whose design and form speaks functionality. It is not a glossy tabloid; it is not a picture book with visual candies to seduce: it is a magazine for reading and not for ‹looking at›. In short, we allowed no non-sense design.

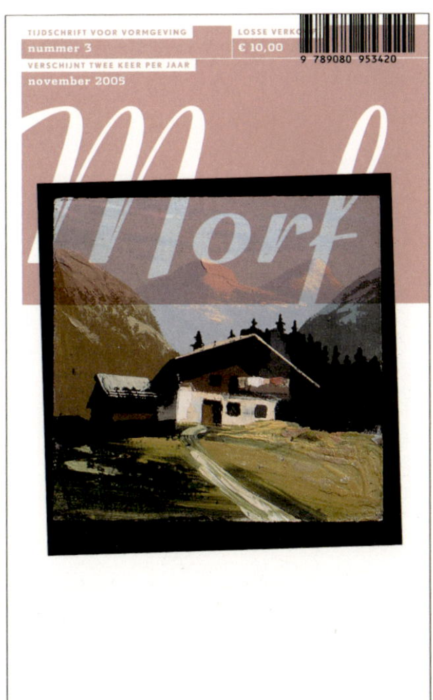

Morf 03: Cosiness, the hidden theme in this issue, has always had an uneasy relation with the design and art movements. In this painting of a Swiss chalet we found a 'cosiness' that is independent of any movements.

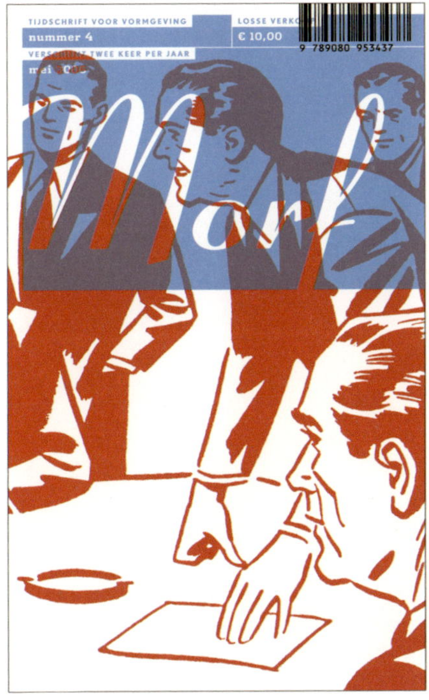

Morf 04: The hidden theme was business in design, with several re-published articles from the post-WWII period. The image on the cover is a 1950s drawing of American men in suits; it illustrates how important decisions are made in meetings that we in our time still benefit and suffer from.

50-80 Lay In—Lay Out

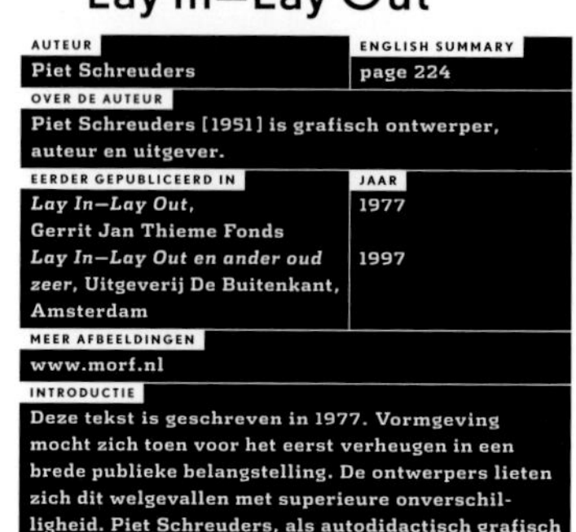

AUTEUR
Piet Schreuders

ENGLISH SUMMARY
page 224

OVER DE AUTEUR
Piet Schreuders [1951] is grafisch ontwerper, auteur en uitgever.

EERDER GEPUBLICEERD IN	JAAR
Lay In—Lay Out, Gerrit Jan Thieme Fonds	1977
Lay In—Lay Out en ander oud zeer, Uitgeverij De Buitenkant, Amsterdam	1997

MEER AFBEELDINGEN
www.morf.nl

INTRODUCTIE
Deze tekst is geschreven in 1977. Vormgeving mocht zich toen voor het eerst verheugen in een brede publieke belangstelling. De ontwerpers lieten zich dit welgevallen met superieure onverschilligheid. Piet Schreuders, als autodidactisch grafisch ontwerper min of meer een buitenstaander, leverde met *Lay In—Lay Out* een niet mis te verstane bijdrage aan de aanzwellende kritiek. Dat was niet de bedoeling! Een erecode was geschonden—ontwerpend Nederland viel over hem heen. Voor de jongere generatie was hij vanaf dat moment uiteraard een held. Met zoveel vuur over vormgeving schrijven is sindsdien helaas zelden meer gebeurd.

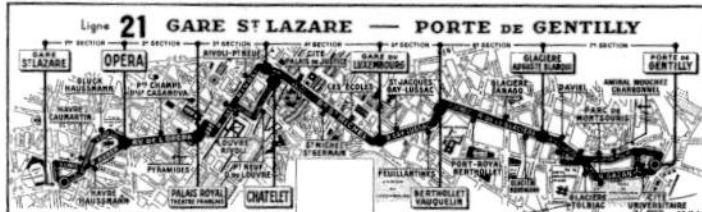

TOPOGRAFISCHE TYPOGRAFIE IS VAAK MOOIE TYPOGRAFIE. DE VORMGEVING VAN DEZE PARIJSE BUSPLATTEGROND (UITGAVE 1972) IS FENOMENAAL, AL HEEFT DE MAKER DAAR MISSCHIEN NIET BIJ STILGESTAAN.

Day in—day out—
Same ol' hoodoo follows me about;
Same ol' pounding in my heart
Whenever I think of you,
And darling, I think of you,
Day in and day out...
—Johnny Mercer
'Day In—Day Out', 1939

Het vak 'grafisch vormgeven' is misdadig en zou eigenlijk niet mogen bestaan. We zullen er een boekje aan wijden. ↵
Het vak bestond honderd jaar geleden nog niet; over honderd jaar bestaat het waarschijnlijk al lang niet meer. Maar vandaag de dag beleeft het een ongekende bloeiperiode. ↵
Iedereen die een brief schrijft en daarbij een linkermarge van vier centimeter aanhoudt, is aan het ontwerpen. Iedereen die de eettafel op een bepaalde manier dekt, is aan het layouten. Iedereen die met grote letters opruiende teksten op muren schildert, bedrijft typografie. In deze zin heeft het vak altijd bestaan zolang de mensen zich van de vormen der dingen bewust waren. Maar doordat het ontwerpen zich in de loop der tijd heeft ontwikkeld tot een commerciële onderneming waarbij tijd geld is en zaken zaken zijn, werd de vormgeving van drukwerk meer een kwestie van efficiency dan van duidelijkheid en schoonheid. Deze branchevervaging leidde er bijvoorbeeld toe dat nieuwe lettertypen niet uit typografische maar uit commerciële overwegingen ontworpen werden. Dergelijke ontwikkelingen zijn eigenlijk alleen maar te vangen onder het begrip 'misdadig'. ↵

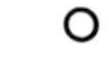

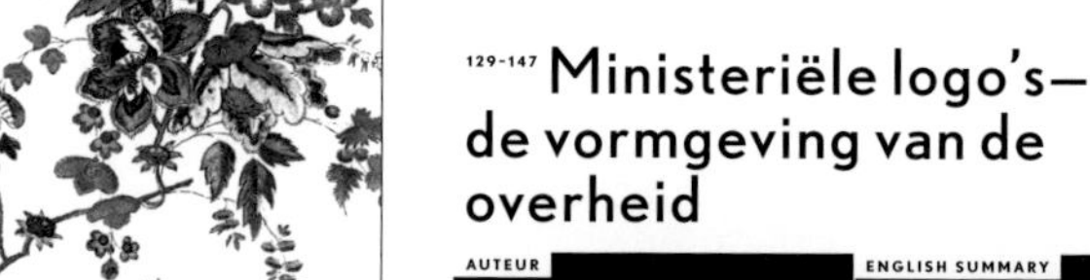

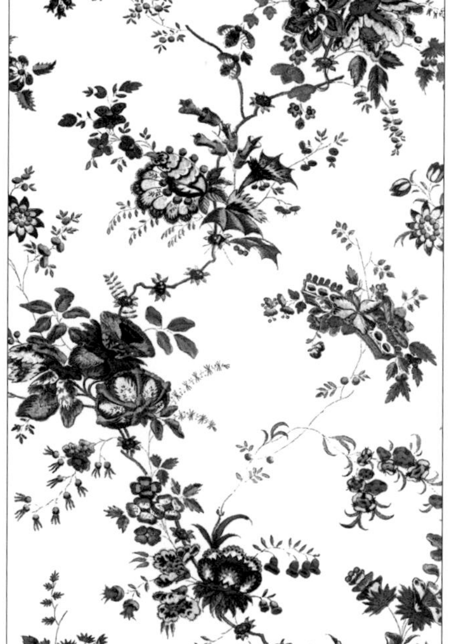

129-147 Ministeriële logo's—de vormgeving van de overheid

AUTEUR
Maurits Vroombout

ENGLISH SUMMARY
page 244

OVER DE AUTEUR
Maurits Vroombout [1981] studeerde in maart van dit jaar af aan Academie St. Joost in Breda, afdeling grafisch ontwerp.

AFBEELDINGEN IN KLEUR
www.morf.nl

INTRODUCTIE
De relatie tussen de overheid en de burger is in een democratisch land als Nederland voortdurend aan verandering onderhevig. De overheid wil gezag uitstralen, maar moet tegelijkertijd ook vertrouwen wekken, zodat de afstand met de burger niet te groot wordt. Sinds ontwerpers medeverantwoordelijk zijn voor het gezicht van de overheid spelen ook modieuze vormspelletjes een rol. Maurits Vroombout nam enkele logo's van ministeries onder de loep en velde zijn oordeel.

Buitenlandse Zaken heeft een regenworm, VROM heeft Engelse drop en bij Sociale Zaken spelen ze graag met streepjes en puntjes. De overheid wil zich sinds de jaren '70 niet meer presenteren als arrogante machtshebber, maar als een transparante organisatie waarbij elke burger zich thuisvoelt. Daarom heeft ze de heraldiek met haar autoritaire bijsmaak aan de kant gezet en is ze gebruik gaan maken van de diensten van grafisch ontwerpbureaus. Ministeries laten zich door

DESSIN VAN ROND 1760 [>P283]

Inside of Morf magazine: from issues 2, 3 (left page) and 4 (right page, two spreads). In the lower right-hand corner is a flipbook animation. A ‹visual essay› with full pages of visuals runs throughout the magazine illustrating the chosen topic.

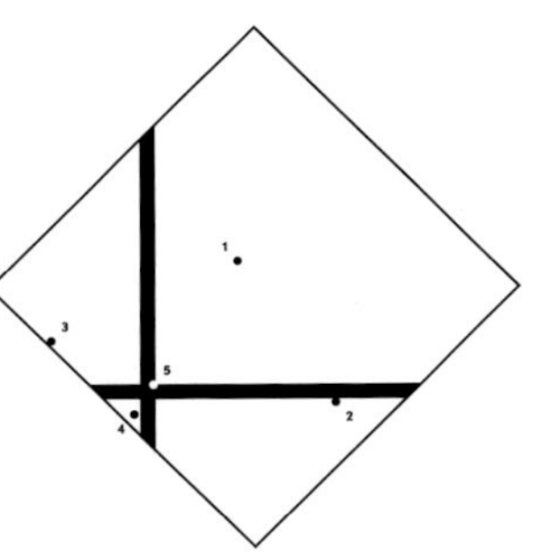

DE MANIFESTATIE *'Holland in vorm'* **VOND PLAATS IN 1987 OP VIJF LOCATIES;**

1 *Stedelijk Museum Amsterdam*
2 *Gemeentemuseum Arnhem*
3 *Haags Gemeentemuseum*
4 *Museum Boijmans Van Beuningen Rotterdam*
5 *Centraal Museum Utrecht*

emoties in keramische objecten vertolkte. Illustratief is een exemplaar met de titel 'Is dood en wordt verbrand'. Het object heeft de vorm van een kruik maar de gebruikelijke halsopening is vervangen door drie 'schoorstenen'. In de wand is onder meer een liggende figuur in een kinderwagen gekrast.* ↵
Een vergelijkbare ontwikkeling kunnen we signaleren in de andere ambachtskunsten. Op alle terreinen begon ambachtelijke virtuositeit plaats te maken voor vrije expressie. De gebruiksfunctie werd hierbij steeds verder losgelaten en weldra zette een deel van de ambachtskunstenaars zijn eerste schreden op het sculpturale pad. In de loop van de jaren zestig breidde het aantal kunstenaars dat een eigen atelier opzette zich snel uit. Aparte vermelding verdienen in dit verband de ontwikkelingen in de glaskunst. ↵
Dat ambachtskunstenaars weer zelfstandig begonnen te werken was op zichzelf geen nieuw fenomeen in Nederland. Ook voor de oorlog kwam het wel voor dat keramisten, textielkunstenaars of edelsmeden in eigen ateliers werkten. De glaskunstenaar was hier echter altijd gebonden geweest aan de smeltovens en de meesterglasblazer van de glasfabriek. Pas nadat de Amerikaanse glaskunstenaar Harvey Littleton een kleine, verplaatsbare glasoven had ontwikkeld, werd de mogelijkheid geschapen zich van de fabriek en de productie van gebruiksvoorwerpen los te maken. De kunstenaar kon het maakproces nu van begin tot eind in eigen hand houden. Het initiatief van Littleton bracht in Amerika de Studio Glass Movement op gang. De beweging waaide over naar Nederland toen Sybren Valkema een oventje voor de Rietveld Academie bouwde en daar in 1969 de werkgroep Glas van start kon gaan. ↵
De nieuwe vrijheid in de ambachtskunsten bracht een grote opbloei van deze kunsttak en een flinke uitbreiding van het aantal zelfstandige beoefenaars met zich mee. De samenwerking met de industrie werd in deze kring steeds minder geambieerd. De industrie had hen dan ook niet veel te bieden. Voor de industriële productie schakelde men bij voorkeur afgestudeerden van de opleidin-

NOOT • Spruyt-Ledeboer 1976, p. 40

Overzicht van de zoomhoogte, ( ) of roklengte,

van westerse vrouwen uit de middenklasse en betere standen over een periode van de laatste tweehonderd jaar in relatie met de gemiddelde ( ) economische groei.

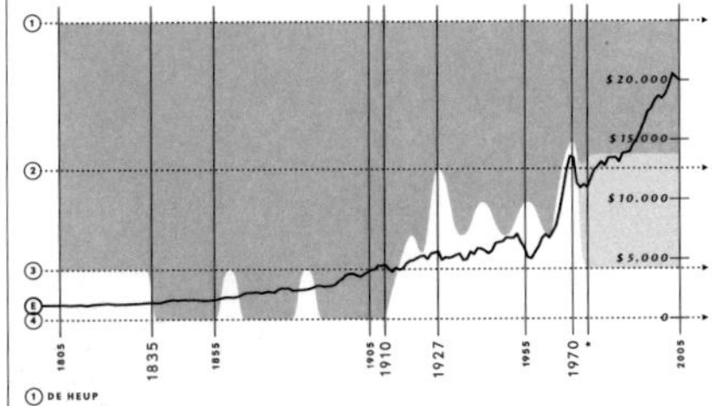

① DE HEUP
② DE KNIE
③ DE ENKEL [OF TOT VIJF CENTIMETER ERBOVEN]
④ DE VLOER

BEREIK TOEGESTANE ROKLENGTE

* SINDS HET MIDDEN VAN DE JAREN ZEVENTIG IS HET BEREIK VAN DE TOEGESTANE ROKLENGTE VEEL RUIMER GEWORDEN: DE MODE SCHRIJFT NIET LANGER EEN ENKELE ROKLENGTE VOOR. VROUWEN KUNNEN KIEZEN UIT VERSCHILLENDE STIJLEN VOOR VERSCHILLENDE GELEGENHEDEN, WAARONDER HET DRAGEN VAN EEN BROEK IN PLAATS VAN EEN ROK OF JURK
BRON: H.C.'S SLIGHTLY SILLY VICTORIAN AND PRE-REGENCY PAGE
WWW.PEMBERLEY.COM/JANEINFO/PEMBFUN/VICTCFSH.HTML.

Ⓔ **REËEL BRUTO NATIONAAL PRODUCT VERENIGDE STATEN 1805-2005. PER HOOFD VAN DE BEVOLKING** [IN DOLLARS UIT 2000]
BRON: ECONOMIC HISTORY SERVICES
WWW.EH.NET

Semantiek Hoe mode als betekenissysteem functioneert, wordt nog duidelijker in de jaren tachtig als de Japanse ontwerpers naar Parijs komen met hun vreemde esthetiek en conceptuele mode. Ook een ontwerper als Jean Paul Gaultier wordt in brede, intellectuele kringen geprezen om het postmoderne spel dat hij met kleding speelt. Hij gooit vaststaande kledingcodes door elkaar door een avondjurk te combineren met sneakers. Ontwerpers als Martin Margiela en Yohji Yamamoto proberen het verstrijken van tijd, 'het gedragene' en de vergankelijkheid van kleding in mode uit te drukken. De inhoud van mode en kunst blijken opeens niet zo ver meer uit elkaar te liggen. Ook mode kan een concept of inhoud hebben en niet slechts een ultiem schoonheidsidaal laten zien. Zo ontstaat er vanuit de musea en de wetenschap plotseling een veel serieuzere belangstelling voor het fenomeen mode. ↵
Opvallend is dat vooraanstaande musea op het gebied van beeldende kunst, zonder eigen modecollectie, hierin het voortouw nemen. Zo nodigt het Stedelijk Museum in 1990 mode-ontwerper Issey Miyake uit voor de groepstentoonstelling 'Energieën'. Miyake ontwerpt hiervoor geen traditionele poppenopstelling, maar maakt een installatie, waarbij de toeschouwer op kousenvoeten over een witte vloer moet lopen met uitsparingen van kleurige plissé-stoffen. Deze museale modepresentaties zijn een voorbeeld voor een nieuwe generatie ontwerpers die van hun modeshows steeds meer kunstperformances gaan maken. Martin Margiela, Hussein Chalayan en Viktor & Rolf doen zo nadrukkelijk de grenzen tussen mode en kunst verder vervagen. Ze verwerken politiek commentaar in hun mode, verkennen de grenzen van wat kleding is en becommentariëren het modesysteem. Anno 2005 beginnen het grote publiek en de commercie conceptuele mode steeds normaler te vinden. ↵
Het een en ander heeft tot gevolg gehad dat mode nog nooit zo in de mode is geweest als vandaag de dag. Via internet, bladen en mondiale televisiezenders worden we direct over alle laatste modenieuwtjes geïnformeerd. In het museale veld is het vanzelfspre-

The Mondriaan Foundation 2004 Annual report
by Lust

The Mondriaan Foundation was created to stimulate visual arts, design and the cultural heritage of the Netherlands. It seeks to strengthen the international position of the contemporary visual arts and design by offering financial support to enable institutions, companies and authorities –both national and international– to reach their audience.

The Annual Report gives information on all of the projects (co-)financed by the Foundation, more than thousand in total, which received funding support of as little as a hundred and as much as several million euros. A typographical system that separates different levels of information in thread form generates the layout of the pages, divided by a three-ring pie chart that graphs exactly what was spent on each project. Each page is printed on a different colour of paper, in a random order that is unique to each copy of the report. There are eight different colours on the cover and more than 20 different colours inside.

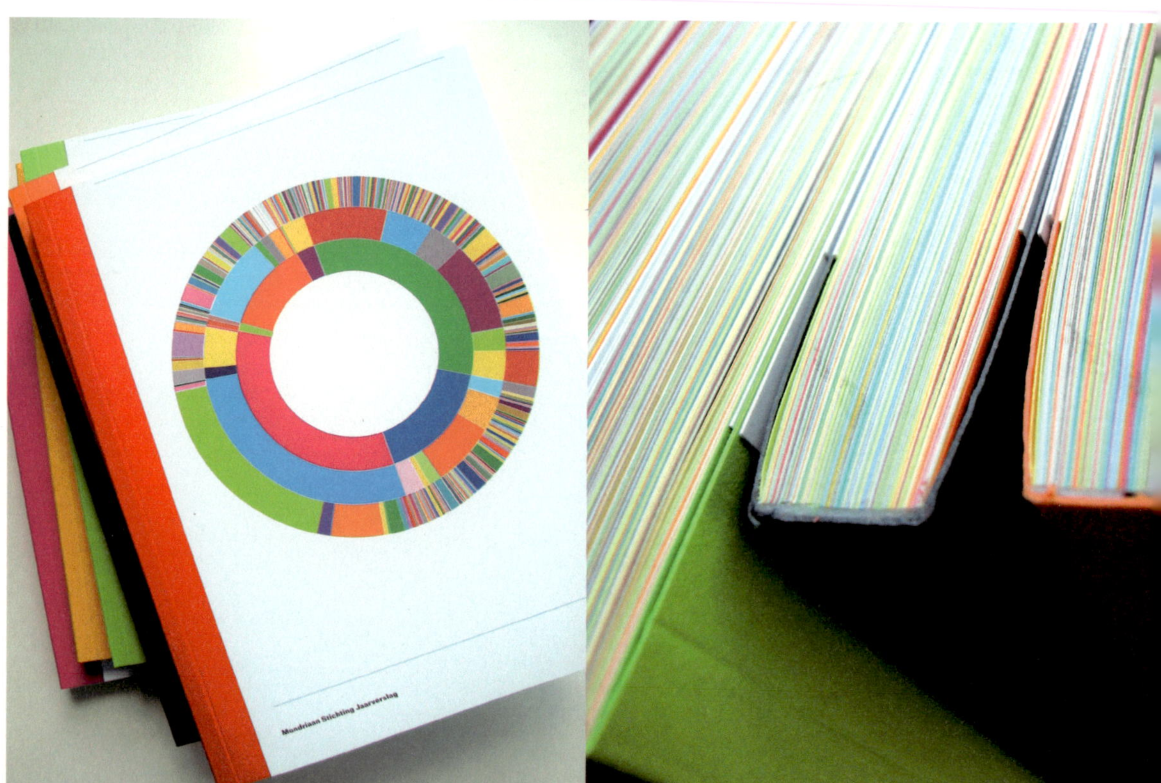

for Mondriaan Foundation, 2005

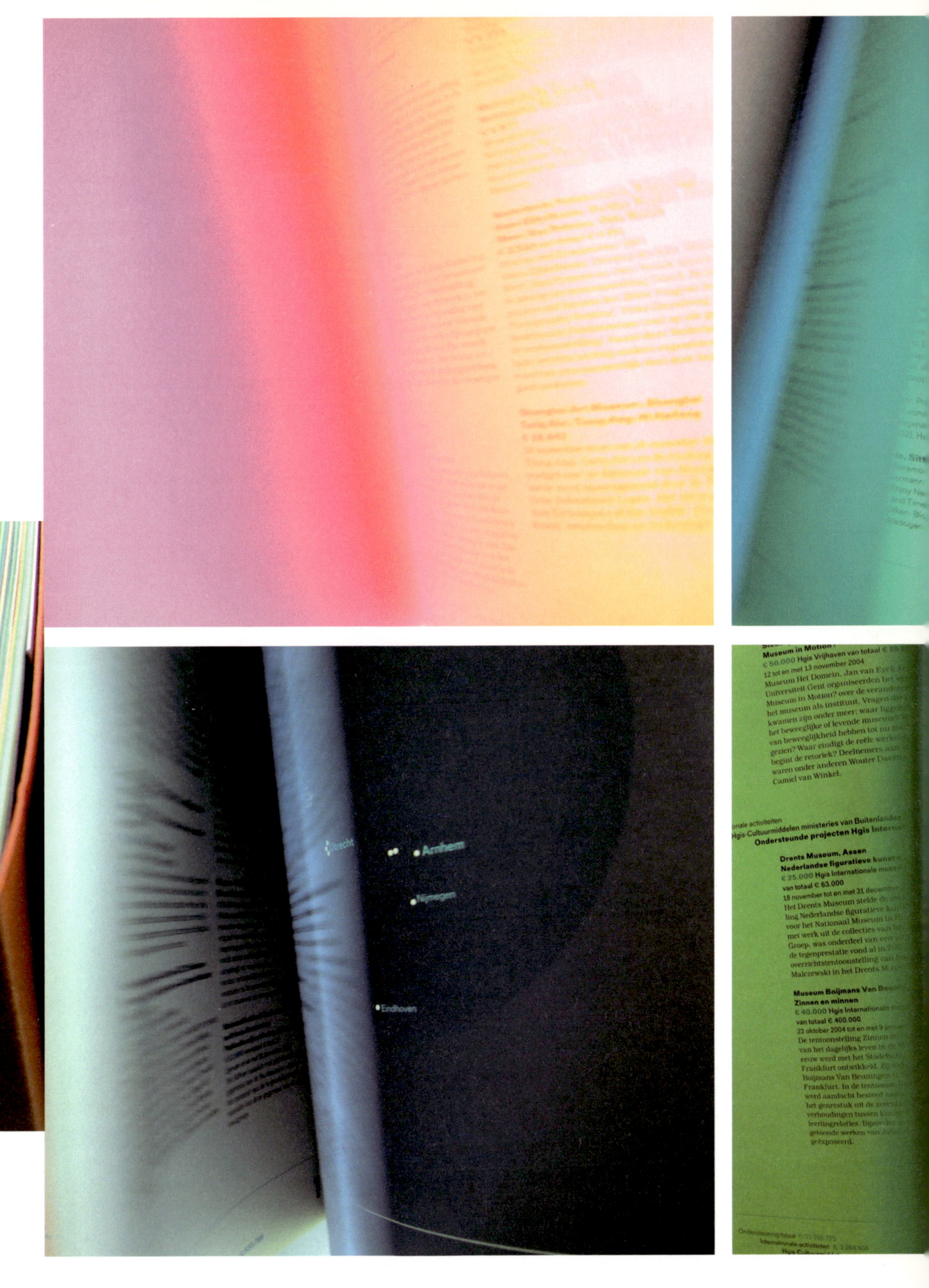
Museum in Motion
€ 50.000 Hgis Vrijhaven van totaal
12 tot en met 13 november 2004
Museum Het Domein, Jan van Eyck
Universiteit Gent organiseerden het
Museum in Motion? over de
het museum als instituut. Vragen
kwamen zijn onder meer: waar
het beweeglijke of levende
van beweeglijkheid hebben tot nu
gezien? Waar eindigt de reële
begint de retoriek? Deelnemers aan
waren onder anderen Wouter
Camiel van Winkel.
onale activiteiten
Hgis-Cultuurmiddelen ministeries van
Ondersteunde projecten Hgis
Drents Museum, Assen
Nederlandse figuratieve
€ 25.000 Hgis Internationale
van totaal € 63.000
18 november tot en met 31
Het Drents Museum stelde
ling Nederlandse figuratieve
voor het Nationaal Museum
met werk uit de collecties
Groep, was onderdeel van
de tegenprestatie vond al
overzichtstentoonstelling
Malczewski in het Drents
Museum Boijmans Van
Zinnen en minnen
€ 40.000 Hgis Internationale
van totaal € 400.000
23 oktober 2004 tot en met
De tentoonstelling
van het dagelijks leven
eeuw werd met het
Frankfurt ontwikkeld.
Boijmans Van Beuningen
Frankfurt. In de
werd aandacht besteed
het genrestuk uit de
verhoudingen tussen
leerlingrelaties.
getoonde werken
geëxposeerd.
Utrecht
Arnhem
Nijmegen
Eindhoven

Paperwaste magazine,
by Julia Müller & Julia Neuroth

‹Paperwaste magazine› is an initiative from young writers in the Netherlands. It features articles about modern art, music history and literature and is intended as a platform for up-and-coming writers. Julia&Julia were asked to design the first issue and were given ‹carte blanche› by the editors.
The magazine contains a variety of very different articles. Each article was given its own sheet and typography and finally all these loose sheets were spread out, forming the yellow ‹in between pages› that run through the magazine and separate one article from the next. Julia&Julia played with contradictions throughout the magazine. On the one hand we have the name of the magazine, which ironically calls itself ‹Paperwaste›, the copied style, the trashy fonts and Post-it-like colours, and on the other hand the size, the layout and the paper, suggesting a glossy fashion magazine rather than a literature magazine. With this combination Julia&Julia embraced and welcomed both glossy and trash!

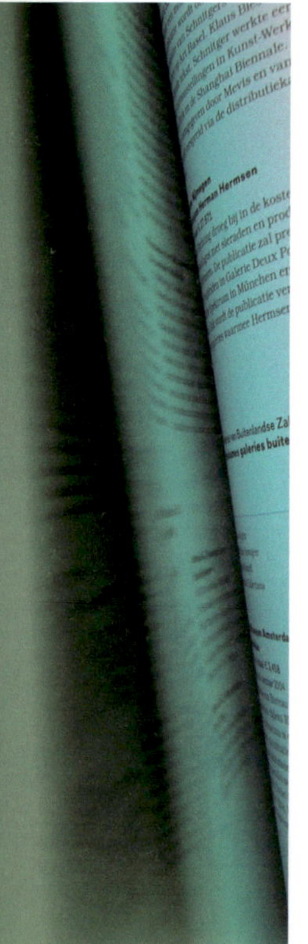

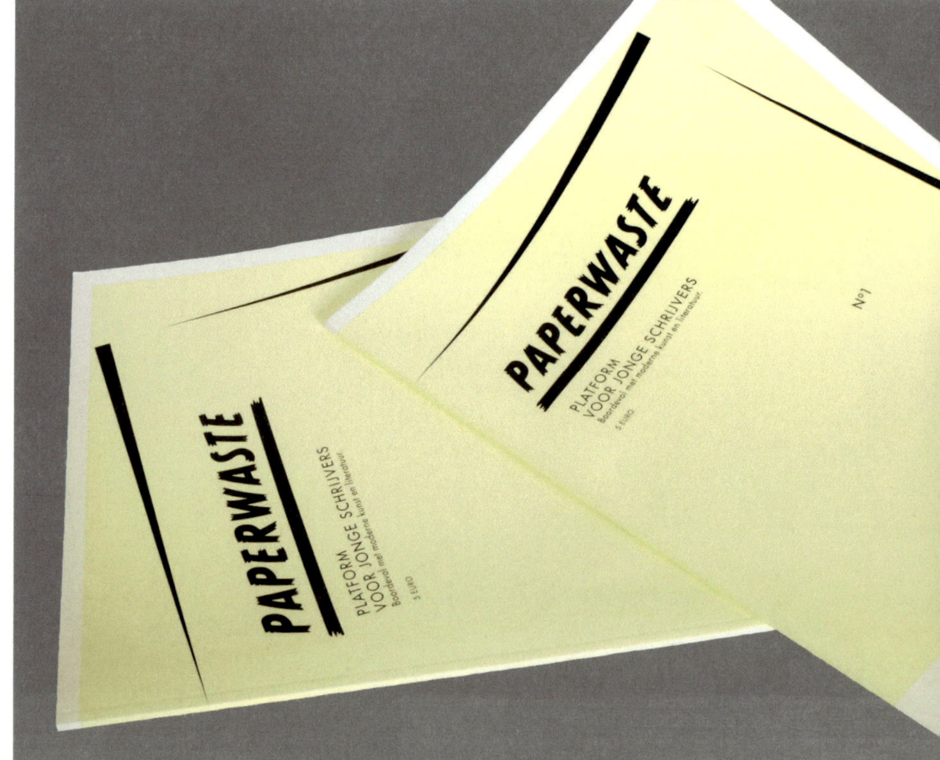

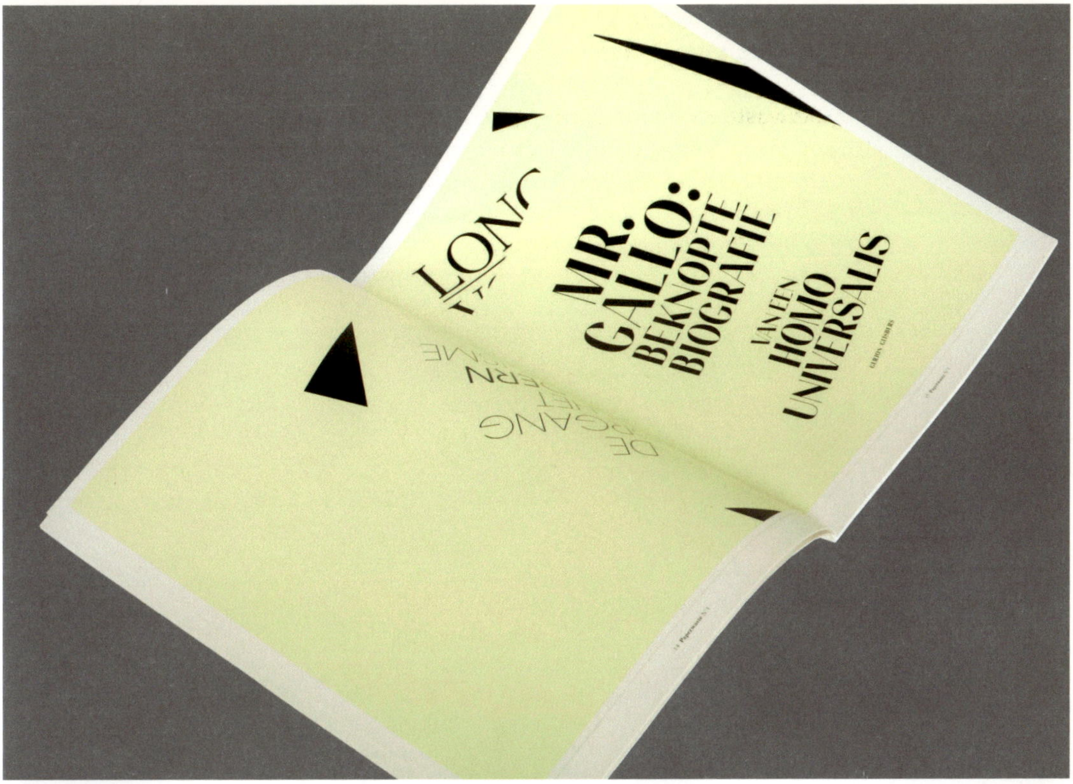

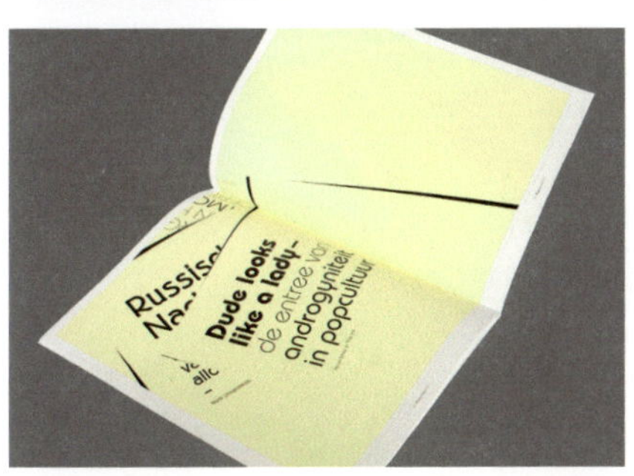
Dude looks
like a lady–

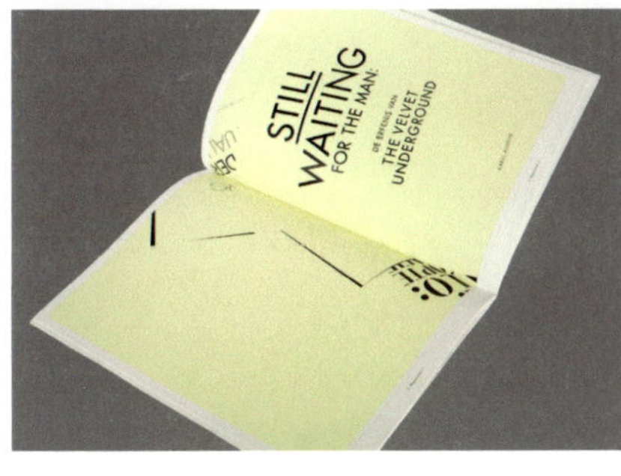
STILL
WAITING
FOR THE MAN:
THE VELVET
UNDERGROUND

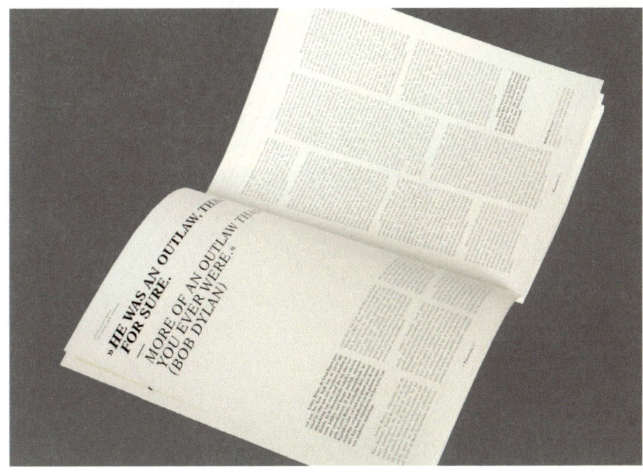
FOR SURE.
YOU EVER WERE.«
(BOB DYLAN)

School brochure
by Julia Müller

Information brochure on educational activities for applicants to the Rietveld Academy in Amsterdam. When the brochure is opened, the pages are uncut, so that only the images can be seen, but can be torn or cut to reveal the text.

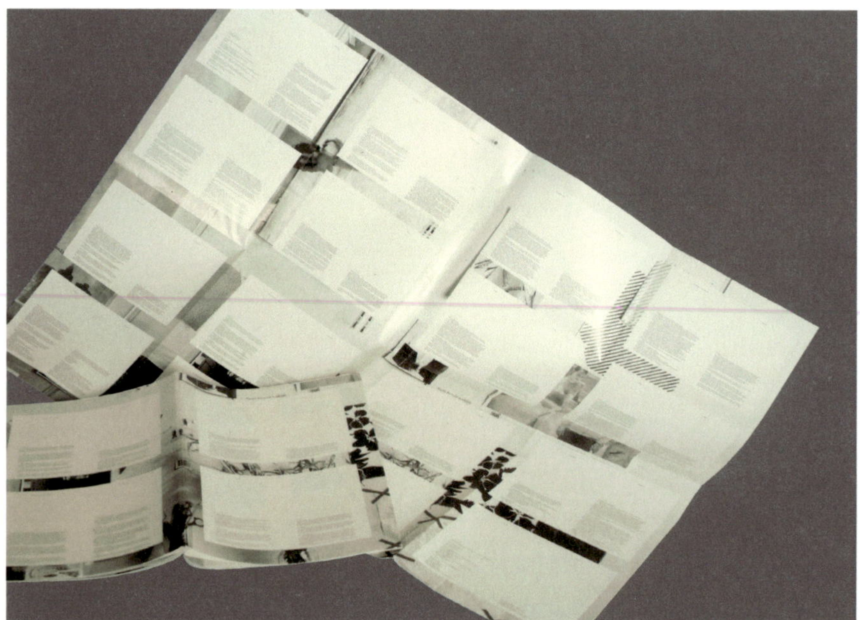

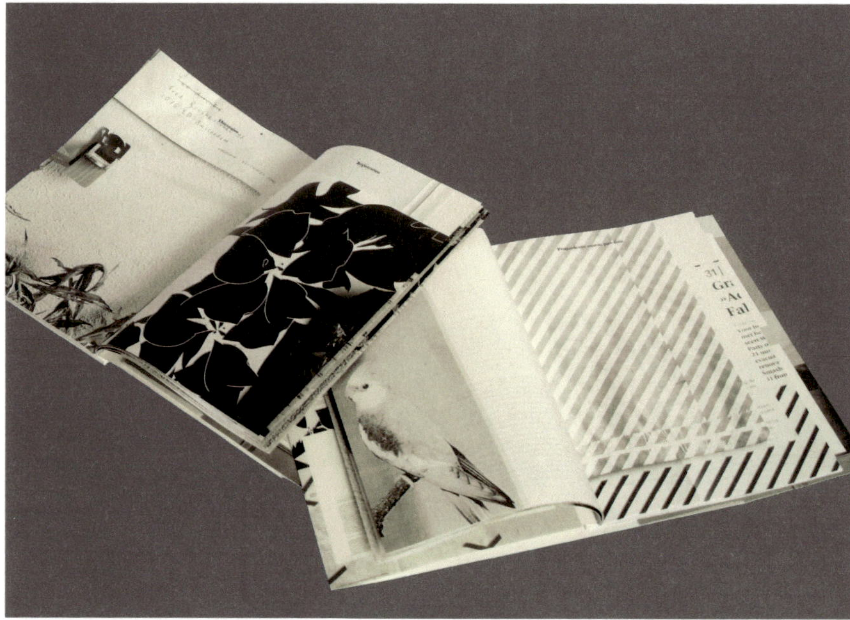

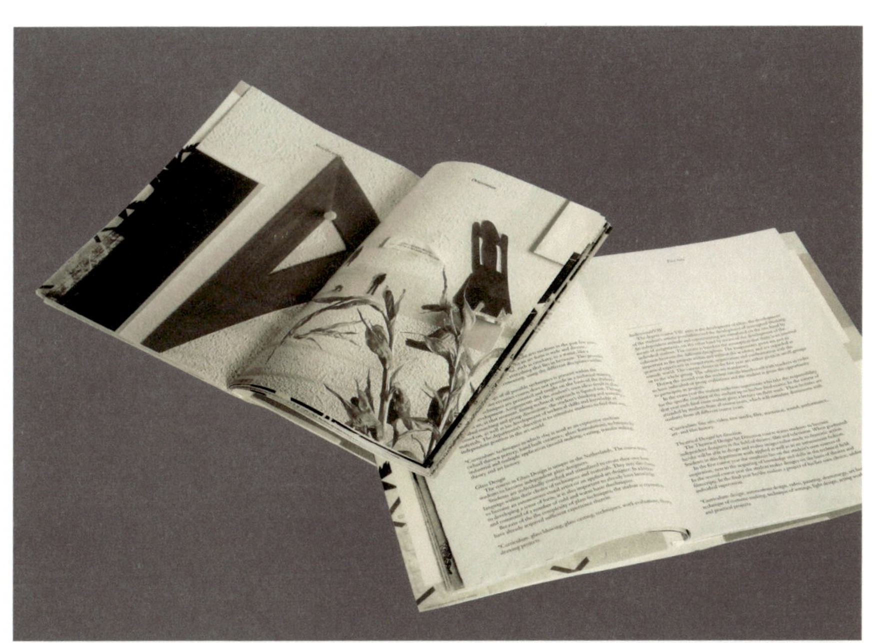

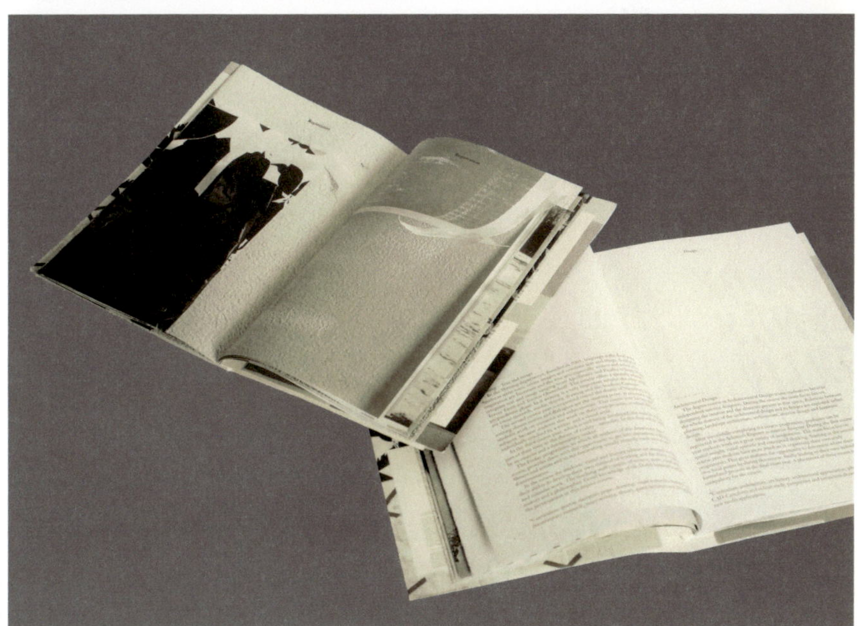

Pages Magazine

by Lust

‹Pages Magazine› was launched in February 2004; a bilingual Farsi/English periodical, it encourages exchanges between Iranian and international authors and artists with critical views on art, culture, urban planning and social issues.

The core idea is to present both languages equally, with no hierarchical preference (i.e. in typography, layout, etc). The magazine this has two ‹front› covers, depending on whether you com to it as a Farsi or an English reader. The English pages are always printed on the right and the Farsi on the left, with the content running parallel so as to avoid repeating images. In other words, the Farsi contents are the mirror (or ‹reverse›) of the English contents, and vice versa.
In order to emphasize the ‹ongoing› aspect of the magazine as a work-in-progress, the pages are numbered progressively, running on from one issue to the next. The first issue ends on page 32, and the second begins with page 33, etc.

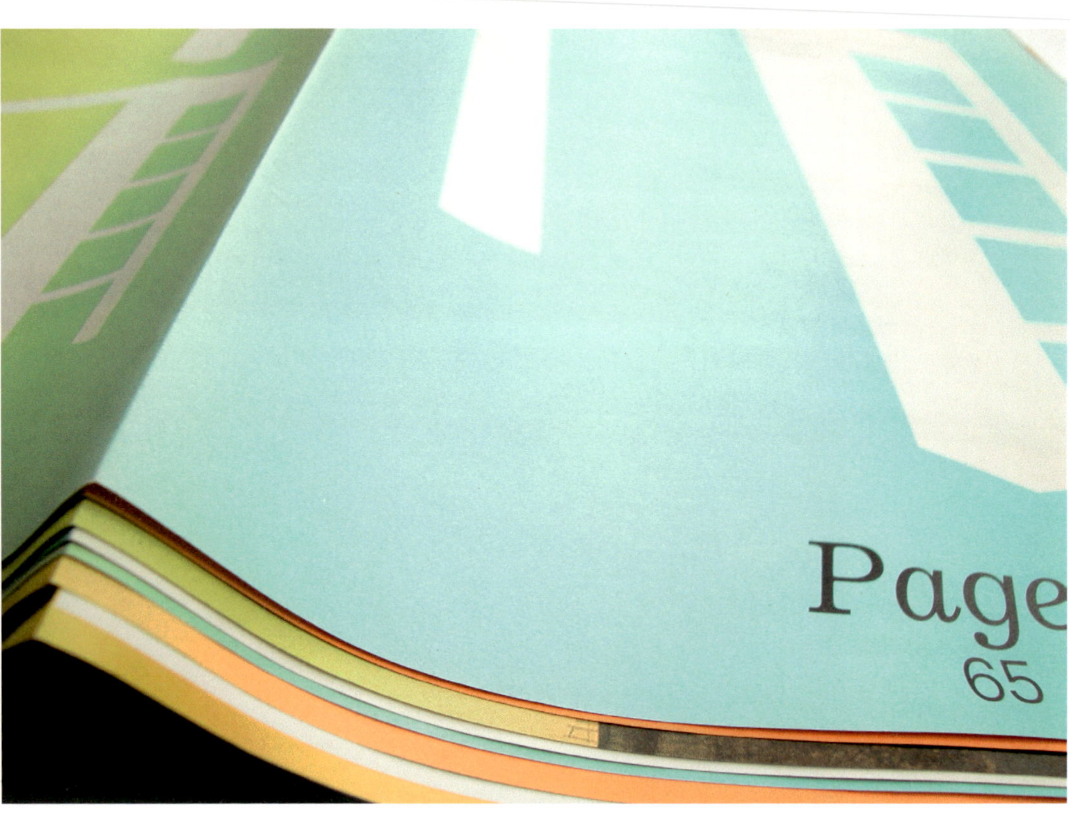

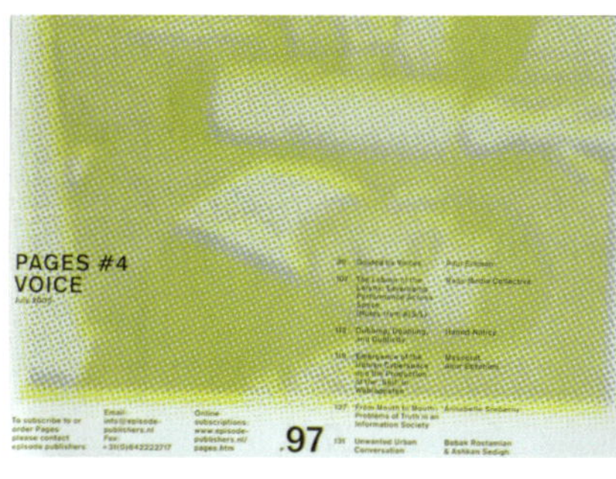

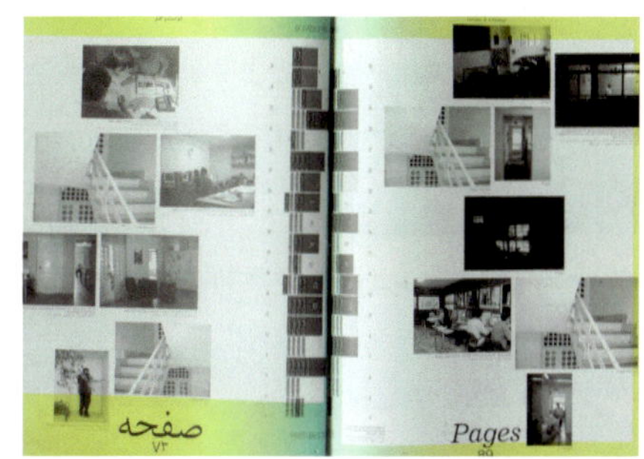

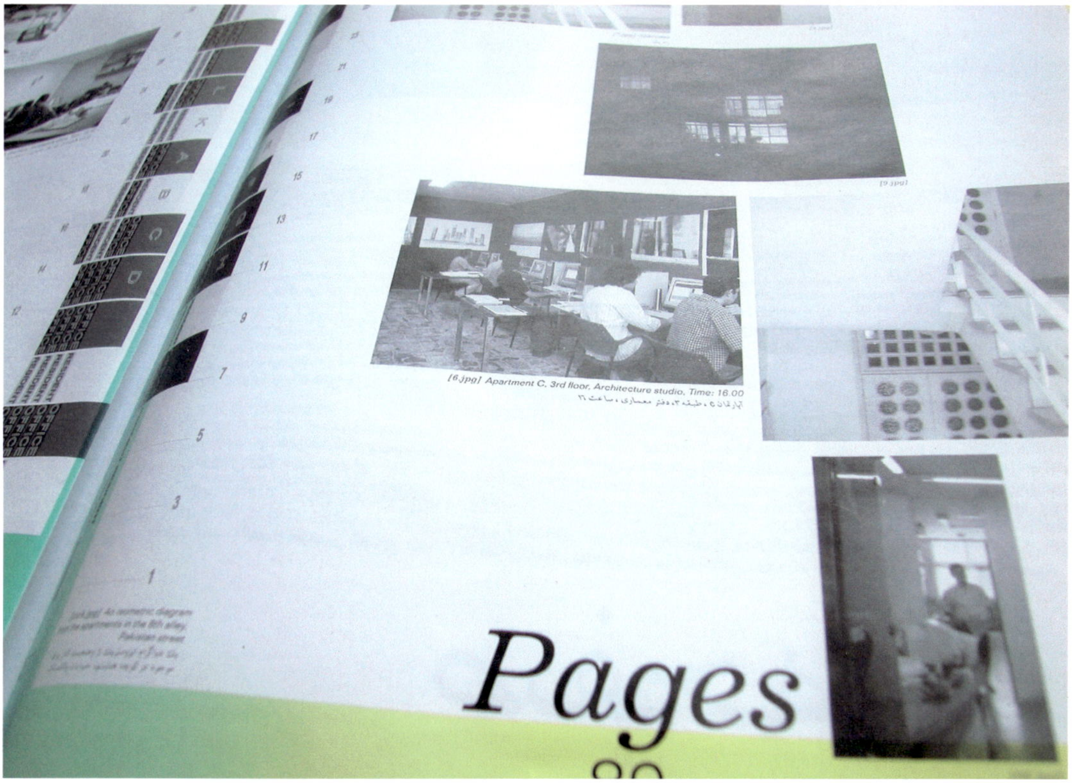

for Pages, 2004-2006

Frame
by Koehorst in't Veld

Koehorst in't Veld is art director of Frame Magazine since #48.

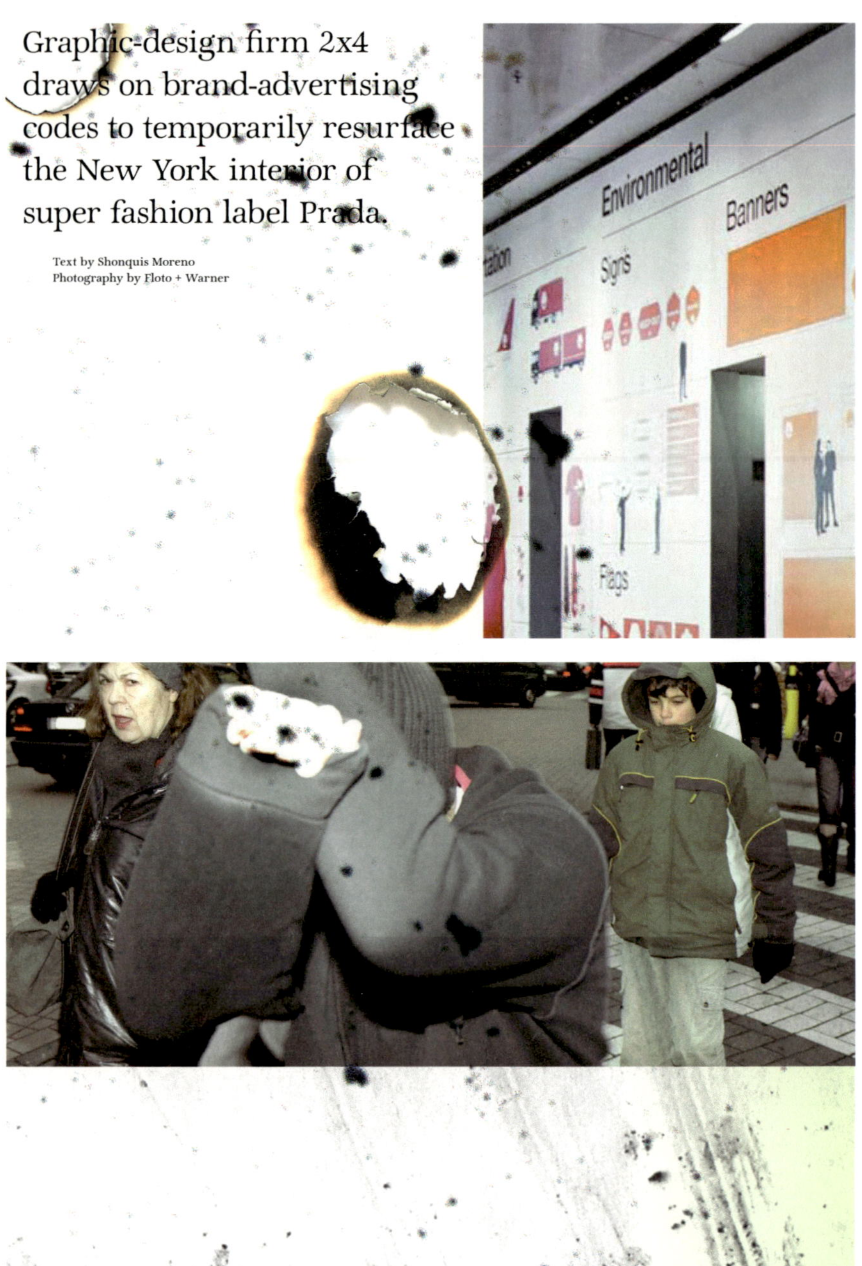

for Frame Magazine, 2006 -

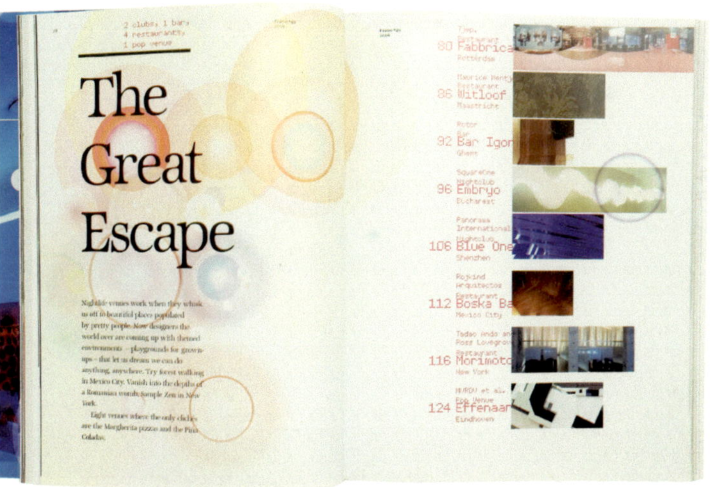
2 clubs, 1 bar,
4 restaurants,
1 pop venue
The Great Escape
Nightlife venues work when they whisk us off to beautiful places populated by pretty people. Now designers the world over are coming up with themed environments – playgrounds for grown-ups – that let us dream we can do anything, anywhere. Try forest walking in Mexico City. Vanish into the depths of a Romanian womb. Sample Zen in New York.
Eight venues where the only clichés are the Margherita pizzas and the Piña Coladas.
Restaurant
80 Fabbrica
Rotterdam
Restaurant
86 Witloof
Maastricht
Rotor
Bar
92 Bar Igor
Ghent
SquareOne
Nightclub
96 Embryo
Bucharest
Panorama
International
Nightclub
106 Blue One
Shenzhen
Rojkind
Arquitectos
Restaurant
112 Boska Ba
Mexico City
Tadao Ando and
Ross Lovegrov
Restaurant
116 Morimoto
New York
Pop Venue
124 Effenaar
Eindhoven

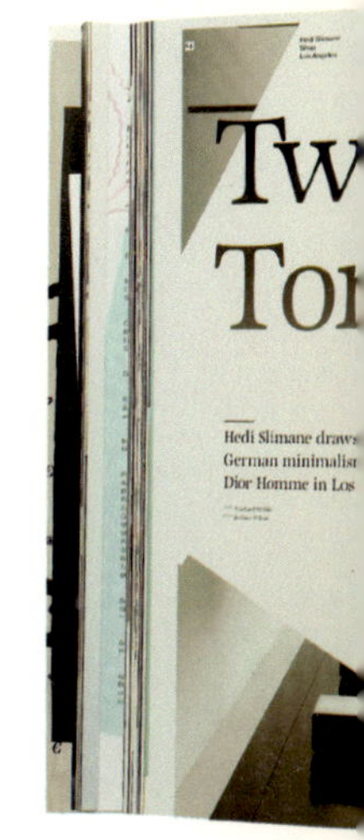
Tw
Tor
Hedi Slimane draws
German minimalism
Dior Homme in Los

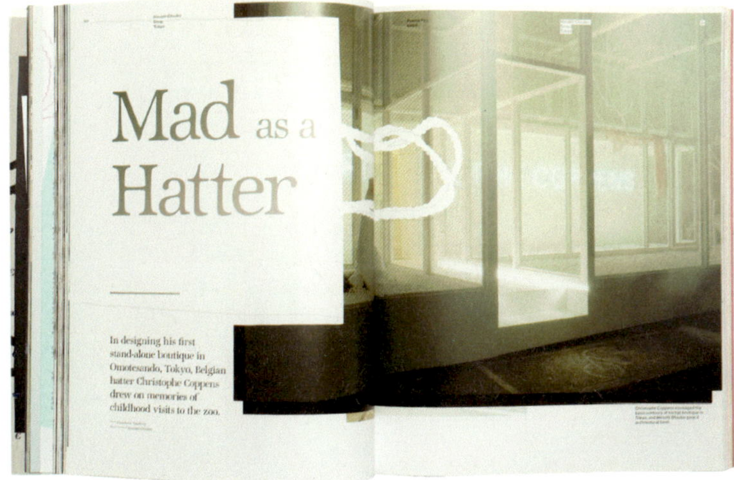
Mad as a
Hatter
In designing his first stand-alone boutique in Omotesando, Tokyo, Belgian hatter Christophe Coppens drew on memories of childhood visits to the zoo.

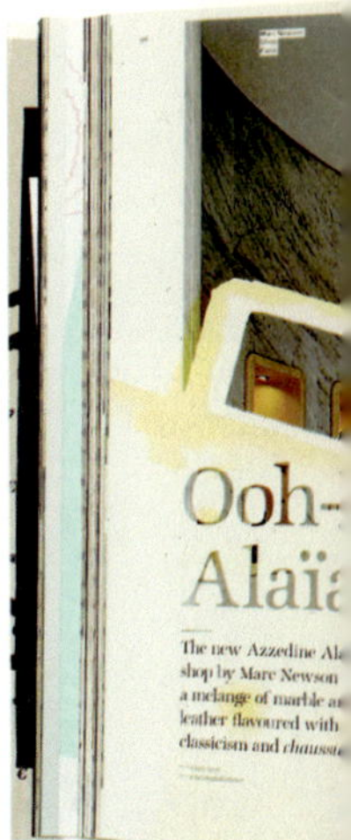
Ooh-
Alaïa
The new Azzedine Ala
shop by Marc Newson
a melange of marble a
leather flavoured with
classicism and chauss

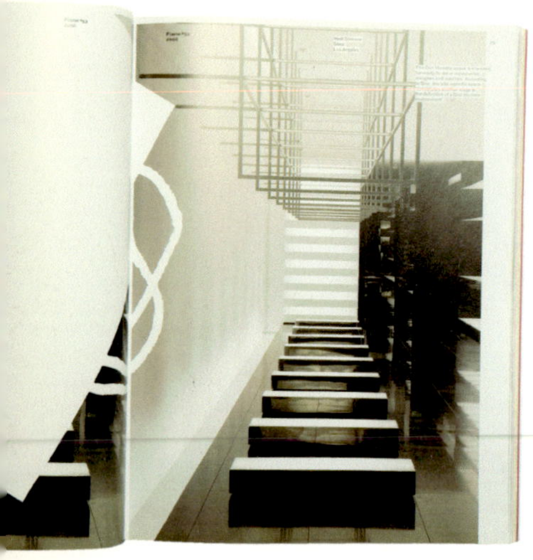

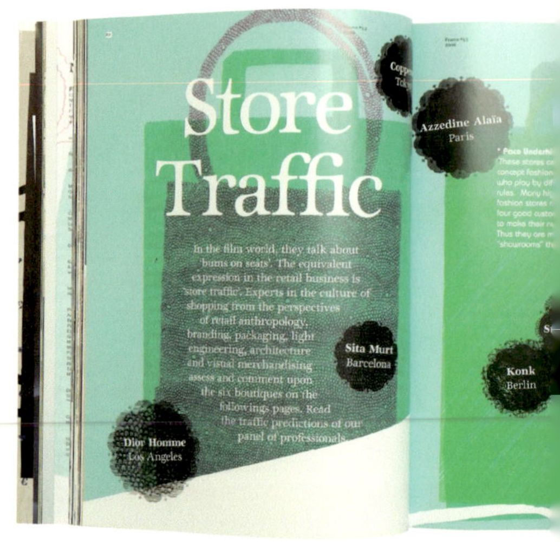
Store Traffic

In the film world, they talk about 'bums on seats'. The equivalent expression in the retail business is 'store traffic'. Experts in the culture of shopping from the perspectives of retail anthropology, branding, packaging, light engineering, architecture and visual merchandising assess and comment upon the six boutiques on the following pages. Read the traffic predictions of our panel of professionals.

Azzedine Alaïa
Paris

Sita Murt
Barcelona

Konk
Berlin

Dior Homme
Los Angeles

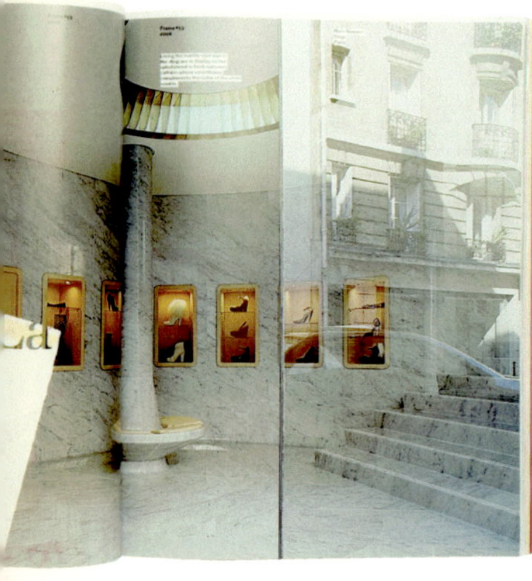

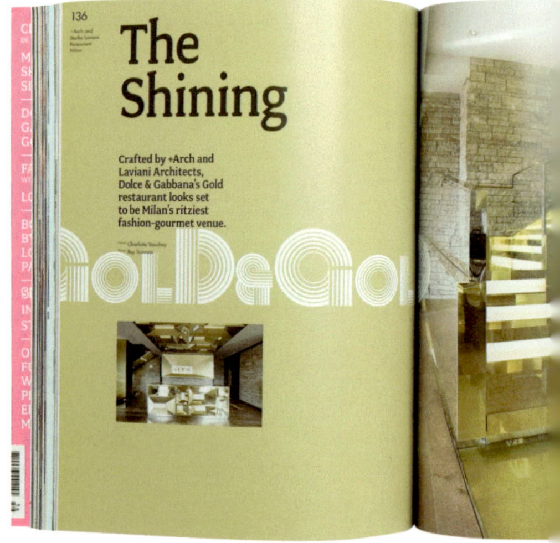
136

The Shining

Crafted by +Arch and Laviani Architects, Dolce & Gabbana's Gold restaurant looks set to be Milan's ritziest fashion-gourmet venue.

243 Code

by Toko

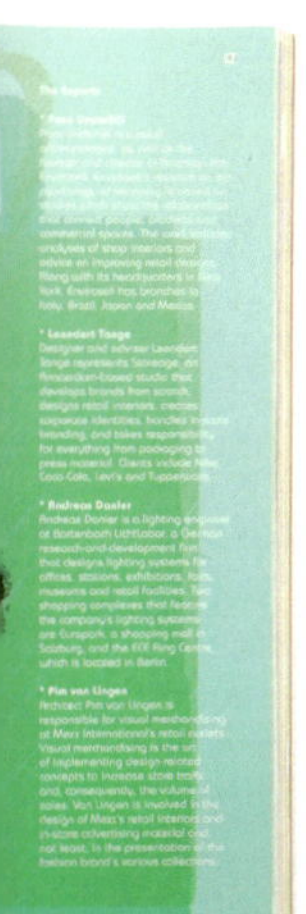

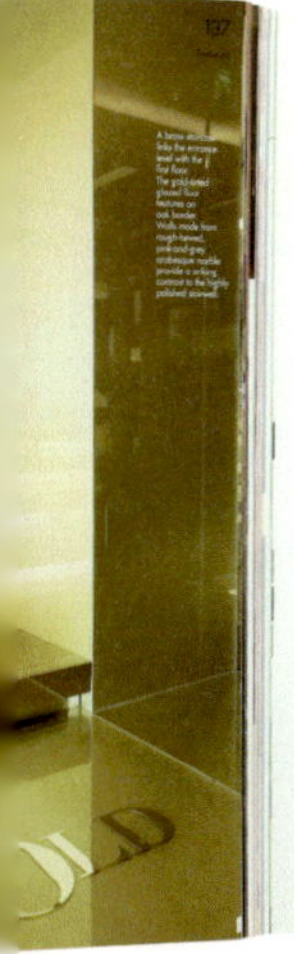

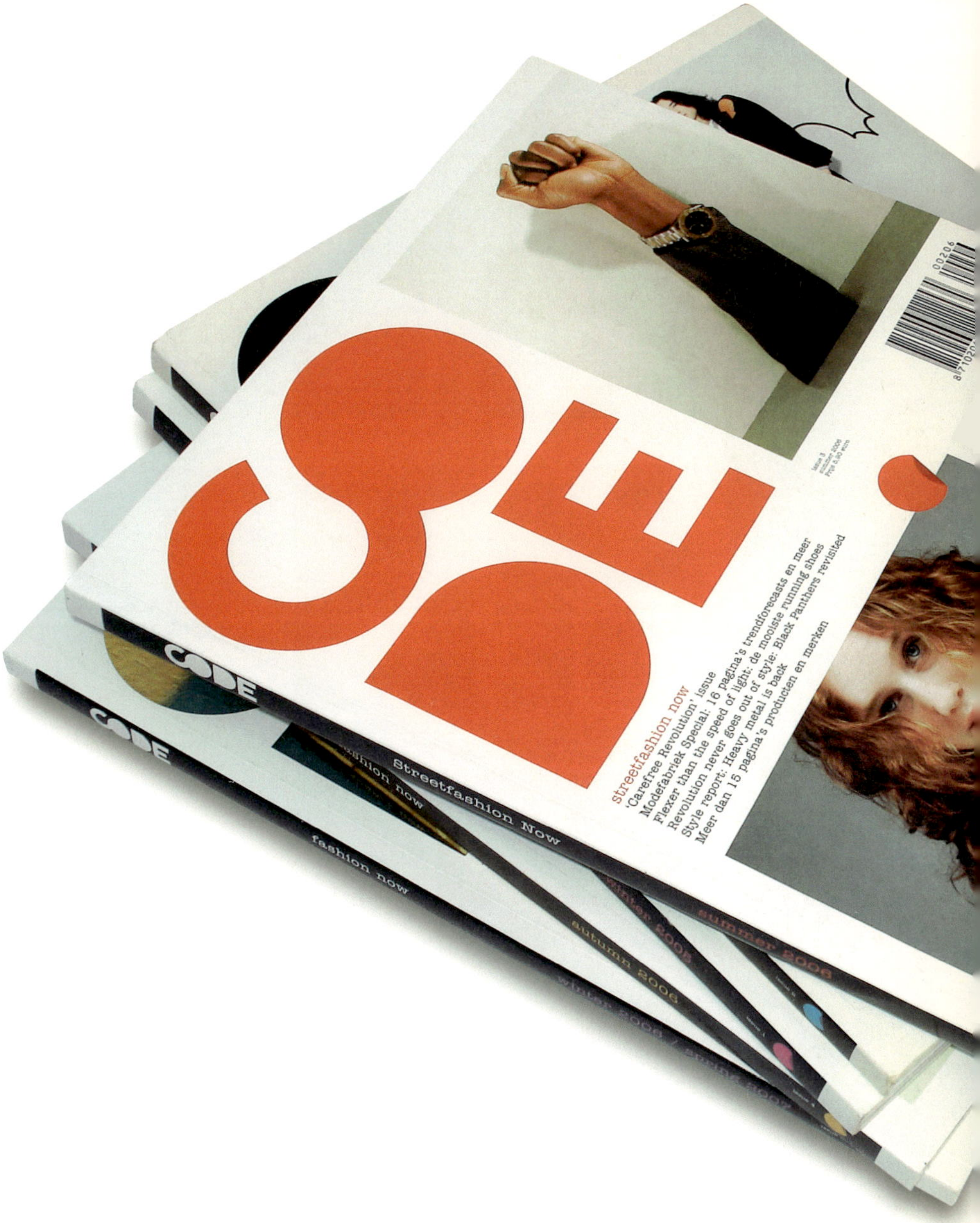

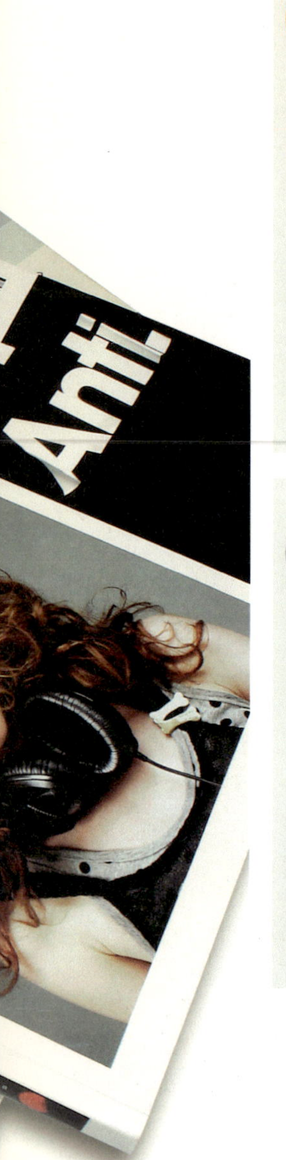
Anti.

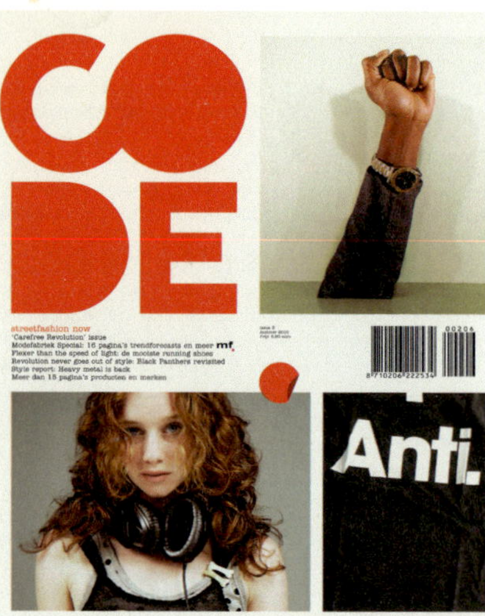
CODE
streetfashion now
'Carefree Revolution' issue
Modefabriek Special: 16 pagina's trendforecasts en meer mf.
Flexer than the speed of light: de mooiste running shoes
Revolution never goes out of style: Black Panthers revisited
Style report: Heavy metal is back
Meer dan 15 pagina's producten en merken
00206
8 710206 222534
Anti.

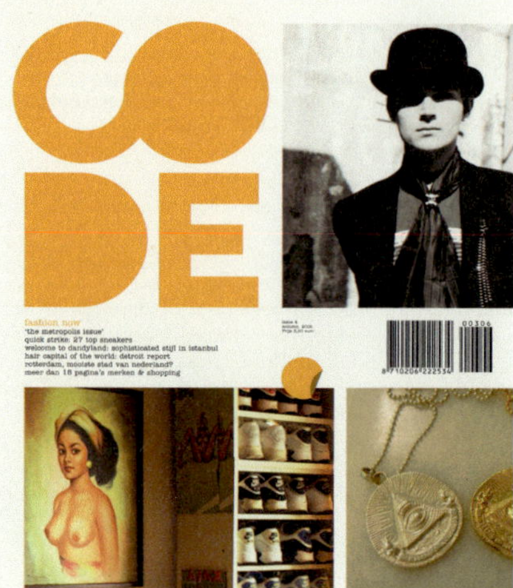
CODE
fashion now
'the metropolis issue'
quick strike: 27 top sneakers
welcome to dandyland: sophisticated stijl in istanbul
hair capital of the world: detroit report
rotterdam, mooiste stad van nederland?
meer dan 18 pagina's merken & shopping
00306
8 710206 222534

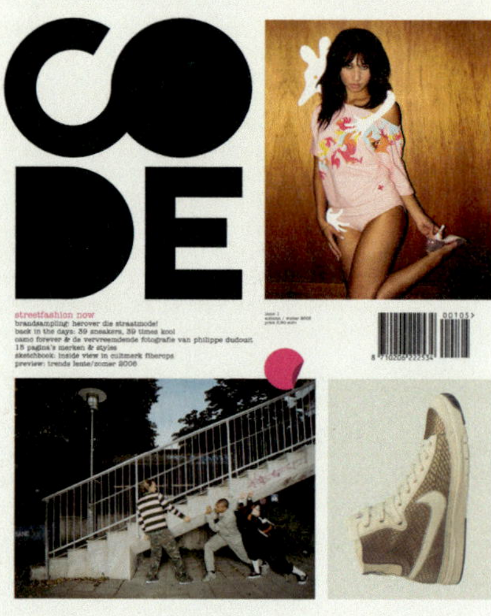
CODE
streetfashion now
brandsampling: herover die straatmode!
back in the days: 39 sneakers, 39 times kool
camo forever & de vervreemdende fotografie van philippe dudouit
15 pagina's merken & styles
sketchbook: inside view in cultmerk fiberops
preview: trends lente/zomer 2006
00105

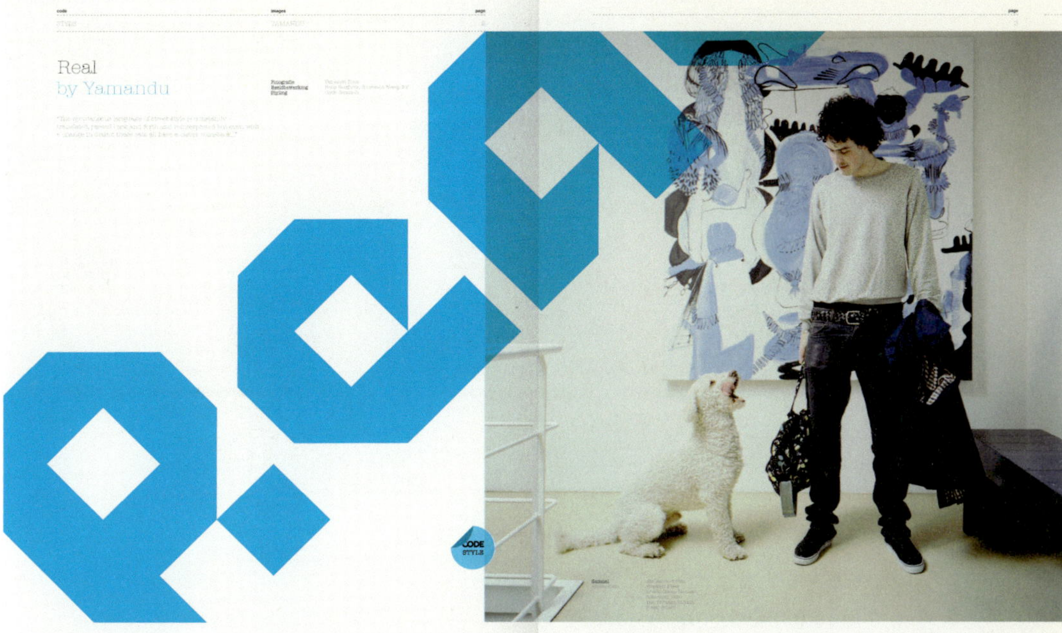

CodeLuxe

Bernhard Willhelm

Na zijn stages bij grote ontwerpers als Walter van Beirendonck, Vivienne Westwood en Alexander McQueen, vond de toen 29-jarige Bernhard Willhelm het tijd om voor zichzelf te beginnen. Tijdens de Parijse modeweek van 1999 lanceerde hij met daverend succes zijn eerste damescollectie. Bernhards ontwerpen waren humoristisch en fantasievol met een heel erg vette knipoog, naar onder andere zijn Duitse roots. Dit bleek in de bloedserieuze modewereld precies de luchtige invalshoek waaraan op dat moment behoefte was.

Toen hij in 2003 ook voor mannen ging ontwerpen bleven de humor en de scherpe blik, maar de collecties waren een stuk draagbaarder en bovenal street credible. Waar zijn vrouwencollecties hier en daar nog wel eens gierend uit de bocht vlogen, zijn de mannencollecties een commentaar op, en een ode aan de straatcultuur en de manier waarop mensen mode in hun dagelijks leven gebruiken. De vermenging van vernieuwende ontwerpen en street-vibes maakt dat hij niet alleen een schare fans heeft onder hardcore fashion victims, maar dat het label ook leeft op de straat.

De mannencollectie voor winter 2006 is geïnspireerd op Nigeriaanse traditionele en hedendaagse kostuums: het relaxte stijlgevoel van de Afrikaanse man en de moderne multiculti vermenging hiervan met sportswearinvloeden. Dus: explosieve prints, flashy kleuren en oversized modellen.
Bernhard Willhelm ontwierp dit jaar voor het eerst ook een schoenencollectie en een speciaal voor de internetwinkel YOOX gemaakte minicollectie met de naam The White Bunch die alleen online te koop is.

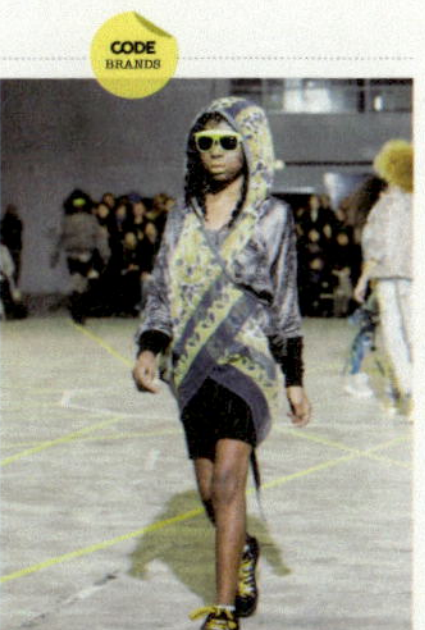

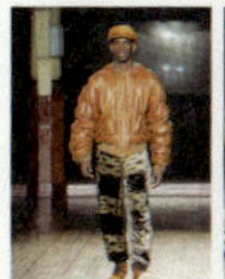

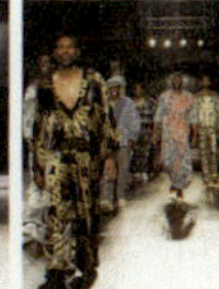

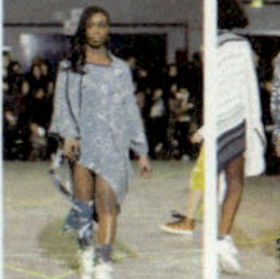

Iovinella

Iovinella werd in 2000 in Rome opgericht door Daniel Iovinella en Fabio di Lorenzo. Uitgerust met kwasten, spuitbussen, verf en scharen leven zij zich uit op hun eigen ontwerpen. Hierdoor ontstaan customized unica, waaronder T-shirts, tanktops, broeken, jeans en hooded sweats. Unica waarvoor je dan wel de hoofdprijs betaalt: 190 euro voor een T-shirt en 415 euro voor een jeans. Het is de kunst deze met verf besmeurde items op de juiste manier te dragen, want anders heb je de look van iemand die midden in een verbouwing zit. Gelukkig heeft Iovinella ook een uitgebreide, reguliere collectie (inclusief accessoires), waarin een T-shirt gemiddeld 90 euro kost. Iovinella brengt collecties voor mannen en vrouwen, waarbij de nadruk momenteel nog op de mannenlijn ligt.

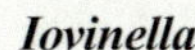

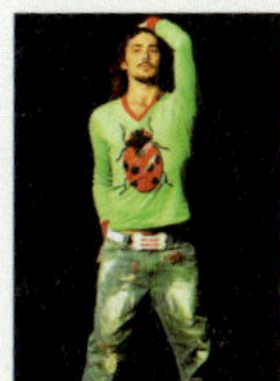

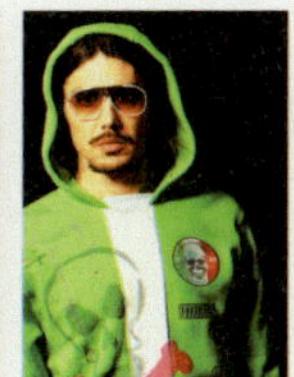

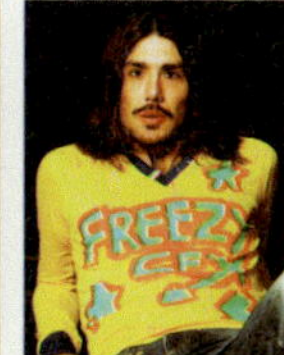

Misericordia

Het is fantastisch en natuurlijk volkomen terecht dat het fair trade-principe ook in de mode een steeds belangrijkere rol speelt. Eén van de leukste initiatieven op dit gebied is de onderneming van de Franse broers Aurelyen en Mathieu: Misericordia.

Het begint allcasual in 2002 als Mathieu een rondreis maakt door Peru en daar in het dorpje Ventanilla in contact komt met de dames van 'Nuestra Senora de Misericordia', de missiezusters die naast een weeshuis en een school ook een naaiatelier runnen waar ze trainingspakken voor de leerlingen van de school vervaardigen. Mathieu ziet wel wat in de grafische belijning en heldere kleuren van de Misericordia sport-outfits. Hij pleegt een paar telefoontjes met zijn vrienden van de winkel Collete in Parijs, en binnen enkele maanden hangt de etalage aan de Rue de Saint Honore vol met de blauw-witte jasjes en broeken.
Drie jaar later is de kleding van de Peruaanse missiezusters te koop in meer dan tachtig winkels over de hele wereld en maken de broers twee collecties per jaar. Naast een mannen- en vrouwenlijn is er sinds dit jaar een kindercollectie en brengen ze ieder seizoen een limited edition uit in samenwerking met een bekende ontwerper. (In het verleden onder meer Bernard Wilhelm en Stephan Schneider.) En het mooie is: het succes van Misericordia betekent voor het dorpje Ventanilla werkgelegenheid, onderwijs en welvaart van voor Peruaanse begrippen ongekend niveau. Check voor meer info

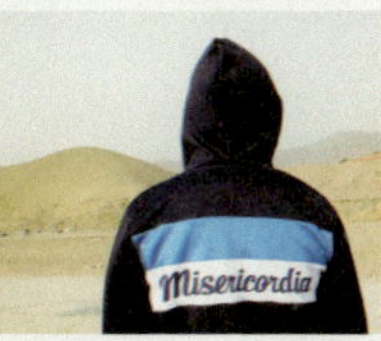

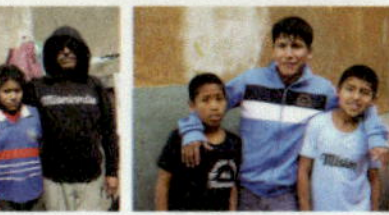

 New Directions
by Toko

Poster for the ‹New Directions› speakers series presented by AGDA. New transcripts of follow-up sessions will be intergrated into this poster. The result, a layerd and unreadable poster which reflexts the complexity of this topic.

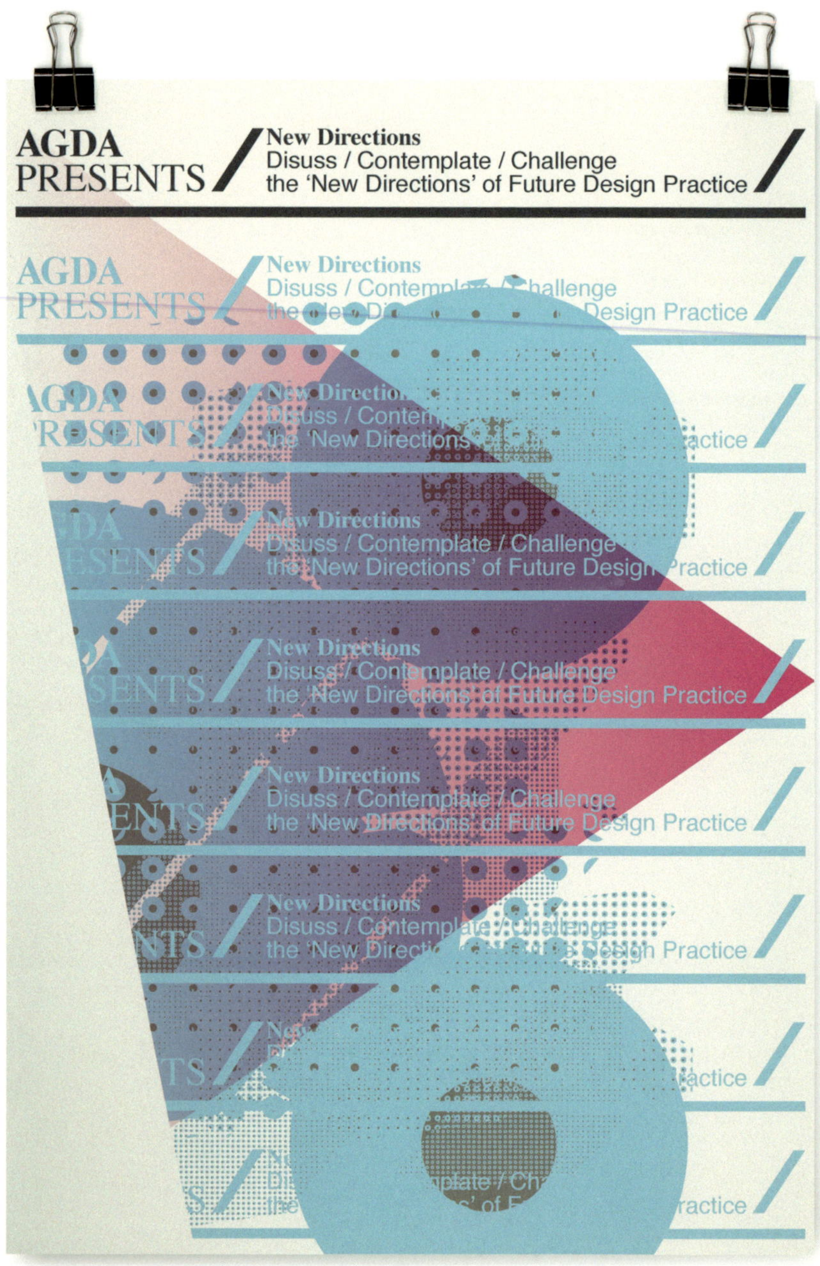

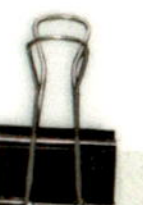

AGDA
PRESENTS /

New Directions
Disuss / Contemplate / Challenge
the 'New Directions' of Future Design Practice /

these are transcripts noted live at the
new directions talks organised by agda australia
this poster will feature all events

New/directi

04 06 '07

transcript 1

session 1
monday
4th june 2007
the australian museum
featuring:
johannes weissenbaeck from play
michael lugmayr from toko
andrew van der westhuyzen and
clemens habicht
from collider

transcript 2

transcript 3

transcript 4

transcript 5

transcript 6

ons/

 Evol Eye Lands End
by Richard Niessen

Selected as one of the best Dutch book designs of 2004, the book consists of eight booklets that are randomly bound. Each booklet is designed in its own way, using one of the four typefaces I designed especially for the project.

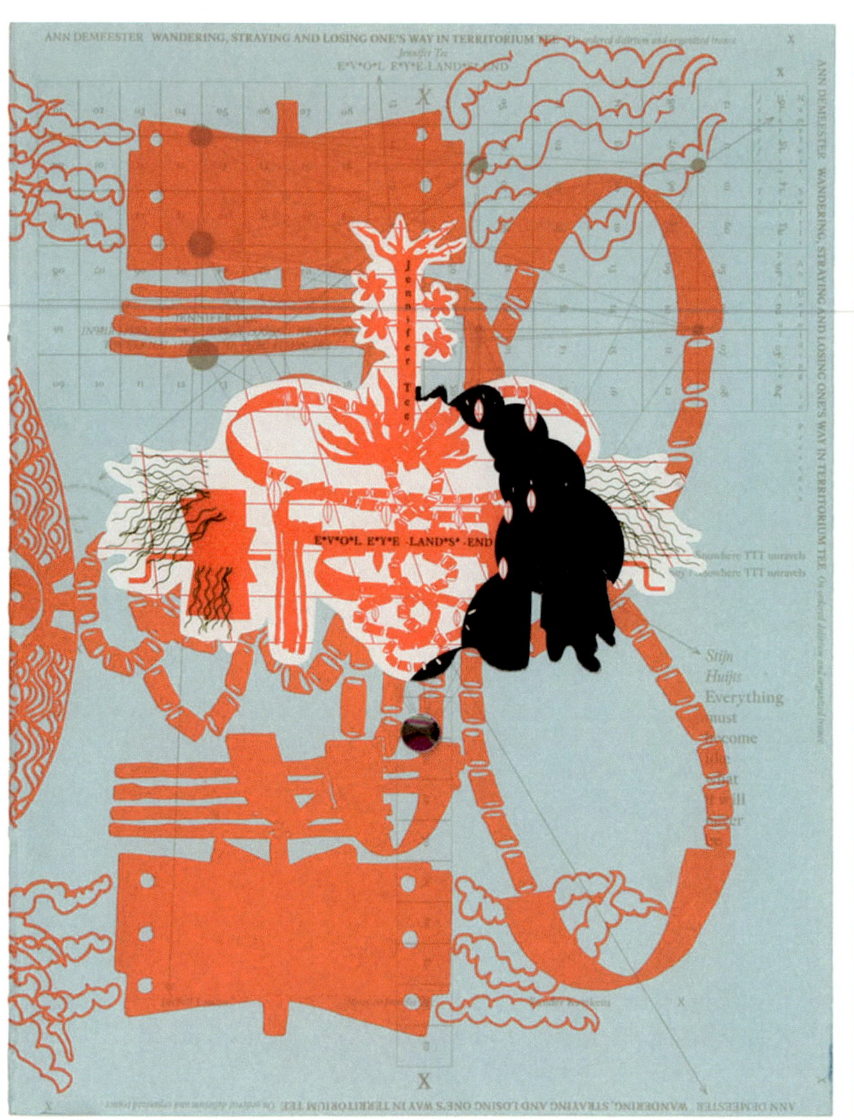

for Jennifer Tee, 2004

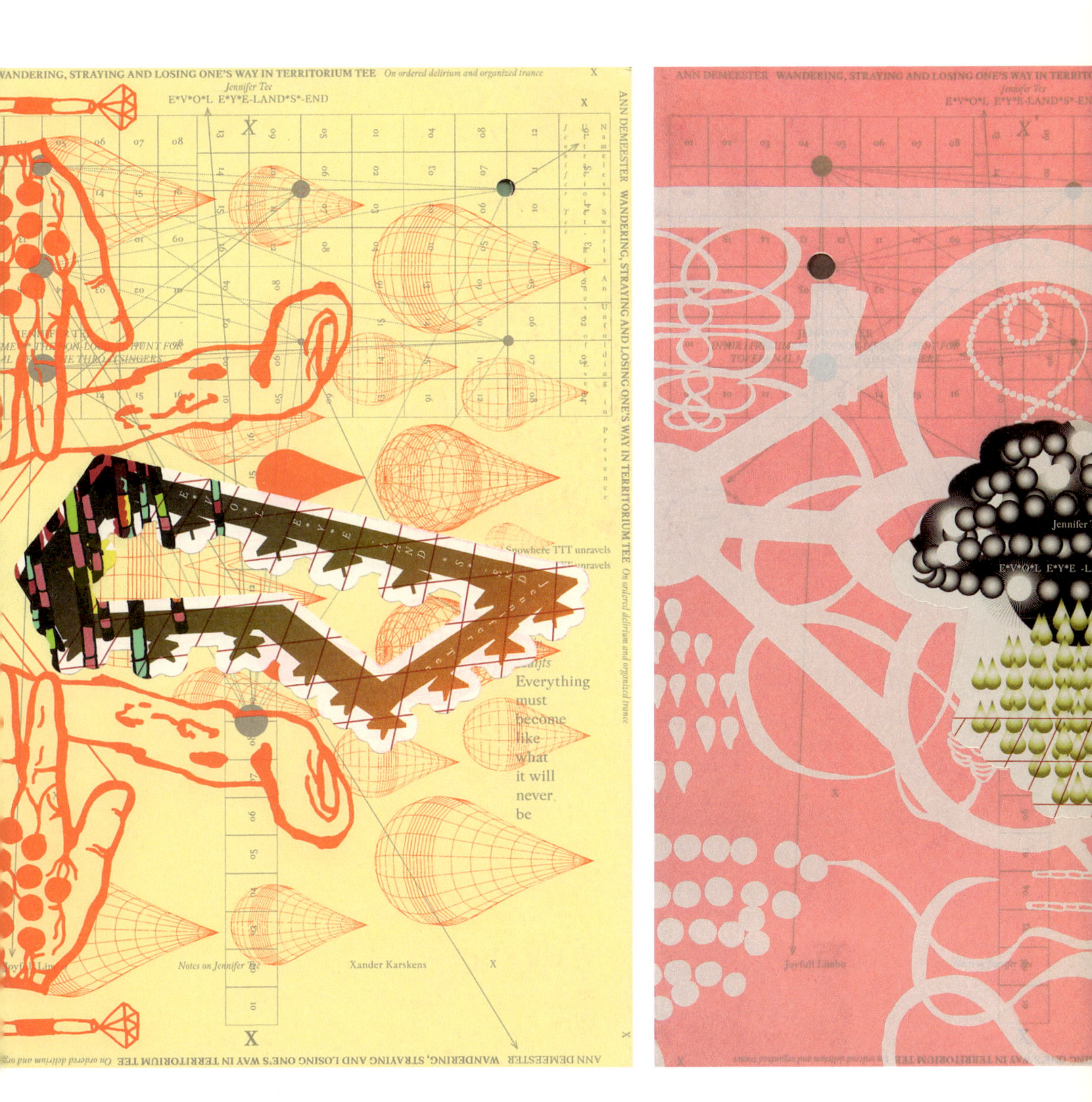

WANDERING, STRAYING AND LOSING ONE'S WAY IN TERRITORIUM TEE On ordered delirium and organized trance
Jennifer Tee
E*V*O*L E*Y*E-LAND*S*-END
Everything
must
become
like
what
it will
never
be
Notes on Jennifer Tee
Xander Karskens
Joyfull Limbo
ANN DEMEESTER WANDERING, STRAYING AND LOSING ONE'S WAY IN TERRITORIUM TEE

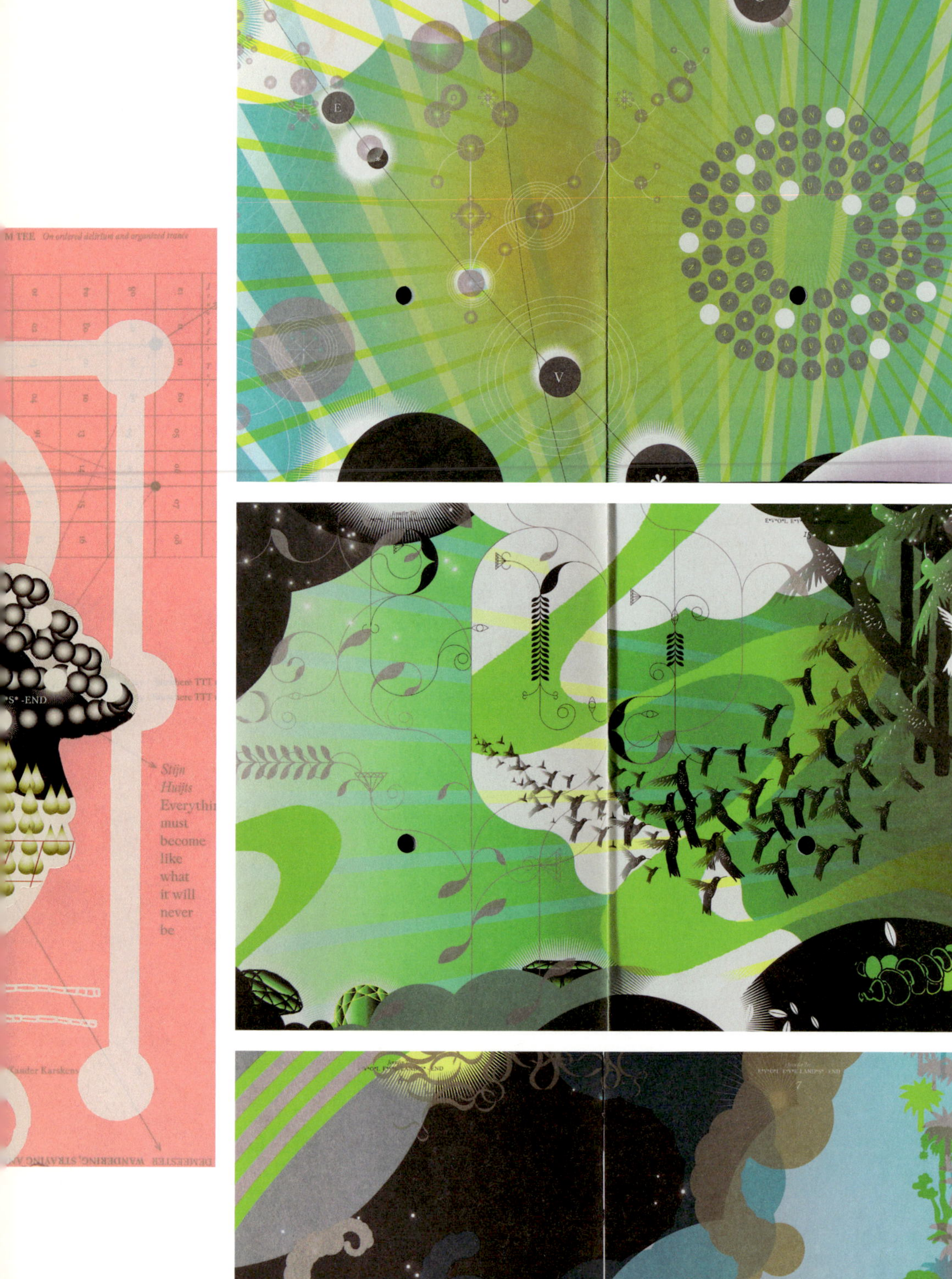
M TEE On ordered delirium and organized trance
Stijn
Huijts
Everythi
must
become
like
what
it will
never
be
Xander Karskens
DEMEESTER WANDERING, STRAYING AN

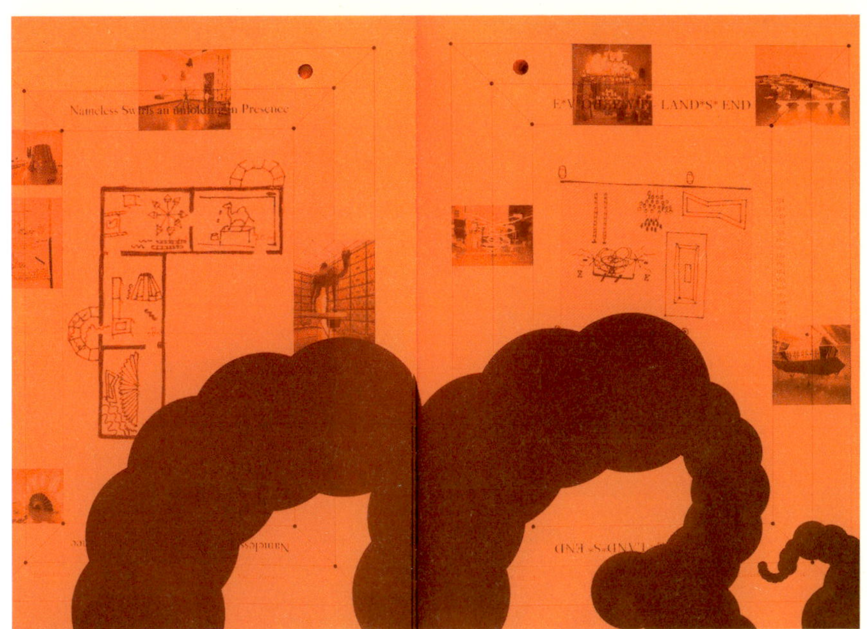

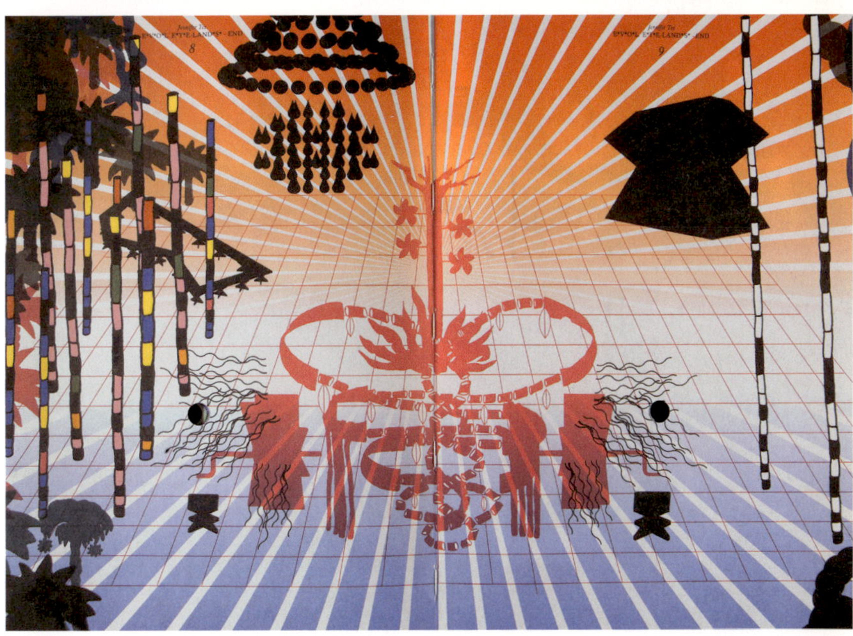

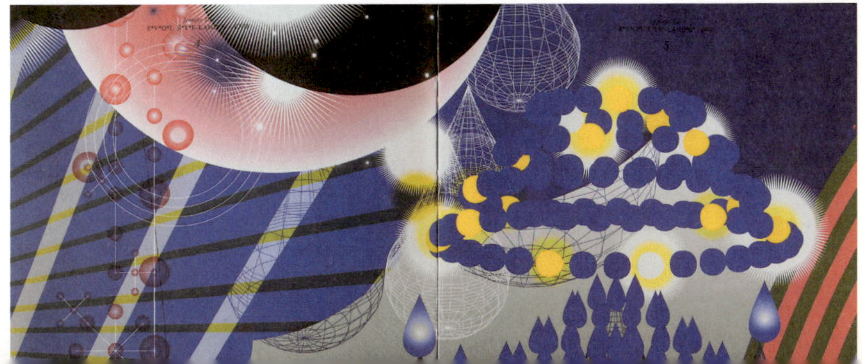

252 Mark
by Machine

Machine did both the design and art direction of this magazine devoted to ‹Another Architecture›.

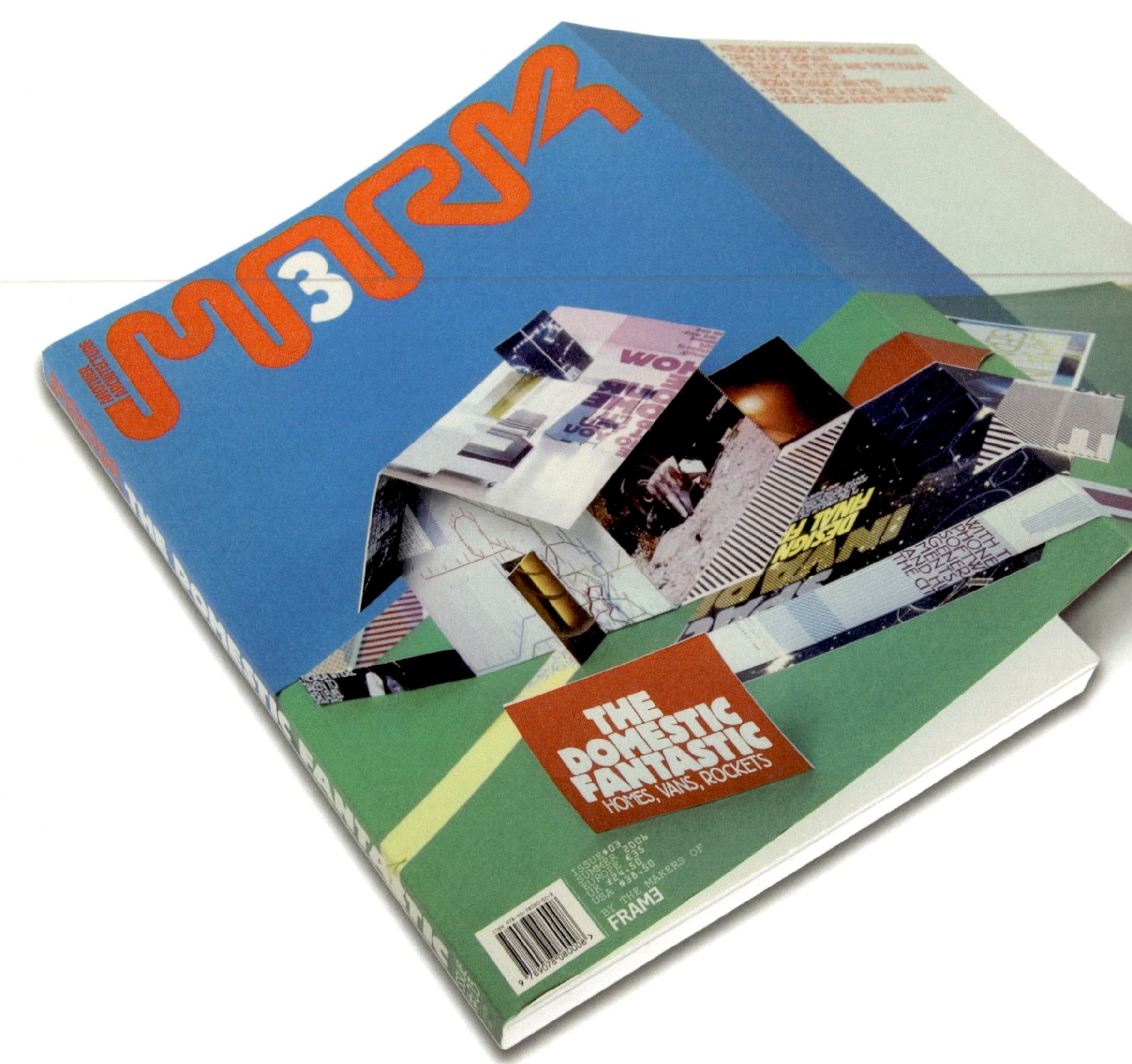

for Frame Publishers, 2005

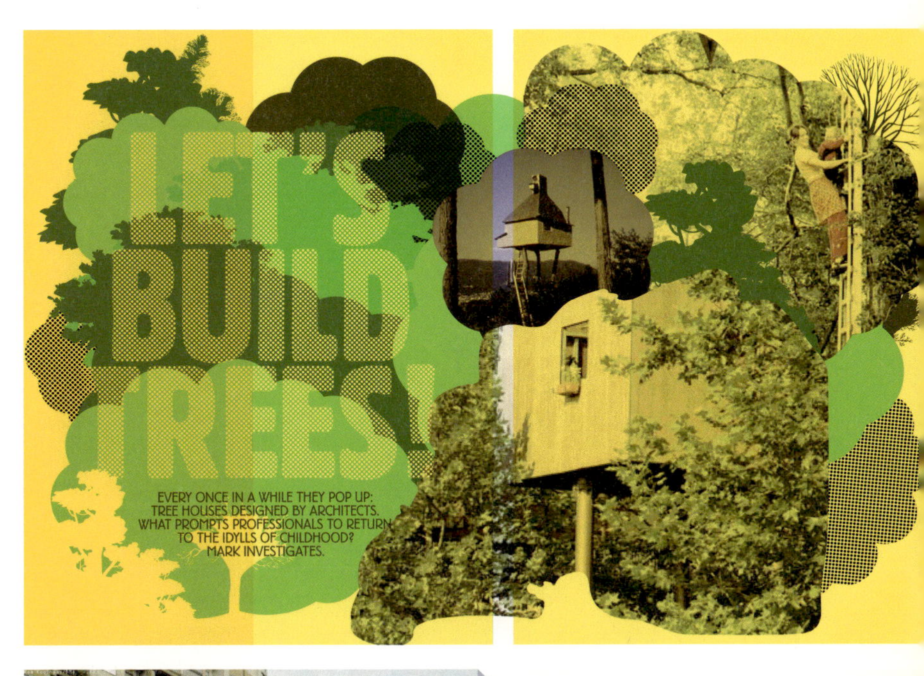
LET'S BUILD TREES!
EVERY ONCE IN A WHILE THEY POP UP: TREE HOUSES DESIGNED BY ARCHITECTS. WHAT PROMPTS PROFESSIONALS TO RETURN TO THE IDYLLS OF CHILDHOOD? MARK INVESTIGATES.

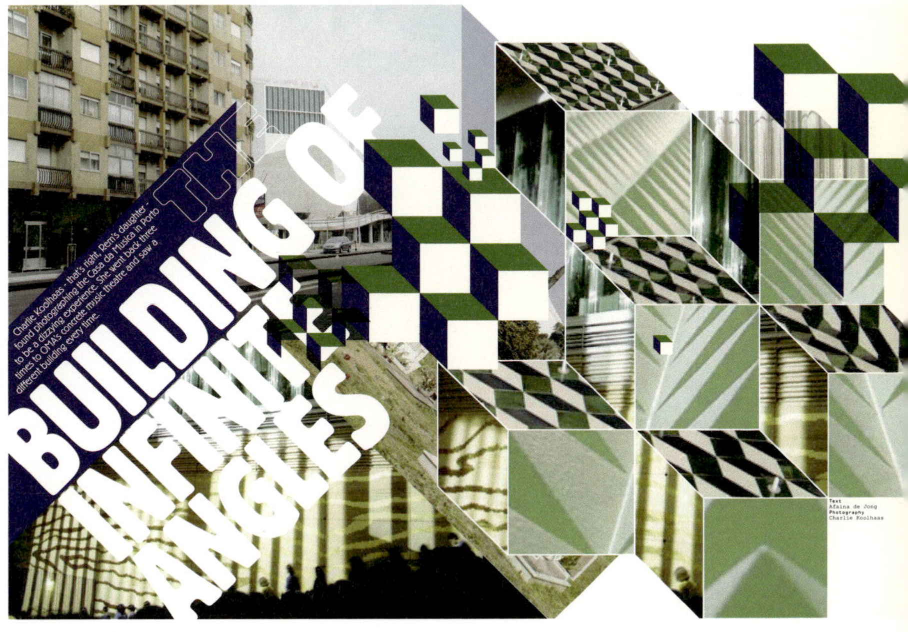
THE BUILDING OF INFINITE ANGLES
Charlie Koolhaas - that's right, Rem's daughter - found photographing the Casa da Musica in Porto to be a dizzying experience. She went back three times to OMA's concrete music theatre and saw a different building every time.
Text
Afaina de Jong
Photography
Charlie Koolhaas

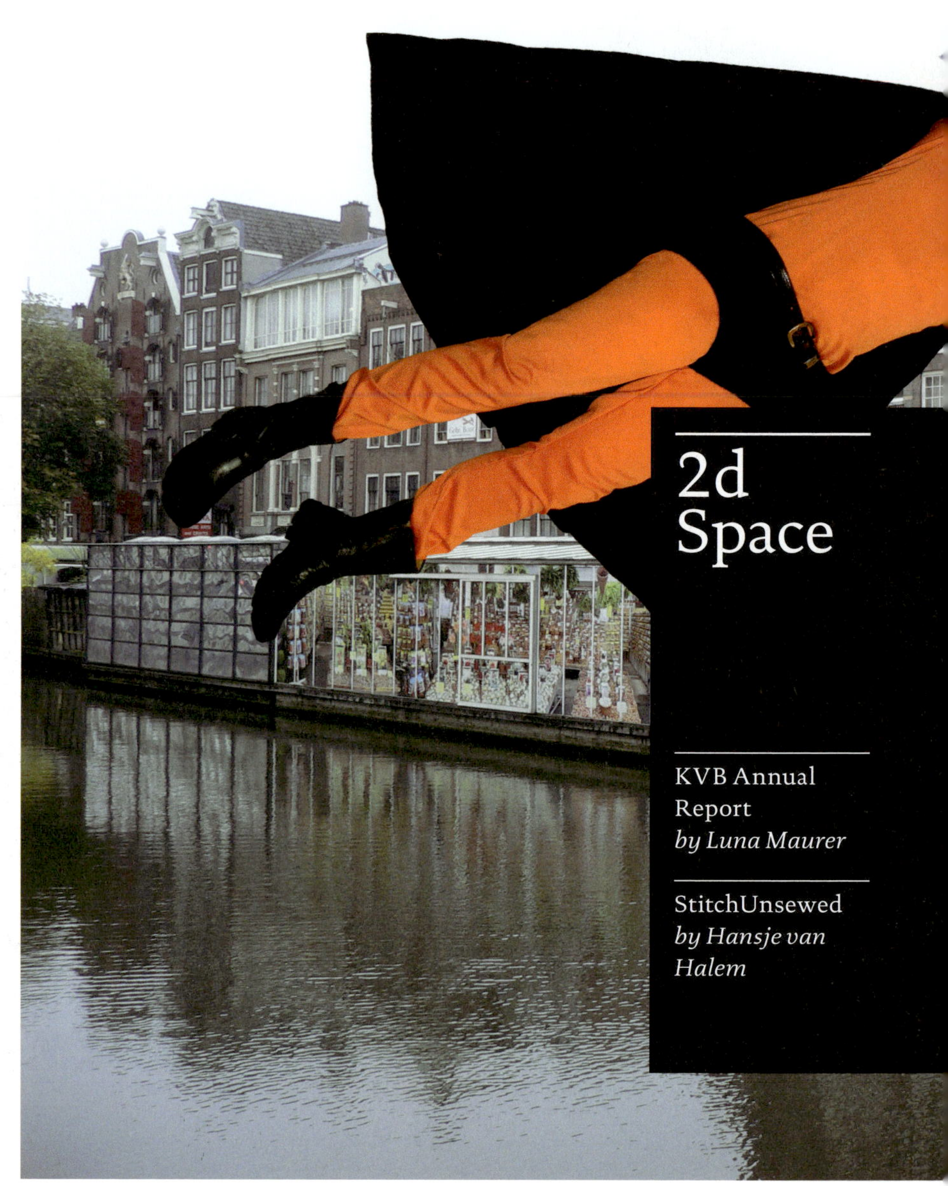
2d
Space
KVB Annual
Report
by Luna Maurer
StitchUnsewed
*by Hansje van
Halem*

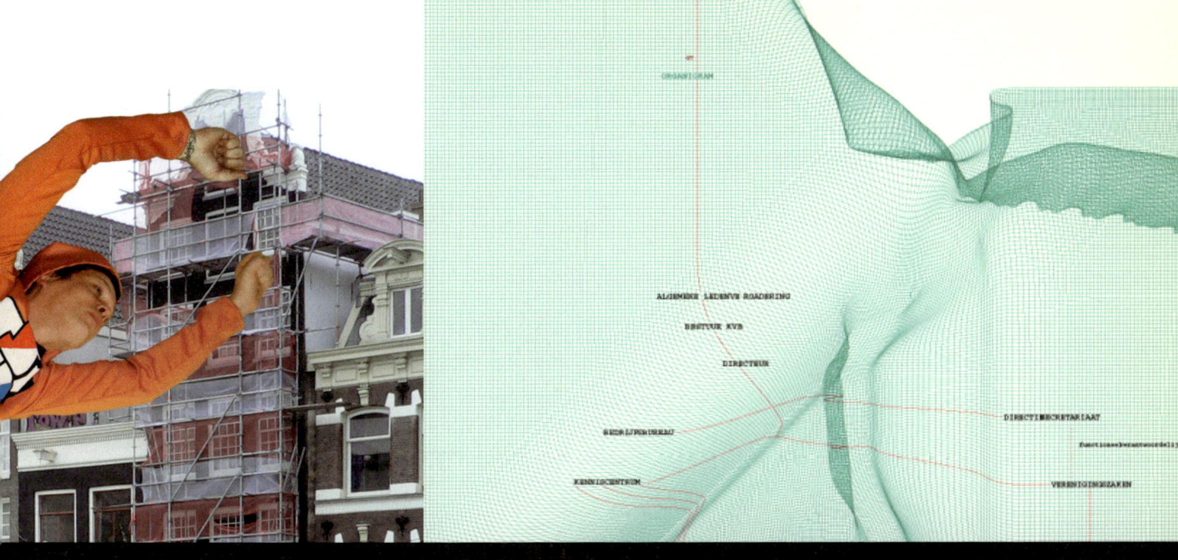

Close Encounters 3
by Catalogtree

Wim Crouwel/ Architectures Typographiques
by Experimental Jetset

SMCS graphic identity
by Experimental Jetset

TuttoBeNe
by Lesley Moore & Silke Spinner

Psychedelic Warfare
by Machine

HEMA packaging office supplies
by Studio Kluif

HEMA packaging, ‹Play with food products'
by Studio Kluif

Nedap Annual Report
by Studio Kluif

Amsterdam ArenA card, David Bowie,
by Studio Kluif

Box with bone-shaped paperclips
by Studio Kluif

KVB Annual Report

by Luna Maurer; dynamics /Jochem van der Spek

The Annual Report of the KVB, Koninklijke Vereniging van het Boekenvak (Royal Dutch Book Trade Association) was produced using an application by Jochem van der Spek. The KVB Annual Report was chosen for the Bestverzorgde Jaarverslagen 2002 award for the year's best Annual Reports.

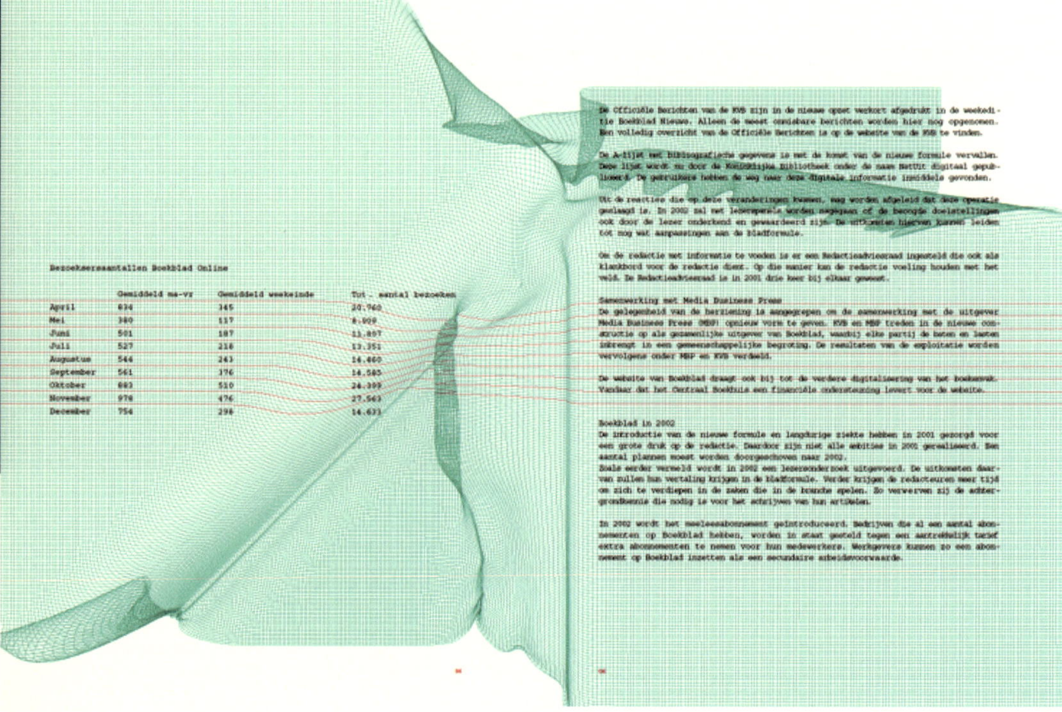

Bezoekersaantallen Boekblad Online

	Gemiddeld ma-vr	Gemiddeld weekeinde	Tot. aantal bezoeken
April	634	345	20.760
Mei	380	117	8.909
Juni	501	187	11.897
Juli	527	218	13.351
Augustus	544	243	14.460
September	561	376	14.585
Oktober	883	510	24.399
November	978	476	27.563
December	754	298	14.633

De Officiële Berichten van de KVB zijn in de nieuwe opzet verkort afgedrukt in de weekeditie Boekblad Nieuws. Alleen de meest openbare berichten worden hier nog opgenomen. Een volledig overzicht van de Officiële Berichten is op de website van de KVB te vinden.

De A-lijst met bibliografische gegevens is met de komst van de nieuwe formule vervallen. Deze lijst wordt nu door de Koninklijke Bibliotheek onder de naam NetUit digitaal gepubliceerd. De gebruikers hebben de weg naar deze digitale informatie inmiddels gevonden.

Uit de reacties die op deze veranderingen kwamen, mag worden afgeleid dat deze operatie geslaagd is. In 2002 zal met lezerspanels worden nagegaan of de beoogde doelstellingen ook door de lezer onderkend en gewaardeerd zijn. De uitkomsten hiervan kunnen leiden tot nog wat aanpassingen aan de bladformule.

Om de redactie met informatie te voeden is er een Redactieadviesraad ingesteld die ook als klankbord voor de redactie dient. Op die manier kan de redactie voeling houden met het veld. De Redactieadviesraad is in 2001 drie keer bij elkaar geweest.

Samenwerking met Media Business Press

De gelegenheid van de herziening is aangegrepen om de samenwerking met de uitgever Media Business Press (MBP) opnieuw vorm te geven. KVB en MBP treden in de nieuwe constructie op als gezamenlijke uitgever van Boekblad, waarbij elke partij de baten en lasten inbrengt in een gemeenschappelijke begroting. De resultaten van de exploitatie worden vervolgens onder MBP en KVB verdeeld.

De website van Boekblad draagt ook bij tot de verdere digitalisering van het boekenvak. Vandaar dat het Centraal Boekhuis een financiële ondersteuning levert voor de website.

Boekblad in 2002

De introductie van de nieuwe formule en langdurige ziekte hebben in 2001 gezorgd voor een grote druk op de redactie. Daardoor zijn niet alle ambities in 2001 gerealiseerd. Een aantal plannen moest worden doorgeschoven naar 2002.
Zoals eerder vermeld wordt in 2002 een lezersonderzoek uitgevoerd. De uitkomsten daarvan zullen hun vertaling krijgen in de bladformule. Verder krijgen de redacteuren meer tijd om zich te verdiepen in de zaken die in de branche spelen. Zo verwerven zij de achtergrondkennis die nodig is voor het schrijven van hun artikelen.

In 2002 wordt het meeleesabonnement geïntroduceerd. Bedrijven die al een aantal abonnementen op Boekblad hebben, worden in staat gesteld tegen een aantrekkelijk tarief extra abonnementen te nemen voor hun medewerkers. Werkgevers kunnen zo een abonnement op Boekblad inzetten als een secundaire arbeidsvoorwaarde.

for KVB, 28 cm x 20 cm, 36 pages, 2002

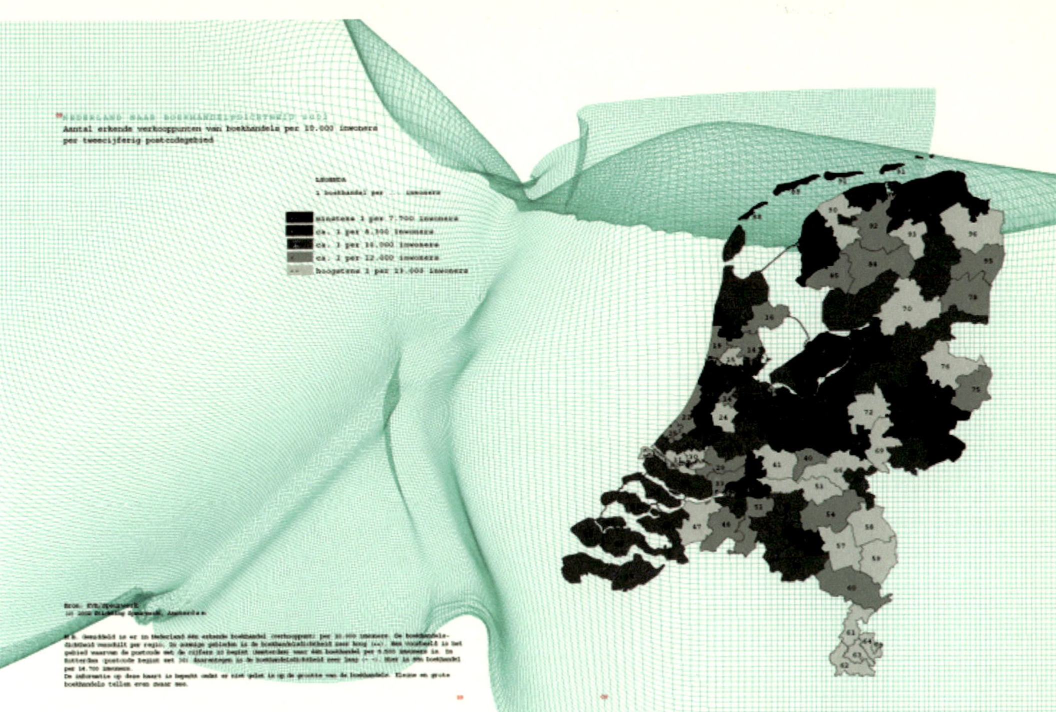

Tabel 4 Kopers van algemene boeken in 2002 naar inkomen

Bruto inkomen van huishouden	Percentage boekenkopers	Koopdichtheid		Segmentaandeel
Meer dan twee keer modaal	32,5% H	179	++	13,3%
Twee keer modaal	24,8% H	136	++	12,8%
Tussen 1 en 2 keer modaal	22,1% H	122	+	23,2%
Bovenmodaal, wil niet zeggen hoeveel	21,9% H	121	+	2,8%
Gelijk aan modaal	15,3% L	84	-	27,1%
Benedenmodaal	13,2% L	73	--	12,6%
Geen antwoord	11,9% L	66	--	8,2%
Totaal	18,1%	100	-	100%

Bron: Boekenlezer-onderzoek van Stichting Speurwerk (veldwerk Interview/NSS) zie toelichting 60

Ruim de helft van de boekenkopers is afkomstig uit huishoudens met een bovenmodaal inkomen.

Tabel 5 Kopers van algemene boeken in het eerste kwartaal 2001 naar dagbladen

Kijkt u het volgende dagblad wel eens in?	Percentage boekenkopers	Koopdichtheid		Segmentaandeel
Algemeen Dagblad	19,8% H	114	+	34,1%
Financieele Dagblad	23,8% H	136	++	14,0%
NRC Handelsblad	33,7% H	193	++	29,6%
Het Parool	26,6% H	152	++	9,3%
De Telegraaf	17,2%	99	-	44,4%
Trouw	29,1% H	167	++	14,5%
De Volkskrant	28,7% H	165	++	39,9%
Een regionaal dagblad	18,1%	104	-	68,3%
Geen van deze	10,4% L	60	--	5,9%
Totaal	17,4%	100	-	*

* omdat het mogelijk is verschillende kranten te lezen, is de som van de percentages groter dan 100%

Bron: Boekenlezer-onderzoek van Stichting Speurwerk (veldwerk Interview/NSS) zie toelichting 60

Ondanks een relatief kleine oplage vormen de lezers van NRC Handelsblad wegens de hoge koopdichtheid een belangrijke groep boekenkopers.

 StitchUnsewed
by Hansje van Halem

As a design solution for the signage of the ‹Go Slow› presentation by Droog Design we embroidered type on perforated hardboard with large stitches within the outlines of the Times New Roman font. For the design of the invitation this system was translated into a double-sided typeface. The back of the stitching is visible on the reverse of the paper.

Because I don't have the technical skills, the letters on the back need to be connected manually, as if the type has been set in one long thread.

Pink: backside
Black: frontside,
2004

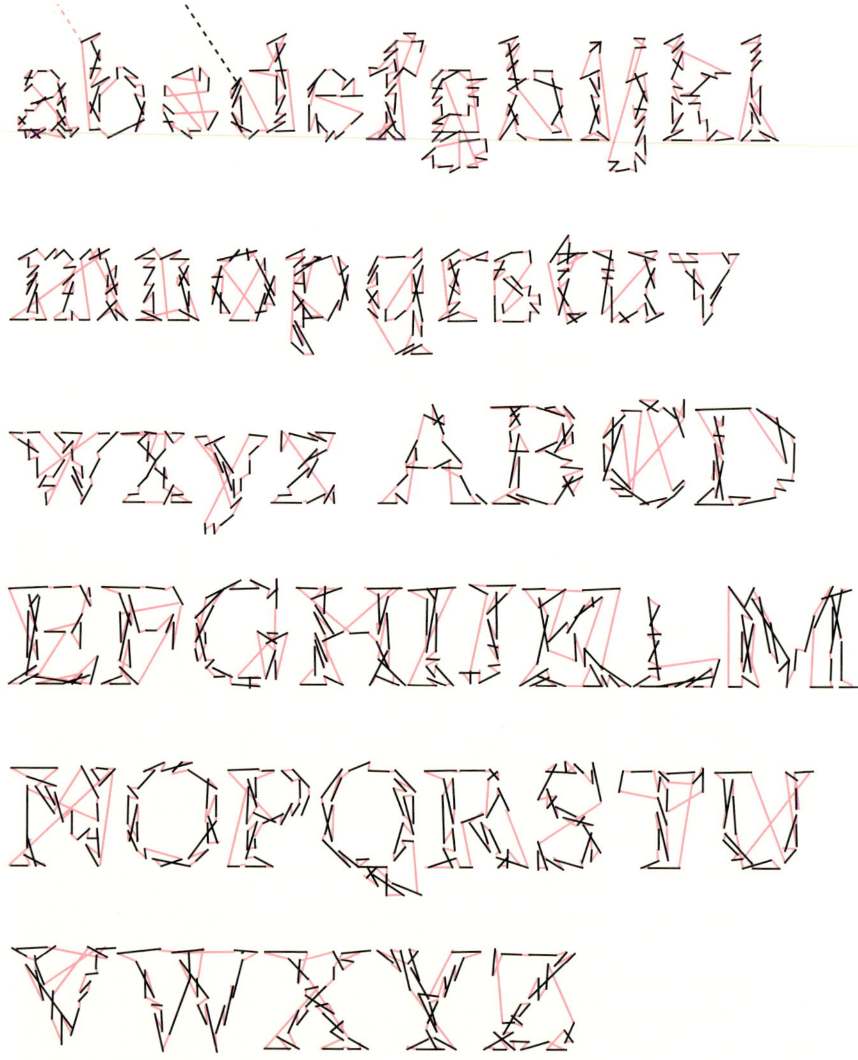

front

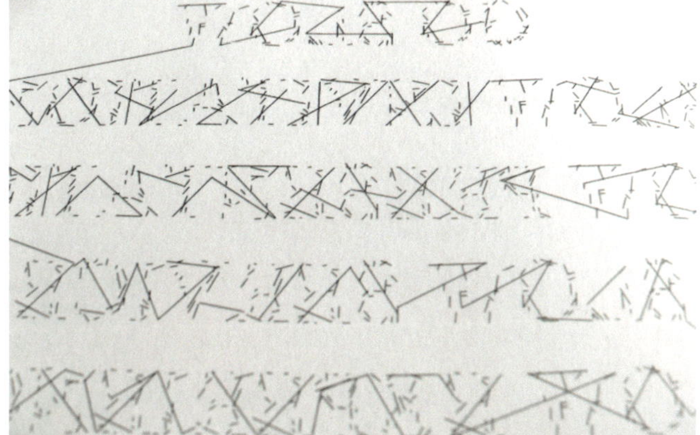

back

‹Go Slow› presentation by Droog Design

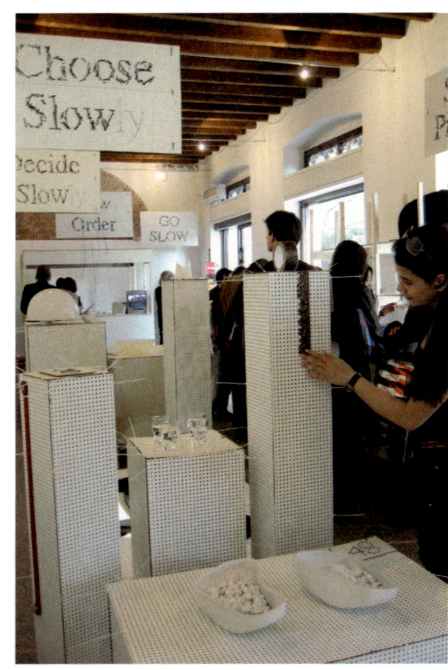

Poster and invitation for arts festival Ypenburg, Den Haag.

CLOSE
ENCOUNTERS
YPENBURG

VANAF 15 30 T/M 22 30 UUR

OP ZATERDAG 9 SEPT 2006

FESTIVAL

MET BEELDENDE KUNST

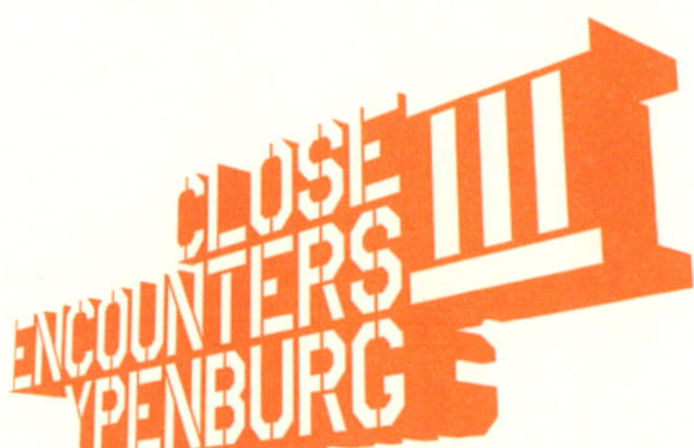

OP EN OM HET
PATRIJSPLANTSOEN
YPENBURG

GRATIS TOEGANG

DEN HAAG

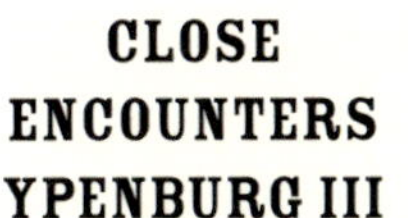

CLOSE ENCOUNTERS YPENBURG III

ZATERDAG 9 SEPTEMBER 2006 15.30 — 22.30 UUR

FESTIVAL MET BEELDENDE KUNST OP EN OM HET PATRIJSPLANTSOEN YPENBURG DEN HAAG

Close Encounters is gratis toegankelijk.

Artoteek Den Haag / 7X11
Denneweg 14a /
Patrijsplantsoen 23
2514 CG Den Haag
info@artoteekdenhaag.nl
info@7X11.nl
070 – 346 5337

Informatie over het festival staat op www.7X11.nl en is verkrijgbaar op de dag zelf bij de informatiestand.

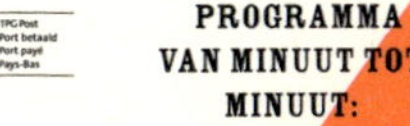

afz. Artoteek Den Haag 2514 CG 14a

TPG Post
Port betaald
Port payé
Pays-Bas

PROGRAMMA VAN MINUUT TOT MINUUT:

15.30
Opening van Close Encounters 3 door de Wethouder van Cultuur en financiën, Jetta Klijnsma

15.45
Presentatie van de Mobiele Volkstuin door Annechien Meier met commentaar van Ronika van der Kaa, schrijver, journalist en tuinier

16.00
Daggeluidswandeling I

16.20
Daggeluidswandeling II

16.30
Draaiorgel Maria uit Delft; verder tot 20.30 uur ieder uur een optreden

16.40
Daggeluidswandeling III

17.00
Daggeluidswandeling IV
- RANDWOORDEN, programma met verhalen en gedichten over randen, grenzen en periferie door randwachter PJ Roggeband en stadsranddichter Jet Crielaard

17.20
Daggeluidswandeling V

17.40
Daggeluidswandeling VI

18.00
Opening van de tentoonstelling 'Het gezicht van Ypenburg', door Albert Wulffers, filmmaker en beeldend kunstenaar, schrijver en curator
- daggeluidswandeling VII

18.20
Laatste daggeluidswandeling VIII

18.30 - 20.00
Borrelen en een warme kunstzinnige maaltijd (tegen een geringe vergoeding), met live muziek van het straatorkest 'Toeters en Bellen'

20.00
Avondgeluidswandeling I

20.15
Aanvang SCHEMERTOUR fietstocht 'Langs de rand van Ypenburg' met o.a. PJ Roggeband, een bewoner van Ypenburg, onverwachte gasten en stadsranddichter Jet Crielaard

20.20
Avondgeluidswandeling II

20.40
Avondgeluidswandeling III

21.00
Avondgeluidswandeling IV

21.20
Avondgeluidswandeling V

21.30
Presentatie van de lichtkrant 'Wit gespikkeld met bruin'. Plaats: Dierenartspraktijk aan de Torenvalklaan 27 – hoek Sperwersingel

21.40
Avondgeluidswandeling VI

22.00
Laatste avondgeluidswandeling VII

22.30
Afsluiting

SOUND SEEING YPENBURG
Ongeplande ontmoetingen in het klanklandschap van de tekentafel

DE MOBIELE VOLKSTUIN

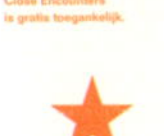

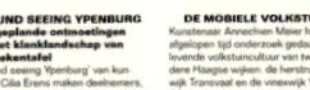

HET GEZICHT VAN YPENBURG

WIT GESPIKKELD MET BRUIN

BEREIKBAARHEID VAN HET PATRIJSPLANTSOEN YPENBURG

COLOFON

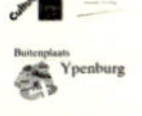

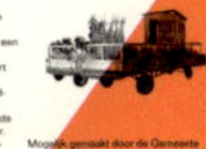

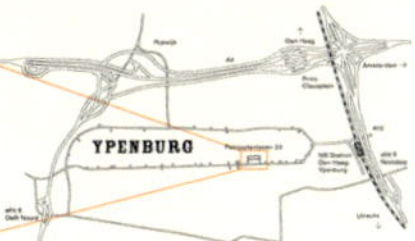

LANGS DE RANDEN VAN YPENBURG

Stroom Den Haag

artoteek den haag

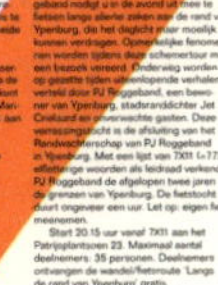

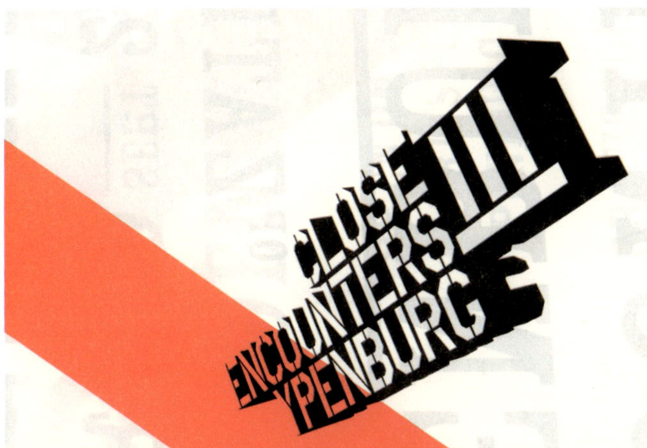

Wim Crouwel /Architectures Typographiques

by Experimental Jetset

We were asked by Galerie Anatome, an art space in Paris, to design the invitation and catalogue for ‹Wim Crouwel: Architectures Typographiques 1956-1976›, an exhibition that ran from February 9 until April 28, 2007.

For this project we photographed Crouwel in our own studio. We constructed a typographic environment, loosely referring to a classic calendar that Crouwel designed in 1963/1964, and photographed Crouwel standing in the middle of this. (The actual photo was taken by photographer Johannes Schwartz).

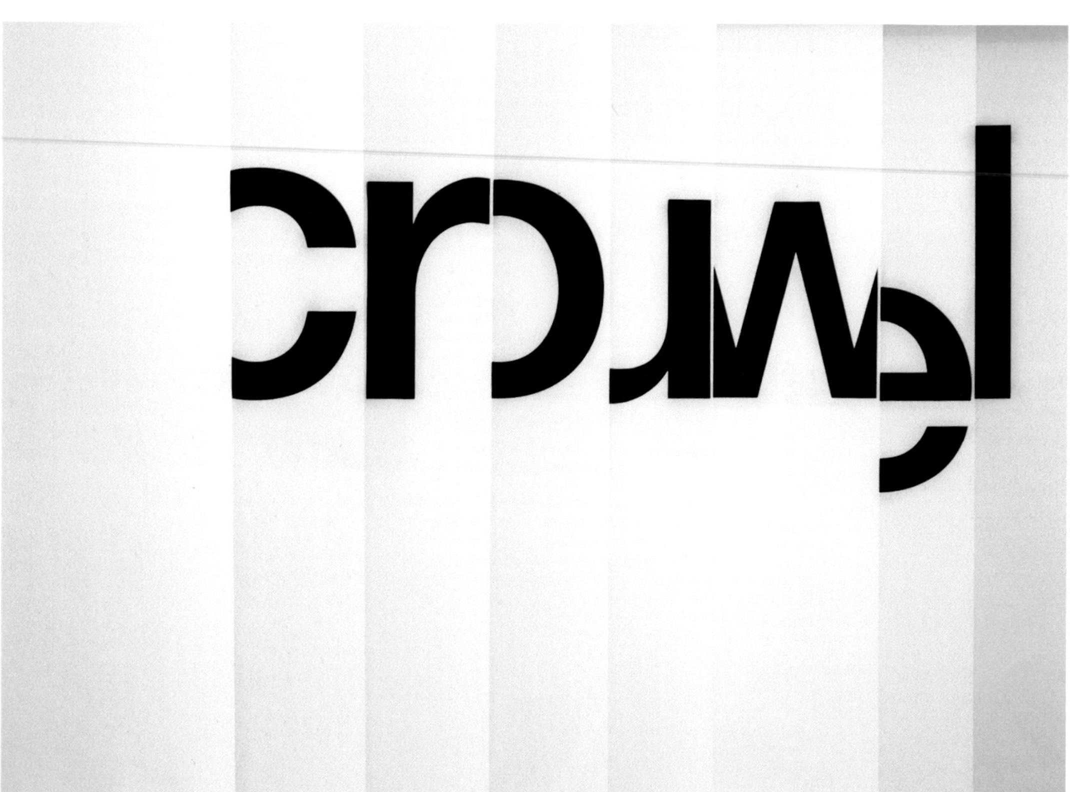

for Galerie Anatome (Paris), 2007

With this photograph, we tried to invoke the title of the exhibition: ‹Architectures Typographiques›. We found the gesture of creating a spatial typographic installation a very fitting way to translate the title of the exhibition.
The question we asked ourselves was simple: how to design an invitation on the subject of Crouwel, without falling into the trap of designing an invitation ‹in the style of› Crouwel? We solved this problem by introducing the photographic element; after all, photography is not something we normally associate with Crouwel's work.

For the photography itself, we worked closely with photographer Johannes Schwartz. We have collaborated with him before, for example on the publications ‹High Noon› (2003), ‹High Nature› (2004), ‹High Light› / ‹High Bold› (2005) and ‹High Rise› (2005).

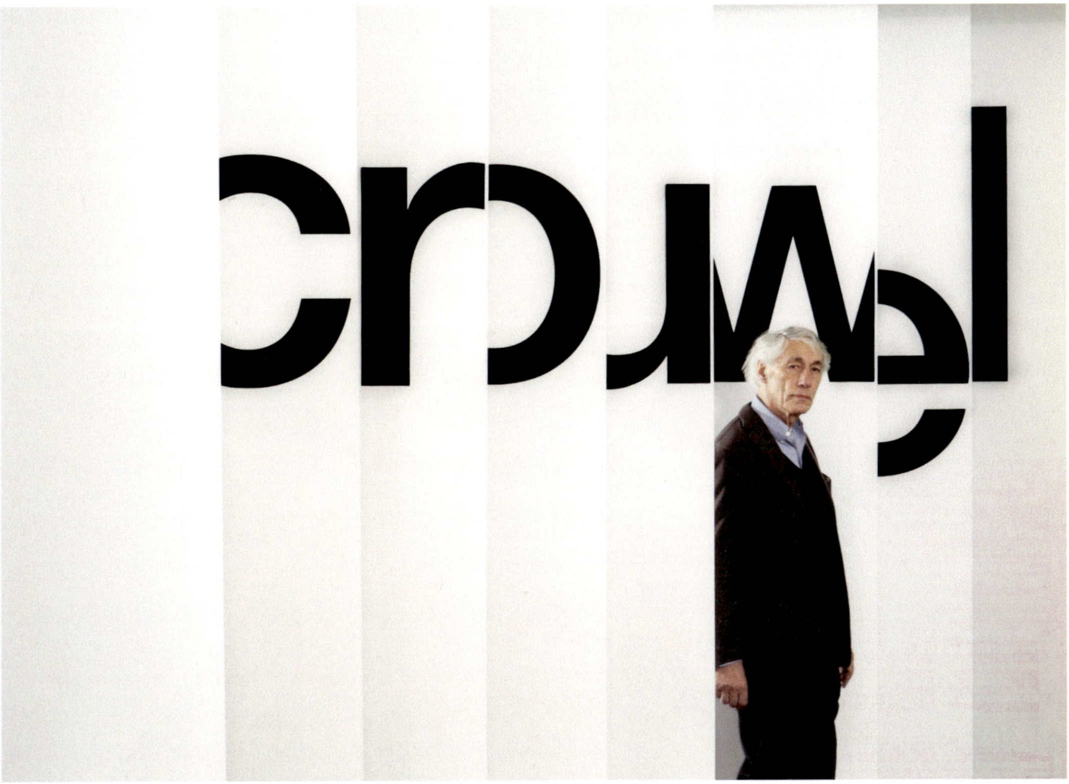

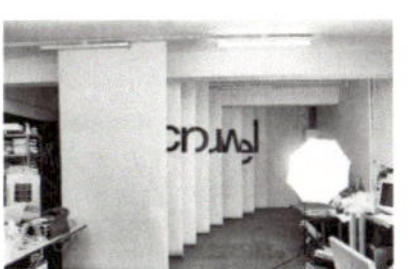

Making of

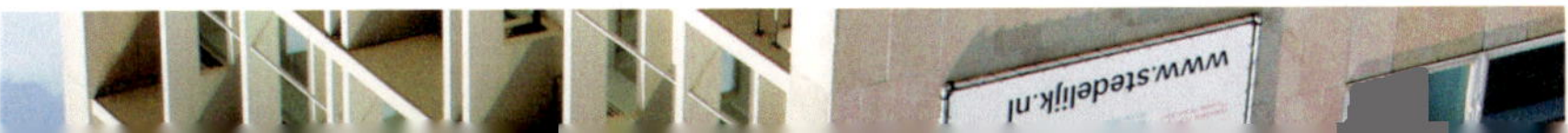

SMCS graphic identity
by Experimental Jetset

From 2004 until 2008, the ‹Stedelijk Museum› is housed in temporary premises. This location used to be the mail distribution centre of the Dutch Post Office (PTT). The logo we designed for ‹Stedelijk Museum CS› refers to the old function of this building: the pattern of blue/red diagonal lines in the SMCS logo resembles the blue/red diagonal lines on international airmail envelopes. At the same time, the SMCS logo points to the history of the ‹Stedelijk Museum›; the typeface (Univers) and the acronym SMCS both refer to the old SM logo, designed in the 1960s by Wim Crouwel.

In other words, we see the logo as a crossroads of two histories: the history of the building (PTT), and the history of the institution (SMCS). In that sense, it's a homage to two cultural institutions that have both played a very important role in the social-democratic landscape of the Netherlands.

For the sign system of the SMCS, we created a grid of more than 2000 plastic A4-sized document-holders, which hang throughout the building. This system proved to be a very easy and flexible way to create signs, emphasizing the sense of temporariness, while at the same time referring to the office-like history of the building.

for Stedelijk Museum CS (SMCS), 2004

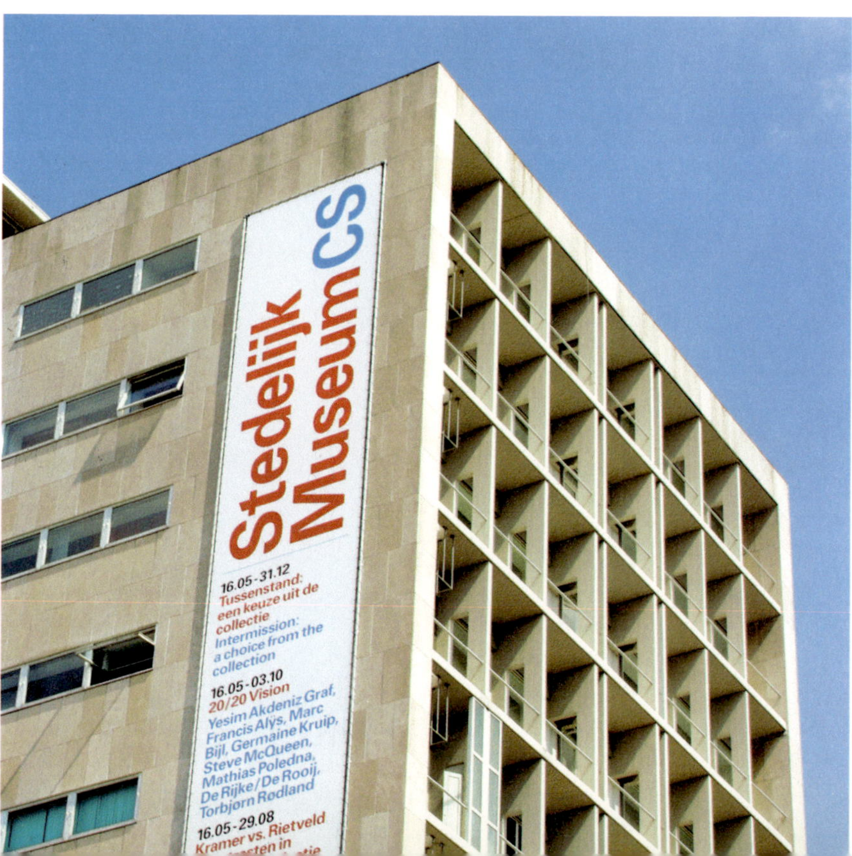

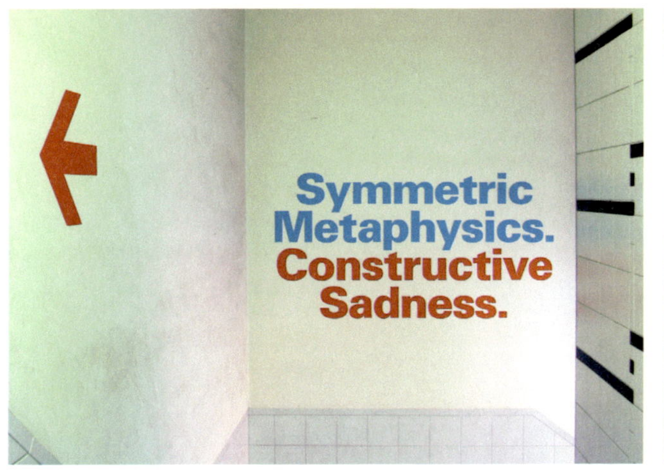
Symmetric
Metaphysics.
Constructive
Sadness.

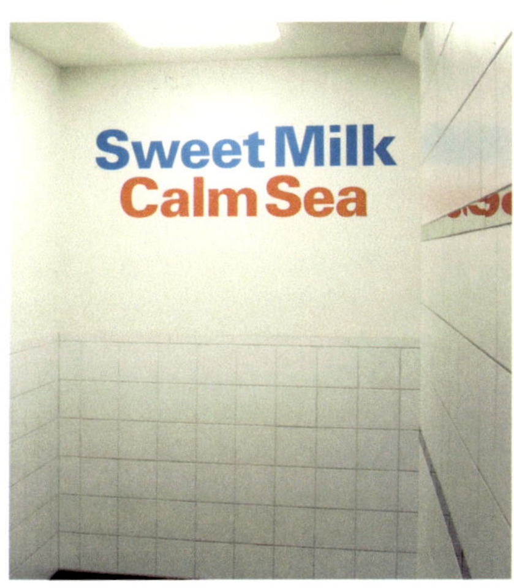
Sweet Milk
Calm Sea

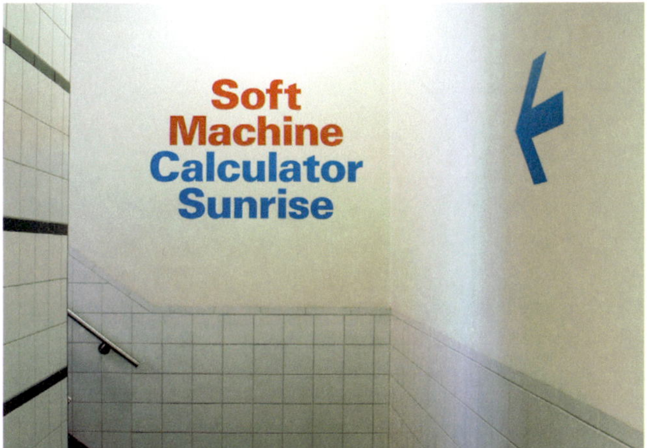
Soft
Machine
Calculator
Sunrise

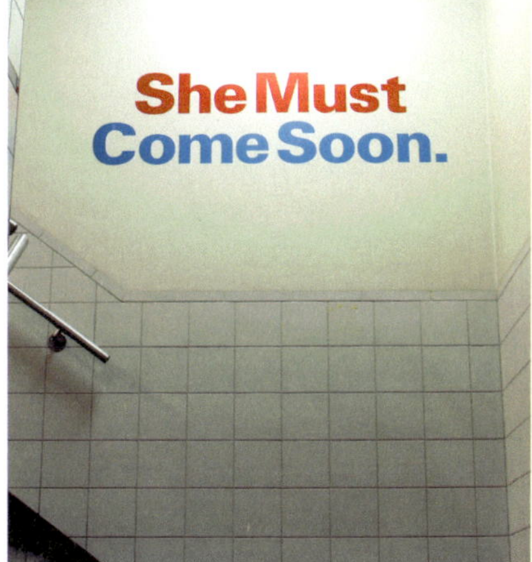
She Must
Come Soon.

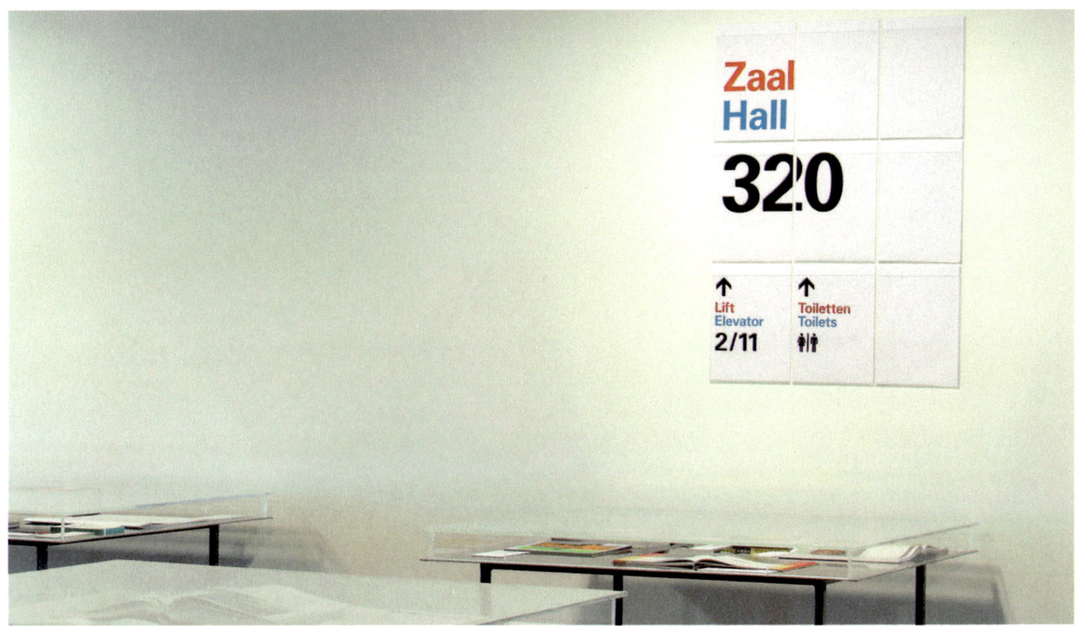
Zaal
Hall
3.20
Lift
Elevator
2/11
Toiletten
Toilets

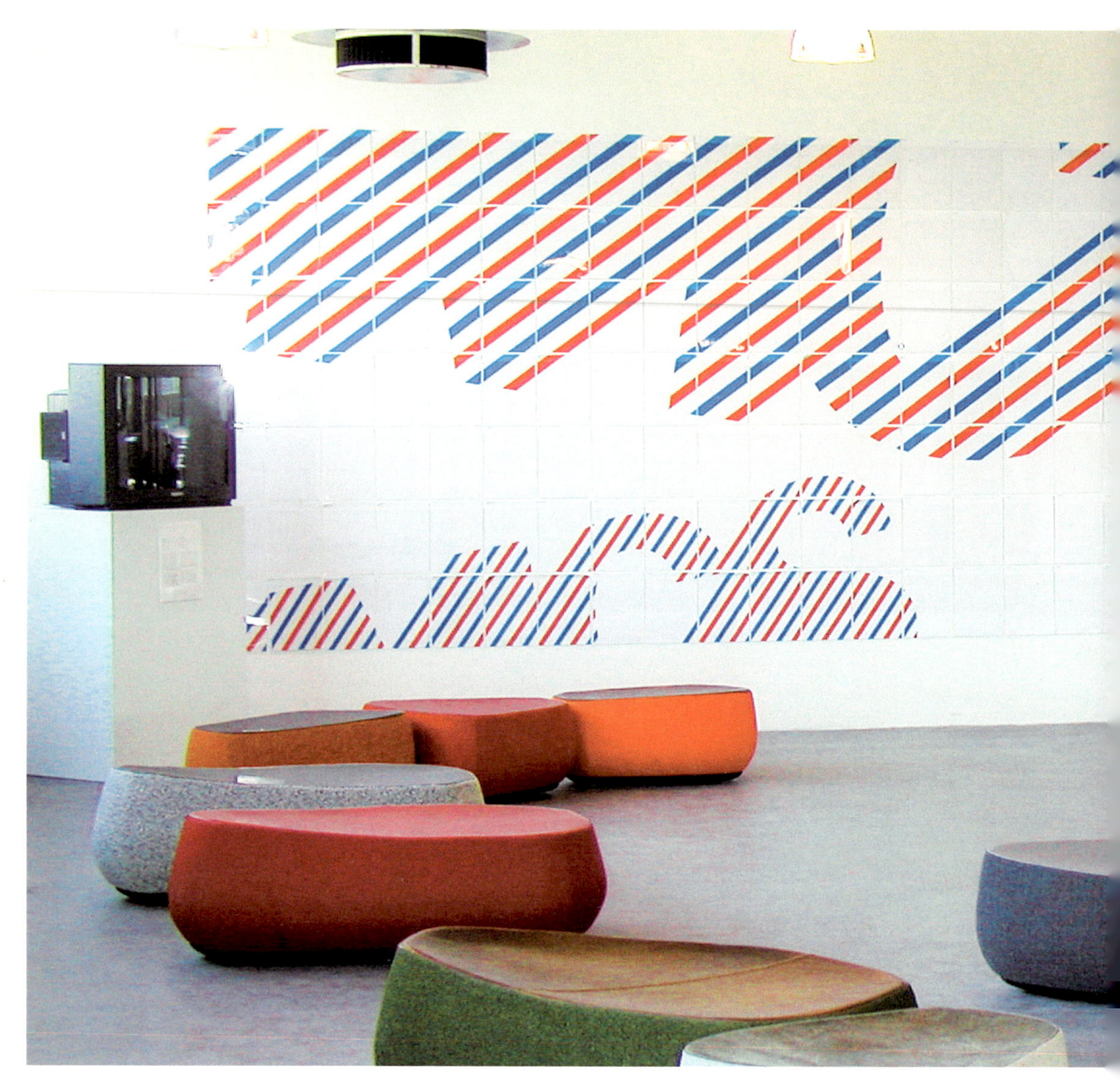

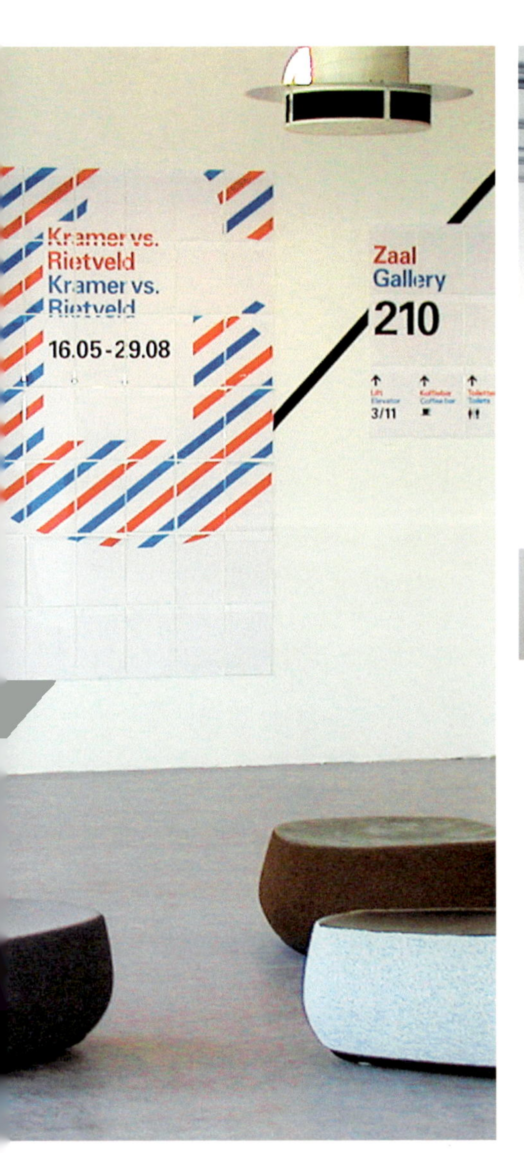
Kramer vs.
Rietveld
Kramer vs.
Rietveld
16.05 - 29.08
Zaal
Gallery
210
3/11

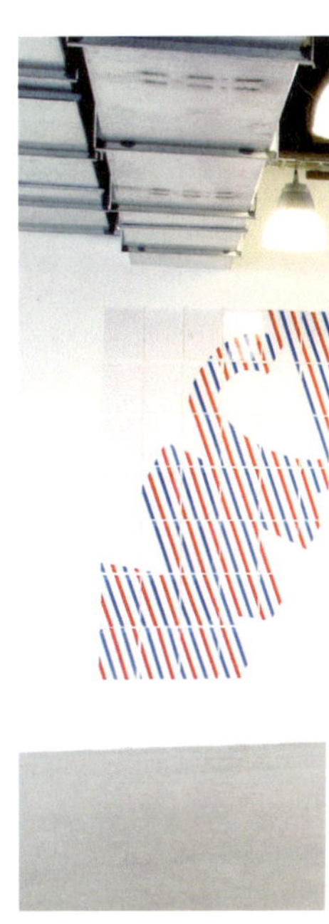

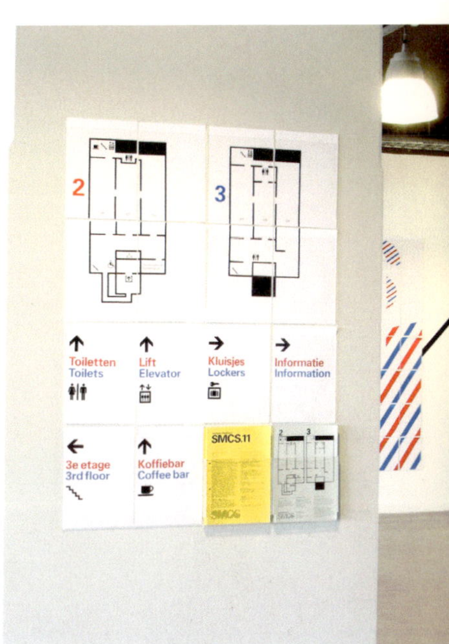
2
3
Toiletten
Toilets
Lift
Elevator
Kluisjes
Lockers
Informatie
Information
3e etage
3rd floor
Koffiebar
Coffee bar
SMCS.11

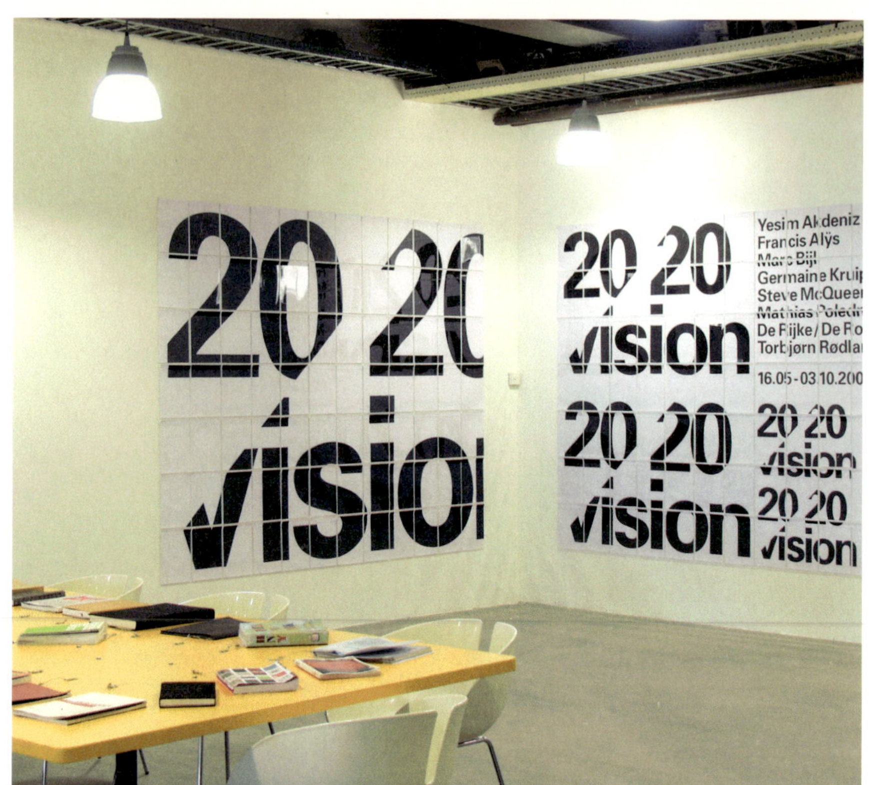
20 20 vision
Yesim Akdeniz
Francis Alÿs

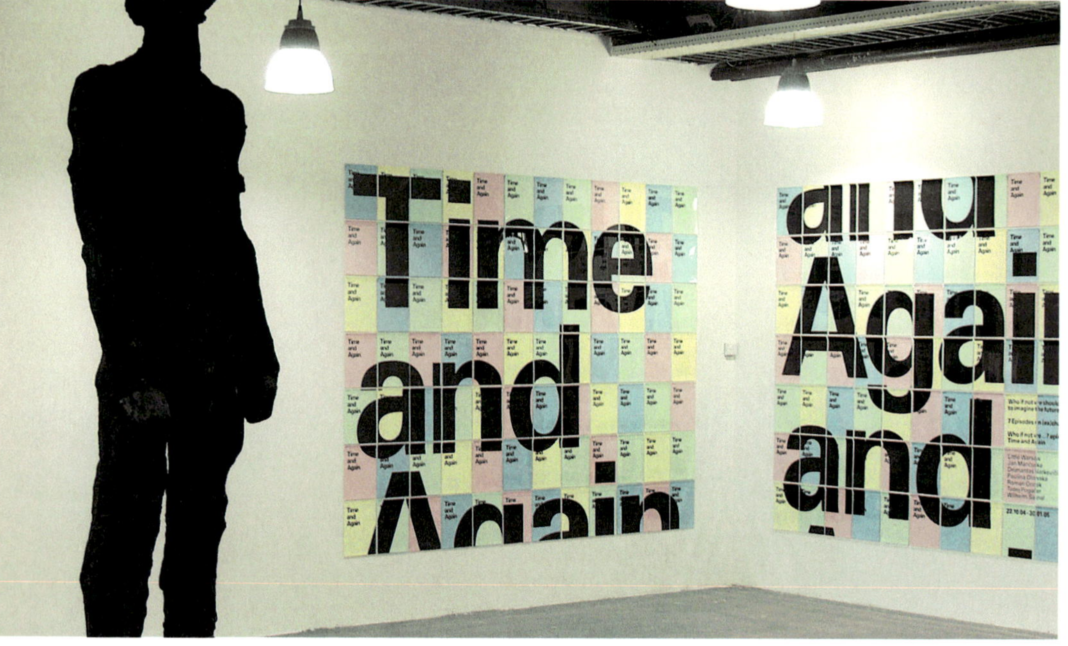
Time and Again

TuttoBeNe presentation
by Lesley Moore & Silke Spinner

‹TuttoBeNe› is an organization whose remit is to help upcoming young designers from Belgium and the Netherlands present themselves to a broader audience. For the 2007 presentation, Lesley Moore came up with the slogan ‹this is the way we see it›, referring to sustainability as a selection criteria for the ‹TuttoBeNe› designers. With ‹sustainability› and ‹low budget› as key words, a ‹less is more› approach was a logical step. The entire presentation was designed with just one ingredient: the ‹TuttoBeNe› ‹all-in-one› newspaper. A handle-like cut-out allowed the newspaper to be hung on the walls of the stand.
A range of functions was created by re-ordering the pages of the newspaper in various ways, including signage, catalogue, flyer, plan, slogan, wallpaper and individual posters for each designer.

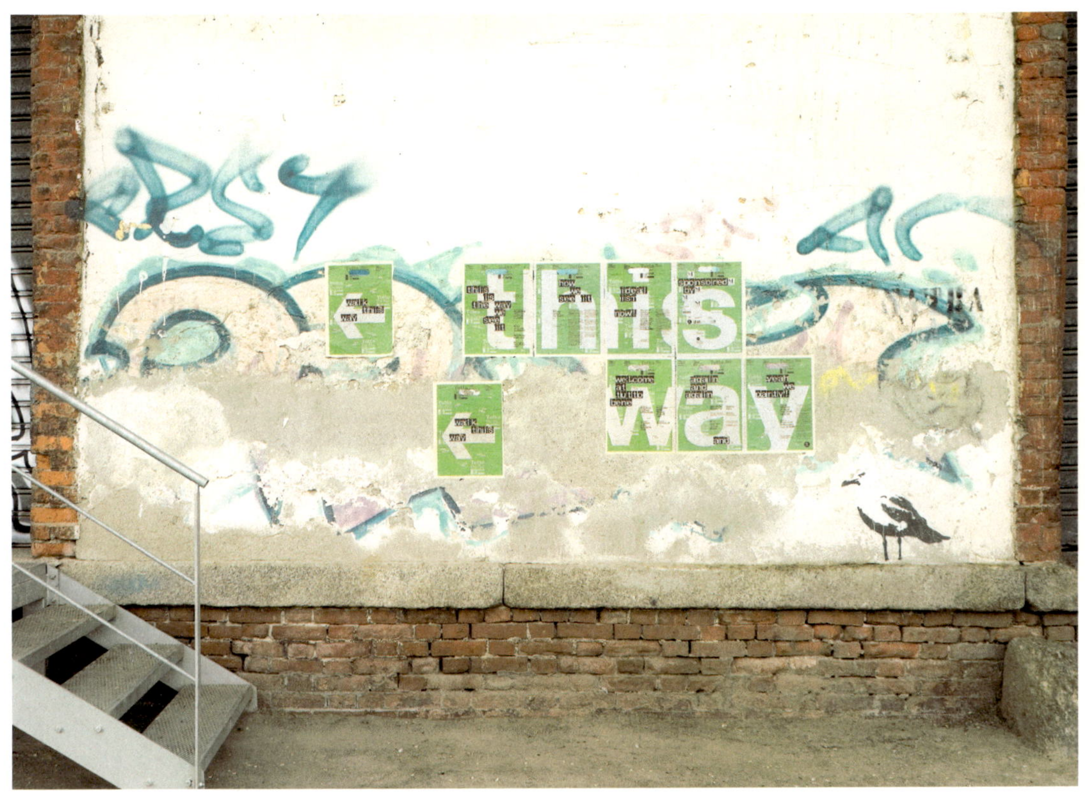

Exhibition by Lesley Moore & Silke Spinner
Photography by Alberto Ferrero, Furniture Fair Milan, 2007

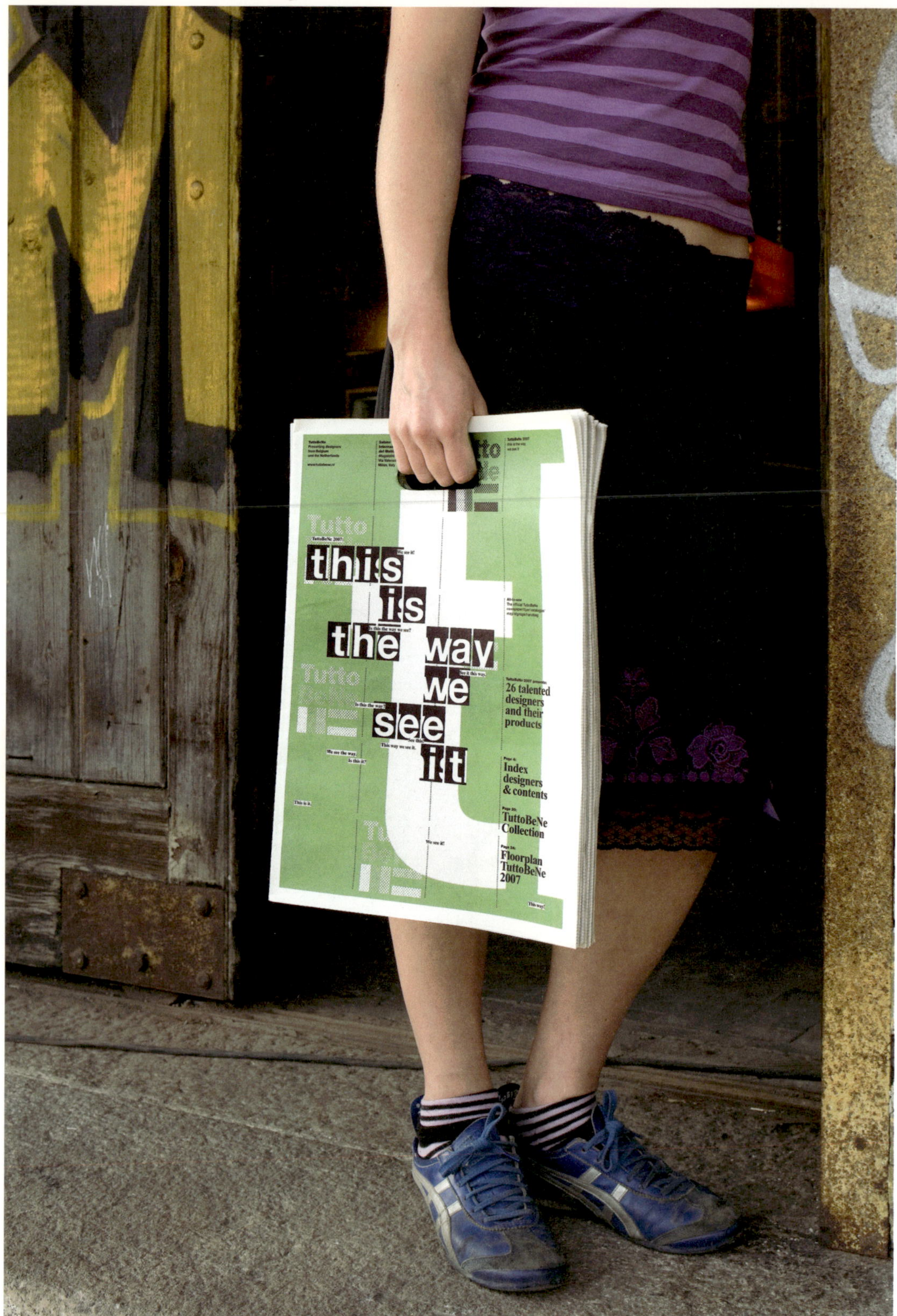
Tutto
this
is
the way
we
see
it
26 talented designers and their products
Index designers & contents
TuttoBeNe Collection
Floorplan TuttoBeNe 2007

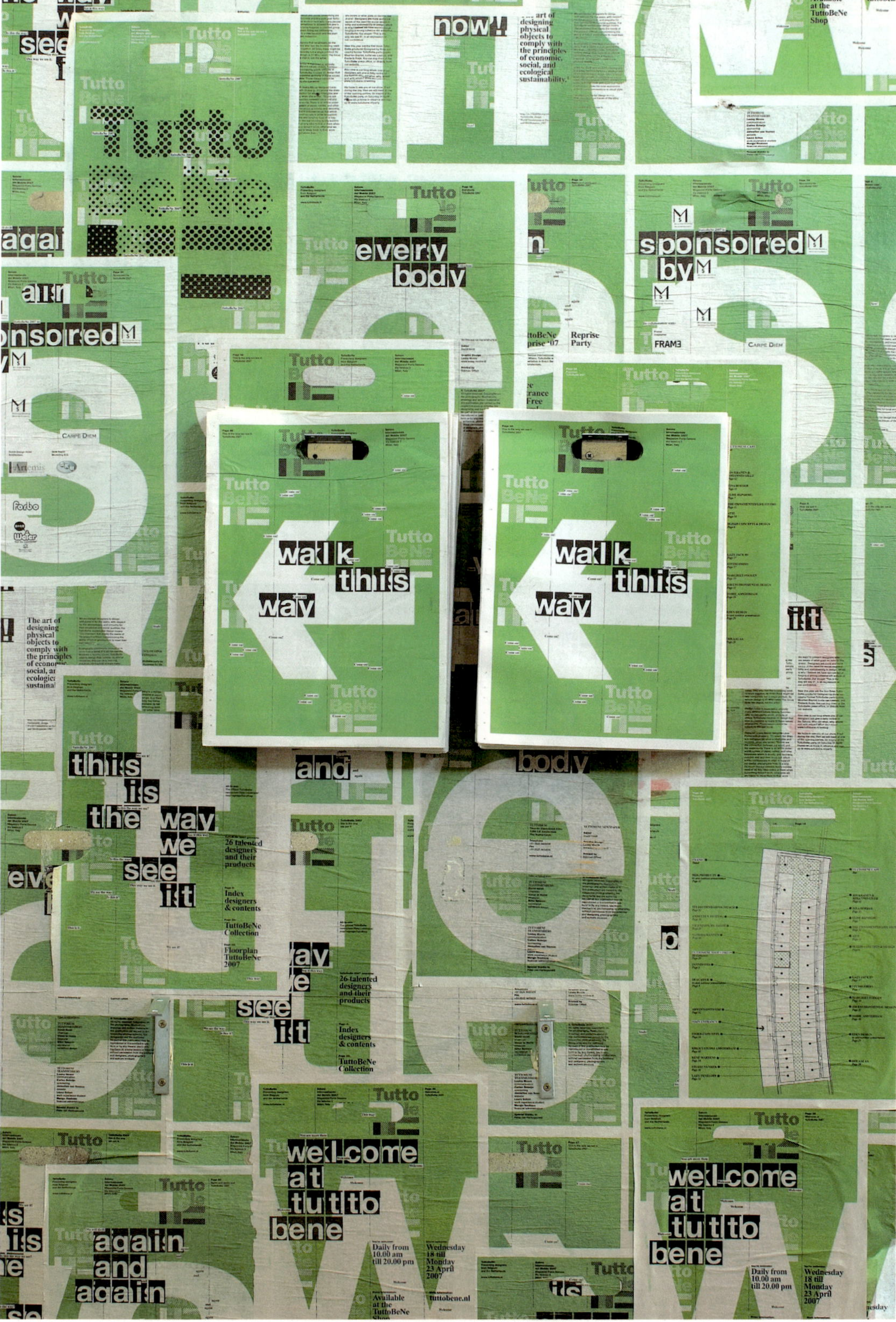

now!
The art of designing physical objects to comply with the principles of economic, social, and ecological sustainability.
Available at the TuttoBeNe Shop
Tutto BeNe
every body
sponsored by
Reprise Party
FRAME
CARPE DIEM
walk this way
walk this way
this is the way we see it
26 talented designers and their products
Index designers & contents
TuttoBeNe Collection
Floorplan TuttoBeNe 2007
and
body
welcome at tutto bene
Daily from 10.00 am till 20.00 pm
Wednesday 18 till Monday 23 April 2007
Available at the TuttoBeNe Shop
tuttobene.nl
again and again
welcome at tutto bene
Daily from 10.00 am till 20.00 pm
Wednesday 18 till Monday 23 April 2007

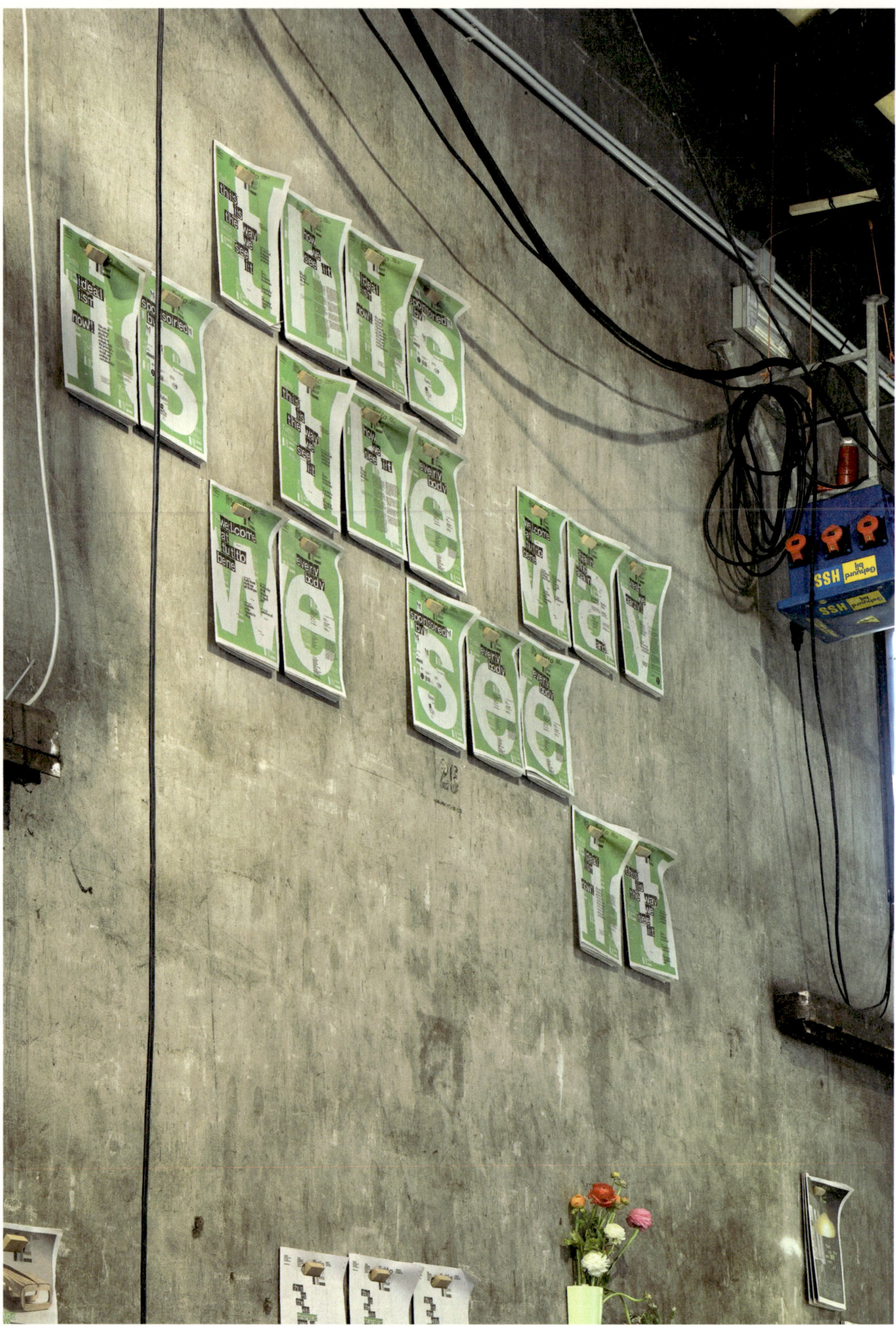
this is the way we see it

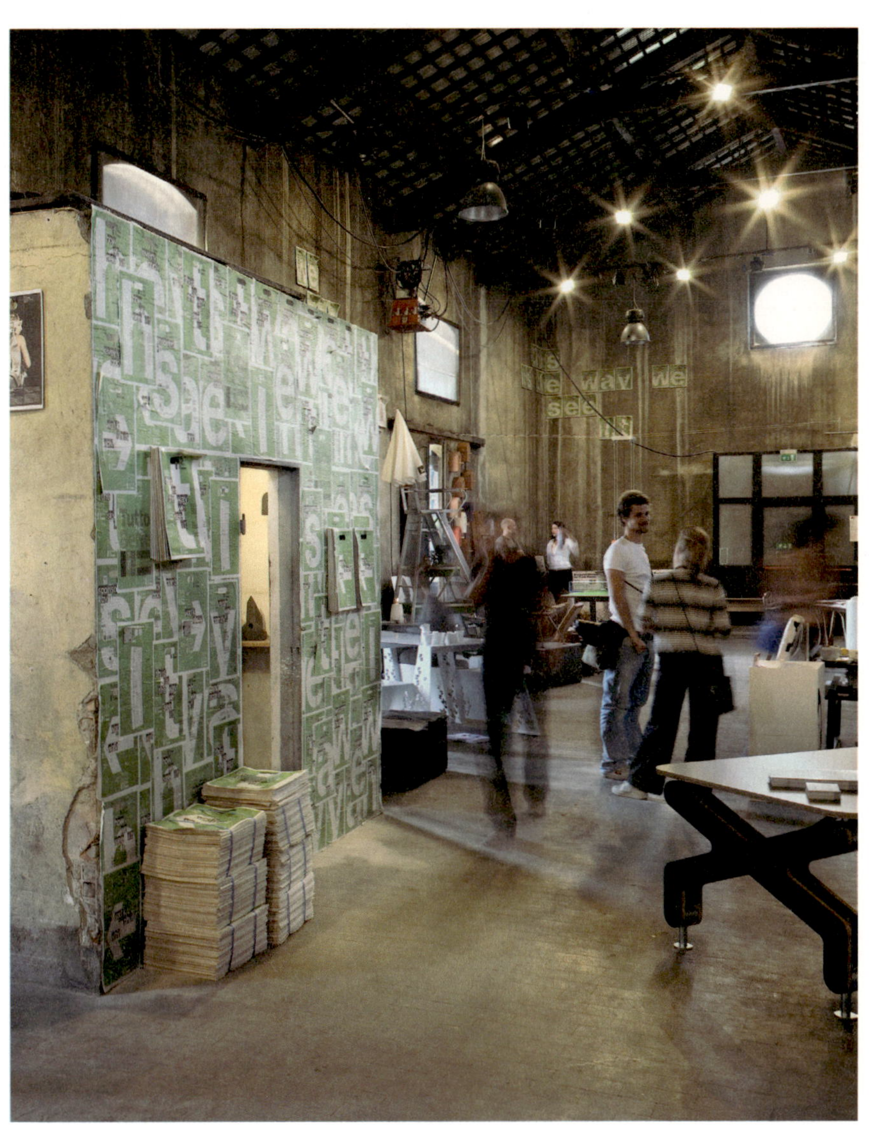
way
we
see

Psychedelic Warfare
by Machine

self-commissioned, 2004

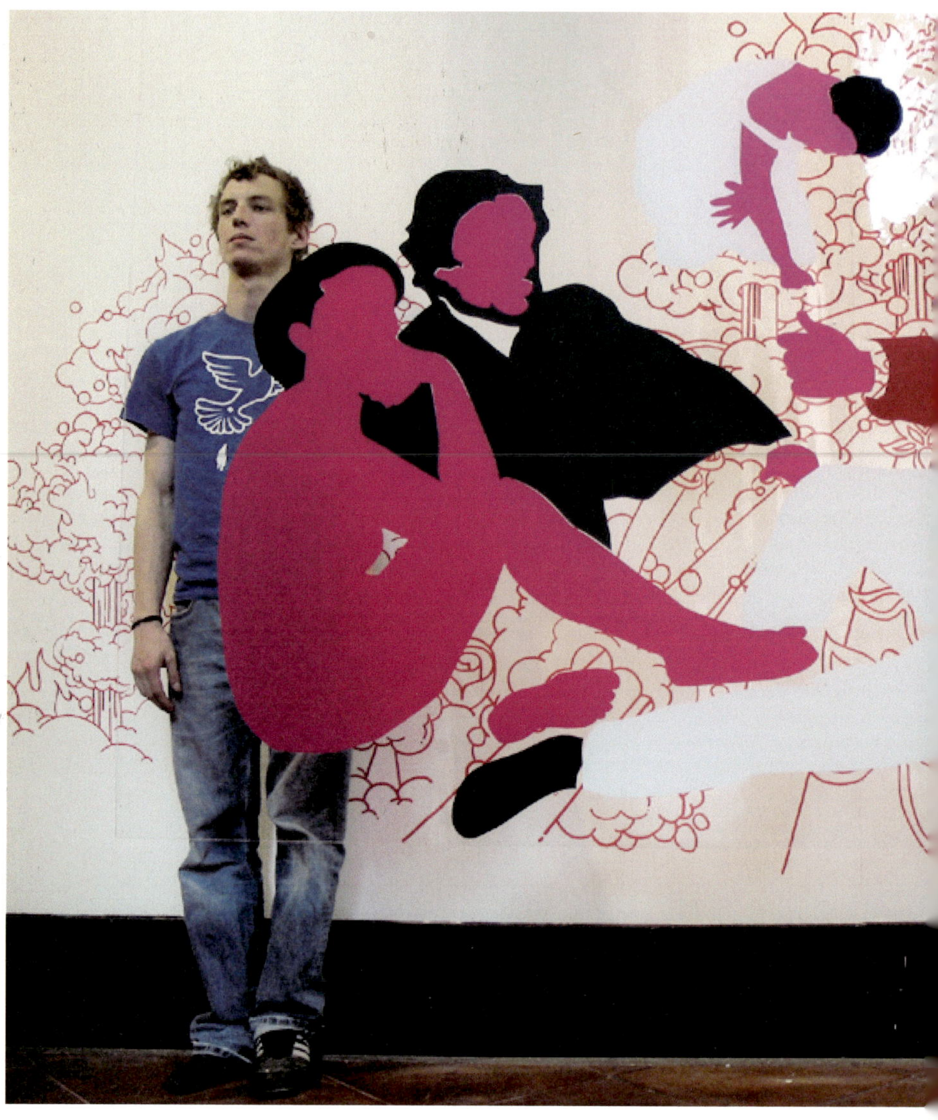

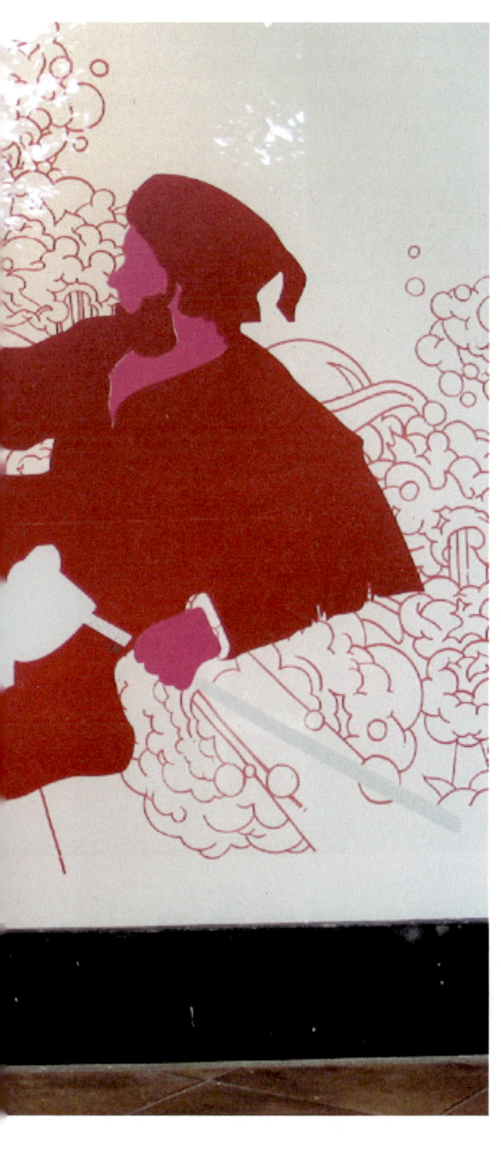

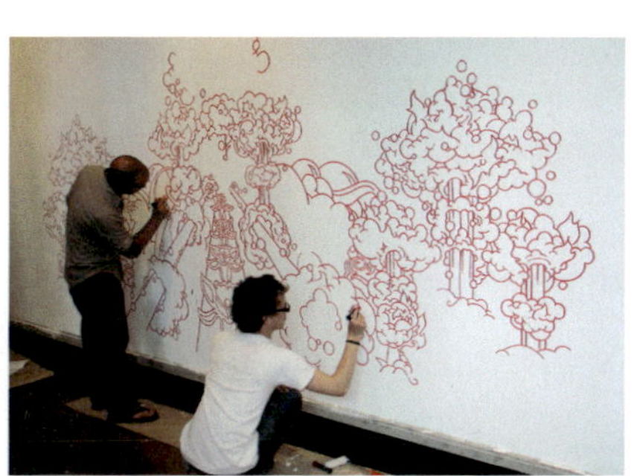

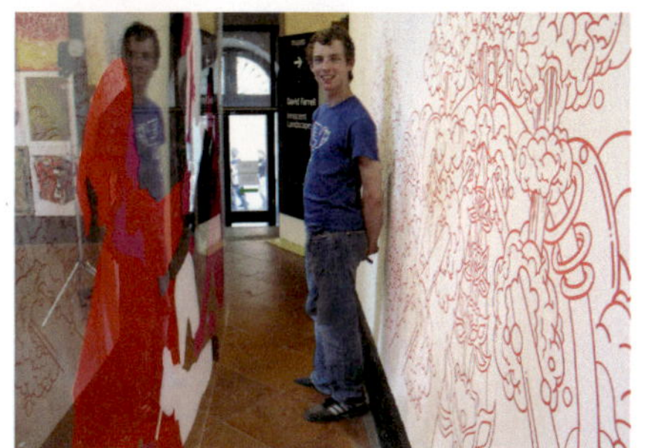

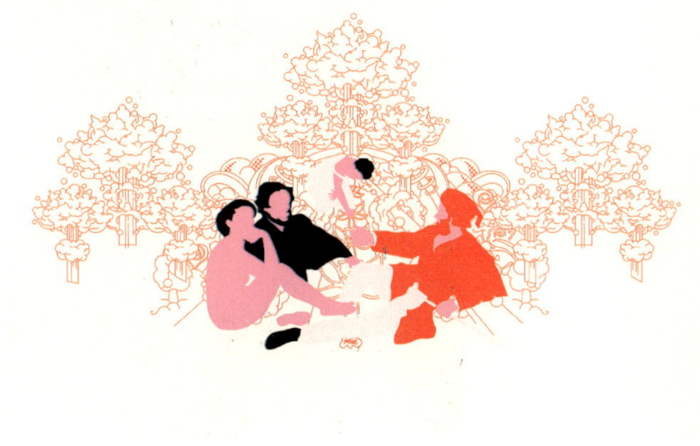

HEMA packaging office supplies
by Studio Kluif

Proposals packaging office supplies. No grey, no silver, no dark blue, no, no, no! Office humour used on office supplies. Very recognizable! Didn't make it to the shops! In our opinion, a missed opportunity.

for HEMA Amsterdam, The Netherlands, 2002

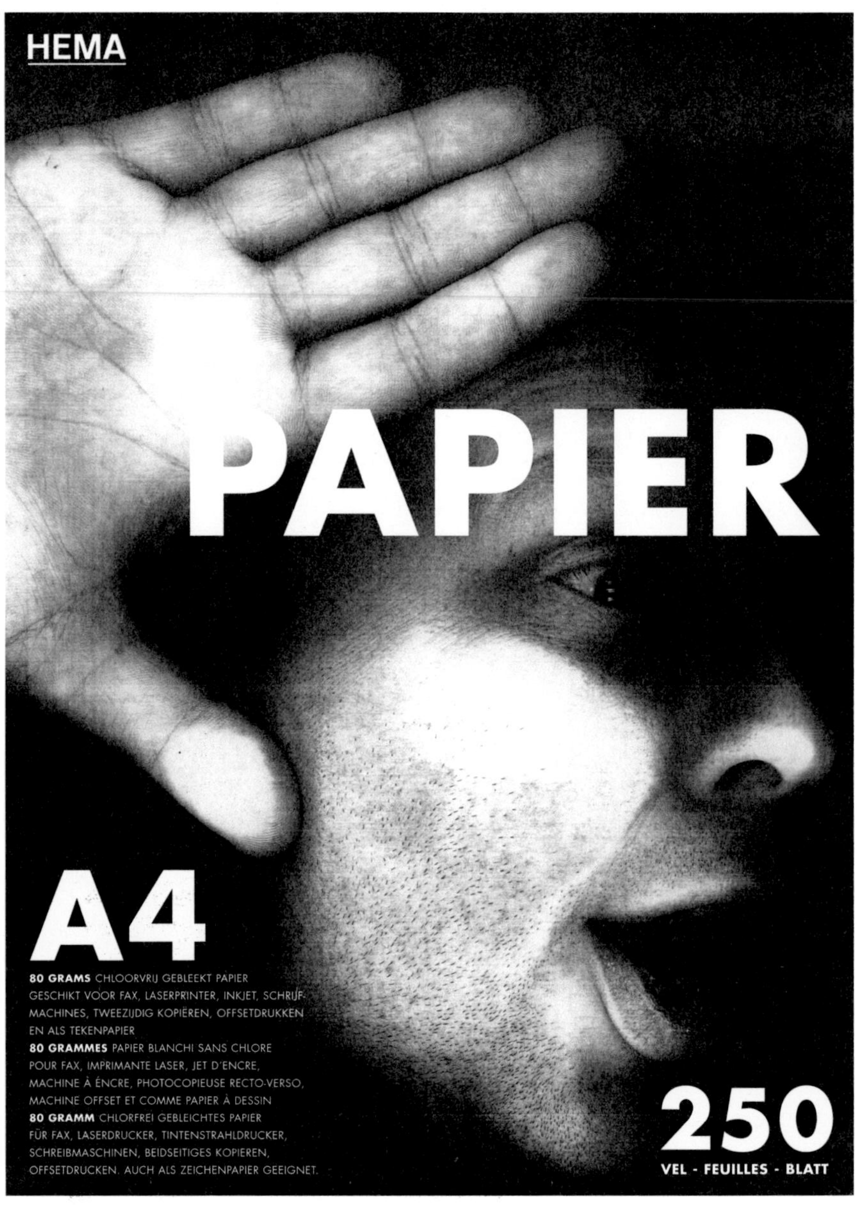

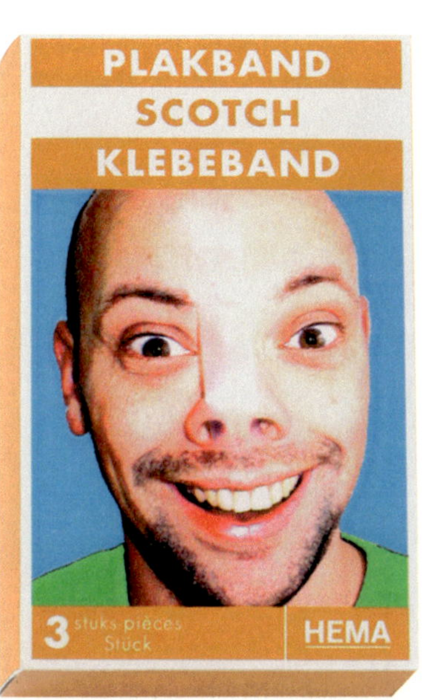
PLAKBAND
SCOTCH
KLEBEBAND
3 stuks-pièces Stück
HEMA

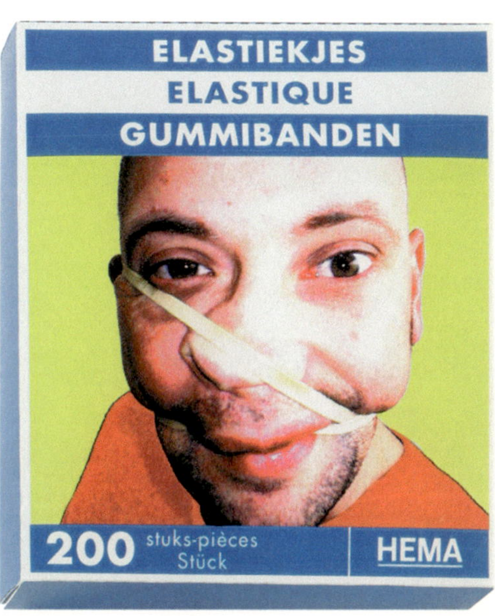
ELASTIEKJES
ELASTIQUE
GUMMIBANDEN
200 stuks-pièces Stück
HEMA

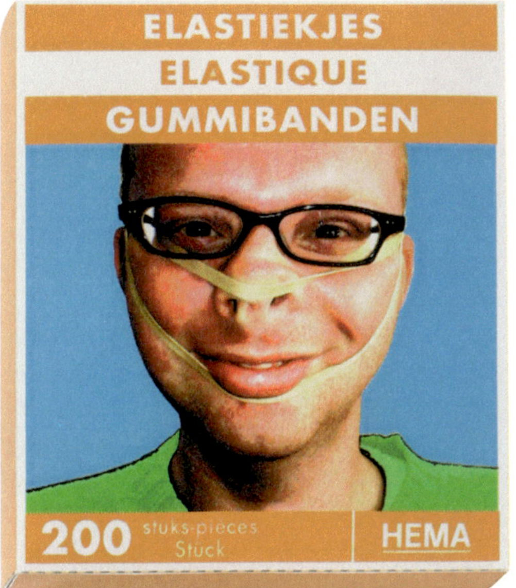
ELASTIEKJES
ELASTIQUE
GUMMIBANDEN
200 stuks-pièces Stück
HEMA

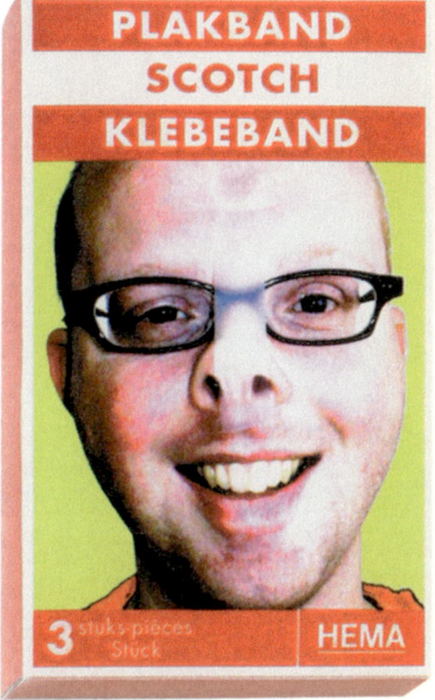
PLAKBAND
SCOTCH
KLEBEBAND
3 stuks-pièces Stück
HEMA

278 HEMA packaging, ‹Play with food products›
by Studio Kluif

Packaging food products for kids. Pirate Food for tough boys, Pretty Pink Food for princesses. Yummy!

for HEMA Amsterdam, The Netherlands, 2005

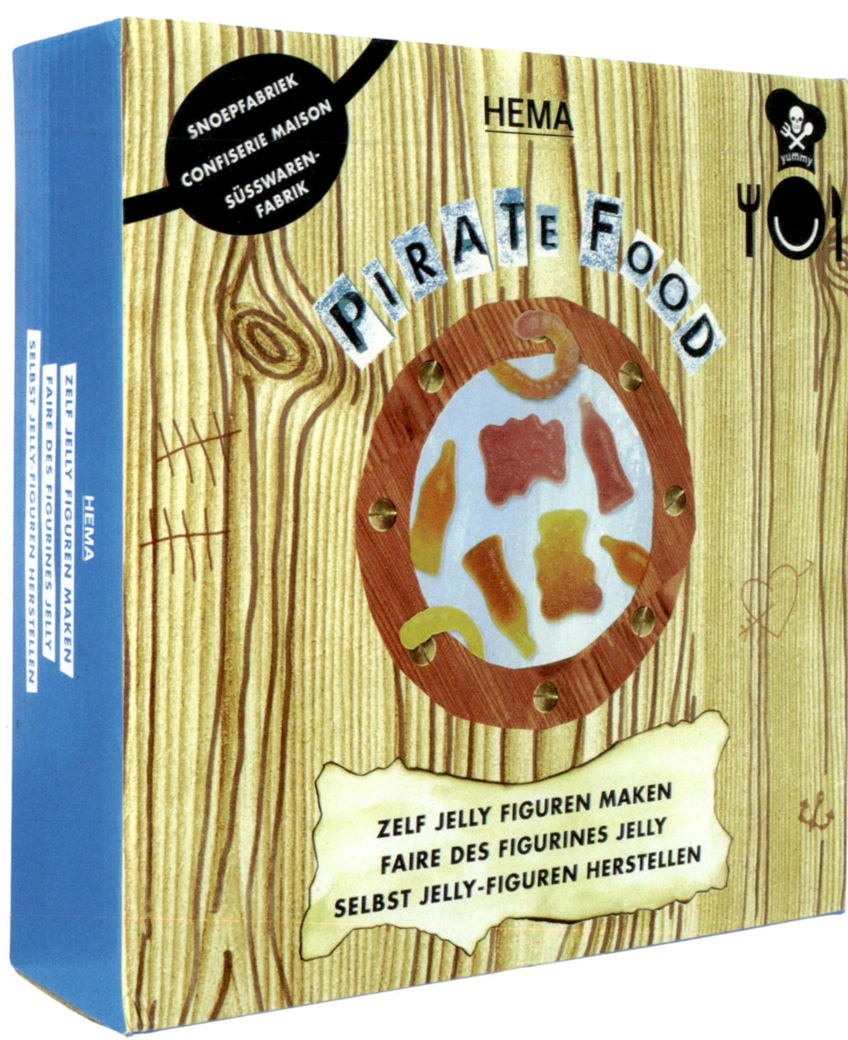

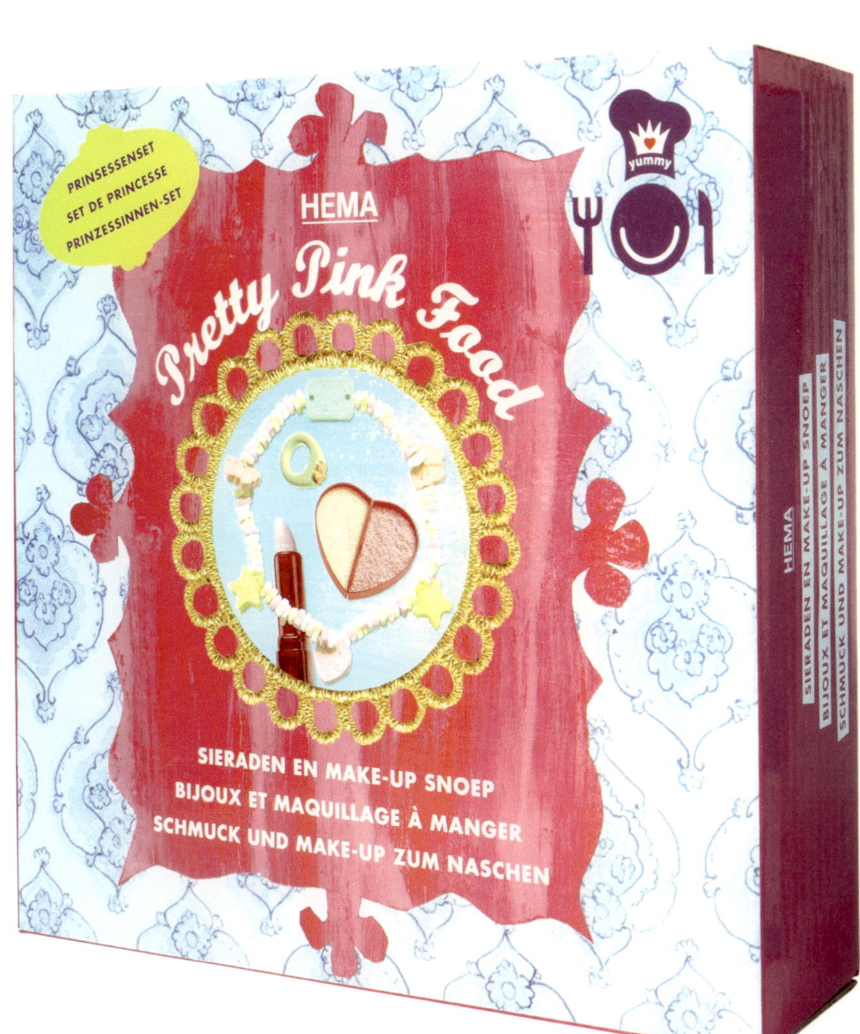
PRINSESSENSET
SET DE PRINCESSE
PRINZESSINNEN-SET
HEMA
Pretty Pink Food
yummy
SIERADEN EN MAKE-UP SNOEP
BIJOUX ET MAQUILLAGE À MANGER
SCHMUCK UND MAKE-UP ZUM NASCHEN
HEMA
SIERADEN EN MAKE-UP SNOEP
BIJOUX ET MAQUILLAGE À MANGER
SCHMUCK UND MAKE-UP ZUM NASCHEN

280 Nedap Annual Report
by Studio Kluif

An Annual Report dealing with the power of imagination. The binding is unique. When people receive the report in their mailbox they can just tear the strip away and open the book. In other words: the box in which the book is sent out in becomes the cover!

for Nedap,
The Netherlands, 2006

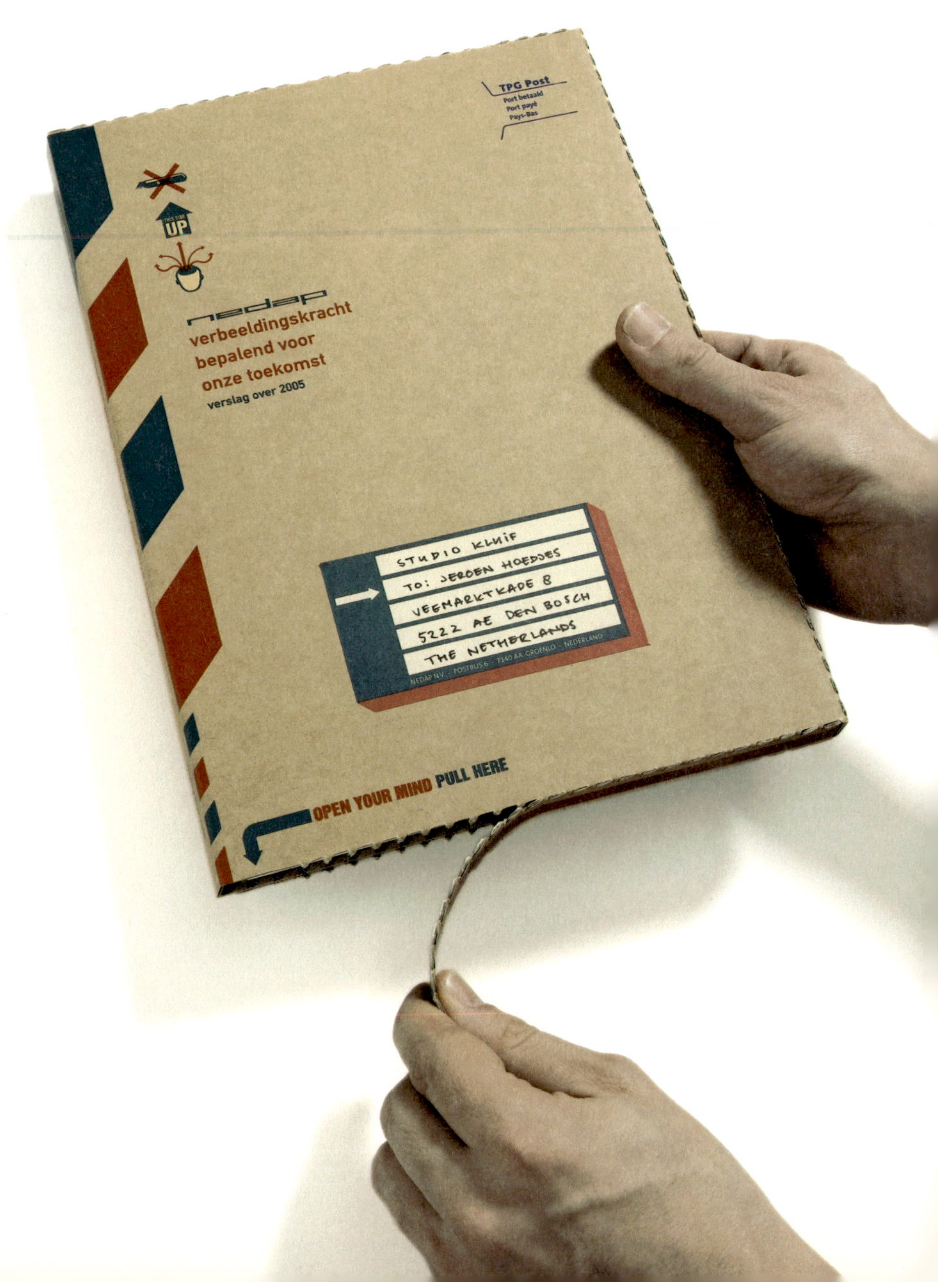

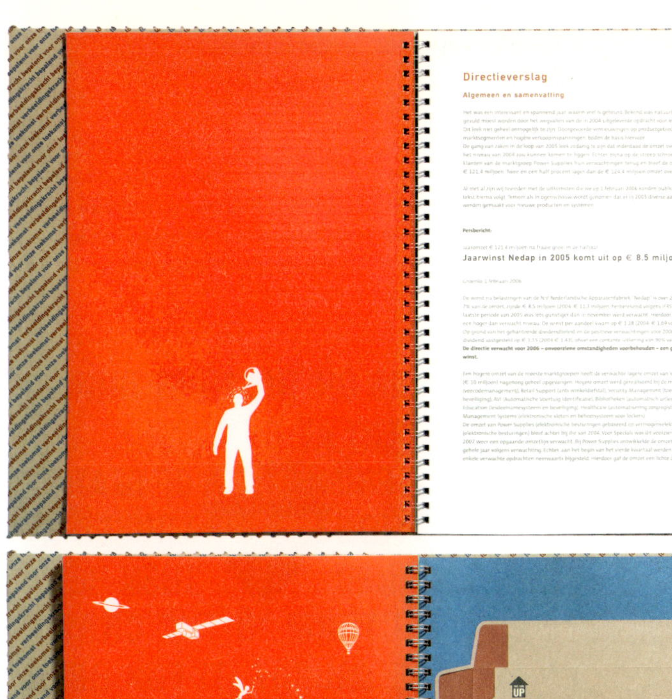

Directieverslag
Algemeen en samenvatting
Persbericht:
Jaarwinst Nedap in 2005 komt uit op € 8.5 miljoen
De directie verwacht voor 2006 – onvoorziene omstandigheden voorbehouden – een groei van omzet en winst.

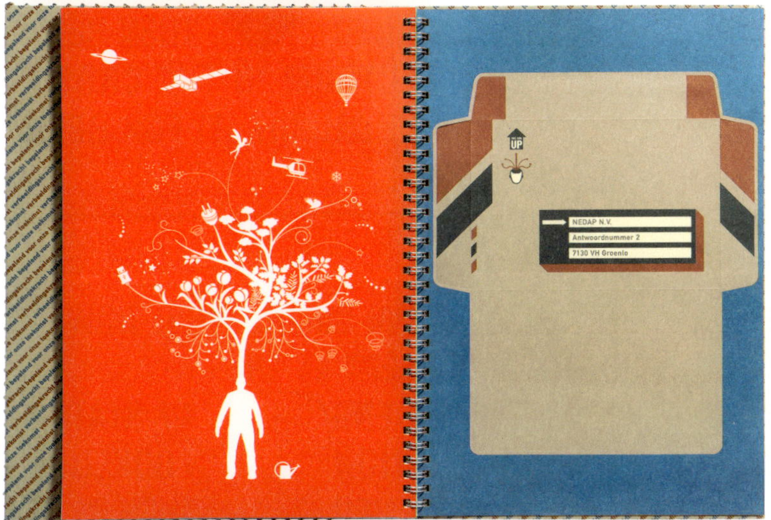

UP
NEDAP N.V.
Antwoordnummer 2
7130 VH Groenlo

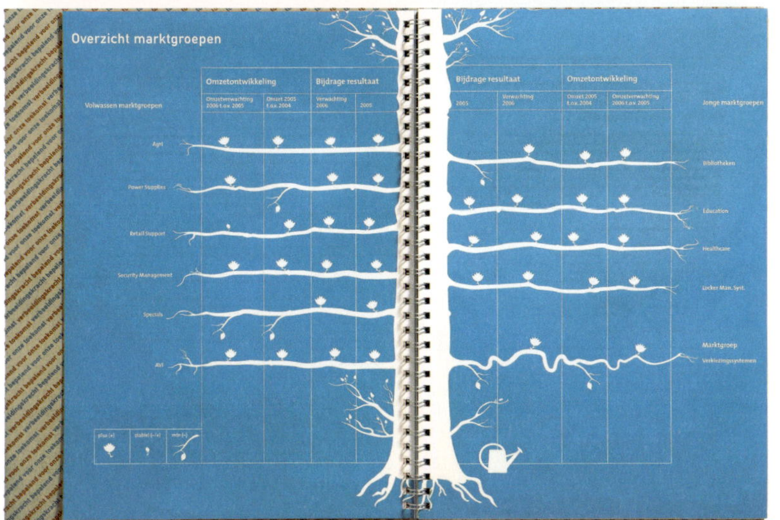

Overzicht marktgroepen
Omzetontwikkeling
Bijdrage resultaat
Volwassen marktgroepen
Agri
Power Supplies
Retail Support
Security Management
Specials
AVI
Bijdrage resultaat
Omzetontwikkeling
Jonge marktgroepen
Bibliotheken
Education
Healthcare
Locker Man. Syst.
Marktgroep
Verkiezingssystemen

 Amsterdam ArenA card, David Bowie
by Studio Kluif

Design for David Bowie's Amsterdam ArenA card (a private payment system for the Amsterdam ArenA). In this proposal the joke is that every buyer of the card has caught Bowie's plectrum. The plectrum can be snapped out of the card, so 20,000 people would have Bowie's plectrum in their wallet...

for Amsterdam ArenA, The Netherlands, 2004

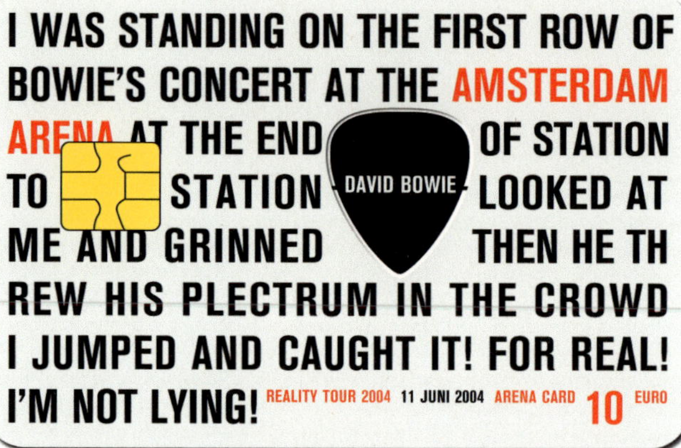

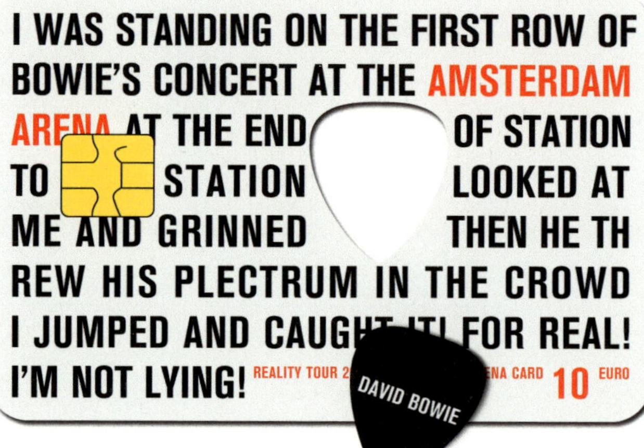

283 Box with bone-shaped paperclips
by Studio Kluif

The Dutch word ‹Kluif›, the name of our studio, means ‹bone›. Our dog Lola was our mascot for years – she is in heaven now... Kluif produced a box with bone-shaped paperclips as a give-away. Bite-sized, for all your business needs!

self-commissioned, 2007

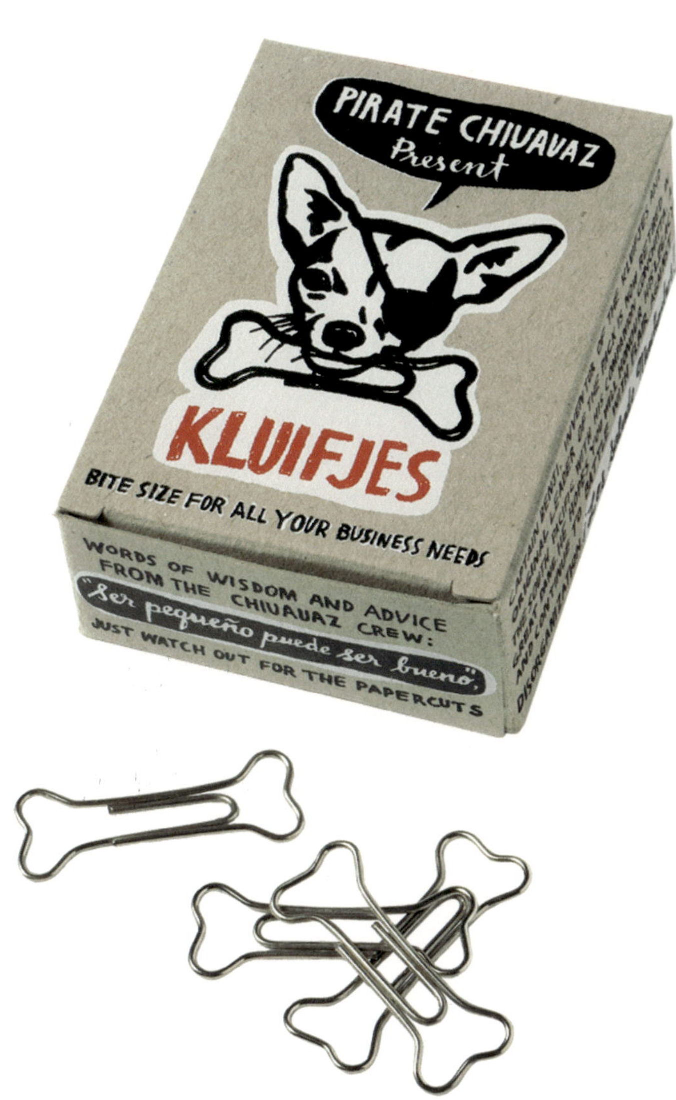

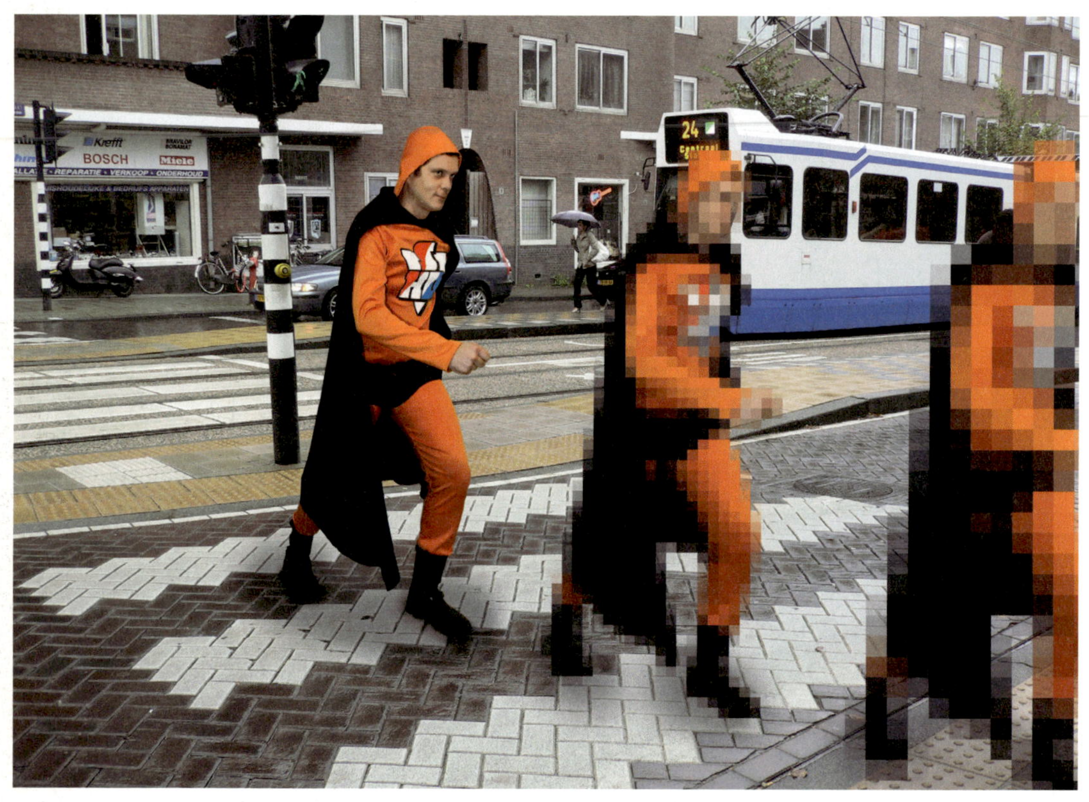
Krefft
BOSCH
Miele
REPARATIE • VERKOOP • ONDERHOUD
24

Behave In Digital Language

Desktop / Desktop-Publishing
by Hans Gremmen

Birthmarks
by Julia Müller, Arjan Groot & Menno Wittebrood

TodaysArt Festival
by Lust

The Argyle Pullover
by Poly-Xelor

Grid in space
by Luna Maurer

Placement/ DIsplacement
by Edo Paulus & Luna Maurer

Genesis
by Lesley Moore

Pulchri Studio
by Studio Dumbar (Dennis Koot)

Desktop / Desktop-Publishing
by Hans Gremmen

The desktop on your computer is based on the ‹perfect› desk: everything you need within easy reach. What happens if you translate this desktop and its tools back into a physical desktop? What would a suitcase of fonts look like? or a folder? or the trashcan? I tried to find an answer by constructing all these items in close collaboration with graphic designer Monique Gofers.

2003

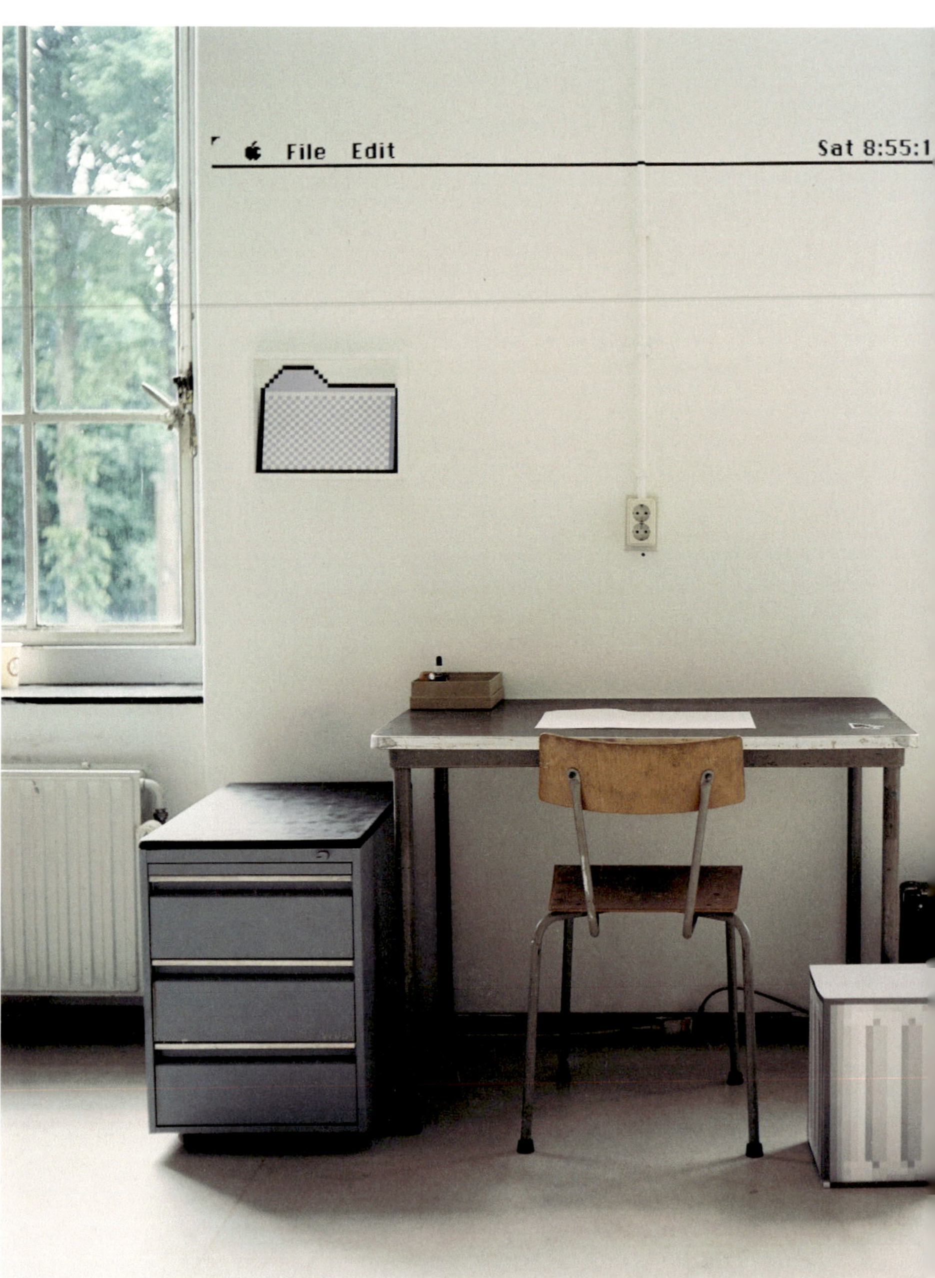

I was also curious how people are organizing their desktop. When I was studying at the Werkplaats Typography in Arnhem I staid one night over and photographed all the desks of my teachers and fellow students, I also made screenshots of all their desktops of the computer. I placed them neext to each-other and made a small publication ‹desktop publishing›.

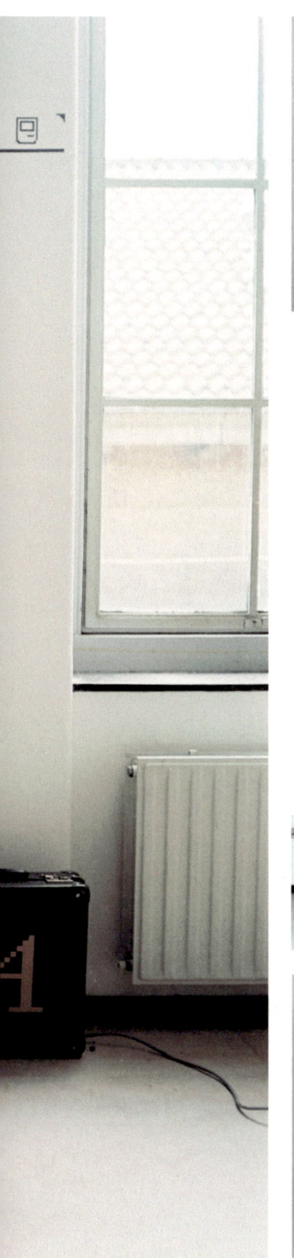

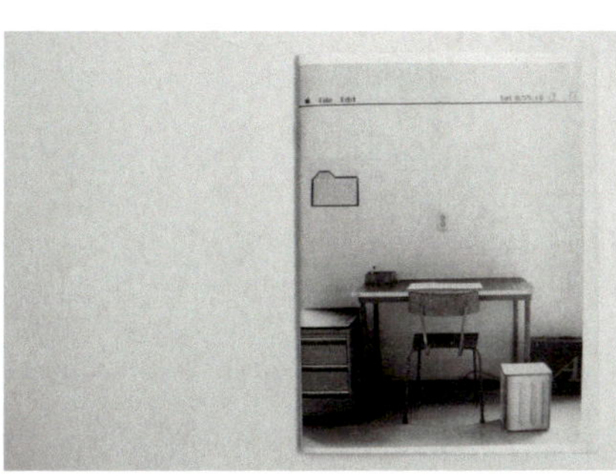

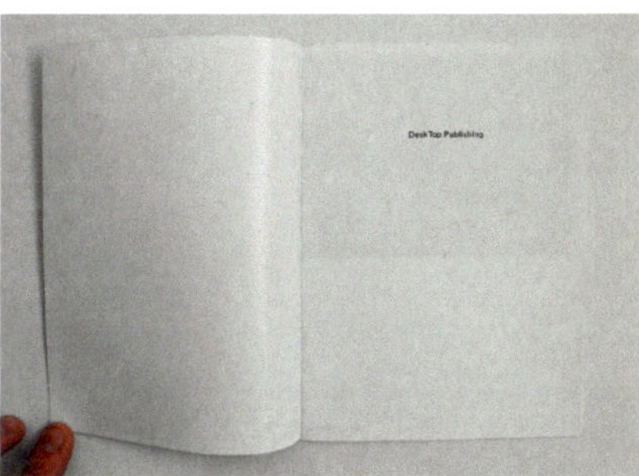

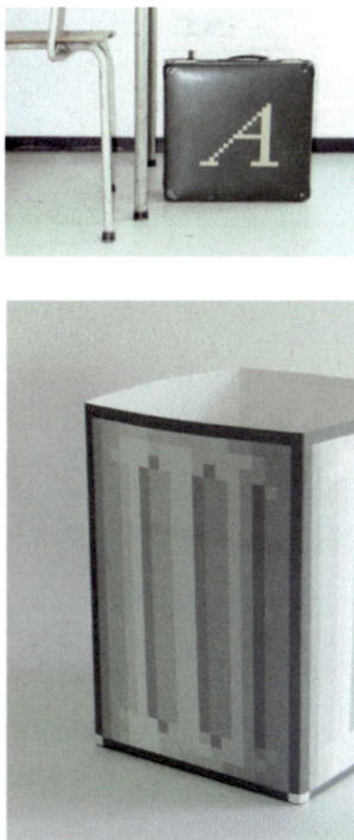

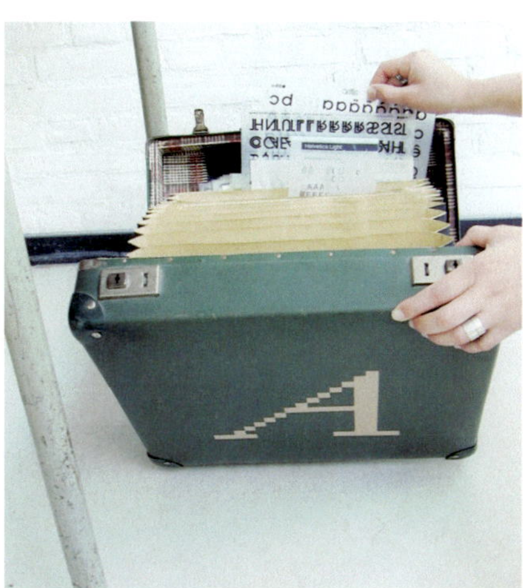

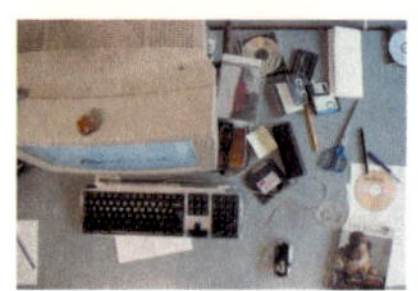

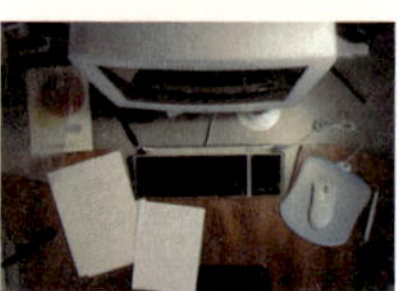

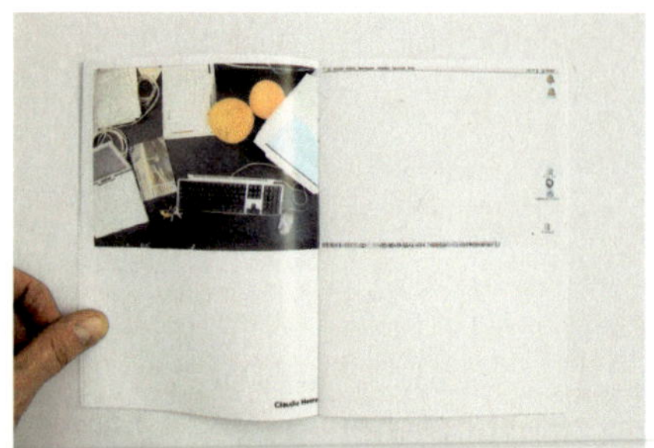

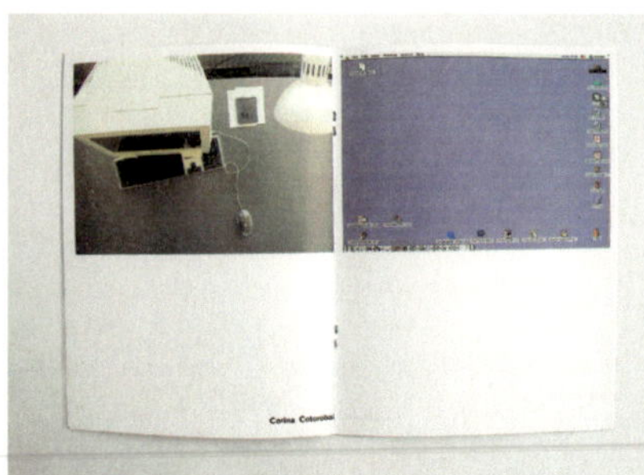

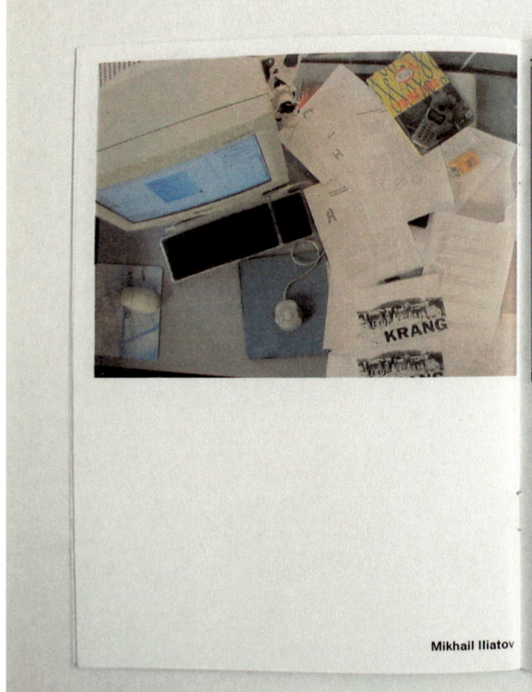
KRANG
Mikhail Iliatov

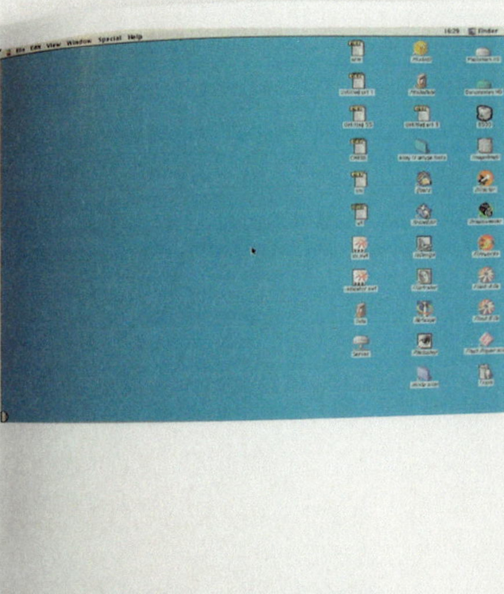
File Edit View Window Special Help
Finder

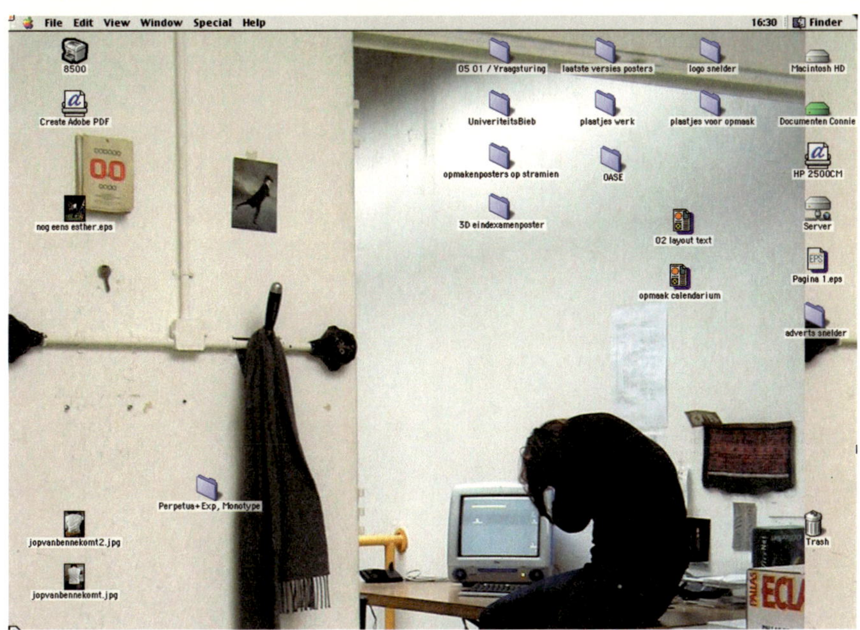

Hans Gremmen

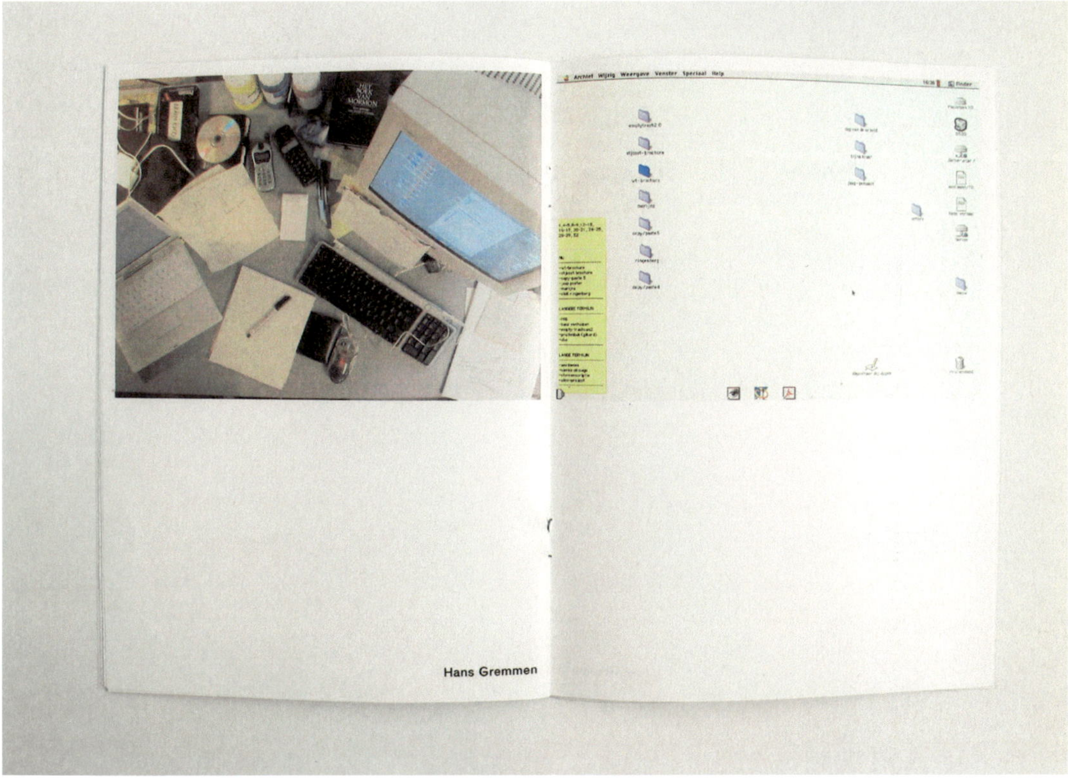

Birthmarks

by Julia Müller & Arjan Groot in collaboration with Menno Wittebrood

Birthmarks, ‹Identity Matters› magazine asked us for a contribution about new ways of tattooing. We came up with ‹birthmarking›, a subtle and very personal form of tattooing.

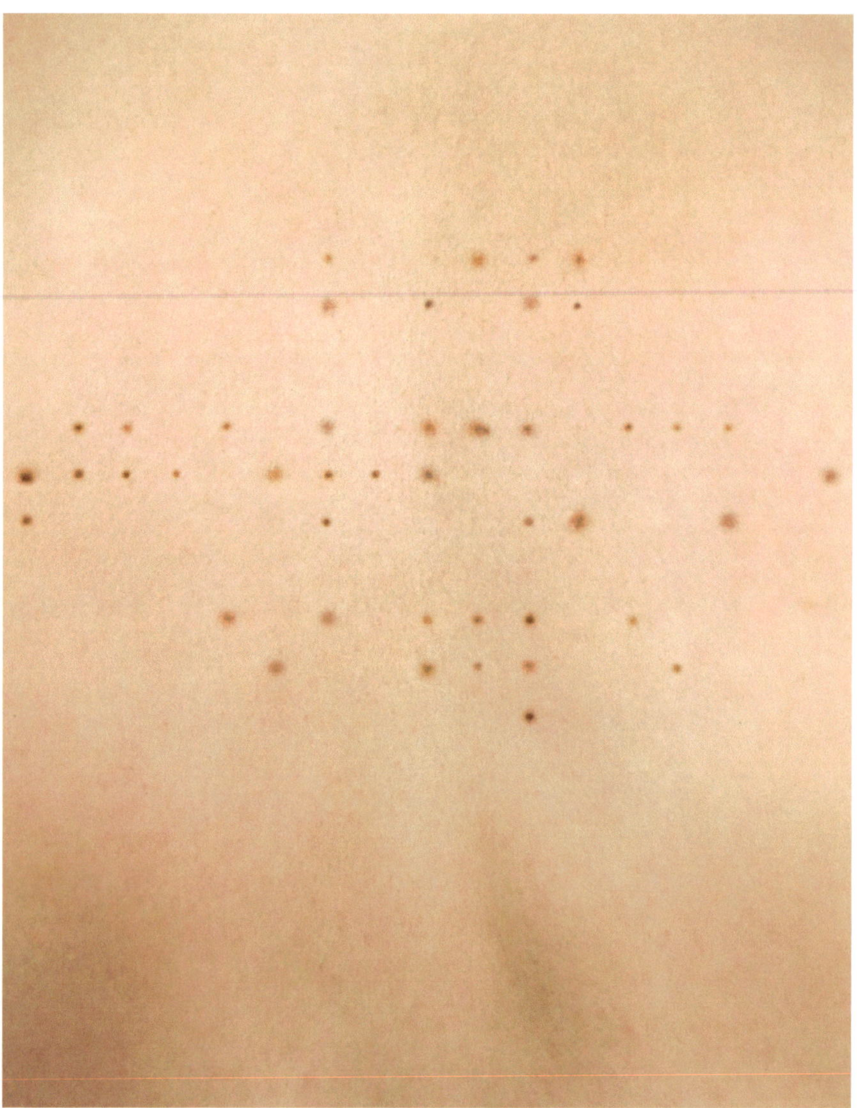

for Identity Matters magazine

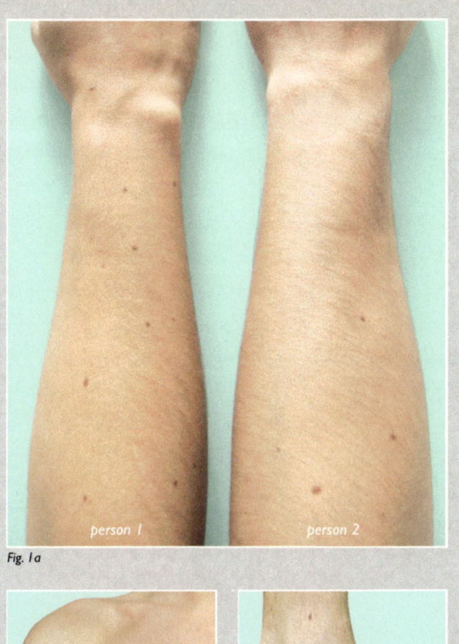

Fig. 1a

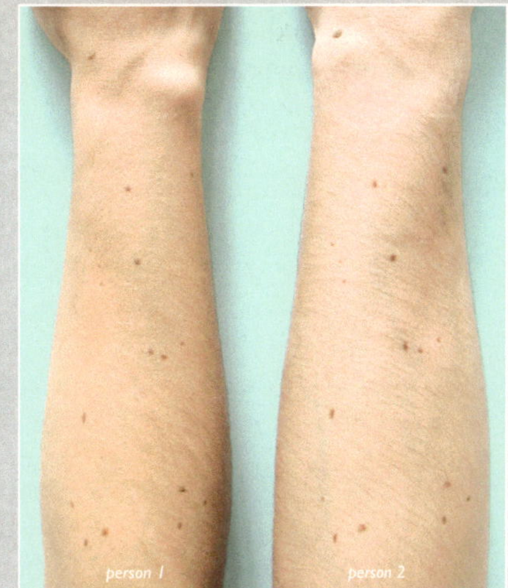

Fig. 1b

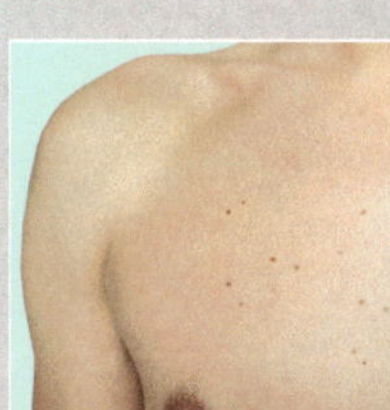
Fig. 2a

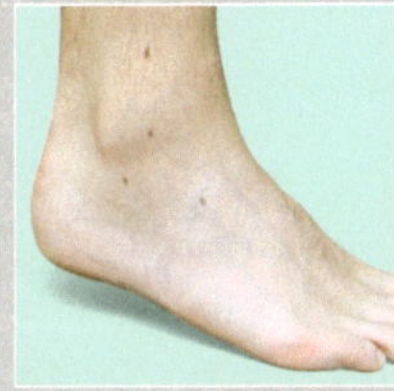
Fig. 2b

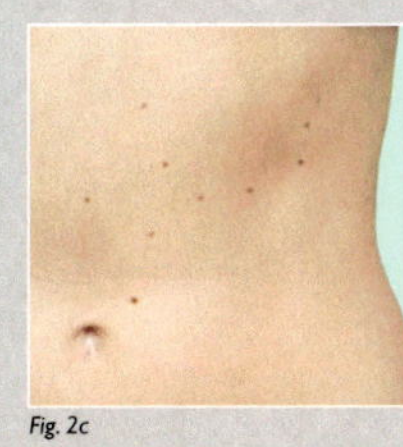
Fig. 2c

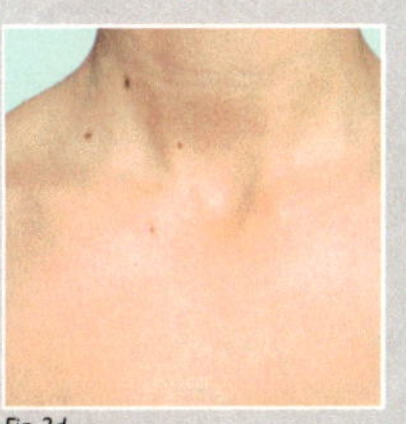
Fig. 2d

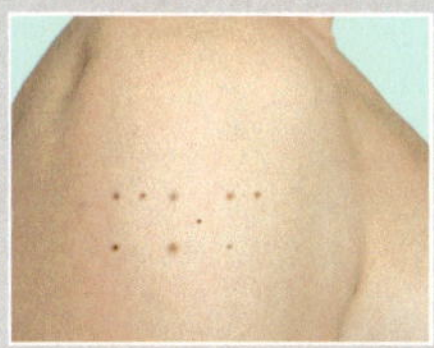
Fig. 3a

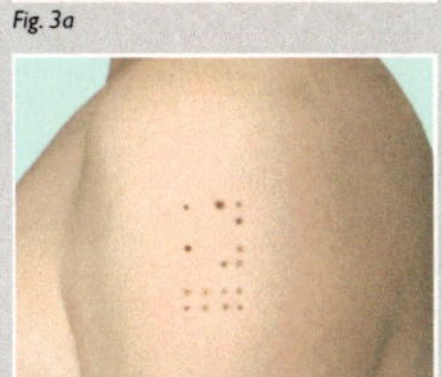
Fig. 3b

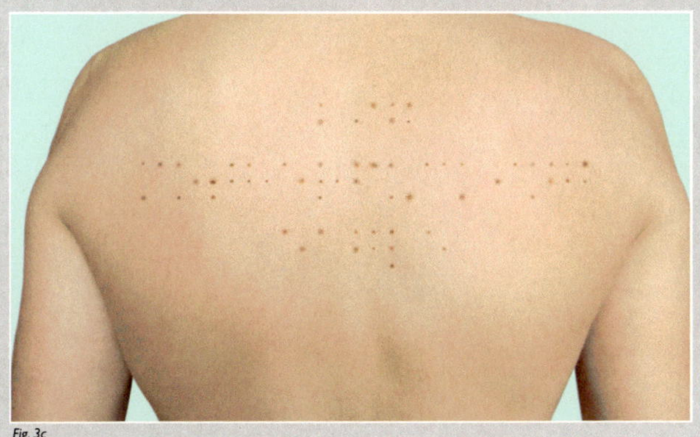
Fig. 3c

'Birthmarking' is a tattooing technique whereby new birthmarks and freckles are added to your skin in combination with existing birthmarks.

Groot/Müller/Wittebrood, 2006

Example 1: Duplication

1a. Two lovers' arms with original birthmarks
1b. After duplicating eachothers freckles, both partners carry identical birthmark patterns

Example 2: Zodiac signs

2a. Sagittarius
2b. Cancer
2c. Virgo
2d. Libra

Example 3: Braille

3a. 'Mom'
3b. '14 10 77'
3c. 'Big motherfucking eagle'

TodaysArt Festival, The Hague
by Lust

Lust puts new technologies at the very centre of its work and explores the ways they can influence and guide the form and look of whatever it is they are creating. In the case of an identity for a festival of art, music and technology, such a strategy seemed particularly appropriate. Taking the idea of a virus as a means of replicating and spreading information as inspiration and organizing principle, Lust created a generative programme that was used to affect and guide every aspect of the festival identity: from the graphic language to the means of disseminating information. The virus resided on the festival website, and could be viewed at all times. Installations throughout the city also served as barometers for the virus. Each generation of the virus was plotted, and in this way the growth of the festival and the spread of information was tracked.

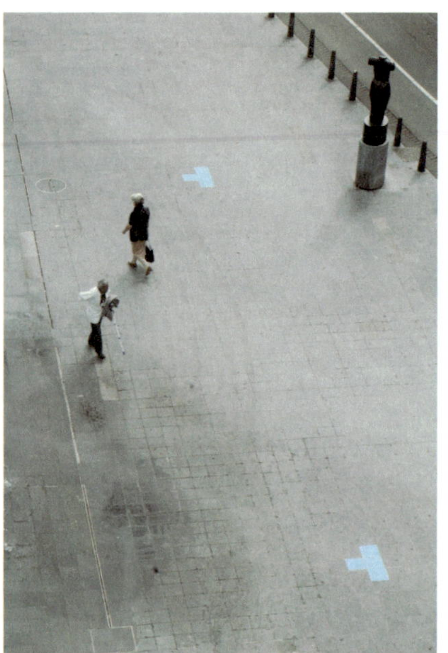

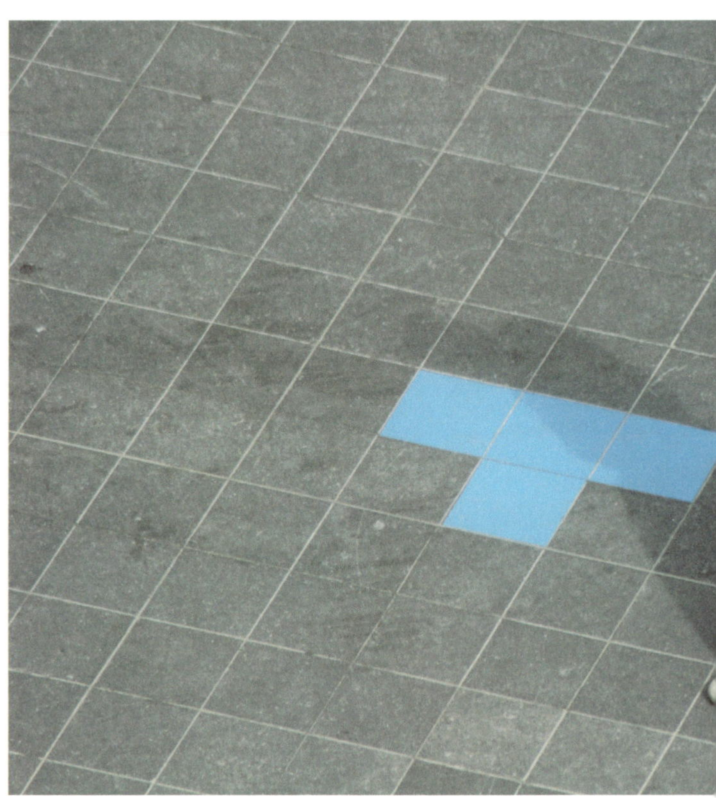

The Hague. Identity, posters, flyers, installations, 2005

The virus was symbolized as a grid –a grid that could be overlaid on the whole city, or on just one building. Various parameters were set up, including hits to the website, number of visitors per venue, number of artists and performances playing and locations of the interventions, and the data affected the grid.

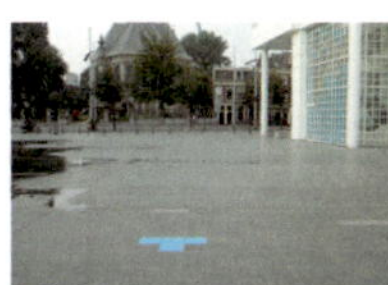

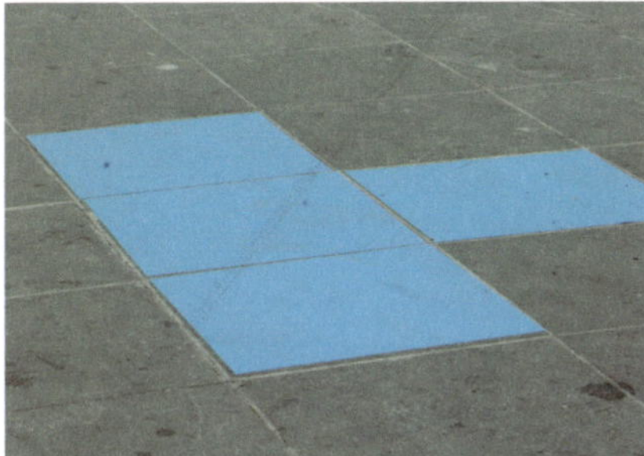

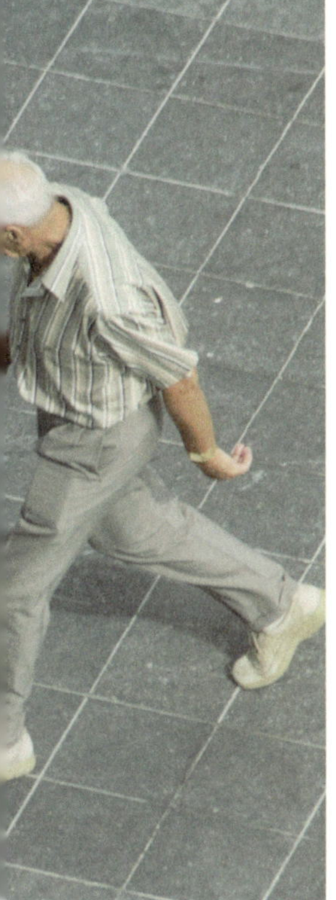

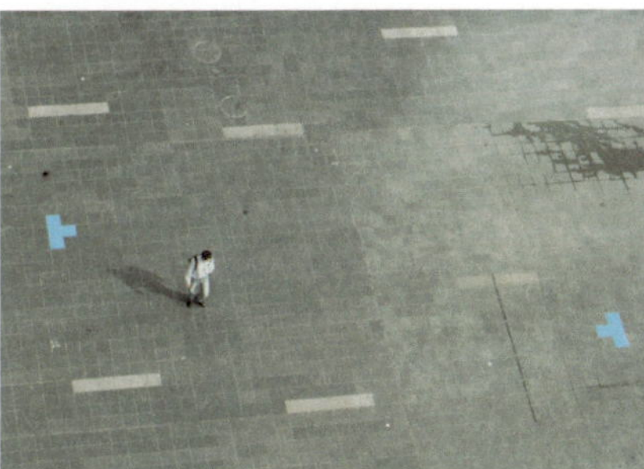

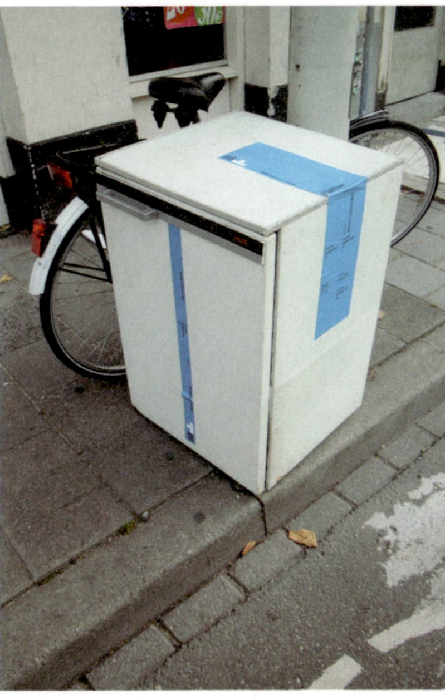

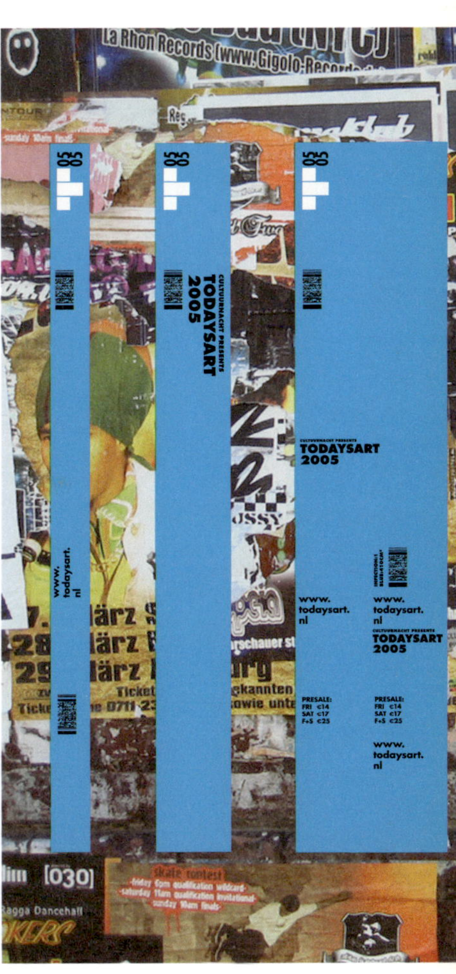

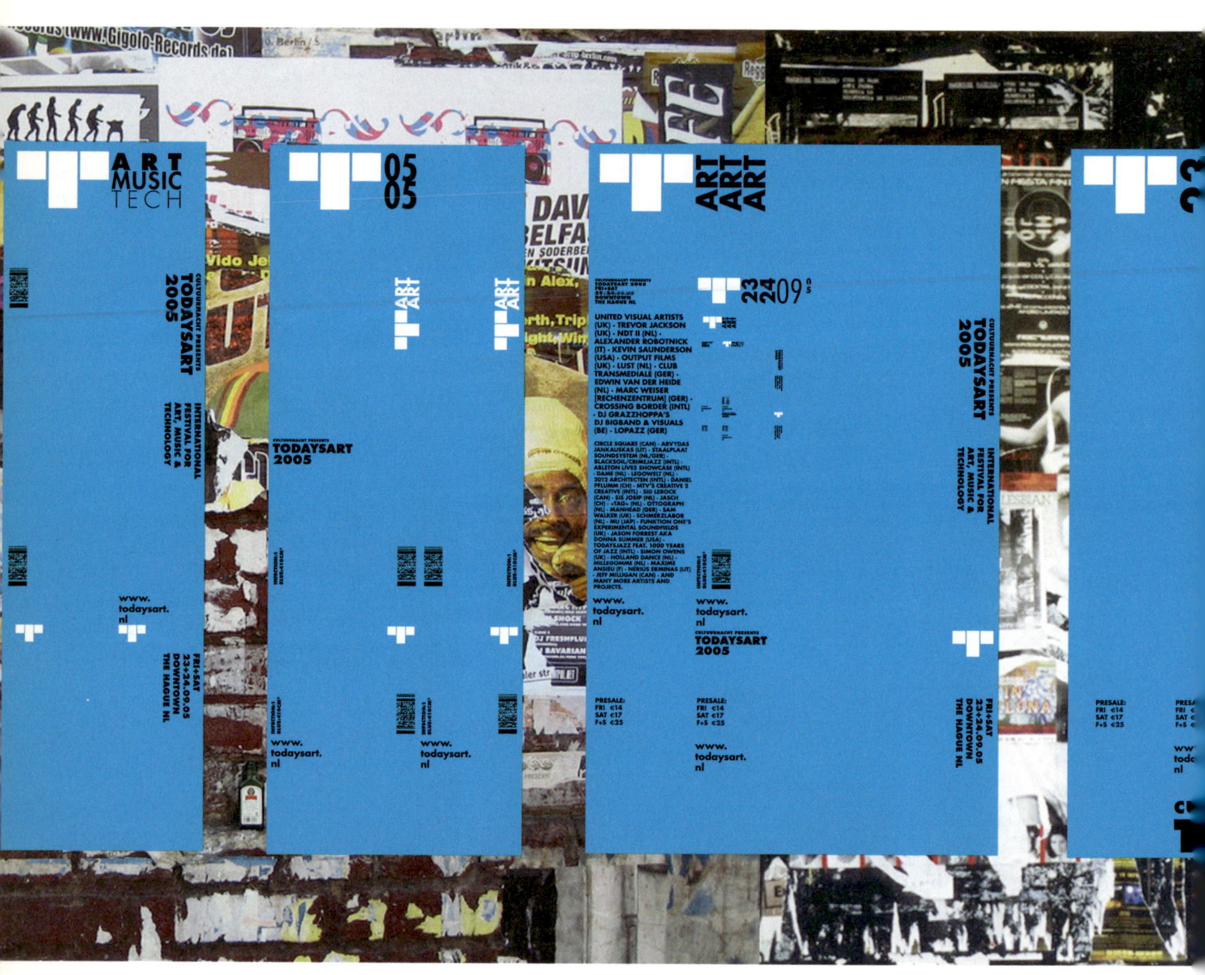

ART
MUSIC
TECH
CULTUURNACHT PRESENTS
TODAYSART
2005
INTERNATIONAL
FESTIVAL FOR
ART, MUSIC &
TECHNOLOGY
www.
todaysart.
nl
FRI+SAT
23+24.09.05
DOWNTOWN
THE HAGUE NL
05
05
ART
ART
CULTUURNACHT PRESENTS
TODAYSART
2005
www.
todaysart.
nl
ART
ART
ART
23
24
09
05
UNITED VISUAL ARTISTS (UK) - TREVOR JACKSON (UK) - NDT II (NL) - ALEXANDER ROBOTNICK (IT) - KEVIN SAUNDERSON (USA) - OUTPUT FILMS (UK) - LUST (NL) - CLUB TRANSMEDIALE (GER) - EDWIN VAN DER HEIDE (NL) - MARC WEISER [RECHENZENTRUM] (GER) - CROSSING BORDER (INTL) - DJ GRAZZHOPPA'S DJ BIGBAND & VISUALS (BE) - LOPAZZ (GER)
CIRCLE SQUARE (CAN) - ARVYDAS JANKAUSKAS (LIT) - STAALPLAAT SOUNDSYSTEM (NL/GER) - BLACKSOIL/CRIMEJAZZ (INTL) - ABLETON LIVES SHOWCASE (INTL) - DAME (NL) - LEGOWELT (NL) - 2012 ARCHITECTEN (INTL) - DANIEL PFLUMM (CH) - MTV'S CREATIVE 2 CREATIVE (INTL) - SID LEROCK (CAN) - SIS JOSIP (NL) - JASCH (CH) - <TAG> (NL) - OTTOGRAPH (NL) - MANHEAD (GER) - SAM WALKER (UK) - SCHMERZLABOR (NL) - MU (JAP) - FUNKTION ONE'S EXPERIMENTAL SOUNDFIELDS (UK) - JASON FORREST AKA DONNA SUMMER (USA) - TODAYSJAZZ FEAT. 1000 YEARS OF JAZZ (INTL) - SIMON OWENS (UK) - HOLLAND DANCE (NL) - MILLEGOMME (NL) - MAXIME ANSIEU (F) - NERIUS ERMINAS (LIT) - JEFF MILLIGAN (CAN) - AND MANY MORE ARTISTS AND PROJECTS.
www.
todaysart.
nl
CULTUURNACHT PRESENTS
TODAYSART
2005
PRESALE:
FRI €14
SAT €17
F+S €25
CULTUURNACHT PRESENTS
TODAYSART
2005
INTERNATIONAL
FESTIVAL FOR
ART, MUSIC &
TECHNOLOGY
FRI+SAT
23+24.09.05
DOWNTOWN
THE HAGUE NL

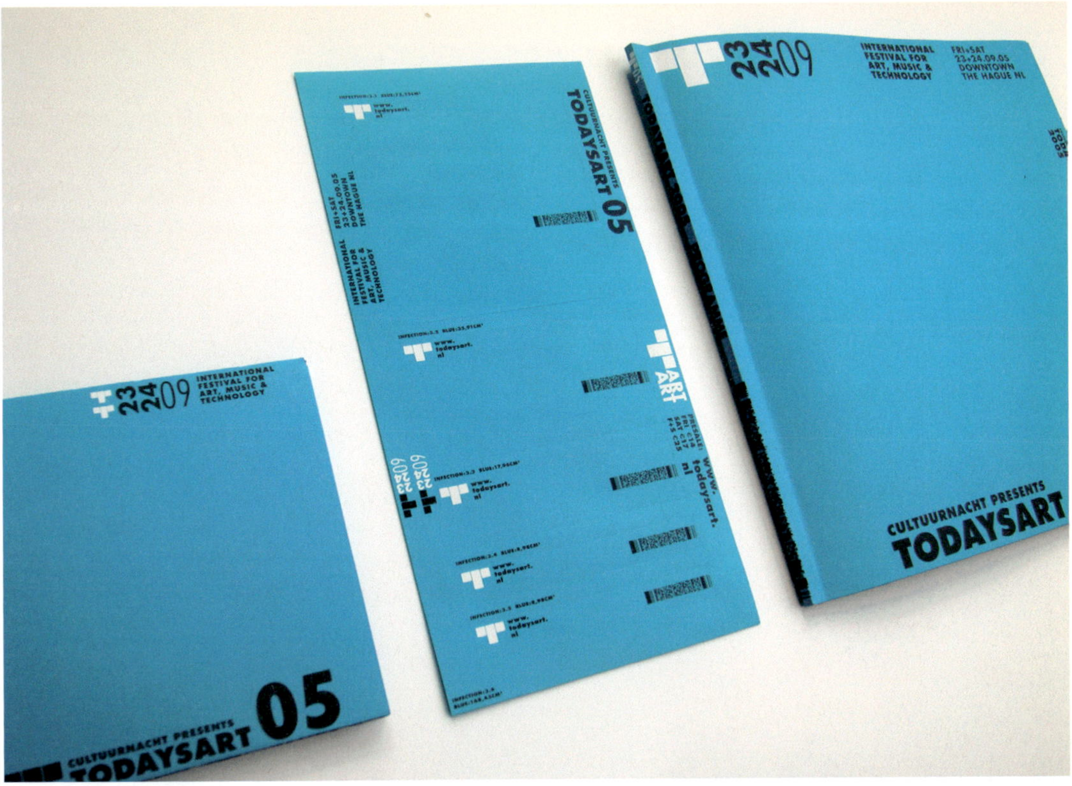

23 24 09
INTERNATIONAL FESTIVAL FOR ART, MUSIC & TECHNOLOGY
CULTUURNACHT PRESENTS
TODAYSART 05
FRI+SAT 23+24.09.05 DOWNTOWN THE HAGUE NL
www. todaysart. nl

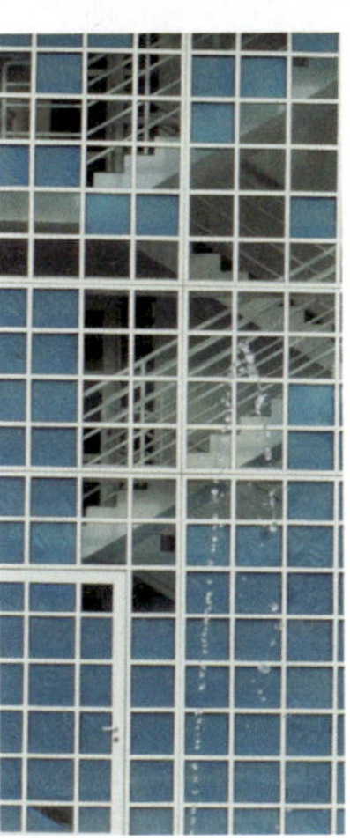

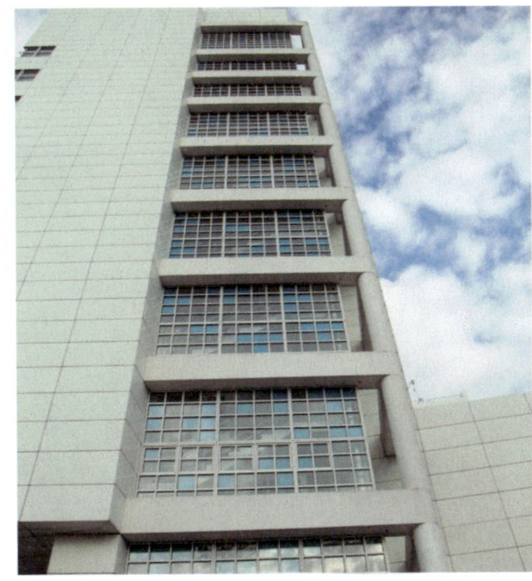

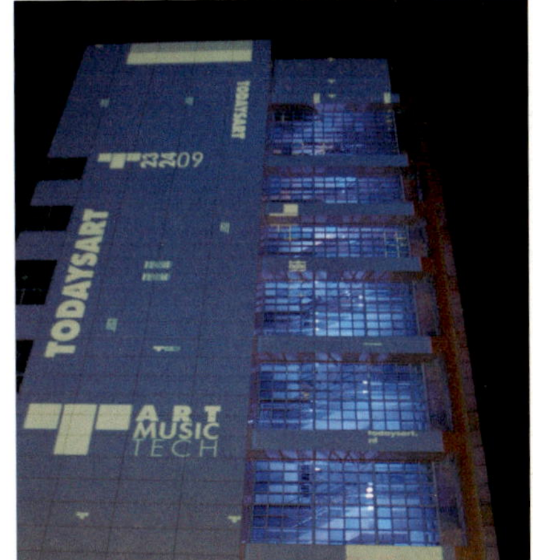

The Argyle Pullover
by Poly-Xelor (Luna Maurer & Roel Wouters)

‹The Argyle Pullovers› were knitted at the Textile Museum, Tilburg, using a digital knitting technique. The traditional Argyle pattern is distorted by capturing the different effects that body postures and movements have on clothes. Five different models of ‹The Argyle Pullovers› were sold in series of 10 during the exhibition.

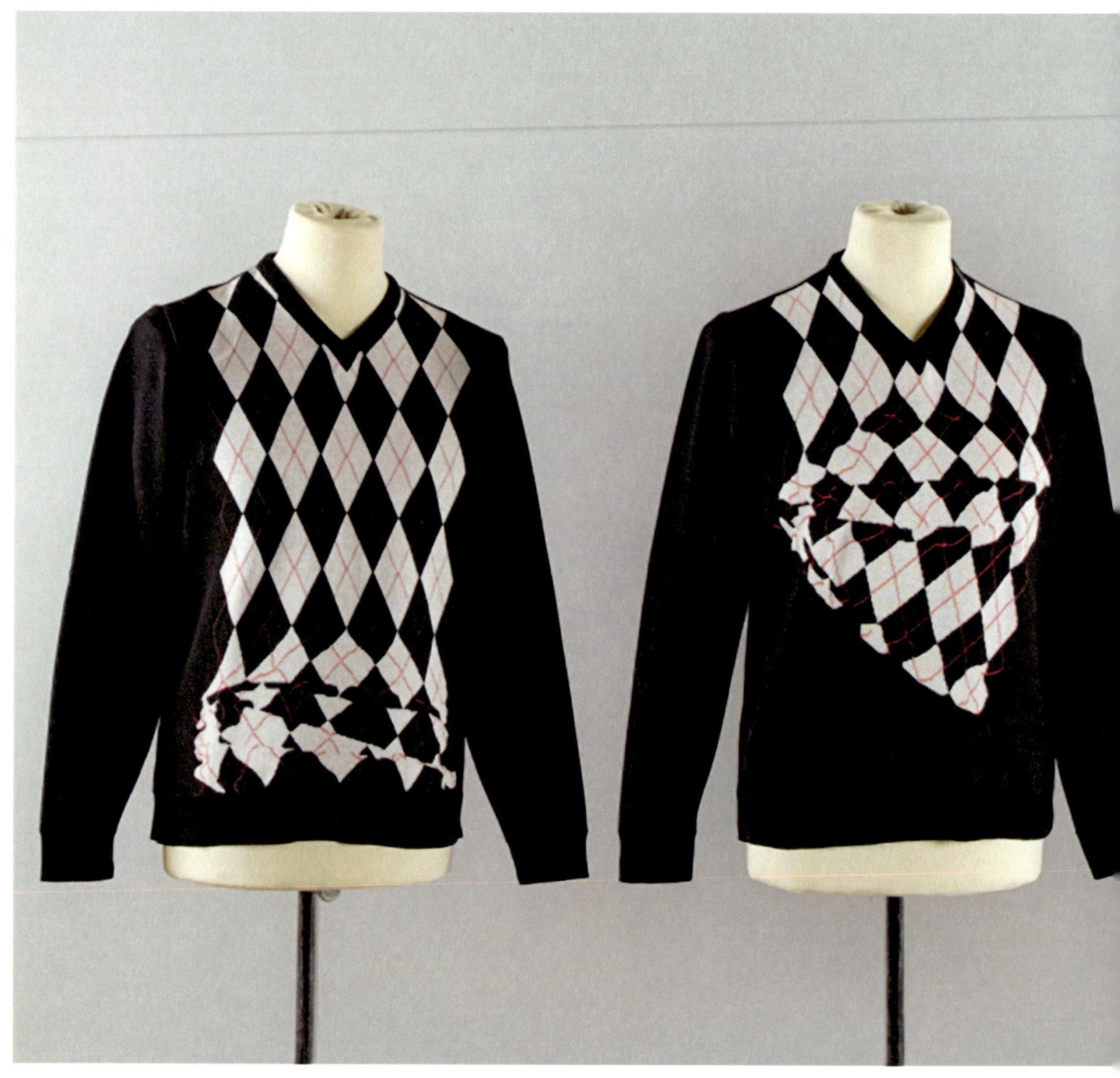

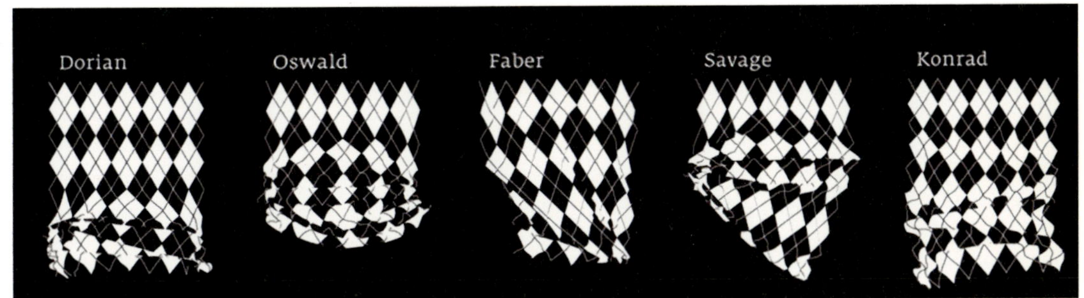

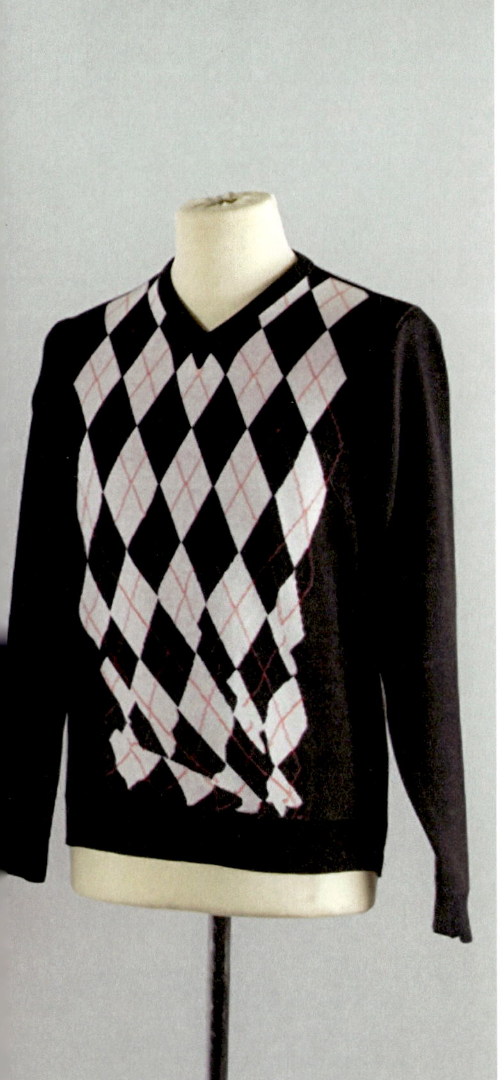

The Argyle Pullover was exhibited in High Tech Low Tech at the Textile Museum, Tilburg, in 2006/07.
Featured (June, 2004) in the exhibition 10 Years Design Sandberg Institute at Post CS, Amsterdam.

 Grid in space
by Luna Maurer

The work nominated for the Art Prize is exhibited in an environment that reflects the underlying idea of the actual work on show. The 3D space becomes 2D. The space is captured by a camera and simultaneously displayed on a monitor. Only on the monitor can you experience yourself in the ‹flat› environment.

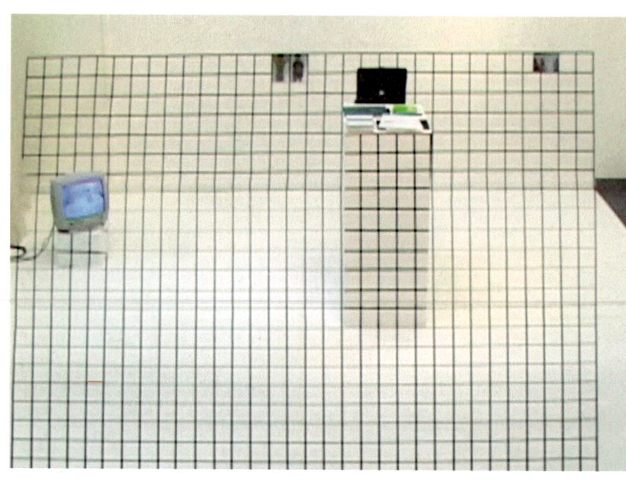

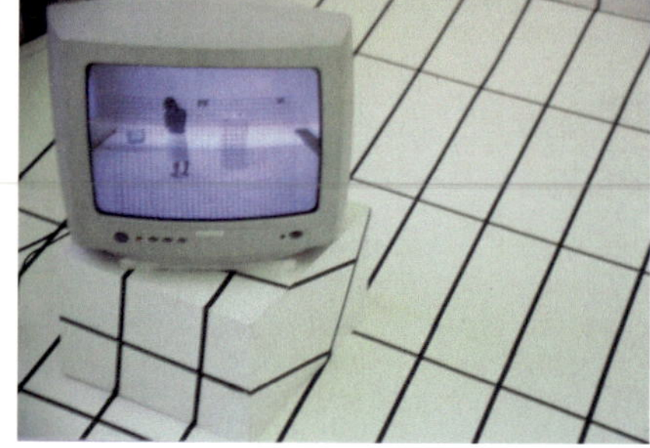

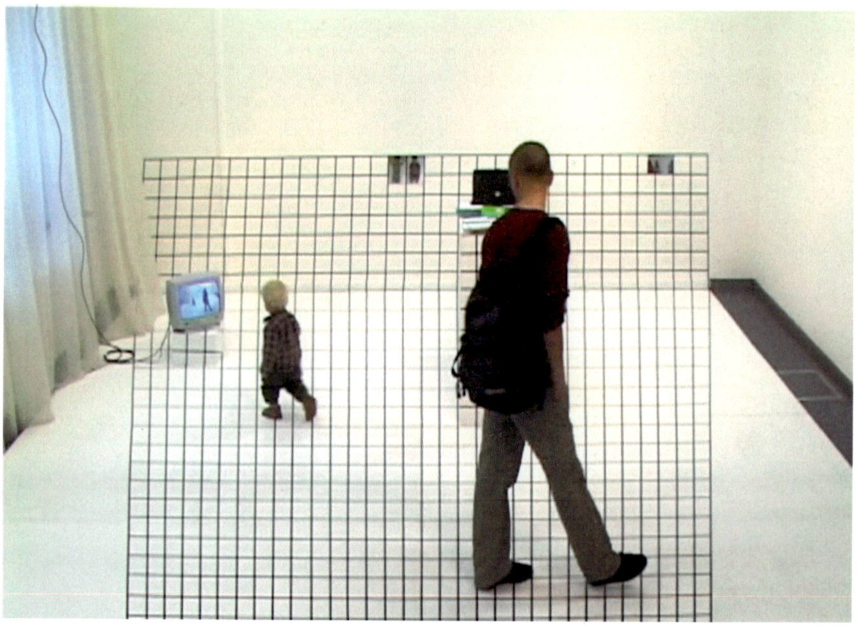

Exhibition: Kunstaanmoedigingsprijs Amstelveen / Netherlands, 2002

Placement / Displacement (seating experiment)

by Edo Paulus & Luna Maurer

‹Placement / Displacement› is a model in which people simulate the logic of a computer system. This living model consists of entities (spectators) that are bound by rules. When the rules cause the individual entities to react on each other, a whole comes into existence that is constantly in motion. You can't design the patterns that emerge beforehand and you can't foresee the result. Especially not when people are executing these rules instead of computers.

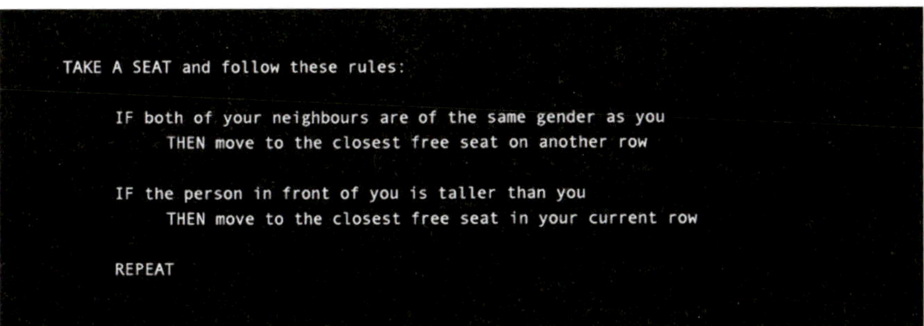

Visual Power Show on Next Nature, Paradiso Amsterdam, 20.01.2005

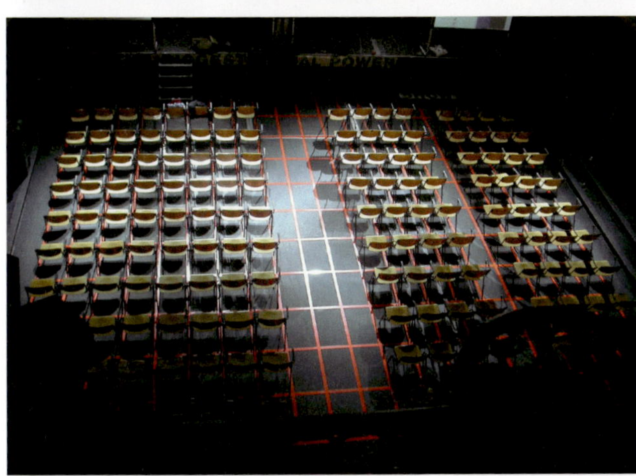

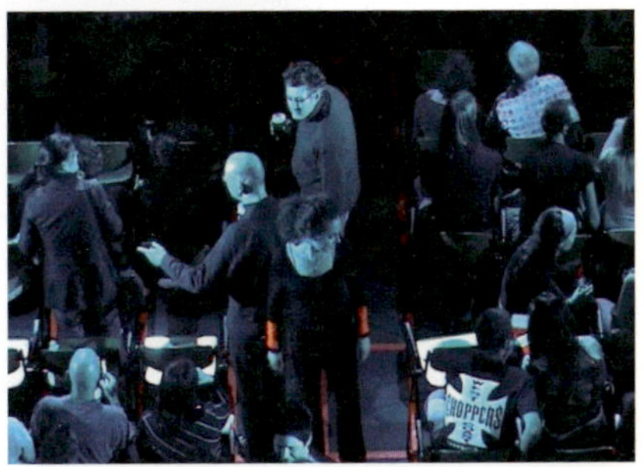

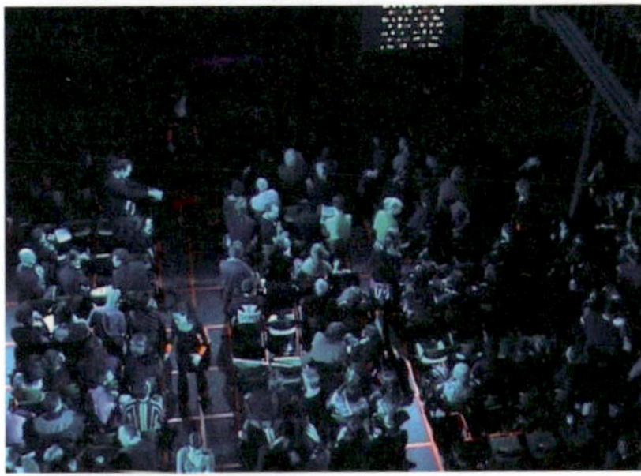

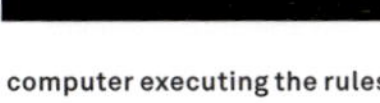

computer executing the rules

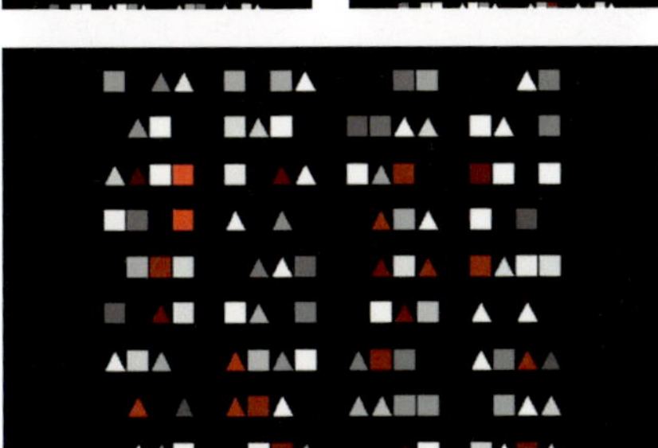

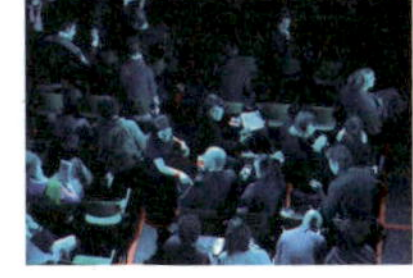

audience executing the rules

300 Genesis
by Lesley Moore

A poster designed for the exhibition ‹Genesis – Life at the End of the Information Age› at Centraal Museum, Utrecht. The exhibition covers the development of gen-technology in art and science, with ‹order› and ‹chaos› as keywords. The poster contains an image that from a distance looks like a butterfly, but dissolves into loose objects as you get closer to it.

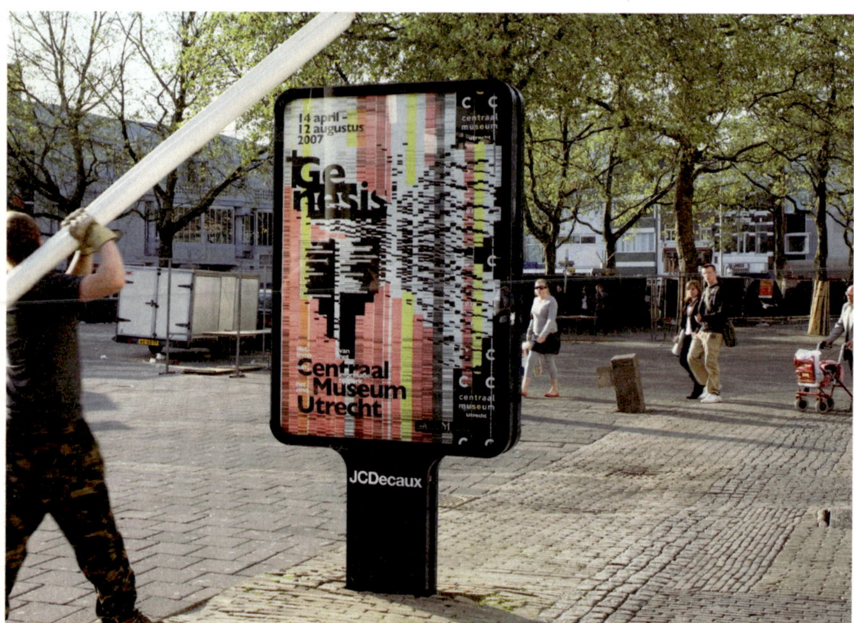

2007

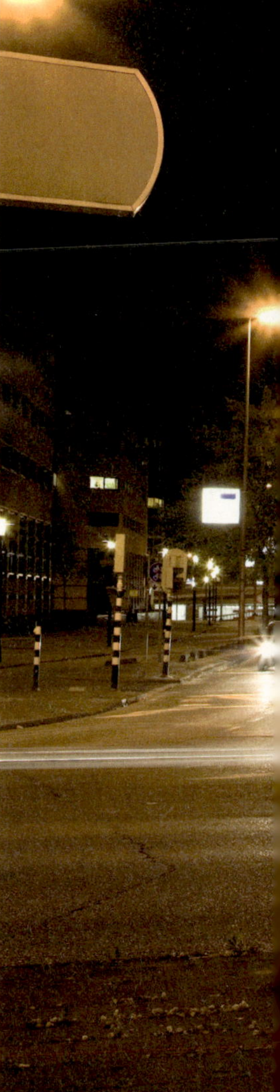

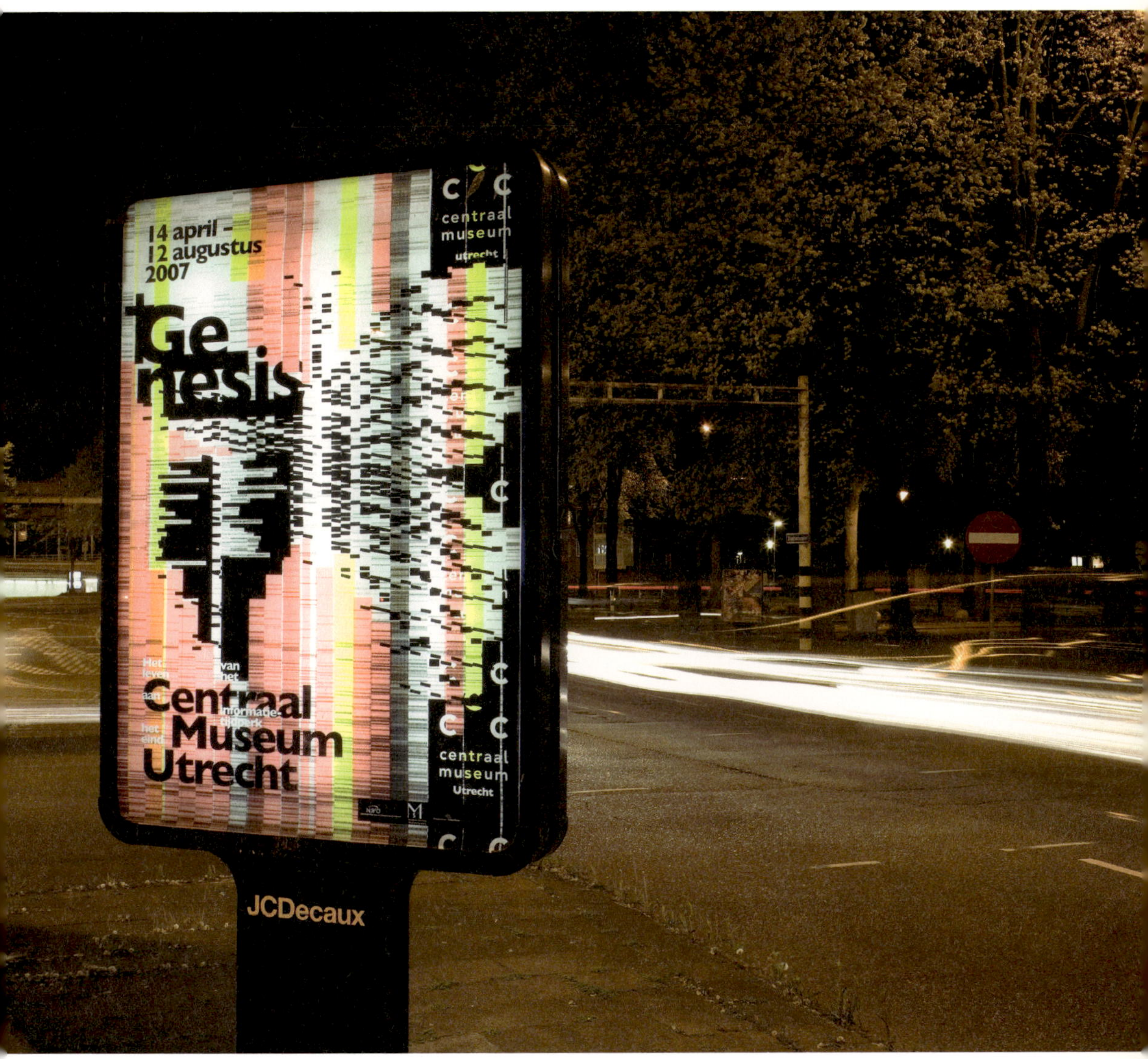

14 april –
12 augustus
2007
Genesis
Het leven aan het eind van het informatietijdperk
Centraal Museum Utrecht
centraal museum utrecht
centraal museum Utrecht
JCDecaux

Pulchri Exhibition Posters
by Studio Dumbar (Dennis Koot)

First established in 1847, this artists' society and exhibition space has found a permanent home on Lange Voorhout, one of the Hague's most lush avenues. The posters promote members' exhibitions in autumn and spring.

for Pulchri Studio, 2007

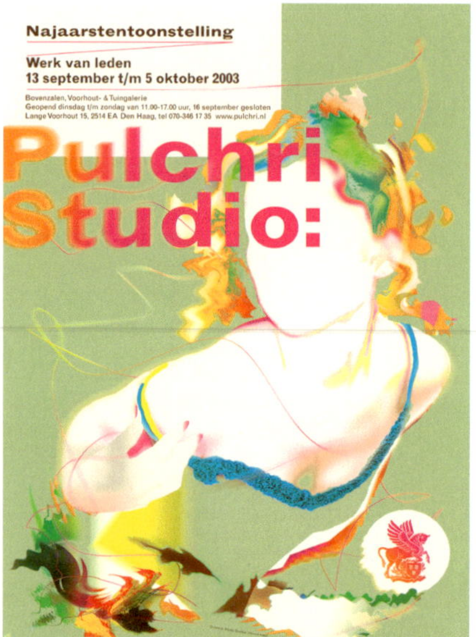

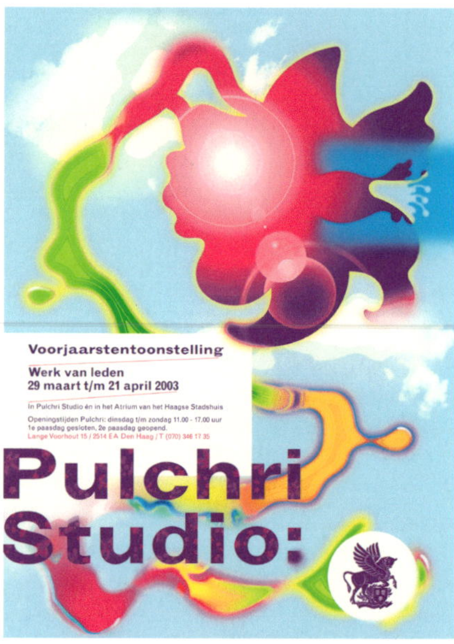

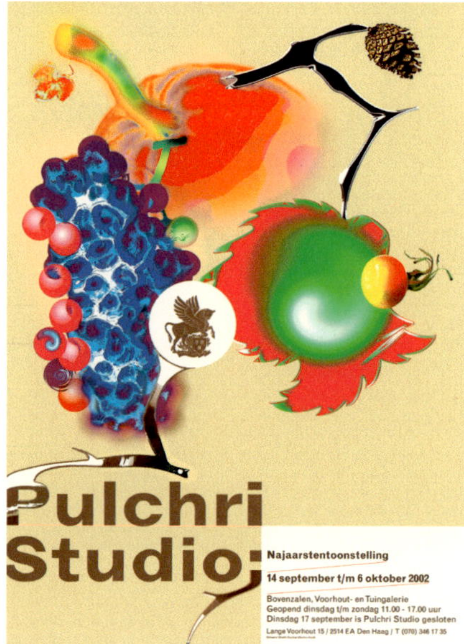

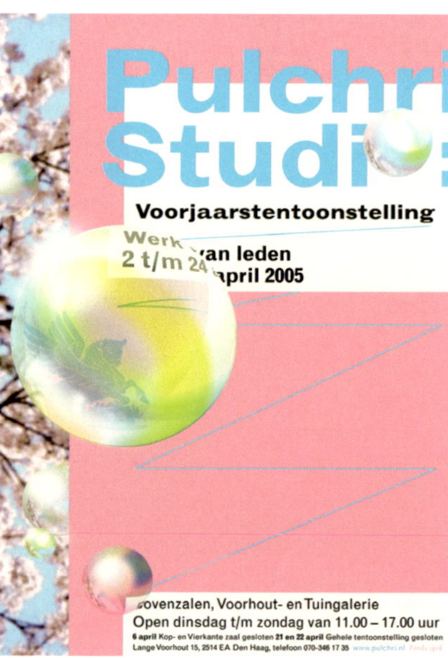

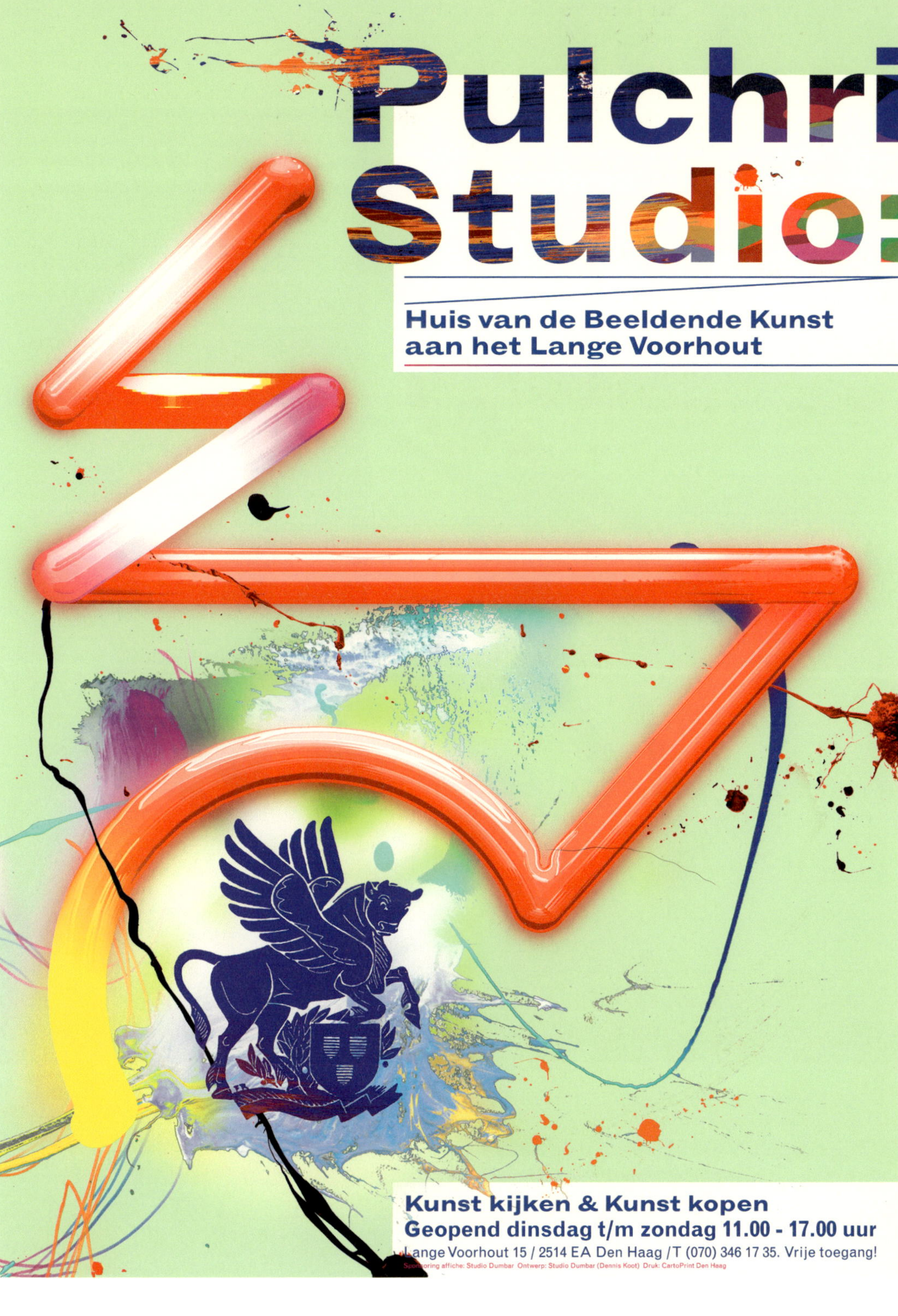
Pulchri
Studio:
Huis van de Beeldende Kunst
aan het Lange Voorhout
Kunst kijken & Kunst kopen
Geopend dinsdag t/m zondag 11.00 - 17.00 uur
Lange Voorhout 15 / 2514 EA Den Haag / T (070) 346 17 35. Vrije toegang!
Sponsoring affiche: Studio Dumbar Ontwerp: Studio Dumbar (Dennis Koot) Druk: CartoPrint Den Haag

Space Design

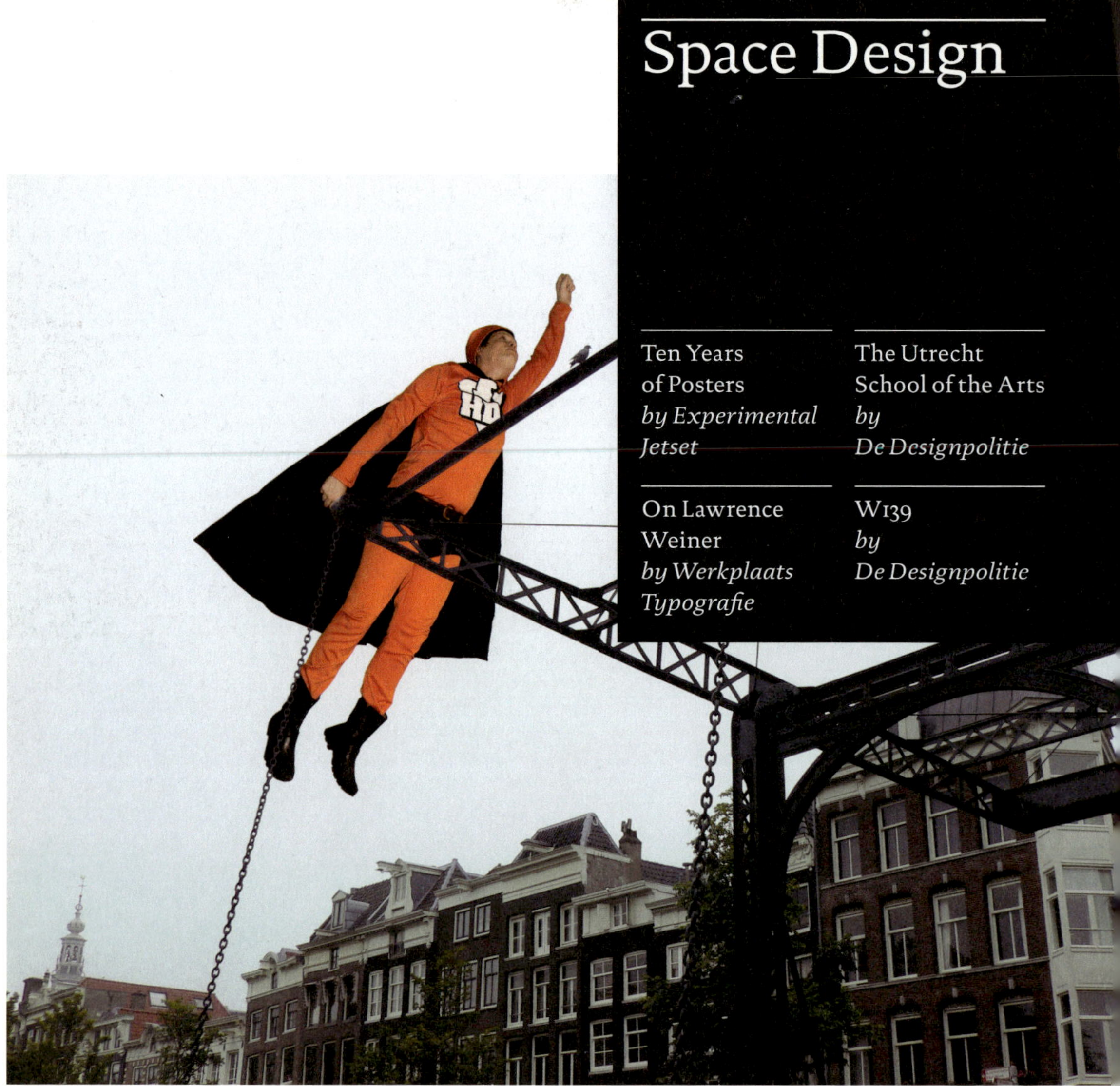

Ten Years of Posters *by Experimental Jetset*

The Utrecht School of the Arts *by De Designpolitie*

On Lawrence Weiner *by Werkplaats Typografie*

W139 *by De Designpolitie*

Fall 2005
Visiting Artist
Lecture Series
by Harmen Liemburg

Uniceflaan
by Richard Niessen

Raadzaal
Zuidoost
by Richard Niessen

TM-City
by Richard Niessen & Esther de Vries

Big Type Says More
by Strange Attractors Design

The Sirens of Venice
by Werkplaats Typografie

Signage graphics for the Nederlands Fotomuseum
by Ping-pong Design

Werck
by Arjan Groot

Pauze
by Lust

Directors' Cuts
by Machine

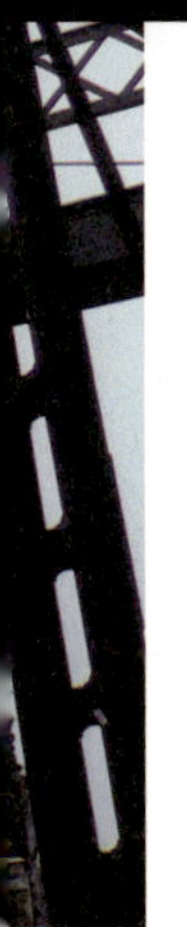

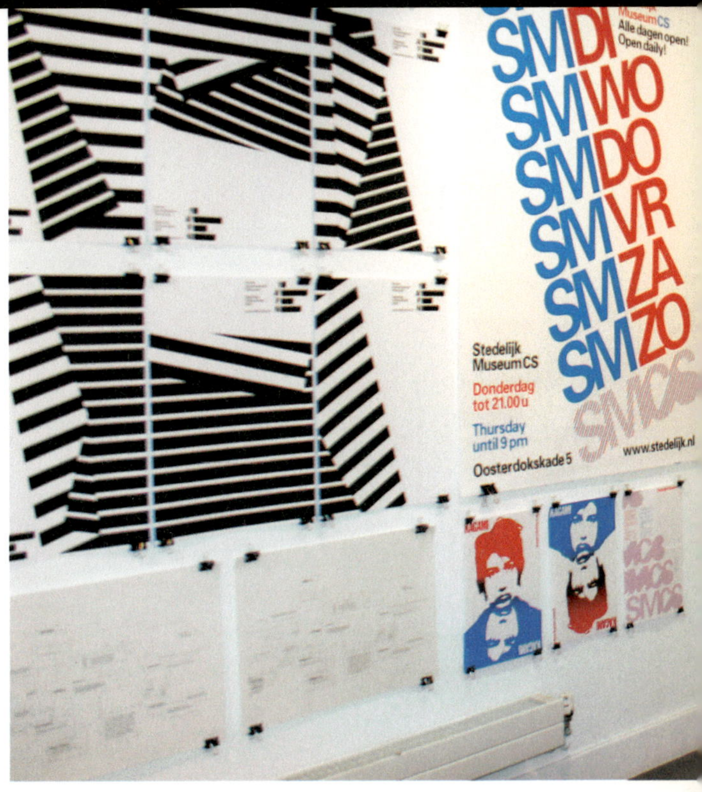

Ten Years of Posters
by Experimental Jetset

In 2006, we were asked to install a solo exhibition at the Kemistry Gallery in London. We didn't have enough time to create a site-specific installation, so we decided just to show a selection of the work we had done over the past ten years. And to make it even easier for ourselves, we opted to show only posters. After all, posters have a very natural relationship with the wall; they fit into almost any environment.

To be honest, we don't think of ourselves as proper poster designers at all; we don't really feel part of this grand tradition of creating overly expressive, painterly ‹affiches›. The posters we design are usually by-products of larger projects; when we're working on an installation, or a catalogue, or a graphic identity, it is usually decided at the last moment that a poster is also needed. In other words, these posters are usually part of a larger whole.

So it was really interesting for us to see how these posters would work when shown together, out of their original context. In that sense, this was a very instructive experience. And a really nice exhibition as well.

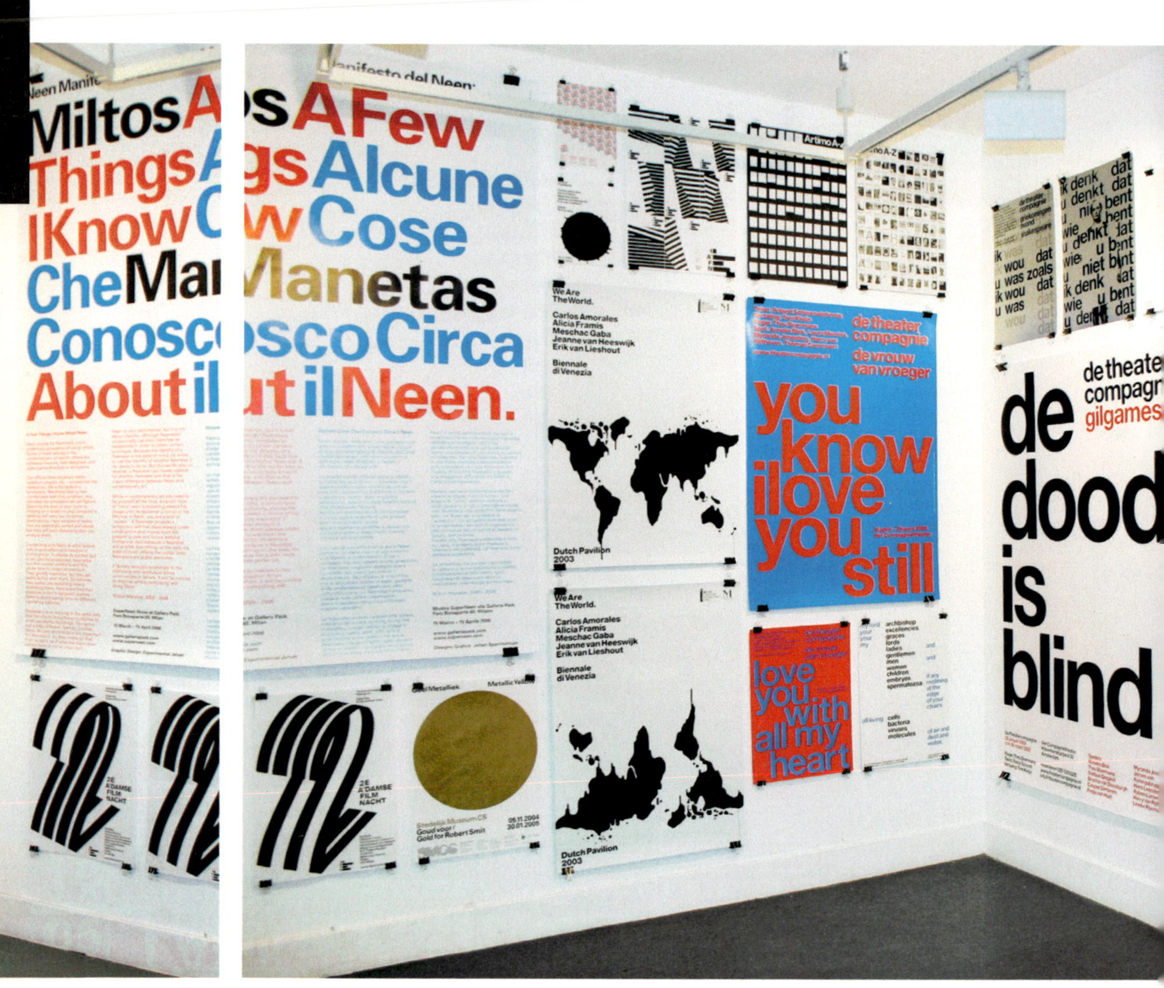

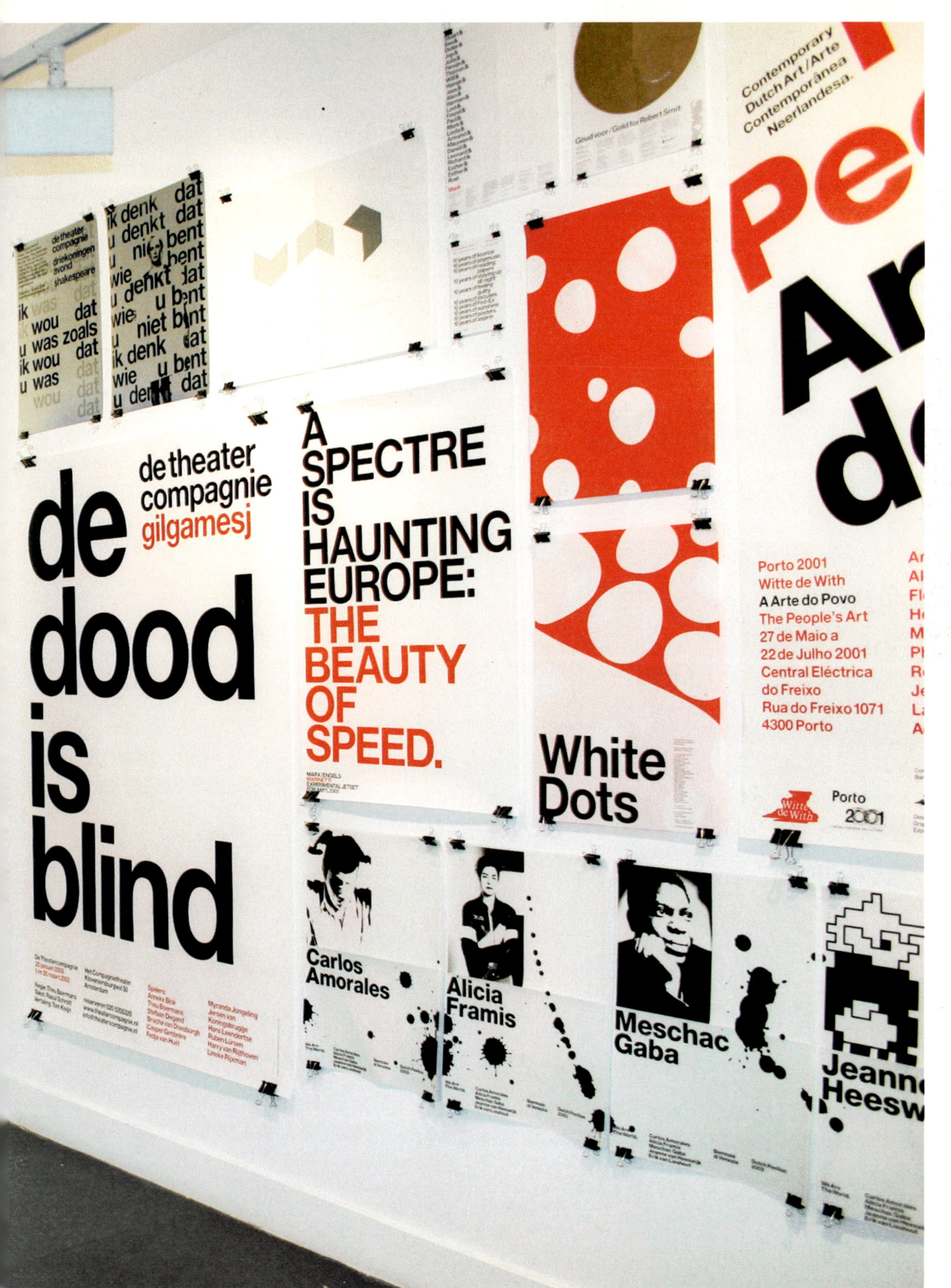

de theater compagnie
driekoningen avond
shakespeare
ik was dat
ik wou dat
u was zoals
ik wou dat
u was dat
wou dat
ik denk dat
u denkt dat
u niet bent
wie denkt dat
u denkt dat
wie u bent
u niet bent
ik denk dat
wie u bent
u denkt dat
Contemporary Dutch Art / Arte Contemporânea Neerlandesa.
Goud voor / Gold for Robert Smit
de theater compagnie
gilgamesj
de dood is blind
A SPECTRE IS HAUNTING EUROPE:
THE BEAUTY OF SPEED.
White Dots
Porto 2001
Witte de With
A Arte do Povo
The People's Art
27 de Maio a
22 de Julho 2001
Central Eléctrica
do Freixo
Rua do Freixo 1071
4300 Porto
Witte de With
Porto 2001
Carlos Amorales
Alicia Framis
Meschac Gaba

On Lawrence Weiner
by Guillaume Mojon / Werkplaats Typografie

For a project initiated by the Werkplaats Typografie, participant Guillaume Mojon transferred quotes by Lawrence Weiner into type installations. He used the spaces of the WT building to make these works with found materials such as boxes, tape, spray paint, etc. In this way he represented the meaning of Weiner's separate works. He documented the spatial translations in a series of five photographs, which were then silk-screened in black, folded and put together in a plastic envelope.

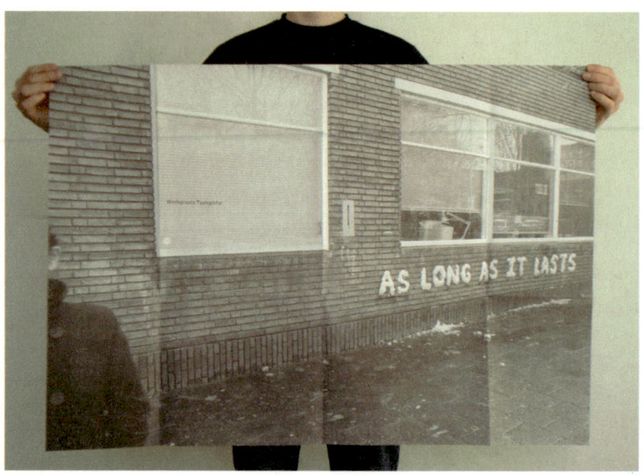

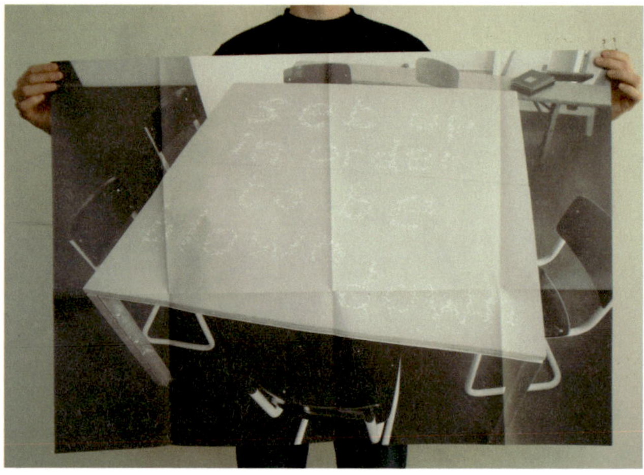

series of 5 posters, 700 x 1000 mm each, 2006

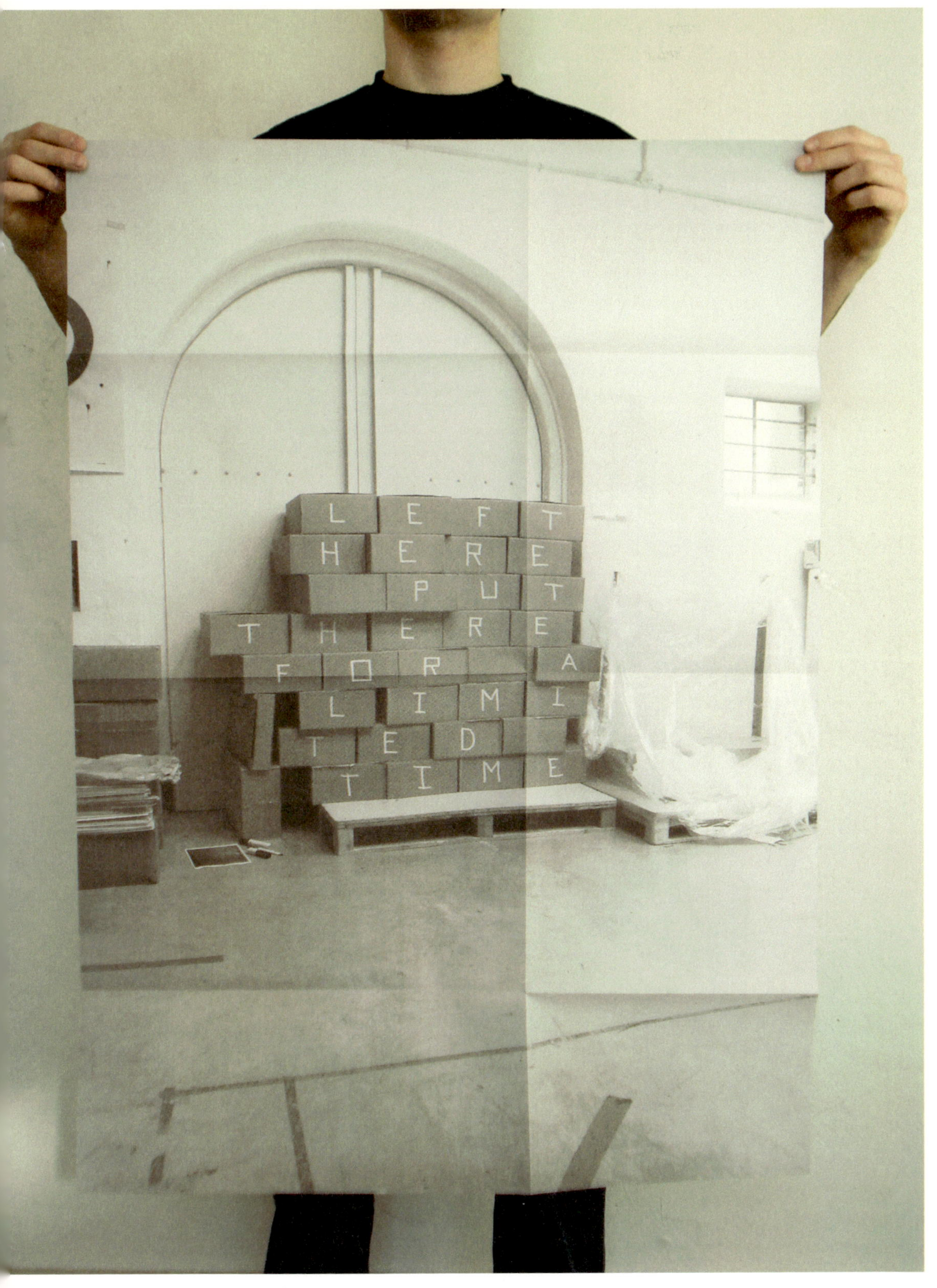
LEFT
HERE PUT
THERE
FOR A
LIMI
TED
TIME

The Utrecht School of the Arts (HKU)

by De Designpolitie

The Utrecht School of the Arts (HKU), the largest art school in The Netherlands, has five faculties: Theatre, Fine Art & Design, Music, Art & Technology and Art & Economy. Over a period of about seven years we worked on various projects, including Annual Reports, catalogues of the Final Exam shows, study guides and various brochures. The biggest project was two student selection and recruitment campaigns, which ran for three years each. A number of designers, photographers and illustrators collaborated on this project. To name a few: Viviane Sassen and Corriëtte Schoenaerts (photography), Herman van Bostelen and Lesley Moore (illustration).

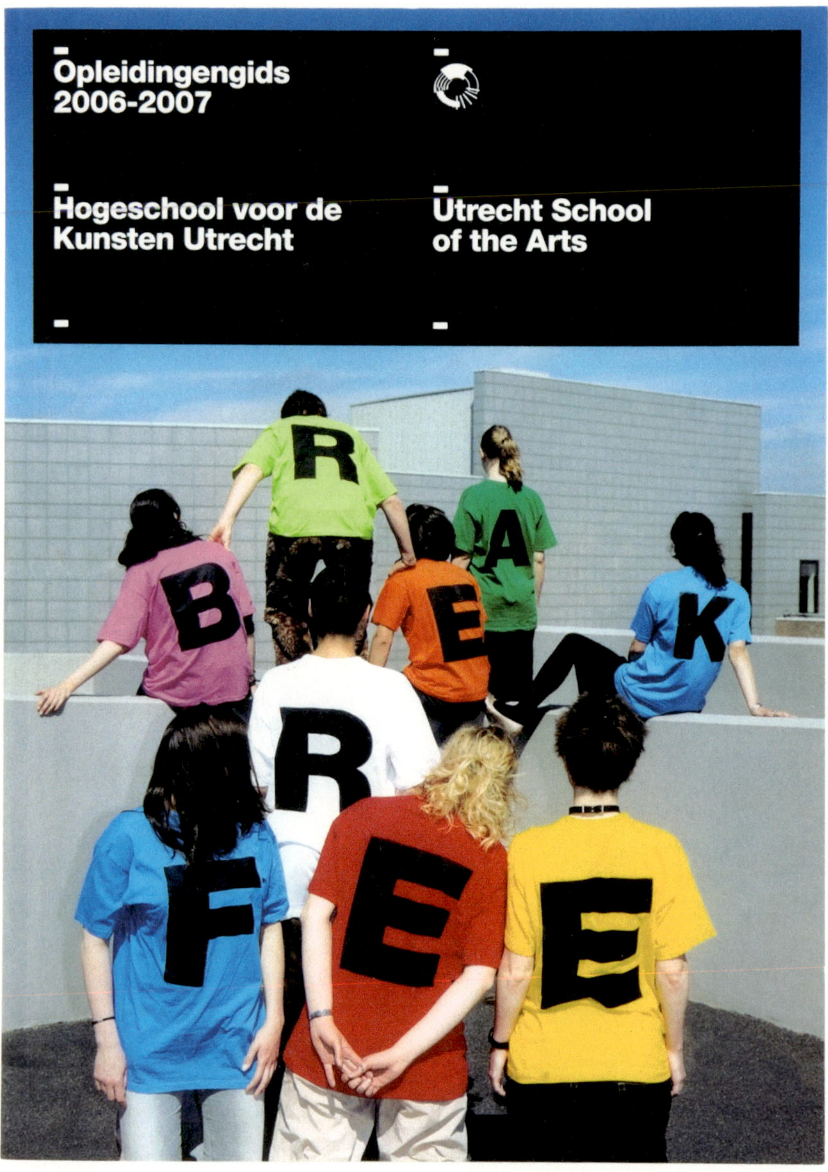

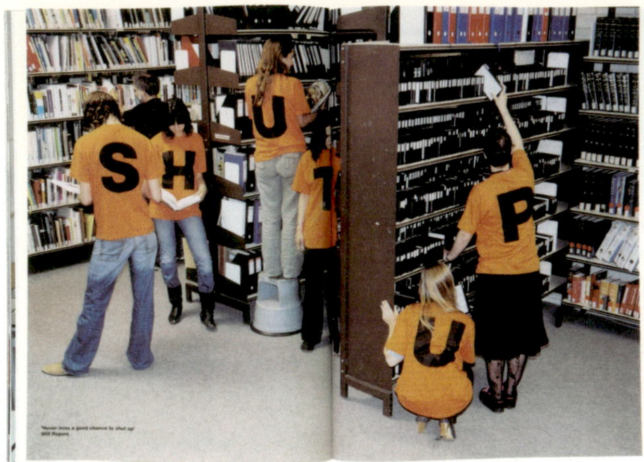

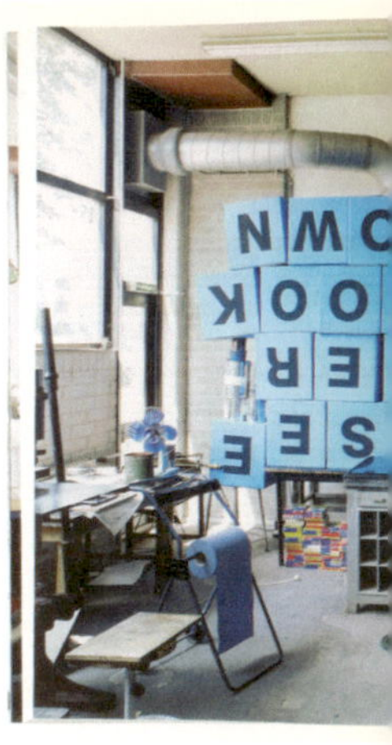

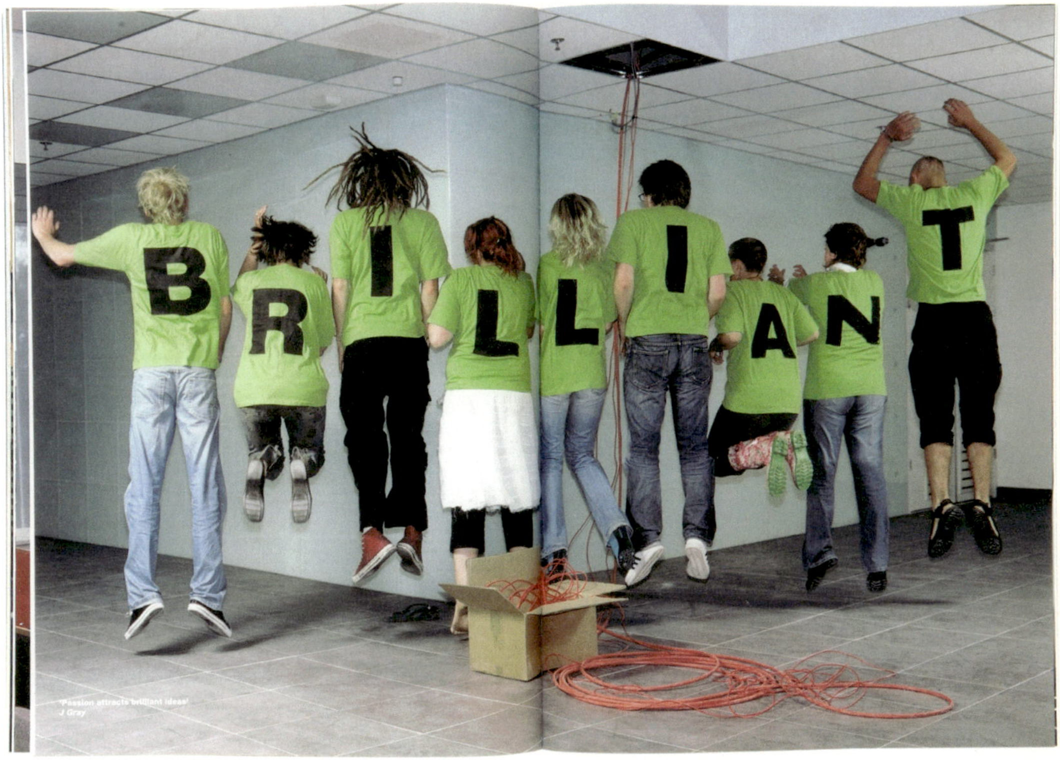

B R I L L I A N T

'Passion attracts brilliant ideas'
J Gray

for HKU, 2006-2007

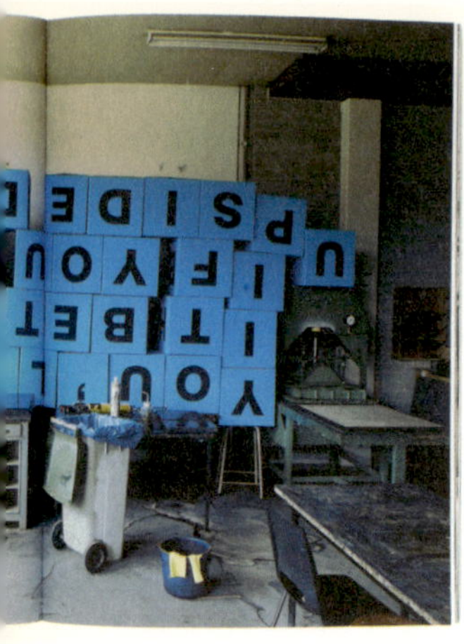

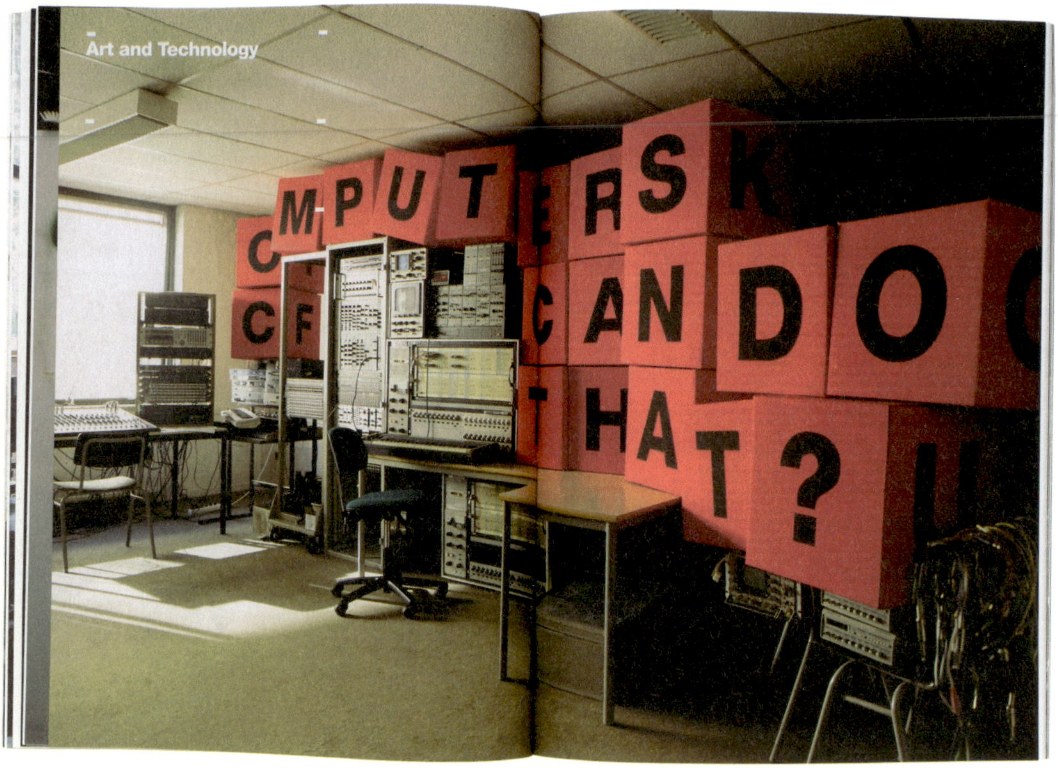

Art and Technology

313 W139
by De Designpolitie

W139 is an avant-garde art gallery in the centre of Amsterdam. For W139 we designed a series of invitations that could also be seen around the city. Empty spaces such as walls, construction sites and building façades were used to position a ‹piece› as it's known in graffiti slang. This typographic piece was the title of the exhibition. After completion of the piece, it was photographed and printed as an invitation card. This card always referred to the original object –for example, with the text ‹This invitation can also be seen at Frederik Hendrikstraat 23›. Some of the pieces are still there two years later!

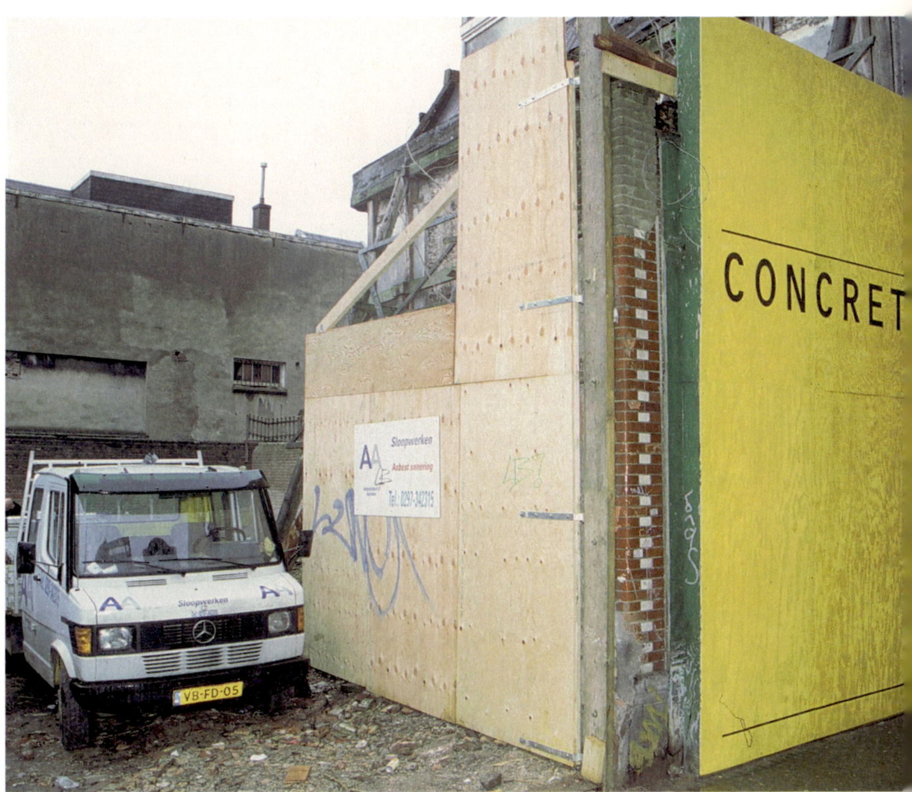

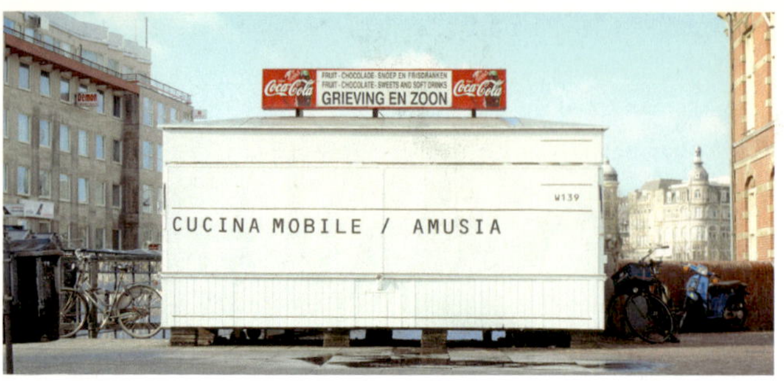

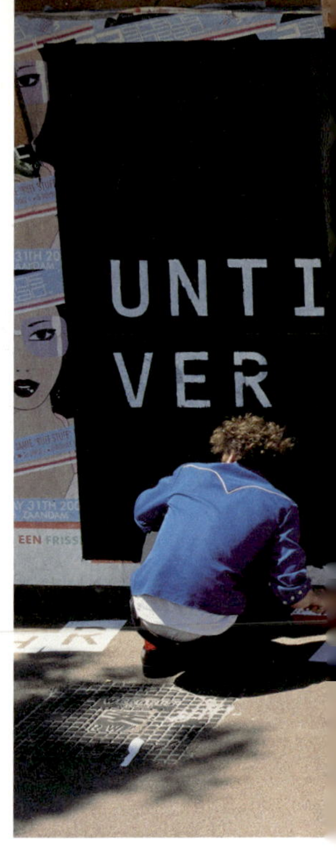

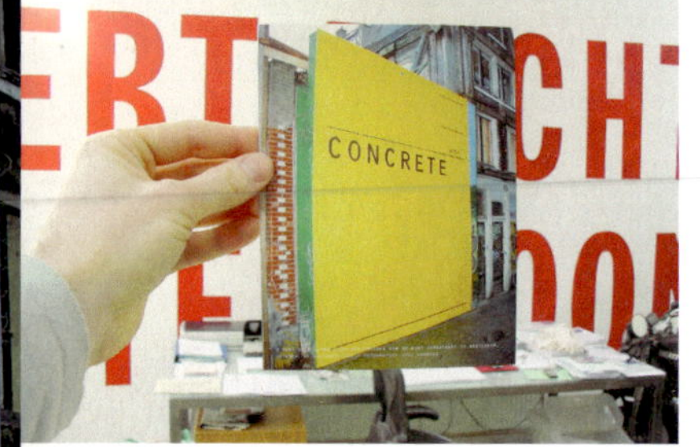

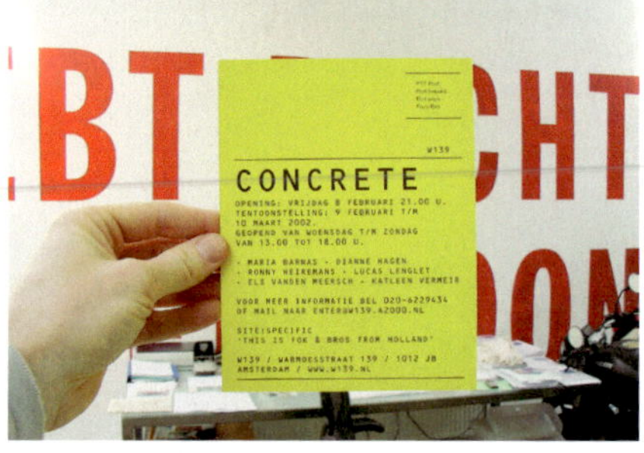

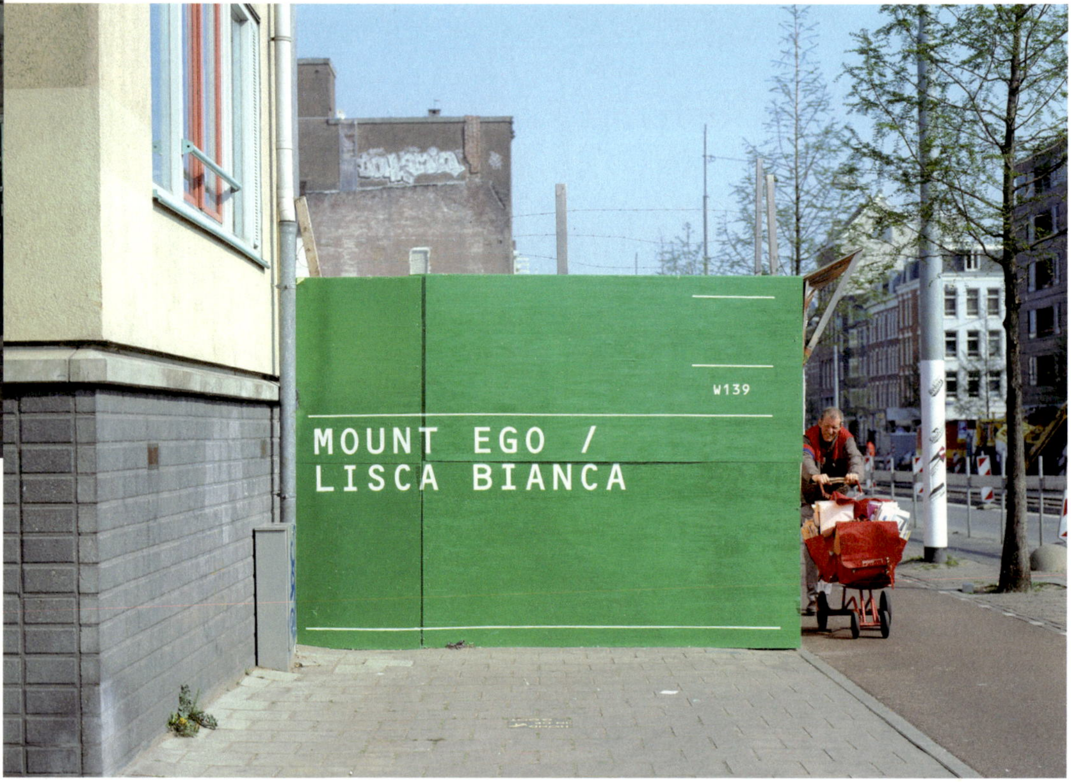

W139

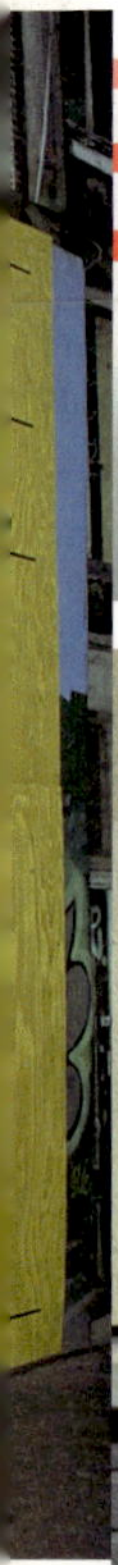

MOUNT EGO /
LISCA BIANCA

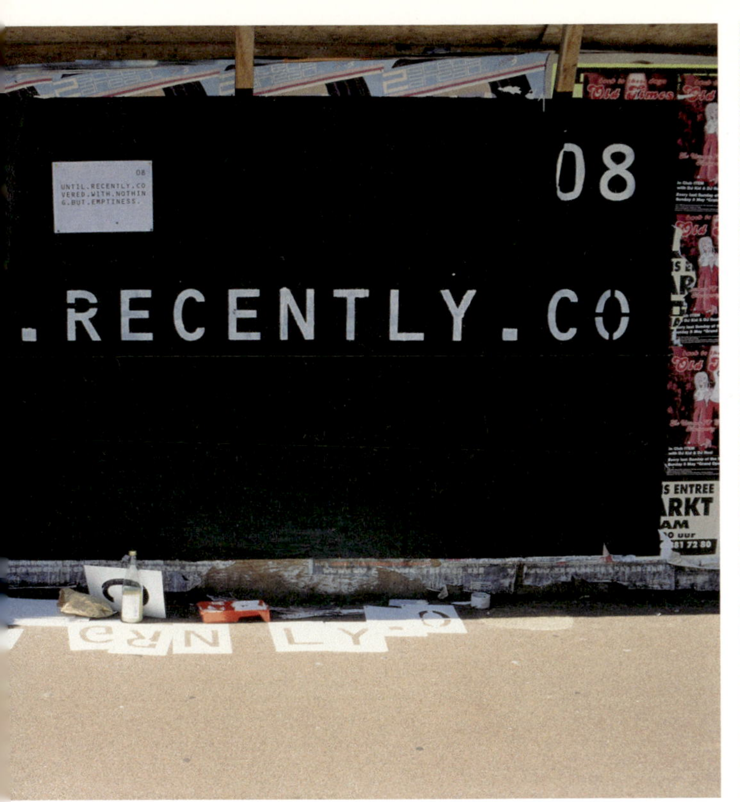
08
UNTIL.RECENTLY.CO
VERED.WITH.NOTHIN
G.BUT.EMPTINESS.
08
.RECENTLY.CO

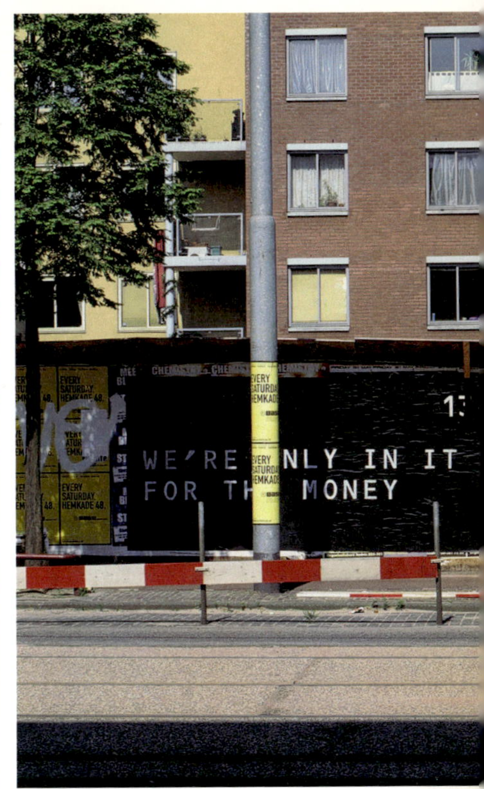
13
WE'RE NLY IN IT
FOR TH MONEY
EVERY SATURDAY HEMKADE 48.

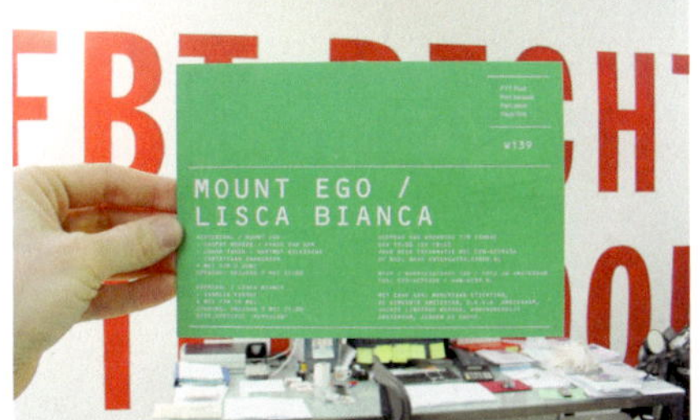
MOUNT EGO /
LISCA BIANCA

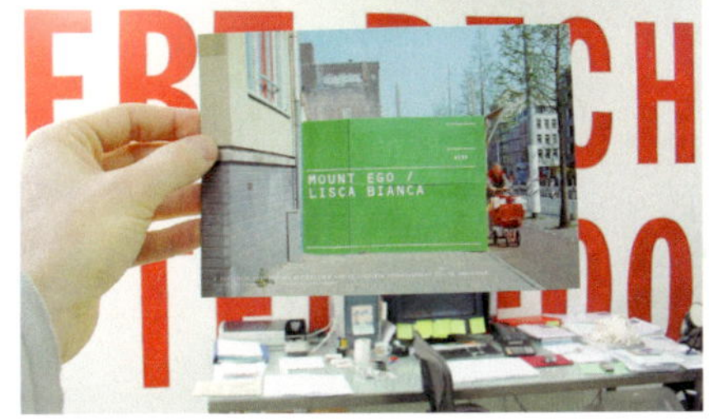
MOUNT EGO /
LISCA BIANCA

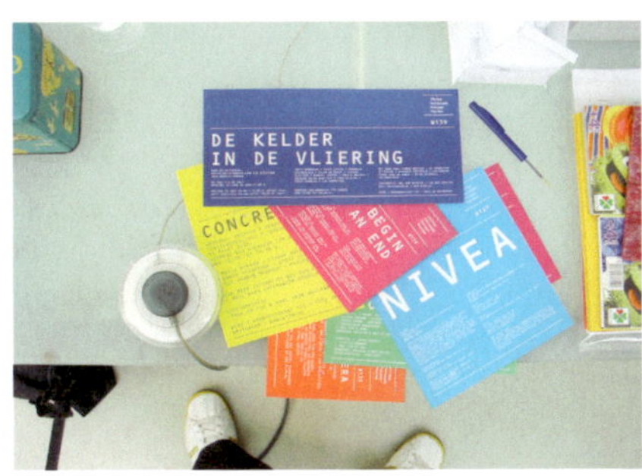
DE KELDER
IN DE VLIERING
CONCRE
BEGIN
AN END
NIVEA

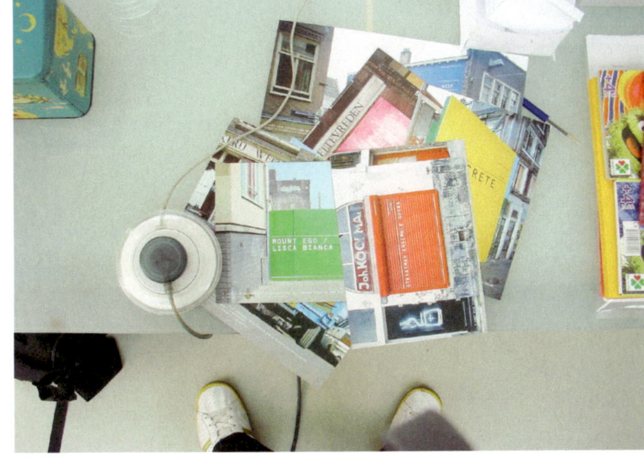
MOUNT EGO /
LISCA BIANCA

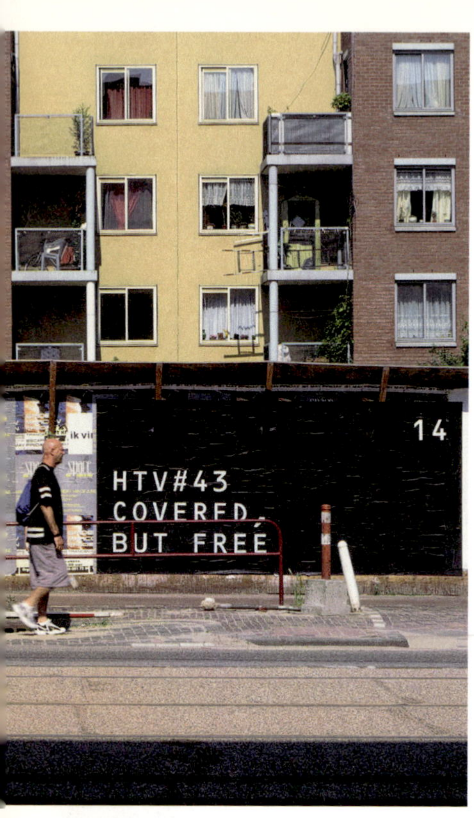
14
HTV#43
COVERED
BUT FREE

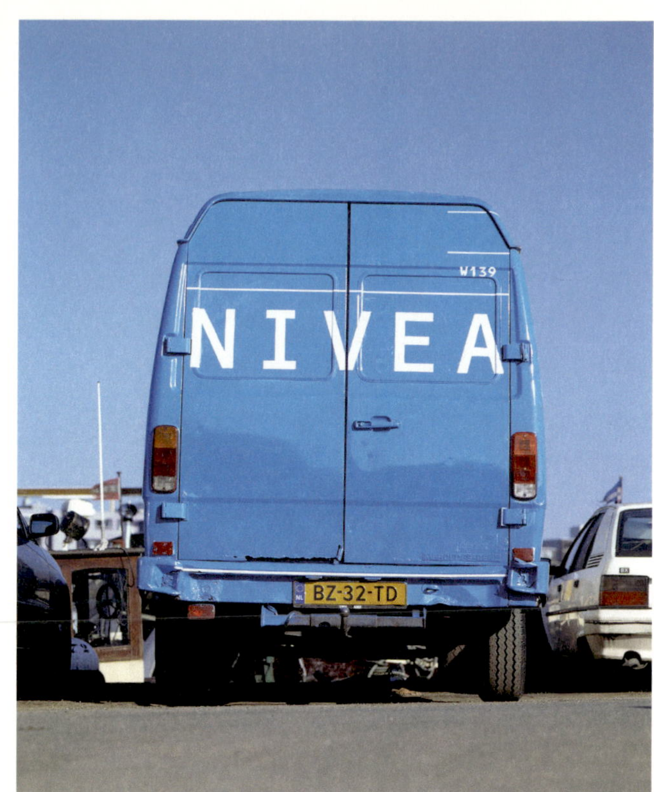
W139
NIVEA
BZ-32-TD

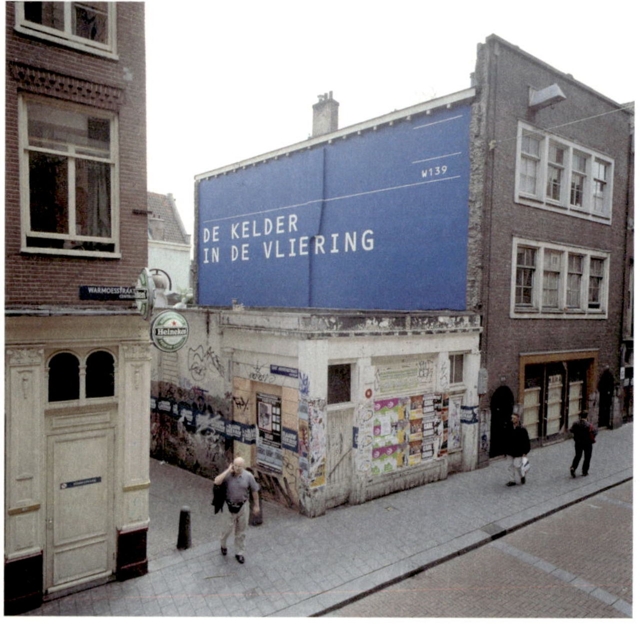
W139
DE KELDER
IN DE VLIERING
Heineken

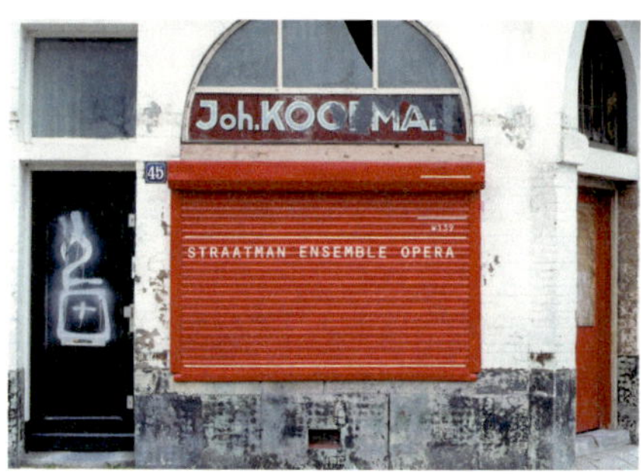
W139
STRAATMAN ENSEMBLE OPERA

Fall 2005 Visiting Artist Lecture Series
by Harmen Liemburg

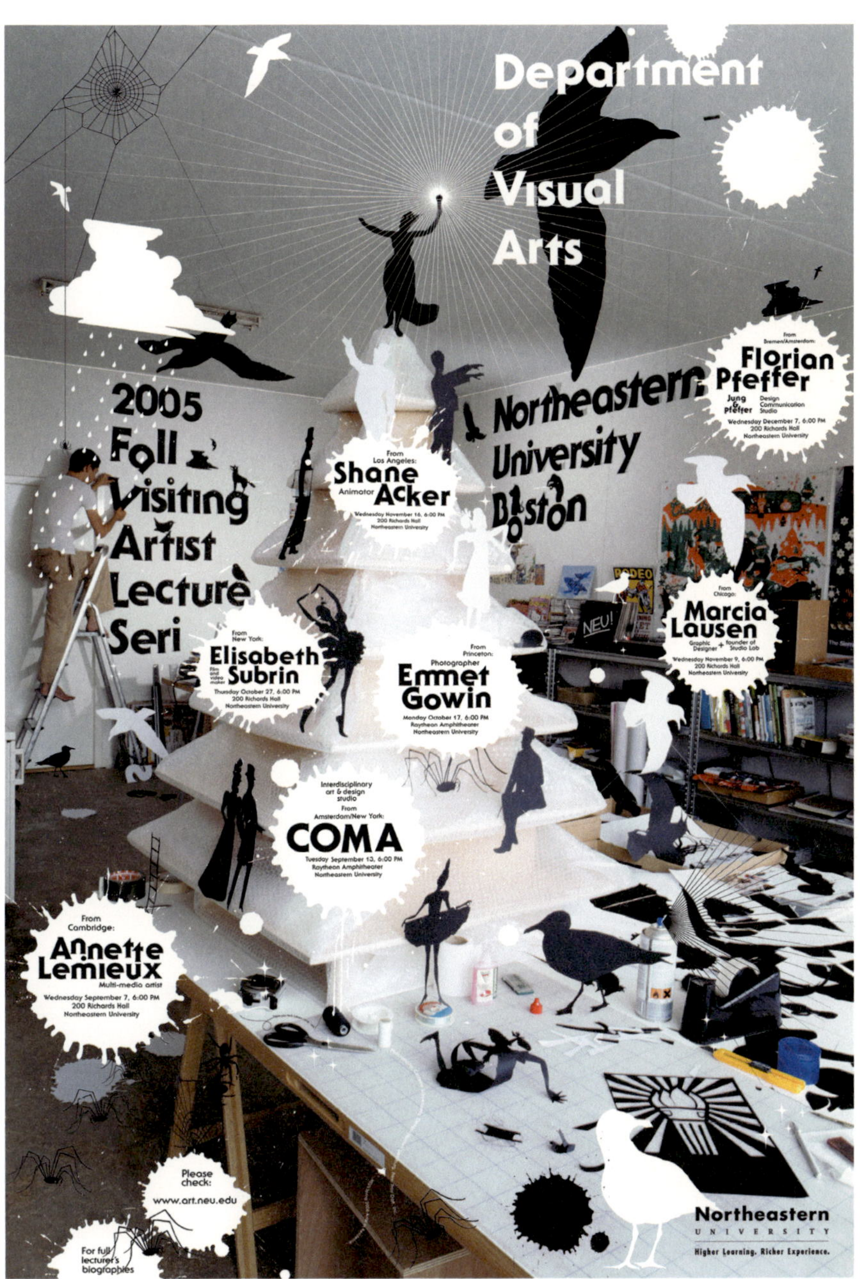

for Northeastern University, Boston, 63 x 97 cm, offset print, 2005

318 Uniceflaan
by Richard Niessen

For a renovated building in Utrecht, I prepared an art-application consisting of a toolkit composed of 24 different parts that can form characters and words. Ceramic tiles on the concrete construction, silk-screened wallpaper at the entrance wall and transparent foil on the glass doors contain these parts. All done in a non-colour format, they make a subtle contribution to the identity of the building.

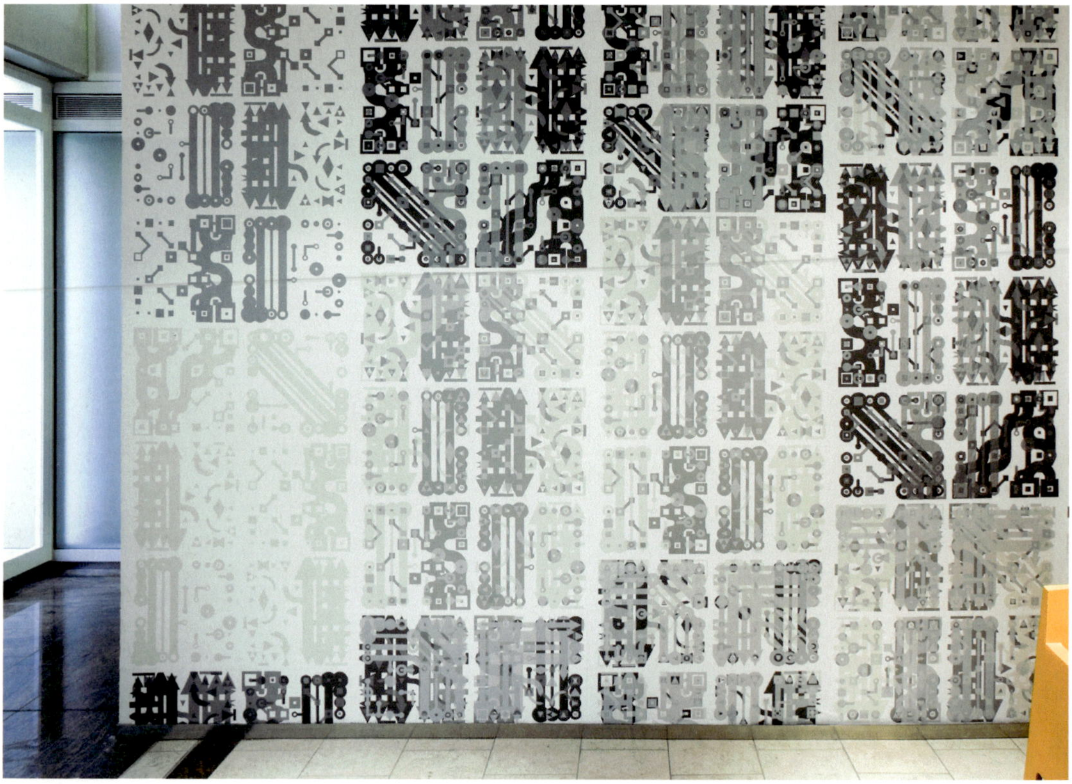

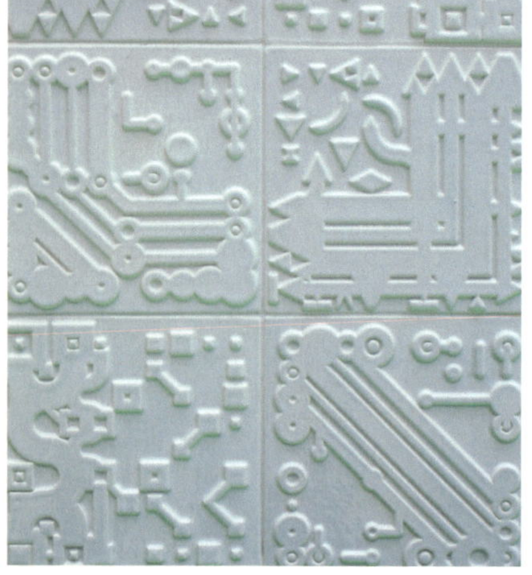

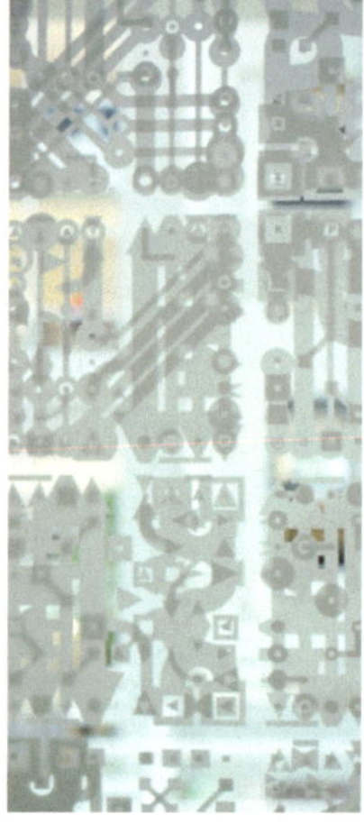

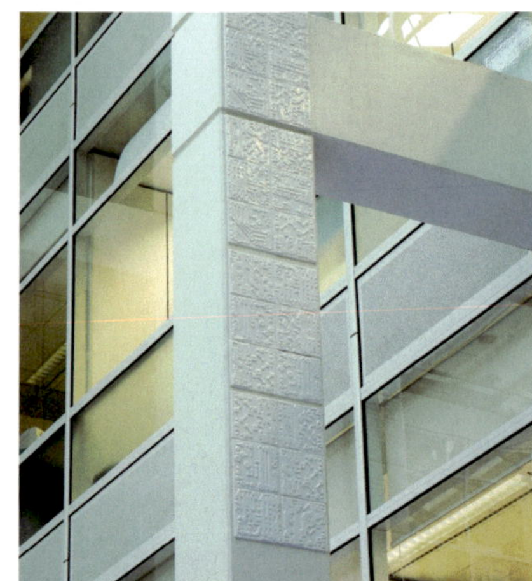

319 Raadzaal Zuidoost
by Richard Niessen & Jennifer Tee

This is a permanent art-work in the City Council headquarters in the south-east of Amsterdam. We designed a secret language to construct the ‹skyline› with, silkscreen printed in a system using six patterns and six colours. In the end, we added neon-light accents.

2006

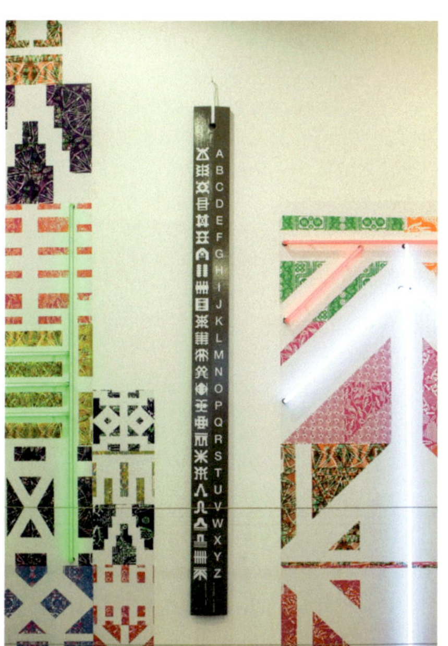

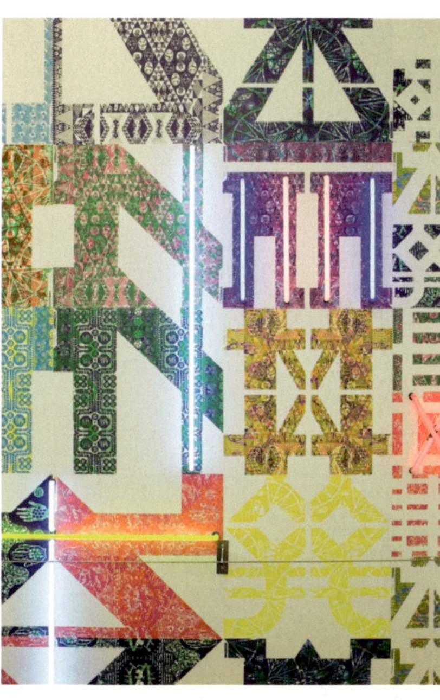

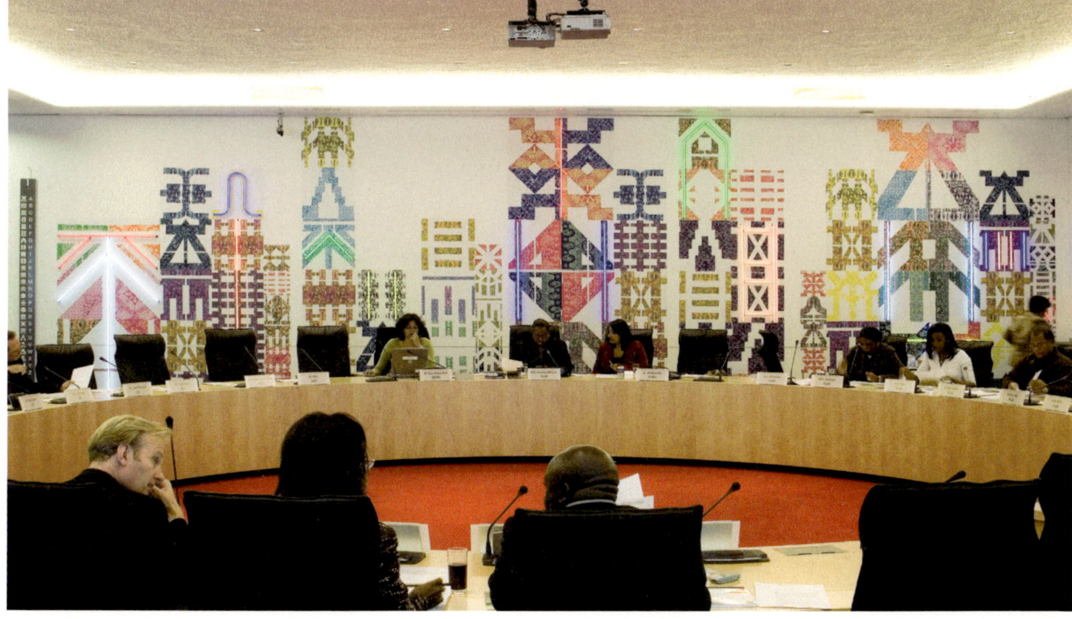

TM-City

by Richard Niessen & Esther de Vries

‹TM-City› has eight neighbourhoods, made out of more than 150 works by the Dutch graphic designer Richard Niessen. Niessen's method can be described as ‹Typo-graphic Masonry› (TM), in that he builds with graphic elements –fonts, shapes and colours. In ‹TM-City›, Niessen takes it all one step further and actually builds a city out of his designs: flyers are stacked to form skyscrapers, posters are laid out to become parks. ‹TM-City› is fully traversable. People can walk down the streets, which are named after Niessen's sources of inspiration, such as Richard Rogers and Eduardo Paolozzi. ‹TM-City› has also been designed to be mobile and easy to transport. Each neighbourhood, individually wrapped in handmade covers, fits inside its wooden base. From 12 May to 24 June 2007, ‹TM-City› formed a ‹gesamtkunstwerk› inside La Chapelle, the Baroque chapel in Chaumont, France. Welcome to ‹TM-City›!

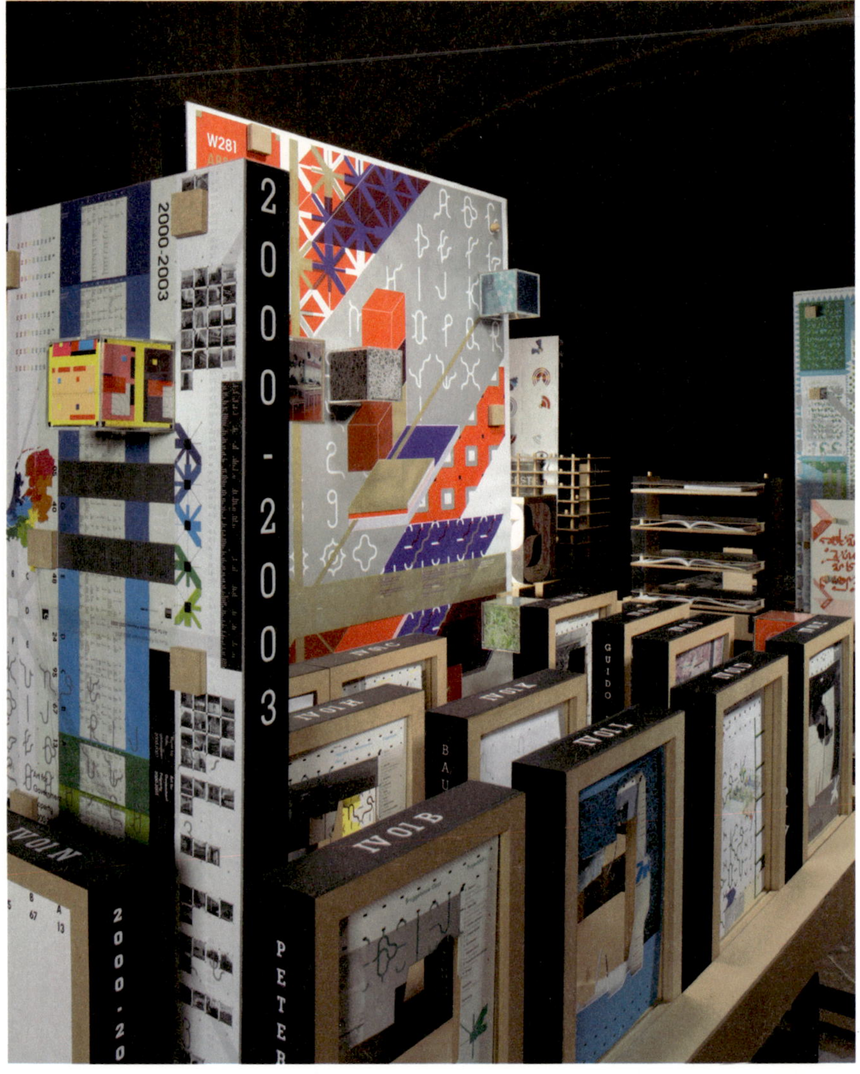

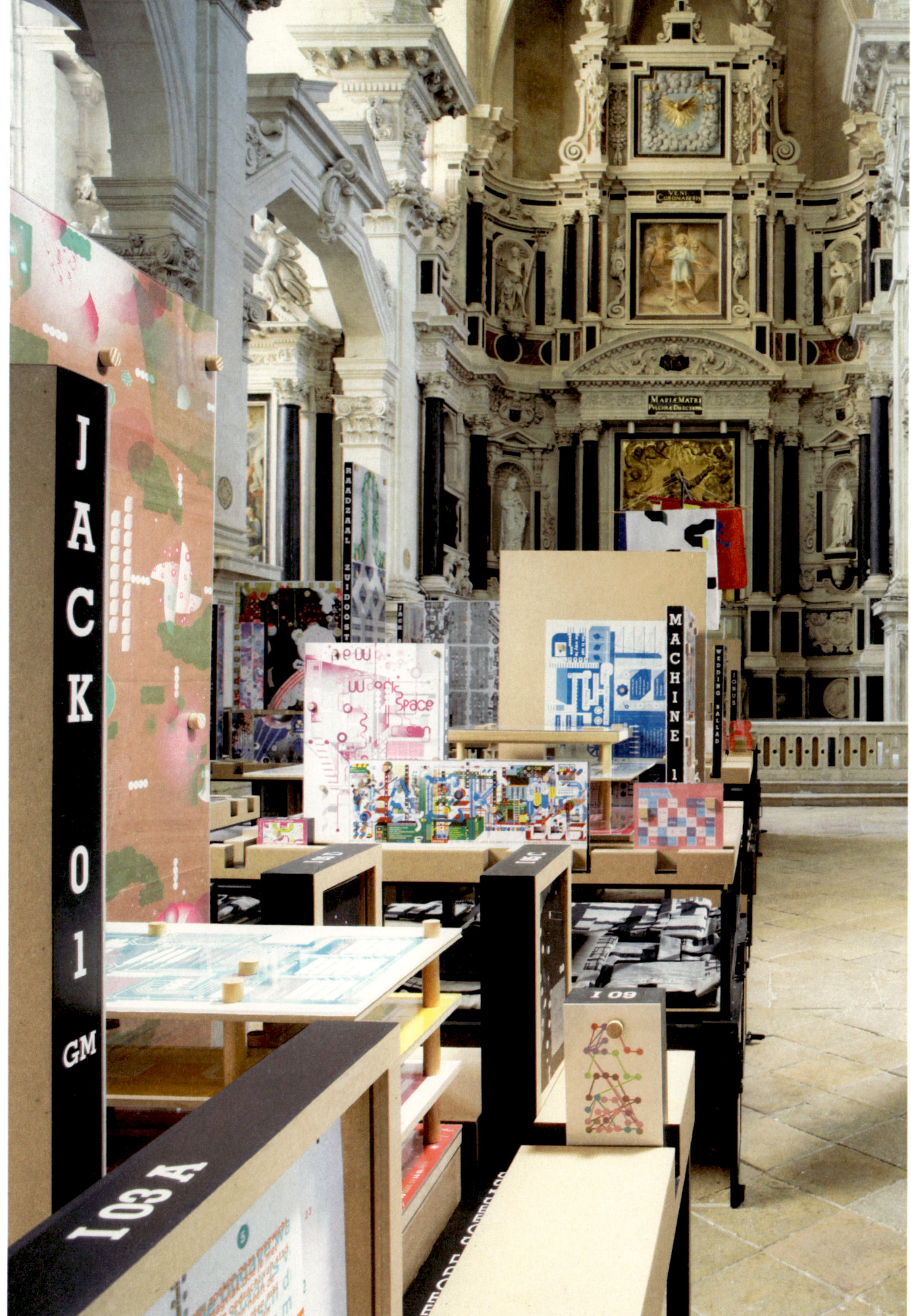
JACK 01
GM
I03 A
RAADZAAL ZUIDOOST
MACHINE 1
WEDDING BALLAD
I09

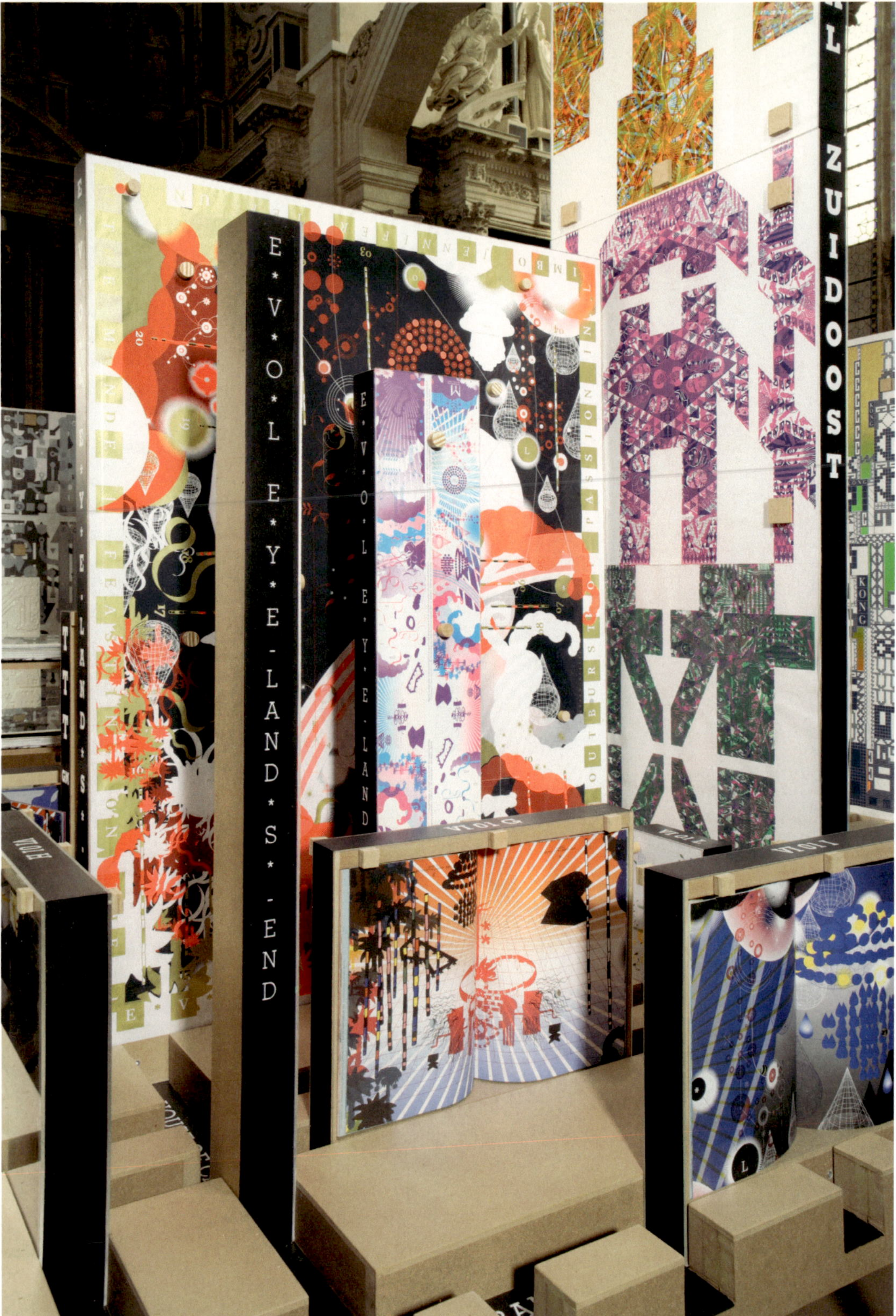
E*V*O*L E*Y*E-LAND*S*-END
ZUIDOOST

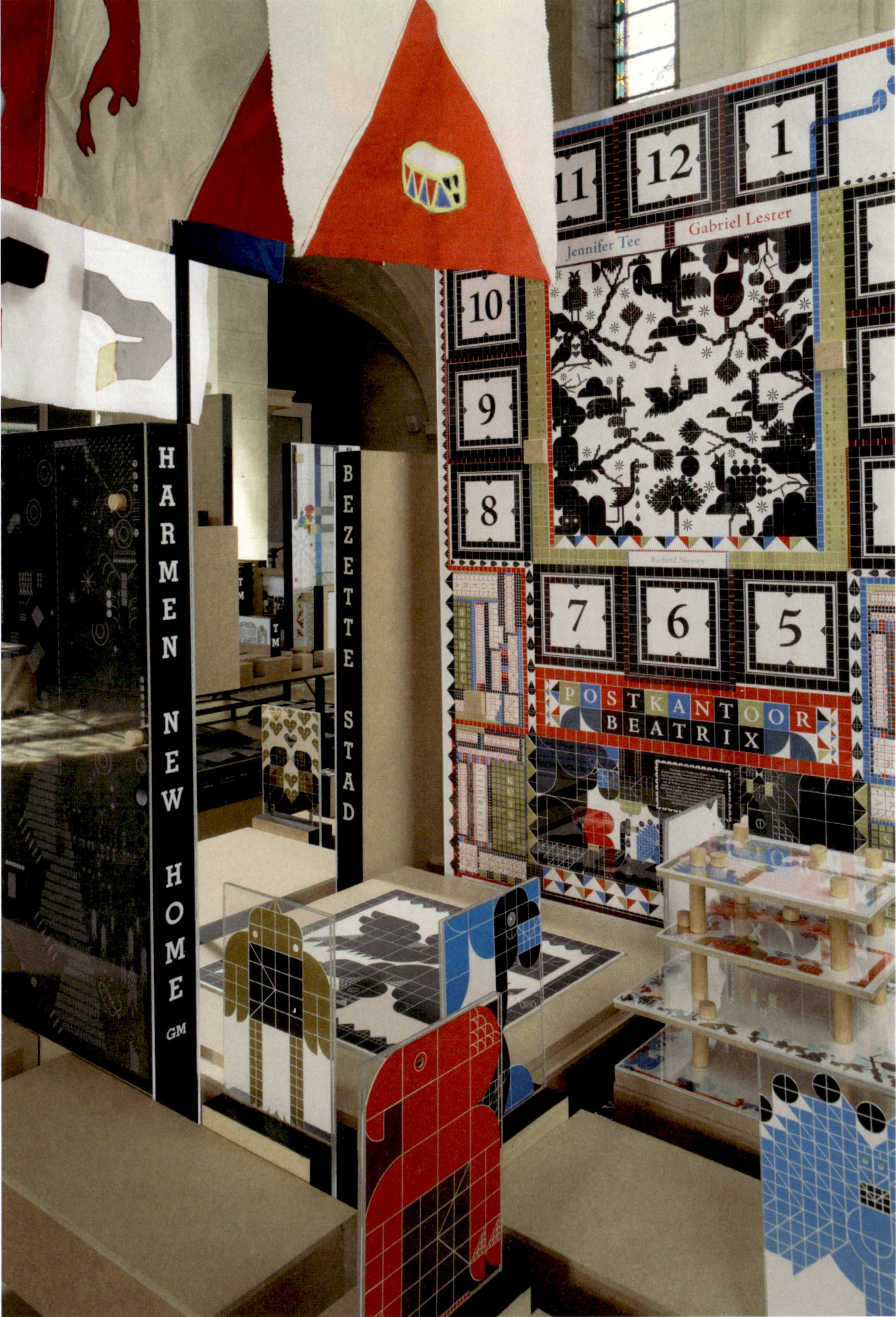

11
12
1
Jennifer Tee
Gabriel Lester
10
9
8
Richard Niessen
7
6
5
POSTKANTOOR
BEATRIX
HARMEN NEW HOME
GM
BEZETTE STAD

Big Type Says More

by Strange Attractors Design

Over the course of 5 weeks, using industrial handheld jigsaws and paint, we manually produced a 5 layer thick, 2.83 metres high, and over 17 metres wide typographic installation as part of the ongoing exhibition ‹Cut for Purpose›, at Museum Boijmans van Beuningen in Rotterdam.

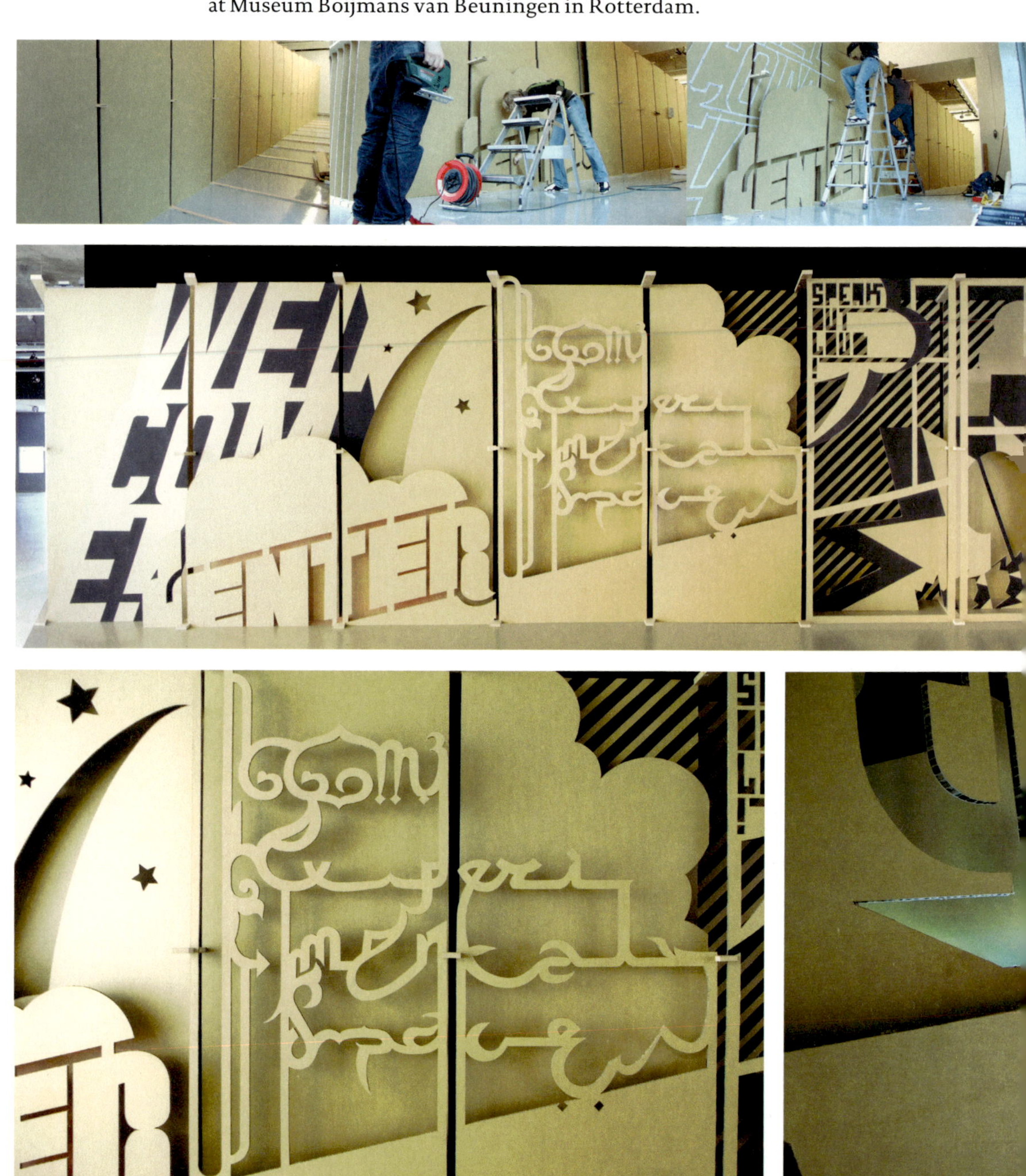

The typographic structure was positioned as the front section of a spatial (honeycomb) cardboard structure (by Stealth.[u]ltd), enticing the viewer from the windows, the glazed entrance, and on approach rewarding them with increasingly complex yet graceful forms.
Our objective was to merge contemporary technology with traditional craftsmanship while representing the diverse, multi-cultural and multi-architectural city of Rotterdam. In the end, custom-programmed microcontrollers sequenced LEDs which were mounted to add a ‹touch of Vegas› to the type that we created specifically for this project.

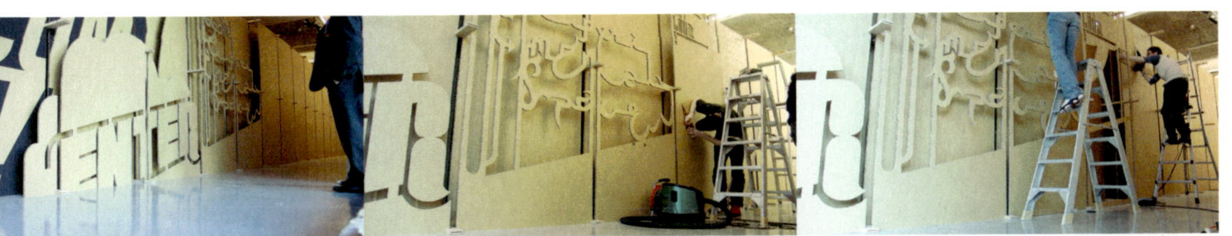

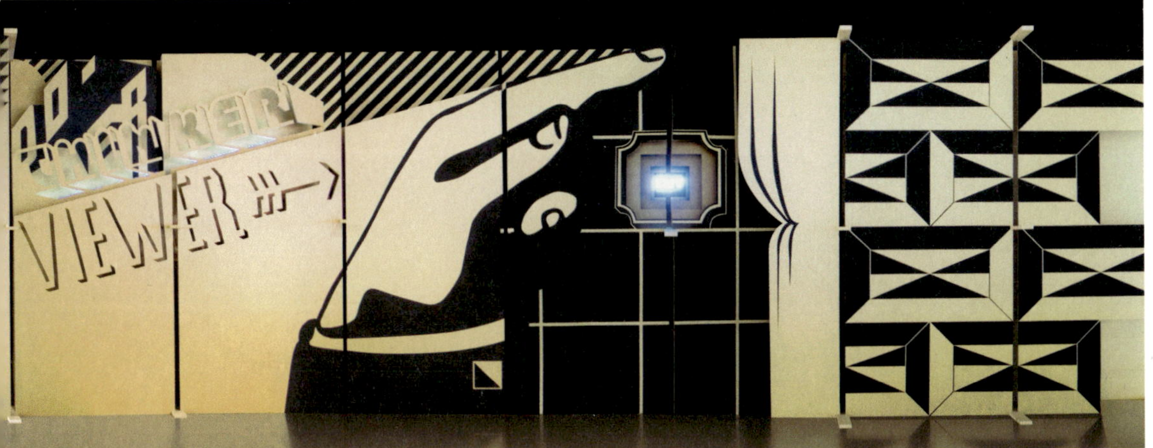

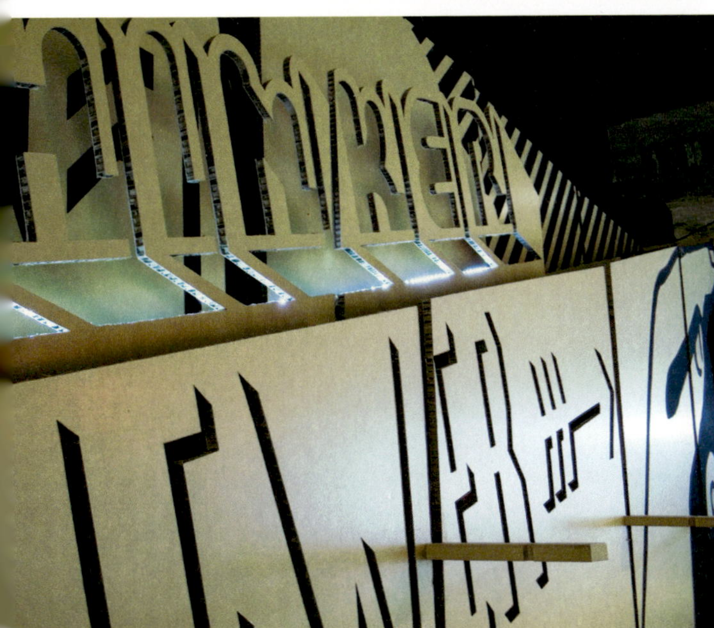

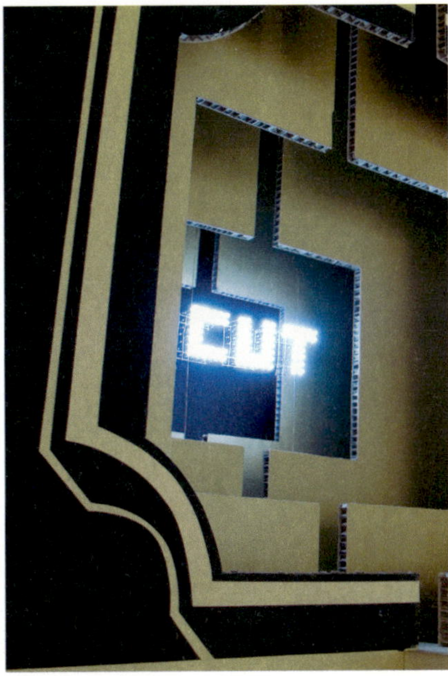

The Sirens of Venice

by Joana Katte, Janna Meeus, Radim Pesko, Willi Schmid, Marie Proyart, Felix Weigand and Paul Elliman / Werkplaats Typografie

The Werkplaats Typografie was invited by the IUAV (University of Venice) to join the Viverevenezia3 workshop. The aim was to devise a new graphic signage system for the city of Venice. Over a period of three months, groups from Arnhem, Bremen, Lausanne, Treviso and Venice worked in Venice on research proposals and projects. Six designers from the Werkplaats Typografie took part under the supervision of Paul Elliman.

We proposed to leave Venice graphically unchanged. Working as the Werkplaats Typografie Audio Sign Unit, we considered instead an audio signage network accessible from mobile phones and computers. We called the system Salvatore, or the Salvatore web. Salvatore is a collection of different voices, male and female, available in several languages, offering a range of information for both locals and visitors. We referred to the film as a sci-fi movie set half an hour into the future, imagining a Venice flooded with wifi signals and inexpensive local-call rates.

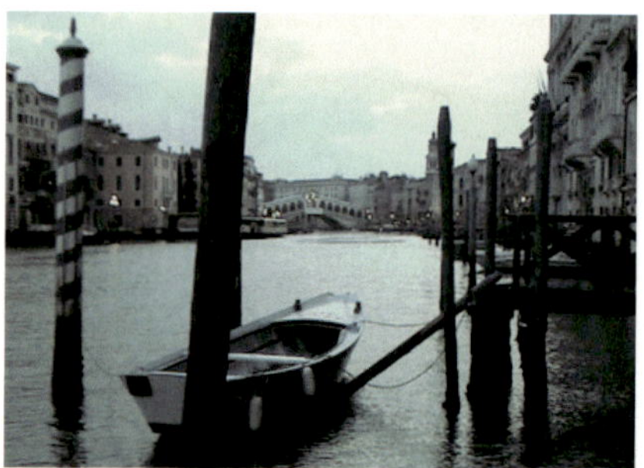

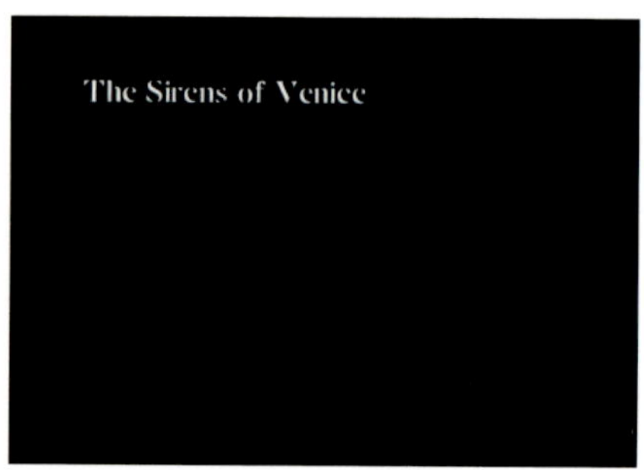

for Viverevenezia3 (IUAV), 2004

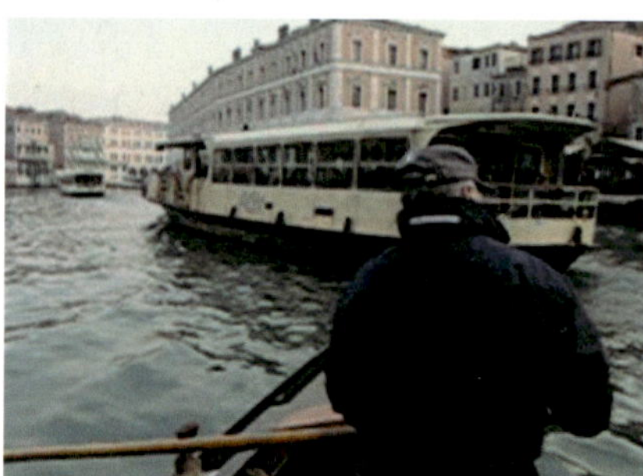

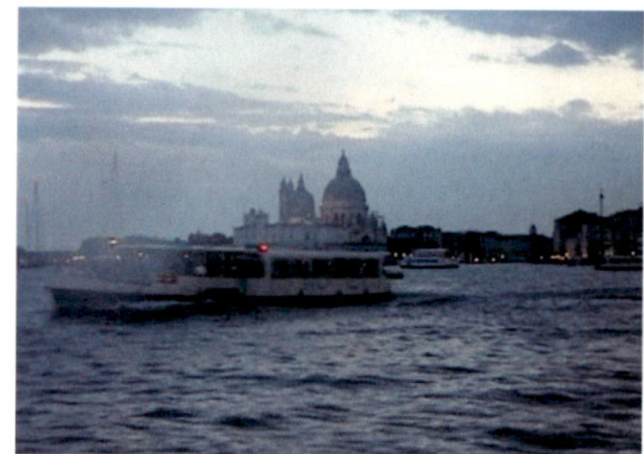

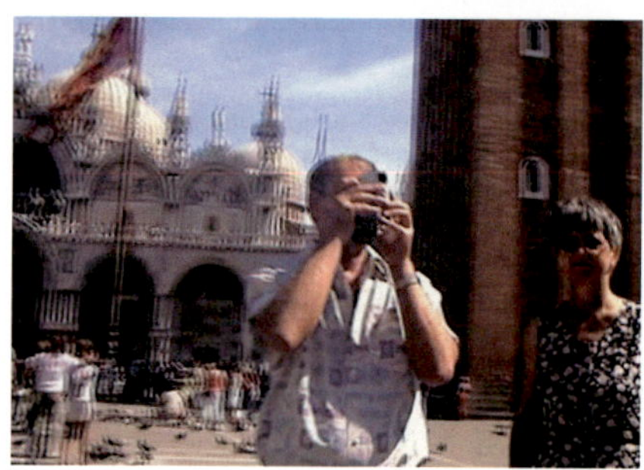

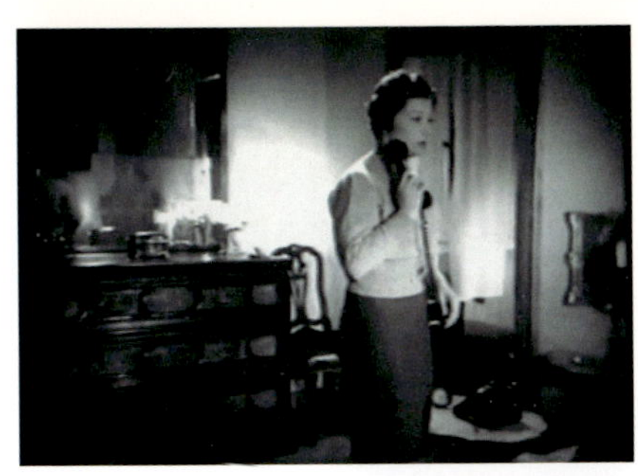
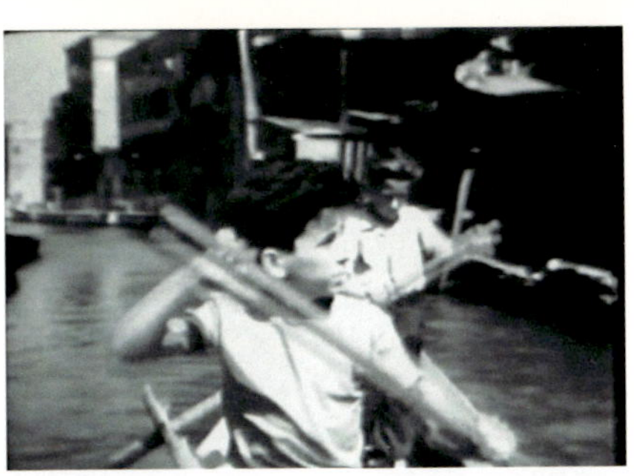
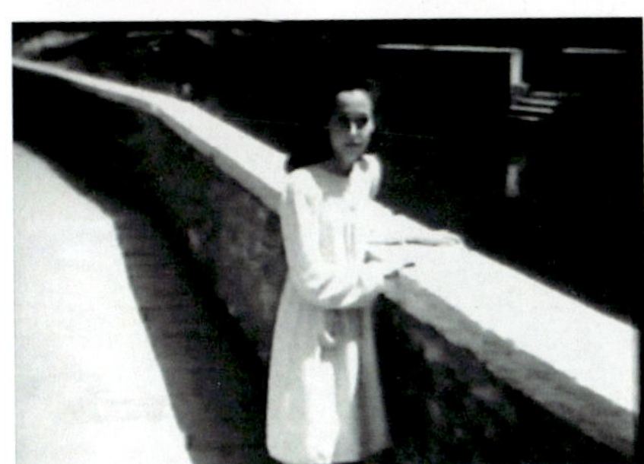
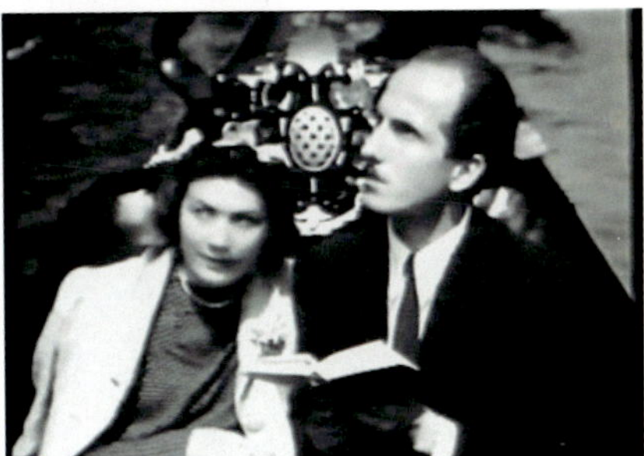
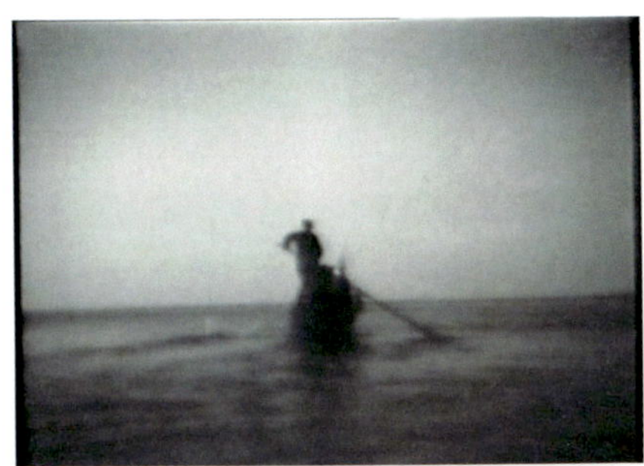
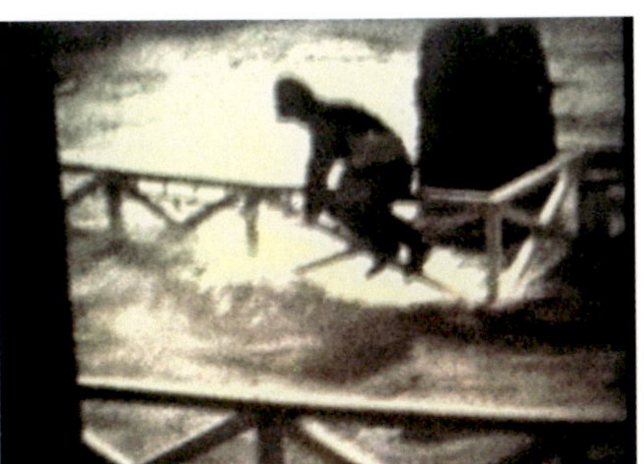
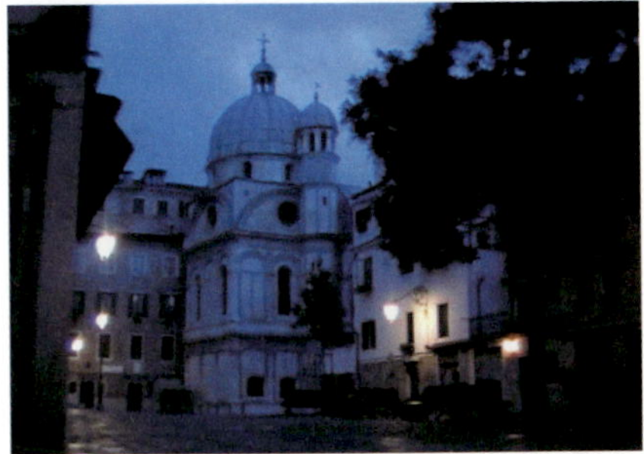

Visual identity and signage graphics for the Nederlands Fotomuseum in Las Palmas
by Ping-pong Design

Ping-pong Design in collaboration with Waac's designed the interior. The signage concept brings ‹glam› to a concrete building. Large colour filters, which temper the light and play with the images on display, divide the exhibition space; extra-large ‹bling› chrome typography refers to the use of photography in the media. Above the entrance a cinema marquee sign shouts out that the exhibition is ‹Live in Las Palmas›, suggesting the inevitable relationship between photography and the moving image.

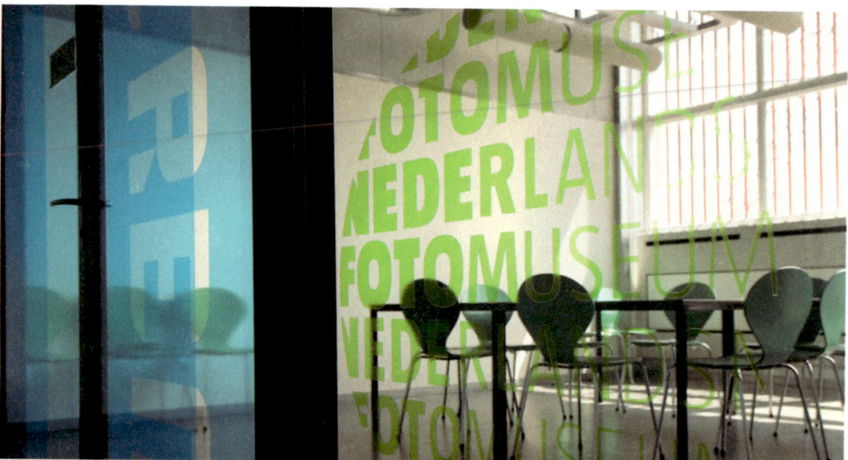

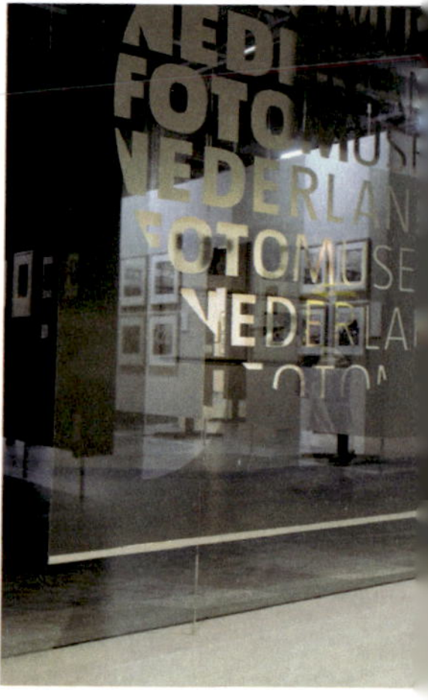

for Nederlands Fotomuseum (Rotterdam),
Signage graphics, 2007

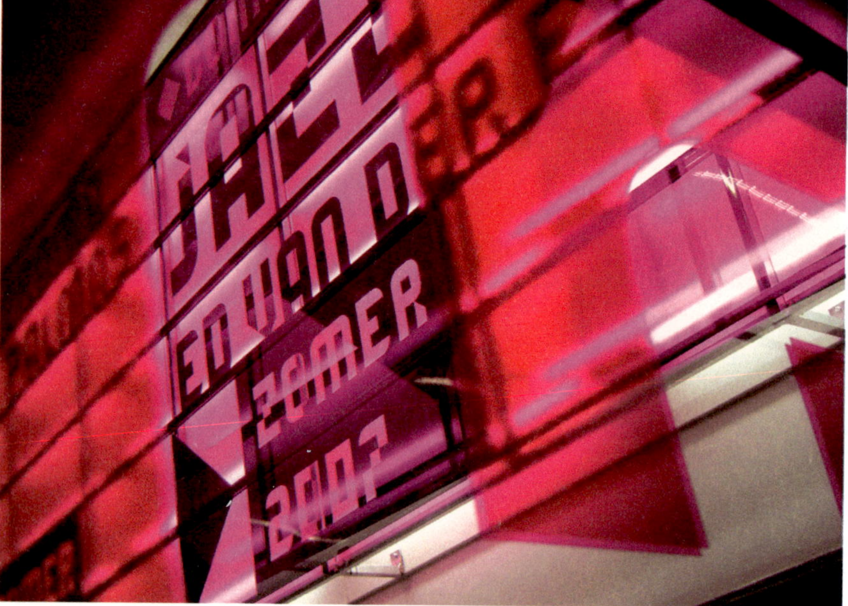

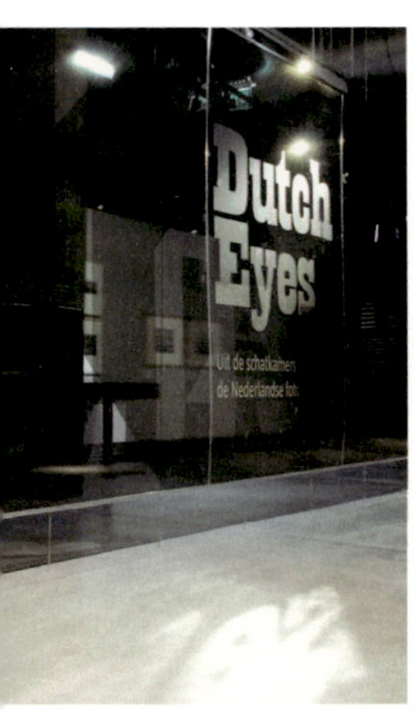
Dutch
Eyes

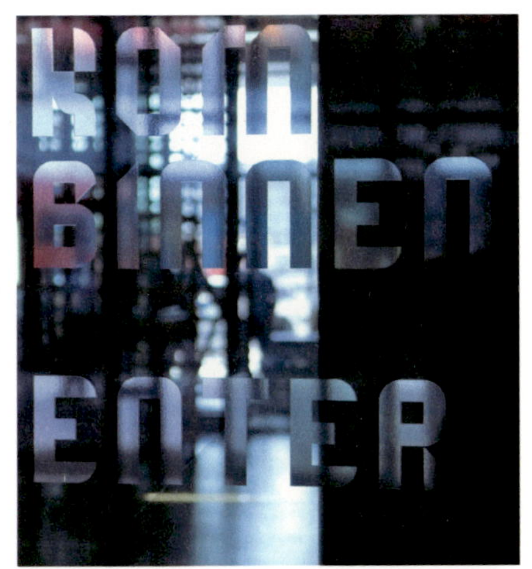
KOM
BINNEN
ENTER

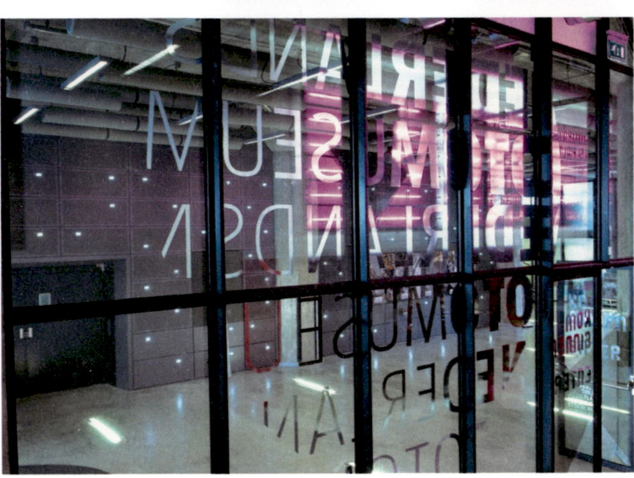

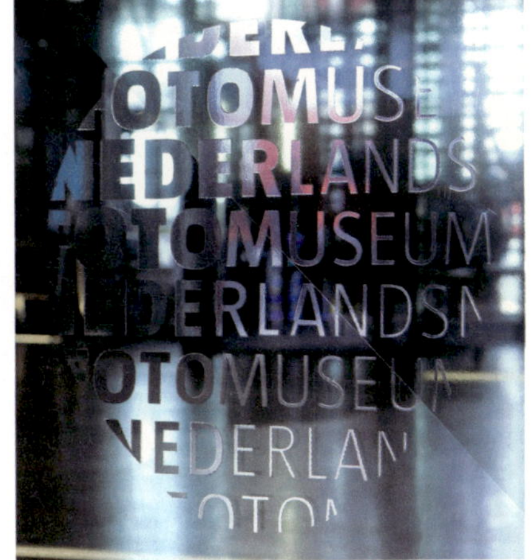
NEDERLANDS

330 Werck

by Arjan Groot

Logo, corporate identity and wall decoration for the Werck restaurant in Amsterdam.

for Werck, 2007

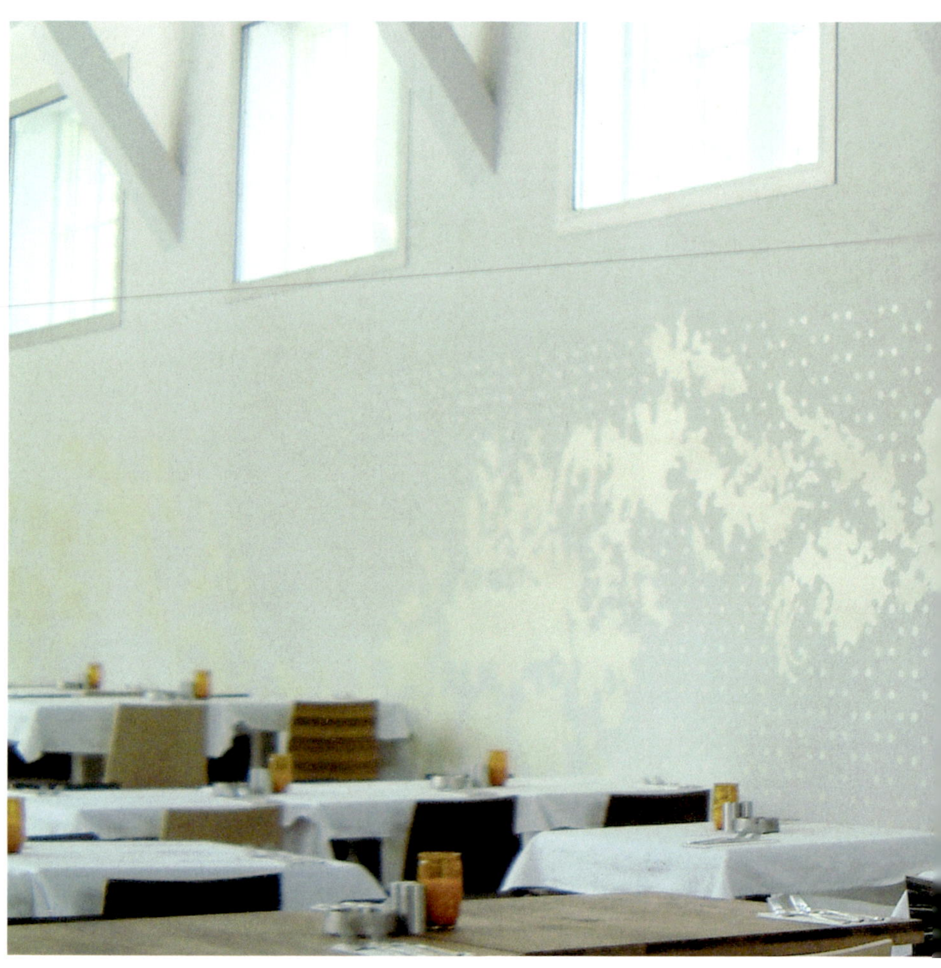

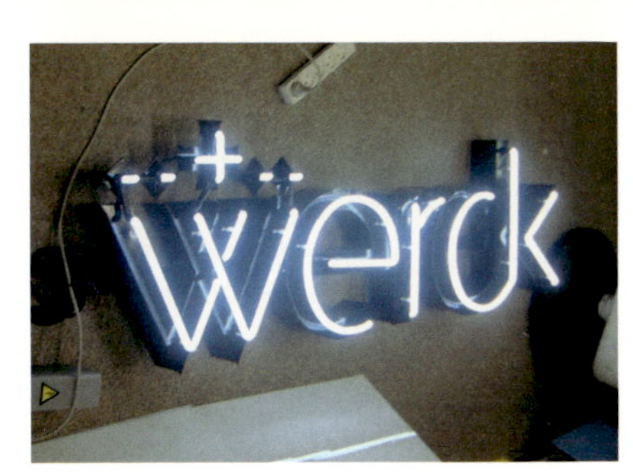
werck

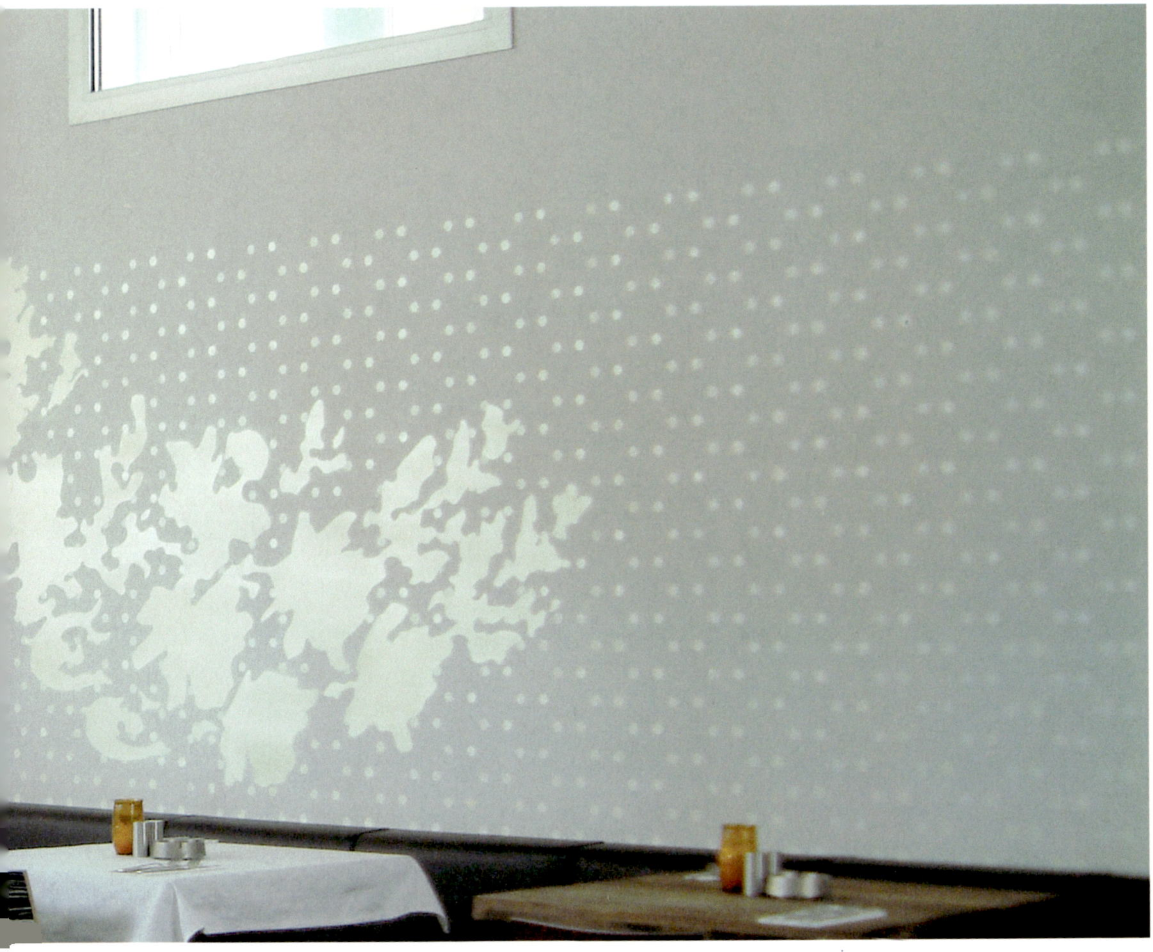

Pauze
by Lust

Exhibition design and installation for ‹In de Tussentijd› for Stroom Den Haag, 2005. In co-operation with RAL2005 (Duzan Doepel, Jan Konings). The exhibition was set up around the presentation of the workshops on mobile urban planning, with the themes of temporary building activities and vacant spaces in the city. We put a giant timeline on the three walls of the room, on which most of the temporary architectural interventions in The Hague since 1860 were plotted. Every ‹intervention› was a bright fluorescent orange sticker, pasted on the walls, that glowed when light was projected onto it. Over the timeline, a film about these projects was shown.

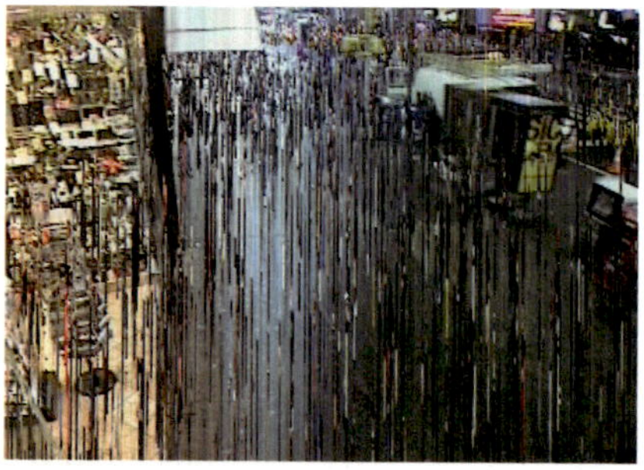

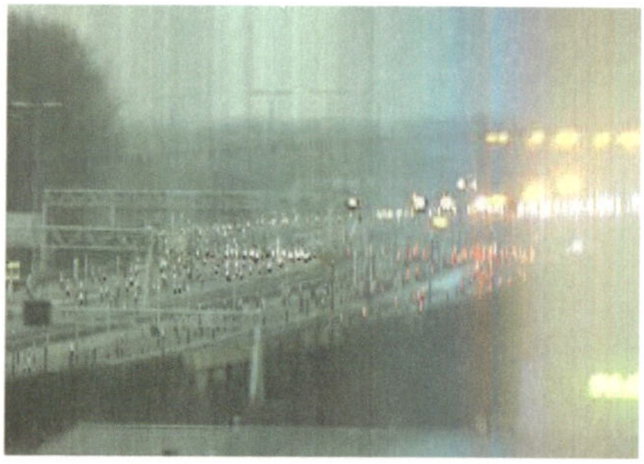

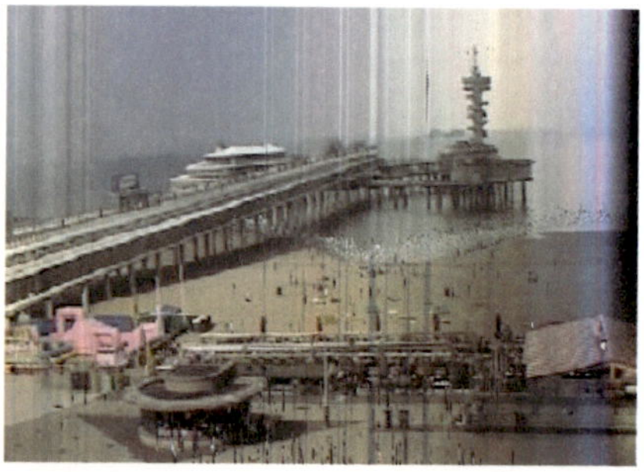

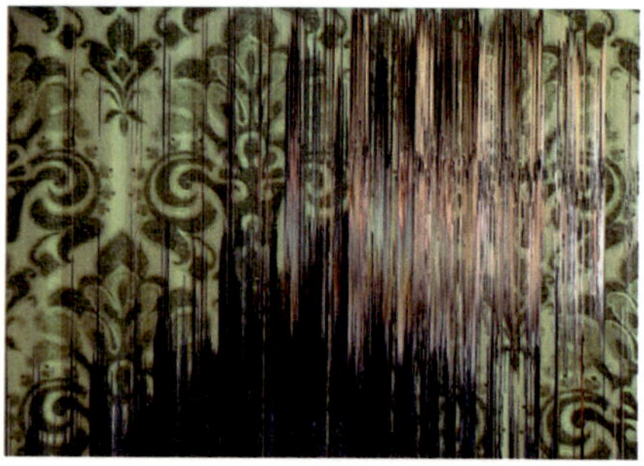

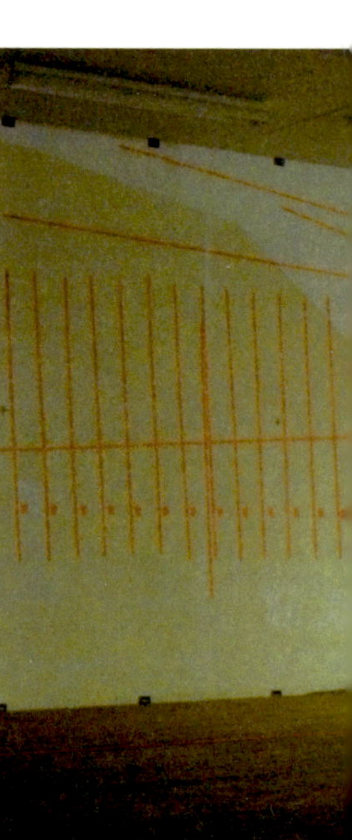

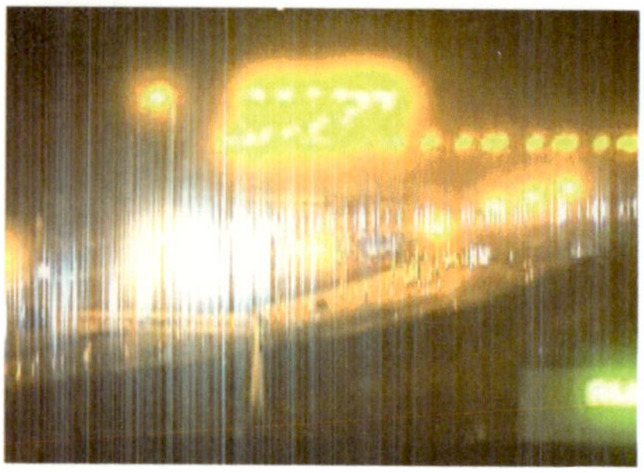

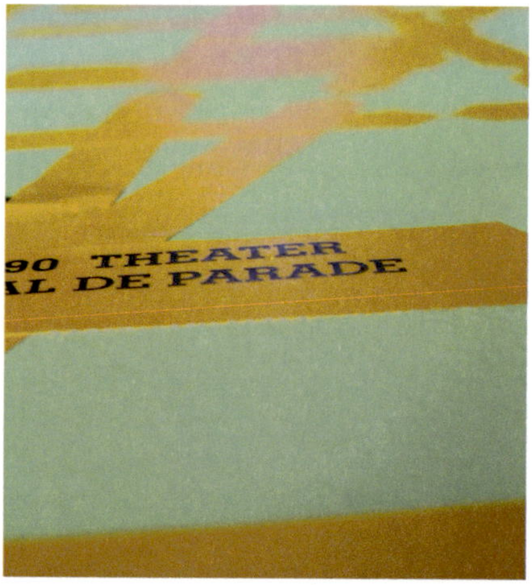

For this exhibition Lust also designed a ‹TimeSlice›, a sort of ‹visual timeline› of changes taking place on the beach of The Hague. This involved ‹scraping› an existing webcam and using a simple programme, which took a pixel from the image at each specified time interval and added it into a new image: see the ebb and flow of the tides. Even the curvature of the Earth could be seen (high and low tides on the horizon).

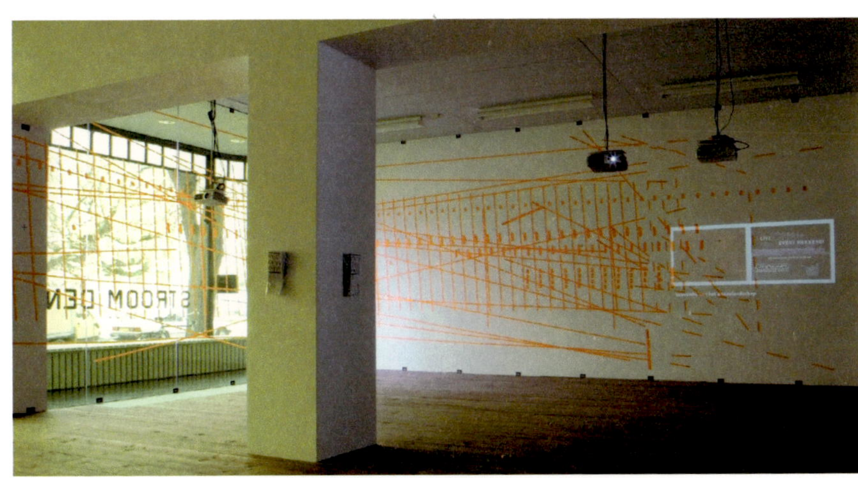

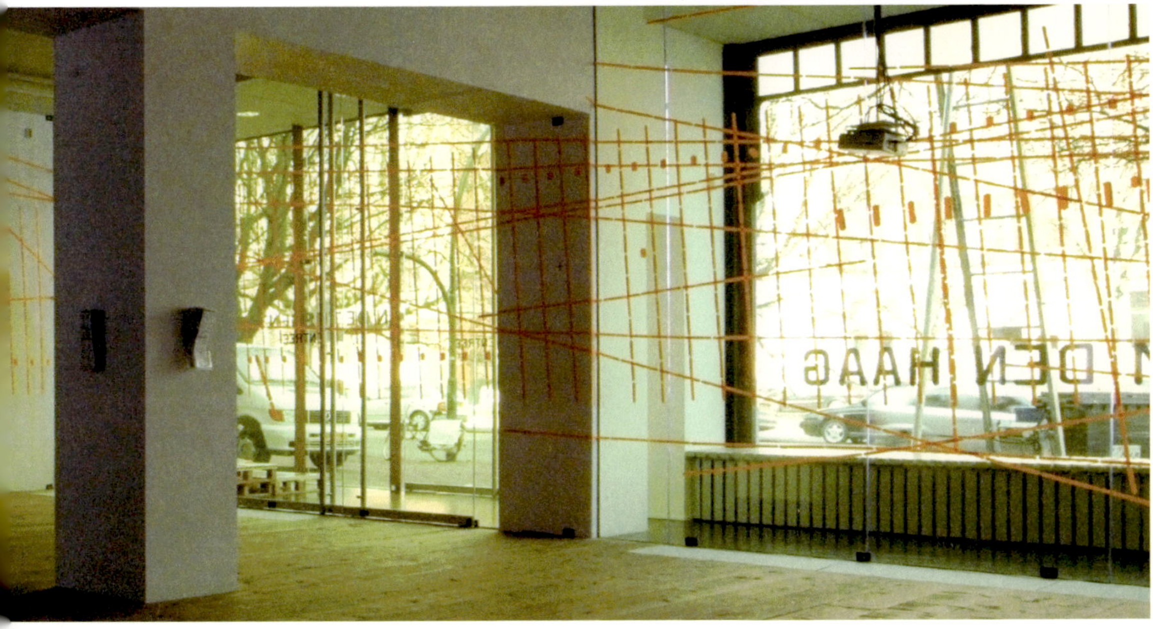

Installation project done in cooperation with teenagers in Amsterdam's Bijlmer district.

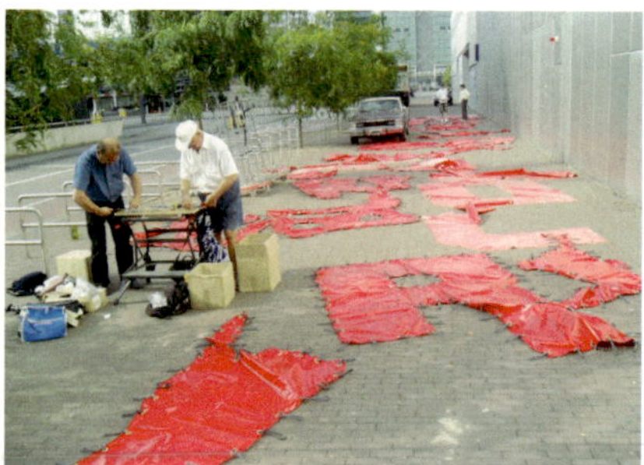

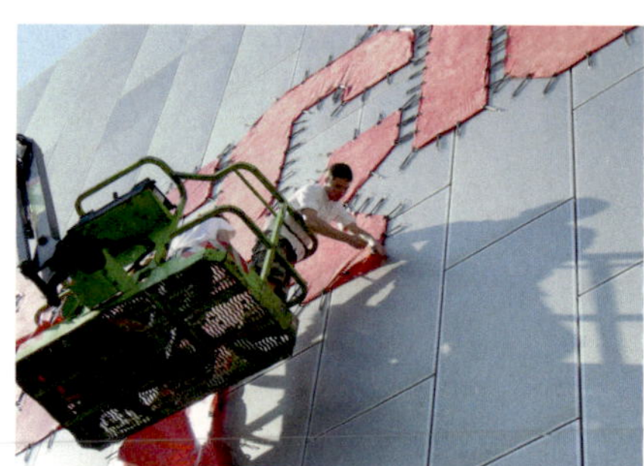

for Compressed Space, 2004

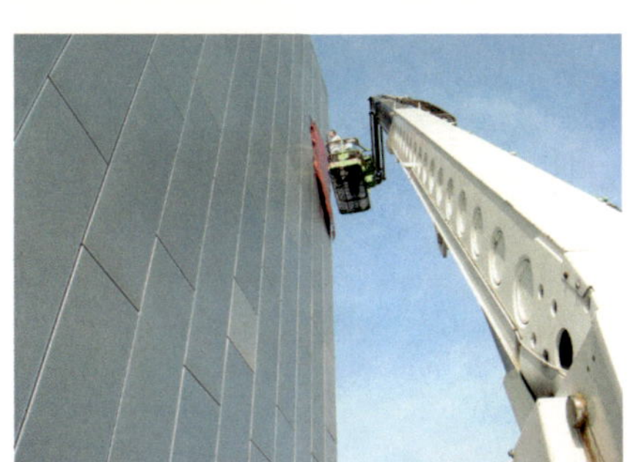

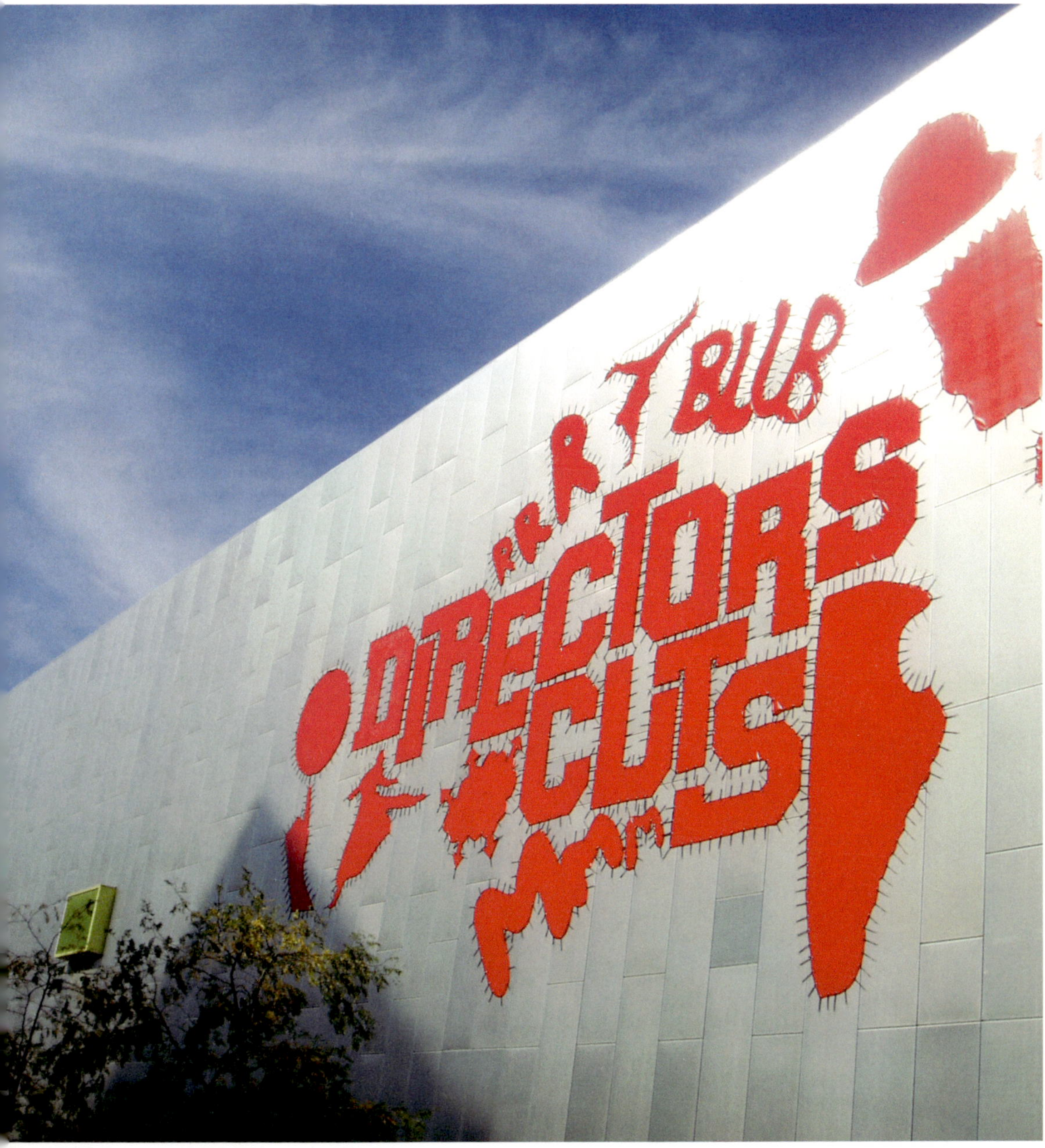

DIRECTORS
CUTS

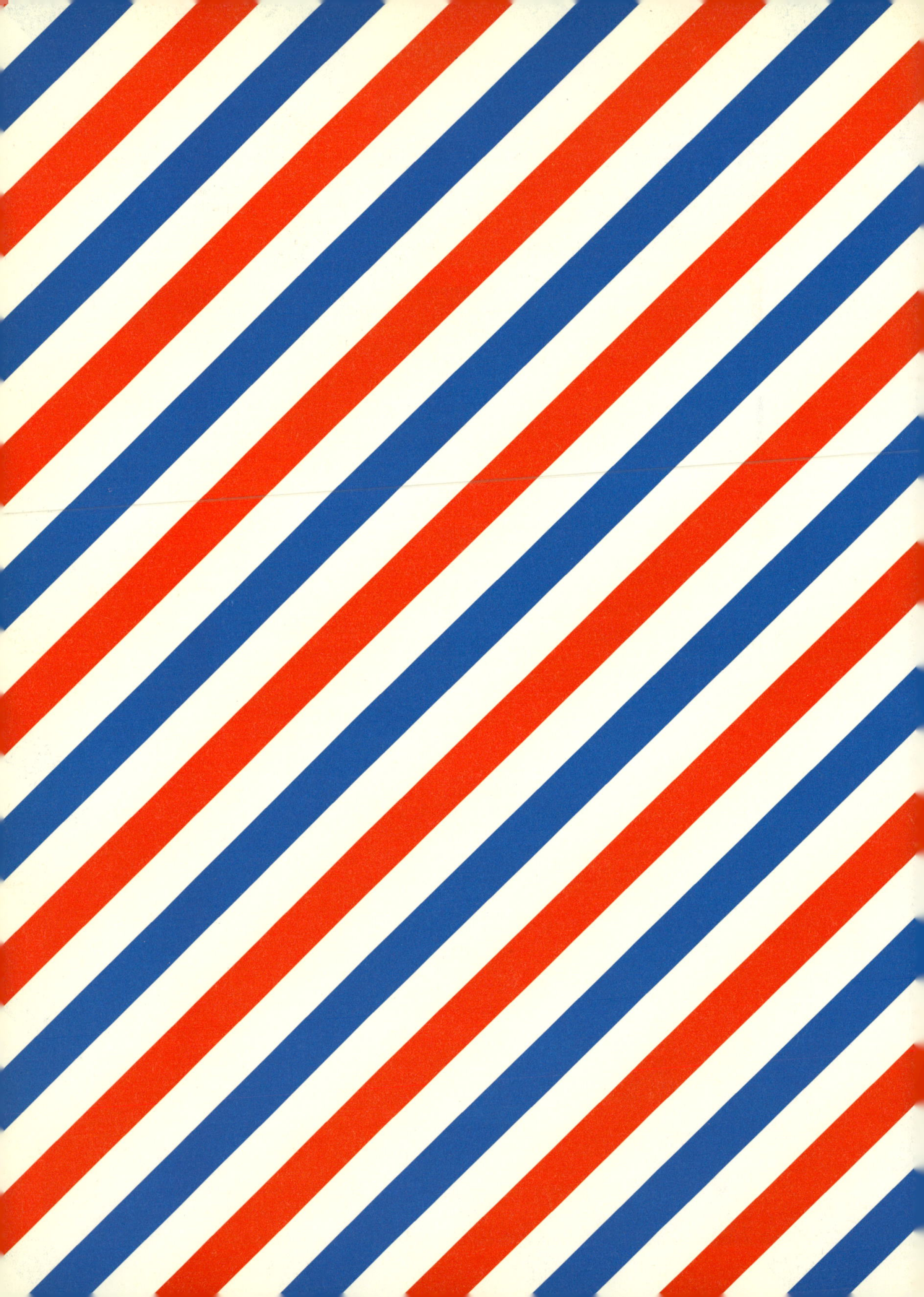

Postcards from Holland

We decided to ask the designers for a little extra collaboration.

"Can you send us a postcard?
It can be bought or hand-made,
and please include a small message.
Also if you have ever designed a postage stamp please include it, we'd love to see them!"

These small crafted graphic design pieces have been all been handed in via conventional mail, nothing digital about them.
Some were personally designed while others were chosen. Some have been damaged others personally stamped and one from the studio Machine got lost on the way...

Herman van Bostelen

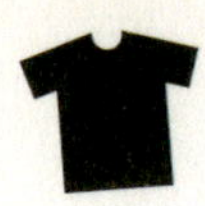

www.patatbetreft.nl
www.hermanvanbostelen.nl
www.volkskrant.nl/gorilla

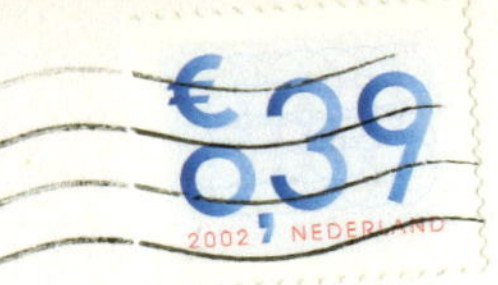

Tomoko Sakamoto
Actar
Roca i Batlle 2
08023 Barcelona
Spain

Kind regards,
Herman van Bostelen

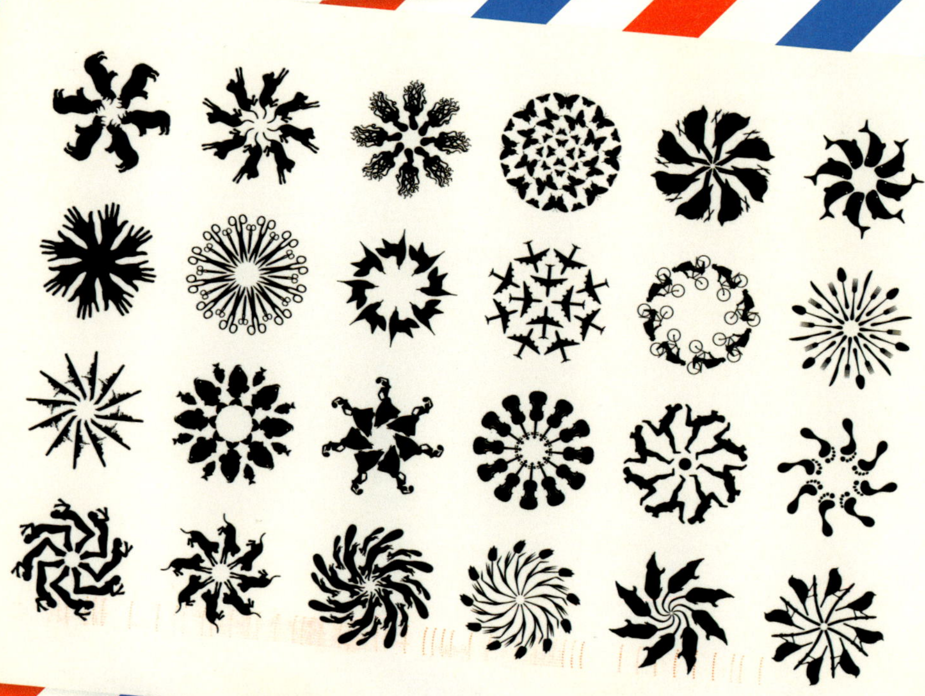

Boomerang supports design.
"It's about the oil, stupid!"
© De Designpolitie
Download free screensaver at www.designpolitie.nl

BOOMERANG

BOOMERANG FREECARDS POSTBUS 763 1000 AT AMSTERDAM WWW.BOOMERANG.NL

TPGPOST PORT BETAALD

koninklijke tpg post
port betaald

Designp

Dear Tomoko,

A piece of old media by De Designpolitie.

Yours, Richard

P.S. STAMPS MADE BY US!

ACTAR
TOMOKO SAKAMOTO
ROCA i BATLLE 2
08023 BARCELONA
SPAIN

Hansje van Halem

I sent this card to all my contacts on the day the stamp was released to present my new stamp. Because I was too subliminal most people thanked me for my moving-card. Some people knew something was ‹wrong› with it, and figured out it was all about the stamp. Instead of learning from my mistakes, I decided to send you this card as well. (Stamps designed by Hansje van Halem)

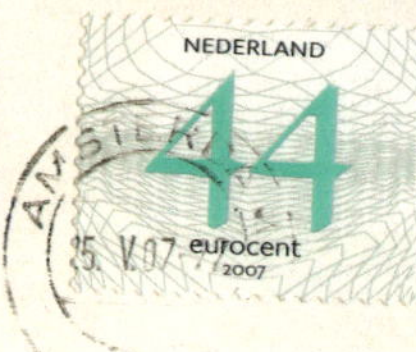

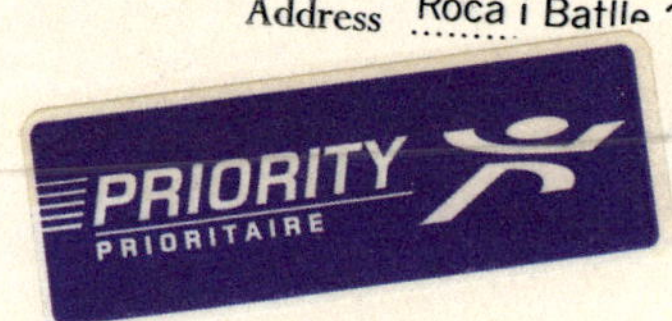

To: Tomoko Sakamoto

Actar

Address Roca i Batlle 2

Post Code: 08023 Barcelona

Country: Spain

Sender.: Hansje van Halem, graphic design
Berberisstraat 16 - 1032 EL AMSTERDAM - NL
+ 31 (0)6 - 412 415 46 - hansje@hansje-net - www-hansje-net

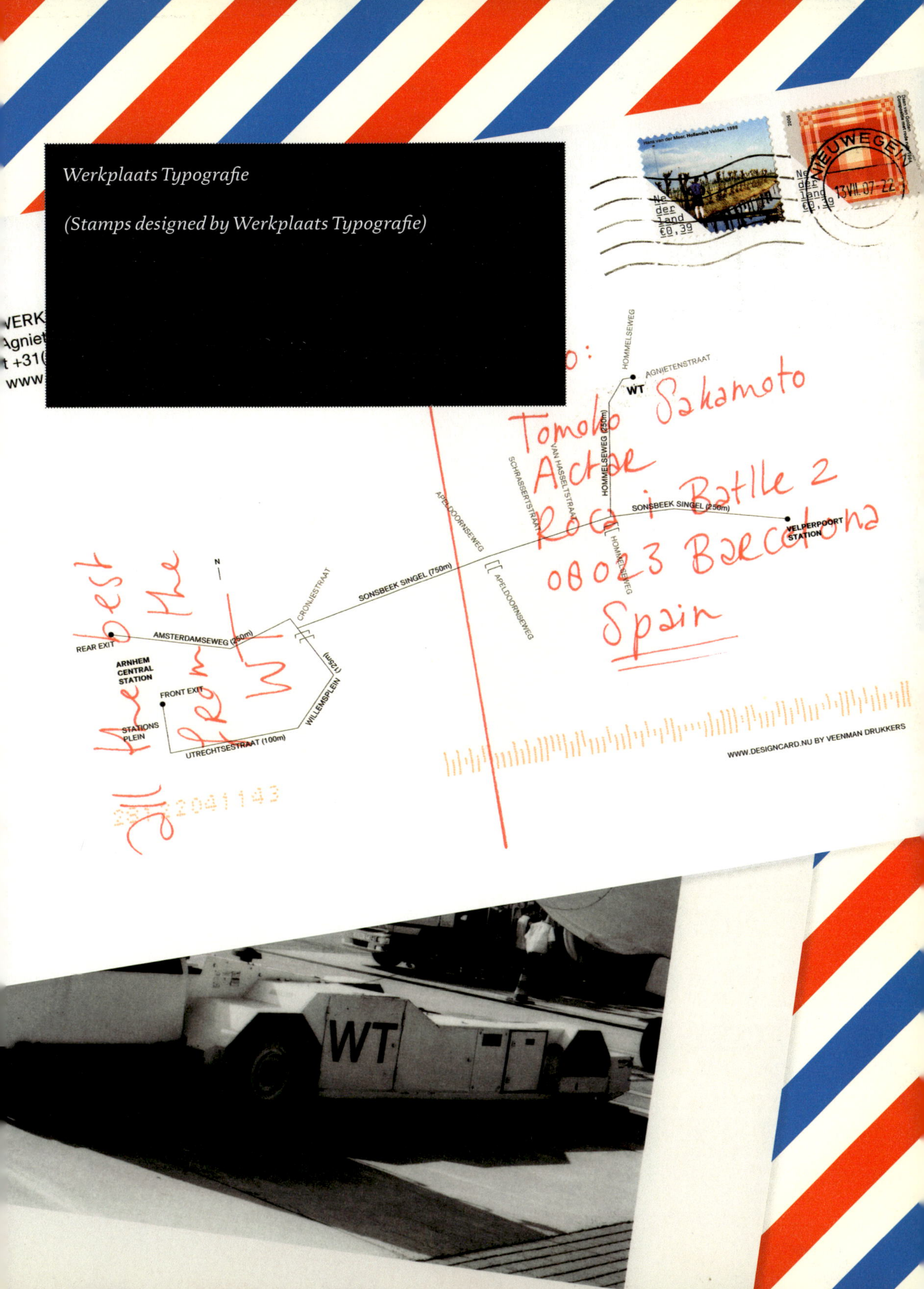

Werkplaats Typografie

(Stamps designed by Werkplaats Typografie)

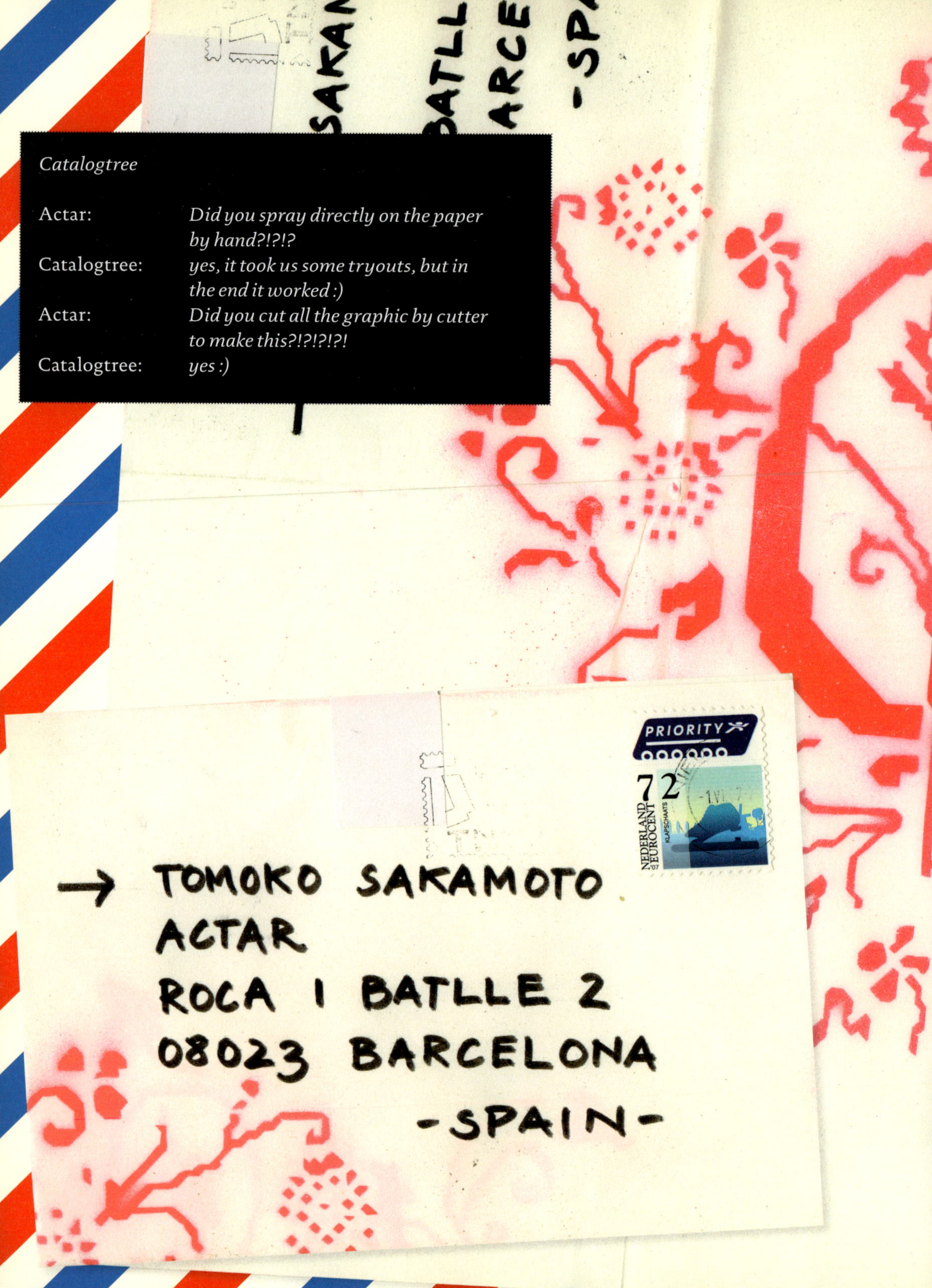

Catalogtree

Actar:	*Did you spray directly on the paper by hand?!?!?*
Catalogtree:	*yes, it took us some tryouts, but in the end it worked :)*
Actar:	*Did you cut all the graphic by cutter to make this?!?!?!?!*
Catalogtree:	*yes :)*

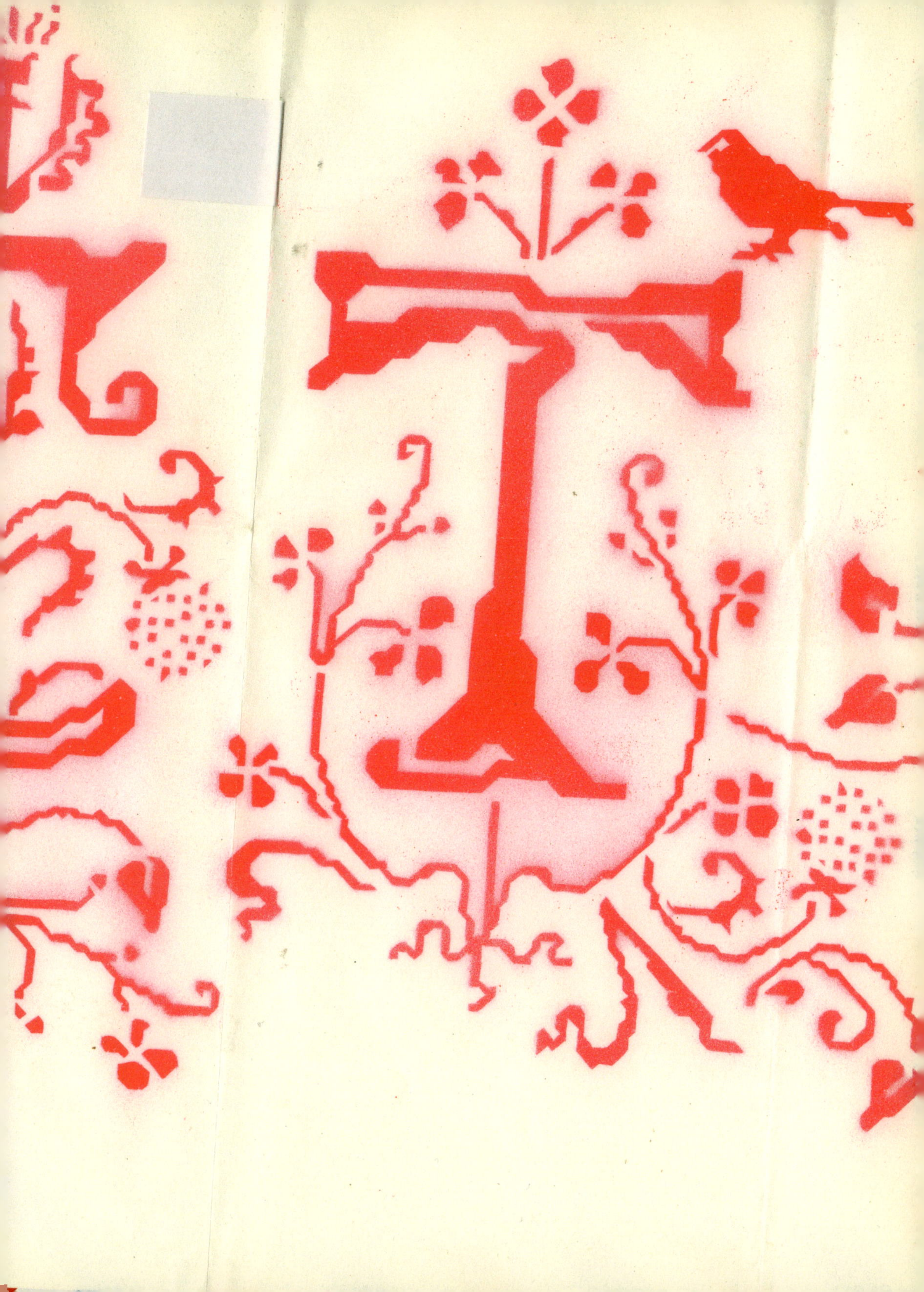

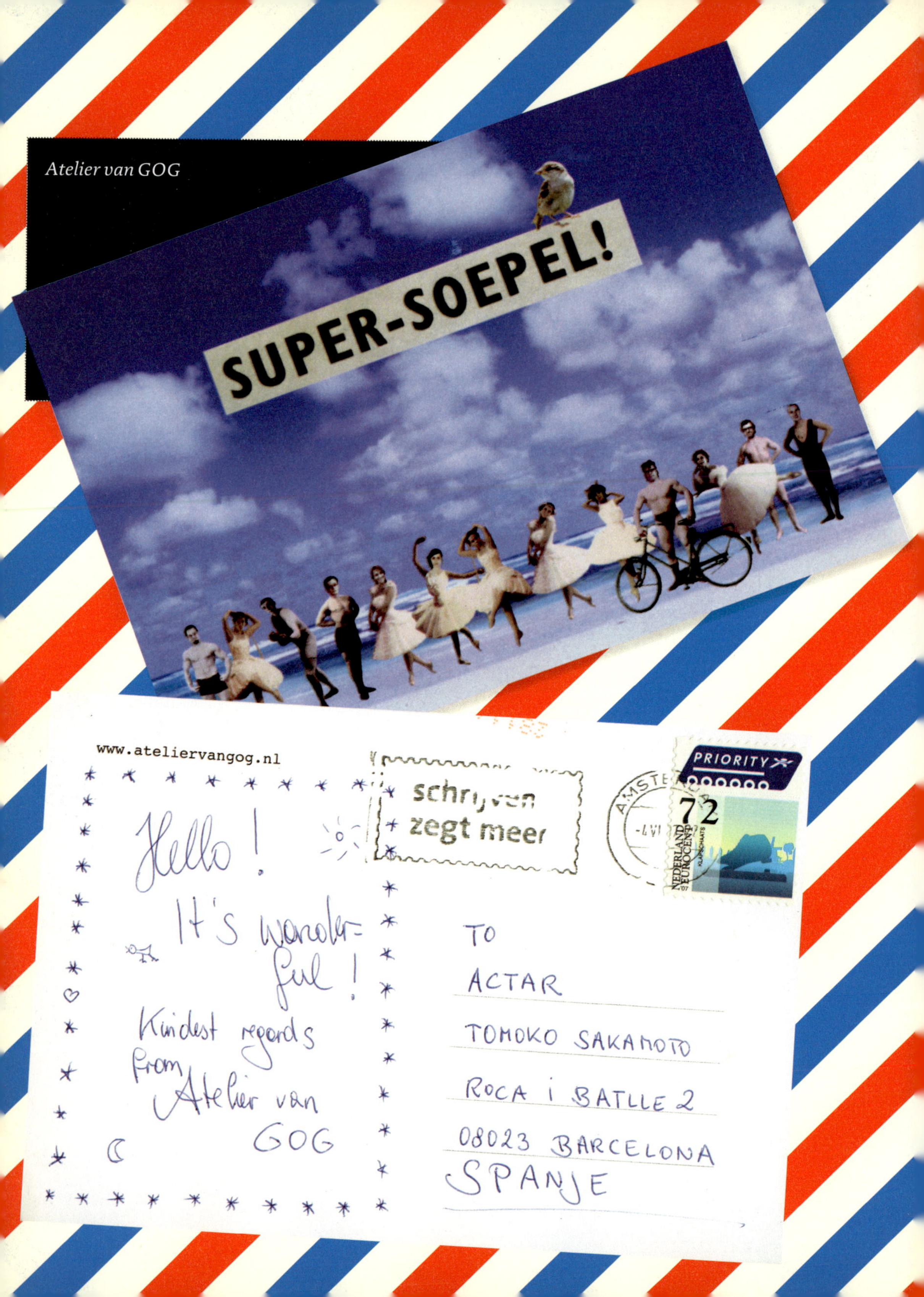

Atelier van GOG

SUPER-SOEPEL!

www.ateliervangog.nl

schrijven zegt meer

Hello!

It's wonderful!

Kindest regards from Atelier van GOG

TO
ACTAR
TOMOKO SAKAMOTO
ROCA I BATLLE 2
08023 BARCELONA
SPANJE

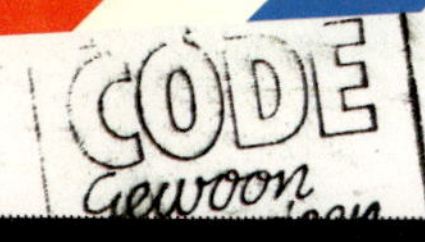
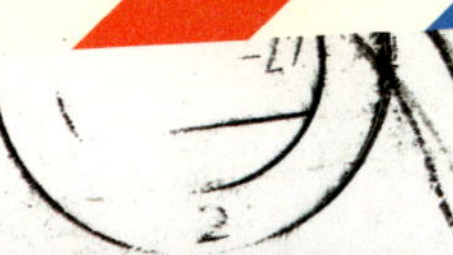
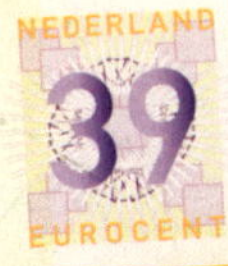
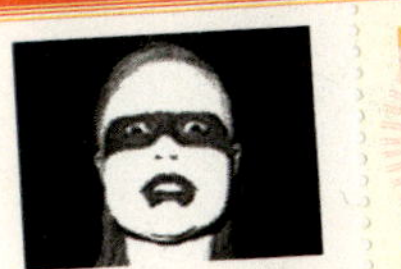
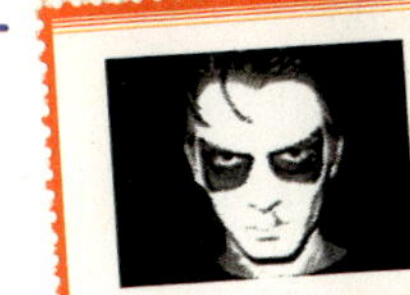

Experimental Jetset

Stamp:
http://www.tntpost.nl/voorthuis/postzegels/eigen-postzegels-maken

Images:
Experimental Jetset self portraits ‹Black Metal Machine› (1998), from an installation in a group exhibition ‹Supernova›, SMBA / Stedelijk Museum Bureau Amsterdam (www.smba.nl/en/exhibitions/supernova/)

Harmen Liemburg

(Stamps designed by Harmen Liemburg & Richard Niessen)

Tomoko Sakamoto
Actar
Roca i Batlle 2
08023 Barcelona
Spanje

1. This is one of the 6 stamps Richard Niessen & me designed in 2001. It's one of the most fun commercial jobs we did, and I'm still proud of it!
2. A new one by Hansje van Halem. Her work is precise & looks computer-like, but is actually very handcrafted.
3. See you in Barcelona, Tomoko!
4. Oh yes, my favourite place must be the library, as it enables me to travel mentally, and, like this card, provides me with the materials for my graphic work.

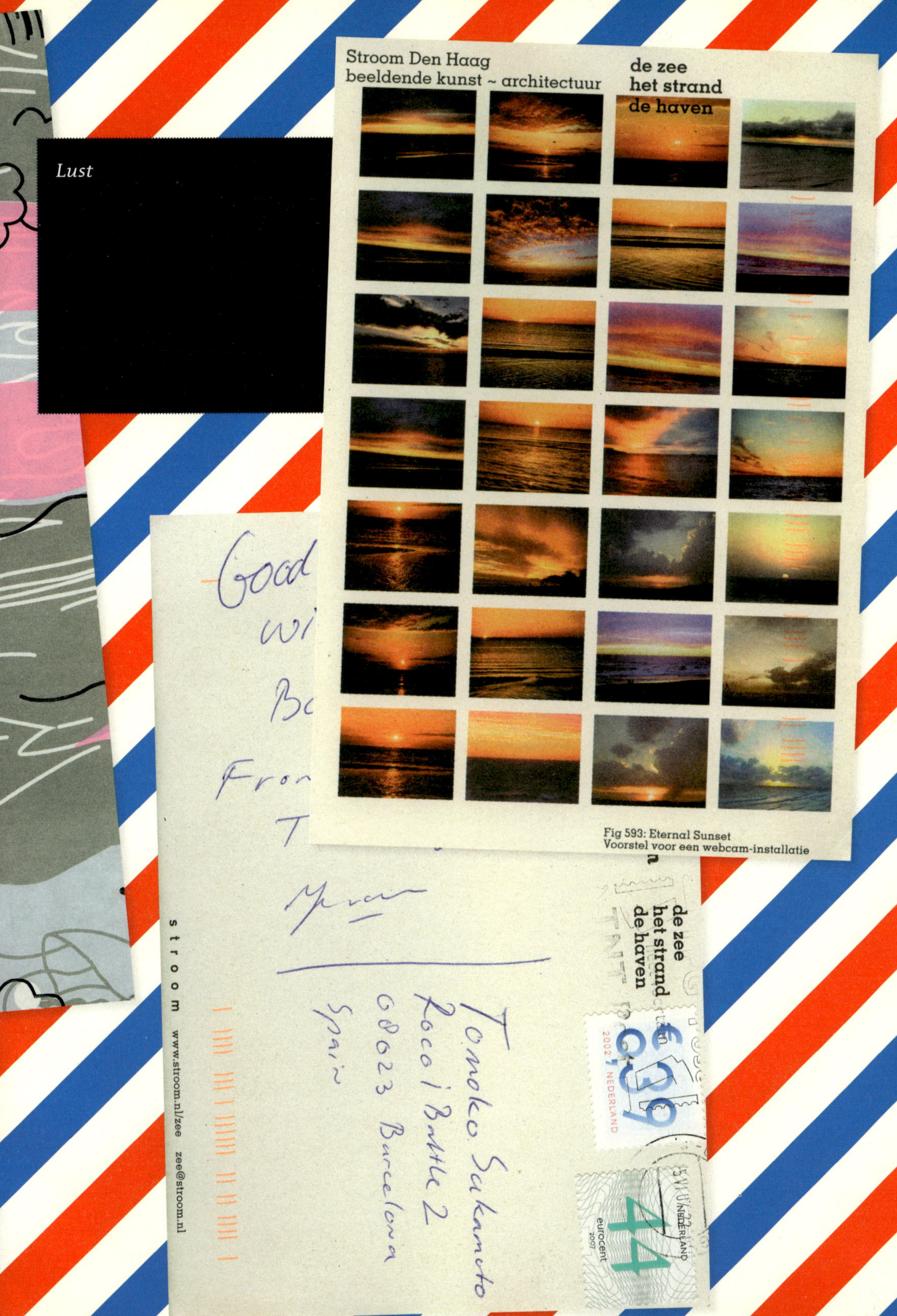
Lust
Stroom Den Haag
beeldende kunst ~ architectuur
de zee
het strand
de haven
Fig 593: Eternal Sunset
Voorstel voor een webcam-installatie
stroom www.stroom.nl/zee zee@stroom.nl
de zee
het strand
de haven
2002 NEDERLAND
€0,39
NEDERLAND
eurocent 2007
44

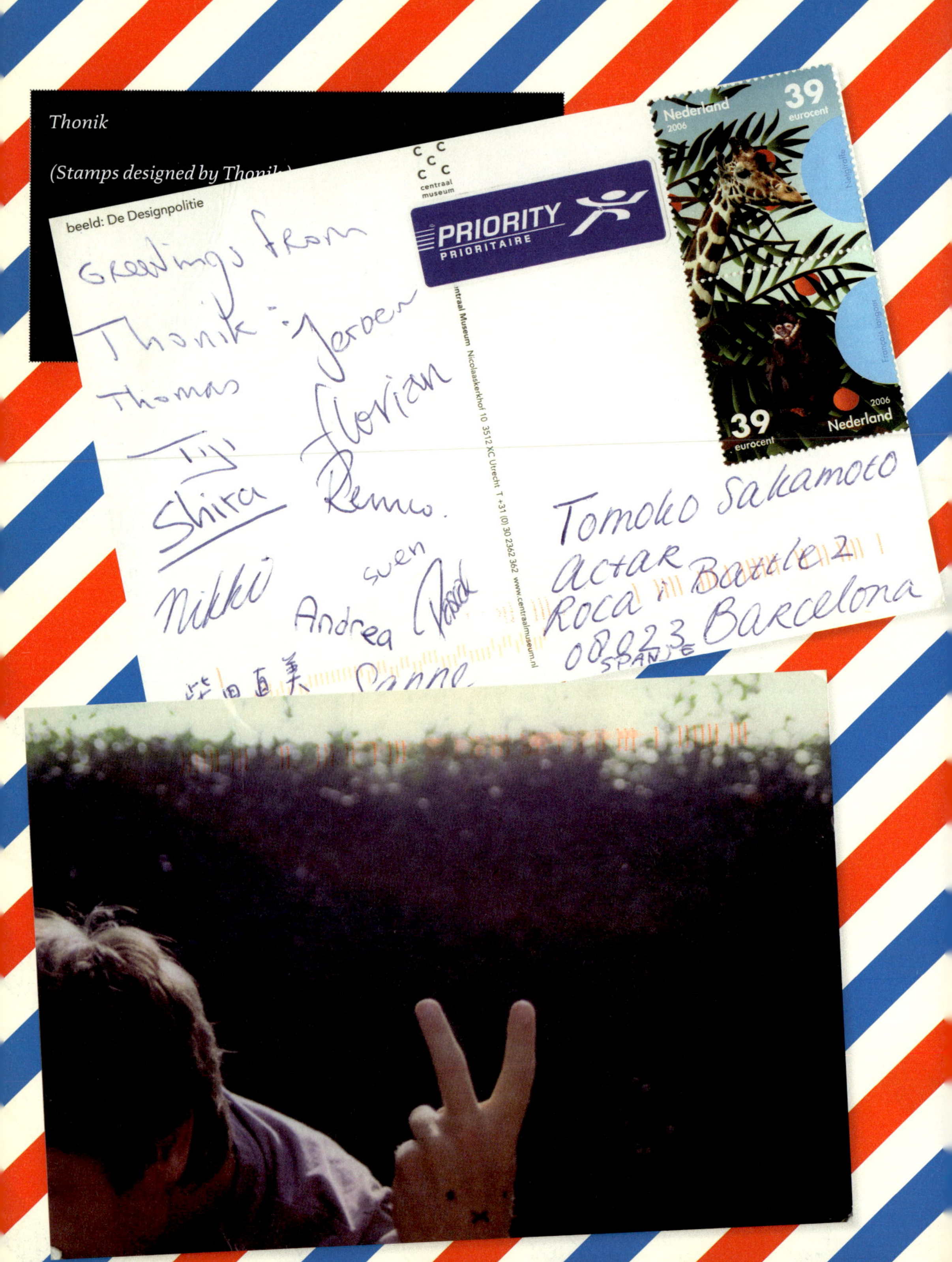

Thonik

(Stamps designed by Thoni

Studio Kluif

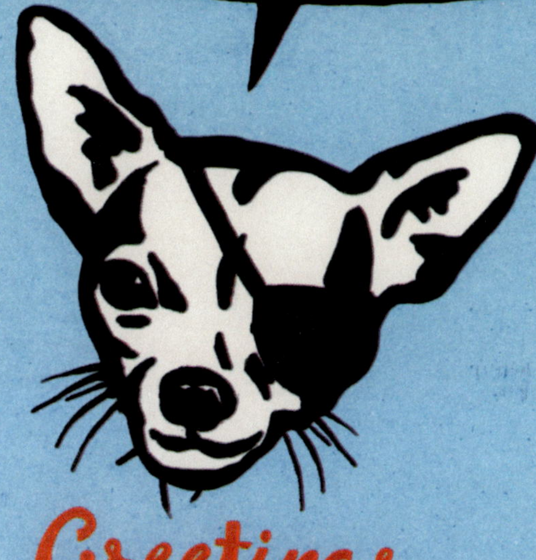

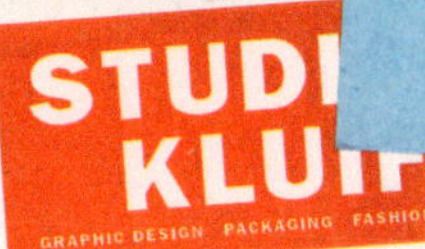

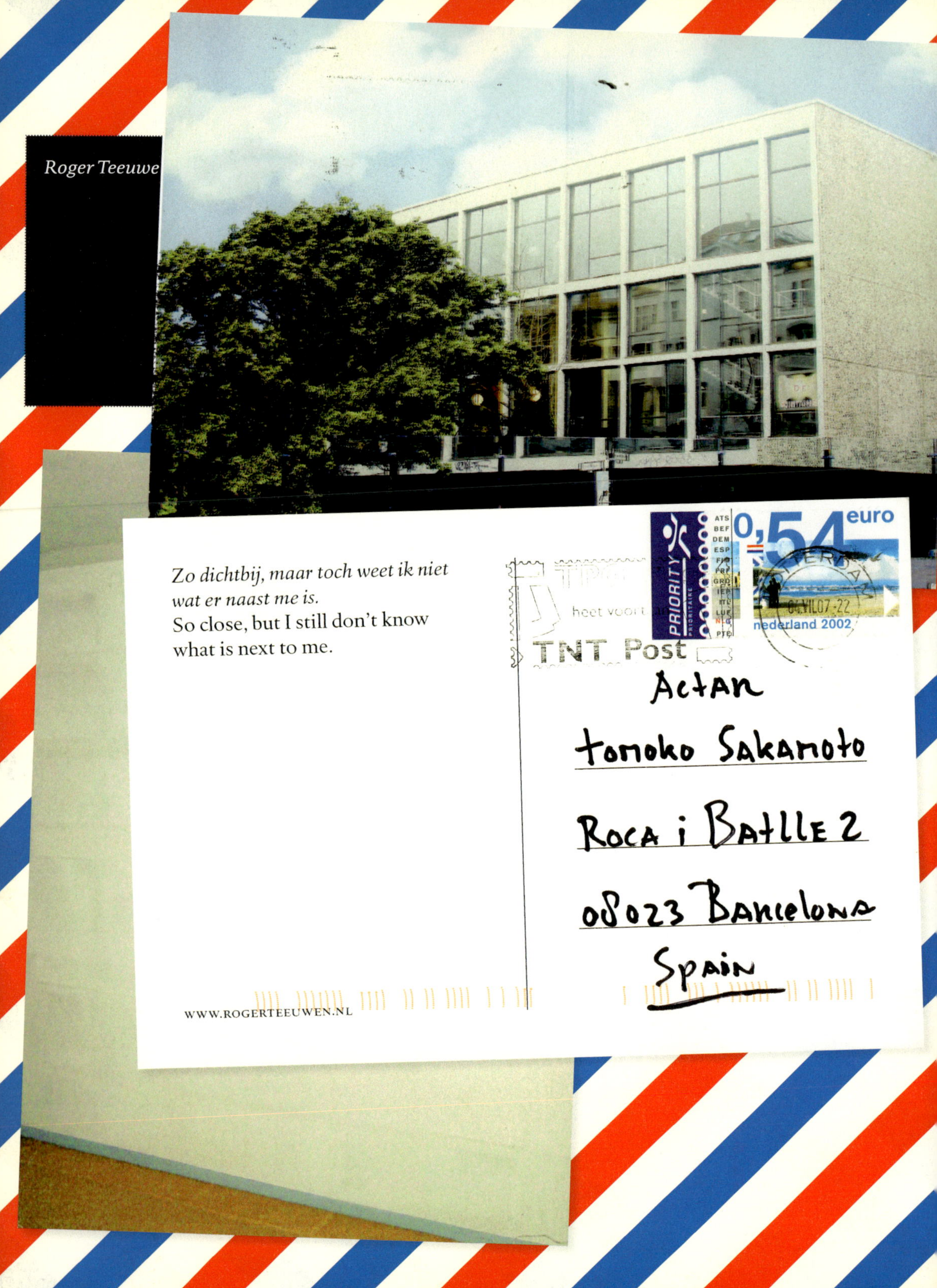
Roger Teeuwe
Zo dichtbij, maar toch weet ik niet wat er naast me is.
So close, but I still don't know what is next to me.
WWW.ROGERTEEUWEN.NL
PRIORITY
0,54 euro
nederland 2002
TNT Post
Actar
tomoko Sakamoto
Roca i Batlle 2
08023 Barcelona
Spain

Minke Themans
Hello T
Sunshine
Rotterd
Best,
Minke
10 years
SMT
www.studiominkethemans.nl

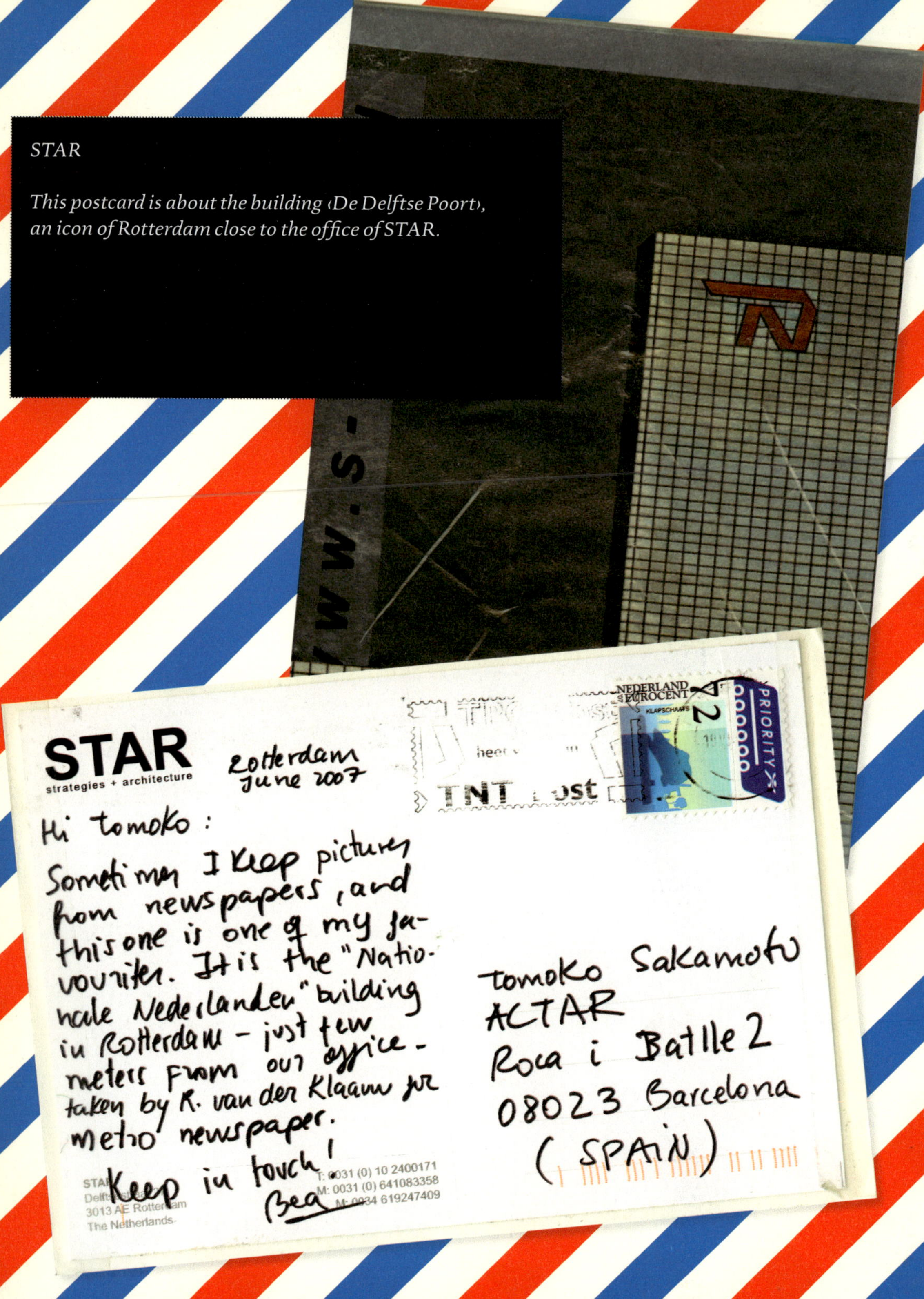

STAR
strategies + architecture

Rotterdam
June 2007

Hi tomoko:

Sometimes I keep pictures from newspapers, and this one is one of my favourites. It is the "Nationale Nederlanden" building in Rotterdam - just few meters from our office - taken by R. van der Klaauw for metro newspaper.

Keep in touch!

Bea

Tomoko Sakamoto
ACTAR
Roca i Batlle 2
08023 Barcelona
(SPAIN)

STAR
Delft...
3013 AE Rotterdam
The Netherlands

T: 0031 (0) 10 2400171
M: 0031 (0) 641083358
M: 0034 619247409

STAR

This postcard is about the building ‹De Delftse Poort›, an icon of Rotterdam close to the office of STAR.

Office of CC

We love these romantic old post cards, aren't they a beauty. We don't recall to whom the post card was addressed to, we only remember it was to someone who lived in the Hague. On the back of the card, we can try to figure out what the small text reads. Sometimes it could be very touching, sweet or very funny messages. We once had this post card of a certain hospital (from the 40's, I think), the card was written by a patient there to his relative, and he was only complaining about the pain he was having.

(Stamps designed by Chris Vermaas in 1992)

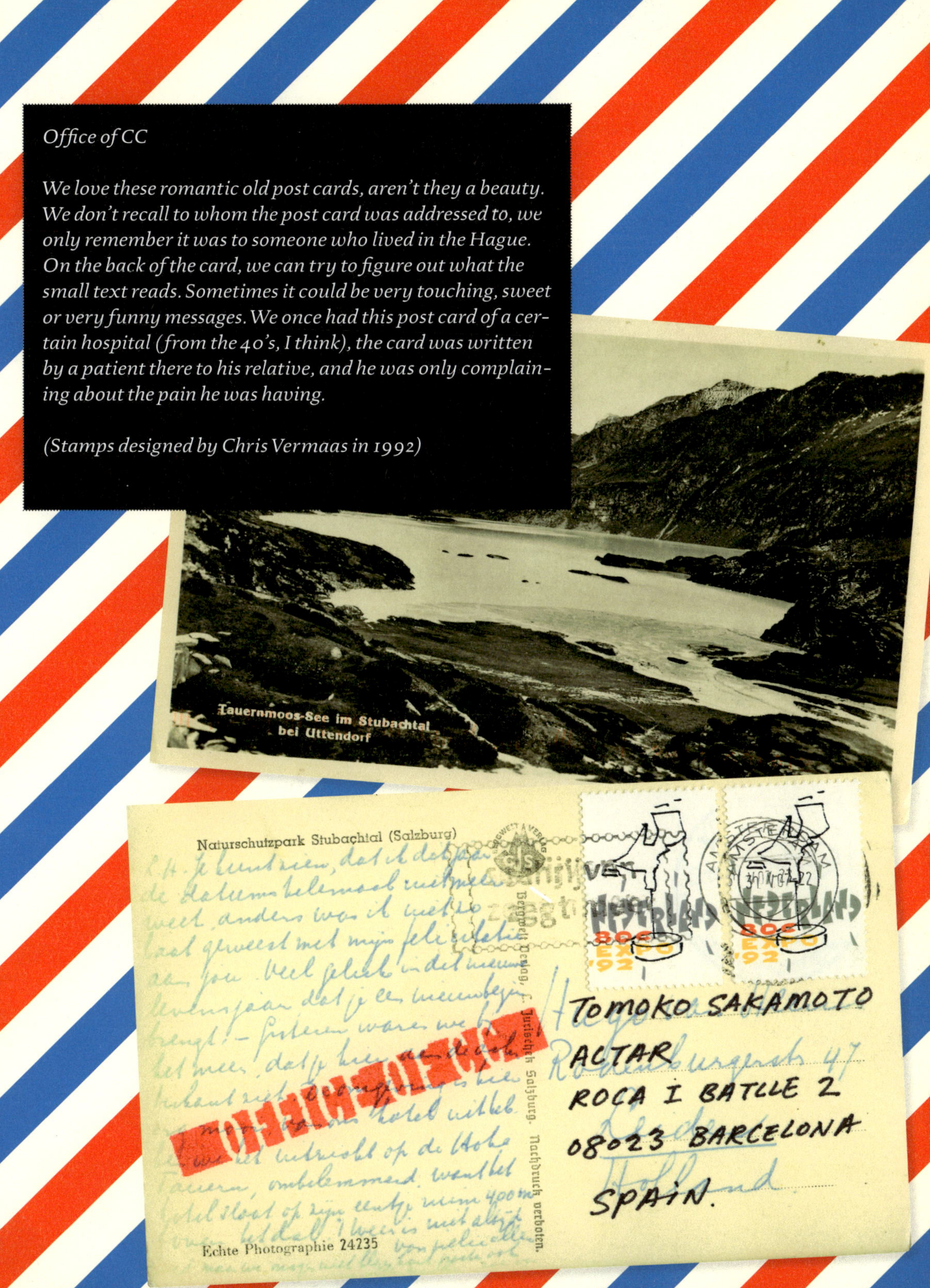

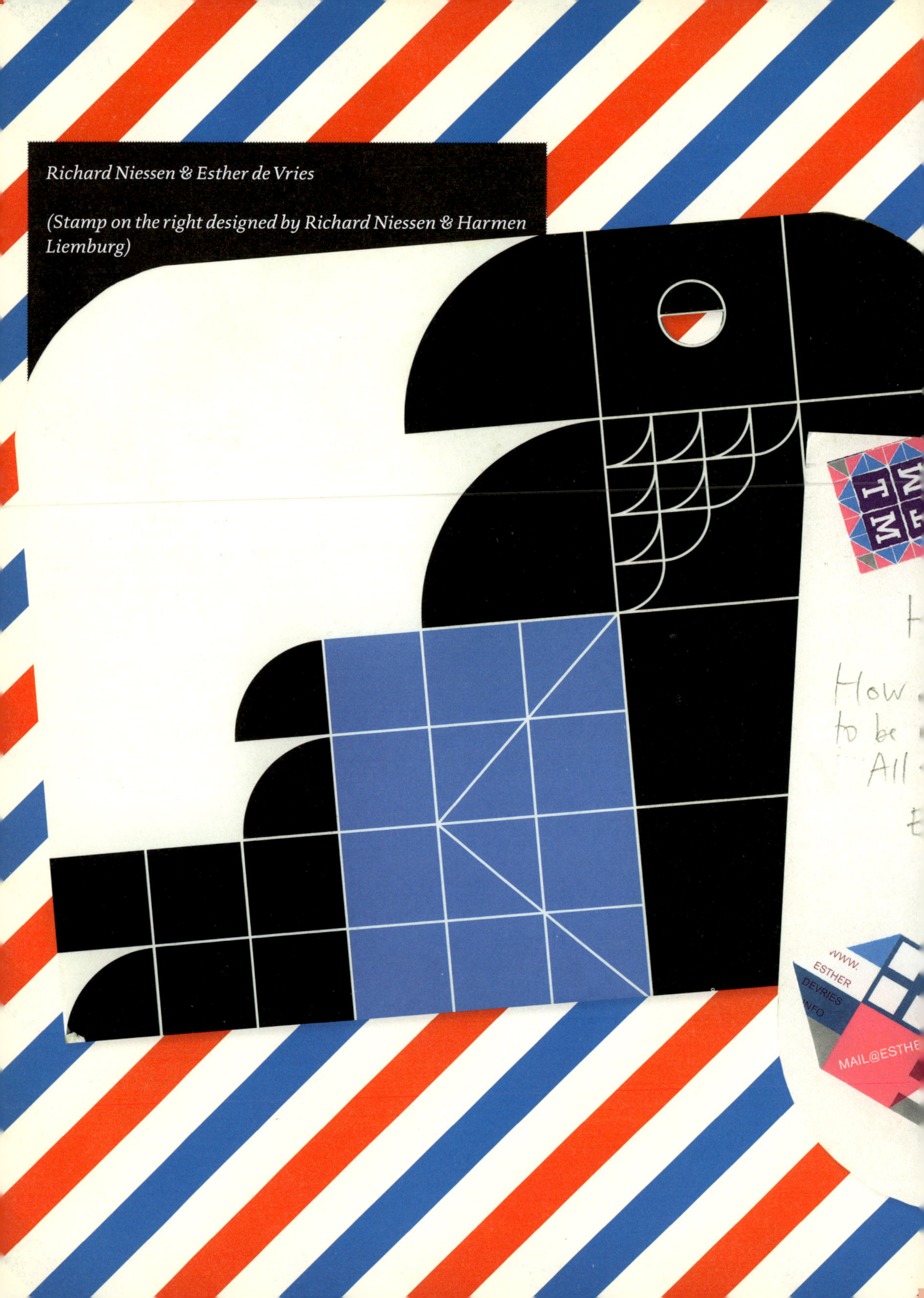

Richard Niessen & Esther de Vries

(Stamp on the right designed by Richard Niessen & Harmen Liemburg)

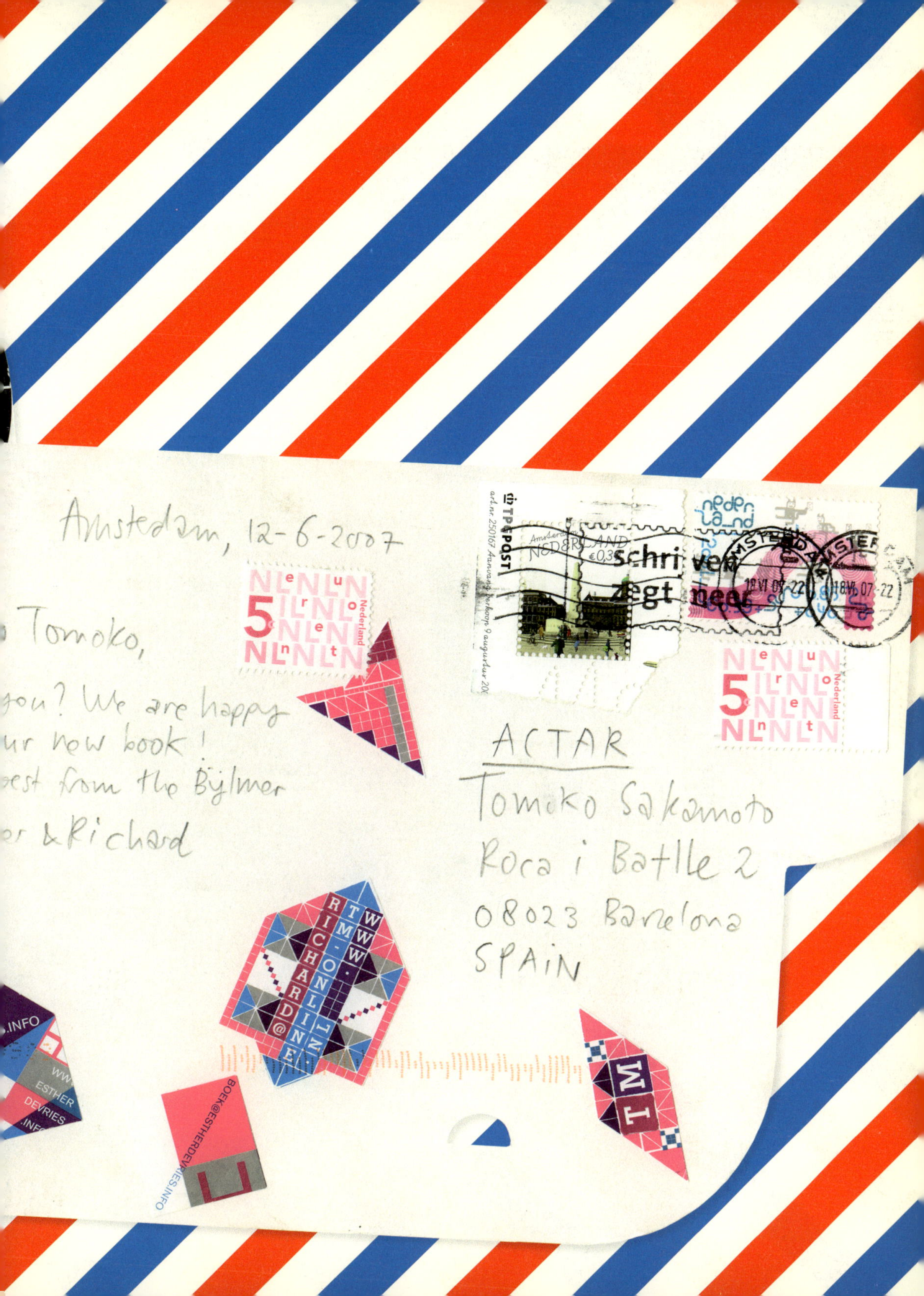
Amsterdam, 12-6-2007
Tomoko,
you? We are happy
ur new book!
best from the Bijlmer
er & Richard
ACTAR
Tomoko Sakamoto
Roca i Batlle 2
08023 Barcelona
SPAIN
TPG POST
Nederland
schrijven zegt meer
BOEK@ESTHERDEVRIES.INFO
WWW.RIM-ONLINE.NL
RICHARD@

zonder titel, nr. 4
Hans Gremmen / Petra Stavast, 2007

5/8

Hans Gremmen

return ticket
Hans Gremmen / Petra Stavast, 2006

1/8

NEDERLAND 44 eurocent 2007

NEDERLAND 44 eurocent 2007

AMSTERDAM

Hello tomoko,

many greetings,

Hans

TOMOKO
SAKAMOTO
ACTAR
ROCA I BATLLE 2
08023
Barcelona, Spain

PRIORITY
PRIORITAIRE

TOMOKO

zonder titel, nr. 6
Hans Gremmen / Petra Stavast, 2007

7/8

... and
more greetings,

Hans

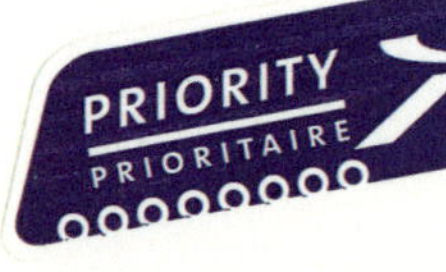

PRIORITY
PRIORITAIRE

... and again ...

Hans

TOMOK
SAKA
ACTA
ROCA
0802

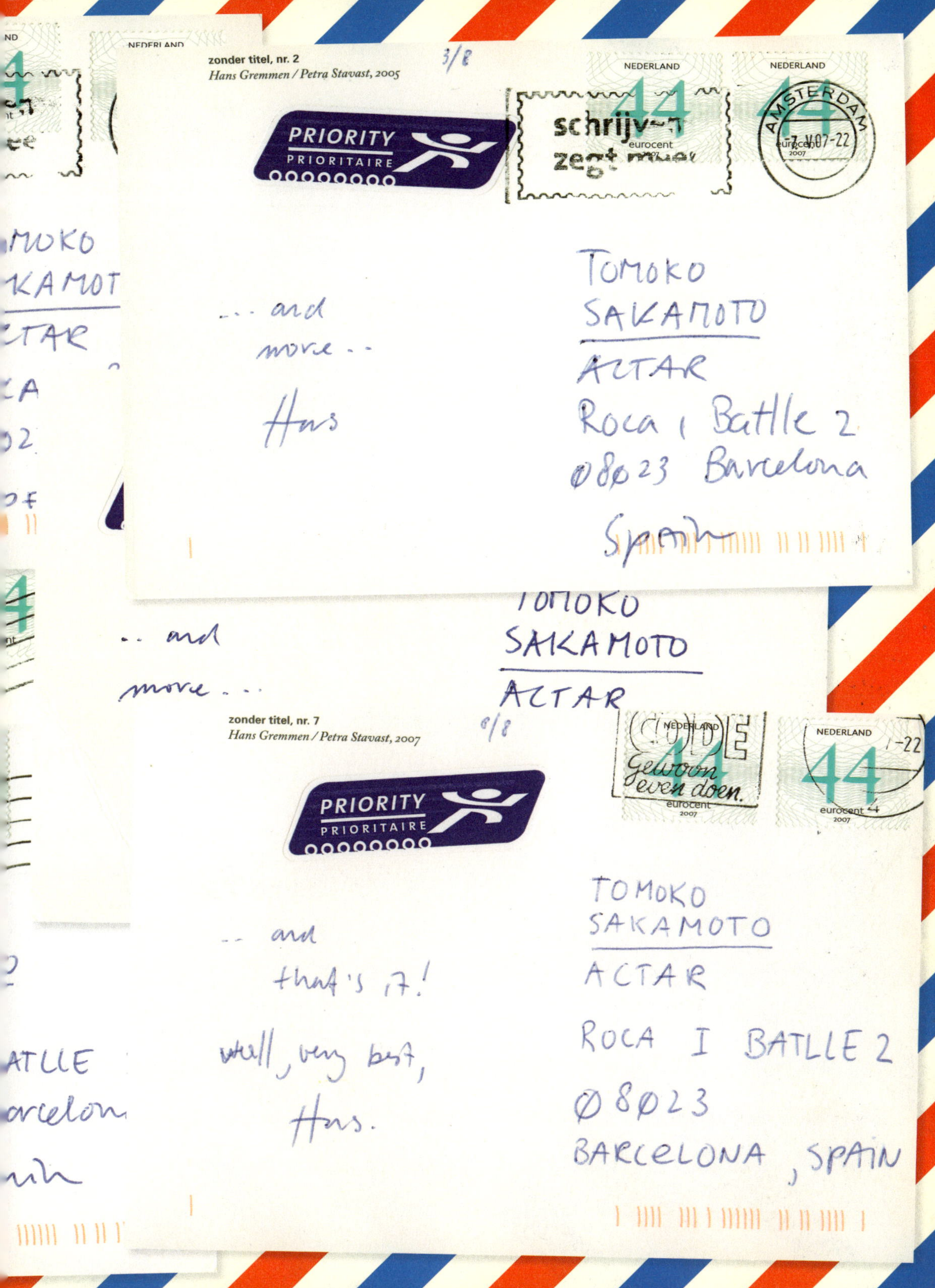
zonder titel, nr. 2
Hans Gremmen / Petra Stavast, 2005
3/8
PRIORITY
PRIORITAIRE
NEDERLAND
NEDERLAND
schrijven
zegt meer
AMSTERDAM
-7.V.07-22
eurocent
2007
... and
more ..
Hans
TOMOKO
SAKAMOTO
ACTAR
Roca i Batlle 2
08023 Barcelona
Spain
TOMOKO
SAKAMOTO
ACTAR
.. and
more ...
zonder titel, nr. 7
Hans Gremmen / Petra Stavast, 2007
8/8
PRIORITY
PRIORITAIRE
NEDERLAND
NEDERLAND
Gewoon
even doen.
eurocent
2007
.. and
that's it!
well, very best,
Hans.
TOMOKO
SAKAMOTO
ACTAR
ROCA I BATLLE 2
08023
BARCELONA, SPAIN

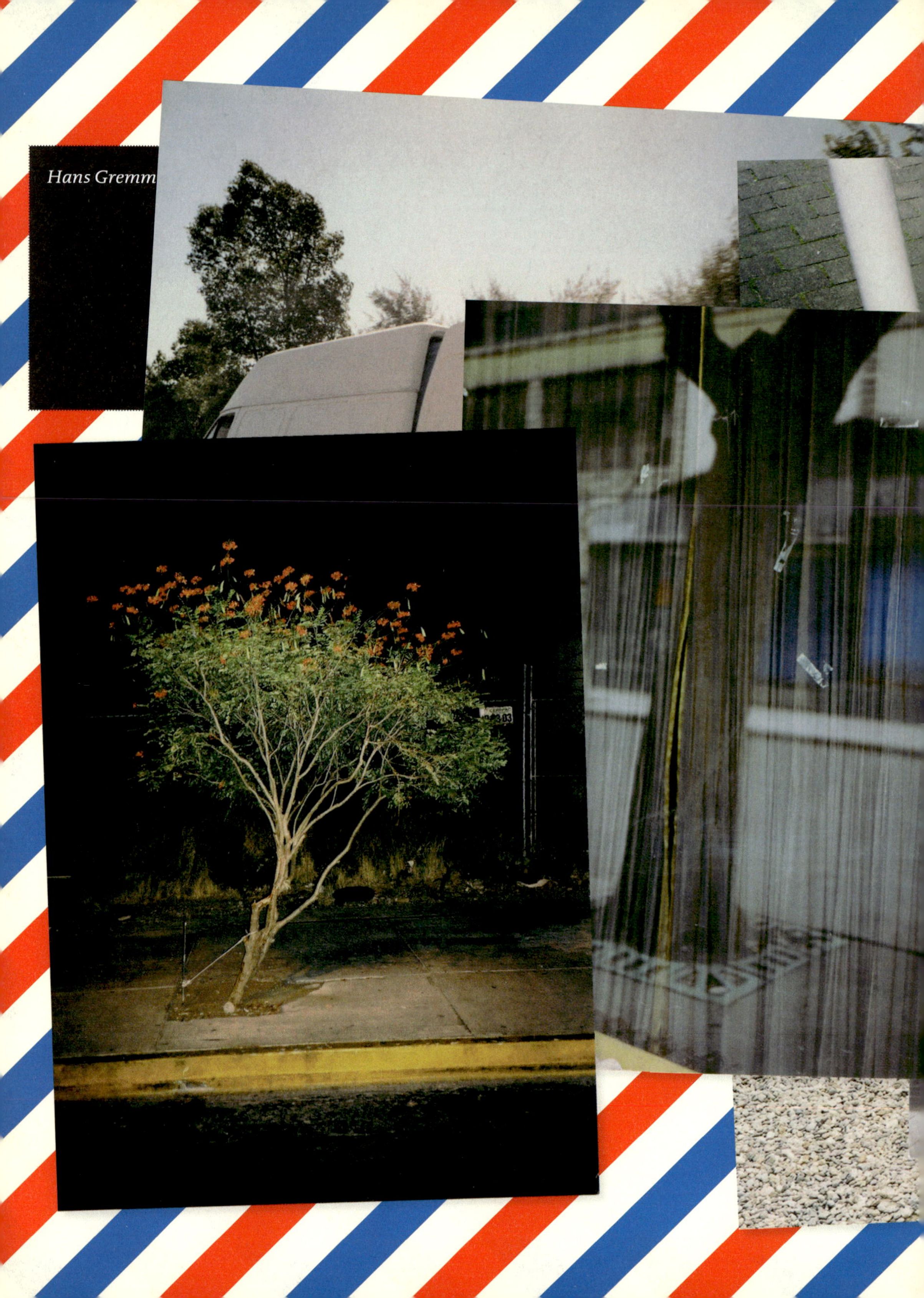
Hans Gremm

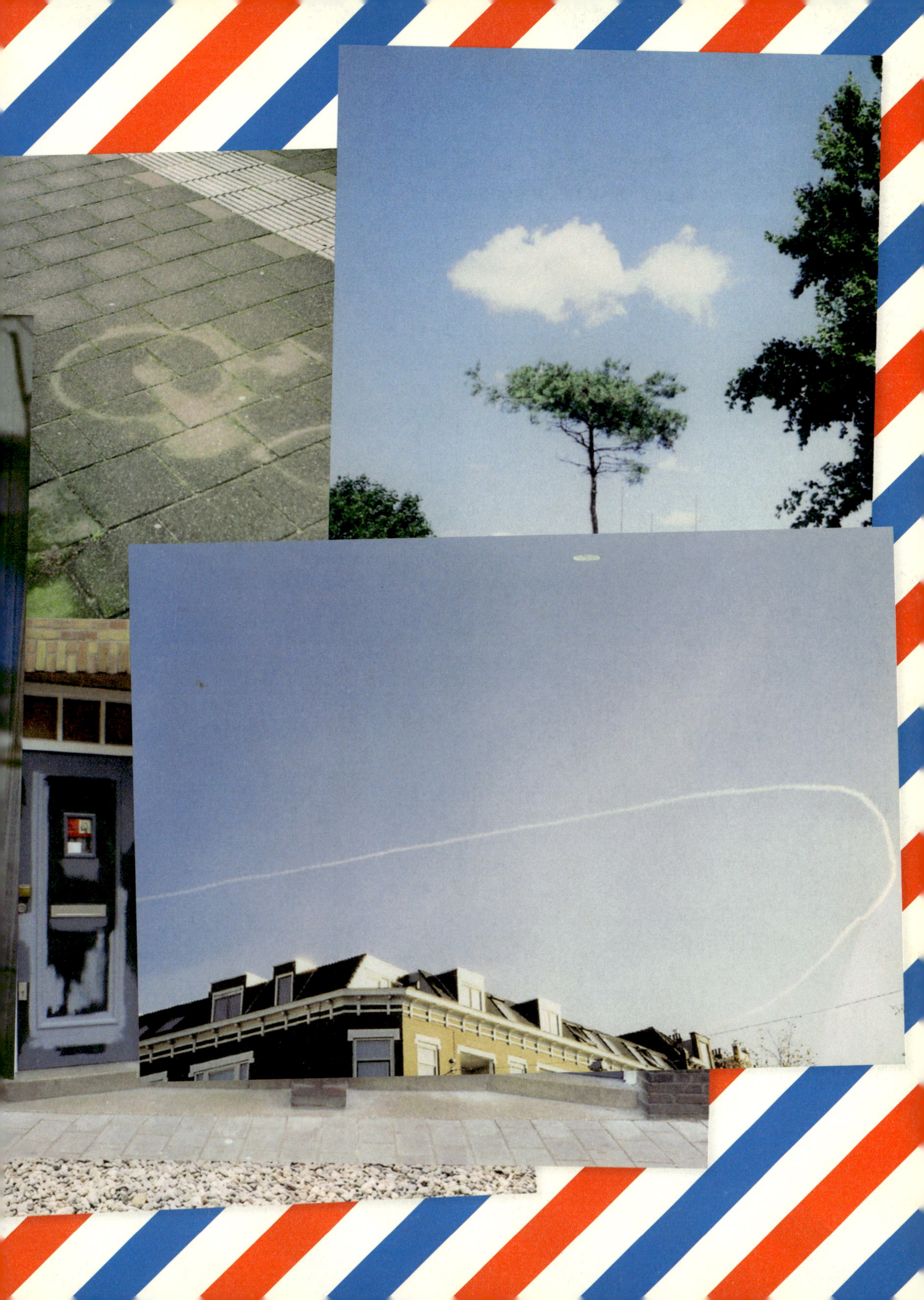

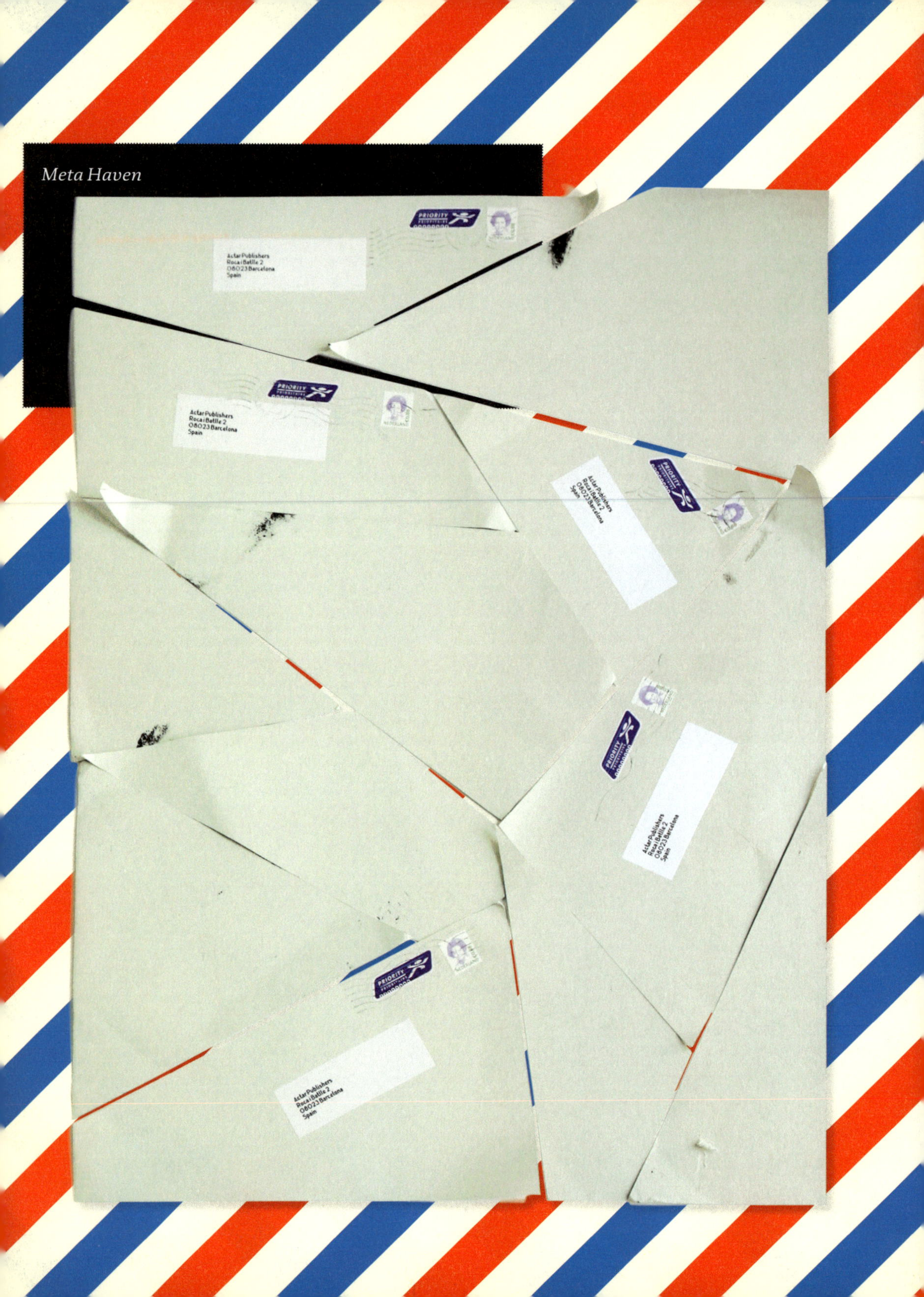
Meta Haven
PRIORITY
Actar Publishers
Roca i Batlle 2
08023 Barcelona
Spain

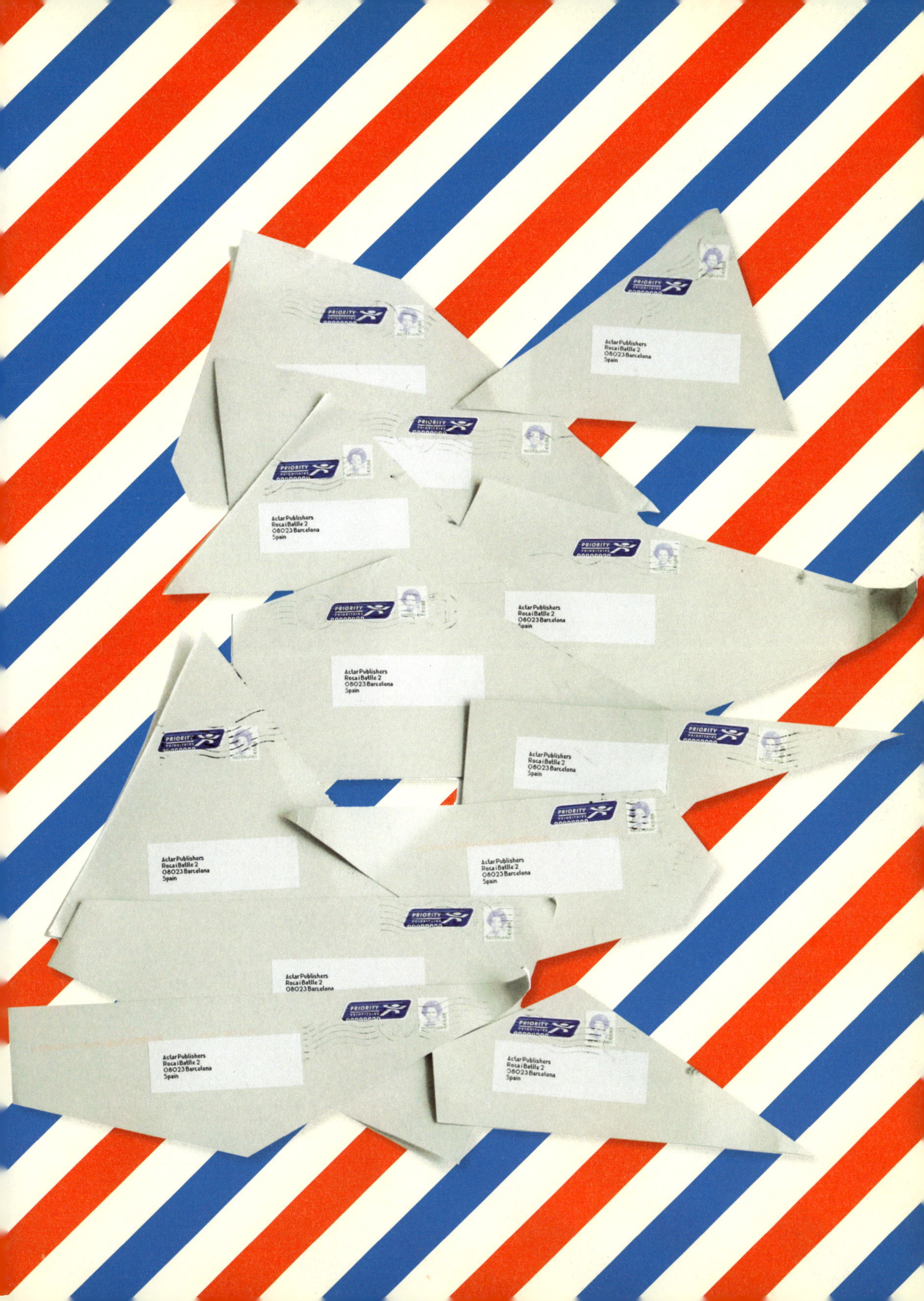
PRIORITY
Actar Publishers
Roca i Batlle 2
08023 Barcelona
Spain

Ping-pong Design

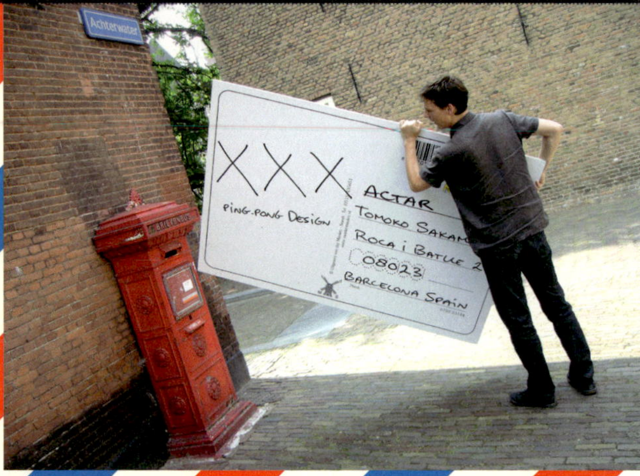

Maarten Brandenburg of Ping-pong posting a card from Rotterdam.

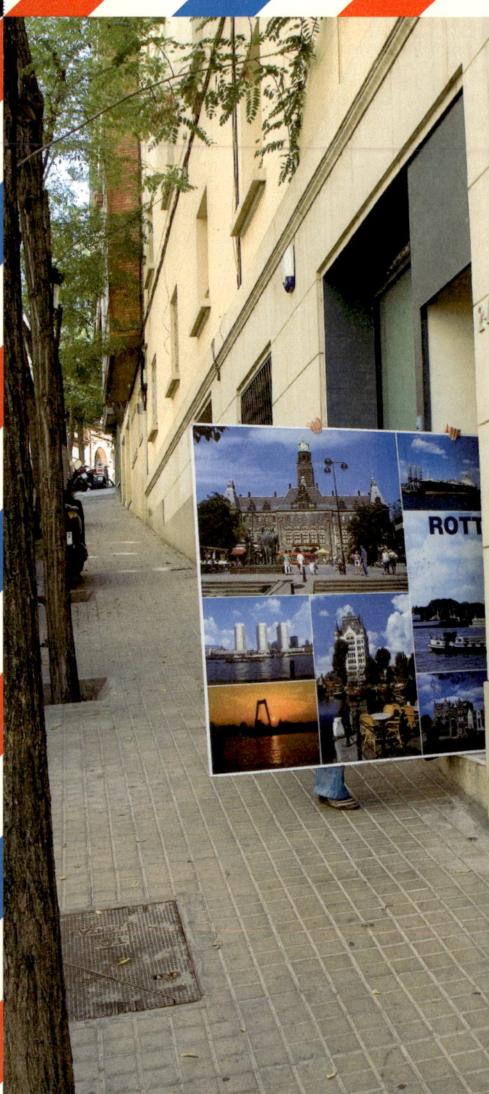

...and arrived to Actar, Barcelona.

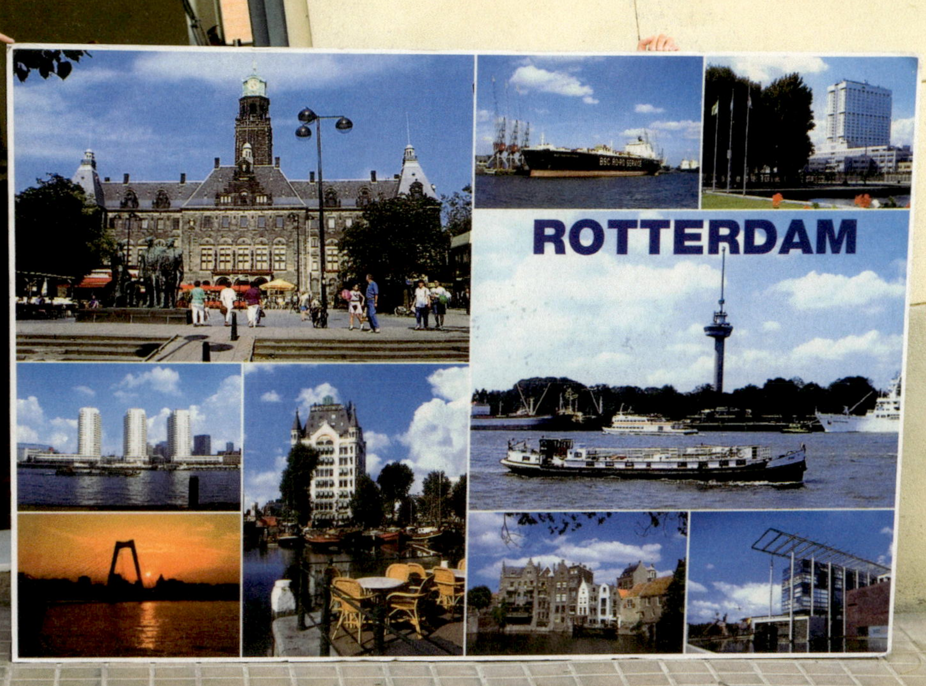
ROTTERDAM

8 712051 1010
EXCELLENT
39 EUROCENT
Nederland
XXX
PING-PONG DESIGN
ACTAR
TOMOKO SAKAMOTO
ROCA I BATLLE 2
08023
BARCELONA SPAIN
© Uitgeverij van der Meulen - Sneek Tel. (0515) 435651
www.vandermeulen.nl
76mk
6750.23144

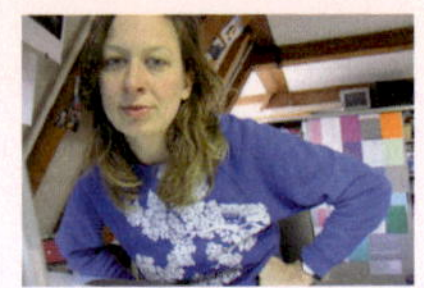

Luna Maurer

Herenmarkt 93B
1013 EC Amsterdam
The Netherlands

T +31 (0)20 6248400

www.poly-luna.com
email@poly-luna.com

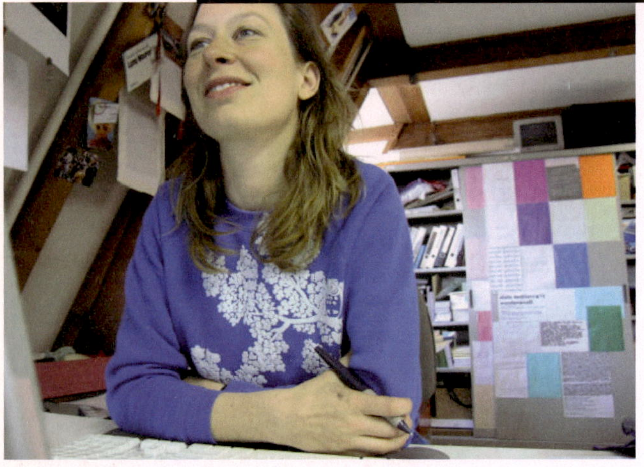

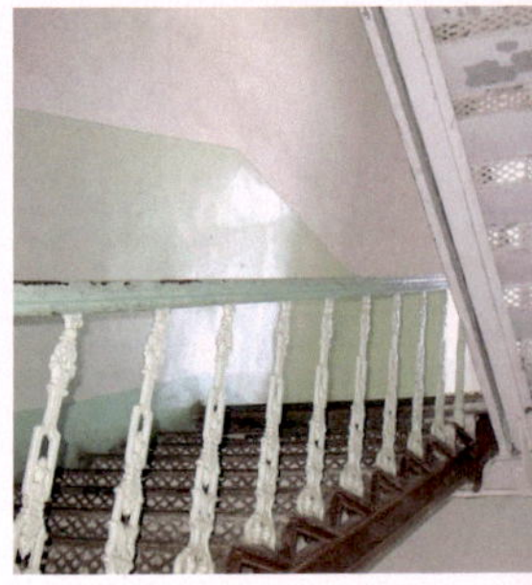

Luna Maurer was born in Stuttgart, Germany, 1972, and studied at Fachhochschule für Gestaltung Pforzheim, Germany (1995-1999), Gerrit Rietveld Academie, Amsterdam (1997-1999) and Sandberg Institute (1999-2001). She opened the studio ‹Luna Maurer› in 2001.

She works with Roel Wouters, Jonathan Puckey, Edo Paulus. She teaches in the Graphic Design dept. at Gerrit Rietveld Academie, Amsterdam, The Netherlands. She was a member of the jury for Graphic Design Municipal Art Acquisitions, Stedelijk Museum Amsterdam, 2004.

Her recent works include: Stedelijk Museum Amsterdam, catalogue ‹Drawing Typologies — Municipal Art Acquisitions›, 2007. Sandberg Institute, website www.sandberg.nl, in collaboration with Edo Paulus. 2007. Predrag Pajdic (independent curator), ‹Infocus, ongoing project across London, UK›; website and exhibition catalogue, www.infocusdialogue.org, 2007. De Balie, ‹Skycatcher›, ongoing project, sky visualizations: web, print and films, www.sky-catcher.nl, 2005-2007. 10 years Lust, ‹City-walk›, in collaboration with Lust, The Hague, 2007.

Selected exhibitions: ‹Graphic Design in the White Cube›, 22nd International Biennale of Graphic Design, Brno, Czech Republic, 2006. ‹Inside Out, werk van jonge grafisch ontwerpers›, Netherlands Foundation for Visual Arts, Design and Architecture, 2006. ‹Grote Kunst voor kleine mensen›, Museum De Paviljoens, Almere, 2005. ‹Recent Graphic Design›, Stedelijk Museum, Amsterdam, 2005. ‹European Design Biennial›, London Design Museum, 2003. ‹Rotterdam Designprijs›, Museum Boijmans van Beuningen, Rotterdam 2003.

Awards: ‹best verzorgde boeken› (Best Dutch Books), 2005. Europrix. 2004. Prix Europa, Interactive Fiction category, 2004. Rotterdam Designprijs, 2003. Kunstaanmoedigingsprijs Amstelveen, 2002.

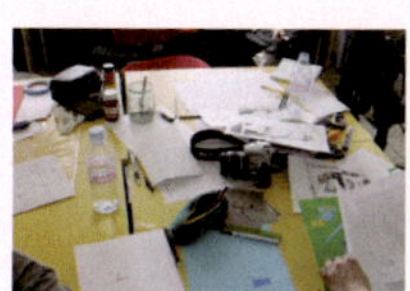

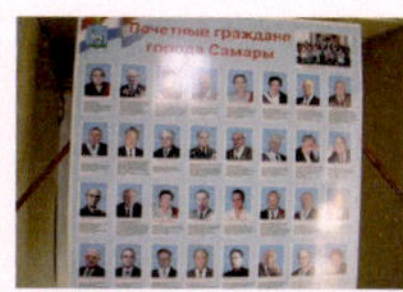

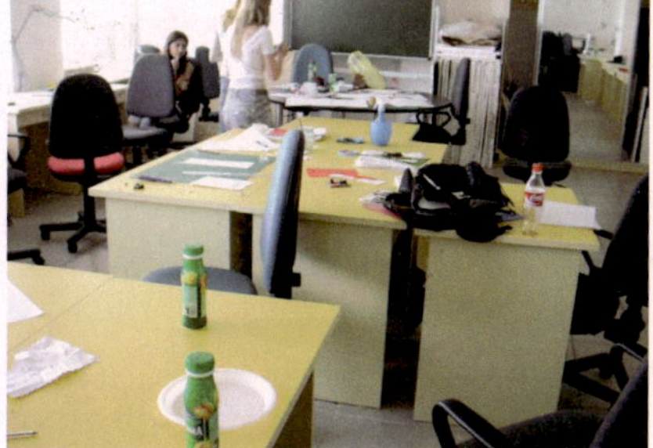

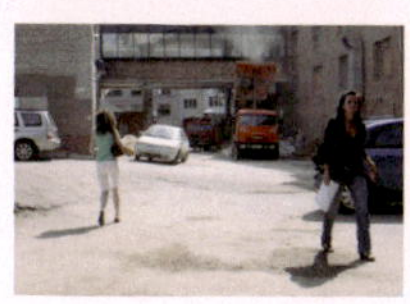

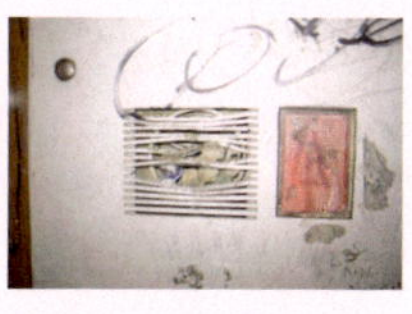

These are impressions of her stay in Samara, Russia.
The university where she runs her workshop is the University for Architecture and Engineering.
They have also a design course.

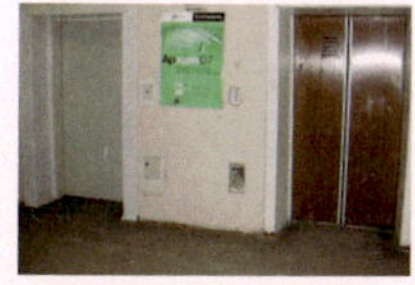

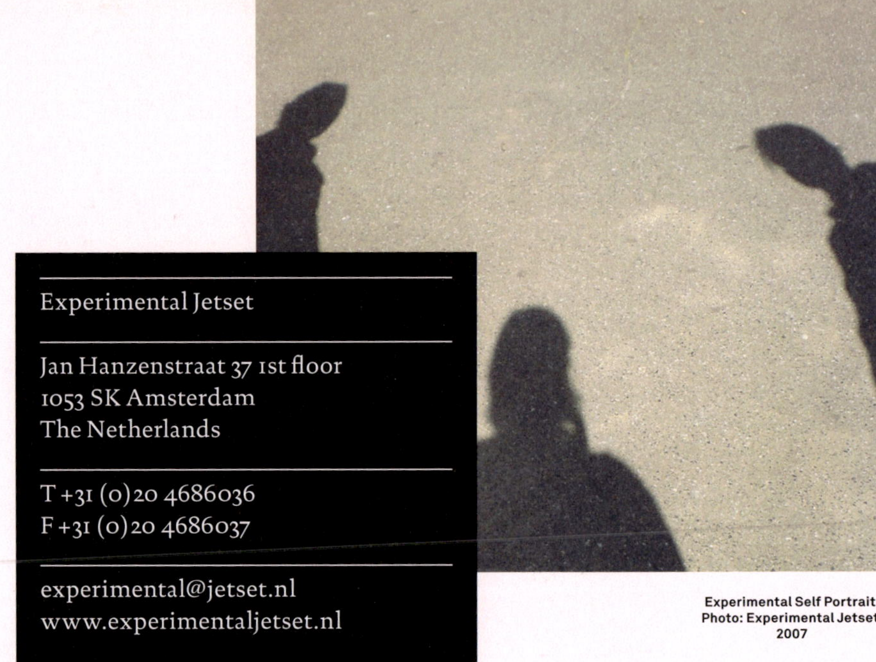

Experimental Jetset

Jan Hanzenstraat 37 1st floor
1053 SK Amsterdam
The Netherlands

T +31 (0)20 4686036
F +31 (0)20 4686037

experimental@jetset.nl
www.experimentaljetset.nl

Experimental Self Portrait,
Photo: Experimental Jetset,
2007

Experimental Jetset is an Amsterdam graphic design unit founded in 1997 by Marieke Stolk, Erwin Brinkers and Danny van den Dungen. Focusing on printed matter and installation work, Experimental Jetset have worked on projects for the Amsterdam Stedelijk Museum (SMCS), Purple Institute, Centre Pompidou, Colette, Dutch Post Group (TPG), Réunion des Musées Nationaux (RMN), De Theatercompagnie, Le Cent Quatre (104) and T-shirt label 2K/Gingham, among many other clients.

Their work has been featured in group exhibitions such as Terminal Five (JFK Airport, New York, 2004) and ‹The Free Library› (Riviera Gallery, New York, 2004). Solo exhibitions have included ‹Kelly 1:1› (Casco Projects, Utrecht, 2002) and ‹Ten Years of Posters› (Kemistry Gallery, London, 2006). In 2007 the MoMA (Museum of Modern Art) acquired a large selection of work by Experimental Jetset for inclusion in its permanent collection.
Since 2000, they have taught at the Gerrit Rietveld Academy (Amsterdam).

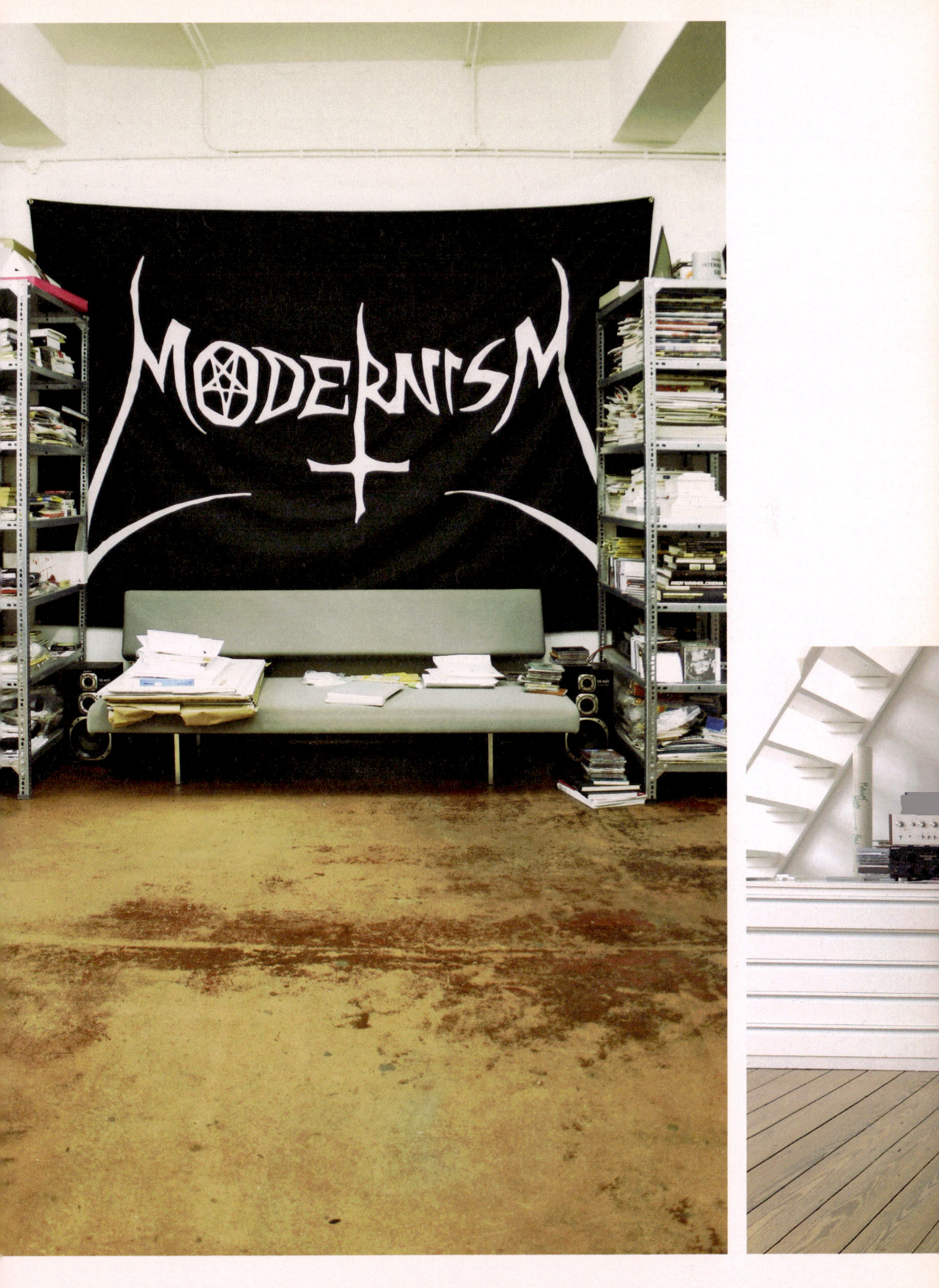
MODERNISM

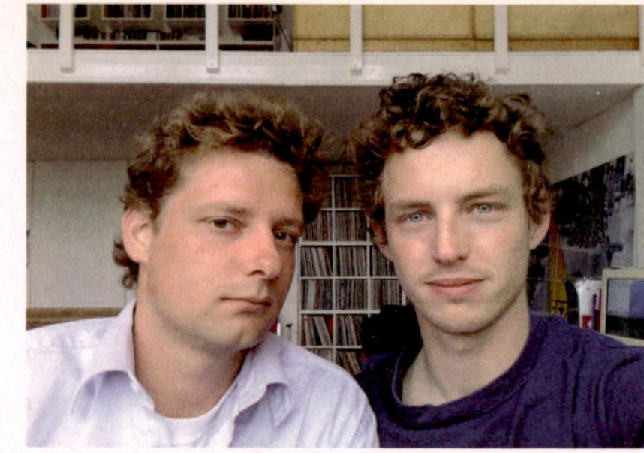

Left: Mark Klaverstijn (1973)
Right: Paul du Bois-Reymond(1974)

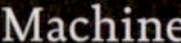

Machine

De Wittenstraat 27
1052 AK Amsterdam
The Netherlands

T +31 (0)20 4862538

we@ourmachine.com
www.ourmachine.com

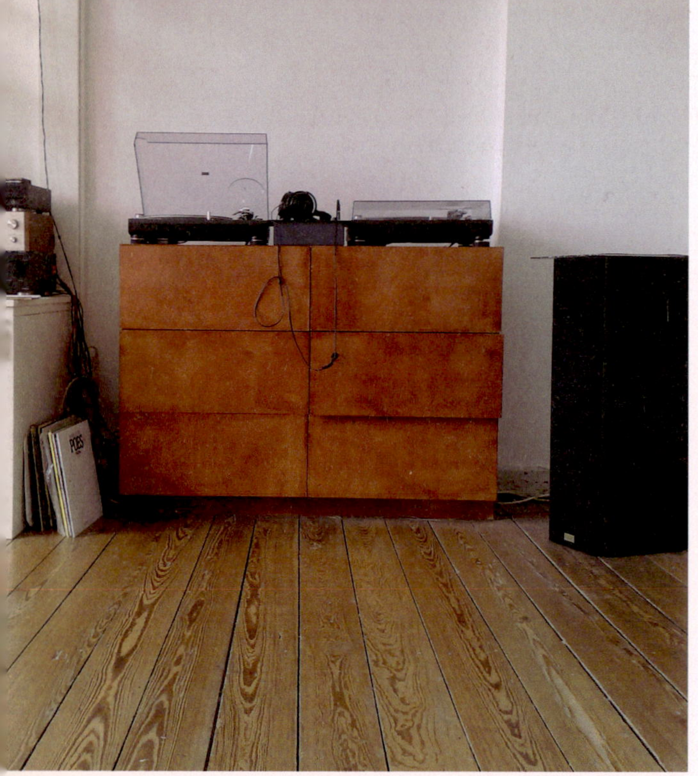

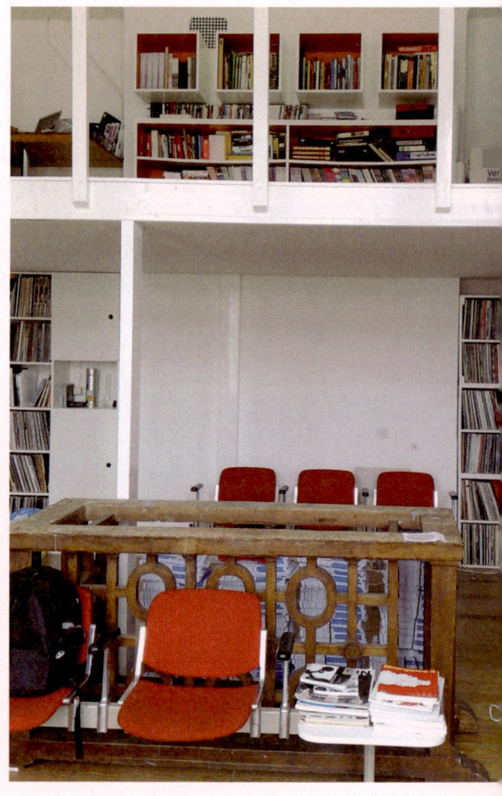

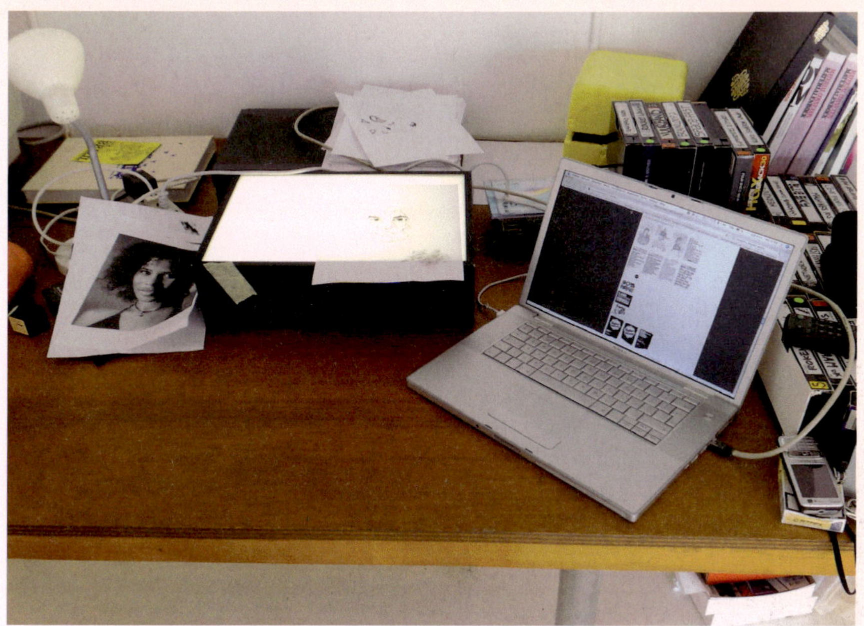

The Machine collective have been active in the field of graphic design and (audio-) visual art since the mid-nineties. The first collective was called DEPT. Operating from Amsterdam, they have worked for numerous clients, large and small, local and foreign. Witnesses to the start of the World Wide Web, working on different types of media has always been a logical consequence for them and others from that time frame: a poster could become a film, a painting could become a T-shirt. The difference in doing independent projects or working for clients is minimal. Their designs are on the edge of being autonomous, and the art they create has a certain directness that is closely related to the approach of graphic designers. Their visual language comes from a variety of backgrounds; inspired by the history of art and design, street culture, political activism and music, Machine seeks to redefine visually and conceptually the different fields it operates in. Machine is tightly connected to the local scene because a lot of its work is music-related. Flyers, logos and posters for numerous club nights have always offered a field with the necessary scope for an experimental approach to defining the look of various musical trends. Another instance of this relationship is the Kindred Spirits record label, exclusively designed by Machine. Having launched Ourmachine Records, Machine's very own label, the Machine Hot Couture line offers the collective a new field of expression.

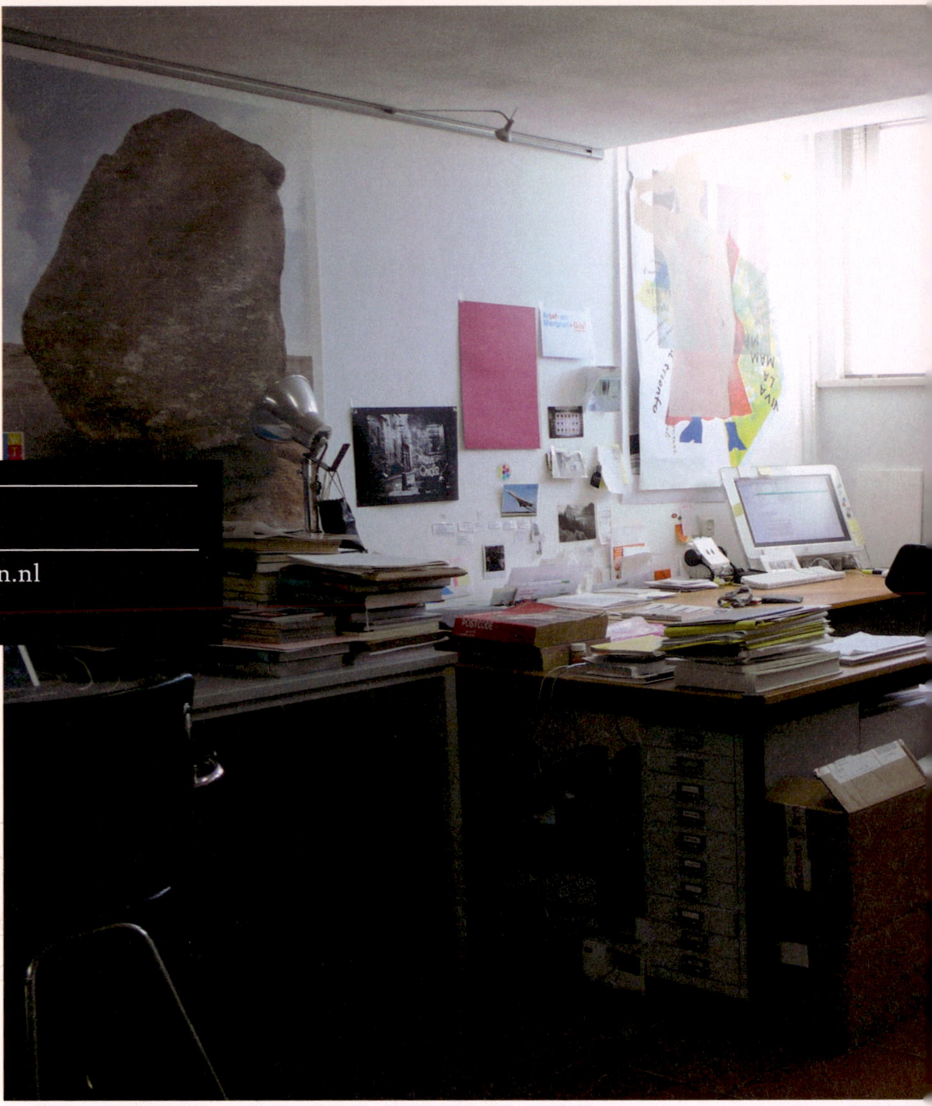

Hans Gremmen

www.hansgremmen.nl

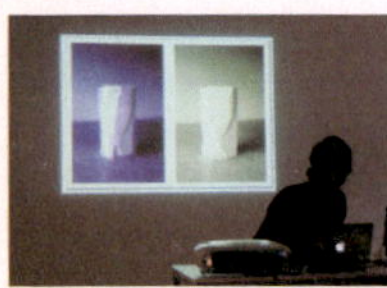

Born in Langenboom, The Netherlands, 1976. Studied at AKV St. Joost, Breda, 1997–2001 and the Werkplaats Typografie, Arnhem, 2001–2003.

Professional graphic designer since 2002.
He works mainly for and with museums, artists, photographers and architects. He teaches project-base in the Photography department at AKV St. Joost, Breda, and is a Typography tutor in the Graphic Design department of the Academy of Arts in Arnhem.

He likes to see designing as thinking about an action that is worth ‹recording› –an action that is continually reacting with the actual content and can addd an extra layer to that content. At its best, a publication becomes part of a project rather than simply documenting it.

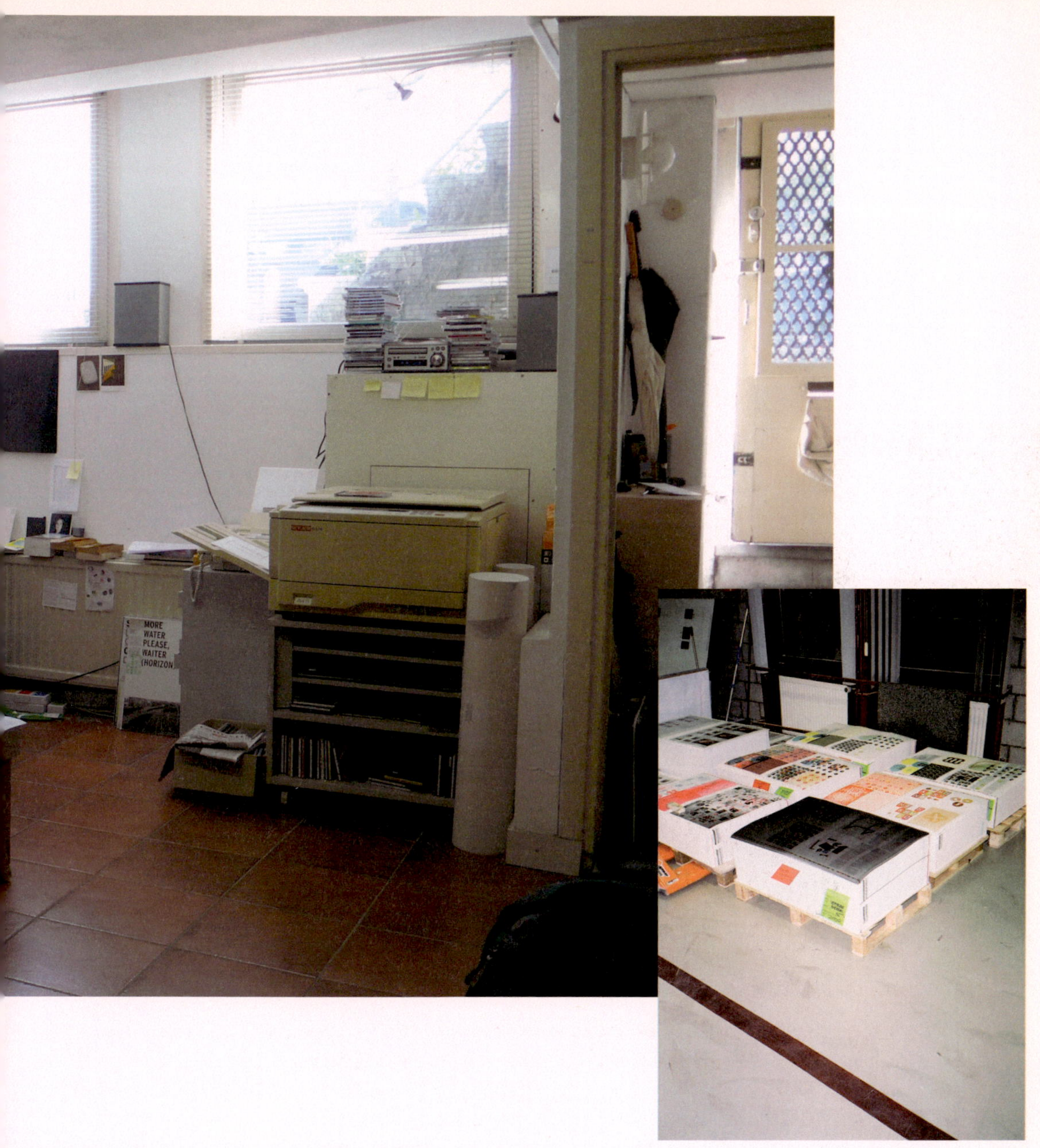

«The most important working space in the design process is at the printer. In this case I was 23 hours non-stop at the press creating and collecting ‹misprints› for the inside cover of Karel Martens' book ‹Counterprint›.»

Lust

Dunne Bierkade 17
2512 BC The Hague
The Netherlands

T +31 (0)70.363 5776
F +31 (0)70.346 9892

lust@lust.nl
www.lust.nl

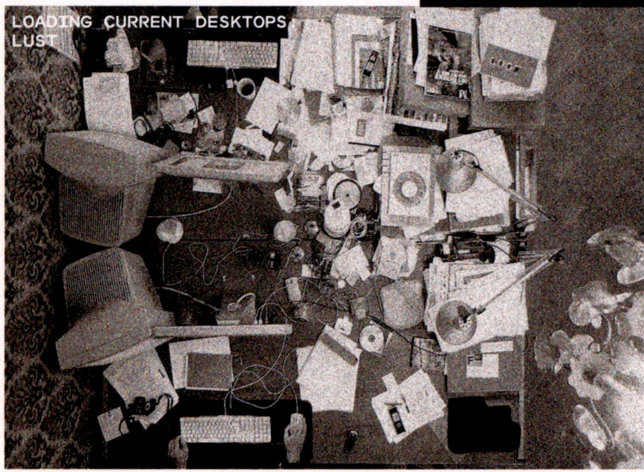

Lust is a graphic practice that seeks to map out new terrains for graphic design, for software, and for new audiences. Lust is a three-person graphic design practice set up by Thomas Castro, Jeroen Barendse and Dimitri Nieuwenhuizen. They work in a variety of media, including print materials, interactive installations and architectural graphics. Lust has been active in the fields of graphic design and new media since 1996. Lust conceives of design as a process. Each design stems from a concept that results from extensive research. In the course of its existence, Lust has developed a design methodology that has been described as process-based or generative systems-based design. This entails developing an analytical process that leads eventually to something that designs itself.

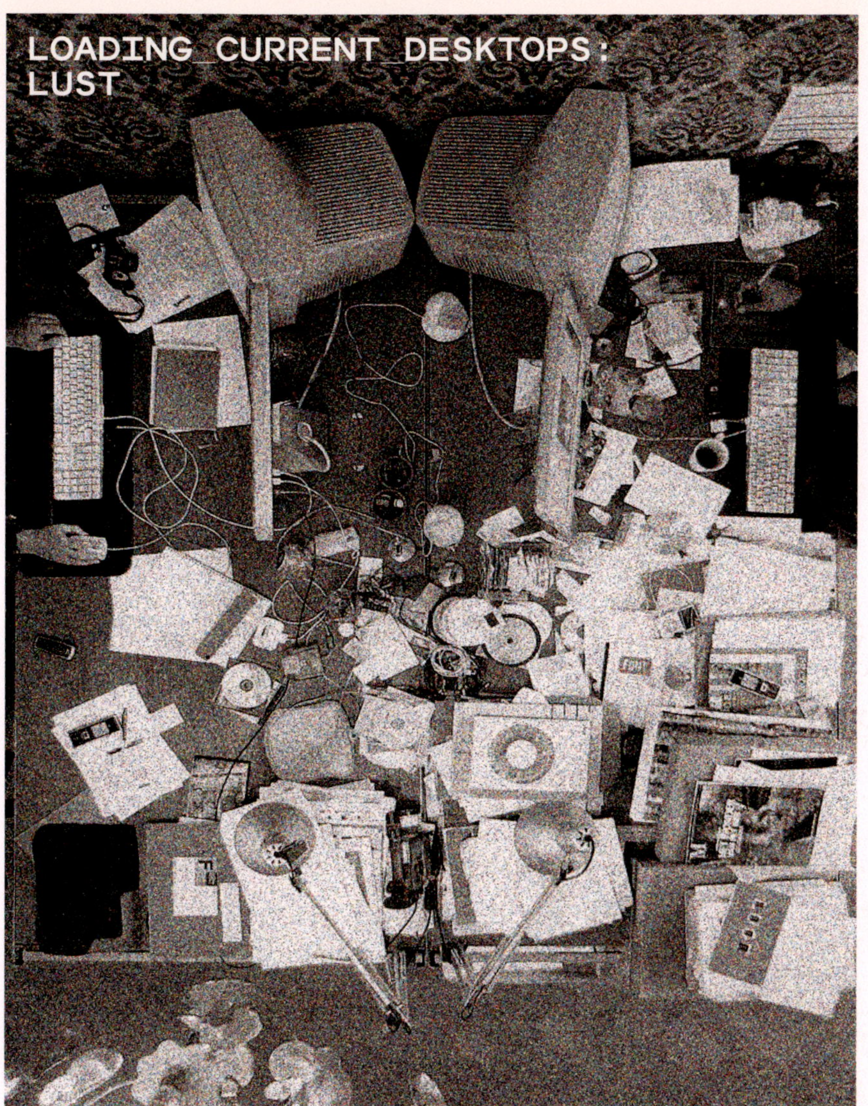

Lust's work is 40% interactive & time-based media, 40% traditional & print media, 10% fonts, and 10% self-initiated projects. Currently, Lust works for architects and town planners, publishers, music groups, galleries, fine art institutions and various small cultural entities, as well as larger institutions, Dutch Ministries and Municipalities and national museums. Lust gives lectures and workshops throughout the world, and Thomas, Jeroen and Dimitri teach at various Dutch academies. Since 2000, Lust has co-sponsored ‹De Program›, the yearly summer workshop of international design students and professionals in The Hague. Since 1998, Lust has also co-organized the ZEFIR7 series of monthly design lectures at Theater Zeebelt in The Hague. During 2005-2007 Lust had a two-year Research Fellowship at The Metropolitan University in Leeds, investigating new cultural possibilities for Leeds.

Catalogtree

Schoolstraat 35
6828 GT Arnhem
The Netherlands

T +31 (0)26 3895655
F +31 (0)26 3637252

www.catalogtree.net

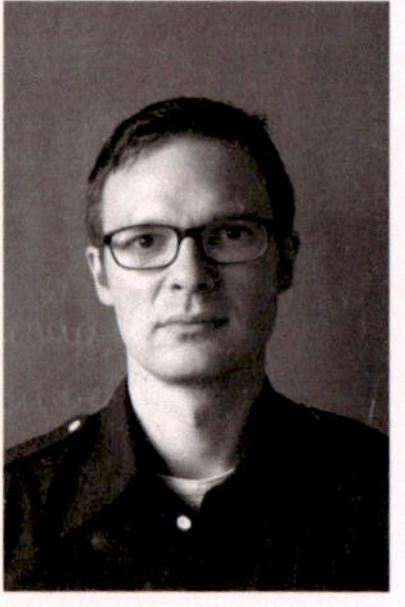

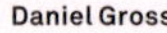

Daniel Gross

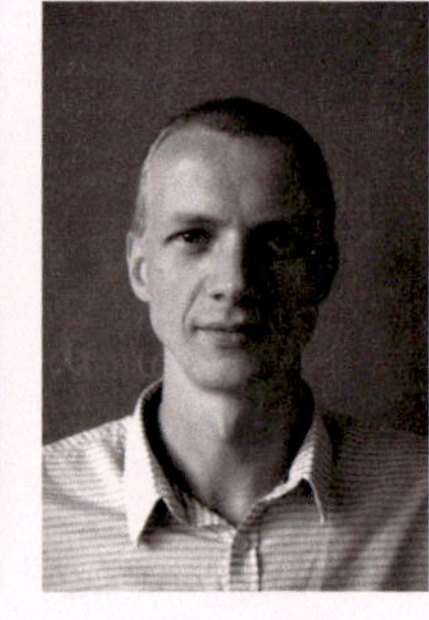

Joris Maltha

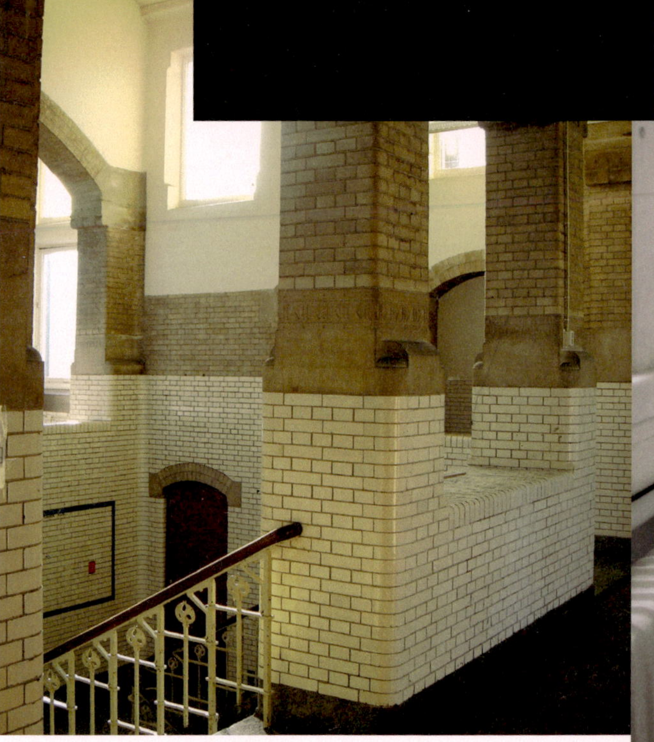

‹Entrance and stairs to our rooms.›

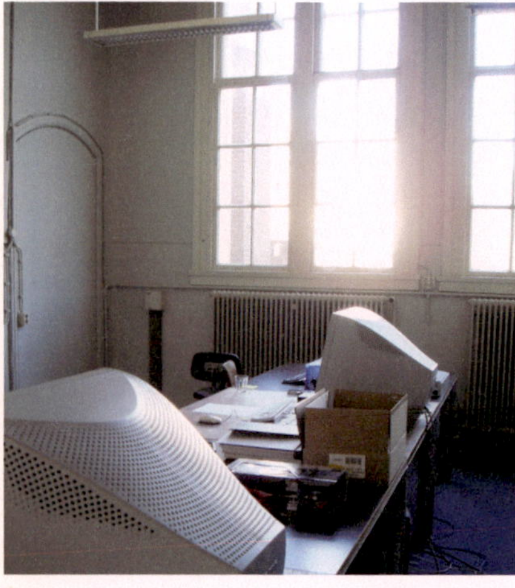

The graphic design studio Catalogtree was founded in 2001 by Daniel Gross (Hamburg, Germany, 1973) and Joris Maltha (Nijmegen, The Netherlands, 1974).
Both studied at the Werkplaats Typografie, Arnhem. Gross graduated in 2001, Maltha graduated in 2000. They have both taught Interactive Design at the Arnhem Academy of Art and Design since 2003.

Clients of the studio include (in alphabetical order): Architects Magazine / Washington DC / USA; Artoteek Den Haag / The Hague / The Netherlands; Bureau Lofvers / Rotterdam; CondeNast / New York; Hogeschool Rotterdam; The Knoxville Voice / Knoxville, TN / USA; Meertens Instituut / Amsterdam; Monadnock architects / Rotterdam; Museum Kurhaus Kleve / Kleve / Germany; The New York Times / New York; NEXT architects / Amsterdam; Plaatsmaken / Arnhem / The Netherlands; Van Bergen Kolpa Architects / Rotterdam; Vlaams Centrum voor Volkscultuur / Brussels / Belgium; VMX architects / Amsterdam; Wieden & Kennedy / Amsterdam.

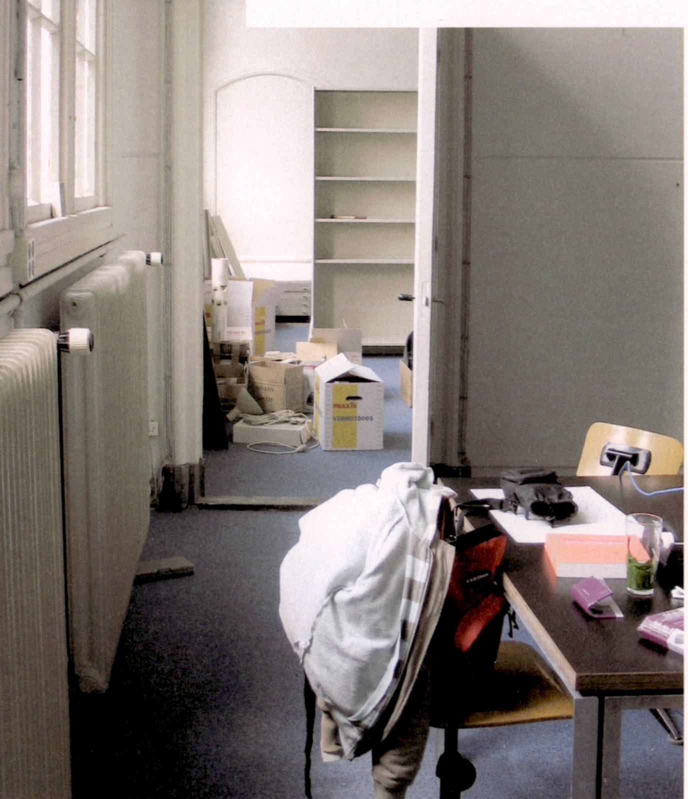

‹Just moved and still a mess.
The school's auditorium is quite big – perfect for remote-controlled dogfights.›

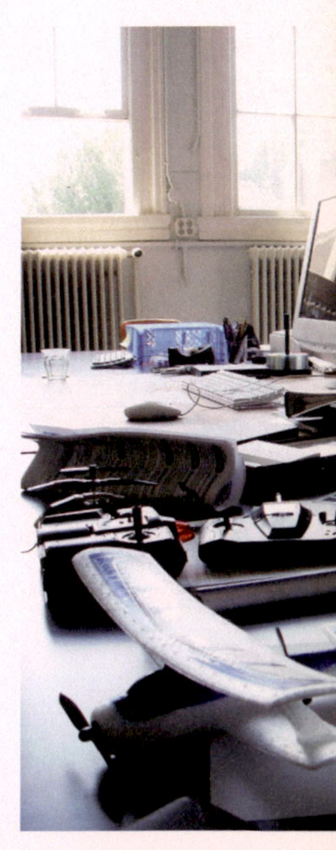

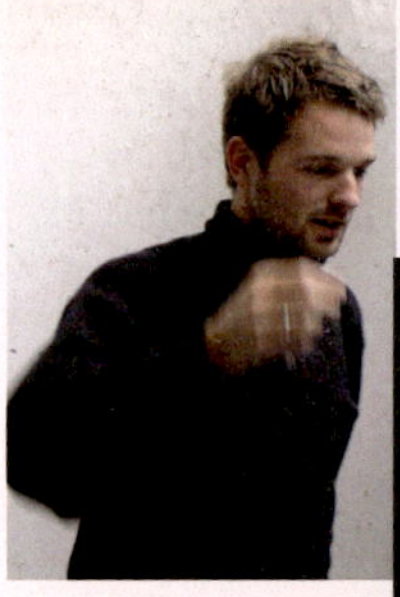

Richard Niessen

Florijn 34
1102 BA Amsterdam
The Netherlands

T +31 (0)20 6633323
M +31 (0)6 24272241

richard@tm-online.nl
www.tm-online.nl

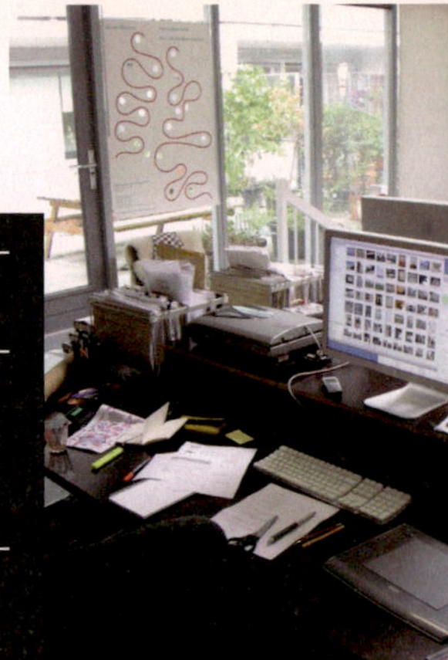

TM - Typographic Masonry

Richard Niessen graduated from the Gerrit Rietveld Academy of Amsterdam in 1996. He has mostly worked alone, but from 1999 to 2002 he collaborated with designer Harmen Liemburg under the name ‹GoldenMasters›. Niessen, also a musician, he designed the packaging, typography and artwork for all of the albums that his band, the Howtoplays has produced. Inspired by the likes of Ettore Sottsass (founder of the Memphis group) and the Scottish-Italian sculptor Eduardo Paolozzi, artists that similarly seek out the tension between structure and going overboard, Niessen developed his own systematic approach to design. He chose the name Typographic Masonry (TM) in 2002, after hearing the term used to describe the work of one of his major influences, Dutch designer and architect Hendrik Th. Wijdeveld.

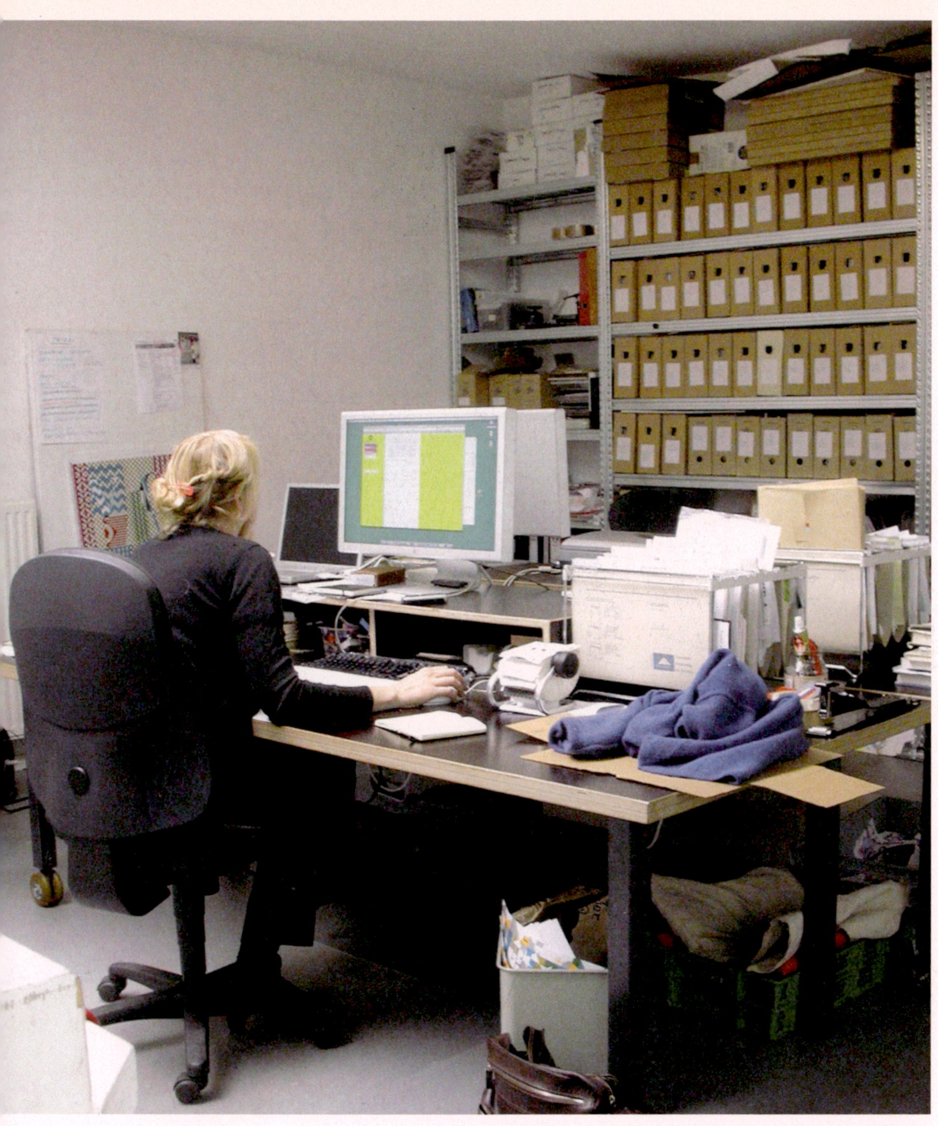

Richard Niessen's work is systematic, grid-like, readable and usable, as much as it is rich in form, shape and colour. Niessen gives projects a distinct language, a secret vocabulary that makes each piece stand out. His consistent oeuvre echoes the seamless integration of typography, calligraphy, imagery and text found in Byzantine and Medieval illuminated manuscripts. Where functionalist design ends, Niessen begins. He has developed the building blocks and the system; but his work comes to life when Niessen starts building with modular elements. He demonstrating can stack them, paste them together, roll them up, fold them in, embed secret messages, and layer the elements until the system itself unfolds into a rich mosaic.

Lesley Moore

Tweede Atjehstraat 60hs
1094 LK Amsterdam
The Netherlands

T +31 (0)20 6635110

mail@lesley-moore.nl
www.lesley-moore.nl

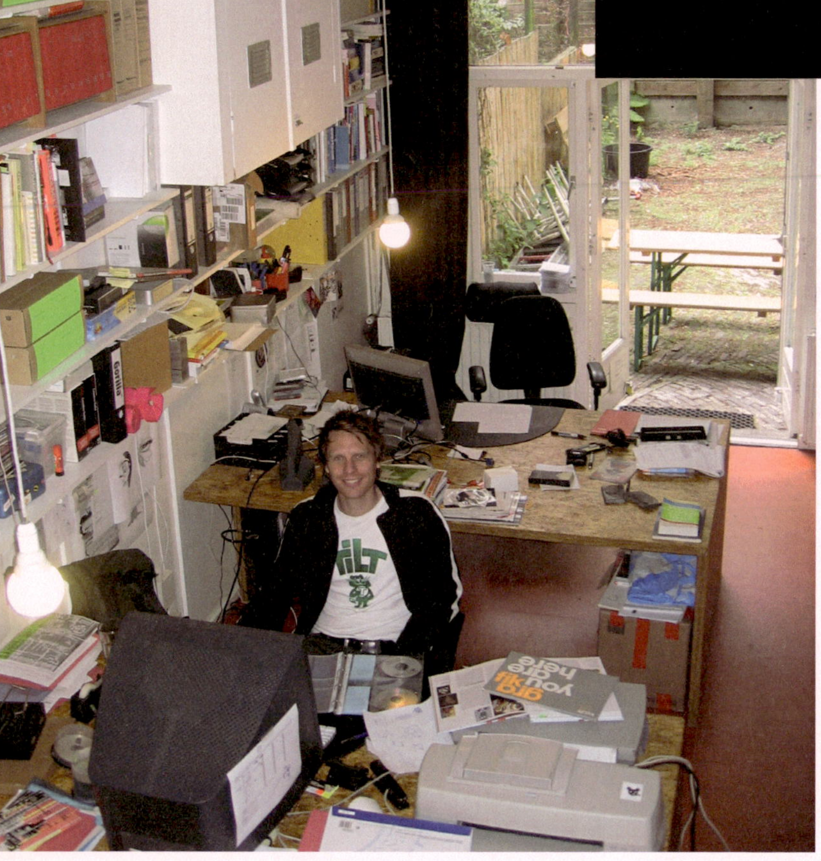

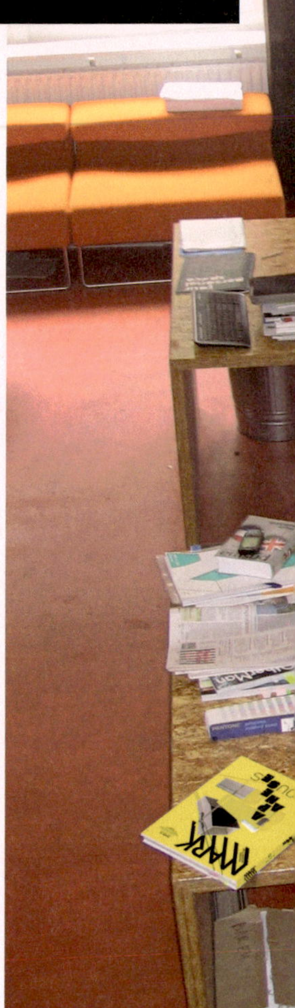

Alex Clay in the Lesley Moore studio

Lesley Moore is an Amsterdam-based graphic design agency founded in May 2004 by Karin (Blerick, The Netherlands, 1975) van den Brandt and Alex Clay (Lørenskog, Norway, 1974).

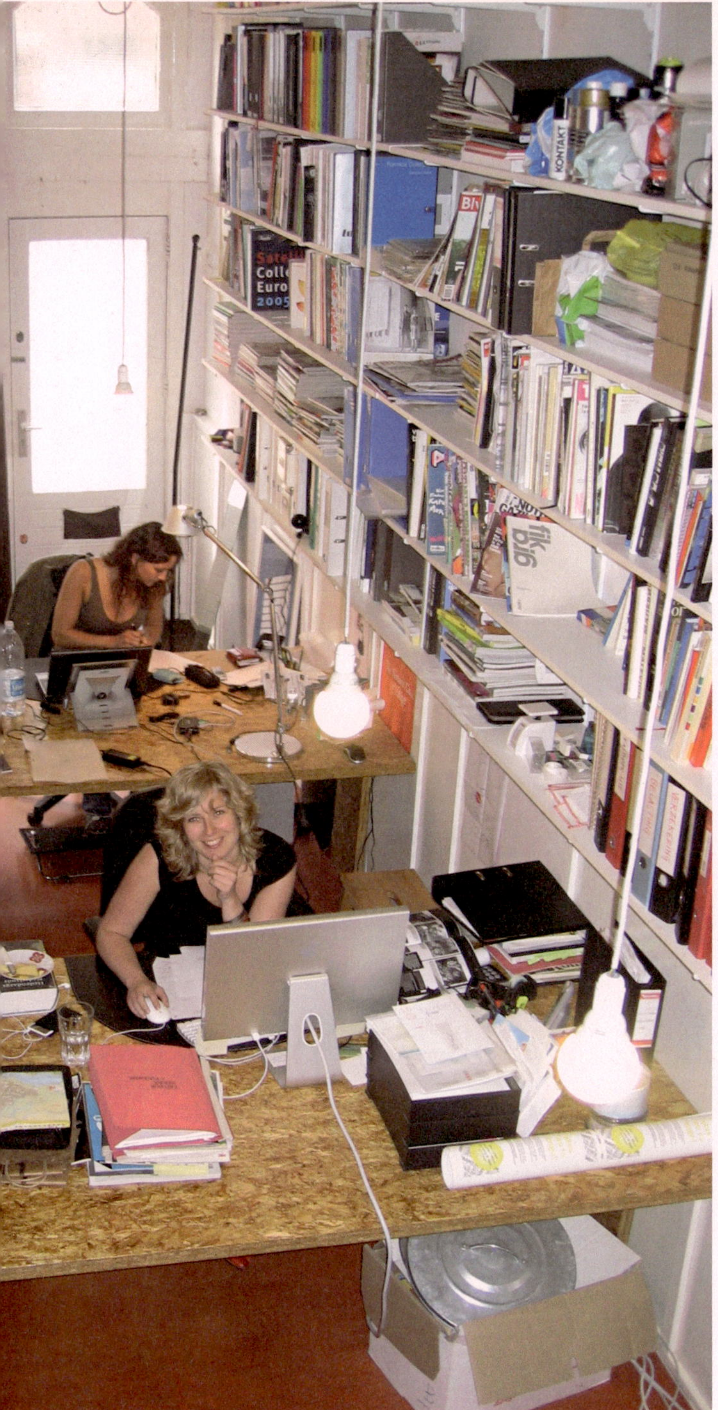

Karin van den Brandt in the Lesley Moore studio, with Silke Spinner in the background

«Lesley Moore is a pseudonym. It derives from ‹less is more›, which fits well with our design mentality. Not formally, but on a conceptual level, our approach is minimalistic.»

Ping-pong Design

Havenstraat 23 A
3024 SG Rotterdam
The Netherlands

T +31 (0) 10 4365744
F +31 (0) 10 4364560

info@pingpongdesign.com
www.pingpongdesign.com

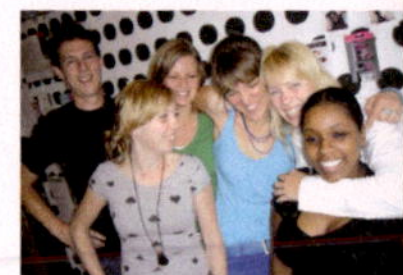

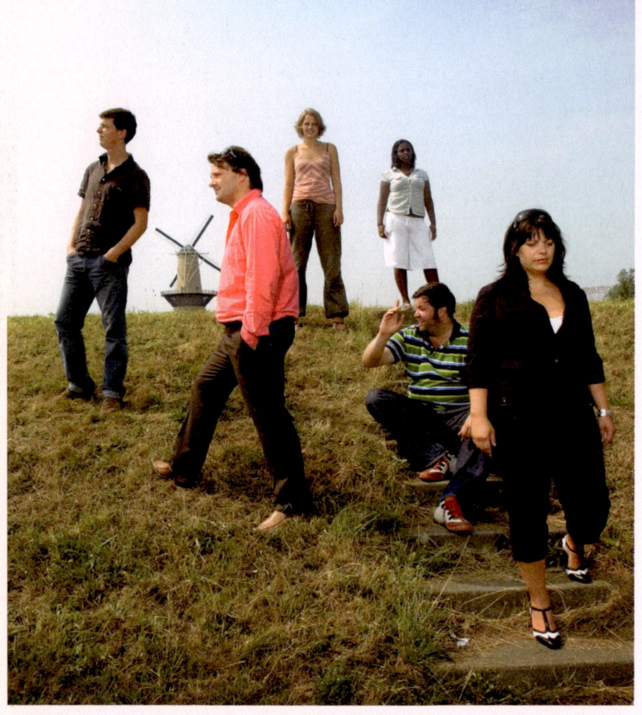

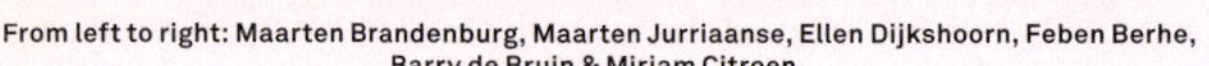

From left to right: Maarten Brandenburg, Maarten Jurriaanse, Ellen Dijkshoorn, Feben Berhe, Barry de Bruin & Mirjam Citroen.

Ping-pong has stood for a lot of things over time.
A game, a sound-effect, diplomacy.

A brief nine months after the turn of the present century,
Ping-pong acquired a new, greater, more expansive definition.

Ping-pong stands for design:
savage, soulful, alive, extravagant, flawed, human, mysterious, magic.

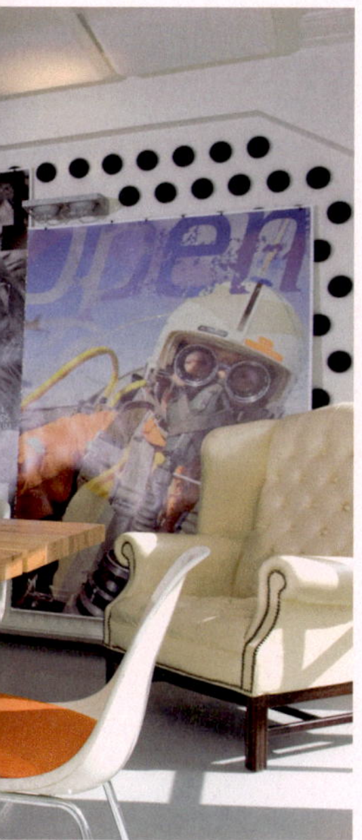

Ping-pong also stands for:
dialogue, exchange, engagement, observation, speculation, performance, people, play.

Ping-pong is a verb:
to make, to do, to be, to want, to build, to dive, to fly, to know, to whistle, to skip, to tell, to try.

It is also a noun:
story, organism, engine, world, fertility, expansion, knife, flower, cloud, rebel, salt, fire, heartbeat.

It is a state of mind:
curious, blunt, bold, sensitive, daring, romantic, assertive, comic, twisted, inspired.

It is also a way of being:
spirited, driven, dramatic, commercial, candid, teachable, defiant, willing, unusual, brilliant.

Ping-pong is a small studio.
We maintain an extensive network of talented minds in the related fields of marketing, media, production, photography, writing, etc. Whatever it takes to make the story complete.

STAR

Delftsestraat 27
3013 AE Rotterdam
The Netherlands

T +31 (0)10 2400171

star@s-t-a-r.nl
www.s-t-a-r.nl

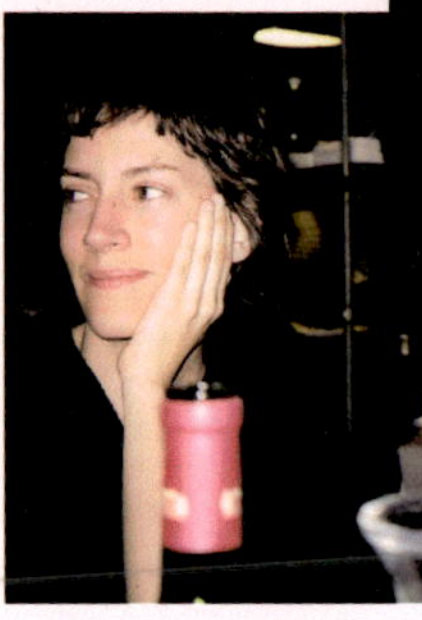

Beatriz Ramo, the director of STAR

This picture was taken at Zinc, a very small restaurant in Rotterdam, on my mother's birthday.

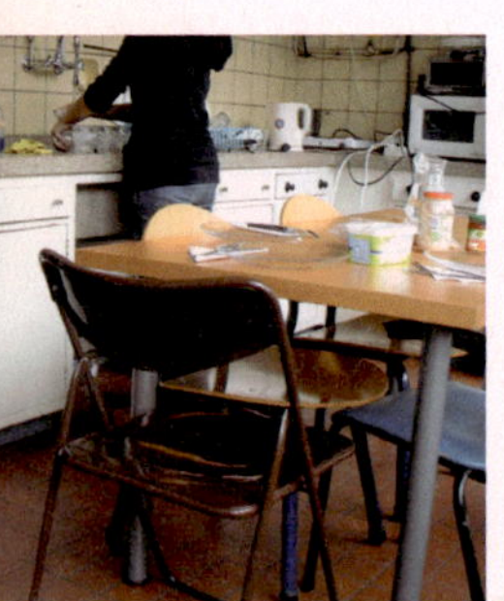

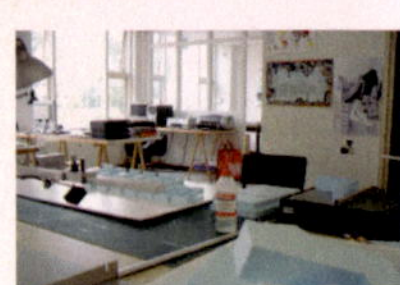

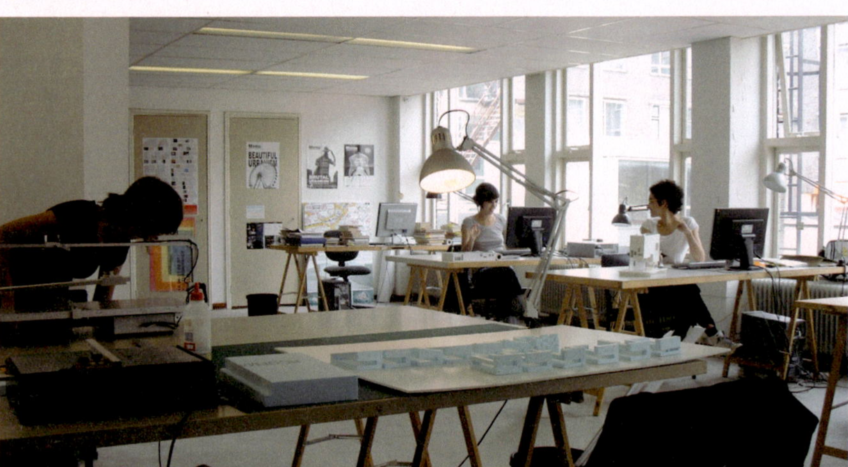

This is the main space of the office. Here we work on the computers and make models.

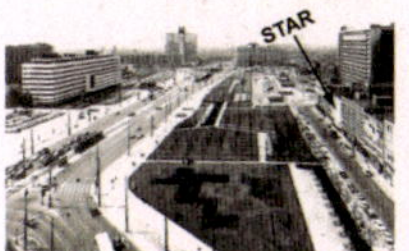

STAR 1968

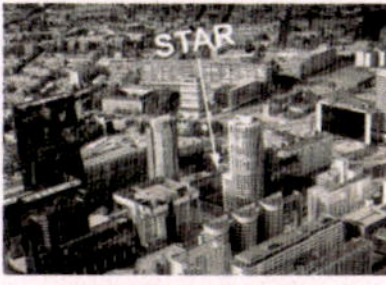

STAR 1997

The office is in the centre of Rotterdam, in a small 1950s building between skyscrapers.

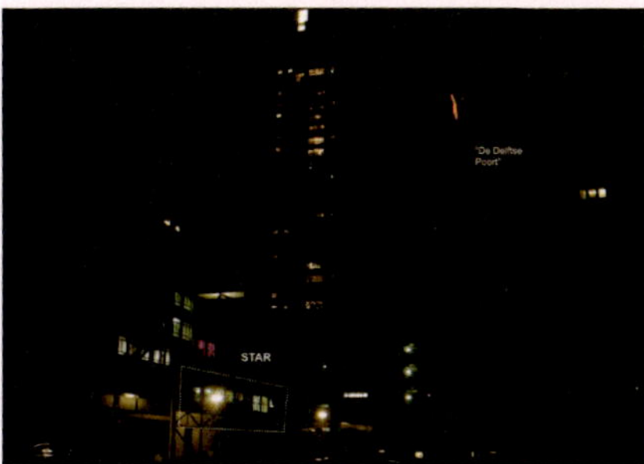

STAR (strategies + architecture) is a Rotterdam-based office of architecture and urban design that analyzes and investigates the relation of architecture and urbanism within their social, cultural, and political context.

Beatriz Ramo is the director of STAR. She studied architecture at the Technical University in Valencia and in Eindhoven before working with Bosch Architects in Amsterdam and OMA (Office for Metropolitan Architecture) in Rotterdam. Beatriz Ramo has lectured at several universities and currently teaches Architecture and Research at Tilburg Academy.

STAR is also interested in areas beyond architecture, and operates in the field of visual journalism. STAR uses simple parameters to produce diagrams and maps that reveal the complexity of our contemporary world. In 2006 STAR was part of the jury of the Malofiej International Infographics awards, and presented its work at the World Congress of the Society for News Design.

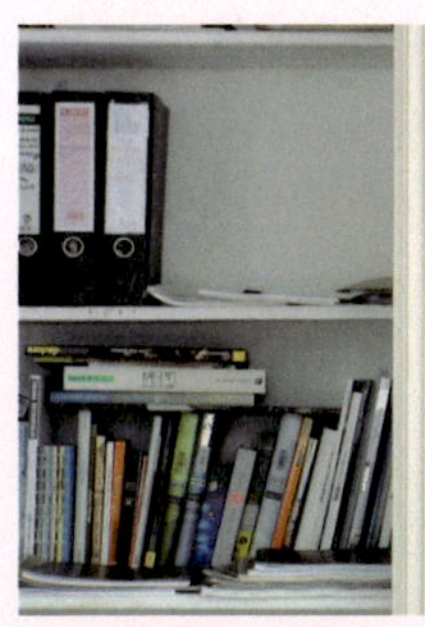
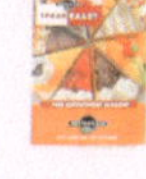
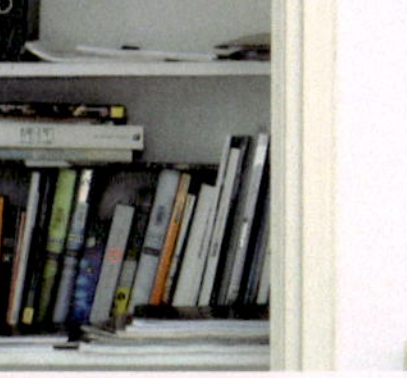
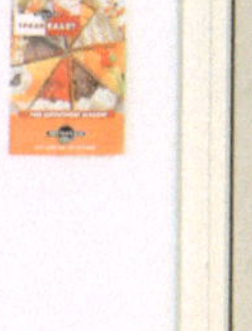
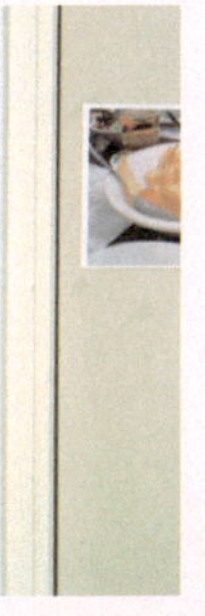
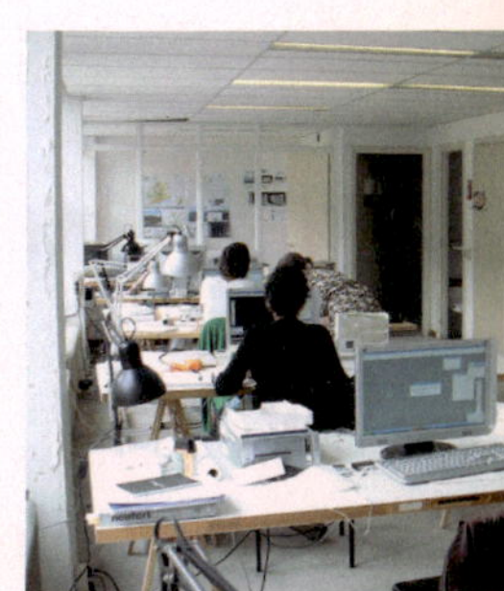

 Harmen Liemburg was born in Lisse, The Netherlands, in 1966. He studied Social Geography/Cartography at Utrecht University and graduated in 1992. While working as a freelance cartographer, and later as a design assistant, he studied Graphic Design at the Gerrit Rietveld Academy in Amsterdam. After an exchange programme with Virginia Commonwealth University's Art Department and an internship at Oven Digital in New York, he graduated in 1998.

In 1998 he started a collaboration with graphic designer Richard Niessen as The Golden Masters. While working for clients, a major part of this period was spent organising the JACK cultural events in Amsterdam. At the same time he was part of the editorial and design team at ‹Sec›, a magazine showcasing the work of young photographers and other image-makers. Since 2003, Liemburg has worked solo or in collaboration with other artists.

After producing a substantial body of work at Interbellum, the screen-printing studio of his former teacher Kees Maas, Liemburg has earned a reputation as an accomplished screen-print artist in his own right, giving workshops at an international level. The technique enables him to produce and publish graphic work independently, and has thus been a major force in his Do It Yourself approach. His work is in the permanent collections of the Stedelijk Museum in Amsterdam, Les Arts Décoratifs in Paris and the Plakat-/Grafiksammlung in Zurich.

Liemburg's work is positioned somewhere between graphic design, illustration, fine art, research and journalism, and has been published in numerous international magazines, books and blogs. While developing his authorial role as an image maker, Liemburg also started publishing articles on visual culture, mainly for the Dutch design magazine ‹ITEMS›. His posters are frequently selected at international poster festivals, and in 2006 he was awarded a bronze medal at Toyama and a silver at Chaumont. Since graduating, his projects have frequently enjoyed the support of the Netherlands Foundation for Visual Arts, Design and Architecture. In 2006 he was inducted as a member of the Phi Beta Delta Honour Society for International Scholars.

Liemburg's work to date has frequently been shown in international group shows, and he had his first solo show as an artist at the Chaumont Poster Festival in 2005. The installation he created there was inspired by the foundation of the festival: the historic Collection Gustave Dutailly. His second solo show was in spring 2007 at the Sieboldhuis in Leiden, where he worked in the footsteps of his Dutch ancestors in Nagasaki.

Though still firmly based in Amsterdam, Liemburg's ambition is to live and work more internationally by means of artist's residencies, teaching, lecturing and travel, sharing his love and enthusiasm for graphic culture past, present and future.

Harmen Liemburg

Oudeschans 59C
1011 KW Amsterdam
The Netherlands

M +31 (0)6 25080766

mail@harmenliemburg.nl
www.harmenliemburg.nl

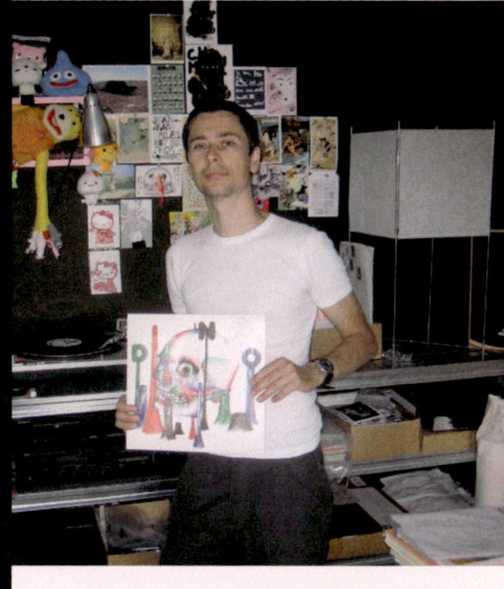

«There's no design or illustration without music. Besides handy iTunes, I love to play vinyl records while working, so at least I get some ‹exercise› every 20 minutes. Dino is published through the Rolax label by Mathias Schweizer, who did this sleeve design. Mathias is one of the most exiting French designers ever, if you ask me!»

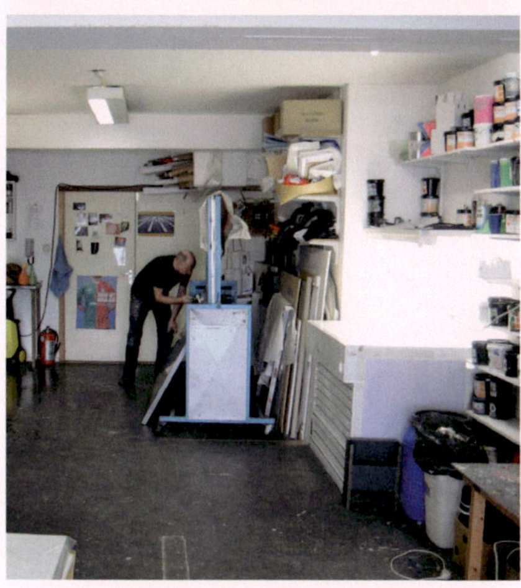

«When I graduated from the Gerrit Rietveld Academy in 1998, my former screen-printing teacher Kees Maas (photo) gave me a great present: the keys to his printing studio. Whenever he's doing other things, I can use it. Besides the practical facilities, the work he has produced for his own publishing house Interbellum is a great source of inspiration to me.»

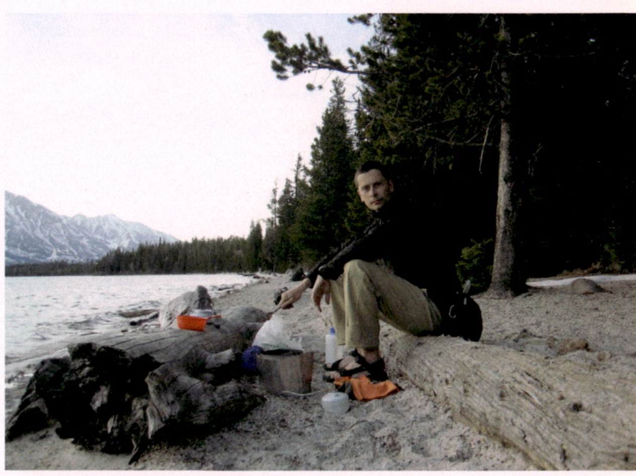

«Like most people, I spend most of my time working inside with my nose to the computer screen, but boy, do I love the outdoors! I'm a big fan of hiking, camping, kayaking and getting away from the consuming crowds. Solitude, silence, fresh air and clean water are going to be the last real luxuries...»

Minke Themans

Taxusstraat 20, Lokaal 7
NL - 3061 HT Rotterdam
The Netherlands

T +31 (0)10 4259810
F +31 (0)10 2762930

info@minkethemans.nl
www.minkethemans.nl

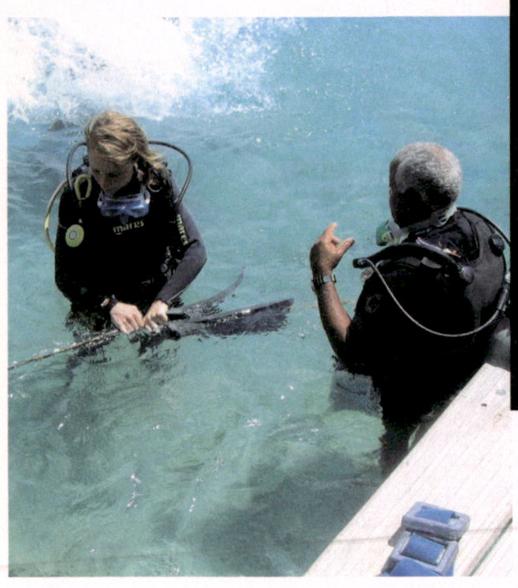

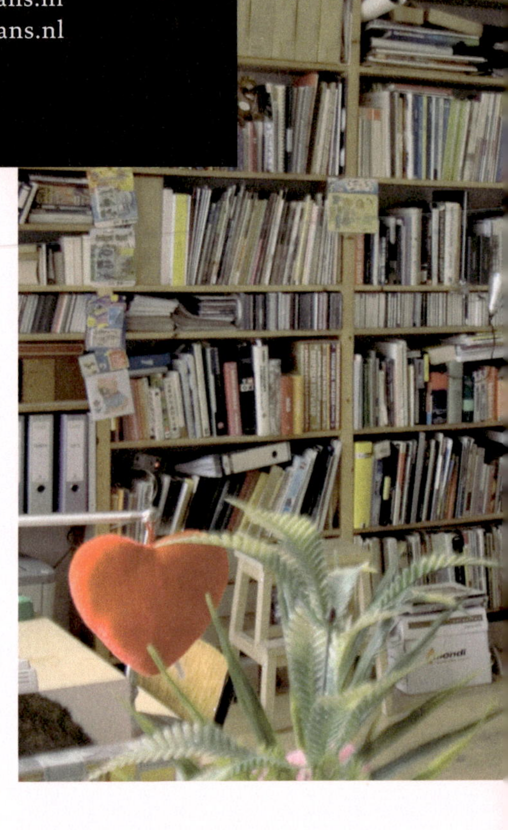

Born in Rotterdam in 1972. Graphic designer. Graduated ‹cum laude› from both the Academy of Visual Arts in Rotterdam and Post St. Joost, a masters course for visual communications in Breda. Since 1997 she has worked as an independent graphic designer for various art and cultural institutes, publishers, museums and architectural offices. She produced and published the book and exhibition ‹New Notational Systems for Urban Situations› in 2000. Nominated for the Dutch Design Prize and the Best Dutch Book Designs the following year. Founded Studio Minke Themans in 2006. The studio designs catalogues, exhibitions and house styles and carries out projects in and about public space.

As opposed to strictly separating the phases of data collection and image generation, SMT's design methodology involves a strategy of intertwining the two in spiral fashion. Assimilating abstract information, personal observation and the development of a legible graphic language are all part of a process.

Besides running the studio, Themans lectures and runs workshops (Rotterdam, Amsterdam, Hamburg, Montreal and Los Angeles) and is a member of several art committees in The Netherlands.

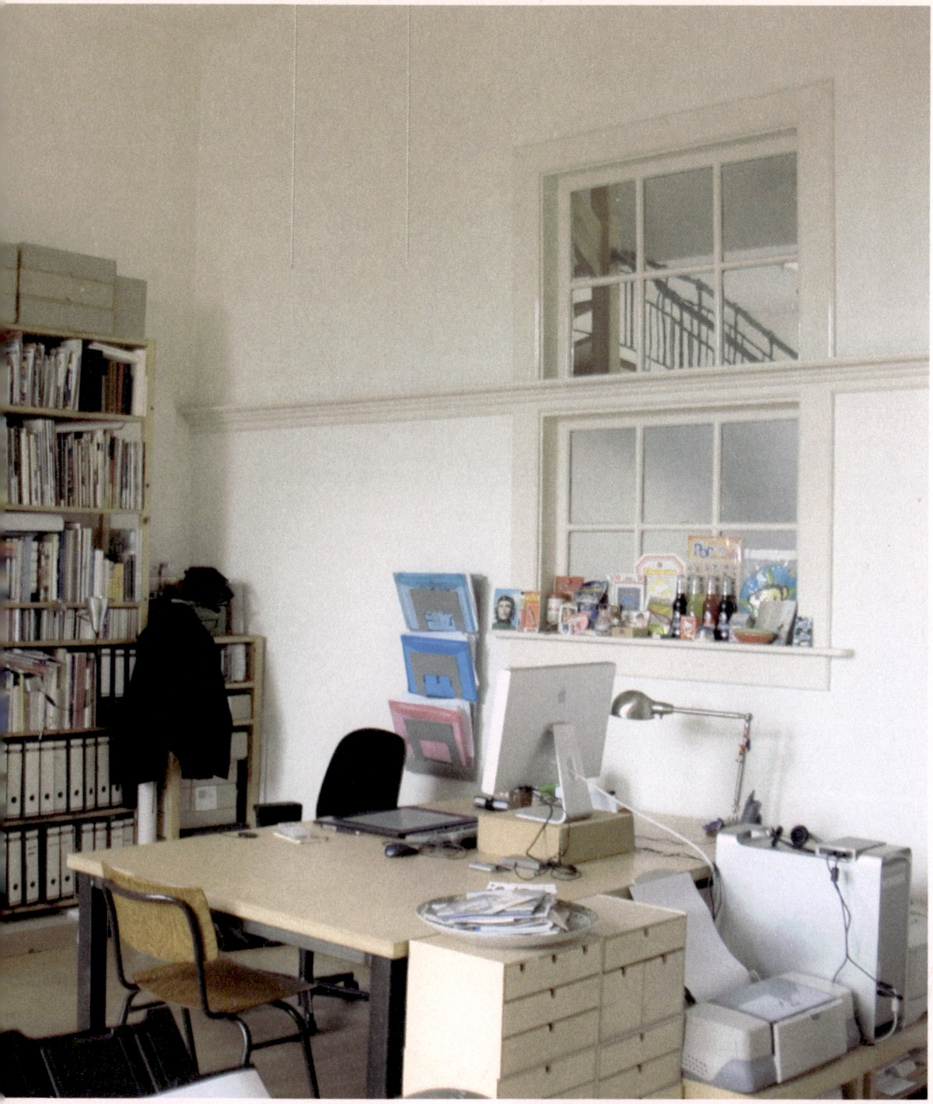

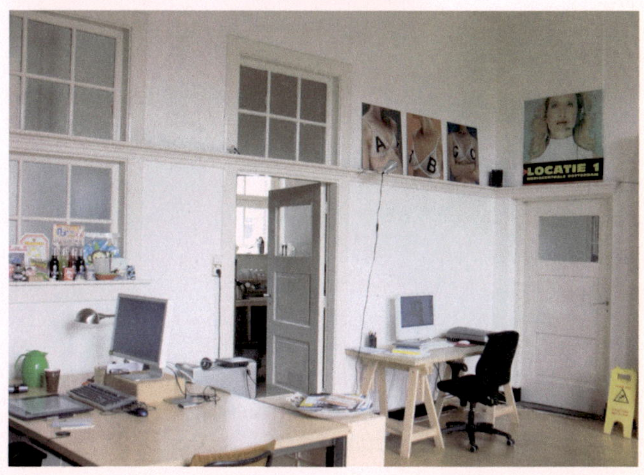
LOCATIE 1

Hansje van Halem

Berberisstraat 16
1032 EL Amsterdam
The Netherlands

T +31 (0)6 41241546

hansje@hansje.net
www.hansje.net

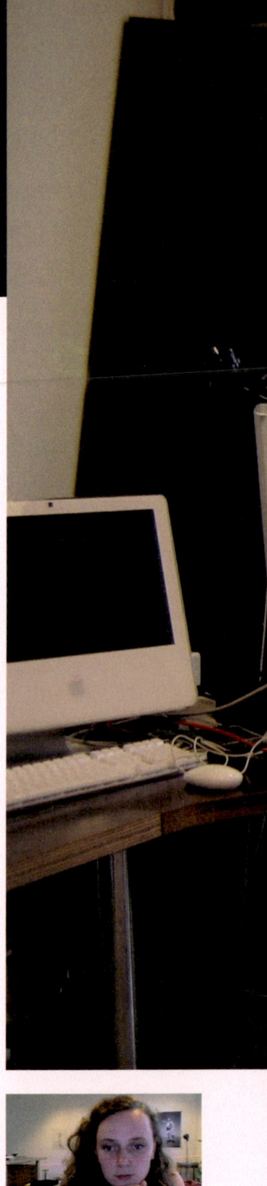

Hansje van Halem (1978), independent graphic designer in Amsterdam, The Netherlands.

She graduated from the Rietveld Academy in 2003 and for the past four years has worked from her studio space in Amsterdam. She specializes in typography, has a great love of paper and hates seeing it get covered with too much ink. She sees books as three-dimensional objects. Through the choice of paper and sometimes through physical alterations to the format, she aims to take on the whole book as her task. She prefers to design for print, but accidentally rolled into exhibition signage as well. In these works she gets the chance to work not solely with paper and ink but to experiment with different materials and techniques such as embroidery on wood, laser-cutting felt or burning type into wood.
Her clients to date have been mainly from the Dutch cultural sector, which is known to allow the designer a great deal of freedom. This freedom has been rewarded with three Most Beautiful Book awards and an honourable mention for Most Beautiful Book in the World, and has helped keep new design opportunities coming in. Even though she mainly works on commissioned assignments, she perceives these as opportunities to add another volume to her bookshelf and forgets that she's not working on a project of her own. When a dull moment crops up she escapes to her type-drawings in Illustrator to attack letter shapes in which those time-consuming drawing systems are welcomed as meditation.

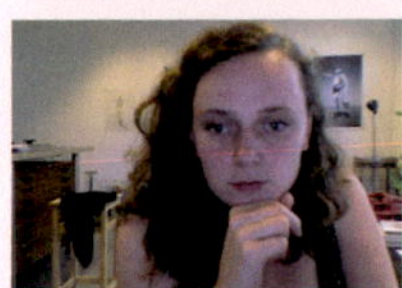

a webcam portrait

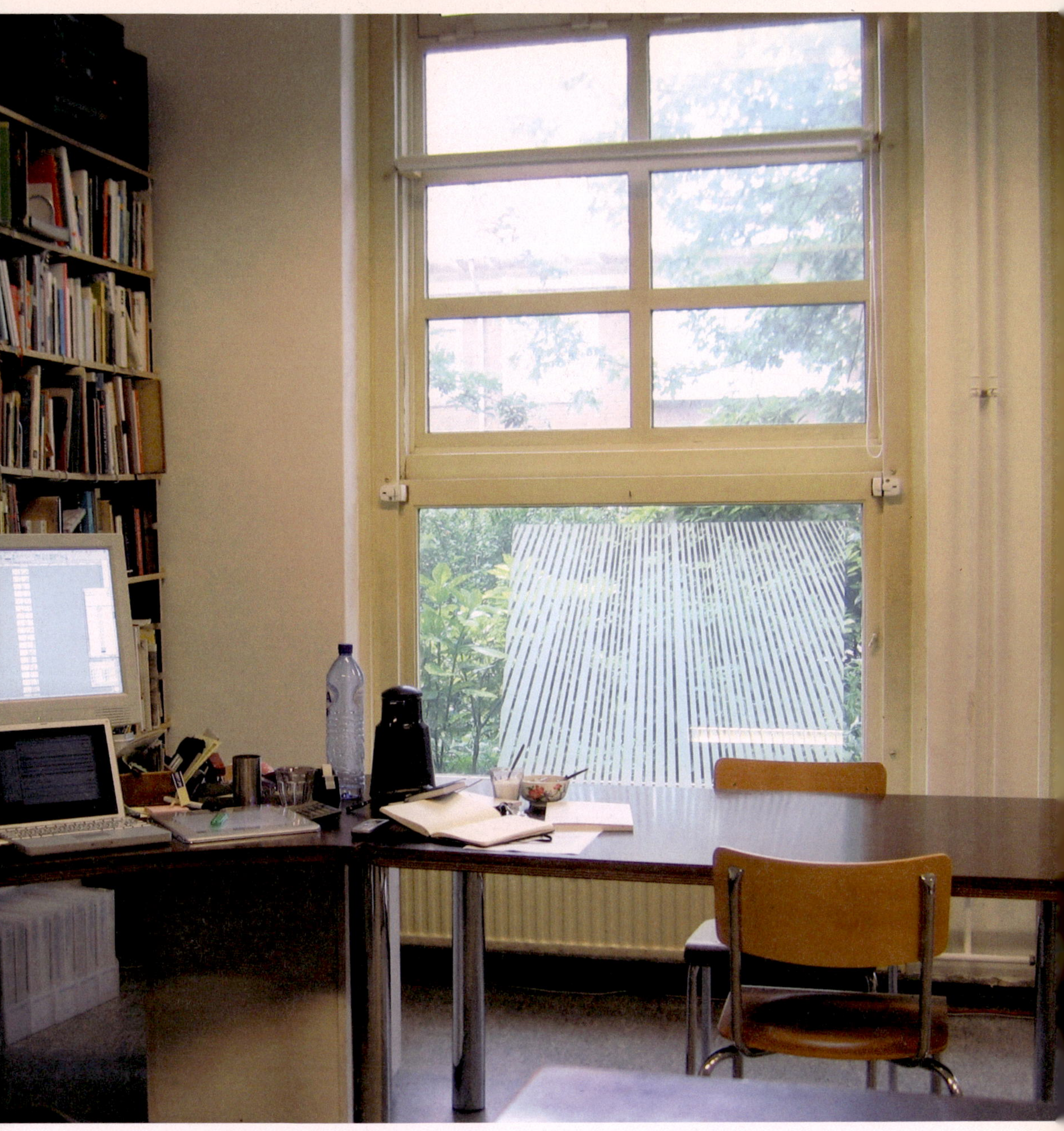

«My studio is in an old Fire Department building in the North of Amsterdam. Every day I have to take a five-minute ferry trip across the river to get there. The nine other studios in this building are filled with artists, documentary makers, sound designers, fashion designers and photographers. I prefer sitting in the garden, on the bench outside my window. Especially when Ed's Snack Car rides through the street every day at 17:38 hrs to sell beers and ice creams. But mainly I'm sat behind the screen. Seeing the picture I realize it looks as if I'm working on three computers at once, but that's not true. The iMac is only there because the DVD-writer on my laptop seems to be broken.»

Thonik

Weesperzijde 79d
1091 EJ Amsterdam
The Netherlands

T +31 (0)20 4683525
F +31 (0)20 4683524

studio@thonik.nl
www.thonik.nl

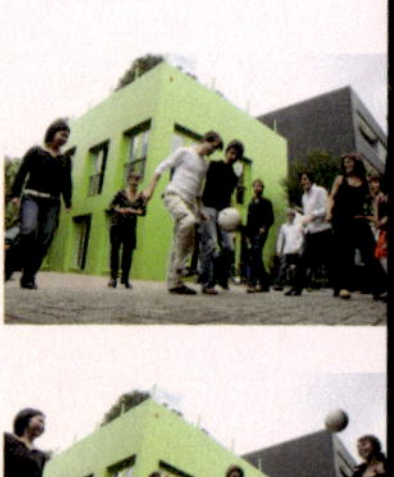

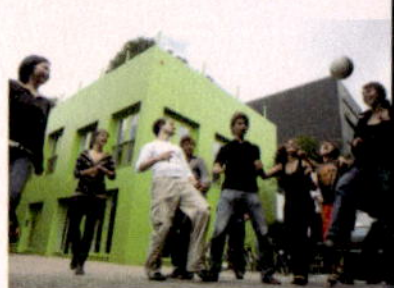

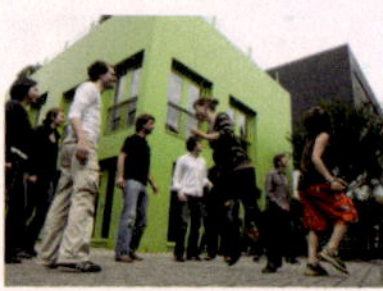

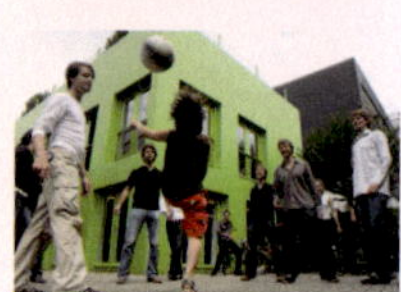

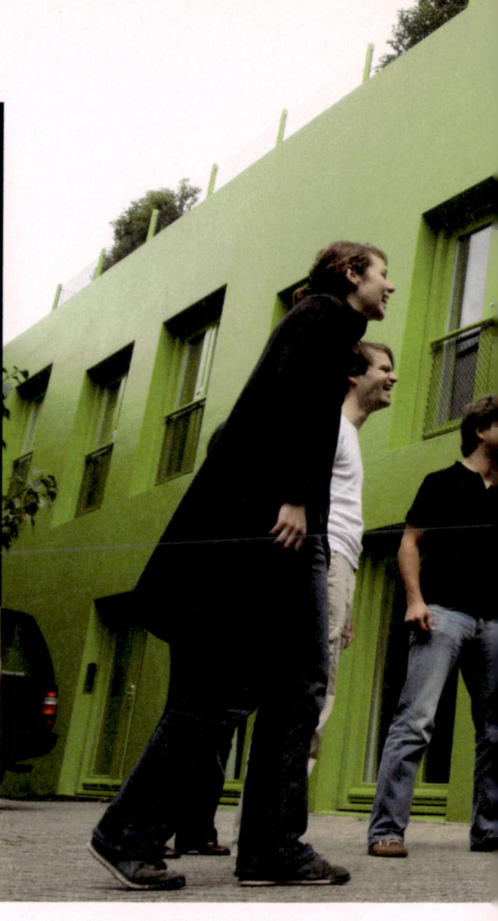

Thonik is a studio for visual communication in Amsterdam. Nikki Gonnissen and Thomas Widdershoven started out as Studio Gonnissen en Widdershoven in 1993. In 2000 they renamed the studio Thonik, a combination of both their first names. Nikki Gonnissen (1967) studied graphic design at the Utrecht School of the Arts. After Thomas Widdershoven (1960) completed his Ph.D. in philosophy at the University of Amsterdam (UvA) he studied graphic design at the Rietveld Academy. At present has, in addition to the two founders, Thonik has a workforce of ten people.

Thonik makes graphic designs (corporate designs, book designs, etc.) and develops communication concepts for publicity campaigns. Thonik has a clear style and a strong conceptual approach. Together with other kindred spirits such as Droog Design and MVRDV, Thonik is widely regarded as one of the leading representatives of Dutch Design.

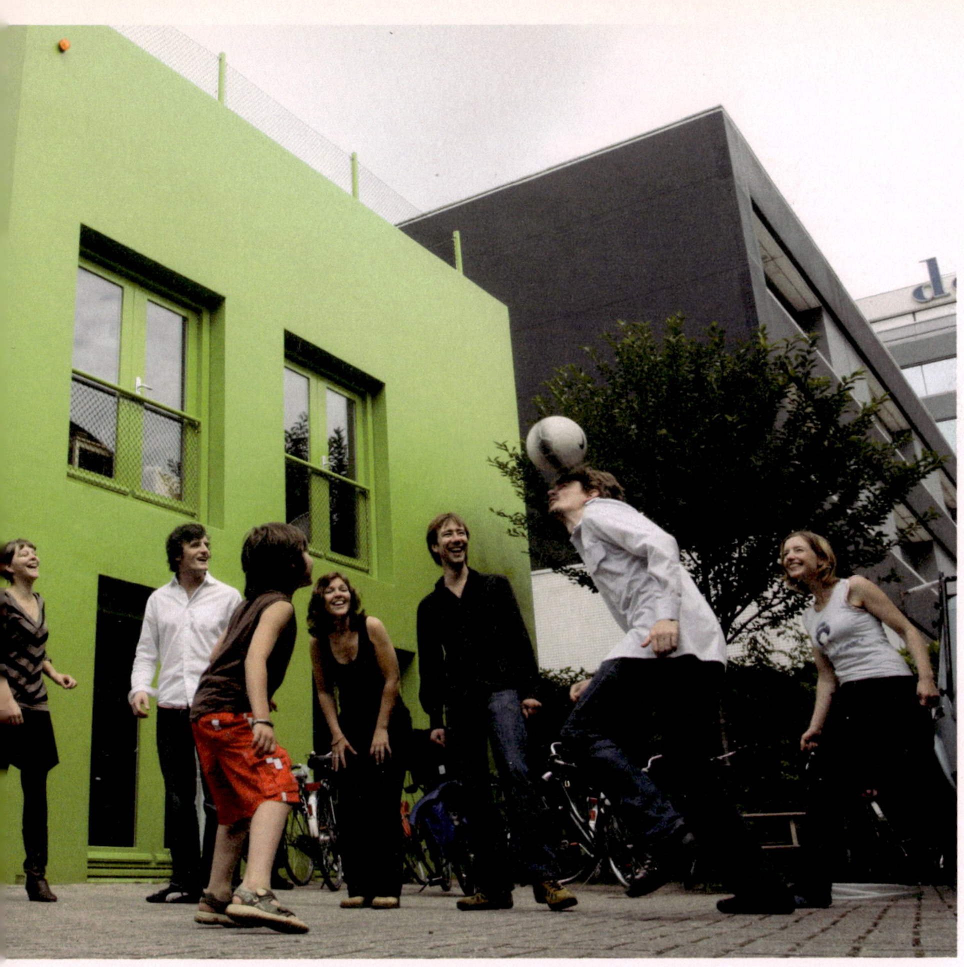

Their campaign for the SP (Socialist Party) won the Dutch Design Prize 2006, the Dutch Corporate Identity Prize 2007, the van Speijk Public Award 2007, the Esprix Public Award 2007 and the Golden Esprix 2007 and has been nominated for the Rotterdam Design Award 2007.

In addition to their design work, Nikki Gonnissen and Thomas Widdershoven are also active in teaching. They also sit on various commissions, for example the Fonds BKVB and the Mondriaanstichting.

In 2001 Bis Publishers brought out ‹Thonik®›, the first title in the series ‹New Dutch Graphic Design›.

Herman van Bostelen

Breedstraat 9A
3512 TS Utrecht
The Netherlands

T +31(0)30 2231424

info@hermanvanbostelen.nl
www.hermanvanbostelen.nl

Herman van Bostelen graduated from the Utrecht School of the Arts in 1996, where he has taught graphic design and typography since 2001.

His clients include: 't Barre Land, Springdance festival, TNT (TPG), KPN, Utrecht School of the Arts, Theater Kikker, de Balie, Nieuw Amsterdam publishers, Zeeland Nazomerfestival, Yo! Operafestival, Bezige Bij publishers, Nijgh & van Ditmar publishers, Spectrum publishers, NAi publishers, ‹De Volkskrant› newspaper, CBK Utrecht & many more.

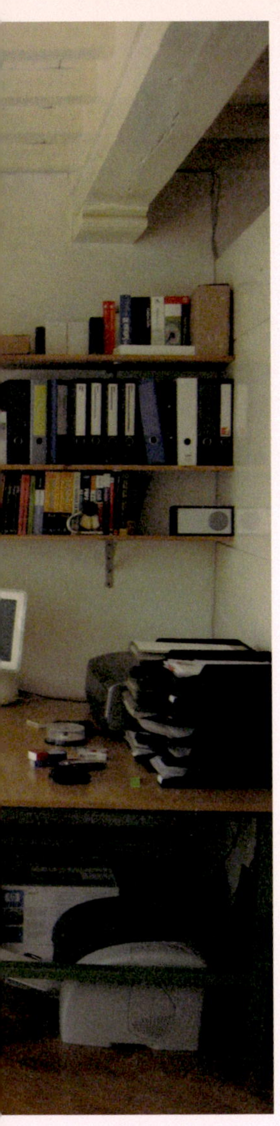

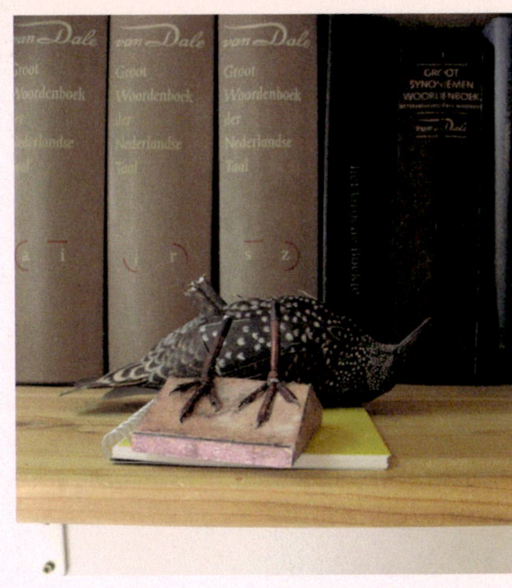

«This is a paper model of a European starling (in Dutch, spreeuw). It was a gift from friends, for designing a card announcing the birth of their first child. It took me about four hours to cut and glue it together and since then it has sitting on top of my computer. A few months ago one of my cats attacked it, and since then the body has been separate from the legs.»

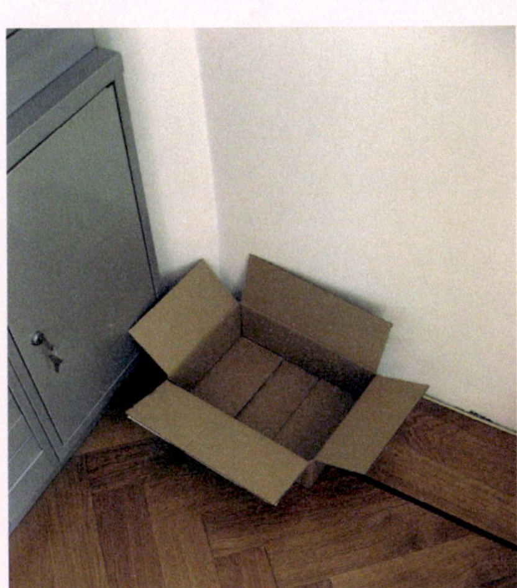

«Whenever I get a box, I leave it open on the floor of my studio. My two cats love to play with it.»

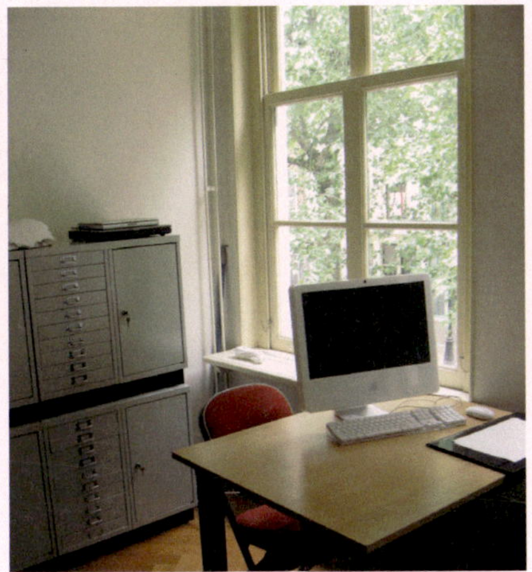

«I work at home. We have a very large living room and my studio is part of it.»

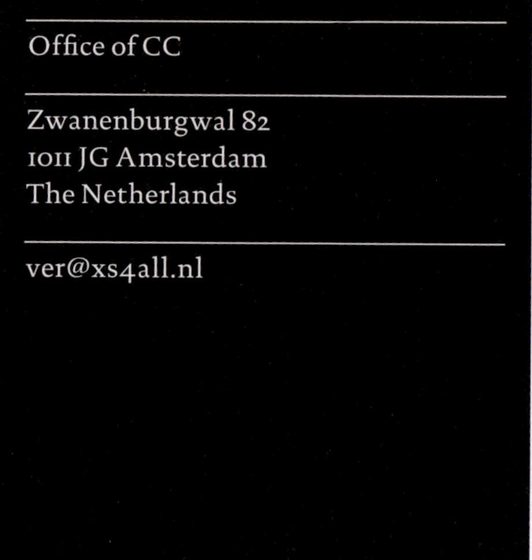

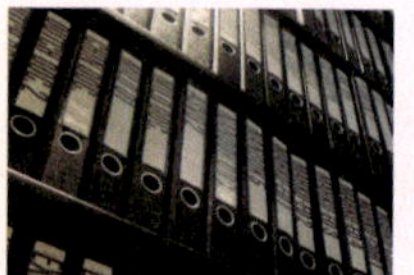
binders

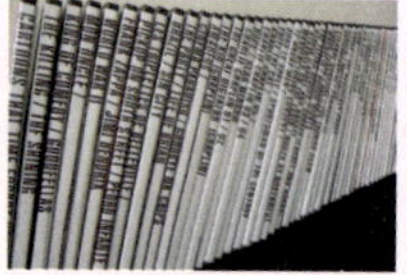
DVD

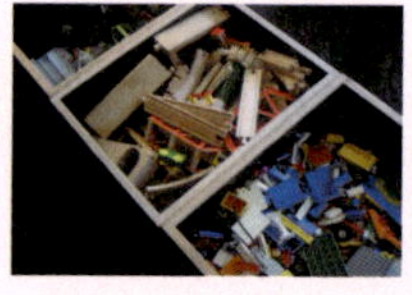
toys

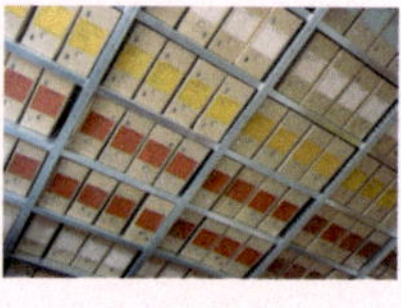
archives

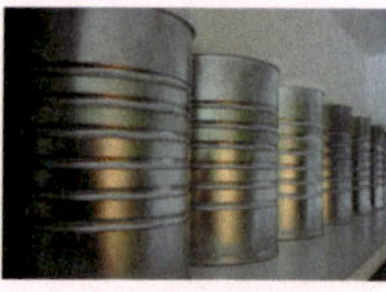
kitchen

After travelling round the world for many years, Chin-Lien Chen (Taiwan, 1973) and Chris H. Vermaas (The Netherlands, 1958) founded their studio, Office of CC in Amsterdam. They work for a wide range of clients, ranging from publishers to lawyers to architects, and specialize in identities, info-graphics, signage systems and books, mixing different media to find the right graphic solution for the problem. Office of CC's articles on design issues have been published in various magazines and books. Chris H. Vermaas has taught at various schools around the world (e.g. RISD, Yale, UDLA-P and DAE), and currently heads MaHKU's Editorial Design graduate programme; he also lectures at the AKI-academy and is a visiting professor at the University of Twente and the Plantin Institute in Antwerp. Chin and Chris have two kids (who have no intention of becoming designers).

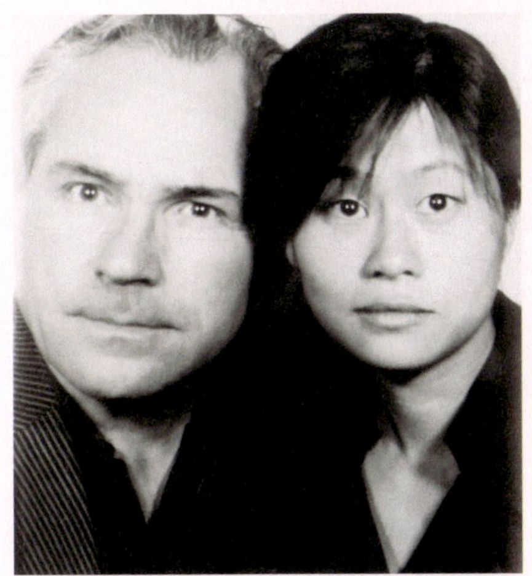

«This photo was taken in a photo booth at the train station. We look a bit serious in the photo, because while we were trying to look ‹nice› outside the booth our two-year old son was lying on the ground screaming and kicking with our eight-year old daughter trying to pick him up and at the same time wanting to strangle him. But there is a good ending to this story. After the photo-shoot was done, we went upstairs to a beautiful 19th-century interior cafe on the platform and had dinner with a view of the trains coming and going, and everyone was happy again (especially the two-year old monster.)»

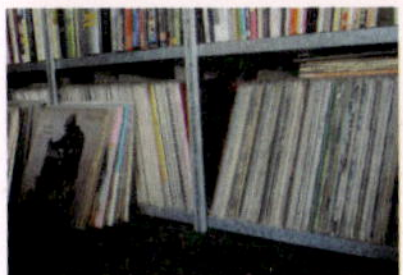

LPs

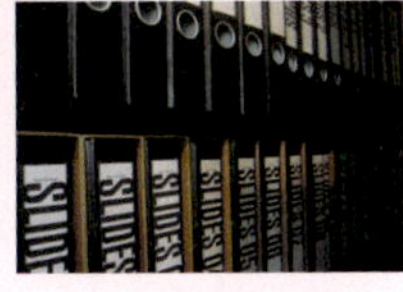

slides

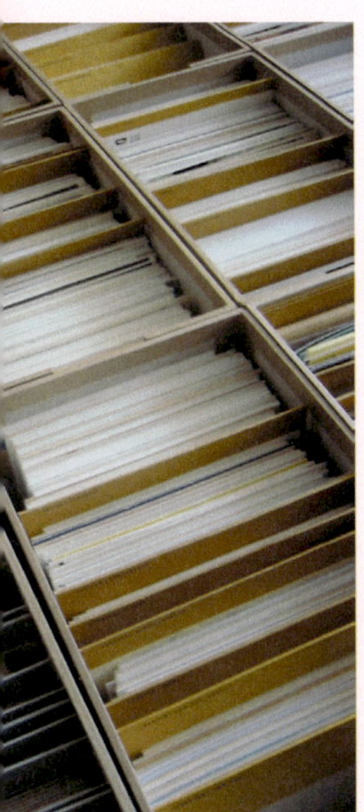

«Our office is located on a typical Amsterdam canal. We work, live and raise children in the same space. It is a small and compact place, overloaded with books and archives.»

«The view from our windows is the Waterlooplein flea market. This market plays a vital part in being one of the sources of our inspirations. For instance, a second-hand book dealer in the market renews his stocks daily with beautiful, strange and funny printed matter such as hundreds of nostalgic postcards from the past.»

De Designpolitie

Graaf Florisstraat 1a
1091 TD Amsterdam
The Netherlands

T +31 (0)20 4686720
F +31 (0)20 4686721

info@designpolitie.nl
www.designpolitie.nl

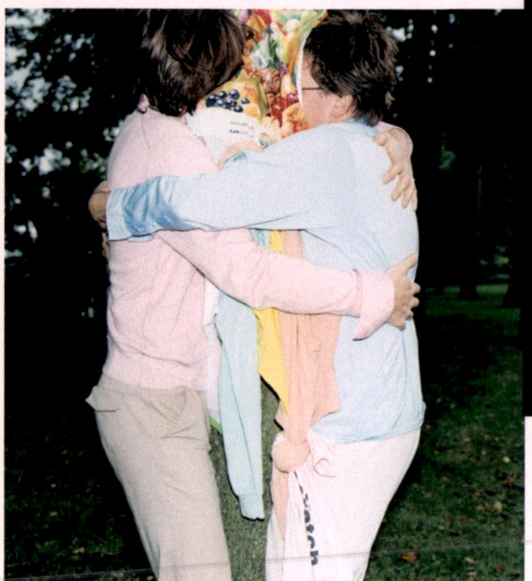

Richard & Pepijn by Viviane Sassen

De Designpolitie is a graphic design agency based in Amsterdam, The Netherlands.
De Designpolitie belongs to the ‹Dutch Design› family. Its members were brought up in the Dutch Design culture and rich tradition of Dutch art, design and tolerance. In keeping with these traditions, De Designpolitie follows simple but ruthlessly strict methods. The agency's working process often ends in a stripped-down image which that is a critical but always communicative solution.

De Designpolitie works for a variety of clients, small and large, in the non-profit and commercial sectors.
De Designpolitie also initiates exhibitions, festivals, books, lectures and workshops.

De Designpolitie consists of a small group of ambitious and talented creative people and was founded by Richard van der Laken (1970) and Pepijn Zurburg (1971) in 1995.
In its twelve years of existence to date, De Designpolitie has received numerous nominations and awards (including the European Design Award 2007). Work and interviews have been published in national (Dutch) and international magazines and books.
At the end of 2007, ‹The ABC of De Designpolitie›, a comprehensive survey of the agency's work, will be published by Valiz Publishers.

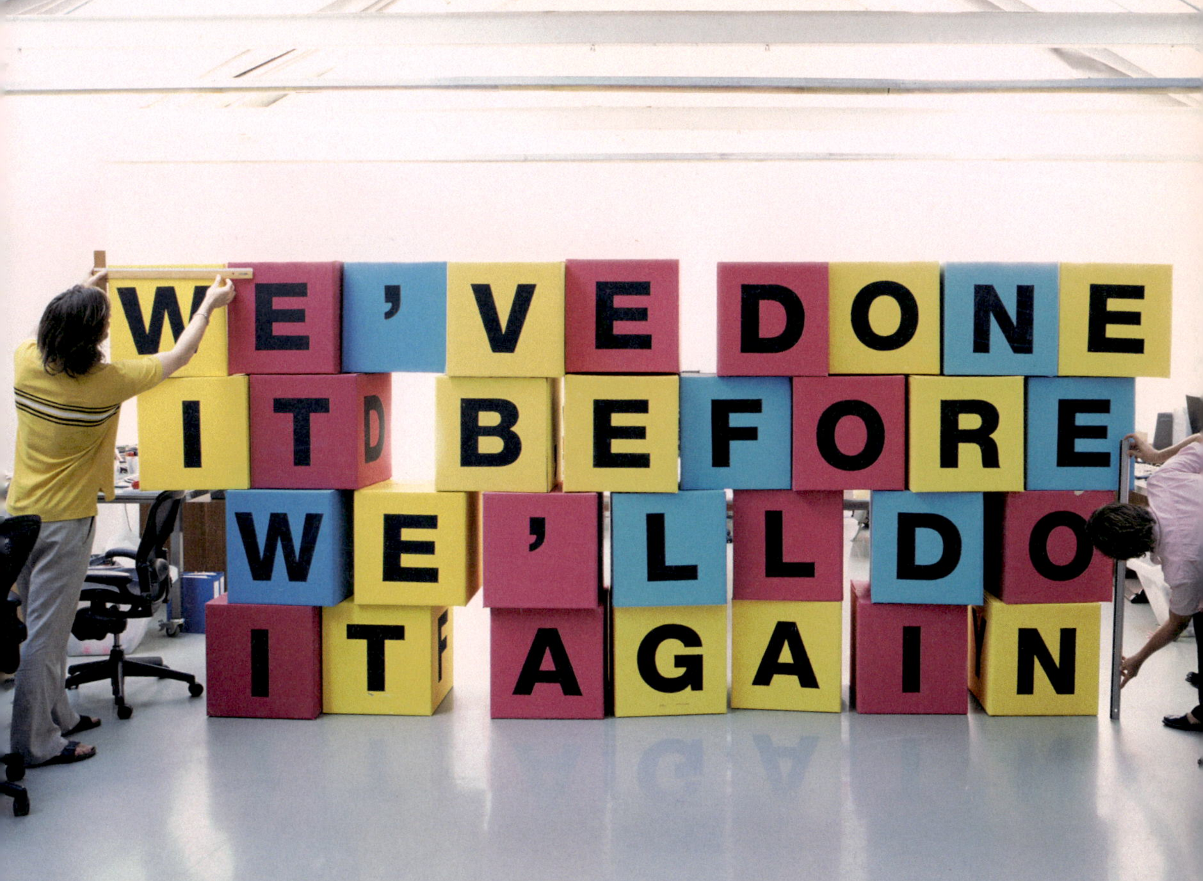
WE'VE DONE
IT BEFORE
WE'LL DO
IT AGAIN

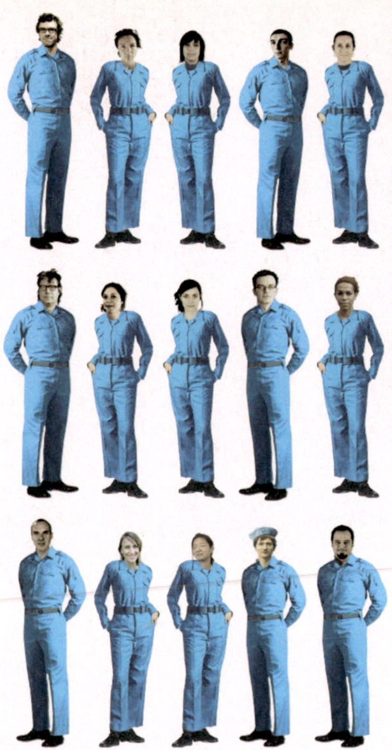

Atelier van GOG

Veemarkt 131
1019 CC Amsterdam
The Netherlands

T +31 (0)20 5606030
F +31 (0)20 6229441

info@ateliervangog.nl
www.ateliervangog.nl

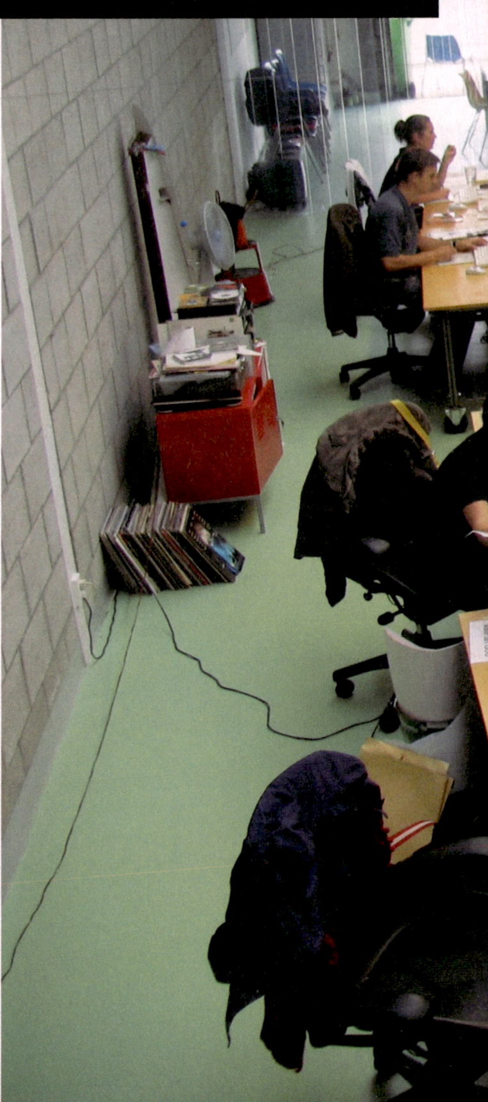

Atelier van GOG focuses on concepts for design and communication.
Our design is functional and follows clear structures.

Van GOG was established in 1994 and consists of Aart, Loïs, Sylvia, Ramon, Ragnhild, Wouter, Jutta, Barbara, Vincent, Salome, Radboud, Marre, Kayuk, Jens and Frank.

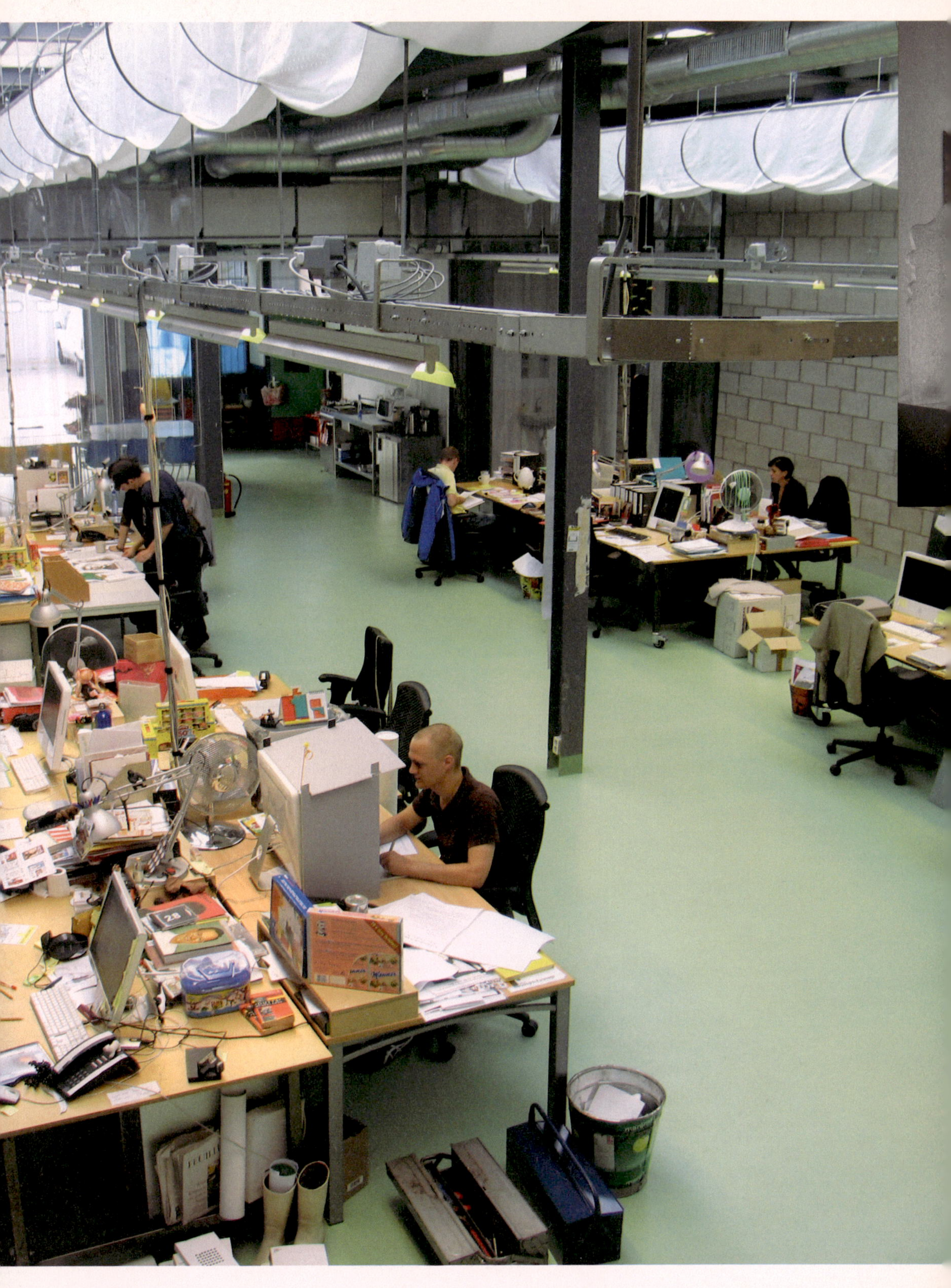

Strange Attractors Design

Paramaribostraat 18-I
2585GN The Hague
The Netherlands

T +31 (0)6 24867799

mail@strangeattractors.com
www.strangeattractors.com

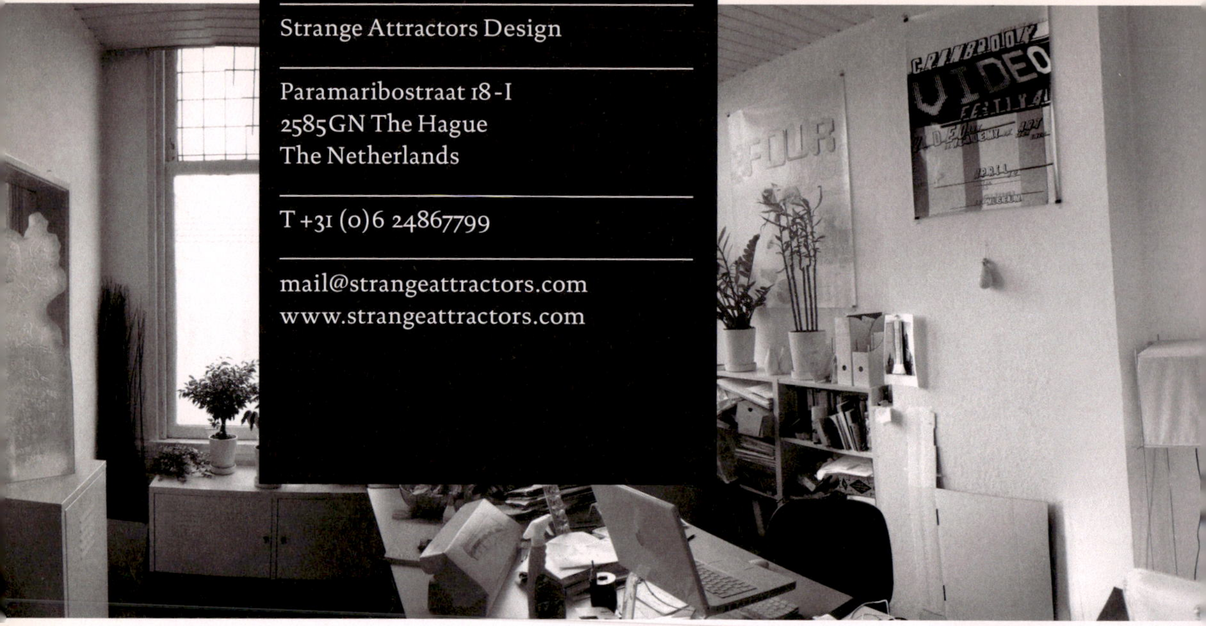

Strange Attractors Design, the international studio of Ryan Pescatore Frisk and Catelijne van Middelkoop, creates innovative ideas and solutions to influence culture and commerce. Using (typography in) new and traditional media, they produce design solutions for contemporary problems and desires.

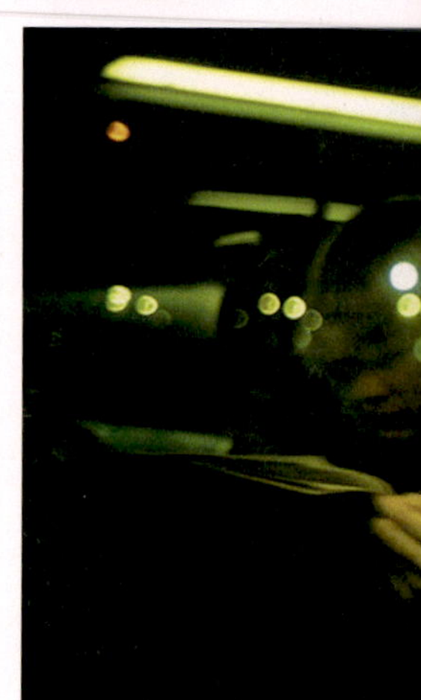

It is our belief that every design problem deserves a unique and custom-drafted solution; therefore, we do not differentiate between cultural and commercial projects.
We seek rich experiences and distinct messages, so we utilize typography as a tool to offer a diversity of custom alternatives to (neo)modernist generic communication and globalist banality.

Our work acts as a bridge, giving form, representation and physical tactility to the intangible, conceptual, digital and ephemeral. Craft, calligraphy, ornament and abundance in concert with technology, history, theory and criticism comprise the common tools we utilize to reach this goal. We believe that communicative experiences are most effective when they seduce and/or provoke the viewer.

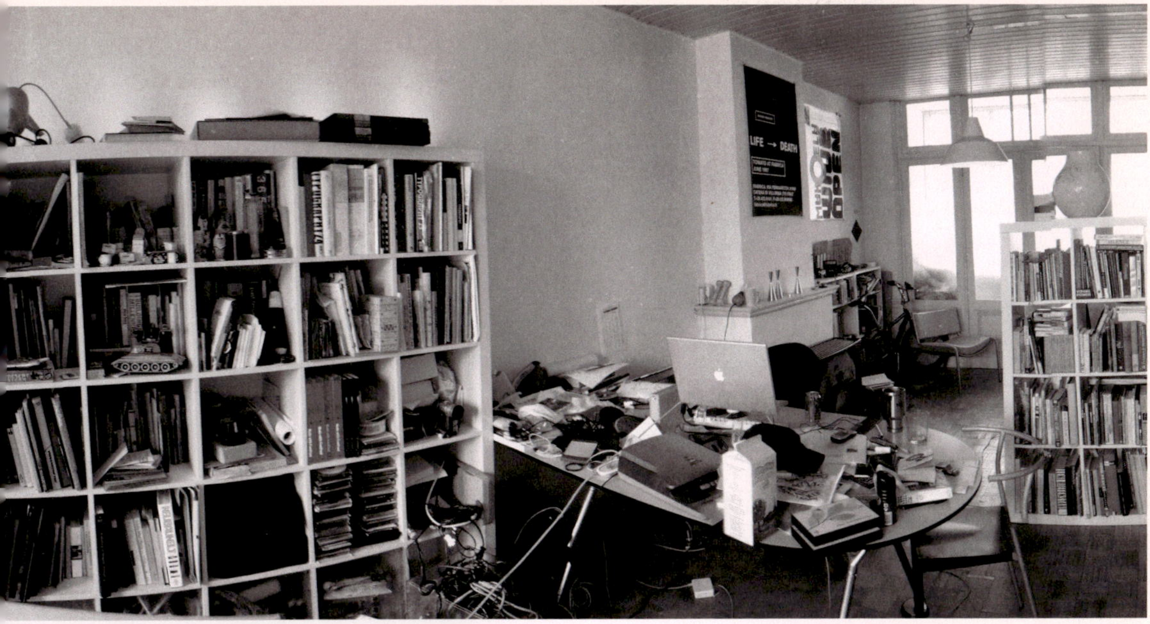

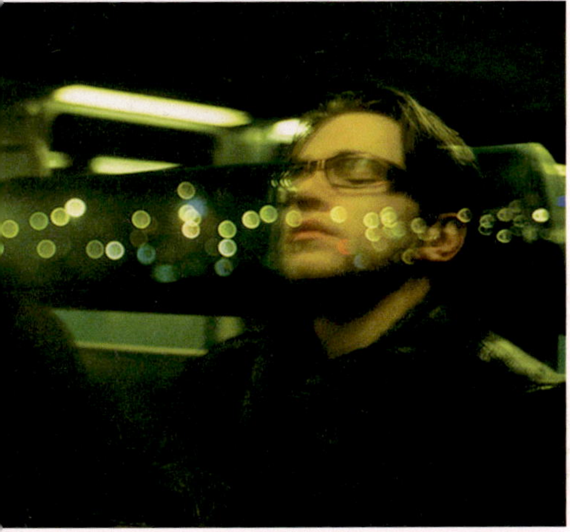

SA on the train

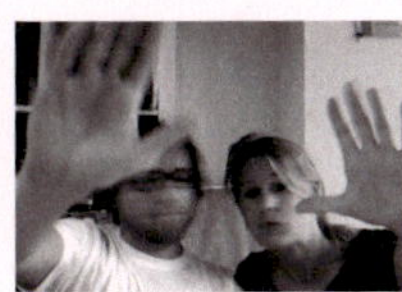

SA in iPhoto

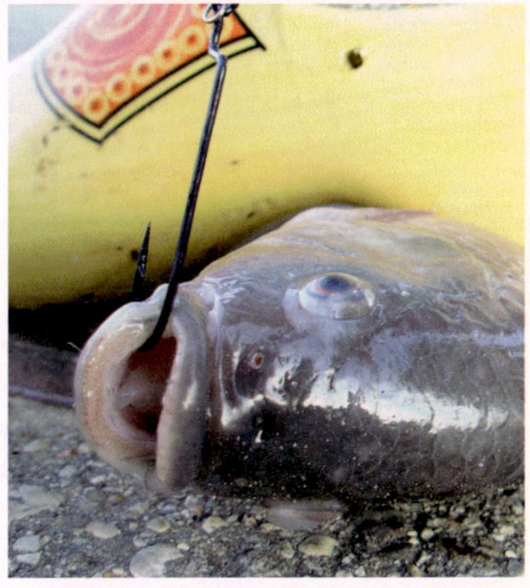

iconic portrait of us: Wooden shoe and a fisherman (Pescatore)

Fish = caught by the fisherman = Pescatore = Ryan
Wooden shoe = Dutch = Catelijne
(Image we took to underline the international
nature of our collaboration) : an iconic portrait...

The Dutch are hooked on the Pescatore!

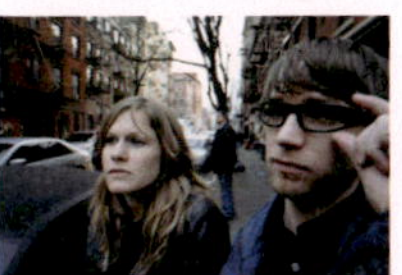

SA at Soho

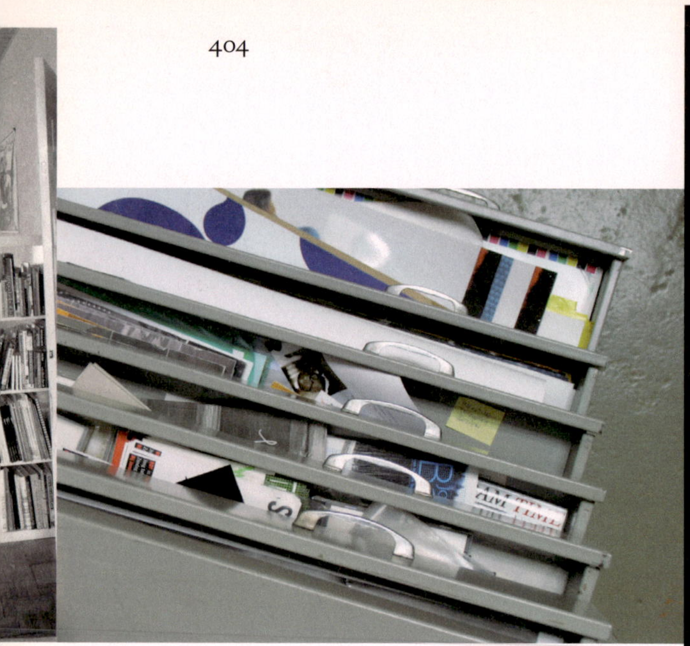

Arjan Groot & Julia Müller

Donker Curtiusstraat 25c
1051 JM Amsterdam
The Netherlands

T +31 (0)20 6848945
F +31 (0)20 6848990

Arjan Groot:
mail@thecoverup.eu
www.thecoverup.eu

Julia Müller:
mail@hellojulia.com
www.hellojulia.com

Arjan Groot

«I was twelve when I discovered the Mecanorma graphic supplies catalogue in a bookstore, and got it as a present for my next birthday. Before that my father had been bringing transfer sheets with alphabets home from work every once in a while. All these different font families intrigued me. Every font had its own personality, and I wanted to familiarize myself with all of them. I'm still trying.»

«Now, many years later, after having quit two graphic design courses (1, 2) and completed a third (3), having worked with three fellow designers in a collective (4), having spent some time in Barcelona (5), having founded an architecture magazine (6) and having collaborated on various projects with my lively friend and colleague from Germany (7), it's time for a new adventure. ‹The Cover-Up› is an ambitious new graphic design conspiracy I hope you will hear about in the near future (8).»

(1) Grafisch Lyceum, Amsterdam, 1990-1991
(2) Hogeschool voor de Kunsten, Utrecht, 1992-1994
(3) Gerrit Rietveld Academie, Amsterdam, 1998-2000
(4) (020) ontwerpers, 1999-2003
(5) January-July 2003
(6) ‹A10 New European Architecture›, founded in 2004 with Hans Ibelings, www.a10.eu
(7) Julia Müller (Frankfurt, 1977)
(8) www.thecoverup.eu

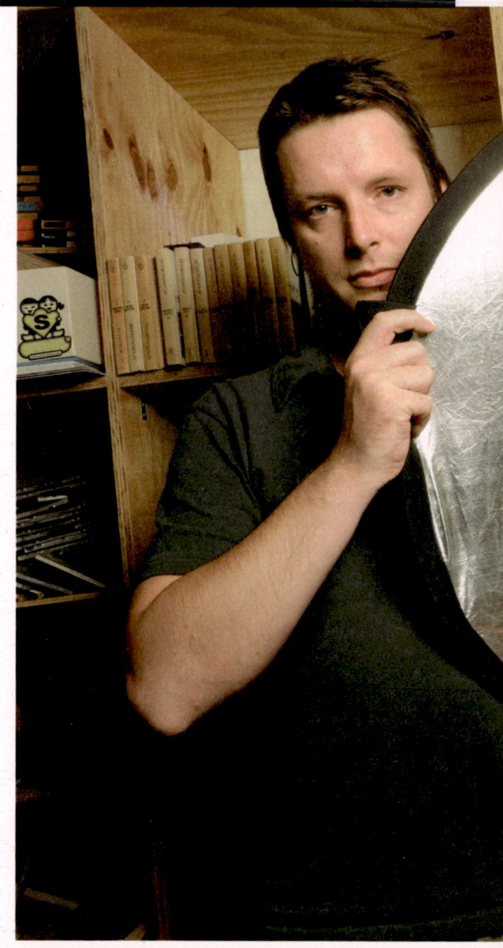

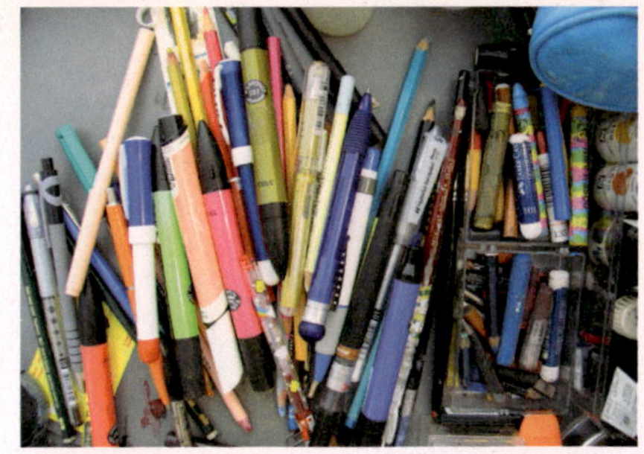

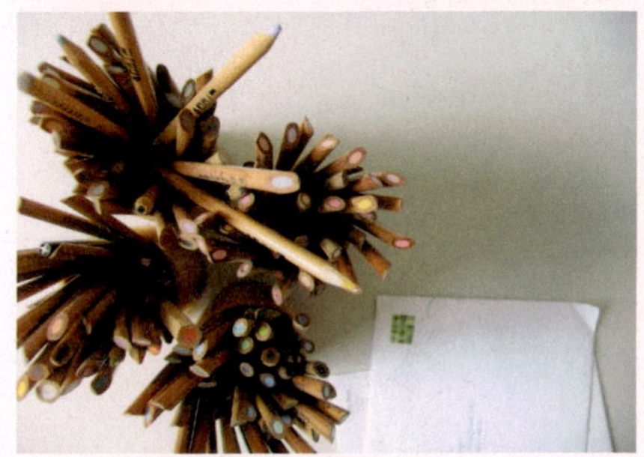

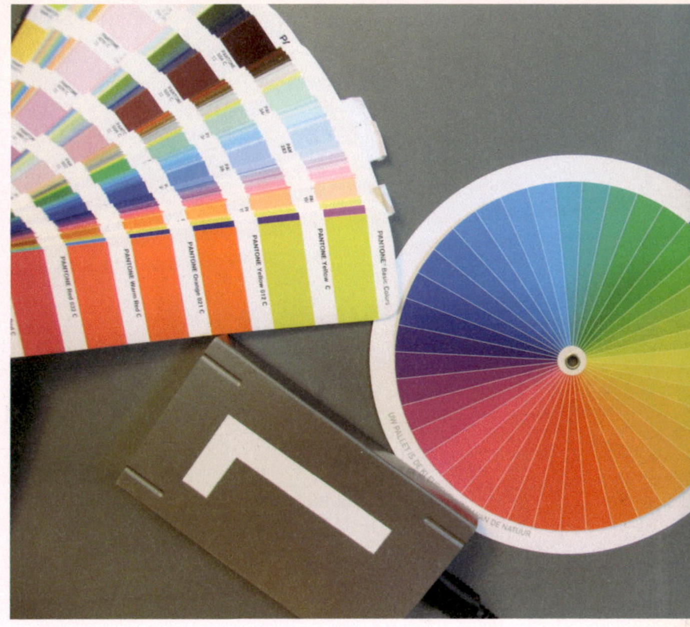

Julia Müller

«After studying Fine Art in Germany (1), I started working as a sound artist. I had some solo exhibitions and one of my works in particular received a great deal of attention (2). This was fantastic, but I still felt I needed more, and exchanged Frankfurt for Amsterdam to study graphic design (3). I realized that my conceptual thinking was also of great use here. Two weeks after I got my diploma, I got on my bike to see one of my favourite designers in Amsterdam (4). We became friends and started to work together and still do. Since then I've also worked with my best friend (5) in Cologne, winning an award (6) for the design of a literary magazine (7) and just being happy with my boyfriend (8) and my cat (9).»

(1) Hochschule für Gestaltung Offenbach, 1999-2002
(2) ‹Plaques›, illegal sound installation, Museum of Modern Art, Frankfurt, 2002
(3) Gerrit Rietveld Academie, Amsterdam, 2002-2004
(4) Arjan Groot (Heerhugowaard, 1972)
(5) Julia Neuroth (Darmstadt, 1980), www.juliajulia.eu
(6) Type Directors Club Awards, New York, 2006
(4) ‹Paperwaste› magazine
(8) Niels Wolf (Oldenburg, 1975), www.swummoq.net
(9) Bambi, 2006

Roger Teeuwen

Willem Buytewechstraat 165a
3024 XG Rotterdam
The Netherlands

T +31 (0)10 4762026
F +31 (0)10 4672029

rtgo@xs4all.nl
www.rogerteeuwen.nl

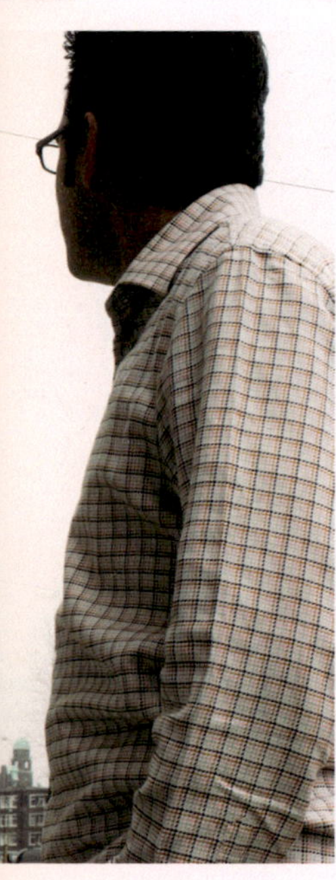

Roger Teeuwen is an independent graphic designer based in Rotterdam, The Netherlands. In his work he plays with additions and redefinitions, simultaneously questioning and offering context to readers and users. He teaches design and is head of the Graphic Design department at the Willem de Kooning Academy. He has also worked for many cultural commissioners including artist Jeanne van Heeswijk, the International Architecture Biennale and the Piet Zwart Institute in Rotterdam.

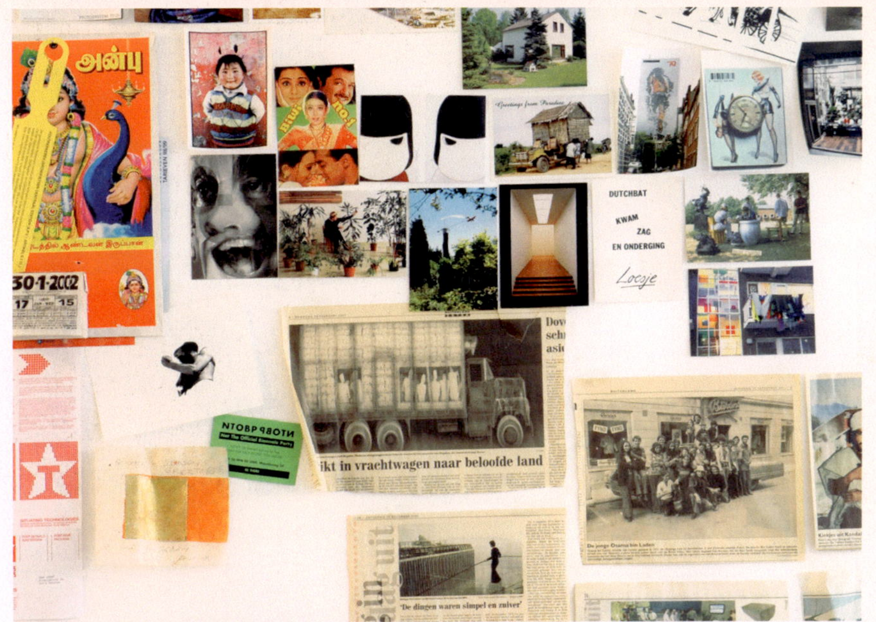
அன்பு
30-1-2002
DUTCHBAT
KWAM
ZAG
EN ONDERGING
ikt in vrachtwagen naar beloofde land
'De dingen waren simpel en zuiver'

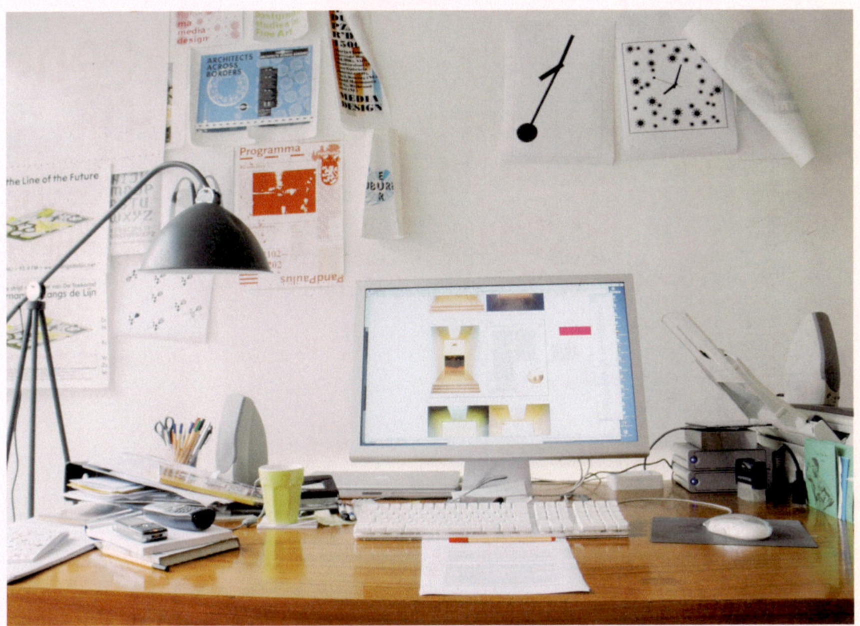
ARCHITECTS ACROSS BORDERS
Programma
the Line of the Future
MEDIA DESIGN

Werkplaats Typographie

Agnietenplaats 2
6822 JD Arnhem
The Netherlands

T +31 (0)26 3535774
F +31 (0)26 3535666

www.werkplaatstypografie.org

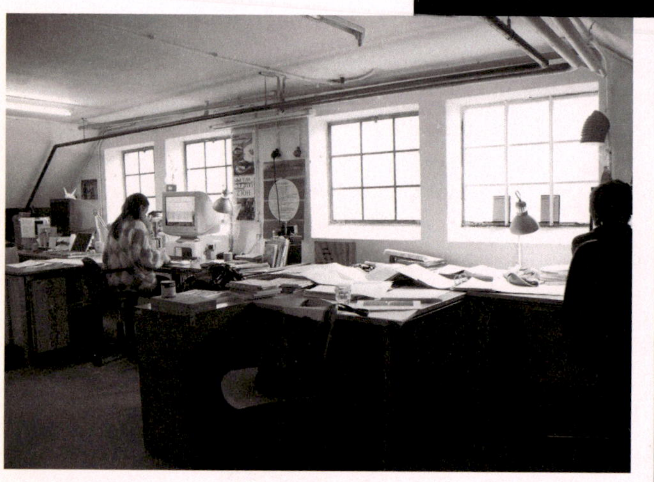

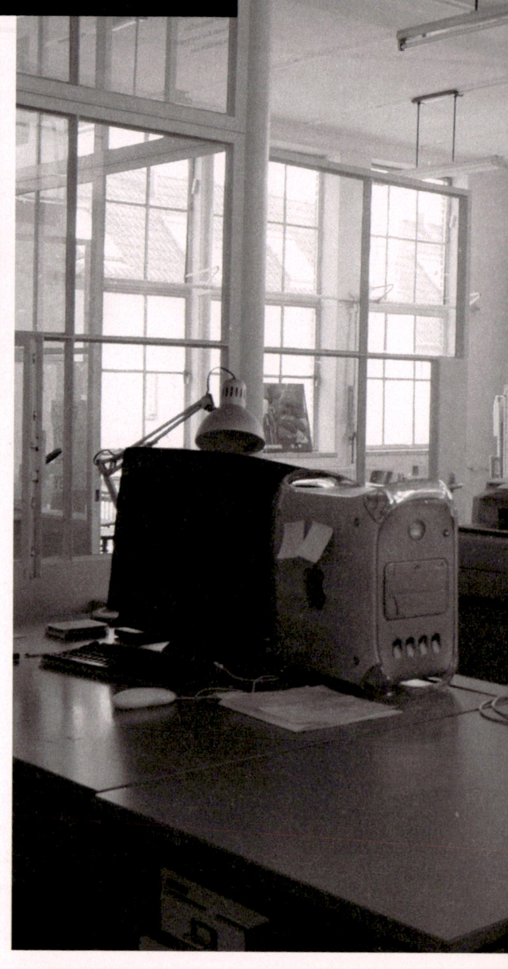

The Werkplaats Typografie (WT) is part of the ArtEZ Institute of the Arts. The WT is a two-year masters programme centred on practical assignments and self-initiated projects. It also serves as a meeting place for graphic designers with regard to research and dialogue.

The WT is supervised by Karel Martens and Armand Mevis. Further guidance is given on a regular basis by Paul Elliman and Maxine Kopsa. Anniek Brattinga and Liesbeth Doornbosch are in charge of co-ordination.

Visiting lecturers are regularly invited to provide individual tutoring and/or to give presentations. Reviews of work, critiques and project participation are informal in character. Participants work in a professionally equipped studio with access 24 hours a day. The WT is open to a maximum of twelve graphic designers who would like to extend their knowledge and skills.

The WT programme stimulates and practices critical reflection on the basis of a broad cultural perspective, with theory playing a supporting role. Participants engage in art research involving content and form, text and image and theory and praxis, in relation to professional practice and supervised by leading designers.

Alongside more theoretical research, participants work on real assignments for external clients. By way of these assignments, participants learn to take a leading role in the process of designing and realizing a final product.
The WT programme broadly consists of three components: 1) Presentations, individual and group critiques, workshops; 2) Practical assignments, and 3) Theoretical orientation in the form of research, excursions and a final thesis. Assignments can be initiated by the WT, by external clients, or by the participants themselves.

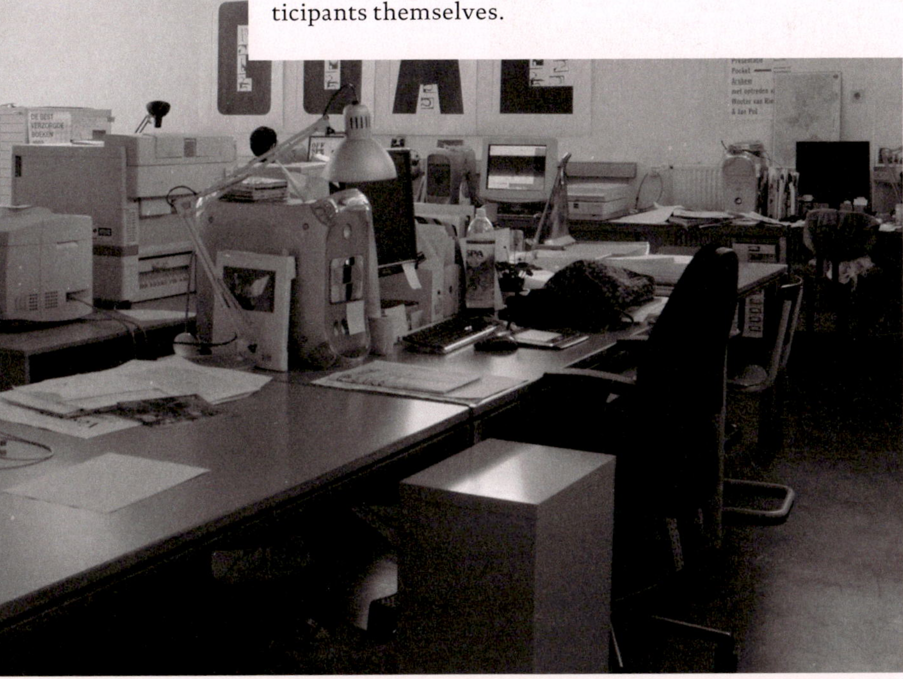

Meta Haven: Design Research

KNSM-laan 32
1019 LL Amsterdam
The Netherlands

T +31 (0)62 4276797

office@metahaven.net
www.metahaven.net

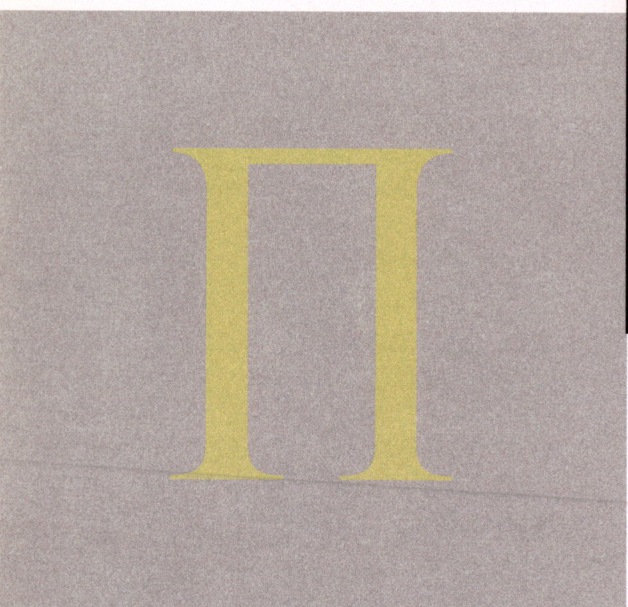

Meta Haven is a collective agency for design research, visual identity and the political, based in Amsterdam. Their work consists of design models, proposals, essays, lectures, conferences and publications. Here is a short interview with its initiators, Daniel van der Velden and Vinca Kruk.

Q: Vinca and Daniel, Meta Haven seems to be the most self-indulgent thing to exist in a country like The Netherlands, which is known for its exceptional quality of commissioned graphic design. Why here and why now?

A: Indeed the freedom that exists in The Netherlands is enormous. Freedom is never absolute, however. It is relative to something else. We might be a new offspring of that freedom, one whose dedication to providing concrete ‹solutions› is less determined by existing assignments than by re-reading the problems that, so to speak, come ‹before› assignments. Whenever we think about commissioned design, to us, the way assignments are formulated is key. However, no history has been written of assignments, which would be a very interesting endeavour to pursue. Even if assignments are not much more than provisory scribblings, they define what must be done. From a potential history of assignments one could learn then also about what was not done, excluded. Recently the freedoms enjoyed in Dutch graphic design practice were, by some, ‹demythologized› as in fact little more than a local oddity of the social-democratic welfare state; one that has brought global fame to its practitioners, but at the same time is difficult if not impossible to export as a condition in the globalized arena of image production.

What we propose however is not that instead a ‹realistic› (read: market-driven) model should be imposed, but instead that design re-orients itself on the issues in the world today. This is why we hope to use design as a means of investigating those, and our work is an account of these investigations. We think there are conditions for making design in an incredibly experimental way, yet outside of the frameworks that have up to now determined the focus of commissioned design.

Q: When you say ‹the political›, what do you mean with that?

A: In short, our interest is in the phenomenon of power. We think that politics is about power, and the political is a means to work with it, in the sense that it determines which collective enacts power upon others, which can be a resistance power as well. Then, the icons of power lead us into the darkest recesses of the mind. The layer of ‹civilized behaviour› in our lives is really rather thin, and so it is for symbols. Primordial visual expressions of power – such as the ones found in armies, on bank notes and coins, and in countless other examples – defy ratio. This is why we think that the essence of the representation of the political lies outside of ratio. If design is considered to be an instrument solely in the service of rational thinking, it can never be political.

Q: Would you be willing to work for a foul government?

A: This is an interesting question. Our first work with Meta Haven was for Sealand, a tiny war platform in the North Sea very near the British Isles. Sealand is the territory of a self-proclaimed nation state, a principality. At the time, 2003-2004, our work for Sealand existed under the somewhat paradoxical name of ‹nation branding›; that's how some people looked at it at least. Our identity for Sealand was compared to a new identity for the tiny state of Liechtenstein. We are far more critical of the phenomenon of ‹branding› than of the phenomenon of foul governments or ‹rogue states›. In a way they are related or juxtaposed; a brand is supposed to emanate certain ‹brand values› while rogue states are supposed to ‹not share our values›. It is entirely dependent from which politico-ideological angle you are looking at the ‹foul› or ‹rogue› state, and at the ‹value›, and whose hegemony this benefits, of course.
Let's say that Meta Haven was naturally built to design for rogue states.

Q: What will you do next?

A: A new team member, Gon Zifroni, has joined us. We are working on a continuation of our engagement with the situation around the so-called ‹House of People›, an enormous building in Bucharest from the Ceausescu era that is at this moment the Romanian palace of parliament. We wish to provide both discussion and scenarios to make this building public. And we are working on an investigation of the 9/11 aftermath and what happened to the remains of the Twin Towers – closely related to the idea of the ruin – in the perspective of the War on Terror. And we're investigating a European search engine, Quaero, together with Gon Zifroni and Tsila Hassine, at the Jan van Eyck Academie. And we're making a book.

Studio Kluif

Veemarktkade 8
5222 AE 's-Hertogenbosch
The Netherlands

T: +31 (0)73 6230707

info@studiokluif.nl
www.studiokluif.nl

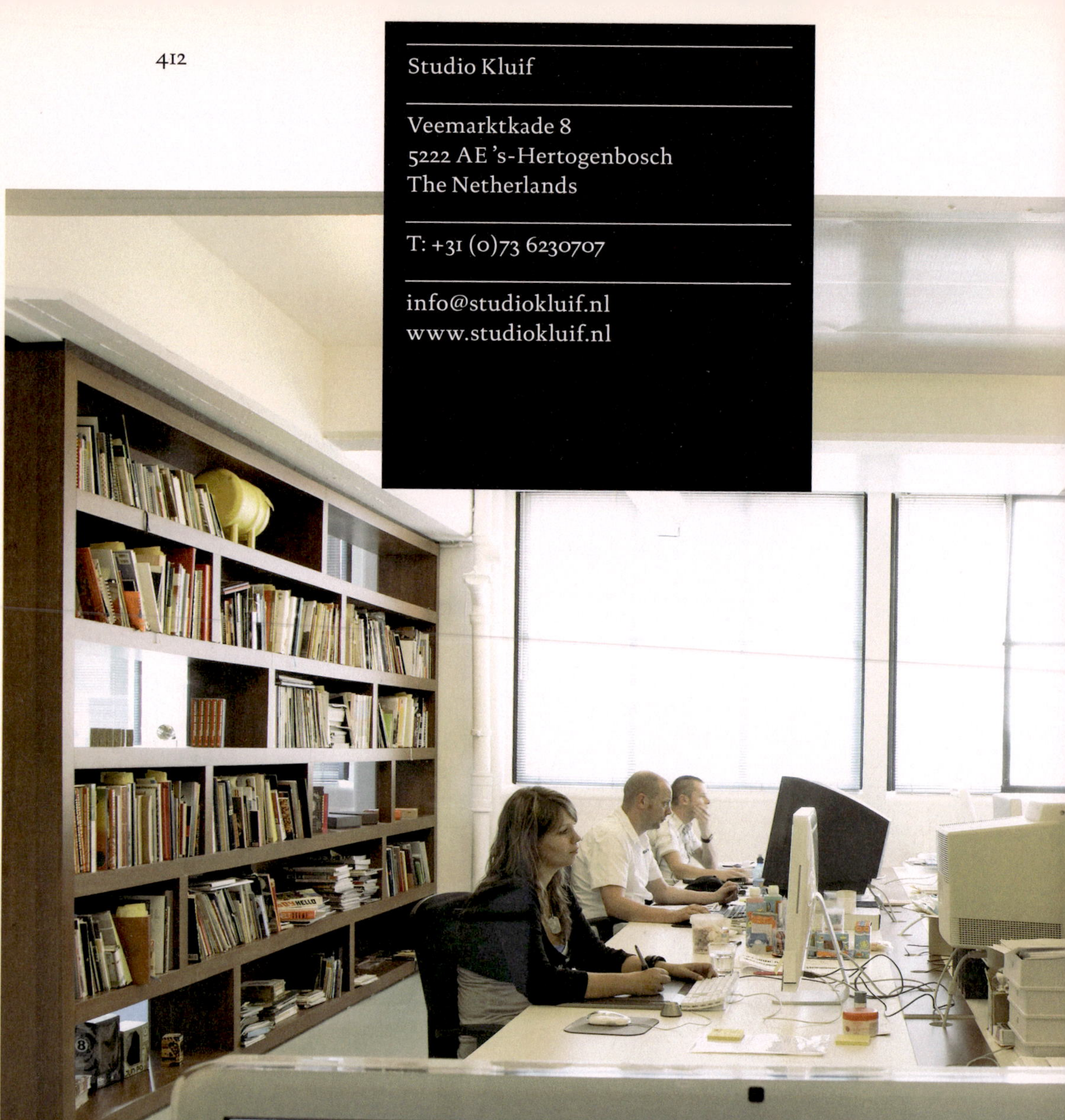

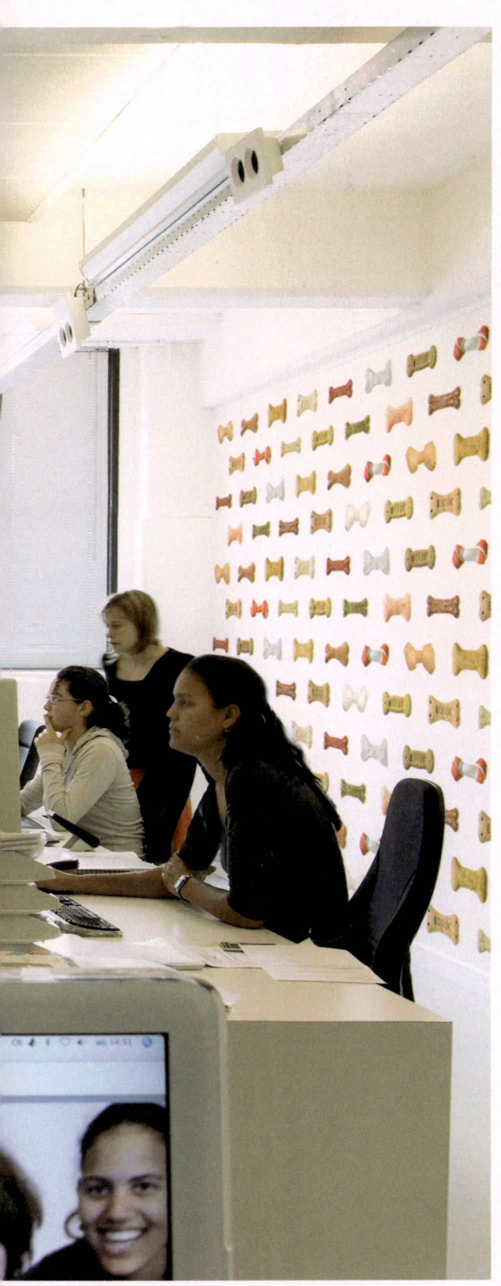

Studio Kluif is a design unit founded by Jeroen Hoedjes and Paul Roeters during the summer of 1999. Nowadays the Kluif team is formed by nine people. All designers.

Kluif is working for exceptionally diverse clients: HEMA (an international retailer), Porsche, Oilily, MTV and many others.

Kluif is designing exceptionally diverse products: condoms packaging, clothing prints, watch collections, business stationery and bike collections to name a few.

Kluif's statement: ‹Having a style is like being in jail›. (David Bowie)

Sander Plug (1969) is a graphic designer and artist.
He graduated in 2004 from Fine Art department at the Sandberg Institute and has shown his work at various exhibitions in Amsterdam, London, Berlin and Barcelona.
He is a regular contributor to BUTT magazine.
Sander works and lives in Amsterdam, The Netherlands.

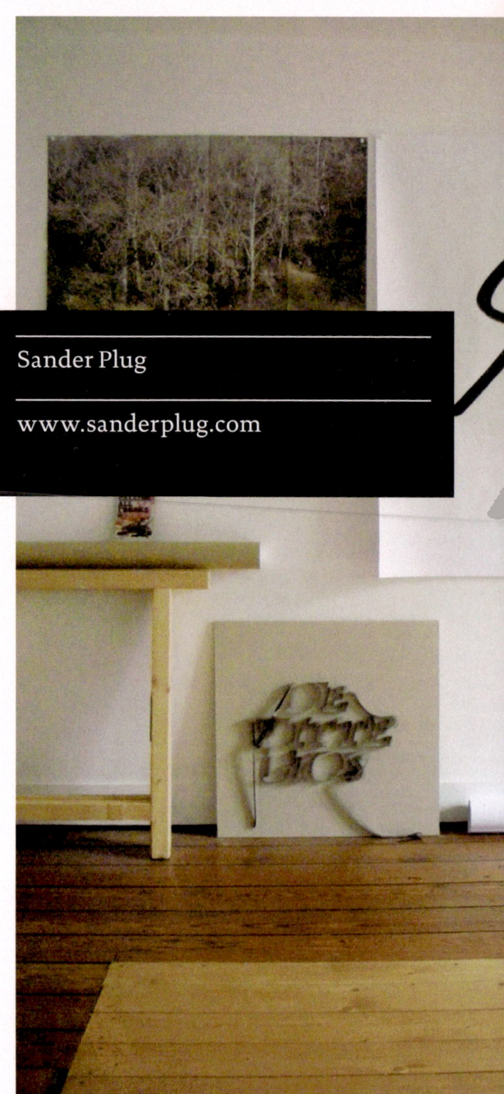

Sander Plug

www.sanderplug.com

Office

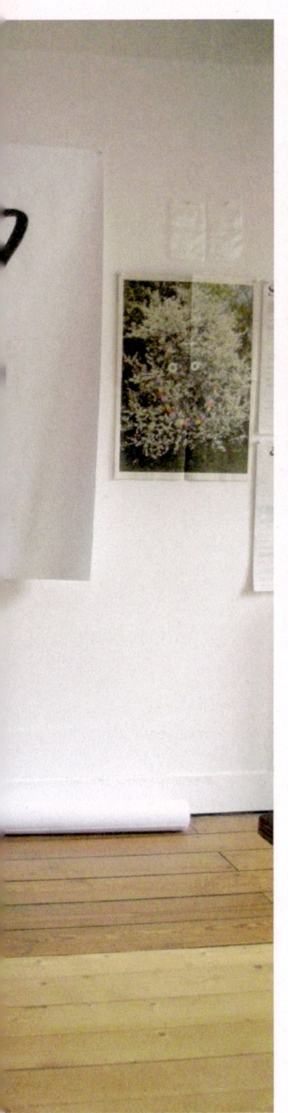

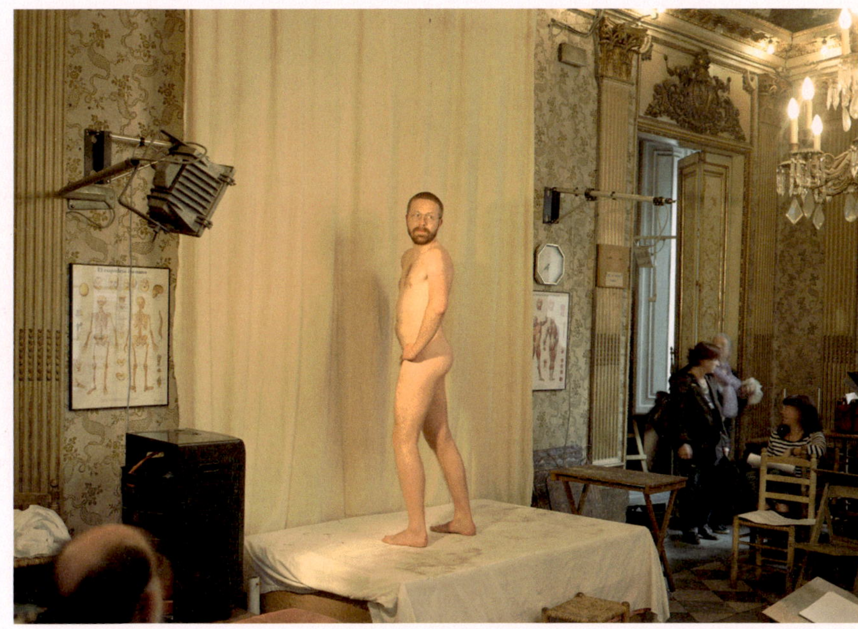

photo: Henk Wildschut

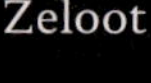

Zeloot

Laan van Meerdervoort 211
2563 AA Den Haag
The Netherlands

zeloot@yahoo.com
www.zeloot.nl

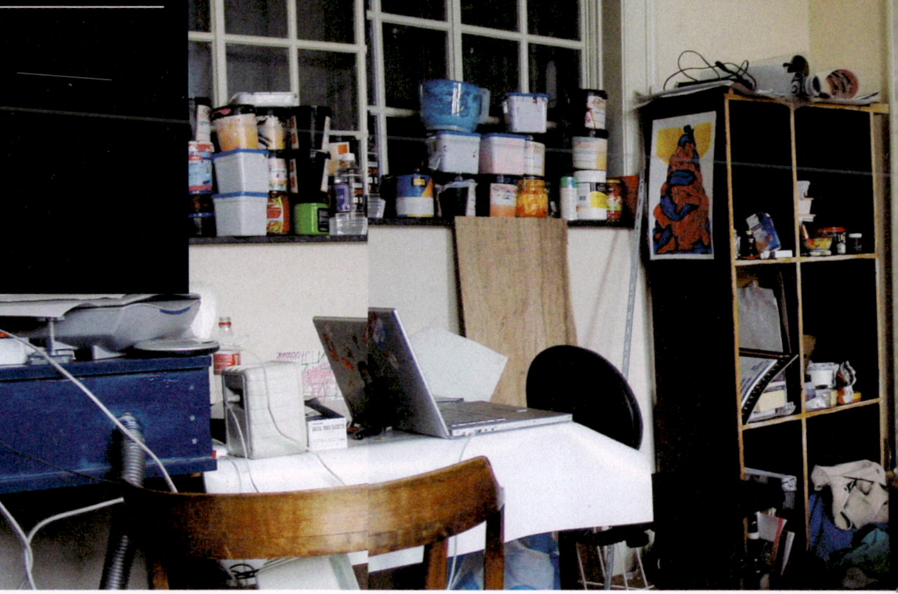

I don't really know what to say about myself…

I organize gigs, nearly every week, for experimental, noise, folk, free-jazz etc musicians in Den Haag with someone by the name of Helbaard and design and silk-screen posters for those. I mainly focus on music-related things such as gig posters and LP/CD-covers because I like to express myself through something as abstract as music. I've been doing this for about 5 years, before that I was a farmer in the south of Europe.

I used to do more commercial work but found it harder and harder to do commissioned work as I get closer and closer to something as self-expression.

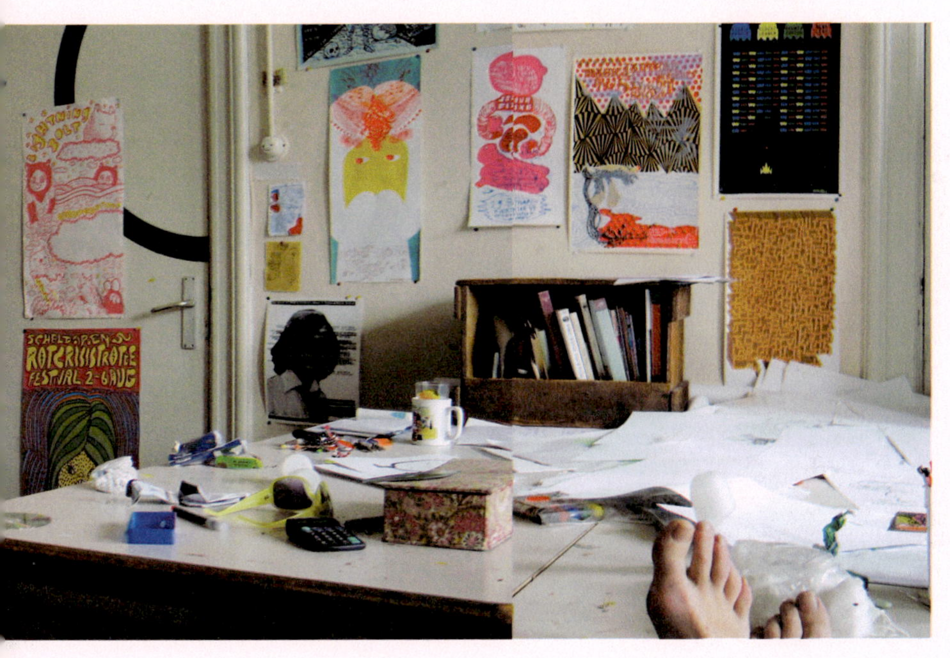
FESTIVAL 2-6AUG

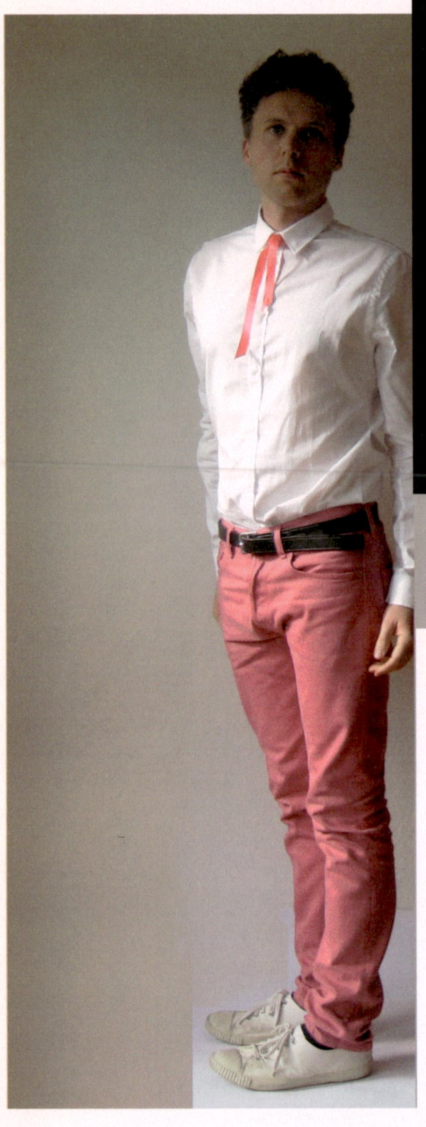

You & McCuskey

T: +31(0)642165553

you@mccuskey.nl
www.mccuskey.nl

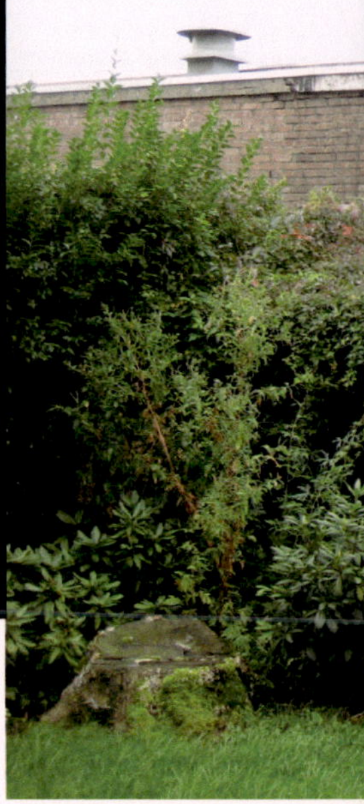

You & McCuskey is the studio for concept, creation and communication founded by Rowan McCuskey.

In enthusiastic cooperation with our clients we bring new life to brands. We therefore find the essence and inspiration within our clients' unique situations, positions, needs and possiblities.

To visualise our ideas we communicate in a wide range of forms, the obvious and the unobvious, applied to branding, advertising, graphic and multimedia design.

Our main interest is in becoming inspired, making money and embracing love.

«The Romantic image of my studio is actually the view I have from my studio window. I always imagine myself being in this house while working. This place houses a great deal of my thoughts. I have worked inside it at different times, in the winter as the cold curls the bones in my toes, the moist curls my paper. But it has everything: electricity, fridge, bird chatter and nice smells.»

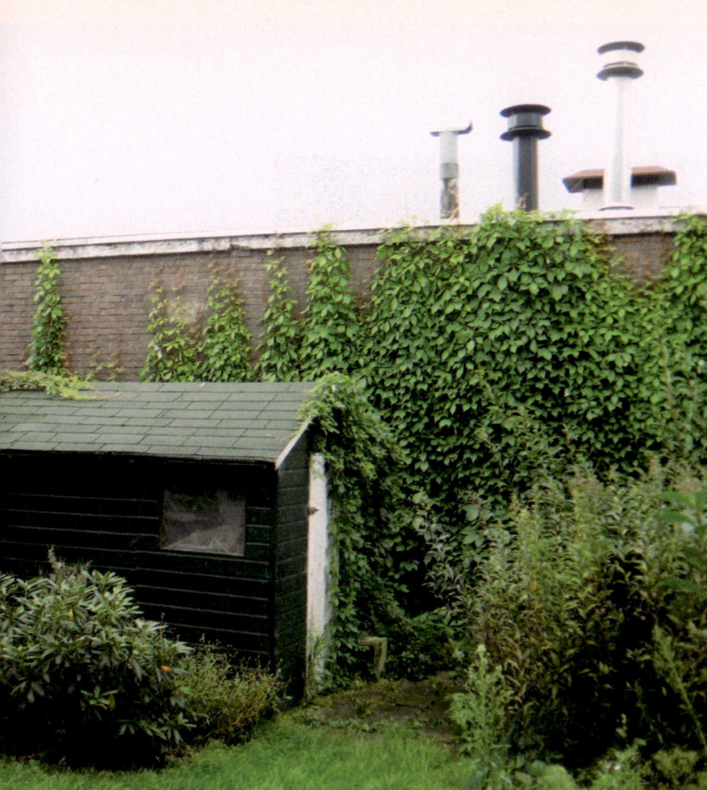

I was born November 14th, 1975 in Middlebury, Vermont, USA, moved to the Netherlands, studied Bewegingtechnologie for a year, graduated in 2001 as a graphic / typographic designer from the Royal Acadamy of Arts, The Hague. After my studies, I worked at a typical Dutch design firm, soon started design firm Propeller VOF, promising myself never to work for a boss again. Bored with standard graphic computer work, ‹FAMC (Frankanne & McCuskey)› was started in 2003 together with artist Martyn Overweel doing exhibitions, performances, lectures, self-titled magazines. In 2004 I decided to quit ‹Propeller VOF› and start ‹You & McCuskey› to focus on a wider scope of design. This has led me to interesting clients and possibilties to develop new aspects of myself, writing, teaching, travelling. Since March 2006 I have been writing and illustrating an article in ‹Items› magazine.
In 2008 ‹Lorenz & McCuskey› will kick off, offering creative self-reflection to businesses and governments. ‹Mccuskey.nl›, ‹Mccuskey.jp›, ‹Famc.nl›, ‹Lorenzand-mccuskey.com› document some of my projects, while ‹Twopoints.Net›, ‹Tag004.nl›, ‹Architectureoffice.net› document some of my support to other people's projects.

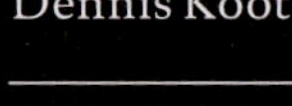

Dennis Koot

Oranjestraat 3
2514 JB Den Haag
The Netherlands

T: +31 (0)6 48795986

dennis@koot.nu
www.koot.nu

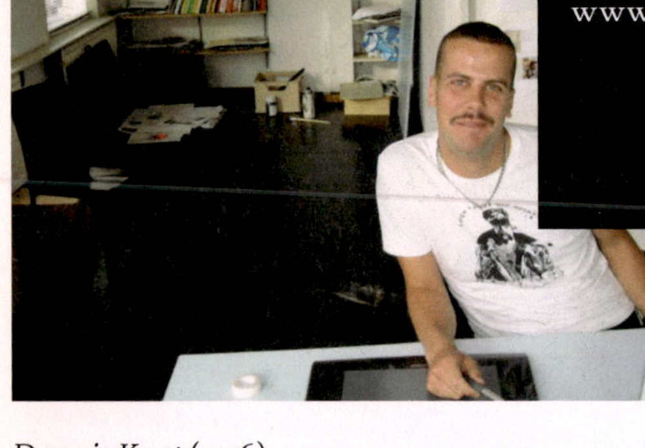

Dennis Koot (1976)
Right after his graduation in 2000 from the Royal Academy in The Hague, Dennis Koot started to work at Studio Dumbar. In 2006 he left Dumbar to start his own studio in The Hague. Koot is a designer and editor for ‹Items›, which is Holland's leading magazine on design and related fields. He also likes to design books and posters. He teaches Graphic Design at the Willem de Kooning Academy in Rotterdam. Together with illustrator Martyn F. Overweel he forms UNISECS, a deejay duo playing ArtPop.

The work of ‹Pulchri› (p.302)was made when he was working at studio Dumbar.

Studio Dumbar
Their projects range from complex assignments for corporations and government agencies to more straightforward assignments for the cultural sector. Ongoing investigation into new forms of visual communication and creative expression guarantees results that are provocative and compelling. Studio Dumbar continually endeavours to break new ground in the field of design.
www.studiodumbar.com

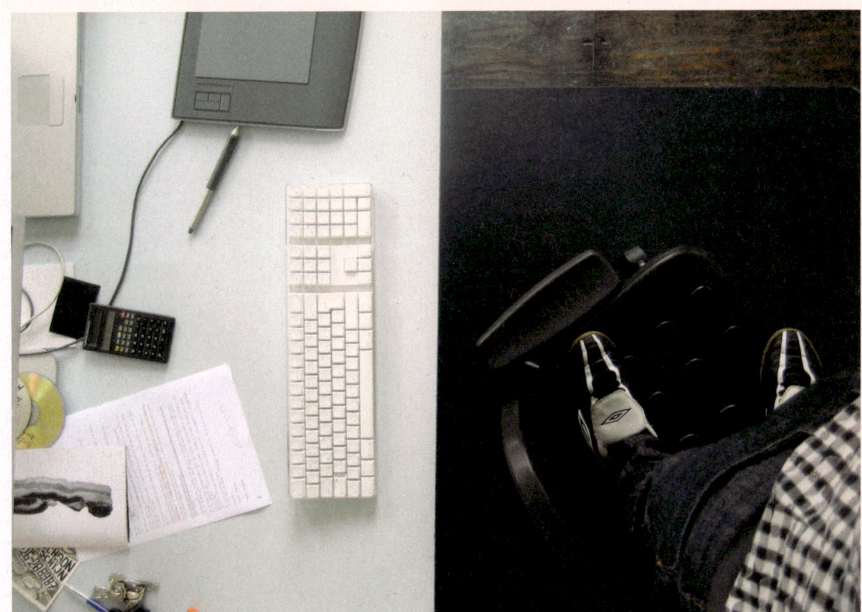

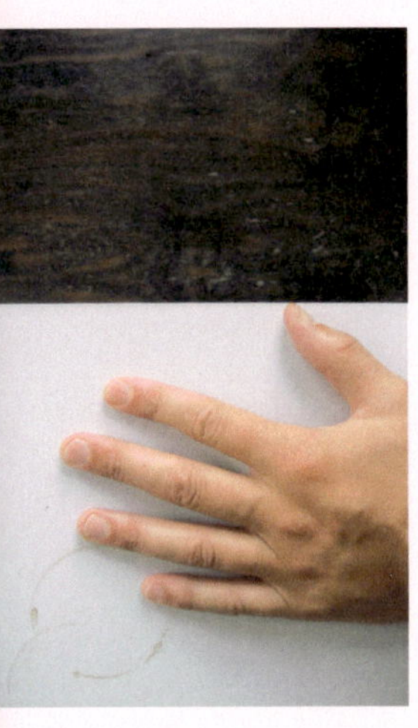

Toko

Level 1
72 Campbell St
2010 NSW
Surry Hills, Sydney
Australia

info@toko.nu
www.toko.nu

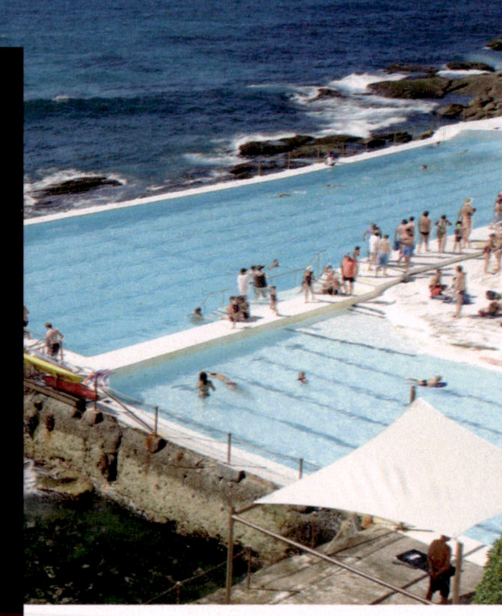

Icebergs Pool

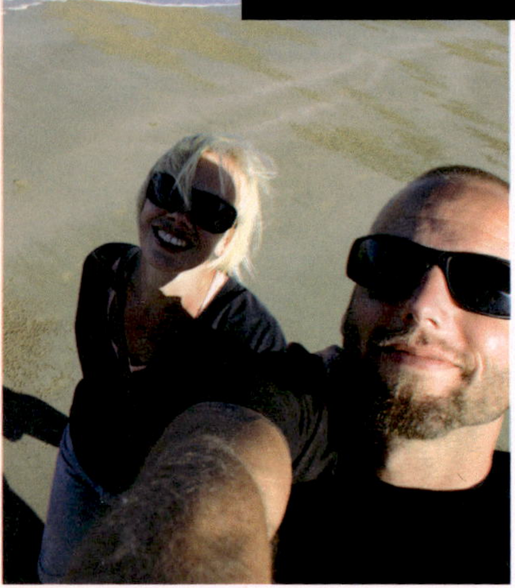

Toko

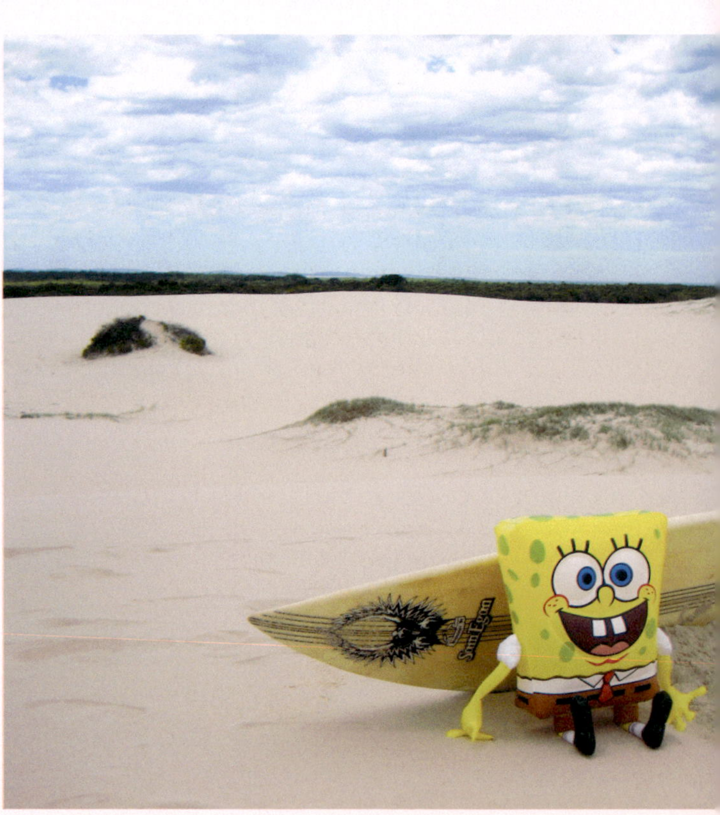

Surfs Up

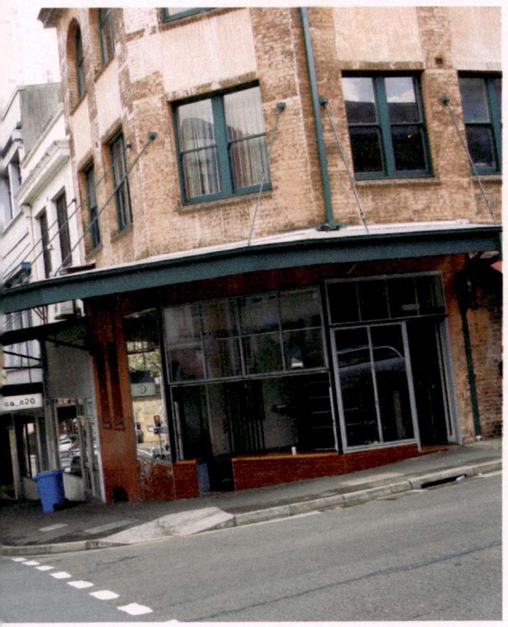

Hang Out

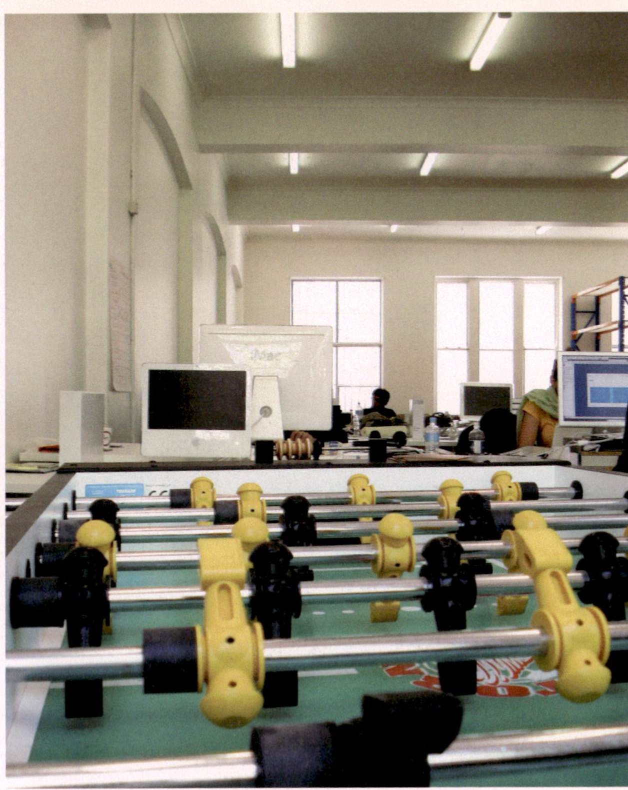

Office

In 2002 Eva Dijkstra and Michael Lugmayr teamed up to found designstudio Toko, a name embedded in Dutch-Asian history that means ‹shop› in Dutch slang. A multidisciplinary design studio with an experimental and conceptual approach with an emphasis on print design. In particular, typography plays a significant role in their design, and they often experiment and create a unique typeface for projects.

Three years ago, they went to Australia for a short holiday and fell in love with the city of Sydney and its lifestyle. They decided to relocate to Sydney in 2006, from where they continue their (geo)graphic adventures for global and local clients from the cities in both the Netherlands and Australia, and for multinational companies from anywhere around the globe.

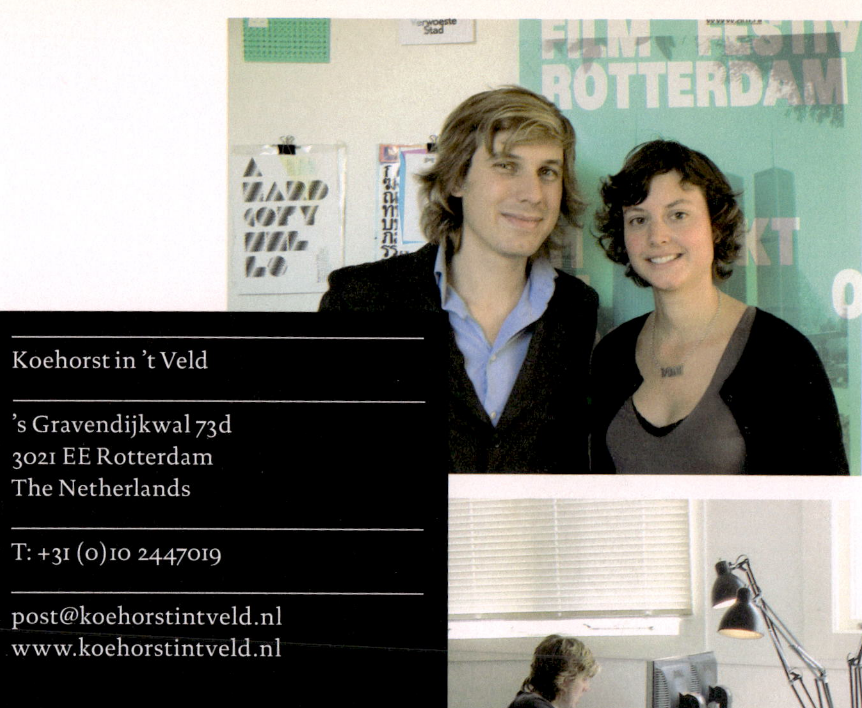

Koehorst in 't Veld

's Gravendijkwal 73d
3021 EE Rotterdam
The Netherlands

T: +31 (0)10 2447019

post@koehorstintveld.nl
www.koehorstintveld.nl

Koehorst in 't Veld is the graphic design studio of Toon Koehorst & Jannetje in 't Veld, based in Rotterdam. They design for both print and digital media.

Koehorst in 't Veld was founded by Jannetje in 't Veld and Toon Koehorst. After finishing the B.A. in graphic design at the Art Academy in Arnhem they went on to do cultural studies at the universities of Rotterdam and Utrecht.
Koehorst in 't Veld teaches graphic design with an emphasis on (new) media at the Willem de Kooning Art Academy in Rotterdam. This accent on cross-mediality is a recurrent theme in their work, both in professional assignments and autonomous projects.

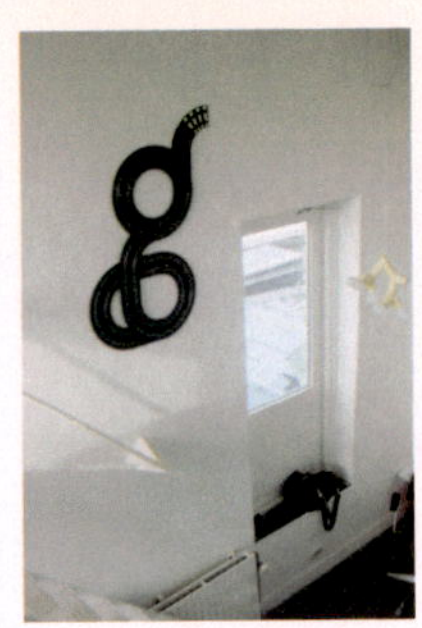

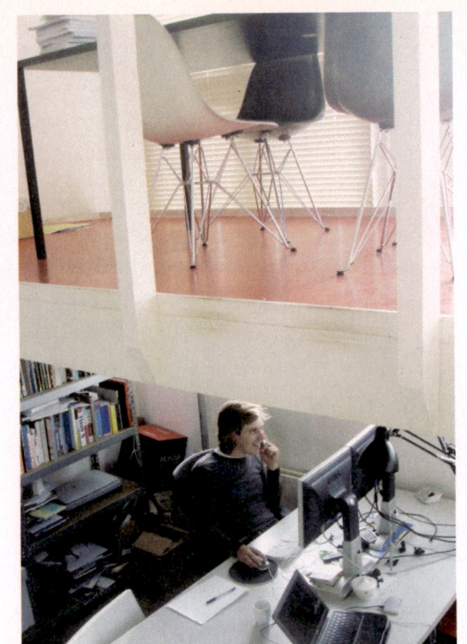

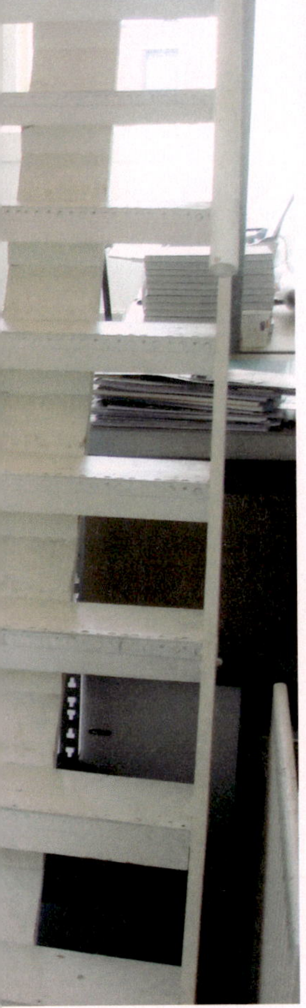

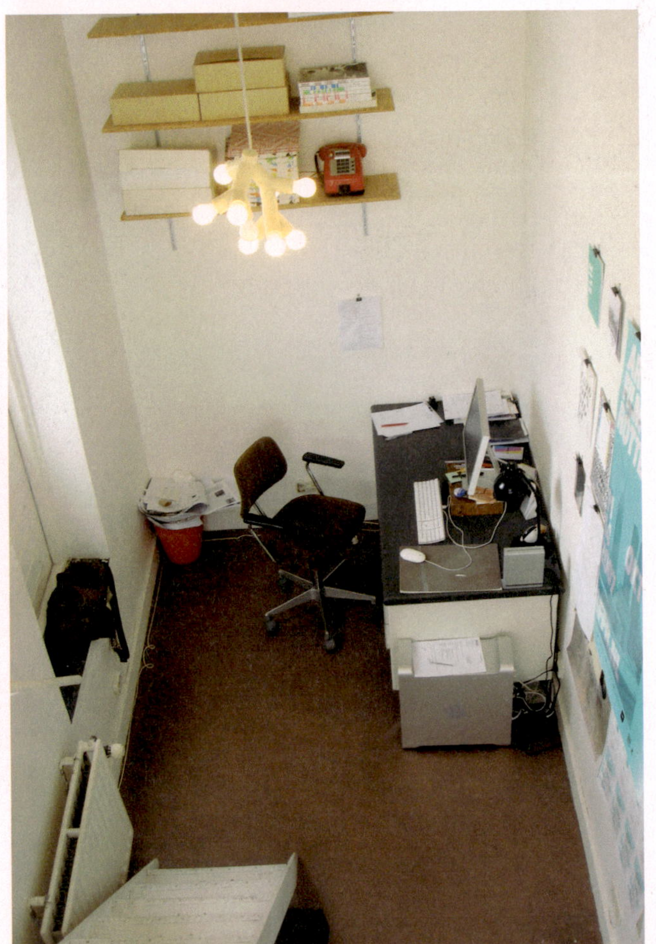

by van Bostelen, Herman

132 Gorilla *(in collaboration with De Designpolitie & Lesley Moore)*

by Catalogtree

60 Postitposter
70 fellows
82 Company logo
88 VINEC 006
90 VINEC 008
108 Transurban
110 VINEC 005
260 Close Encounters 3

by Office of CC

98 General Electricville /GOOD
100 The Expanding Universe of Wikipedia /GOOD
102 Drink up /GOOD
103 Buying a Brand /GOOD
104 Homeless /GOOD
228 Morf

by De Designpolitie

132 Gorilla *(in collaboration with Herman van Bostelen & Lesley Moore)*
310 The Utrecht School of the Arts (HKU)
313 W139

by Experimental Jetset

80 RMN logo
262 Wim Crouwel /Architectures Typographiques
264 SMCS graphic identity
306 Ten Years of Posters

by Atelier van GOG

38 Back-to-school-package
192 GOG e-cards

by Gremmen, Hans

26 PHS-manual
182 MLB
184 LPCD 2004
286 Desktop /Desktop-Publishing

by Groot, Arjan
40 Oh Pedro *(in collaboration with Julia Müller)*
290 Birthmarks *(in collaboration with Julia Müller & Menno Wittebrood)*
330 Werck

by van Halem, Hansje
52 DecoLetters
54 ScratchedLetter
56 GridLetter
58 WireLetter
59 PostageStamp
258 StitchUnsewed

by Studio Kluif
33 Newrulez
200 The Murder Game
204 Mees Goal-den boys
206 Blockheads Central Park Guerilla Campaign
208 Nedap annual report
276 HEMA packaging office supplies
278 HEMA packaging, ‹Play with food products›
280 Nedap Annual Report
282 Amsterdam ArenA card, David Bowie
283 Box with bone-shaped paperclips

by Koehorst in't Veld
240 Frame

by Dennis Koot
302 Pulchri Exhibition Posters *(Studio Dumbar)*

by Lesley Moore
78 The Wall is the Landscape
132 Gorilla *(in collaboration with Herman van Bostelen & De Designpolitie)*
188 Lesley Moore corporate identity
269 TuttoBeNe presentation *(in collaboration with Silke Spinner)*
300 Genesis

by Liemburg, Harmen
16 Crispy Cloud Kombini
18 To Oceans Of Joy
19 Kikiriki Souvenir poster
20 The Recordshow
21 Speed
22 At Random
220 Heavenly Leader
317 Fall 2005 Visiting Artist Lecture Series

by Lust
92 Margeting: Inventing a Different Marketing Language - book
94 Margeting: Inventing a Different Marketing Language - pages
106 Marking Europe High Speed
196 Digital Depot
232 The Mondriaan Foundation 2004 Annual report
238 Pages Magazine
292 TodaysArt Festival, The Hague
332 Pauze

by Machine
31 Therapy Praful Pyramid
36 Outsiders
140 Untitled
194 www.ourmachine.com
252 Mark
274 Psychedelic Warfare
334 Directors' Cuts

by Maurer, Luna
118 Living Agenda
256 KVB Annual Report *(in collaboration with Jochem van der Spek)*
296 The Argyle Pullover *(in collaboration with Roel Wouters)*
298 Grid in space
299 Placement / Displacement *(in collaboration with Edo Paulus)*

by Meta Haven
150 Sealand Identity Project
158 PostCom Grids
160 PostCom North Korea, Ryungyong - Forbidden Icon
162 Quaero Design Research, Quaero Logo

by Müller, Julia
40 Oh Pedro *(in collaboration with Arjan Groot)*
218 Music scandals *(in collaboration with John Heymans)*
234 Paperwaste magazine *(in collaboration with Julia Neuroth)*
236 School brochure
290 Birthmarks *(in collaboration with Arjan Groot & Menno Wittebrood)*

by Richard Niessen
34 Five stationaries
210 Wedding Design *(in collaboration with Esther de Vries)*
222 Wedding tablecloth *(in collaboration with Esther de Vries)*
248 Evol Eye Lands End
318 Uniceflaan
319 Raadzaal Zuidoost *(in collaboration with Jennifer Tee)*
320 TM-City *(in collaboration with Esther de Vries)*

by Ping-pong Design
24 Poster series for the Nederlands Fotomuseum in Las Palmas
43 A telling
45 BKOR
190 Volksuniversiteit
216 Cultural Posters
328 Visual identity and signage graphics for the Nederlands Fotomuseum in Las Palmas

by Sander Plug
28 The Good Body

by STAR
112 Een nieuwe wereldkaart / Potenciales Estados Nación (Potential Nation States)
114 Wereld ball/ La bola del mundo (World-ball)
126 Los edificios más altos de cada país (The Tallest Buildings in the World)
128 La Historia de las Expos (The History of the Expos)
164 The Image of Europe - ‹EU-History ring› *(in collaboration with OMA/AMO)*

by Strange Attractors Design
83 Vive le Papier Électronique
324 Big Type Says More

by Teeuwen, Roger
29 World Wide Westwijk
75 Face Your World
120 Mare Nostrum *(in collaboration with Minke Themans)*

by Themans, Minke
116 Map of Maps
120 Mare Nostrum *(in collaboration with Roger Teeuwen)*

by Thonik
68 Lemmer
72 Power
73 BNA
146 SP

by Toko
84 Confused Type
243 Code
246 New Directions

by You & McCuskey
48 Concrete web magazine
62 Brombeeren identity
64 Tape
66 Dans

by Werkplaats Typografie
185 KaAp Generale Posters
226 WT Magazines
308 On Lawrence Weiner
326 The Sirens of Venice

by Zeloot
214 Pelt
215 Final Milks

Published
by Actar Barcelona / New York

Edited
by Tomoko Sakamoto, Ramon Prat in collaboration with David Lorente, Reinhard Steger, Hector Sos, Anna Tetas, Christian Schärmer & Twopoints.Net

Design & Illustration (Cover, p.1-13)
by Twopoints.Net

Assisted
by Marieke Bielas (Actar)

Super HD Model
Bob Groen

Photography
by Oriol Rigat (Model) & Tomoko Sakamoto (Landscape)

Production Management
by Dolors Soriano & Leandre Linares

Digital Production
by Oriol Rigat & Carmen Galán

Copy Editing
by Graham Thomson & Tonya Gates

Printed
by Ingoprint S.A.

Printed and bound in the EU

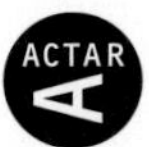

ISBN 978-84-96954-19-9
DL B-49291-2007

Distributed
by Actar D
Roca i Batlle, 2
08023 Barcelona, Spain
T: +34 93 418 7759
F: +34 93 418 6707
office@actar-d.com
www.actar.com

Distributed in the United States
by Actar D USA
158 Lafayette Street, 5th Fl.
New York, NY 10013
T: 212-966-2207
F: 212-966-2214
officeusa@actar-d.com
www.actar-d.com